FAST TRACK TO A 5

Preparing for the AP® European History Examination

To Accompany
Western Civilization
9th and 10th Editions
by Jackson J. Spielvogel

Susie Gerard
Lewis and Clark High School, Spokane, Washington

Patti Harrold
Edmond Memorial High School, Edmond, Oklahoma

Richard VerWiebe
Onondaga Community College, Syracuse, New York

Pamela Wolfe
The Yeshiva of Greater Washington, Silver Spring, Maryland

CENGAGE
Learning·

Australia • Brazil • Mexico • Singapore • United Kingdom • United States

AP® is a trademark registered and/or owned by the College Board, which was not involved in the production of, and does not endorse, this product.

National Geographic Learning/Cengage Learning is pleased to offer our college-level materials to high schools for Advanced Placement®, honors, and electives courses. To contact your National Geographic Learning representative, please call us toll-free at **1-888-915-3276** or visit us at **http://ngl.cengage.com**.

For permission to use material from this text or product, submit all requests online at **www.cengage.com/permissions** Further permissions questions can be emailed to **permissionrequest@cengage.com**.

ISBN: 978-1-337-29334-1

Cengage Learning
20 Channel Center Street
Boston, MA 02210
USA

Cengage Learning is a leading provider of customized learning solutions with office locations around the globe, including Singapore, the United Kingdom, Australia, Mexico, Brazil, and Japan. Locate your local office at: **www.cengage.com/global**.

Cengage Learning products are represented in Canada by Nelson Education, Ltd.

To learn more about Cengage Learning Solutions, visit **www.cengage.com**.

To find online supplements and other instructional support, please visit **www.cengagebrain.com**.

AP® is a trademark registered and/or owned by the College Board, which was not involved in the production of, and does not endorse, this product.

Printed in the United States of America
Print Number: 03   Print Year: 2017

CONTENTS

PREFACE

AP® European History is an exciting course. Spanning some seven centuries, it is filled with dramatic events, personalities, ideas, artistic creations, discoveries, and inventions. Fascinating in its own right, it is especially interesting for us because the European experience has often informed—and been informed by—our American experience.

Some of the most important learning can happen during review, when you step back and look at the broad arc of the history covered in the course. This book, designed to help you review the huge amount of material covered in an AP® European History course and prepare you for the AP® exam, is not a substitute for your textbook and what you learn in the classroom. The content in this book is condensed, but we are confident that it covers most of what you will see on the AP® exam.

We are deeply indebted to John Naisbitt and Louis Gallo, who reviewed our material and gave us their invaluable insights on both European history and the workings of our course and the Advanced Placement exam. We especially want to thank our families and friends, who gave us so much encouragement, support, and understanding throughout the writing process. Finally, we thank our students. Smart, hardworking, enthusiastic, they make teaching a deeply rewarding profession. Posing hard questions and offering nuanced reflections, they make us lifelong students.

Susie Gerard
Patti Harrold
Richard VerWiebe
Pamela Wolfe

September 2016

ABOUT THE AUTHORS

SUSIE GERARD is Social Studies Department Leader at Lewis and Clark High School in Spokane, Washington, where she has taught since 1984. Beginning with AP® European History in 1985, she now teaches three other Advanced Placement classes—U.S. History, World History, and U.S. Government and Politics. She received the Spokane Public Schools Distinguished Teacher Award in 2003 and National Board certification in 2007. A 2001 Gates Foundation Teacher Leadership Grant and a 2014–15 Microsoft Innovative Educator Grant allowed her to develop technology applications for curriculum development; she is technology mentor for her school district and teaches several district online courses. An AP® examination reader and now table leader since 1996, she is a presenter at College Board conferences nationwide. Materials she developed have been published by the College Board in *AP® European History Teachers' Guide* (1999), *AP® European History Special Focus: Whose History Is It?* (2007), and *AP® European History Professional Development Curriculum Module: Capitalism in Early Modern Europe* (2013).

PATTI HARROLD, a National Board Certified Teacher, began her career in 1975. She is Social Studies Department Chair at Edmond Memorial High School in Edmond, Oklahoma, where she has taught AP® European History, AP® Art History, AP® World History, and AP® U.S. History. Among the awards she has received are the Southwestern Region AP® Award (1997) and the National Council for the Social Studies Teacher of the Year (2004–2005). A College Board consultant who began presenting at national, regional, state, and local Pre-AP® and AP® workshops in 1992, she has been an AP® examination reader since 2004.

RICHARD VERWIEBE was a legislative assistant in Washington, D.C., for several years before earning two master's degrees and beginning work on a doctoral degree. He began teaching in 1995 at Tompkins Cortland Community College in Dryden, New York, where he was an instructor of western civilization and American history. From 2003 to 2006 he taught AP® European History at Skaneateles High School in Skaneateles, New York, before returning to the college level, again in the State University of New York system, as instructor of western civilization and American history at Onondaga Community College in Syracuse. He has served as a reader for the AP® European History exam since 2008.

PAMELA WOLFE is the History and Social Studies Department Chair at the Yeshiva of Greater Washington in Silver Spring, Maryland where she has taught since 1980. With a bachelor's degree in French and Secondary Education, she was originally hired to teach French and served as Chair of the Foreign Language Department. Since completing her master's degree in European History at the University of Maryland College Park, she has been teaching AP® European history for 28 years. She served as an AP® reader for European history for fifteen years and as a table leader for six years. She was on the AP® test development committee and runs College Board programs in AP® European History and AP® Human Geography. She teaches AP® summer institutes for teachers in both subjects at schools such as Manhattan College, Goucher College, Rutgers University, University of South Florida, the College of William and Mary, and Penn State University. She has served as a consultant for textbook companies by reviewing and writing texts and online programs for AP® students.

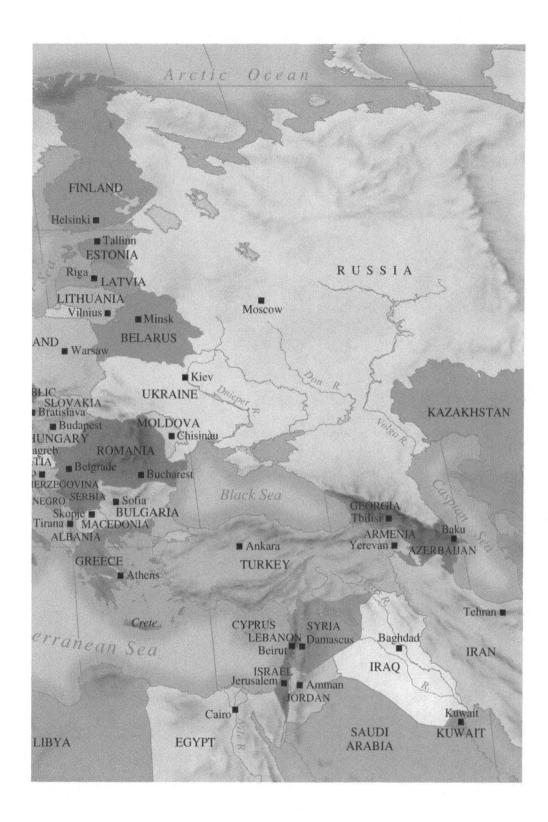

Part I

Strategies for the AP® Examination

PREPARING FOR THE AP®* EXAM

Whether you are taking an AP® course at your school or working on AP® independently, the stage is set for a great intellectual journey. As you progress and you burrow deeper and deeper into the coursework, you can see the broad concepts, events, conflicts, resolutions, and personalities that have shaped the history of our complex world. Examining the cultural, political, and economic developments that have brought great change, while at the same time acknowledging the continuities that remain throughout European history, is a thrilling task. Fleshing out those forces of change and continuity in European history is exciting. More exciting still is recognizing references to those forces when you hear about them in the media and understanding how history has shaped current world events.

But as spring approaches and the College Board examination begins to loom on the horizon, Advanced Placement® can seem quite intimidating, given the enormous scope and extent of the information you need to know. If you are intimidated by the College Board examination, you are certainly not alone.

The best way to approach an AP® examination is to master it, not let it master you. If you manage your time effectively, you will eliminate one major obstacle—learning a considerable amount of factual material. In addition, if you can think of the AP® test as a way to show off how your mind works, you have a leg up: attitude *does* help. If you are not one of those students, there is still much you can do to sideline your anxiety. This book is designed to put you on a fast track. Focused review and practice time will help you master the examination so that you can walk in with confidence and get a 5.

WHAT'S IN THIS BOOK

This book is keyed to the ninth and tenth editions of *Western Civilization*, by Jackson J. Spielvogel, but because it follows the College Board Curriculum Framework, it is compatible with all textbooks. It is divided into three sections. Part I offers suggestions for getting yourself ready, from signing up to take the test and sharpening your pencils to organizing a long-essay response. At the end of Part I, you will find a Diagnostic Test. When you go through the answers at the end of the test, a cluster of wrong answers in one area will show you where you are weak and thus where you should spend extra time studying. Page

---

AP® is a trademark registered and/or owned by the College Board, which was not involved in the production of, and does not endorse, this product.

references at the end of the Diagnostic Test indicate where you will find the discussion on that particular point in both the ninth and tenth editions of *Western Civilization*. There is a sample essay for the document-based question and a sample essay for a long-essay question. Scoring is explained, so you will have a better understanding of the results you achieved.

Part II is made up of fifteen chapters that follow the course of European history beginning with the fourteenth century. These chapters are not a substitute for your textbook and class discussion; they simply provide a brief review of the content of the course. At the end of each chapter, you will find ten content review questions that help you to internalize details that you will need to use in your essays and short-answer responses, six multiple-choice questions that model the style of the AP® examination, two short-answer questions, and two long-essay questions based on the material in that chapter. Again, you will find page references at the end of each chapter directing you to the discussion on that particular point in *Western Civilization*.

Part III has two complete AP® European History practice examinations. At the end of each test, you will find the answers, explanations, and references to *Western Civilization* for the fifty-five multiple-choice questions, as well as comments on what your essays for the four short-answer questions, the document-based question (DBQ), and the long-essay question should cover.

At the end of this book is a glossary. It provides short definitions of many of the terms you will encounter in your study of European history.

SETTING UP A REVIEW SCHEDULE

If you have been steadily doing your homework and keeping up with the coursework, you are in good shape. The key to preparing for the examination is to begin as early as possible; do not wait until the exam is just a week or two away to begin your studying. But even if you have done all that—or if it is too late to do all that—there are more ways to get it all together. This introduction to the exam will familiarize you with the types of questions you will see.

To begin, read Part I of this book. You will be much more comfortable going into the test if you understand how the test questions are designed and how best to approach them. Then, take the Diagnostic Test and see where you stand right now.

Take out a calendar and set up a schedule for yourself. If you begin studying early, you can chip away at the review chapters in Part II. You will be surprised—and pleased—by how much material you can cover with half an hour a day of study for a month or so before the test. Look carefully at the sections of the Diagnostic Test; if you missed a number of questions in one particular area, allow more time to review the chapters that cover that area of the course. The practice tests in Part III will give you more experience with the various kinds of multiple-choice questions and the wide range of short-answer and long-essay questions.

If time is short, skip reading the extended review. Instead, look at the Key Concepts at the beginning of each chapter to make sure you know the broad concepts, and then work on the content review and stimulus-based multiple-choice questions, the short-answer questions, and the long-essay questions at the end of each review. These will give you a good idea of your understanding of the topics. From there go on to the tests in Part III.

If time is *really* short, go straight from Part I to Part III. Taking practice tests over and over again is the fastest, most practical way to prepare.

BEFORE THE EXAM

By February, long before the exam, you need to make sure that you are registered to take the test. Many schools take care of the paperwork and handle the fees for their AP® students, but check with your teacher or the AP® coordinator to make sure that you are on the registration list. (If you have a documented disability and need test accommodations, talk with your teacher or AP® coordinator in the fall or as early as possible.) If you are studying AP® independently, call AP® Services at the College Board for the name of the local AP® coordinator, who will help you through the registration process.

The evening before the exam is not a good time for cramming. If you like, look over class notes or drift through your textbook, but concentrate on the broad outlines, not the small details, of the course. You might also want to skim through this book and read the Key Concepts and AP® Tips. Be sure to sharpen a fistful of no. 2 pencils with good erasers for the multiple-choice section of the test; set out several black or blue ballpoint pens for the document-based question, short-answer, and long-essay questions; get a watch if you don't have one (cell phones are not allowed in the testing room), and turn off its alarm; get a piece of fruit or a snack bar and a bottle of water for the break. Then relax. And get a good night's sleep. An extra hour of sleep is more valuable than an extra hour of study.

On the day of the examination, make certain to eat well to provide fuel for the brain. Studies show that students who eat a good meal before testing get higher grades. You will be given a ten-minute break between Section I and Section II; the European history exam lasts for over three hours, so be prepared for a long afternoon. You do not want to be distracted by a growling stomach or hunger pangs. Be sure to wear comfortable clothes, taking along a sweater in case the heating or air-conditioning is erratic. When you get to the testing location, make certain to comply with all security procedures. Cell phones are not allowed, so leave yours at home or in your locker. A watch might be a helpful item to bring to help you keep track of time; however, be sure that you turn off all alarms and beepers, or the watch will not be allowed in the testing room. Be careful not to drink a lot of liquids, necessitating trips to the bathroom, which take up valuable test time.

Remember, preparation is key, even on the fast track. Best wishes on your journey to success—go get that 5!

TAKING THE AP® EUROPEAN HISTORY EXAMINATION

The AP® European History exam consists of four parts in two sections. Section I includes Parts A and B. Section I Part A consists of 55 multiple-choice questions that you will have 55 minutes to answer; all questions will be organized into sets of two to five questions that follow an item of stimulus material (a primary or secondary source). Section I Part B consists of four short-answer questions that you will answer in 50 minutes. Section II includes its own Part A and Part B. Section II Part A contains a document-based question assessing a particular skill, such as Causation or Patterns of Continuity and Change Over Time, as well as your ability to apply your understanding of the documents using the historical thinking skills. You will be given 55 minutes to read the documents and answer the question. Section II Part B consists of two long-essay questions that both focus on the same historical thinking skill as it applies to two different time periods; you will choose to respond to one of these in the allotted 35 minutes. Keep an eye on your watch. Watch alarms are not allowed.

Here is a chart that shows the breakdown of the exam:

	Multiple-Choice Questions	Short-Answer Questions	Document-Based Question (Essay)	Long-Essay Question (Essay)
Weight	40% of exam	20% of exam	25% of exam	15% of exam
Number of Questions	55	4	1	Long-Essay Question: Choose one of two questions.
Time Allowed	55 minutes	50 minutes	90 minutes for reading and writing	
Suggested Pace	Approx. 45 seconds per question	Approx. 10 minutes per question	Suggested time: 15 minutes for reading and planning and 40 minutes to write	35 minutes to plan and write

THEMES IN AP® EUROPEAN HISTORY

The College Board has identified five themes that run through the AP® European History course: Interaction of Europe and the World (INT)—the interactions between Europeans and other parts of the world and the impact that those encounters had on European and non-European societies; Poverty and Prosperity (PP)—the development of economic systems and systems of production, the causes and consequences of economic and social inequality, and the responses of individuals,

6

groups, and the state to economic and social inequality; Objective Knowledge and Subjective Visions (OS)—the ways in which European thinkers began to arrive at methods for discerning objective truths and how they moved from reliance on absolute truth toward more subjective interpretations of the world; States and Other Institutions of Power (SP)—the development of different forms of European governments, the impact of warfare on European political systems, and the emergence of the concept of a balance of power; Individual and Society (IS)—the organization of family, class, and social groups in European society, tensions between the individual and society, and the ways in which the status of specific groups has changed over time. A theme won't appear in every chapter of the textbook, but it will turn up over and over again in the course. For example, Objective Knowledge and Subjective Visions evolved throughout the Renaissance era, in the Scientific Revolution, during the Enlightenment era, in the nineteenth century, as Romanticism began to challenge the rationalism of the Enlightenment era, and throughout the twentieth century as discoveries in the sciences began to cause people to adopt relativism in values and emphasize subjective sources of knowledge, expressing these ideas in philosophical and artistic genres. The themes can give you a real assist in writing long essays; they provide the big idea, which you support with your historical facts.

HISTORICAL THINKING SKILLS

Besides themes, the College Board has also identified nine historical thinking skills. You will need to demonstrate mastery of these skills while answering exam questions. The questions on the AP® test all involve application of one or more of these historical thinking skills, so reviewing the use of the skills will help you score better on the AP® exam.

I. Analyzing Historical Sources and Evidence	II. Making Historical Connections	III. Chronological Reasoning	IV. Creating and Supporting a Historical Argument
Analyzing Evidence: Content and Sourcing	Comparison	Causation	Argumentation
Interpretation	Contextualization	Patterns of Continuity and Change Over Time	
	Synthesis	Periodization	

Skill type I, Analyzing Historical Sources and Evidence, includes the skills of Analyzing Evidence: Content and Sourcing, and Interpretation. In order to demonstrate the ability to analyze evidence for its content and sourcing, you must be able to analyze a wide variety of documents, determining the intended audience, purpose, historical context, and point of view of the author and then draw credible conclusions, based upon the evidence. Interpretation requires you to exhibit the ability to analyze diverse interpretations of historical events, to consider the structure, evidence, and influences on varying interpretations of past events, and to evaluate the strength of those arguments. It also requires you to analyze and evaluate historical arguments, based on accessible evidence.

Skill type II, Making Historical Connections, includes the skills of Comparison, Contextualization, and Synthesis. Comparison requires you to analyze similarities and differences over place and time and to analyze differing interpretations of a historical event, while Contextualization requires you to connect specific movements and events to broader national, international, and global movements happening at the same time. Synthesis requires you to apply insights about the past to different contexts, including the present. You will need to make connections between a historical event or movement and other historical events, movements, ideas from other times, places, disciplines (such as geography, psychology, anthropology, etc.) or themes. For example, you might be writing an essay on the French Revolution and compare an aspect of it to the Russian Revolution or the American Revolution.

Skill type III, Chronological Reasoning Skills, includes Causation, Patterns of Continuity and Change Over Time, and Periodization. Causation requires you to analyze multiple short- and long-term causes and effects and differentiate among correlation, causation, and coincidence. Patterns of Continuity and Change Over Time requires you to recognize the changes that occurred over distinct periods of time and the continuity that existed among the different time periods. You will also need to connect those patterns of continuity and change to larger historical processes. To demonstrate mastery of Periodization, you must analyze events and processes, specifically dividing history into discrete eras. Specifically, you must be able to evaluate whether an event should be considered a turning point in European history and support your conclusion with evidence.

Skill type IV, Creating and Supporting a Historical Argument, requires you to demonstrate the skill of Argumentation and to support your argument with relevant historical evidence. Argumentation requires you to create an argument with an analytical thesis and pertinent and diverse historical evidence that addresses a historical question. It requires you to apply a specific historical thinking skill within your argument, based upon the prompt, and it expects you to examine the relationships among multiple sources as you develop your argument and support your thesis. Finally, it also requires you to use disparate evidence to synthesize new understandings of the past.

STRATEGIES FOR THE MULTIPLE-CHOICE SECTION

Here are some rules of thumb to help you work your way through the multiple-choice questions:

- **Multiple-choice scoring.** Each correct answer is worth 1 point; you will not lose points for incorrect answers. Therefore, it is worthwhile to answer every question, even if you have to guess. There are four possible answers for each question. If you cannot narrow down the choices at all, you have a 25 percent chance of guessing correctly. If you can eliminate even just one response, it will always improve your chances of guessing correctly. Your best strategy is to go through the entire multiple-choice section, answering all questions to which you know the answers. If you skip a question, be careful to skip that line on the answer sheet as well. Then go back and work on the questions you skipped. Leave yourself enough time to fill in answers—even if they are guesses— for all unanswered items before the time expires.

- **Read the question carefully.** Pressured for time, many students make the mistake of reading the questions too quickly or merely skimming them. By reading a question carefully, you may immediately have some idea about the correct answer. You can then look for it in the responses. Careful reading is especially important in EXCEPT or NOT questions because, unlike the typical multiple-choice question, all the answers are right except for one.

- **Eliminate any answer that you know is wrong.** You can write on the multiple-choice questions in the test book. As you read through the responses, draw a line through any answer you know is wrong.

- **Read all of the possible answers, then choose the most accurate response.** AP® exams are written to test your precise knowledge of a subject. Sometimes there are a few probable answers but one of them is more accurate. For example, a question dealing with the Berlin Conference of 1885 may have an answer that seems correct: "It was a conference of European nations." There may be an even better answer, however, one that is more specific to the topic: "It allowed European nations to carve up Africa for their economic gain."

- **Avoid absolute responses.** These answers often include the words "always" or "never." For example, the statement "Great Britain always led in the race for industrial growth" is an overstatement because although Britain led in industrialization during the nineteenth century, it gradually gave way to the United States.

- **Mark and skip tough questions.** If you are hung up on a question, mark it in the margin of the question book and go back to it later. (Do not forget to skip that question on your answer sheet too.) But be sure to answer all of the questions before the time is up, because there is *no penalty for incorrect answers.*

TYPES OF MULTIPLE-CHOICE QUESTIONS

There are various kinds of multiple-choice questions and all will require you to review a primary or secondary source and to answer questions drawn from the source and from your knowledge of European history.

It is important to remember that the answers to these questions may not be directly answered in the documents you are given. To answer these questions correctly, you have to draw on your knowledge related to the document—including historical context—and apply the historical skills you have learned in this course.

Here are some suggestions for how to approach each kind of stimulus.

Photograph/Illustration/Cartoon Questions

These questions require you to interpret a picture in order to gain information in a different way. **A good approach is to examine the picture before you read the question and possible responses.** Look for symbolism in the image; symbols are especially used in cartoons and paintings. Ask yourself what the artist or photographer is trying to convey. For example:

Source: Rijksmuseum, Amsterdam//DEA Picture Library/Getty Images

1. Which of the following statements is the most accurate description of Rembrandt's *The Night Watch*, above?
   (A) The painting shows that the Dutch Republic was controlled by the urban gentry and rural estate owners who promoted trade and commerce.
   (B) These Puritans are preparing to leave for the New World.
   (C) This play being performed by the Amsterdam Theater Company shows the importance of theater in Dutch society.
   (D) This painting shows that Dutch women were not involved in business.

Answer: **(A)** This painting shows one of Amsterdam's local militias. The focus on the protection of Amsterdam and its merchant oligarchy emphasizes the importance of the urban gentry and the prosperity created by trade and commerce in the Netherlands. Although their dress might lead you to assume they are Puritans (English Calvinists), they are not; they are probably Dutch Reformed, another Calvinist faith.

CHART/GRAPH QUESTIONS

These questions require you to examine the data on a chart or graph. While these questions are not difficult, spending too much time interpreting a chart or graph can slow you down. To avoid this, **first read the question and all of the possible answers so that you know what you are looking for. Before you look at the chart, you may be able to eliminate some obviously incorrect responses.** For example, analyze this chart on emigration:

	1876–1880	1881–1885	1886–1890	1891–1895	1896–1900	1901–1905	1906–1910
Europe	94	196	213	185	147	271	322
Ireland	650	1,422	1,322	988	759	743	662
Great Britain	102	174	162	119	88	127	172
Denmark	157	380	401	338	117	292	275
Norway	432	1,105	819	597	312	903	746
Sweden	301	705	759	587	249	496	347
Germany	108	379	207	163	47	50	44
Belgium	—	—	86	50	23	57	69
Netherlands	32	136	111	76	25	45	58
France	8	14	49	14	13	12	12
Spain	—	280	437	434	446	391	758
Portugal	258	356	423	609	417	464	694
Italy	396	542	754	842	974	1,706	1,938
Austria	48	90	114	182	182	355	469
Hungary	—	92	156	134	205	437	616
Russia	6	13	42	47	32	63	67

Source: Robert Gildea, *Barricades and Borders: Europe, 1800–1914* (Oxford, 1987), p. 283.

1. Which of the following statements does the above table best support?
   (A) The rate of emigration from northern Europe fell dramatically between 1876 and 1910.
   (B) Compared with other European nations, Russia saw the greatest growth in the rate of emigration between 1876 and 1910.
   (C) The overall number of emigrants from Germany dropped because of the impact of World War I.
   (D) During the late nineteenth century, Irish emigration reflected the country's independence from Great Britain.

ANSWER: **(B)** After analyzing the table, option A can be eliminated because emigration in the north actually grew during this time. Option C is incorrect because World War I did not begin until 1914, four years after the table's timeframe. Option D is incorrect because the Irish during this time were fleeing restrictive British policies and various waves of economic downturns caused by potato famines; Ireland did not become independent of Great Britain until the twentieth century. Because Russia's emigration rate grew over 1,000 percent, much more than that of any other country in the table, option B is the correct answer.

INTERPRETING A MAP

For history students, maps are used to describe not just geography but social and political organization as well. **Asked to interpret a map, you can pick up a lot of information just by looking at the key.**

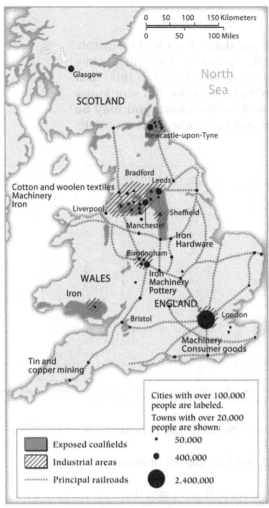

© Cengage Learning

1. This map of Great Britain in 1850 shows
   (A) how poor Scotland was at that time.
   (B) that very large cities grew only where there were rich coal deposits.
   (C) that the Irish produced cotton and woolen textiles.
   (D) the dependence on coal as fuel in the growth of industrial areas.

ANSWER: **(D)** The map shows the importance of coal as an energy source for British factories during the Industrial Revolution. As Britain shifted from water to coal as a source of power, factories no longer had to be situated along rivers and streams. Thus, factories and the towns that built up around them could be located near the new source of power. Although some large cities grew near coal deposits, they grew in other places as well.

INTERPRETING A PRIMARY TEXT SOURCE

Primary sources provide a historian's best window on the past and should be read carefully. Particularly when dealing with sources from the sixteenth or seventeenth century, be sure that you understand the author's meaning. Give careful consideration to the intended audience and, if you are familiar with the author listed, keep in mind their actions, beliefs, and motivations. Take any dates given to help you place the passage in context.

David Davies, The Case of Labourers in Husbandry Stated and Considered

The depriving of all landed property has beggared multitudes. It is plainly agreeable to sound policy, that as many individuals as possible in a state should possess an interest in the soil; because this attaches them strongly to the country and its constitution, and makes them zealous and resolute in defending them. But the gentry of this kingdom seem to have lost sight of this wise and salutary policy. Instead of giving to labouring people a valuable stake in the soil, the opposite measure has so long prevailed, that but few cottages, comparatively, have now any land about them. Formerly many of the lower sort of people [had land on which] they raised for themselves a considerable part of their subsistence. . . . But since these small parcels of ground have been swallowed up in the contiguous farms and enclosures, and the cottages themselves have been pulled down, the families which used to occupy them are crowded together in decayed farmhouses, with hardly ground enough about them for a cabbage garden; and being thus reduced to be mere hirelings, they are of course very liable to come to want. . . .

Thus an amazing number of people have been reduced from a comfortable state of partial independence to the precarious condition of hirelings, who, when out of work, must immediately come to their parish [for welfare]. And the great plenty of working hands always to be had when wanted, having kept down the price of labour below its proper level, the consequence is universally felt in the increased number of dependent poor.

Source: From David Davies, *The Case of Labourers in Husbandry Stated and Considered* (London, 1795), pp. 55–56.

1. Which of the following changes in 18th-century England was most likely the topic of Davies's concern?
   (A) Migration to rural areas
   (B) Immigration to England from colonial holdings
   (C) Enclosure of common lands
   (D) Starvation of English city dwellers

ANSWER: **(C)** In this passage, Davies is discussing the hardships created for small farmers by the enclosure of common lands by English noblemen. Between 1604 and 1914, the British Parliament enacted over 5,200 individual enclosure acts that effectively ended the use of common lands, forcing many farming families off of the land and into growing cities where many survived as factory workers. Answer choices A and B are incorrect. Although choice D sounds logical, the significant change that led to the growing poverty of the small farmers was C, the enclosure of common lands.

INTERPRETING A SECONDARY SOURCE

Secondary sources reveal historians' thoughts about the past, and often present an argument about causes or impacts of historical events. When presented with one or two sources, first identify the author's argument, then try to contextualize the issue. What era is being discussed? What was happening at that time?

> *This chapter must be one of pessimism. The Treaty includes no provisions for the economic rehabilitation of Europe—nothing to make the defeated Central Empires into good neighbors, nothing to stabilize the new States of Europe, nothing to reclaim Russia; nor does it promote in any way a compact of economic solidarity amongst the Allies themselves; no arrangement was reached at Paris for restoring the disordered finances of France and Italy, or to adjust the systems of the Old World and the New.*

> **Source**: John Maynard Keynes, British economist, *The Economic Consequences of the Peace*, 1920.

1. Leaders of which of the following nations would have been least likely to agree with the perspective advanced by John Maynard Keynes?
   (A) France
   (B) Germany
   (C) The United States
   (D) England

ANSWER: **(A)** In this document, John Maynard Keynes advanced the argument that the Treaty of Versailles did not provide the basis for a lasting peace in Europe. Since the nation that most vehemently wanted to punish Germany for World War I was France, French leaders would have been the most likely to disagree with the statement by Keynes.

SHORT-ANSWER QUESTIONS

You are required to write responses to a total of four short-answer questions in the provided 50 minutes. Your score on this portion will count for 20 percent of your final exam score. Each question will consist of three parts, and at least two of the four questions will contain elements of internal choice, allowing you to demonstrate the content that you know best. Each question will require you to use your knowledge about European history to respond to a stimulus such as a primary or secondary source, a map or image, or a general statement (without a stimulus) about European history. **You do not need to develop and defend a thesis—however, bulleted answers will automatically receive a zero.** Be sure to write legibly so that you earn credit for your responses. Instead, focus on answering the questions fully (**and in complete sentences**) and on including evidence or examples to support your response. The questions are designed to give you the freedom to choose from a wide range of possible examples. This means that you can pick from what you might have studied in depth in class or what you might have read more about, rather than worrying about knowing one, specific fact or event.

For example, you might be asked to answer a short-answer question such as the following:

1. Compare England and France in the 17th century.
   A) Briefly explain ONE political difference between England and France in the 17th century.
   B) Briefly explain ONE economic similarity between England and France in the 17th century.
   C) Briefly explain ONE reason for the political difference you identified in Part A.

ANSWER: A good answer to Part A would identify the fact that while France was consolidating power and moving toward absolutism in the 17th century, England was moving toward a Constitutional monarchy. The answer to this part should explain that the two politically divergent systems were well-established by the end of the 17th century and should be written in three to four full sentences.

A good answer to Part B would explain that while the two nations differed politically in the 17th century, both pursued an economy based on mercantilism. The answer to this part should point out the colonization of the New World and the role of mercantilism in the prosperity of both nations. This answer should also be written in three to four full sentences.

A good answer to Part C would explain that the development of a Constitutional monarchy in England occurred as a result of the growing power of an assertive Parliament and the long tradition of Parliamentary power, dating back to the Magna Carta, while absolutism in France resulted from a search for order following the French religious wars of the 16th century. This answer should also be written in three to four full sentences.

See the short-answer questions found at the end of each chapter for more information about how to answer these questions.

STRATEGIES FOR SECTION II

You are required to write essays for one document-based question and one long-essay question in Section II of the AP® European History examination. Section II Part A presents the Document-Based Question. It is mandatory and will count as 25 percent of your final score. For the DBQ, you are given 55 minutes to read the documents, organize your answer, and write your response. The essay will ask you to use your historical thinking skills in addition to analysis of one or more of the themes of European History. In Section II Part B, you will respond to one of two Long-Essay Questions, both of which will focus on the same historical thinking skill as applied to different time periods. You will be asked to choose one question to answer in the given 35-minute time period. Your score on this portion will count for 15 percent of your final score.

> **AP® Tip**
>
> For each essay in Section II, you need to take a few minutes to plan your response. Time spent on good notes or an outline is important for a number of reasons:
>
> - It provides you with an opportunity to brainstorm before writing.
> - It allows you to determine your analytical thesis after seeing the evidence you can gather to support your argument.
> - It lets you organize your thinking and helps you determine the groupings you will use in your DBQ essay.
>
> Once you have outlined your essay, it is time to write. Remember that examination readers are looking for a clear thesis backed up with specific evidence for support. Concentrate on setting out accurate information in straightforward, concise prose. Readers can spot efforts to mask vague information with flowery prose.

THE DOCUMENT-BASED QUESTION (DBQ)

The DBQ is considered by many students to be the most complex and challenging component of the AP® examination. As its name implies, the DBQ presents you with a wide variety of primary-source information in the form of a series of seven documents. Primary sources are contemporaneous with a time period or event and include everything from maps, political cartoons, photographs, and illustrations to speeches, essays, books, documentaries, and editorials. In order to earn the highest scores, DBQ essays must incorporate outside information that is not included in the documents.

Both the long-essay and the document-based question essay require you to utilize your knowledge of the topic. But with the DBQ, your essay needs to be grounded in the documents as well. Your goal is to demonstrate your ability to analyze the purpose, point of view, and substance of each document, and then combine this information with your own general knowledge in an analytical essay.

The document-based question is worth up to 7 points. Be sure to write legibly, so that readers can give you credit for your response.

A quality DBQ essay, according to the AP® European History rubric, does all of the following:

- **Thesis and Argument Development (0–2 points).** The points in this category are earned by writing an acceptable thesis (1 point) and developing and supporting a solid argument that accounts for historical complexity (1 point). An acceptable thesis is one that makes an analytical argument that responds specifically to what the prompt is calling for you to address in the DBQ. You must not simply restate the question; your thesis must reflect your analysis of the documents. A generic statement such as "There were many political, economic, and social causes of..." would not be an acceptable thesis. As well, your thesis does not have to be stated in one sentence. Writing a "thesis paragraph" is an excellent way to show the full range of your thesis. Remember that your thesis must directly address all parts of the prompt; addressing only some parts of it will not earn you this point. The thesis point is an important one to earn: you need a solid thesis to guide your essay. The second point in this category is equally important, because your essay needs to illustrate your ability to make a logical argument that supports your thesis and your ability to support that argument with evidence from the documents and from outside information. A well-supported argument will show your understanding of the complexities of the documents and the differing perspectives presented on the topic of your essay.

■ **Document Analysis (0-2 points).** To earn the first point in this category, you must use at least 6 documents to support your thesis or argument. To get credit for using a document, you cannot simply list the document number in a sentence or make a laundry list that does nothing more than summarize the content of each document; you must talk about each document individually and must use the documents as supporting evidence. To earn the second point in this category, you must provide a deeper analysis of at least four of the documents by addressing not only the content, but also one of the following: intended audience, purpose, historical context, or point of view. Although you can earn one point for analyzing the content of at least six of the documents, you can earn two points for analyzing both the content and either the intended audience, the purpose, the historical context, or the point of view of at least four of the documents.

To earn the second point in this category, it is essential that you consider how characteristics such as class, gender, nationality, profession, and the like shaped the views of a document's author. The type of document or purpose of the document can also be important in determining the point of view and the reliability of the author. For example, a diary entry might be more truthful than a public document because the diarist would not expect the entry to be subject to public scrutiny. It is not enough to say what point of view you see presented in a document; you must also account for *why* that point of view exists in the source. In addition, ask yourself how the point of view affects the document's content. A good place to begin looking for clues to the point of view is the source line of the document. The source line indicates the author or speaker in the document and the date of the document and helps you place the document in a larger historical context. It is also important to consider how that historical context impacts the content, perspective, and purpose of the document. The source line often has other important pieces of information about the document. *Read and analyze the source line BEFORE you read the document!* That will help you more easily write about the point of view rather than just write about the gist of what the document says.

■ **Using Evidence Beyond the Documents (0-2 points).** You can earn up to two points for incorporating outside information into your essay: one for analyzing outside evidence to support the thesis or a relevant argument and another for contextualization. To earn the point for outside evidence, you will need to support your argument with at least one fact or piece of evidence that was not found in or suggested by any of the documents (0–1 point). For example, if you were writing a DBQ on the causes of the French Revolution and the documents all suggested political causes, you could discuss the debt and the tax burden placed upon the third estate as economic causes to earn the outside evidence point. To earn the point for contextualization, you must explicitly connect historical events to the broader historical context in which they occurred (0–1 point). For example, when analyzing a historical event, **discuss other things that were happening around the same time that might have had an impact on the reasons why the event occurred or the ways that people reacted to it.**

■ **Synthesis (0–1 point).** To earn this point, your essay must extend the thesis/argument by connecting the topic of the question to other time periods, geographic regions, contexts or circumstances, or other disciplines. For example, if your thesis/argument compared the economic differences between the 19th and 20th centuries in Russia, analyzing a political difference between Russia in those centuries could count for synthesis. **A QUICK MENTION of a connection is NOT ENOUGH—you must provide a several sentence analysis of how the items connect in order to earn the point!**

AP® Tip

In order to earn all of the points for the DBQ, you cannot "double dip." For example, the information you use for contextualization cannot be the same piece of information that you use for the historical context of one of the documents, the analysis of outside evidence, or the synthesis. Earning each of the different points requires the use of your knowledge of the time period and some outside evidence, but you must use different examples for each point to successfully earn all of the points.

Take a look at this DBQ, which contains seven documents.

1. Using the documents, evaluate the responsibility of various nations for the outbreak of World War I.

Document 1

Source: Europe in 1914.

© Cengage Learning

Document 2

Source: Telegram from Kaiser Wilhelm II of Germany to Tsar Nicholas II of Russia, July 31, 1914.

...While this action was proceeding your troops were mobilized against Austro-Hungary, my ally, thereby, as I have already pointed out to you, my mediation has been made almost illusory....I now receive authentic news of serious preparations for war on my Eastern frontier. Responsibility for the safety of my empire forces preventive measures of defence upon me. In my endeavours to maintain the peace of the world I have gone to the utmost limit possible. The responsibility for the disaster which is now threatening the whole civilized world will not be laid at my door. In this moment it still lies in your power to avert it. Nobody is threatening the honour or power of Russia....

Document 3

Source: "How Germany Attacked Our Commerce," in *The Great War Magazine: The Standard History of the All-Europe Conflict,* Part 11, October 31, 1914.

The greatest war of modern times, and perhaps in the whole history of the human race, was begun by Germany using the crime of a schoolboy as an excuse.

Document 4

Source: German Chancellor Theobald von Bethmann-Hollweg in a speech to the Reichstag, August 1914.

Where the responsibility in this greatest of all wars lies is quite evident to us. Outwardly responsible are the men in Russia who planned and carried into effect the general mobilization of the Russian army. But in reality and truth the British Government is responsible. The London Cabinet could have made war impossible if they had unequivocally told Petersburg that England was not willing to let a continental war of the Great Powers result from the Austro-Hungarian conflict with Serbia. . . . Therefore, England, together with Russia (I have spoken about Russian on the 4th of August), is answerable before God and man for this catastrophe which has come over Europe and over mankind.

Document 5

Source: Article 231, The Versailles Treaty, June 28, 1919.

The Allied and Associated Governments affirm and Germany accepts the responsibility of Germany and her allies for causing all the loss and damage to which the Allied and Associated Governments and their nationals have been subjected as a consequence of the war imposed upon them by the aggression of Germany and her allies.

Document 6

Source: Sidney Bradshaw Fay, American historian, *The Origins of the World War*, 1928, revised edition 1930.

None of the Powers wanted a European War. Their governing rulers and ministers, with very few exceptions, all foresaw that it must be a frightful struggle, in which the political results were not absolutely certain. . . . Nevertheless, a European war broke out. Why? Because in each country political and military leaders did certain things, which led to mobilizations and declarations of war, or failed to do certain things which might have prevented them. In this sense, all the European countries, in a greater or lesser degree, were responsible.

Document 7

Source: *The Constitution of the Ujedinjenje ili Smrt—Unification or Death* (Terrorist organization more commonly known as the Black Hand), May 1911.

I. Purpose and Name

Article 1. For the purpose of realising the national ideals—the Unification of Serbdom—an organization is hereby created, whose members may be any Serbian irrespective of sex, religion, place or birth, as well as anybody else who will sincerely serve this idea.

Article 2. The organisation gives priority to the revolutionary struggle rather than relies on cultural striving, therefore its institution is an absolutely secret one for wider circles.

Article 3. The organization bears the name: "Ujedinjenje ili Smrt".

Article 4. In order to carry into effect its task the organization will do the following things:

(1) Following the character of its raison d etre it will exercise its influence over all the official factors in Serbia—which is the Piedmont of Serbdom—as also over all the strata of the State and over the entire social life in it:

(2) It will carry out a revolutionary organisation in all the territories where Serbians are living:

(3) Beyond the frontiers, it will fight with all means against all enemies of this idea:

(4) It will maintain friendly relations with all the States, nations, organisations, and individual persons who sympathise with Serbia and the Serbian race:

(5) It will give every assistance to those nations and organisations who are fighting for their own national liberation and unification.

> ## AP® Tip
>
> *Do not wait until you've read the documents to develop your own personal knowledge.* Even before reading the documents, take a few minutes to brainstorm information that you can recall about the topic. If time permits, organize this information so that you can construct the essay while incorporating the documents into the essay. When the document information is similar to what you have brainstormed, present that knowledge as it is expressed in the documents. Possibly the document material can be used to help you analyze other issues.

Your first step is to brainstorm the information that you know about the prompt and then analyze each document in order to come up with evidence to create your thesis. What is the meaning of the document? What or who is the source, and how does that affect his point of view? The source provides important clues to the position being put forth in the document. As you analyze the meaning or significance of the document, jot down margin notes—generalizations that relate to the document, the prompt, or the point of view in the document. For example:

- **Margin note for Document 1** Shows the alliances that existed on the eve of World War I. Did these alliances affect actions taken in the days before war broke out?
- **Margin note for Document 2** Shows the German Kaiser attempting to maintain peace and blaming the imminent outbreak of war on Russian mobilization. He might be biased because he doesn't want Germany to be blamed for the war.
- **Margin note for Document 3** Clearly blames Germany for the war—biased because it is a patriotic weekly magazine that probably would have been running articles written to gather public support for the war. Is it propaganda?
- **Margin note for Document 4** Clearly blames England and Russia for the war. This document and Document 2, both German, might exhibit the hidden agenda of justifying German actions surrounding the outbreak of war.
- **Margin note for Document 5** Clearly blames the war on Germany and the Triple Alliance—probably biased because it was written by the winners of the war and used to justify the reparations imposed on Germany. The winners would not have blamed themselves for the war. This document is similar to Document 3.
- **Margin note for Document 6** Written a decade after the war ended, this source blames all of the great powers for the war. This author might be more unbiased because he was an American and an historian who was using hindsight to understand, not justify, the actions of the various nations.
- **Margin note for Document 7** Written during a time of unrest in the Balkan region, this source clearly demonstrates that at least some Serbians supported the organization that was responsible for

the assassination of Archduke Franz Ferdinand. The organization directly stated that it would support national liberation movements in other nations.

Once you have analyzed the documents, combine the evidence from the documents with the information you have brainstormed to create your thesis and arguments. Often the prompt may give you a hint to help you figure out the arguments that you can use to address the prompt. Here the prompt suggests that one way to group the documents is to categorize them by which country or countries they blame for the war. For example, Documents 3 and 5 blame Germany, an Alliance power; Documents 2, 4, and 7 blame Serbia, England and Russia, which were Entente powers. Each of these groups contains two or more logically connected documents that are relevant to the prompt, so these groups of documents suggest two arguments that could be used to build your thesis. What should go in a third argument? You have several choices. You could create a third argument by connecting Documents 1 and 6. Document 6 assigns responsibility to all of the great powers; Document 1 indicates that this assumption could be true because all of the major powers had formed entangling alliances before the war. Another possibility for the third group would be to connect Document 6 with Documents 4, 5, and 7. In this case, the assumption that all of the great powers contributed to the outbreak of war would be corroborated by the accusations and statements made in Documents 4, 5, and 7. Remember that usually there are many ways to group the documents to form convincing arguments; you just need to be sure that your groups are logical and explicit and appropriate to the prompt.

After identifying the arguments that can be created from the documents and combining them with outside evidence, you need to address the intended audience, purpose, historical context, or point of view for each of the documents that you use in your essay. For example, you could point out that Bethmann-Hollweg, speaking before the Reichstag and probably asking the legislature for money to fight the war, wanted to convince the Reichstag that the war was necessary in order to maintain German honor and security. He would need to blame England and Russia for the war and paint them as threats to Germany. Just stating that Bethmann-Hollweg used his speech to blame England and Russia for the war does not adequately define the purpose or demonstrate point of view. You must analyze the particular perspective or purpose of the author and also explain the reasons for that viewpoint in order to get credit for this portion of the document analysis. A good strategy is to analyze the intended audience, purpose, historical context, or point of view of all of the documents, ensuring you have reasonable attempts for all or all but one of the documents, because you want to earn as many points as possible for analysis and argumentation.

Once you have analyzed the documents and constructed your groups, you should use this information to help you write an analytical thesis. *Make sure your thesis answers the prompt with an argument, and does not just repeat the prompt.* For example, the thesis "Various powers were responsible for the outbreak of World War I" would not be acceptable. Here is a better one: "There are various perspectives concerning which nations should be assigned responsibility for the outbreak of World War I. Members of the winning Triple Entente often blamed Germany and her allies, assigning blame and demanding reparations, while members of the losing Triple Alliance claimed that the war was actually perpetrated by members of the Triple Entente. Finally, from hindsight, some historians have concluded that all of the great powers shared responsibility for the catastrophe that raged across the European continent from 1914 to 1918." This thesis paragraph suggests a variety of evidentiary claims and demonstrates the range of the documentary sources, providing the reader with a roadmap that is much more than a simple restatement of the prompt. With good planning at the beginning, your DBQ should be in great shape.

There are three DBQs in this book, one in the Diagnostic Test and one in each of the practice tests. There are also sample DBQs in the appendix of the textbook. Use these questions to get practice analyzing writing document-based question essays.

LONG-ESSAY QUESTIONS

The AP® European History exam concludes by asking students to write one long essay. You will be required to choose one question for your long-essay response from two possible prompts. The key to choosing a question is to determine how much evidence you can provide in the essay. Plan to devote 35 minutes to this essay.

Like the DBQ, there is no single "correct" answer for these essay questions; however, unlike the DBQ, you will not be given any documents upon which to base your answer. Your essay will come from your own store of knowledge of European history.

Also like the DBQ, there is not a required length for the long-essay. A good rule of thumb is to write a standard four to five paragraph essay that directly addresses all parts of the prompt thoroughly.

You will be given your choice of two long-essay prompts. Choose the one that you know you can answer well. The two prompts will focus on the same historical thinking skill and will focus on either Causation, Patterns of Continuity and Change Over Time, Periodization, or Comparison.

An essential aspect of writing an effective essay is understanding the tasks required. The following is a list of terms often used in prompts. These terms have shades of meaning that suggest how to construct your essay.

- **Analyze:** Break the topic into its parts and determine the relationship between those parts.
- **Assess:** Determine a judgment regarding a specific claim or statement, prompting you to take sides on a topic.
- **Compare:** Discuss both similarities and differences.
- **Contrast:** Discuss differences, although similarities may be noted.
- **Describe:** Give an account that presents a detailed word picture.
- **Discuss:** Present an argument that examines different sides or opinions regarding a specific topic.
- **Evaluate:** Discuss the advantages and disadvantages, the positive and negative aspects of a topic.
- **Explain:** Clarify a topic by presenting a cause or reason.
- **To what extent:** Argue a topic in terms of "how much."

Unlike the DBQ, the long-essay is graded on a scale from 0 to 6. Once you have selected your questions, keep the following in mind as you write:

- **Manage your time:** Try to split your time evenly between the two essays, allowing thirty-five minutes for each.
- **Address the entire prompt:** Make sure that you answer ALL parts of the question, even if you have little evidence.
- **Create a strong thesis:** A strong thesis will give you points toward your overall score. In addition, it will provide the structure for the rest of your essay.
- **Do not simply restate the question when writing your introductory paragraph:** You need to make an argument and support that argument within your essay.
- **Write legibly:** If the reader has insurmountable difficulty reading your work, you will lose points.
- **Pay attention to chronology:** If you provide a wealth of information about the wrong time period, you will not have addressed the prompt and will not receive points for your effort.
- **Organize your essay so it flows from point to point:** Write a balanced essay, trying to devote each paragraph in the body of your essay to a single idea and supporting that idea with relevant evidence.

Finally, remember that it is "quality, not quantity" when it comes to a good essay. Each assertion should be backed up by some evidence, and more is better. But some information presented effectively and clearly is better than a lot of information presented haphazardly.

A quality Long Essay, according to the AP® European History rubric, does all of the following:

- **Thesis (0–1 point):** Contains a thesis that directly addresses all parts of the question and does more than restate the question.
- **Argument Development: Using the Targeted Historical Thinking Skill (0–2 points):** Describes the required information in the context of the historical skill (0–1 point) and explains the reasons for the developments described (0–1 point). For example, a description of similarities and differences in a comparison essay would earn one point while an analysis of the reasons for those similarities and differences and/or an analysis of their relative importance would add a second point.
- **Argument Development: Using Evidence (0–2 points):** Addresses the topic of the question and/or supports the stated thesis (or makes a relevant argument) using specific evidence (0–1 point). Supports the stated thesis (or makes a relevant argument) using specific evidence, clearly and consistently stating how the evidence supports the thesis or argument, and establishing clear linkages between the evidence and the thesis or argument (0–1 more point). In this case, if you earn the first point for providing relevant specific evidence, then you can earn a second point for establishing clear linkages between the evidence and the thesis.

- **Synthesis (0–1 point):** Extends the argument by connecting it to another theme or appropriate analytical category, another time period or region, or another discipline. The connection must be explained well and must be more than a brief mention of a possible connection.

THEMATIC LEARNING OBJECTIVES

As indicated earlier, the College Board has identified five themes, or topics, that can guide our exploration of history. They have also identified a series of learning objectives, categorized by theme, to help identify important understandings that they expect students to grasp. As you study European History, refer often to these themes and objectives and ensure that you can offer analysis and factual details for each. On the AP® exam, every question will measure your understanding of one of these objectives. For a few weeks prior to the exam, it would be a good idea to thoroughly study the themes and objectives so that you can see the big picture.

INTERACTION OF EUROPE AND THE WORLD (INT)

Essential Understanding	In particular, students can…
Students demonstrate understanding of the reasons that Europeans sought contact and interaction with other parts of the world.	INT-1: Assess the relative influence of economic, religious, and political motives in promoting exploration and colonization.
	INT-2: Analyze the cultural beliefs that justified European conquest of overseas territories and how they changed over time.
Students demonstrate understanding of the political, technological, and intellectual developments that enabled European contact and interaction with other parts of the world.	INT-3: Analyze how European states established and administered overseas commercial and territorial empires.
	INT-4: Explain how scientific and intellectual advances—resulting in more effective navigational, cartographic, and military technology—facilitated European interaction with other parts of the world.
Students demonstrate understanding of the ways in which encounters between Europe and the world shaped European culture, politics, and society.	INT-5: Evaluate the impact of the Columbian Exchange—the global exchange of goods, plants, animals, and microbes—on Europe's economy, society and culture.
	INT-6: Assess the role of overseas trade, labor, and technology in making Europe part of a global economic network and in encouraging the development of new economic theories and state policies.
	INT-7: Analyze how contact with non-European peoples increased European social and cultural diversity and affected attitudes toward race.
	INT-8: Evaluate the United States' economic and cultural influence on Europe and responses to this influence in Europe.

Essential Understanding	In particular, students can…
Students demonstrate understanding of the impact that contact with Europe had on non-European societies.	**INT-9**: Assess the role of European contact on overseas territories through the introduction of disease, participation in the slave trade and slavery, effects on agricultural and manufacturing patterns, and global conflict.
	INT-10: Explain the extent of and causes for non-Europeans' adoption of or resistance to European cultural, political, or economic values and institutions, and explain the causes of their reactions.
	INT-11: Explain how European expansion and colonization brought non-European societies into global economic, diplomatic, military, and cultural networks.

Poverty and Prosperity (PP)

Essential Understanding	In particular, students can…
Students demonstrate understanding of the ways in which capitalism developed as an economic system.	**PP-1**: Explain how and why wealth generated from new trading, financial, and manufacturing practices and institutions created a market and then a consumer economy.
	PP-2: Identify changes in agricultural production and evaluate their impact on economic growth and the standard of living in preindustrial Europe.
	PP-3: Explain how geographic, economic, social, and political factors affected the pace, nature, and timing of industrialization in western and eastern Europe.
	PP-4: Explain how the development of new technologies and industries—as well as new means of communication, marketing, and transportation— contributed to expansion of consumerism and increased standards of living and quality of life in the nineteenth and twentieth centuries.
	PP-5: Analyze the origins, characteristics, and effects of the post-World War II "economic miracle" and the economic integration (the Euro zone).
Students demonstrate understanding of the ways in which the organization of society changed as a result of or in response to the development and spread of capitalism.	**PP-6**: Analyze how expanding commerce and industrialization from the sixteenth through the nineteenth centuries led to the growth of cities and changes in the social structure, most notably a shift from a landed to a commercial elite.
	PP-7: Explain how environmental conditions, the Agricultural Revolution, and industrialization contributed to demographic changes, the organization of manufacturing, and alterations in the family economy.
	PP-8: Analyze socialist, communist, and fascist efforts to develop responses to capitalism and why these efforts gained support during times of economic crisis.
Students demonstrate understanding of the causes and consequences of economic and social inequality.	**PP-9**: Assess how peasants across Europe were affected by and responded to the policies of landlords, increased taxation, and the price revolution in the early modern period.

Essential Understanding	In particular, students can…
	PP-10: Explain the role of social inequality in contributing to and affecting the nature of the French Revolution and subsequent revolutions throughout the nineteenth and twentieth centuries.
	PP-11: Analyze the social and economic causes and consequences of the Great Depression in Europe.
	PP-12: Evaluate how the expansion of a global consumer economy after World War II served as a catalyst to opposition movements in Eastern and Western Europe.
Students demonstrate understanding of the ways in which individuals, groups, and the state respond to economic and social inequality.	**PP-13**: Analyze how cities and states have attempted to address the problems brought about by economic modernization, such as poverty and famine, through regulating morals, policing marginal populations, and improving public health.
	PP-14: Explain how industrialization elicited critiques from artists, socialists, workers' movements, and feminist organizations.
	PP-15: Analyze efforts of government and nongovernmental reform movements to respond to poverty and other social problems in the nineteenth and twentieth centuries.
	PP-16: Analyze how democratic, authoritarian, and totalitarian governments of the left and right attempted to overcome the financial crises of the 1920s and 1930s.

OBJECTIVE KNOWLEDGE AND SUBJECTIVE VISIONS (OS)

Essential Understanding	In particular, students can…
Students demonstrate understanding of the roles traditional sources of authority (church and classical antiquity) played in the creation and transmission of knowledge and factors that altered those roles.	**OS-1**: Account for the persistence of traditional and folk understandings of the cosmos and causation, even with the advent of the Scientific Revolution.
	OS-2: Analyze how religious reform in the sixteenth and seventeenth centuries, the expansion of printing, and the emergence of civic venues such as salons and coffeehouses challenged the control of the church over the creation and dissemination of knowledge.
	OS-3: Explain how political revolution and war from the seventeenth century on altered the role of the church in political and intellectual life and the response of religious authorities and intellectuals to such challenges.
Students demonstrate understanding of the reasons why and the ways in which Europeans came to rely on the scientific method and reason in place of traditional authorities.	**OS-4**: Explain how a worldview based on science and reason challenged and preserved social order and roles, especially the roles of women.
	OS-5: Analyze how the development of Renaissance humanism, the printing press, and the scientific method contributed to the emergence of a new theory of knowledge and conception of the universe.

Essential Understanding	In particular, students can…
	OS-6: Explain how European exploration and colonization were facilitated by the development of the scientific method and led to a reexamination of cultural norms.
	OS-7: Analyze how and to what extent the Enlightenment encouraged Europeans to understand human behavior, economic activity, and politics as governed by natural laws.
	OS-8: Explain the emergence, spread, and questioning of scientific, technological, and positivist approaches to addressing social problems.
	OS-9: Explain how new theories of government and political ideologies attempted to provide a coherent explanation for human behavior and the extent to which they adhered to or diverged from traditional explanations based on religious beliefs.
Students demonstrate understanding of the reasons why and the ways in which Europeans came to value subjective interpretations of reality.	**OS-10**: Analyze the means by which individualism, subjectivity, and emotion came to be considered a valid source of knowledge.
	OS-11: Explain how and why religion increasingly shifted from a matter of public concern to one of private belief over the course of European history.
	OS-12: Analyze how artists used strong emotions to express individuality and political theorists encouraged emotional identification with the nation.
	OS-13: Explain how and why modern artists began to move away from realism and toward abstraction and the non-rational, rejecting traditional aesthetics.

STATES AND OTHER INSTITUTIONS OF POWER (SP)

Essential Understanding	In particular, students can…
Students demonstrate understanding of the forms European governments have taken and how they have changed over time.	**SP-1**: Explain the emergence of civic humanism and new conceptions of political authority during the Renaissance, as well as subsequent theories and practices that stressed the political importance and rights of the individual.
	SP-2: Explain the emergence of and theories behind the New Monarchies and absolutist monarchies, and evaluate the degree to which they were able to centralize power in their states.
	SP-3: Trace the changing relationship between states and ecclesiastical authority and the emergence of the principle of religious toleration.
	SP-4: Analyze how the new political and economic theories from the seventeenth century and the Enlightenment challenged absolutism and shaped the development of constitutional states, parliamentary governments, and the concept of individual rights.
	SP-5: Assess the role of colonization, the Industrial Revolution, total warfare, and economic depressions in altering the government's relationship to the economy, both in overseeing economic activity and in addressing its social impact.

Essential Understanding	In particular, students can...
	SP-6: Explain how new ideas of political authority and the failure of diplomacy led to world wars, political revolutions, and the establishment of totalitarian regimes in the twentieth century.
Students demonstrate understanding of the reasons why and the ways in which European governments moved toward or reacted against representative and democratic principles and practices.	SP-7: Explain the emergence of representative government as an alternative to absolutism.
	SP-8: Explain how and why various groups, including communists and fascists, undermined parliamentary democracy through the establishment of regimes that maintained dictatorial control while manipulating democratic forms.
	SP-9: Analyze how various movements for political and social equality—such as feminism, anti-colonialism, and campaigns for immigrants' rights—pressured governments and redefined citizenship.
Students demonstrate understanding of the ways in which civil institutions develop apart from governments and the impact they have had upon European states.	SP-10: Trace the ways in which new technologies from the printing press to the Internet have shaped the development of civil society and enhanced the role of public opinion.
	SP-11: Analyze how religious and secular institutions and groups attempted to limit monarchical power by articulating theories of resistance to absolutism and by taking political action.
	SP-12: Assess the role of civic institutions in shaping the development of representative and democratic forms of government.
Students demonstrate understanding of the reasons for and the ways in which changes in warfare affected diplomacy, the European state system, and the balance of power.	SP-13: Evaluate how the emergence of new weapons, tactics, and methods of military organization changed the scale and cost of warfare, required the centralization of power, and shifted the balance of power.
	SP-14: Analyze the role of warfare in remaking the political map of Europe and in shifting the global balance of power in the nineteenth and twentieth centuries.
Students demonstrate understanding of the ways in which the concept of a balance of power emerged, developed, and eventually became institutionalized.	SP-15: Assess the impact of war, diplomacy, and overseas exploration and colonization on European diplomacy and balance of power until 1789.
	SP-16: Explain how the French Revolution and the revolutionary and Napoleonic wars shifted the European balance of power and encouraged the creation of a new diplomatic framework.
	SP-17: Explain the role of nationalism in altering the European balance of power, and explain attempts made to limit nationalism as a means to ensure continental stability.
	SP-18: Evaluate how overseas competition and changes in the alliance system upset the Concert of Europe and set the stage for World War I.
	SP-19: Explain the ways in which the Common Market and collapse of the Soviet Empire changed the political balance of power, the status of the nation-state, and global political alliances.

INDIVIDUAL AND SOCIETY (IS)

Essential Understanding	In particular, students can...
Students demonstrate understanding of the forms that family, class, and social groups have taken in European history and the ways in which they have changed over time.	**IS-1:** Explain the characteristics, practices, and beliefs of traditional communities in preindustrial Europe and how they were challenged by religious reform.
	IS-2: Explain how the growth of commerce and changes in manufacturing challenged the dominance of corporate groups and traditional estates.
	IS-3: Evaluate the role of technology, from the printing press to modern transportation and telecommunications, in forming and transforming society.
	IS-4: Analyze how and why the nature and role of the family has changed over time.
	IS-5: Explain why and how class emerged as a basis for identity and led to conflict in the nineteenth and twentieth centuries.
Students demonstrate understanding of the reasons why and the ways in which tensions have arisen between the individual and society over the course of European history.	**IS-6:** Evaluate the causes and consequences of persistent tensions between women's role and status in the private versus the public sphere.
	IS-7: Evaluate how identities such as ethnicity, race, and class have defined the individual in relationship to society.
	IS-8: Evaluate how the impact of war on civilians has affected loyalty to and respect for the nation-state.
Students demonstrate understanding of the reasons why and the ways in which the status of specific groups within society changed over time.	**IS-9:** Assess the extent to which women participated in and benefited from the shifting values of European society from the fifteenth century onward.
	IS-10: Analyze how and why Europeans have marginalized certain populations (defined as "other") over the course of their history.

A Diagnostic Test

Section I
Part A: Multiple-Choice Questions
Time: 55 minutes
Number of questions: 55
Percent of examination score: 40%

DIRECTIONS: The multiple-choice section consists of question sets organized around a stimulus material—a primary or secondary source, a historian's argument, or a historical problem. For each question, select the best response.

Questions 1–4 refer to the following quotation:

> *Descend, O Liberty, daughter of Nature:*
> *The People have recaptured their immortal*
> *power;*
> *Over the pompous remains of age-old*
> *imposture*
> *Their hands raise thine altar.*
> *Come, vanquisher of kings, Europe gazes*
> *upon you;*
> *Come, vanquish the false gods.*
> *Thou, holy Liberty, come dwell in this*
> *temple;*
> *Be the goddess of the French.*

Source: P. H. Beik, *The French Revolution* (New York: Walker & Co., 1970).

1. The poem above is most likely the work of
   (A) a Catholic monk decrying France's turning away from the Church.
   (B) the Revolutionary government's religious leaders celebrating the return to nature worship and paganism.
   (C) a supporter of Louis XVI.
   (D) a revolutionary who loves liberty above all else.

2. The quotation reflects
   (A) Napoleon's belief in liberty as the most important Enlightenment ideal.
   (B) the de-Christianization of France.
   (C) the French belief that Europe would watch as France put Louis XVI to death.
   (D) the belief among French commoners that Liberty was a goddess who deserved worship.

3. Which of the following would be most likely to agree with the sentiments of the poem?
   (A) Rousseau
   (B) Voltaire
   (C) Robespierre
   (D) Louis XVI

GO ON TO NEXT PAGE

Questions 4–7 refer to the following image.

Source: HIP/Art Resource, NY

4. Which of the following was a major goal of this man and the French monarchy in the seventeenth century?
   (A) Promoting religious toleration in France
   (B) Developing a strong diplomatic relationship with Spain
   (C) Strengthening the power of the Bourbon monarchy
   (D) Expanding the power of the French nobility

5. All of the following are ways in which Cardinal Richelieu limited the power of the French nobility EXCEPT
   (A) elimination of private armies.
   (B) crushing of aristocratic conspiracies.
   (C) elimination of fortified cities of the Huguenots.
   (D) elimination of conspiracies among the intendants.

6. Which of the following is true of French religious policies in the early seventeenth century?
   (A) They supported the Protestant forces in the Thirty Years' War.
   (B) They closed down all Huguenot schools.
   (C) They rescinded all religious freedom for the Huguenots in France.
   (D) They supported the Catholic forces in the Thirty Years' War.

7. Which of the following statements best describes the impact of Cardinal Richelieu's policies?
   (A) Although he employed a network of spies, Cardinal Richelieu failed to eliminate most major threats to royal authority.
   (B) Due to international war and fiscal inefficiency, Cardinal Richelieu increased the national debt.
   (C) Although he eliminated corruption among the intendants, Cardinal Richelieu was forced to turn to the nobility for loyal and well-educated administrators.
   (D) Due to the outbreak of the first Fronde, Cardinal Richelieu was forced to make compromises with the French nobility.

Questions 8–10 refer to the following image.

Source: British Library, London, UK/Bridgeman Images

8. The drawing above illustrates the benefits of
   (A) factory work.
   (B) the Enclosure Movement.
   (C) allowing women to work outside the home.
   (D) cottage industry.

9. The first businesses to industrialize and bring about the Early Industrial Revolution were
   (A) the textile industry and mining.
   (B) mining and chemical manufacturing.
   (C) shoe-making and leather-working.
   (D) shipbuilding and gunmaking.

10. Much early manufacturing work was done by women because
    (A) they had so much free time around the house.
    (B) it was a logical extension of the work they already did for the family home.
    (C) it was believed that women were not capable of doing other jobs.
    (D) it was against the law to have children working.

Questions 11–14 refer to the following map.

Source: © Cengage Learning

11. Which statement regarding Italy's participation in World War I is true?
    (A) Previously allied with Germany, Italy chose to remain neutral.
    (B) Previously allied with Russia and France, Italy chose to join with Germany.
    (C) Previously allied with Germany, Italy chose to join with the Allied Powers.
    (D) Previously allied with Britain and France, Italy chose to remain neutral.

12. All of the following are true about post-war Italy EXCEPT
    (A) economic turmoil and political disorder made it difficult for the existing government to survive in Italy in the early 1920s.
    (B) the general insecurity and fear stemming from World War I created conditions that facilitated the rise of fascist dictator Benito Mussolini.
    (C) Italy acquired Trieste and South Tyrol as a result of World War I.
    (D) Italy acquired Trieste, South Tyrol, and Yugoslavia as a result of World War I.

13. All of the following were problems that helped propel Benito Mussolini and the fascists into power in the 1920s EXCEPT
    (A) difficulty governing the Yugoslavian territories that Italy had gained as a result of World War I.
    (B) high unemployment, especially among veterans, that created huge groups of dissatisfied men.
    (C) widespread industrial and agricultural strikes that created a climate of class warfare and continual violence.
    (D) high post-war inflation that undermined middle-class security.

14. In an attempt to gain support from conservatives and military men, Benito Mussolini did which of the following?
    (A) He supported the socialist call for a left-wing revolution.
    (B) He published a socialist newspaper that opposed the old regime.
    (C) He formed bands of armed Fascists to attack socialists and put down strikes.
    (D) He set up a social welfare system to aid the poor.

GO ON TO NEXT PAGE

Questions 15–17 refer to the following quotation:

Pico della Mirandola, Oration on the Dignity of Man

At last the best of artisans [God] ordained that that creature to whom He had been able to give nothing proper to himself should have joint possession of whatever had been peculiar to each of the different kinds of being. He therefore took man as a creature of indeterminate nature, and assigning him a place in the middle of the world, addressed him thus: "Neither a fixed abode nor a form that is yours alone nor any function peculiar to yourself have we given you, Adam, to the end that according to your longing and according to your judgment you may have and possess what abode, what form, and what functions you yourself desire. The nature of all other beings is limited and constrained within the bounds of laws prescribed by Us. You, constrained by no limits, in accordance with your own free will, in whose hand We have placed you, shall ordain for yourself the limits of your nature. We have set you at the world's center that you may from there more easily observe whatever is in the world. We have made you neither of heaven nor of earth, neither mortal nor immortal, so that with freedom of choice and with honor, as though the maker and molder of yourself, you may fashion yourself in whatever shape you shall prefer. You shall have the power to degenerate into the lower forms of life, which are brutish. You shall have the power, out of your soul's judgment, to be reborn into the higher forms, which are divine."

Source: From _The Renaissance Philosophy of Man_ by Ernst Cassirer, Paul Kristeller, and John Randall, Jr. Copyright © 1948 by University of Chicago Press. Reprinted by permission of the publisher.

15. In the "Oration on the Dignity of Man," Pico della Mirandola made which of the following claims?
    (A) Man was created by God and owes complete allegiance to the Church.
    (B) Man is an amazing creature with unlimited potential.
    (C) Man is a limited creature who can never fully understand the world.
    (D) Man's thinking is wholly controlled by the Church.

16. Who among the following would most likely have supported the argument of Pico della Mirandola?
    (A) A humanist
    (B) A clergyman
    (C) A nobleman
    (D) A peasant

17. Pico della Mirandola would most likely have disapproved of which of the following?
    (A) Humanist education
    (B) Individualism
    (C) Clerical educational curriculum
    (D) Civic humanism

Questions 18–20 refer to the following image of Saltaire, a model town built by Titus Salt in 1851.

Source: HIP/Art Resource, NY

18. The model town in the illustration above is
    (A) dominated by a grand palace.
    (B) located on a canal to provide transportation for raw materials and factory products.
    (C) using new methods to produce little pollution.
    (D) surrounded by lush fields tended by peasant farmers.

19. The reason that this illustration is called a "model town" is that
    (A) it is a scale model, not a real town.
    (B) its founder modeled it after other factory towns like Leeds and Manchester.
    (C) it was seen as an ideal model of what a factory town should be like.
    (D) it was founded by Chartists to model their ideals of equality.

20. A town similar to Saltaire would be
    (A) Robert Owen's factory town in New Lanark, Scotland.
    (B) Count Henri de Saint Simon's utopian community.
    (C) an industrial center such as Manchester or Leeds.
    (D) the city of London.

GO ON TO NEXT PAGE

Questions 21–23 refer to the following quotation:

First and foremost, then, the document stated the city of Kinsay to be so great that it hath a hundred miles of compass. And there are in it twelve thousand bridges of stone, for the most part so lofty that a great fleet could pass beneath them. . . .

The document aforesaid also stated that the number and wealth of the merchants, and the amount of goods that passed through their hands, was so enormous that no man could form a just estimate thereof. . . .

All the streets are paved with stone or brick. . . .

In this part [of the city] are ten principal markets, though besides these there are a vast number of others. . . . there is always an ample supply of every kind of meat and game, as of roebuck, red-deer, fallow-deer, hares, rabbits, partridges, pheasants, francolins, quails, fowls, capons, and of ducks and geese an infinite quantity . . .

Those markets make a daily display of every kind of vegetables and fruits; and among the latter there are in particular certain pears of enormous size, weighing as much as ten pounds apiece. . . .

Now Messer Marco heard it stated by one of the Great Khan's officers of customs that the quantity of pepper introduced daily for consumption into the city of Kinsay amounted to 43 loads, each load being equal to 223 lbs.

The houses of the citizens are well built and elaborately finished; and the delight they take in decoration, in painting and in architecture, leads them to spend in this way sums of money that would astonish you.
Source: H. Yule, ed., trans., *The Book of Ser Marco Polo*, vol. I (London: John Murray, 1903), pp. 185–193, 200–208.

21. Which of the following was an important impact of the distribution of *The Travels of Marco Polo*?
    (A) Europeans began to fear the dangers of traveling to foreign lands.
    (B) Europeans began to wish they could travel to foreign lands.
    (C) Europeans desired the wealth of foreign lands such as China.
    (D) Europeans began to believe that exploration was too dangerous and did not support it.

22. All of the following were motives for European exploration of the New World EXCEPT
    (A) descriptions of Asia by medieval European travelers appealed to merchants.
    (B) the hope of economic gain appealed to Europeans.
    (C) the desire to Christianize the natives led missionaries to take an interest in the New World.
    (D) the desire to take over more land for agricultural purposes appealed to European farmers.

23. Which of the following was an important result of the popularity of travel literature, such as *The Travels of Marco Polo*?
    (A) Europeans began to establish colonial empires in China.
    (B) Europeans began to expand the Silk Road.
    (C) Europeans increased trade with China.
    (D) Rich Europeans began to travel to China in large numbers.

Questions 24–27 refer to the following image of a poster with the closing words of The Communist Manifesto: "Proletarians of the World, Unite!"

Source: Deutsches Historisches Museum, Berlin/ © DHM/The Bridgeman Art Library

24. In what way did the European socialist parties of the late nineteenth century differ from the vision of Karl Marx?
    (A) They believed that the proletariat was exploited by the bourgeoisie.
    (B) They organized themselves into mass political parties that competed in national elections.
    (C) They believed that the proletariat would triumph over the bourgeoisie.
    (D) They espoused revolutionary communist rhetoric.

25. Which of the following Marxist ideas is represented by the image?
    (A) Theory of surplus value
    (B) Creation of a classless society
    (C) Creation of a Marxist society worldwide
    (D) The dialectical process.

26. All of the following factors caused the German Social Democratic Party to advocate evolutionary socialism EXCEPT
    (A) the workers' conditions were declining, so they believed gradual change was the most effective way to support them.
    (B) their observations of the operation of moderate English socialism and the British parliamentary system convinced them that gradual reform was possible.
    (C) the expansion of the middle class was occurring in opposition to Marxist assertions.
    (D) the workers were experiencing a higher standard of living than previous years, making violent revolution unlikely.

27. Which of the following was a divisive issue for international socialism?
    (A) Poor working and living conditions for the working class in European nations
    (B) Refusal of some socialist leaders to participate in strikes and mass labor demonstrations promoted by the Second International
    (C) Opposition to socialism from European governments
    (D) Nationalist differences and antagonisms

GO ON TO NEXT PAGE

Questions 28–31 refer to the following image.

Source: Deutsches Historisches Museum, Berlin/© DHM/The Bridgeman Art Library

28. All of the following are reasons that Stalin blockaded Berlin EXCEPT
    (A) by February, 1948, the United States, France, and England made plans to unify their three sections of Germany into a united West German state.
    (B) Stalin hoped to gain economic control of all of Berlin.
    (C) Stalin wanted to stop the Western allies from creating a separate West German state.
    (D) Stalin wanted to halt the construction of a new autobahn linking the western zones of Berlin to the Western sectors of Germany.

29. All of the following are reasons that the Western allies staged an airlift to supply Berlin with supplies during the Berlin Blockade EXCEPT
    (A) they wanted to avoid a war with the USSR.
    (B) they wanted to try out new American planes to see how they performed at low altitudes.
    (C) they wanted to maintain control of West Berlin.
    (D) they wanted to show that they could not be pushed around by Stalin.

30. All of the following are reasons that 1949 is considered to be a turning point in the Cold War EXCEPT
    (A) the Berlin Blockade and Airlift occurred.
    (B) the USSR successfully tested an atomic bomb.
    (C) the Korean War began.
    (D) NATO was formed.

31. Which of the following policies was illustrated in the Berlin Airlift and became the cornerstone of American Cold War policy toward the USSR?
    (A) containment
    (B) Westernization
    (C) peaceful coexistence
    (D) detente

Questions 32–34 refer to the following quotation.

Petition for Higher Pay by a Group of Third-Class Constables (1848)

Men joining the Police service as 3rd Class Constables and having a wife and 3 children to support on joining, are not able properly to do so on the pay of 16/8d. Most of the married men on joining are somewhat in debt, and are unable to extricate themselves on account of rent to pay and articles to buy which are necessary for support of wife and children.

Complaints from Constables of D Division of the London Metropolitan Police

We are not treated as men but as slaves we englishmen do not like to be terrorized by a set of Irish Sergeants who are only lenient to their own countrymen we the D division of Paddington are nearly all ruled by these Irish Sergeants after we have done our night-Duty may we not have the privilege of going to Church or staying at home to Suit our own inclination…..another thing we want to know who has the money that is deducted out of our wages for fines and many of us will be obliged to give up the duty unless we can have fair play as to the stationing of us on our beats why cannot we follow round that may all and each of us go over every beat and not for the Sergeants to put their favorites on the good beats and the others kept back their favorites are not the best policemen but those that will spend the most with them at the public house there are a great many of these things to try our temper.

Source: From Clive Emsley, *Policing and Its Context, 1750–1870* (London: Palgrave Macmillan, 1983).

32. The establishment of police forces in England
    (A) was a reform called for by the workers and peasants who were most often the victims of crime.
    (B) was part of wave of reforms in the mid-nineteenth century that included prison reforms and the Factory Acts.
    (C) was called for by women, along with anti-prostitution legislation and the fight for the right to vote.
    (D) was done in the early 1700s as part of the Enlightenment, but reforms of the system needed to be made after a century or more.

33. The documents above suggest that
    (A) the job of policeman was a respected and well-paying one.
    (B) policemen, like other workers of the period, were not well paid and suffered at the hands of their superiors.
    (C) policemen did not have to go to church.
    (D) policemen only patrolled during the day.

34. An important reason for some of the problems discussed in these documents could be
    (A) the nationalistic animosity between the English and Irish police.
    (B) the growth of atheism.
    (C) the freedom to unionize that workers experienced during this period.
    (D) the fact that policemen were discouraged from marrying and having families.

GO ON TO NEXT PAGE

Questions 35–37 refer to the following quotation.

Isaac Newton, Rules of Reasoning in Philosophy

Rule 1

We are to admit no more causes of natural things than such as are both true and sufficient to explain their appearances.

To this purpose the philosophers say that Nature does nothing in vain, and more is in vain when less will serve; for Nature is pleased with simplicity, and affects not the pomp of superfluous causes.

Rule 2

Therefore to the same natural effects we must, as far as possible, assign the same causes.

As to respiration in a man and in a beast; the descent of stones in Europe and in America; the light of our culinary fire and of the sun; the reflection of light in the earth and in the planets.

Rule 3

The qualities of bodies, which admit neither intensification nor remission of degrees, and which are found to belong to all bodies within the reach of our experiments, are to be esteemed the universal qualities of all bodies whatsoever.

For since qualities of bodies are only known to us by experiments, we are to hold for universal all such as universally agree with experiments; and such as are not liable to diminution can never be quite taken away.

Rule 4

In experimental philosophy we are to look upon propositions inferred by general induction from phenomena as accurately or very nearly true, notwithstanding any contrary hypotheses that may be imagined, till such time as other phenomena occur, by which they may either be made more accurate, or liable to exceptions.

This rule we must follow, that the argument of induction may not be evaded by hypotheses.

Source: Newton, *The Mathematical Principles of Natural Philosophy* (London, 1803), pp. 160–162.

35. In his rules of reasoning, Newton
    (A) rejected empiricism as unreliable.
    (B) rejected rationalism.
    (C) supported the superiority of church authority.
    (D) supported the deductive method.

36. Newton's discovery of natural laws of the universe and their dissemination in his book *Principia* impacted Europe by
    (A) convincing most people that only scientists would be able to understand the physical world.
    (B) sparking a backlash against Newton, since he challenged traditional views of the universe.
    (C) causing his condemnation and house arrest by the Roman Catholic Church.
    (D) sparking an increase in intellectual investigation as thinkers attempted to discover natural laws to govern politics, society, and economics.

37. All of the following statements are true of Sir Isaac Newton EXCEPT
    (A) Newton created a mechanistic view of the universe that dominated western thinking until the mid-twentieth century.
    (B) although he rejected accepting scientific knowledge without proof, Newton was active in aspects of the occult, including his studies in alchemy.
    (C) Newton's work was the culmination of the ideas of Ptolemy, Kepler, and Galileo.
    (D) Newton was an active member and president of the English Royal Society.

Questions 38–41 refer to the following image.

Source: Private Collection/The Bridgeman Art Library

38. Based on the image, which of the following statements best describes Tsar Nicholas II's relationship with the people?
   (A) Tsar Nicholas hoped to preserve autocratic traditions in Russia and appealed to the aristocracy.
   (B) Tsar Nicholas hoped to appeal to the Russian middle class and enacted military parades to gain their political support.
   (C) Tsar Nicholas was in touch with the common people of Russia and often walked through the streets to ask them for their views on political issues.
   (D) Tsar Nicholas hoped that if he went out into the streets with the people, political threats to his power might diminish.

39. All of the following are true statements about Russian industrialization at the turn of the twentieth century EXCEPT
   (A) although Russia's industrialization got a late start, Russia was the fourth-largest steel producer in the world by 1900.
   (B) Sergei Witte believed that industrialization was crucial to Russia's national strength, especially the development of railroads.
   (C) in response to poor working and living conditions, the working class formed several democratic parties that participated in legislative decisions and worked for reform.
   (D) Socialist parties developed in response to the poor working and living conditions of the industrial workers, but they were forced underground by government repression.

40. All of the following were important causes of the Russian Revolution of 1905 EXCEPT
   (A) the Russian loss to Japan in the Russo-Japanese War.
   (B) Marxist ideology.
   (C) unrest among members of the working class due to poor conditions in the cities and unrest among peasants, who still suffered from famine and a lack of land.
   (D) Bloody Sunday.

41. The Revolution of 1905 ended with the proclamation of the October Manifesto. The most important change created by the October Manifesto was
   (A) the adoption of broad urban reforms that satisfied the working class.
   (B) the granting of civil liberties by Tsar Nicholas II.
   (C) the abolition of the tsarist secret police.
   (D) the creation of the Duma, an elected legislative body that satisfied the middle class.

GO ON TO NEXT PAGE

Questions 42–44 refer to the following image.

Source: Jonathan Poore

42. Balthasar Neumann's eighteenth-century Pilgrimage Church of the Fourteen Saints can be seen as an example of
(A) the focus on plain living found in Calvinist churches.
(B) the lessening of importance of religion due to Deist tendencies.
(C) the focus on symmetrical exteriors and ornate interiors found in Rococo architecture.
(D) the power of the absolute monarchs to promote pilgrimages.

43. As illustrated in the photographs above, the architecture of the late eighteenth and early nineteenth centuries was influenced by
(A) the dignity and simplicity of the aristocracy.
(B) the wealth and power of the Catholic Church and the upperclass.
(C) a delicate, refined, and decorative ideal that came to Europe from Asia.
(D) the linear, rationalist views of the scientific revolution.

44. Besides seeing the building of beautiful churches during the time of the Enlightenment, religion was impacted when philosophes encouraged religious change by
(A) pushing people to remain loyal to the Roman Catholic Church.
(B) speaking against Deism, the religion of the French royal family.
(C) offering a philosophy centered on multiple gods rather than a single god.
(D) advocating belief in God's existence as a creator but no involvement in the world he created

Questions 45–47 refer to the following quotation.

Hence, in order that the social pact shall not be an empty formula, it is tacitly implied in that commitment— which alone can give force to all others—that whoever refused to obey the general will shall be constrained to do so by the whole body, which means nothing other than that he shall be forced to be free; for this is the condition which, by giving each citizen to the nation, secures him against all personal dependence, it is the condition which shapes both the design and the working of the political machine, and which alone bestows justice on civil contracts—without it, such contracts would be absurd, tyrannical and liable to the grossest abuse.

Source: Jean-Jacques Rousseau, *The Social Contract*, trans. M. Cranston (London: Penguin Classics, 1968).

45. The selection above by Jean-Jacques Rousseau best illustrates
(A) his belief in the triumph of emotion over reason.
(B) his wish for the abolition of slavery.
(C) his belief that governments should grant rights and freedoms to the governed.
(D) his assertion that women should play no role in politics.

46. Rousseau's ideas of the Social Contract would most agree with the theory of
    (A) Voltaire's enlightened despotism.
    (B) Locke's civil government.
    (C) Bossuet's absolutism.
    (D) Machiavelli's prince.

47. Although an Enlightenment philosophe, Rousseau also held beliefs that would lead to the nineteenth-century intellectual movement known as Romanticism. Which of his beliefs showed his Romantic tendency?
    (A) The Old Order must be not only questioned but totally removed.
    (B) Education is essential to improving society.
    (C) People should be actively involved in their government.
    (D) It is important to have a balance of reason and emotion.

48. Pamphlets that included woodcuts became popular among reformers for which of the following reasons?
    (A) Only about 4–5% of the people in Germany were literate, so woodcuts provided an effective way for reformers to communicate with the population.
    (B) Reformers realized that it was difficult for artists to make a living in Germany and offered jobs to artists who could produce the woodcuts.
    (C) Woodcuts were expensive, so including woodcuts in their pamphlets allowed reformers to appeal to wealthy princes who could afford to buy the works.
    (D) Woodcuts provided a more effective way for reformers to communicate their ideas than sermons, which many common people didn't understand.

Questions 48–51 refer to the following woodcut.

Source: bpk, Berlin/Kupferstichkabinett, SMB/Jörg P. Anders/Art Resource, NY

GO ON TO NEXT PAGE

49. The woodcut shown on the previous page would probably have been created by someone opposed to which of the following religious practices?
(A) Daily prayer
(B) The use of music as a means to teach the Gospel
(C) The translation of the Bible into the vernacular
(D) The sale of indulgences

50. The two panels of the woodcut seen on the previous page represent which of the following?
(A) Illiterate vs. literate religious congregations
(B) Informal vs. formal religious services
(C) Support for Lutheran practices vs. an attack on papal greed
(D) Support for Roman Catholic practices vs. an attack on Luther's reform ideas

51. The spread of Lutheranism and the decline of Catholicism in many parts of Germany were aided by all of the following EXCEPT
(A) economic benefits enjoyed by German noblemen who rejected the Roman Catholic faith.
(B) corruption within the Roman Catholic Church.
(C) the splintered nature of the Holy Roman Empire that allowed many princes to become relatively independent of imperial authority.
(D) the fact that the reformation was strongest in rural areas.

Questions 52–55 refer to the following map.

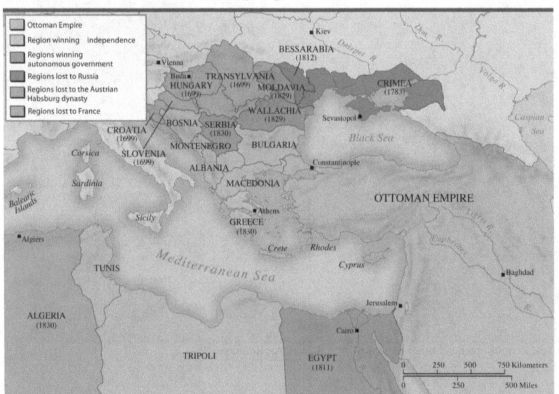

Source: Cengage Learning

52. All of the following contributed to the nineteenth-century decline of the Ottoman Empire EXCEPT
    (A) a nationalist revolt in Greece that led to Greek independence.
    (B) Serbian demands for autonomy, which led to the independence of Serbia.
    (C) establishment of a Russian protectorate over Moldavia and Wallachia.
    (D) the loss of Hungary and Transylvania to the Hapsburgs.

53. Which of the following factors best explains the decision of Britain and France to support the Ottomans in their fight against Russia in the Crimean War?
    (A) They feared the expansion of the Austrian Empire into the Balkan peninsula, posing a threat to French trade routes in eastern Europe.
    (B) They feared the expansion of Russia into Ottoman territory, posing a threat to British naval control of the eastern Mediterranean.
    (C) They wanted to support the right to national self-determination of the ethnic groups in the Balkans.
    (D) They wanted to take over the Bosphorus and Dardanelles.

54. Which of the following was an important impact on women of nineteenth-century wars?
    (A) Many women began to suffer due to food shortages, and had a hard time feeding their families while their husbands were fighting in the war.
    (B) Due to the efforts of newspaper reporters, many women learned to read so they could follow the war in the newspaper while their husbands were fighting in the war.
    (C) Due to the efforts of Florence Nightingale, nursing became an admirable profession for middle-class women.
    (D) Many women began to go to work in munitions factories to help supply the armies with arms.

55. Which of the following makes the Crimean War an important turning point in European history?
    (A) It shattered the Concert of Europe, realigning alliance systems.
    (B) It revealed the weakness of the Ottoman Empire.
    (C) It awarded Russia control of the straits, making it a Mediterranean power.
    (D) It was the final step in German unification.

STOP
END OF SECTION I, PART A

IF YOU FINISH BEFORE TIME IS CALLED, YOU MAY CHECK YOUR WORK ON THIS SECTION. DO NOT GO ON TO SECTION I PART B UNTIL YOU ARE TOLD TO DO SO.

GO ON TO NEXT PAGE

AP® EUROPEAN HISTORY EXAMINATION
Section II
Part B: Short-Answer Questions
Time: 50 minutes
Number of questions: 4
Percent of examination score: 20%

DIRECTIONS: Part B of the examination contains four questions. You will have 50 minutes to respond to all questions. You are not required to develop and support a thesis statement in your response. Rather, focus on directly answering each question using evidence from your study of history.

1. Answer Parts A, B, and C by comparing and contrasting France under Louis XIV with Poland in the seventeenth century. Answer Parts A, B, and C by comparing and contrasting France under Louis XIV with Poland in the seventeenth century.
    A) Briefly describe ONE challenge faced by both Louis XIV and the Polish monarchs.
    B) Briefly describe ONE domestic difference between France under Louis XIV and Poland in the seventeenth century.
    C) Briefly describe ONE foreign difference between France under Louis XIV and Poland in the seventeenth century.

Question 2 refers to the following quote:

The object of this Essay is to assert one very simple principle, as entitled to govern absolutely the dealings of society with the individual in the way of compulsion and control, whether the means used be physical force in the form of legal penalties, or the moral coercion of public opinion. That principle is, that the sole end for which mankind are warranted, individually or collectively, interfering with the liberty of action of any of their number, is self-protection.....

But there is a sphere of action in which society, as distinguished from the individual has, if any, only an indirect interest; comprehending all that portion of a person's life and conduct which affects only himself, or if it also affects others, only with their free, voluntary and undeceived consent and participation. . . . This then is the appropriate region of human liberty. It comprises, first, the inward domain of consciousness; demanding liberty of conscience in the most comprehensive sense; liberty of thought and feeling; absolute freedom of opinion and sentiment on all subjects, practical or speculative, scientific, moral, or theological. . . .

The peculiar evil of silencing the expression of an opinion is, that it is robbing the human race; posterity as well as the existing generation; those who dissent from the opinion, still more than those who hold it. If the opinion is right, they are deprived of the opportunity of exchanging error for truth: if wrong, they lose, what is almost as great a benefit, the clearer perception and livelier impression of truth, produced by its collision with error.

Source: John Stuart Mill, *Utilitarianism, On Liberty, and Representative Government* (New York: Viking Press, 1914).

2. Answer Parts A, B, and C of the following question about the excerpt above from John Stuart Mill's book *Utilitarianism, On Liberty, and Representative Government*.
    A) Briefly explain Mill's philosophy of liberty.
    B) In what way does the excerpt above exemplify this philosophy?
    C) Briefly explain why this philosophy would be popular with middle class liberals in the 1800s.

3. Answer Parts A, B, and C about the Versailles War Guilt Clause.
   A) Briefly explain the Versailles War Guilt Clause.
   B) Provide ONE piece of evidence and briefly explain how it justifies the War Guilt Clause
   C) Provide ONE piece of evidence and briefly explain how it shows the injustice of the War Guilt Clause.

4. Choose two laws passed during the early 19th century that were used to improve quality of life for the working class.
   A) Explain the first law you chose.
   B) Explain the second law you chose.
   C) Which one do you think is more important? Explain your answer.

STOP
END OF SECTION I

IF YOU FINISH BEFORE TIME IS CALLED, YOU MAY CHECK YOUR WORK ON THIS SECTION. DO NOT GO ON TO SECTION II UNTIL YOU ARE TOLD TO DO SO.

AP® EUROPEAN HISTORY EXAMINATION
Section II: Free-Response Essays
Part A: Document-Based Question (DBQ)
Suggested writing time: 55 minutes
Percent of examination score: 25%

DIRECTIONS: The following question is based on the accompanying Documents 1–7. The documents have been edited for the purposes of this exercise. This question is designed to test your ability to apply several historical thinking skills simultaneously, including historical argumentation, appropriate use of relevant historical evidence, contextualization, and synthesis. Your response should be based on your analysis of the documents and your knowledge of the topic.

Write a well-integrated essay that does the following:

- States an appropriate thesis that directly addresses *all parts* of the question.
- Supports the thesis or an appropriate argument with evidence from all or all but one of the documents AND knowledge of European history beyond/outside the documents.
- Analyzes a majority of the documents in terms of such features as their intended audience, purpose, point of view, format, argument, limitations, and/or social context as appropriate to the argument.
- Places the argument in the context of the broader regional, national, or global process.

QUESTION 1. Analyze the different views of, the causes of, course of, and responses to the Irish Famine of 1845–1851.

Document 1

Source: Parliamentary Proceedings, "The State of Famine and Disease in Ireland," February 18, 1846.

Mr. O'CONNELL then rose and said—The calamity with which Ireland is now threatened is not owing to any default of the people, it is not owing to any sterility of the soil, it is not even owing to any want of the abundance of the harvest. It is owing to a dispensation of Providence, which man cannot control. Our duty is to submit to the will of an All-disposing power and to perform the part of charitable Christians by endeavoring to mitigate the evils as they arise.

Document 2

Source: Editorial, *London Times,* September 22, 1846.

The worst symptoms of the Irish famine … have begun to show themselves in the way of popular gatherings and processions, which at present are only turbulent, but may soon become outrageous….

Alas! the Irish peasant had tasted of famine and found that it was good…. He wrapped himself up in the ragged mantle of inert expediency and said that he trusted to Providence. But the deity of his faith was the Government….

[T]here are ingredients in the Irish character which must be modified and corrected before either individuals or Government can hope to raise the general condition of the people.

Document 3

Source: *London Times,* news articles, January 11, 1847.

FOOD RIOTS IN DUBLIN

Before 8 o'clock this morning a mob consisting of between 40 and 50 persons, many of them boys, commenced an attack upon the bakers' shops in the neighborhood of Summer Hill, Britain Street and Abbey Street…. The rioters had the appearance of country people….

OUTDOOR RELIEF

Balrothery union … resolution: "That the workhouse being now fully occupied, there being no fewer than 499 inmates (the house being calculated for only 400 … [if] a destitute person may present himself, … before sending such person away to give him a meal….

Document 4

Source: *The Cork Examiner,* Irish newspaper, "Scenes of Misery," January 11, 1847.

TRACTON—Stretched on a bed of straw lies a dying husband and father; and grouped around that couch are a wretched wife and children, who devour wild weeds themselves, that they might leave the only remaining morsel of food to the dying man!

Is this tide of horror to roll on unchecked? Will the Imperial rulers of this slavish province wait until one-half of the 'Irish savages' be swept away? For to this it will soon come.

GO ON TO NEXT PAGE

Document 5

Source: Queen Victoria, Letter to His Grace the Archbishop of Canterbury, January 13, 1847.

Whereas a large portion of the population in Ireland, and in some districts in Scotland, is suffering severe distress, owing to the failure of the ordinary supplies of food; and whereas many of our subjects have entered into voluntary subscriptions for their relief....

We ... being always ready to give the best encouragement and countenance to such humane and charitable undertakings, [direct] ministers in each parish [to] effectively excite their parishioners to a liberal contribution....

Document 6

Source: Charles Trevelyan, Assistant Secretary to the Treasury in charge of the administration of government relief to the victims of the Irish Famine, published comments, 1848.

The judgement of God sent the calamity to teach the Irish a lesson, that calamity must not be too much mitigated.... The great evil with which we have to contend is not the physical evil of the famine but the moral evil of the selfish, perverse and turbulent character of the people.

"Mitigate" means "lessen."

Document 7

Source: *Punch,* British satirical journal, "Here and There; or, Emigration a Remedy," July 15, 1848.

HERE AND THERE;
OR, EMIGRATION A REMEDY

From Getty Images:
http://www.gettyimages.com/detail/news-photo/or-emigration-a-remedy-cartoon-from-punch-london-news-photo/113490080
Image ID: 113490080

END OF DOCUMENTS FOR PART A.
GO ON TO THE NEXT PAGE.

AP® EUROPEAN HISTORY EXAMINATION
Section II: Free-Response Essays
Part B: Long-Essay Questions
Suggested planning and writing time: 35 minutes
Percent of examination score: 15%

DIRECTIONS: You are to choose ONE question from the two questions below. Make your selection carefully, choosing the question that you are best prepared to answer thoroughly in the time permitted. You should spend 5 minutes organizing or outlining your answer. Write your answer to the question on the lined pages of the Section II free-response booklet, making sure to indicate the question you are answering by writing the appropriate question number on the top of each page.

Write an essay that:

- has a relevant thesis.
- addresses all parts of the question.
- supports your thesis with specific evidence.
- is well organized.

QUESTION 1. To what extent was the Scientific Revolution a truly revolutionary time period in European history?

QUESTION 2. To what extent was the Italian Renaissance a truly revolutionary time period in European history?

END OF EXAMINATION

ANSWERS FOR SECTION I, PART A: MULTIPLE-CHOICE QUESTIONS

ANSWER KEY FOR PART A: MULTIPLE-CHOICE QUESTIONS

1. D	12. D	23. C	34. A	45. C
2. B	13. A	24. B	35. B	46. B
3. C	14. C	25. C	36. D	47. D
4. C	15. B	26. A	37. C	48. A
5. D	16. A	27. D	38. A	49. D
6. A	17. C	28. D	39. C	50. C
7. B	18. B	29. B	40. B	51. D
8. D	19. C	30. C	41. D	52. D
9. A	20. A	31. A	42. C	53. B
10. B	21. B	32. B	43. B	54. C
11. C	22. D	33. B	44. D	55. A

EXPLANATIONS FOR PART A: MULTIPLE-CHOICE ANSWERS

1. **(D)** This poem sees "Liberty" as an ideal that should be worshiped like a goddess (*Western Civilization*, 9th ed., p. 583 / 10th ed., p. 580; Historical Thinking Skills—Analyzing Evidence: Content and Sourcing; Learning Objective SP-11; Key Concept 2.1).

2. **(B)** This is from a hymn sung in the Temple of Reason, a reflection of the de-Christianization effort (*Western Civilization*, 9th ed., p. 583 / 10th ed., p. 580; Historical Thinking Skills—Analyzing Evidence: Content and Sourcing; Learning Objective SP-11; Key Concept 2.1).

3. **(C)** Robespierre, as one of the leaders of the French Revolution, would be most likely to agree with the sentiments found in this poem (*Western Civilization*, 9th ed., p. 583 / 10th ed., p. 580; Historical Thinking Skills—Analyzing Evidence: Content and Sourcing, Synthesis; Learning Objective SP-11; Key Concept 2.1).

4. **(C)** Cardinal Richelieu, the chief advisor for King Louis XIII, was responsible for strengthening the power of the monarchy at the expense of the nobility (*Western Civilization*, 9th ed., pp. 444–45 / 10th ed., pp. 440–41; Historical Thinking Skills—Contextualization; Learning Objectives SP-2; Key Concept 2.1).

5. **(D)** Cardinal Richelieu strengthened the power of the crown by eliminating the ability of the nobles to threaten the monarchy. The intendants, royal civil servants, were generally loyal, since they owed their jobs to the crown (*Western Civilization*, 9th ed., pp. 444–45 / 10th ed., pp. 440–41; Historical Thinking Skills—Causation; Learning Objectives SP-2, IS-7; Key Concept 2.1).

6. **(A)** Although he contained the ability of the Huguenots to threaten the power of the king, Cardinal Richelieu allowed limited religious freedom to French Huguenots. He decided to support the protestant forces in the Thirty Years' War because he believed that weakening the Hapsburgs was more important than concerning himself with the religious beliefs of their opponents (*Western Civilization*, 9th ed., pp. 444–45 / 10th ed., pp. 440–41; Historical Thinking Skills—Causation; Learning Objectives SP-2, SP-3; Key Concept 2.1, 2.3).

7. **(B)** Since many benefited from corruption within the French financial system, Richelieu found it nearly impossible to institute reform. This problem, combined with large expenditures in the Thirty Years' War, increased the French national debt (*Western Civilization*, 9th ed., pp. 444–45 / 10th ed., pp. 440–41; Historical Thinking Skills—Contextualization; Learning Objectives SP-2; Key Concept 2.1).

8. **(D)** These women are participating in cottage industry, which would have allowed them to make a little extra money at home, being paid by the piece by an entrepreneur (*Western Civilization*, 9th ed., pp. 552–53 / 10th ed., pp. 548–49; Historical Thinking Skills—Periodization, Analyzing Evidence: Content and Sourcing, Synthesis; Learning Objective PP-2; Key Concept 2.2).

9. **(A)** The textile industry, which was incredibly time-consuming to do at home, was first along with the mining industry, which was something that could never have been done at home (*Western Civilization*, 9th ed., pp. 552–53 / 10th ed., pp. 548–49; Historical Thinking Skills—Causation, Periodization; Learning Objective PP-3; Key Concept 2.2).

10. **(B)** Women had always been responsible for much of the productive work around the house, making all the clothes, soap, candles, etc. as well as preserving food (*Western Civilization*, 9th ed., pp. 552–53 / 10th ed., pp. 548–49; Historical Thinking Skills—Causation, Periodization, Contextualization; Learning Objective PP-2; Key Concept 2.2).

11. **(C)** Italy joined the Allied Powers based on the promise that it could acquire Austrian territory after the war (*Western Civilization*, 9th ed., p. 769 / 10th ed., p. 785, 765; Historical Thinking Skills—Patterns of Continuity and Change Over Time; Learning Objectives SP-14, SP-17, SP-18; Key Concept 4.1).

12. **(D)** Italy switched sides in the war in an attempt to acquire Austrian lands. After the war, Italy gained Trieste and South Tyrol (*Western Civilization*, 9th ed., p. 806 / 10th ed., p. 802; Historical Thinking Skills—Patterns of Continuity and Change Over Time; Learning Objectives SP-14, SP-17, SP-18; Key Concept 4.1).

13. **(A)** Choices B, C, and D all are factors that led to the rise of fascism in the 1920s in Italy. Italy did not receive Yugoslavian lands as a result of World War I, and anger over the limited amount of territory that Italians received was another contributing factor in the rise of Mussolini (*Western Civilization*, 9th ed.,

p. 806 / 10th ed., p. 802; Historical Thinking Skills—Patterns of Continuity and Change Over Time; Learning Objectives SP-6, SP-8, SP-17, SP-18; Key Concept 4.1, 4.2).

14. (C) Fascism was an extreme right-wing ideology that appealed to disgruntled veterans and conservatives. To gain their continuing support, Mussolini attacked the left-wing socialists, violently put down strikes, and created squads of armed fascists (*Western Civilization*, 9th ed., p. 806 / 10th ed., p. 806; Historical Thinking Skills—Causation; Learning Objectives SP-6, SP-8, SP-17, SP-18; Key Concept 4.1, 4.2).

15. (B) Pico della Mirandola was a Neo-Platonist who believed in the unbridled power of the mind to comprehend the universe (*Western Civilization*, 9th ed., pp. 347–48 / 10th ed., pp. 346–47; Historical Thinking Skills—Analyzing Evidence: Content and Sourcing; Learning Objective OS-2; Key Concept 1.1).

16. (A) A humanist would most likely have supported the ideas of Pico della Mirandola because his belief in the unlimited potential of the human mind was a hallmark of humanism (*Western Civilization*, 9th ed., pp. 347–48 / 10th ed., pp. 346–47; Historical Thinking Skills—Analyzing Evidence: Content and Sourcing; Learning Objective OS-5; Key Concept 1.1).

17. (C) As a humanist, Pico della Mirandola would have supported and promoted humanist education and ideals; therefore, he would most likely have disapproved of the educational curriculum promoted by the Catholic Church (*Western Civilization*, 9th ed., pp. 347–48 / 10th ed., pp. 346–47; Historical Thinking Skills—Analyzing Evidence: Content and Sourcing; Learning Objective OS-2; Key Concept 1.1).

18. (B) At the center of Saltaire is the factory, surrounded by shops and factory housing. It was built on a waterway, the canal between Manchester and Leeds, to facilitate transportation of raw materials and finished goods (*Western Civilization*, 9th ed., pp. 611–12 / 10th ed., pp. 607–09; Historical Thinking Skills—Analyzing Evidence: Content and Sourcing; Learning Objective OS-9, PP-8; Key Concept 3.1).

19. (C) This is called a model town because it was built to show what a factory town should be like, as a model to others (*Western Civilization*, 9th ed., pp. 611–12 / 10th ed., pp. 607–09; Historical Thinking Skills—Patterns of Continuity and Change Over Time, Analyzing Evidence: Content and Sourcing, Contextualization; Learning Objective OS-9, PP-8; Key Concept 3.3).

20. (A) Another "ideal town" along these lines would be New Lanark, Scotland, built by Robert Owen. Leeds, Manchester, and London were all manufacturing centers but they grew up haphazardly and were not planned at all. St. Simon's utopian community was not planned around a factory but instead relied on cottage industry (Western Civilization, 9th ed., p. 620 / 10th ed., pp. 632, 634; Historical Thinking Skills—Periodization, Analyzing Evidence: Content and Sourcing, Comparison, Contextualization; Learning Objective OS-9, PP-8; Key Concept 3.3).

21. **(B)** Enticed by the lure of fantastic lands, Europeans wished to see other worlds, such as the lands described by Marco Polo (*Western Civilization*, 9th ed., pp. 404–06 / 10th ed., pp. 400–01; Historical Thinking Skills—Causation; Learning Objective SP-15; Key Concept 1.4).

22. **(D)** The Polos' accounts of their travels to Asia sparked an interest in exploration among European merchants who wanted to gain sea access to Asia's treasures. Economic opportunities and religious zeal also increased interest in exploration. The desire for agricultural expansion, however, was not a motivation (*Western Civilization*, 9th ed., pp. 404–06 / 10th ed., pp. 400–01; Historical Thinking Skills—Analyzing Evidence: Content and Sourcing; Learning Objective INT-1; Key Concept 1.4).

23. **(C)** Renewed interest in China, sparked by *The Travels of Marco Polo*, led European merchants to increase trade with China. After the disintegration of the Silk Road, the merchants began looking for overseas routes to establish more direct access to the spice trade described by Marco Polo (*Western Civilization*, 9th ed., pp. 404–06 / 10th ed., pp. 400–01; Historical Thinking Skills—Causation, Analyzing Evidence: Content and Sourcing; Learning Objective INT-1; Key Concept 1.4).

24. **(B)** Karl Marx did not believe that communist goals could be achieved through reform and advocated the inevitability of violent revolution. The European socialist parties, realizing that a Marxist revolution was not feasible in the immediate future, tried to achieve socialist reforms through the legislative process (*Western Civilization*, 9th ed., pp. 698–701 / 10th ed., pp. 693-96; Historical Thinking Skills—Comparison; Learning Objectives PP-14, OS-8, OS-9, SP-1, SP-7, SP-9, SP-12, IS-5, IS-7; Key Concept 3.3).

25. **(C)** As seen on the labels on the banners and in the faces of the people in the image, the socialists who created this poster were hoping for the unity of workers worldwide and international support for socialist goals (*Western Civilization*, 9th ed., pp. 698–701 / 10th ed., pp. 693–96; Historical Thinking Skills—Comparison; Learning Objectives PP-14, OS-8, OS-9, SP-1, SP-7, SP-9, SP-12, IS-5, IS-7; Key Concept 3.3).

26. **(A)** The condition of the working class was actually slowly improving, making evolutionary socialism a more feasible option than revolutionary change (*Western Civilization*, 9th ed., pp. 698–701 / 10th ed., pp. 693–96; Historical Thinking Skills—Comparison; Learning Objectives PP-14, OS-8, OS-9, SP-1, SP-7, SP-9, SP-12, IS-5, IS-7; Key Concept 3.3).

27. **(D)** As socialist parties began to participate in their governments, national interests began to overshadow the goals of international socialism. After World War I broke out, socialist leaders and members of the working class tended to support their nations' war efforts, destroying the possibility of success for an international socialist movement (*Western Civilization*, 9th ed., pp. 698–701 / 10th ed., pp. 693–96; Historical Thinking

Skills—Comparison; Learning Objectives PP-14, OS-8, OS-9, SP-1, SP-7, SP-9, SP-12, IS-5, IS-7; Key Concept 3.3).

28. (**D**) An autobahn built in the 1930s already linked West Berlin to the West German sectors (*Western Civilization*, 9th ed., pp. 841–43 / 10th ed., pp. 866–67; Historical Thinking Skills—Causation; Learning Objectives SP-13; Key Concept 4.1).

29. (**B**) The most important reason that the western powers chose to stage an airlift was that they didn't want to risk a war with the USSR (*Western Civilization*, 9th ed., pp. 841–43 / 10th ed., pp. 866–67; Historical Thinking Skills—Causation; Learning Objectives SP-13; Key Concept 4.1).

30. (**C**) The Korean War began in 1950. All of the other events, along with the communist revolution in the People's Republic of China, occurred in 1949 (*Western Civilization*, 9th ed., pp. 841–43 / 10th ed., pp. 866–67; Historical Thinking Skills—Periodization; Learning Objectives SP-13; Key Concept 4.1).

31. (**A**) Containment became the cornerstone of American foreign policy during the Cold War, as the America tried to contain Soviet aggression and protect her Western allies (*Western Civilization*, 9th ed., pp. 841–43 / 10th ed., pp. 866–67; Historical Thinking Skills—Causation; Learning Objectives SP-13; Key Concept 4.1).

32. (**B**) There were no police forces before the 1800s. Middle-class liberals called for this reform, along with prison reform and other social reforms. Women, workers, and peasants had no political power when it came to getting laws passed (*Western Civilization*, 9th ed., pp. 648–49 / 10th ed., pp. 642–44; Historical Thinking Skills—Causation, Analyzing Evidence: Content and Sourcing; Learning Objective IS-7; Key Concept 3.3).

33. (**B**) The first document complains of the low pay while the second discusses the problems of superior officers (*Western Civilization*, 9th ed., pp. 648–49 / 10th ed., pp. 642–44; Historical Thinking Skills—Analyzing Evidence: Content and Sourcing; Learning Objective IS-7; Key Concept 3.3).

34. (**A**) The writer of the second document repeatedly makes reference to the Irish sergeants, who treat the English constables badly. The fact that most of the Irish would have been Catholic could also be an issue, but atheism definitely was not. Unions were not allowed at this period and the first document discusses the fact that many of the policemen have wives and children to support on meager salaries (*Western Civilization*, 9th ed., pp. 648–49 / 10th ed., pp. 642–44; Historical Thinking Skills—Causation, Analyzing Evidence: Content and Sourcing; Learning Objective IS-7; Key Concept 3.4).

35. (**B**) By calling upon scientists and thinkers to use experiments to learn about the qualities of bodies, he inadvertently rejected rationalism (*Western Civilization*, 9th ed., pp. 483–86 / 10th ed., pp. 482–84; Historical Thinking Skills—Analyzing Evidence:

Content and Sourcing; Learning Objectives OS-5, OS-7; Key Concept 2.3).

36. **(D)** Enlightenment thinkers began to look for natural laws to govern society, believing that if a rational person (such as Newton) could discover the natural laws that governed the physical world, then they would be able to apply the rules of reasoning to other issues and find the natural laws that would help them improve their world (*Western Civilization*, 9th ed., pp. 483–86 / 10th ed., pp. 482–84; Historical Thinking Skills— Causation, Analyzing Evidence: Content and Sourcing; Learning Objectives OS-5, OS-7; Key Concept 2.3).

37. **(C)** Newton's cosmology was the synthesis of the ideas of Copernicus, Kepler, and Galileo (*Western Civilization*, 9th ed., pp. 483–86 / 10th ed., pp. 482–84; Historical Thinking Skills— Patterns of Continuity and Change Over Time, Analyzing Evidence: Content and Sourcing; Learning Objectives OS-5; Key Concept 2.3).

38. **(A)** As seen in his dress and the attire of his wife and daughters, it is clear that Tsar Nicholas valued Russian autocratic traditions and hoped to appeal to the aristocracy (*Western Civilization*, 9th ed., pp. 742–43 / 10th ed., pp. 738–39; Historical Thinking Skills—Analyzing Evidence: Content and Sourcing, Contextualization; Learning Objectives PP-10, IS-5; Key Concept 3.3, 3.4).

39. **(C)** The tsarist government did not tolerate any resistance to its policies; as a result, political parties were forced underground and became revolutionary (*Western Civilization*, 9th ed., pp. 742–43 / 10th ed., pp. 738–39; Historical Thinking Skills— Contextualization; Learning Objectives PP-3, PP-10, IS-5; Key Concept 3.1, 3.3, 3.4).

40. **(B)** Marxist ideology did not play a role in the Russian Revolution of 1905 (*Western Civilization*, 9th ed., pp. 742–43 / 10th ed., pp. 738–39; Historical Thinking Skills—Causation; Learning Objectives PP-10, SP-4, IS-5; Key Concept 3.3, 3.4).

41. **(D)** Although the October Manifesto did provide for the protection of some civil liberties, the most important result was the creation of the Duma, which satisfied the middle-class moderates. By satisfying the middle class, the tsar gained their support in his repression of workers' revolts (*Western Civilization*, 9th ed., pp. 742–43 / 10th ed., pp. 738–39; Historical Thinking Skills—Causation; Learning Objectives PP-10, SP-4, IS-5; Key Concept 3.3, 3.4).

42. **(C)** The incredibly ornate interior design with a more plain exterior is a hallmark of Rococo architecture, which is more of a reaction to Deism and the resurgence of religion at the end of the nineteenth century. A Calvinist church would not be named after 14 saints, and rulers did not promote pilgrimages any longer (*Western Civilization*, 9th ed., pp. 517–18 / 10th ed., pp. 513–14; Historical Thinking Skills—Periodization, Contextualization,

Analyzing Evidence: Content and Sourcing, Synthesis; Learning
Objective OS-13; Key Concept 2.3).

43. **(B)** Wealthy members of the upper class and absolute monarchs
were patrons of the arts in the 18th and early 19th centuries, as
was the still-powerful Catholic Church. Rococco style developed
to showcase the strength and power of these elites. (*Western
Civilization*, 9th ed., pp. 517–18 / 10th ed., pp. 513–14; Historical
Thinking Skills—Contextualization, Analyzing Evidence: Content
and Sourcing, Synthesis; Learning Objective OS-13; Key Concept 2.3).

44. **(D)** One of the ideals of the Enlightenment and a belief of most
of the philosophes was Deism, that God had created the world
to run by laws of nature and then left it to run on its own
without interference—like a gigantic clock (*Western Civilization*,
9th ed., pp. 507–08 / 10th ed., p. 506; Historical Thinking Skills—
Contextualization; Learning Objective OS-11; Key Concept 2.3).

45. **(C)** Rousseau's argument that the government's job is to act as
a general will to guarantee the rights and equality of all men is
evident in this passage. While all the other answers are also
beliefs of Rousseau, they are not discussed in the work given
(*Western Civilization*, 9th ed., pp. 511–12 / 10th ed., pp. 508–10;
Historical Thinking Skills—Argumentation, Analyzing Evidence:
Content and Sourcing; Learning Objective OS-7; Key Concept 2.3).

46. **(B)** Rousseau's *The Social Contract* is similar to John Locke's
Two Treatises on Civil Government, in which he argues for the
inalienable natural rights of man and the government's job to
uphold those rights (*Western Civilization*, 9th ed., pp. 505, 511–
12 / 10th ed., pp. 501–02, 508–10; Historical Thinking Skills—
Periodization, Comparison, Argumentation; Learning Objective
OS-7; Key Concept 2.3).

47. **(D)** Rousseau believed that pure reason and logic had caused
society to become less moral over time. He advocated the
tempering of logic with emotion (*Western Civilization*, 9th ed.,
pp. 511–12 / 10th ed., pp. 508–10; Historical Thinking Skills—
Patterns of Continuity and Change Over Time, Comparison;
Learning Objective OS-7; Key Concept 2.3).

48. **(A)** Since only a small percent of the German population was
literate and since these literate people were mainly concentrated in
urban areas, the woodcuts were a useful way to spread the
reformation ideas (*Western Civilization*, 9th ed., pp. 375–76 / 10th
ed., pp. 372–73; Historical Thinking Skills—Causation; Learning
Objective IS-3; Key Concept 1.1).

49. **(D)** The woodcut gives a negative view of the Catholic Church's
sale of indulgences within church on the right while the left
side, showing a Lutheran Church service, is a positive view of
the beliefs of Lutherans such as having only two sacraments
and a pastor teaching directly from God's Word. (*Western
Civilization*, 9th ed., pp. 375–76 / 10th ed., pp. 372–73; Historical
Thinking Skills—Analyzing Evidence: Content and Sourcing;
Learning Objective OS-5; Key Concept 1.1).

50. **(C)** Although the woodcut is filled with many images, making it somewhat difficult to interpret, the panel on the left clearly shows Jesus attending a Lutheran religious service while the panel on the right shows an angry God looking down on the papal sale of indulgences. Thus, answer choice C is the correct answer to this question (*Western Civilization*, 9th ed., pp. 375–76 / 10th ed., pp. 372–73; Historical Thinking Skills—Analyzing Evidence: Content and Sourcing; Learning Objectives OS-2, OS-11; Key Concept 1.3).

51. **(D)** Many of the leaders of the many territorial entities in the Holy Roman Empire benefited greatly from the Reformation. Those princes who rejected the Roman Catholic faith and seized church lands benefited from greater wealth and territorial expansion. Due to the close relationship between the Catholic Church and the Holy Roman Empire, some princes supported the Reformation in an attempt to gain greater political autonomy. Finally, corruption within the Roman Catholic Church convinced some people concerned with the need for religious reform to join with Luther. Answer choice D is the correct answer, since the Reformation was initially centered in cities, where it was easy for converted clergymen to work with ruling elite (*Western Civilization*, 9th ed., pp. 375–77 / 10th ed., pp. 372–74; Historical Thinking Skills—Causation; Learning Objective SP-3; Key Concept 1.3).

52. **(D)** Although the loss of Hungary and Transylvania to the Hapsburgs in Austria significantly weakened the Ottoman Empire, those losses occurred in 1699 and had nothing to do with the nineteenth-century decline of their empire (*Western Civilization*, 9th ed., pp. 660–62 / 10th ed., pp. 656–58; Historical Thinking Skills—Patterns of Continuity and Change Over Time; Learning Objectives SP-13, SP-14, SP-17; Key Concept 3.2, 3.4).

53. **(B)** Fearing that the Russians would try to capitalize on Ottoman weakness and expand their naval power in the eastern Mediterranean, and also fearing that the collapse of the Ottomans could allow for the growth of Russian influence in the Balkans, Britain and France supported the Ottomans in the Crimean War (*Western Civilization*, 9th ed., pp. 660–62 / 10th ed., pp. 656–58; Historical Thinking Skills—Causation; Learning Objectives SP-13, SP-14, SP-17; Key Concept 3.1, 3.2, 3.4, 3.5).

54. **(C)** Since approximately 60% of the deaths associated with the Crimean War resulted from disease and poor quality medical care for wounded soldiers, the British allowed Florence Nightingale to lead a group of nurses to take care of soldiers. Her efforts led many middle-class women to become nurses (*Western Civilization*, 9th ed., pp. 660–62 / 10th ed., pp. 656–58; Historical Thinking Skills—Causation; Learning Objectives OS-4, IS-6, IS-10; Key Concept 3.3).

55. **(A)** The war was a turning point, since it broke up the Concert of Europe, the alliance system that had been created by the Congress of Vienna. Since Russia felt betrayed by Austria's lack of support in the war, their friendship ended, effectively

destroying the alliance and leading to future diplomatic reorganizations (*Western Civilization*, 9th ed., pp. 486–88 / 10th ed., pp. 623–28, 656–58; Historical Thinking Skills—Periodization; Learning Objectives SP-13, SP-14, SP-17; Key Concept 3.1, 3.2, 3.4, 3.5).

ANSWERS FOR SECTION I, PART B: SHORT-ANSWER QUESTIONS

QUESTION 1

A) One challenge faced by both Louis XIV and the seventeenth-century Polish monarchs was that Polish monarchs, elected by the nobility, and Louis XIV all faced challenges to their power from the aristocracy. When Louis XIV became king, French nobles rebelled against him in the Fronde, hoping to regain some of the privileges and powers taken from them by Louis XIII and Cardinal Richelieu. Elected by assemblies of nobles who carefully limited royal power, the Polish monarchs also had to protect their sovereignty from ambitious nobles.

B) One domestic difference between France under Louis XIV and Poland in the seventeenth century was that while the nobles of Poland demanded that the kings share power with the Sejm, a legislative body of nobles and powerful townspeople, Louis XIV found ways to limit the power of the nobility and assert his sovereign power. While Polish monarchs were forced to share power over taxation, foreign and military policy, and appointment of state officials and judges, Louis XIV managed to take away much of the actual political and economic power of the nobility. For example, Louis established the intendant system to govern the provinces, while he moved many nobles to Versailles where he was able to entertain them and make them feel privileged while actually taking away their ruling power.

C) One major foreign difference between France under Louis XIV and Poland in the seventeenth century was that Louis XIV increased the military power of France, making it a strong European power with a fearsome army and good fortifications, while the disunity within Poland added to the military weakness of the nation and its declining international status. While Louis XIV was able to maintain the defense of France, involve France in four major wars in which he gained some European territory, and successfully colonize parts of the New World, Polish kings ruled over a nation that had little unity and became a battleground for foreign powers.

(*Western Civilization*, 9th ed., pp. 453–56 / 10th ed., pp. 440–47, 455–56; Historical Thinking Skills—Comparison; Learning Objectives SP-1, SP-2, IS-7; Key Concept 2.1)

QUESTION 2

The idea of utilitarianism is that people have the right to do as they wish as long as it does not harm others. Thoughts and opinions never harm others and therefore should not be regulated by the government. Actions that are potentially harmful must be weighed to see whether they help more people than they harm. For this reason, middle-class liberals liked utilitarianism because it allowed them great freedoms when it came to running their factories and their social lives. Indeed, keeping a factory running provided jobs for the poor which, even if hours were long and pay was low, was better than having no job at all.

(*Western Civilization*, 9th ed., pp. 636–38 / 10th ed., pp. 631–32; Historical Thinking Skills—Patterns of Continuity and Change Over Time, Periodization, Argumentation; Learning Objective PP-8, PP-10; Key Concept 3.3)

QUESTION 3

A) Article 231 of the Versailles treaty, often called the War Guilt Clause, blamed Germany for causing World War I and was one of the most controversial parts of the treaty. Assigning the blame for the war to Germany provided justification for requiring reparation payments from Germany. Since the victors of the war wrote the treaty, they wanted to make sure that they were not perceived as contributing to the outbreak of war in any way. Therefore, they added the War Guilt Clause to exonerate themselves from responsibility and justify the reparations that they demanded from Germany.

B) One of the most significant pieces of evidence that justified the War Guilt Clause was the German blank check. On July 6, 1914, Germany sent a telegram to Austria-Hungary in which German officials offered any and all help necessary to punish Serbia for the assassination of the Archduke Franz Ferdinand. Counting on support from Germany, Austro-Hungarian officials were bold enough to issue an ultimatum to Serbia on July 23rd that they knew Serbia would not be able to accept. Although Serbia was an ally of Russia, Austria did not fear war with Serbia or Russia, because they knew they had the backing of Germany; therefore, the German blank check provides evidence that the War Guilt Clause was justified.

C) One piece of evidence that illustrates the injustice of the War Guilt Clause was Russia's support of Serbia. Russia and Serbia had an alliance. When the Archduke Franz Ferdinand was assassinated by Gavrillo Princip, a Bosnian nationalist, Austria-Hungary blamed Serbian political and military officials for their support of Princip. Serbian support of the Black Hand was reckless and endangered the peace just as much as the German blank check. Although Serbia claimed that they were not involved, evidence showed that they probably knew more than they admitted. Serbia received support from Russia and, consequently, was less inclined to fully cooperate with Austrian demands. In defense of Serbia, Russia mobilized and was the first nation to do so. Due to the expense and work involved in mobilization in the early 1900s, mobilization was almost equivalent to a declaration of war. Thus, Russia's support of Serbia shows that the War Guilt Clause was not justified.

(*Western Civilization*, 9th ed., pp. 762–65 / 10th ed., pp. 758–62. 786–87; Historical Thinking Skills—Argumentation; Learning Ol SP-6, SP-18; Key Concept 4.1)

QUESTION 4

In this question, you are being asked to make a judgment based on historical evidence of your own choosing. This idea of argumentation is one of the historical thinking skills critical to doing well on the AP® Exam. As long as you choose two laws and make a clear argument, your answer cannot be wrong, but you have to make the argument to prove your point. The Factory Act of 1833, for example, made it illegal to employ children under the age of nine in textile mills. The Mines Act took women and children out of the pits, although they could still work above ground in the breakers, sorting rooms, etc. The Ten Hours Act limited the hours women and children could work. Drawbacks of the Factory Act were many. It was limited to textile mills only and was very difficult to enforce. Who was to say that the malnourished waif standing for 13 hours a day at a spinning jenny wasn't nine years old like she claimed to be? While the Mines Act took women and children out of the most dangerous part of the mine, the other parts of the mining industry were also unsafe and unsanitary. The Ten Hours Act, while a step in the right direction, was bad, since it cut the hours women and children could work but did not affect their pay, thus cutting the amount of money they could earn. It had the benefit of forcing factory owners to hire more men, who were paid higher wages.

(*Western Civilization*, 9th ed., p. 621 / 10th ed., p. 617; Historical Thinking Skills—Comparison, Argumentation, Synthesis; Learning Objective SP-5; Key Concept 3.2)

ANSWER FOR SECTION II, PART A: DOCUMENT-BASED QUESTION (DBQ)

THE DOCUMENTS

Below are short analyses of the documents. As you read the documents, you should be looking for not only what the document actually says but also other important things about it. Does it indicate change or continuity over time? What is the opinion of the writer and WHY might he hold this opinion? How is the document affected by its format or intended audience? The italicized words suggest what your margin notes might include:

DOCUMENT 1 This speaker says that it is not the fault of the Irish but, instead, of God (Providence). He also says that Parliament should help the Irish. *Because he is probably an Irish delegate, O'Connell deals with both cause and response from an Irish point of view of looking to the British for support. Since this is a record of parliamentary proceedings, it is evident that the famine is a large enough problem even in February of 1946 that the British government is investigating it.*

DOCUMENT 2 This editorial holds that a cause of the famine was Irish laziness. It notes that in response to the famine, the Irish are holding gatherings that could escalate. It finishes by indicating that the Irish will have to change before they can be helped. *This editorial in the* London Times *offers both a cause and a response from the British point of view.*

DOCUMENT 3 This document shows that mobs were becoming more violent. We also see, however, that a union is providing for its struggling members by providing a workhouse, which is already filled to more than capacity. *These news articles from the* London Times *deal with two responses to the famine, but since they are published in a British newspaper, they are written for a British audience and are more likely writing what the British public wants to hear. It is also important to note that the Irish were trying to help themselves, although there is little evidence that the British government is doing anything yet.*

DOCUMENT 4 This document describes a family that eats weeds so their dying father can have the last of their food, offering an account of the course of the famine. *The* Cork Examiner *offers an Irish point of view as it discusses both the course and response, clearly blaming the British.*

DOCUMENT 5 This document comments on both the course of and responses to the famine. Queen Victoria writes of the suffering of the Irish and the Scots and of the lack of food supplies. She also discusses her subjects' responses, telling her Anglican ministers to collect donations for the Irish in their churches. *As the ruler of an empire, Queen Victoria has a specific point of view about the famine. She comments on both the course of and responses to the famine, showing compassion to those in need. She does not, however, discuss any government aid but instead expects charitable contributions and voluntary subscriptions to take care of the problem. It is also important to note that, as a noblewoman and ruler of a country, she would not have seen or experienced any of the horrors of the famine firsthand.*

DOCUMENT 6 This document states that God caused the famine because of Irish selfishness and that therefore little should be done. *The man in charge of the British relief effort, Trevelyan, discusses both cause and response from a strongly British point of view. It is important to note too that this document, written in 1848, finally shows that the British government is starting to do something to alleviate the famine, fully two years after it had begun.*

DOCUMENT 7 *This sketch offers a British response to the famine: emigration was the solution. Since it was published in a journal that often satirized the British government, the point of view of the cartoonist can be interpreted to mean that sending the Irish elsewhere instead of helping them was part of the British government's plan. The cartoon can also be seen as satire in that immigrants' lives were not substantially better in their new lands, where they often ended up working in factories or sweatshops.*

The clearest way to organize the documents is to put them in three groups—cause, course, and impact. Then, within each group you can note the author's point of view as you juxtapose the comments.

#	POV	Cause	Course	Response
1	I	Not the fault of the Irish. God's fault		Parliament should help.
2	B	Lazy Irish.		Gatherings could become outrageous. Irish can't be helped until they fix themselves.
3	B			Mob attacked bakers' shops for food. Union workhouses used to house and feed.
4	I		Eating wild weeds. Horror of deaths.	British not doing enough. "Imperial rulers." Possible genocide?
5	B		Irish and Scots suffering. Failure of food supplies.	British subjects donating. Victoria sets up church collections.
6	B	God angry because of Irish selfishness and perversity.		Do not do much to lessen God's interaction.
7	B			Irish should emigrate to America.

For this question, the main historical thinking skill being assessed is Causation; in employing this skill, you will also be using the skill of Patterns of Continuity and Change over Time. Other document-based questions may focus on other historical thinking skills. All document-based questions will also assess the historical thinking skills of Argumentation, Analyzing Evidence: Content and Sourcing, Contextualization, and Synthesis.

A Sample Essay for the Document-Based Question

The Irish Potato Famine began with a potato blight, a fungus that attacked Ireland in the fall of 1845. During the Industrial Revolution, British landowners had bought up Irish land, enclosing it for livestock and forcing the Irish farmers to grow potatoes on rocky hillsides. As the blight spread, waned, and returned, the Irish, as part of the United Kingdom (which included England, Scotland, and Wales), were devastated by a famine that led to approximately one million deaths. In both Ireland and England, a wide variety of strategies were used to provide the needed help for the starving Irish. Arguments ensued about what and who caused the famine, and what should be done to end it. The views on the Irish Famine were generally divided between those who felt compelled to help the Irish and those who did not. Many people commented on causes, some blaming God, some blaming the Irish themselves, and some blaming the British. Responses changed over time as the famine and its horrors grew worse.

There were several reasons offered for why the famine occurred. Some people blamed the Irish for their suffering. An editorial in the *London Times* held the Irish responsible, saying that their character would have to be corrected before they could be helped. This clearly was a British point of view in that the Irish had been a thorn in the side of the British for several centuries. Queen Elizabeth and James I had sent Protestants to help them tame the Irish, and there had been periodic Irish rebellions ever since. Indeed, the nationalism of the first half of the nineteenth century had caused many Irish to call for Irish home rule. Mr. O'Connell, as an Irishman speaking in the British Parliament, said that the famine came from God (Providence), and was not based on any fault of the Irish people themselves. It seems that he might have said this in response to the attacks on the Irish themselves as the cause. As a representative of the Irish, he would not want to place any blame on them but instead would defend them.(1) Even two years after the famine started, Charles Trevelyan, the man in charge of the British government relief to the famine victims, implied the cause was the weak character of the Irish when he spoke of their selfish, perverse character. There were several people who wrote of the course of the famine and the horror of people's lives. An Irish newspaper, the Cork Examiner, told of a family that ate wild weeds so that the little food they had could be given to their dying father. Their view is colored by the compassion for fellow Irish, which can even be seen in the title of the article, "Scenes of Misery."(6) The British themselves were not unaware of what was happening, as seen in an editorial published in the London Times in 1846. The writer, however, seems to be more concerned about the Irish people gathering to protest, which could evolve into riots. He further comments that the Irish were waiting for the British government to help them instead of helping themselves. Queen Victoria herself showed concern about the situation in Ireland. In a letter to the Archbishop of Canterbury, she spoke of the severe distress her Irish and Scottish subjects were dealing with because of the lack of food. As a ruler, the queen would clearly be concerned about the welfare of her subjects, but she would also be influenced by the fact that riots by hungry Irish were causing problems in her kingdom.(7)

Although various opinions were offered on the causes and course of the famine, the greatest disparity in opinions was in the types of responses suggested and enacted. The responses tended to be divided along national lines, with the British generally looking to the Irish to fix themselves, and the Irish looking more for positive solutions. An editorial in the London Times said that there could be no help offered to the Irish until they changed, because the Irish essentially thought that the famine was good and they were just waiting for government help.(4) And, again, the man in charge of British aid to the Irish, who should have shown compassion, seemed callous as he said that because the famine was God teaching the Irish a lesson, the famine should not be mitigated. On the other hand, many spoke of the need to offer support. O'Connell spoke to Parliament about the importance of its taking action.(1) A quite radical view was offered by the Cork Examiner. It wondered if the British "Imperial rulers" were doing nothing, waiting for the Irish to leave or die. This belief in a virtual British genocide of the Irish was not uncommon among the Irish.(6) The fact that many Irish did leave their land to go to work in British factories or join the British military could be used to show that the British had good reason to do nothing to stop the famine. It did benefit them by providing a desperate workforce who would not complain about long hours and low pay in the factories. Another mention of food being given was in a more direct, personal manner. A union in Ireland, when its workhouse filled beyond capacity, still offered meals to the destitute members who needed help. This is an especially interesting viewpoint because it reflected the growing importance of unions in people's lives as the Industrial Revolution grew.(5) Queen Victoria encouraged Anglican churches to collect money to help the suffering Irish, beginning her request by noting that many British had already given voluntarily to the Irish. As the leader of the church, she could marshal the resources of the church to provide financial, non-governmental support to the Irish. It is interesting to note that she is not pushing her government to help, but her church.

Finally, there were those who spoke of more direct action. Some looked at retaliation as an answer. The editorial in the London Times noted that people were having gatherings and processions that could become "outrageous." This editor was definitely warning his fellow countrymen of the mood of the Irish.(4) Violence was reported in a story about food riots in Dublin, detailing a large number of people who attacked bakers' shops. Emigration of the Irish was the final action taken, one that involved thousands of Irish moving to the United States, Canada, and Australia. Punch, a British satirical journal, encouraged Irish emigration through a drawing showing a destitute family in Ireland juxtaposed with a well-off family in America. Its pro-emigration and hard work bias is clearly seen, especially with the subtly placed shovel in the "There" image, indicating the hard work necessary for success in America.

There was a wide variety of views about the Irish Famine, with blame being placed by some on the Irish themselves, by some on the British, and by some on God. As the famine went on, people pointed out the tremendous suffering. Views on how to respond also changed as many offered food and financial support or suggested revolt or immigration as a solution. The Irish Potato Famine can be clearly seen within the context of the nineteenth-century British Empire. Nationalistic feelings, which had been present in Ireland since it was taken by the British centuries before, were exacerbated by the famine. The taking of Irish lands by British landowners and enclosure of those lands to raise sheep for the British woolen mills were seen as a major cause by the Irish, who then had to immigrate to Britain or America to work in those very factories.

(*Western Civilization*, 9th ed., pp. 610–11 / 10th ed., pp. 606–07; Historical Thinking Skills—Causation, Patterns of Continuity and Change Over Time, Argumentation, Analyzing Evidence: Content and Sourcing, Synthesis; Learning Objective PP-3, IS-7; Key Concept 3.1, 3.2)

COMMENT This essay uses all of the documents effectively and accurately to analyze the differing views on the Irish Famine. The three topics—cause, course, and response—are dealt with separately, yet tied together through analysis. The essay looks at the issues of Change Over Time and Causation, also bringing in necessary outside information about the effects of nationalism and the industrial revolution on the Irish. It securely places the essay in the context of early nineteenth-century Britain, while noting the importance of immigration to America as well.

SCORING This question is worth 7 points. It earns 1 point for thesis in the introductory paragraph (sometimes called a thesis paragraph) and another point for using all or all but one of the documents to support the thesis. It gets 3 points for understanding and all of the documents individually and specifically with reference to their intended audience, point of view, format, argument, limitations, and/or social context. It gets 1 point for providing relevant outside information and another point for placing the argument in the context of the nineteenth century by discussing nationalism, industrialization, and immigration.

The DBQ essay counts for 25 percent of the examination score.

ANSWERS FOR SECTION II, PART B: LONG-ESSAY QUESTIONS

A SAMPLE ESSAY FOR QUESTION 1

Although scientists of the period continued to believe in such things as alchemy, witchcraft, and astrology, the Scientific Revolution was a revolutionary period when seen in the context of what was believed previously about the universe and man. It is also revolutionary in that it contributed to the Enlightenment in its emphasis on the use of reason to understand the world. Its impact was felt in the political realm as philosophes looked to natural law in the creation of better systems of government. Some philosophes applied these ideas of natural law to social issues, such as encouraging equal rights. Finally, economics was viewed through the lens of reason as many called for laissez-faire.

Before the Scientific Revolution, knowledge of the universe was based on the theories of the classical writers Ptolemy and Galen and seen through a lens of religious belief and superstition. It was thought that the universe was geocentric—that it had all been created to revolve around man. Both the universe and man were believed to be made up of four elements, which all had their proper place. Movement occurred when an element was not in its proper place, and sickness occurred when the elements or humors were unbalanced in the body.

Scientists such as Copernicus and Galileo advanced heliocentric theory, asserting that the earth (and man) was not the center of creation. Vesalius published an anatomy book, *On the Structures of the Human Body*, and scientists like William Harvey studied circulation of the blood. Von Leeuwenhoek, who used the microscope to see cells, disproved the theory of the four humors. In all, a new period of scientific thinking using logic, reason, and experimentation was ushered in, leading to the Enlightenment.

Politically, the Enlightenment offered a variety of responses to the old order that were directly rooted in the ideas of scientists like Isaac Newton and the political philosophy of John Locke. Newton's belief in a world that could be logically analyzed and Locke's theory that people had natural rights that should be protected led philosophers to analyze contemporary governments as they looked for the type most in line with natural rights and reason. The Baron de Montesquieu, for example, after studying the English system, said that power should be divided so that no one person or group could gain too much power. His system of separation of powers along with balance of power should, therefore, protect the rights of the individual. Voltaire, as well, having lived in England, looked to that country's system of a limited monarchy and freedom of the press as offering a logical political system that would protect people's rights.

Enlightened philosophes, such as Voltaire, also applied the ideas of the Scientific Revolution and Locke to social issues. Voltaire offered not only political theories but also social ones. Applying logic to religion, Voltaire expressed concern with the power of the Catholic Church and its dogmatic beliefs. He sought a faith that would be reasonable and protective of people's true liberties. Mary Wollstonecraft went beyond most philosophes in espousing a belief that not only should the rights of men be protected, but those of women should, too. She believed that it was reasonable to see that men and women had equal rights, including the right to an education. Because of his belief in *tabula rasa*, or the blank slate, Locke had encouraged education virtually a century before as the foundation of a good society. David Hume also based his work on these same beliefs as he wrote of a "science of man" and the importance of studying man to create a better world.

Finally, the enlightened economic philosophy had its roots in the work of the Scientific Revolution and Locke. The physiocrats, led by François Quesnay, believed that man's natural economic rights were most logically protected by laissez-faire. The system of free enterprise would allow people great economic freedom through the removal of mercantilistic controls. Adam Smith described this new discipline of economics in *The Wealth of Nations*, which laid the foundation for a new, more logical system of economics.

The Scientific Revolution, in spite of the fact that some old beliefs remained, was a major break with the past and directly influenced the work of the philosophes during the Enlightenment to promote the use of reason to understand and better the world and the importance of education in building that new world.

(*Western Civilization*, 9th ed., pp. 477–90 / 10th ed., pp. 474–88; Historical Thinking Skills—Periodization, Causation, Patterns of Continuity and Change Over Time, Argumentation, Synthesis: Learning Objective 1.1; Key Concept 1.1, 2.2).

QUESTION 2

This question, like the one above it, asks you to assess how much of a change occurred during a particular period of European history, in this case the Renaissance. It does not specify art as a topic, although your answer should include the arts and how they reflected their time, specifically Renaissance ideals. Your essay could also include other ways in which the Renaissance was a revolutionary time period, such as the emphasis on logical thinking (seen in the essay above and evinced by Copernicus, Galileo, and Vesalius). Your essay must also include some arguments for things that did NOT change. Women actually lost rights during the Renaissance and while serfdom had disappeared in much of Western Europe, peasants still labored on noble-owned property in most places. The Catholic Church, although weakened by growing secular interests, still held great power and influence.

You should begin your essay with a quick overview of the period before the Renaissance, one in which the emphasis was on society as a whole and one's place in it. The idea of the serf in his village, the noble in his castle, and the townsman in his city was to survive and to be a good Christian until death took him to the afterlife. In contrast to this bleak view, the Renaissance was a time of bettering oneself. One ideal you should discuss is humanism, one of the major facets of the Renaissance. Because humanism was a belief in the importance of education and literature in the improvement of man, you should cite works of literature and art that illustrate those points. You could discuss the writings of humanists, such as Castiglione's *The Courtier*, and paintings, such as Raphael's portrait of Castiglione. The ideal of Individualism is another ideal you should address. The respect for the individual, which was in direct contrast with the focus on the group during the Middle Ages, can be shown through such works as Titian's *Portrait of a Man*, Cellini's *Autobiography*, or Castiglione's *The Courtier*.

You should also discuss secularism, the growing focus on people's lives outside of the Catholic Church. Point out that secularism did *not* mean that people were not religious, but that they looked at their everyday lives in addition to their religious lives. Da Vinci's *Last Supper* and Michelangelo's painting of the ceiling of the Sistine Chapel, as well as his sculpture of Moses and his *Pièta*, would provide you with excellent examples of the importance of faith in Renaissance art, but examples of secular portraits such as the *Mona Lisa* and classically influenced works like Petrarch's poems and Raphael's *School of Athens* show the importance of the classical world in painting.

Finally, you should include a paragraph on things that did not change, such as the fact that women actually lost rights that they had enjoyed during the Middle Ages. Castiglione's *Book of the Courtier* makes plain that a woman's job is to help her husband become the man of virtue. While some women did flourish in this time, like Christine de Pisan, Isabella d'Este, and Caterina Sforza, it was within the confines of what was allowed of them. Peasants, while no longer serfs, were still poor, owed many feudal dues to their lords, and had few rights.

You should have a clearly structured essay that is organized by ideals and that does not simply focus on the arts to the virtual exclusion of a discussion of the ideals. Each topic must provide significant examples that are tied to the topic through analysis as you build your argument. Your conclusion should come back to the prompt by pointing out that although there were major changes during the Renaissance, there were also things that did not change.

(*Western Civilization*, 9th ed., pp. 335–57 / 10th ed., pp. 332–54; Historical Thinking Skills—Periodization, Causation, Patterns of Continuity and Change Over Time, Argumentation, Synthesis; Learning Objective OS-5, OS-10, SP-1, IS-3, IS-6, IS-9; Key Concept 1.1)

Part II

A Review of AP® European History

Period 1: 1450–1648

Period 1 of the AP® European History framework examines the changes that occurred as Europeans emerged from the Middle Ages and struggled with divisive social, political, and religious issues. Beginning with the Renaissance, continuing through the Reformation period, and culminating in the early modern wars of religion, this era marked a turning point in the history of Europe and its relationship with the New World. Renaissance thinkers began to challenge the authority of traditional religious and scientific beliefs, unified Christendom began to collapse with the rise of new monarchies and sovereigns who controlled everything in their realms, and technological advances allowed Europeans to venture further, gaining control of an expanding global economy. The following charts outline the learning objectives and topics from the content outline that fit into this era.

THEMATIC LEARNING OBJECTIVES FOR PERIOD 1

INTERACTION OF EUROPE AND THE WORLD

Learning Objectives—Students are able to…	Relevant Topics in the Concept Outline
INT-1: Assess the relative influence of economic, religious, and political motives in promoting exploration and colonization.	1.4.I—Commercial and religious motivations 1.4.III—Competition for trade
INT-2: Analyze the cultural beliefs that justified European conquest of overseas territories and how they changed over time.	1.4.I—Christianity
INT-3: Analyze how European states established and administered overseas commercial and territorial empires.	1.4.II—Technological advances 1.4.III—Commercial networks
INT-4: Explain how scientific and intellectual advances—resulting in more effective navigational, cartographic, and military technology—facilitated European interaction with other parts of the world.	1.4.II—Technological advances
INT-5: Evaluate the impact of the Columbian Exchange—the global exchange of goods, plans, animals, and microbes—on Europe's economy, society, and culture.	1.4.IV—Shift of economic power to Atlantic states; economic opportunities
INT-6: Assess the role of overseas trade, labor, and technology in making Europe part of a global economic network and in encouraging the development of new economic theories and state policies.	1.4.I—Access to gold, spices, and luxury goods; mercantilism 1.4.III—Commercial and trading networks 1.4.IV—Columbian Exchange
INT-7: Analyze how contact with non-European peoples increased European social and cultural diversity and affected attitudes toward race.	1.4.IV—Expansion of slave trade

76

Learning Objectives—Students are able to…	Relevant Topics in the Concept Outline
INT-9: Assess the role of European contact on overseas territories through the introduction of disease, participation in the slave trade and slavery, effects on agricultural and manufacturing patterns, and global conflict.	1.4.IV—Columbian Exchange
INT-11: Explain how European expansion and colonization brought non-European societies into global economic, diplomatic, military, and cultural networks.	1.4.I—European motives and mercantilism 1.4.III—Establishment of empires 1.4.IV—Slave trade and new goods 1.5.I—Money economy

POVERTY AND PROSPERITY

Learning Objectives—Students are able to…	Relevant Topics in the Concept Outline
PP-1: Explain how and why wealth generated from new trading, financial, and manufacturing practices and institutions created a market and then a consumer economy.	1.4.IV—Rise of mercantilism
PP-2: Identify changes in agricultural production and evaluate their impact on economic growth and the standard of living in preindustrial Europe.	1.5.II—Commercialization of agriculture; codification of serfdom
PP-6: Analyze how expanding commerce and industrialization from the sixteenth through the nineteenth centuries led to the growth of cities and changes in the social structure, most notably a shift from a landed to a commercial elite.	1.2.I—Commercial and professional groups gained in power 1.5.I—New social patterns 1.5.III—Expansion of cities; challenges to traditional political and social structures
PP-7: Explain how environmental conditions, the Agricultural Revolution, and industrialization contributed to demographic changes, the organization of manufacturing, and alterations in the family economy.	1.5.IV—Family was primary social and economic institution
PP-9: Assess how peasants across Europe were affected by and responded to the policies of landlords, increased taxation, and the price revolution in the early modern period.	1.5.II—Commercialization of agriculture and abolition of traditional rights
PP-13: Analyze how cities and states have attempted to address the problems brought about by economic modernization, such as poverty and famine, through regulating morals, policing marginal populations, and improving public health.	1.5.III—Government regulation of public morals

OBJECTIVE KNOWLEDGE AND SUBJECTIVE VISIONS

Learning Objectives—Students are able to…	Relevant Topics in the Concept Outline
OS-1: Account for the persistence of traditional and folk understandings of the cosmos and causation, even with the advent of the Scientific Revolution.	1.1.IV—Continued appeal of alchemy and astrology; oral culture of peasants 1.5.V—Popular culture

Learning Objectives—Students are able to…	Relevant Topics in the Concept Outline
OS-2: Analyze how religious reform in the sixteenth and seventeenth centuries, the expansion of printing, and the emergence of civic venues such as salons and coffeehouses challenged the control of the church over the creation and dissemination of knowledge.	1.1.I—New methods of scholarship and new values 1.1.II—Invention of printing 1.3.I—Protestant and Catholic reformations
OS-3: Explain how political revolution and war from the seventeenth century on altered the role of the church in political and intellectual life and the response of religious authorities and intellectuals to such challenges.	1.2.I—New political systems and secular systems of law 1.2.II—Concept of the balance of power 1.3.III—Conflicts among religious groups
OS-4: Explain how a worldview based on science and reason challenged and preserved social order and roles, especially the roles of women.	1.5.IV—Renaissance and Reformation debates
OS-5: Analyze how the development of Renaissance humanism, the printing press, and the scientific method contributed to the emergence of a new theory of knowledge and conception of the universe.	1.1I—Revival of classical texts; new methods of scholarship 1.1.II—Invention of the printing press 1.1.III—Visual arts of the Renaissance 1.1.IV—Science based on observation, experimentation, and mathematics
OS-6: Explain how European exploration and colonization were facilitated by the development of the scientific method and led to a reexamination of cultural norms.	1.4.II—Advances in navigation, cartography, and military technology
OS-9: Explain how new theories of government and political ideologies attempted to provide a coherent explanation for human behavior and the extent to which they adhered to or diverged from traditional explanations based on religious beliefs.	1.1.I—Secular models for political behavior 1.2.I—Concept of sovereign state and secular systems of law
OS-10: Analyze the means by which individualism, subjectivity, and emotion came to be considered a valid source of knowledge.	1.1.I—Humanists valued the individual
OS-11: Explain how and why religion increasingly shifted from a matter of public concern to one of private belief over the course of European history.	1.1.I—Humanist secular models for individual and political behavior 1.3.I—New interpretations of Christian doctrine and practice 1.3.III—Adoption of religious pluralism

STATES AND OTHER INSTITUTIONS OF POWER

Learning Objectives—Students are able to…	Relevant Topics in the Concept Outline
SP-1: Explain the emergence of civic humanism and new conceptions of political authority during the Renaissance, as well as subsequent theories and practices that stressed the political importance and rights of the individual.	1.1.I—Civic humanism and secular theories 1.1.III—Art in service of the state 1.2.I—Growth of sovereign nation-state

Learning Objectives—Students are able to...	Relevant Topics in the Concept Outline
SP-2: Explain the emergence of and theories behind the New Monarchies and absolutist monarchies, and evaluate the degree to which they were able to centralize power in their states.	1.2.I—New Monarchs and the rise of nation-state 1.2.III—Absolutism and its challengers 1.3.II—Control over religion 1.3.III—Religious wars
SP-3: Trace the changing relationship between states and ecclesiastical authority and the emergence of the principle of religious toleration.	1.1.I—Secular political theories 1.2.I—State control over religion 1.3.II—Reformation and religious conflict 1.3.III—Religious wars
SP-5: Assess the role of colonization, the Industrial Revolution, total warfare, and economic depressions in altering the government's relationship to the economy, both in overseeing economic activity and in addressing its social impact.	1.4.I—Colonization and mercantilism
SP-7: Explain the emergence of representative government as an alternative to absolutism.	1.2.III—Limits to absolutism
SP-10: Trace the ways in which new technologies from the printing press to the Internet have shaped the development of civil society and enhanced the role of public opinion.	1.1.II—Printing press
SP-11: Analyze how religious and secular institutions and groups attempted to limit monarchical power by articulating theories of resistance to absolutism and by taking political action.	1.2.III—English Civil War and nobles 1.3.II—Religious minorities 1.3.III—Religious war and religious pluralism
SP-13: Evaluate how the emergence of new weapons, tactics, and methods of military organization changed the scale and cost of warfare, required the centralization of power, and shifted the balance of power.	1.2.II—Early modern military revolution 1.4.II—Exploration and colonization
SP-15: Assess the impact of war, diplomacy, and overseas exploration and colonization on European diplomacy and balance of power until 1789.	1.2.II—Peace of Westphalia and balance of power 1.4.III—Colonial empires

INDIVIDUAL AND SOCIETY

Learning Objectives—Students are able to...	Relevant Topics in the Concept Outline
IS-1: Explain the characteristics, practices, and beliefs of traditional communities in preindustrial Europe and how they were challenged by religious reform.	1.1.IV—Alchemy and astrology 1.5.I—Hierarchy and social status 1.5.II—Subsistence agriculture 1.5.IV—Family economy, gender roles, European marriage pattern 1.5.V—Folk culture and communal norms

Learning Objectives—Students are able to…	Relevant Topics in the Concept Outline
IS-2: Explain how the growth of commerce and changes in manufacturing challenged the dominance of corporate groups and traditional estates.	1.2.I—Rise of commercial and professional groups 1.5.I—Financial and commercial innovations 1.5.II—Price revolution and commercial agriculture 1.5.III—Urban expansion and problems
IS-3: Evaluate the role of technology, from the printing press to modern transportation and telecommunications, in forming and transforming society.	1.1.II—Printing press—Renaissance and Reformation 1.4.II—Exploration and colonization
IS-4: Analyze how and why the nature and role of the family has changed over time.	1.5.IV—Family, gender roles, and marriage patterns
IS-6: Evaluate the causes and consequences of persistent tensions between women's role and status in the private versus the public sphere.	1.5.IV—Family economy; Renaissance and Reformation debates on women 1.5.V—Communal norms and enforcement
IS-7: Evaluate how identities such as ethnicity, race, and class have defined the individual in relationship to society.	1.4.IV—Slave trade 1.5.I—New economic elites and hierarchy
IS-9: Assess the extent to which women participated in and benefited from the shifting values of European society from the fifteenth century onward.	1.5.IV—Renaissance and Reformation
IS-10: Analyze how and why Europeans have marginalized certain populations (defined as "other") over the course of their history.	1.3.II—Religious minorities 1.4.I—Colonial conquest 1.5.III—Urban migrants and regulation of morals 1.5.V—Communal norms and witchcraft

KEY CONCEPTS FROM THE COLLEGE BOARD

1.1 The worldview of European intellectuals shifted from one based on ecclesiastical and classical authority to one based primarily on inquiry and observation of the natural world.

1.2 The struggle for sovereignty within and among states resulted in varying degrees of political centralization.

1.3 Religious pluralism challenged the concept of a unified Europe.

1.4 Europeans explored and settled overseas territories, encountering and interacting with indigenous populations.

1.5 European society and the experiences of everyday life were increasingly shaped by commercial and agricultural capitalism, notwithstanding the persistence of medieval social and economic structures.

The Renaissance: 1350–1550

The Renaissance was a period of change following the crises that ultimately transformed the civilization of the late medieval world. Wars, the Black Death, and demographic changes such as the growth of towns and trade led to intellectual, artistic, social, economic, and political changes that collectively shaped this new era, the age of the Renaissance.

Key Terms

alchemy

astrology

cinquecento

city-states

Civic Humanism

Great Schism

Hanseatic League

humanism

individualism

National (New) Monarchies

Naturalism

patronage

primogeniture

quattrocento

Renaissance

secularism

vernacular

Chapter Key Concepts

- Recovering from the conflicts of the late medieval period, including the Hundred Years' War, some regions in Europe were organized into National (New) Monarchies. Political leaders imposed their will on surrounding areas, forming the modern nation states of France, Spain, and England. Italy did not form a national monarchy at the time, but instead was a collection of city-states, each ruled by a powerful family.

- Italy, the geographical gateway between East and West, had a cultural and economic advantage over the rest of Europe and traded extensively. The Italian city-states soon became the trade and cultural centers of Renaissance Europe.

- The rediscovery of classical science and scholarship, led by Byzantine and Islamic scholars, spawned a renewal of interest in the study of art, science, philosophy, and the classical world and launched intellectual pursuits that began in Italy and spread over Northern and Southern Europe from about 1350 to 1550. The dissemination of this new learning was accelerated by late medieval and Renaissance writings that were produced in the vernacular, and by the invention of the printing press in the 1450s.

For a full discussion of the Renaissance, see *Western Civilization,* 9th and 10th editions, Chapters 11 and 12.

WHAT WAS THE RENAISSANCE?

The Renaissance was a unique period in European history. It began in Italy in about 1350 and spread throughout most of Southern and Northern Europe, culminating in the recovery from the crises of the fourteenth century, the renewal of interest in the classical civilizations of the Greeks and Romans, the development of a new appreciation of the abilities of the individual, and the creation of new styles of art. Although much of what characterizes the Renaissance actually began in the late medieval period—such as the growth of towns and the breakdown of the feudal system—it was during the Renaissance that these trends became dominant and widespread. The Renaissance can therefore be considered a distinct historical period.

RENAISSANCE ECONOMIC AND SOCIAL STRUCTURES

The seed for the Renaissance sprouted in Italy with the revival of trade with the Near East in the eleventh century. Italian cities quickly developed into vibrant urban societies, and Italian merchants became masters of bookkeeping, finding new markets, and securing monopolies on trade commodities. During the thirteenth and fourteenth centuries, these moneyed Italian cities expanded into the surrounding countryside to become powerful city-states that dominated the economic and political life around them, thriving as a result of the emergence of the merchant class.

Italian dominance in commerce was hurt during the fourteenth century by competition with the powerful merchants of the Hanseatic League, a commercial and military alliance of more than 100 North German cities and guilds that dominated Baltic Sea trade. As a result, the Italians began to lose their dominant position in commerce. Also afflicted by the plague, Italian merchants soon lost economic ground in Northern Europe. This recession in trade, however, was temporary. The Italian city-states' trade revived once again in the fifteenth century with the decline of the Hanseatic League, and it economically fueled the Renaissance. The wool trade in Flanders and Florence expanded again, as did the sale of new luxury trade items, such as silks and glassware. At the same time, the mining industry began to develop.

The growth of trade and new industries required economic and commercial support, so banking became a vast source of wealth, spawning powerfully rich families, including the Medici in Florence. The Medici banking house became the largest in Europe, financing the political rise of that family in both the city-state of Florence and the Roman Catholic Church.

Although the feudal system gave way to the system of National (New) Monarchies in many areas of Europe, the basic social structure, based on three estates, remained largely in place during the Renaissance. Members of the First Estate, the clergy, enjoyed clerical privilege and were subject only to the laws of the Church. Most also paid no taxes. This estate consisted of upper clergy, such as the pope, cardinals, bishops, and archbishops; and the lower clergy, such as the parish priests and friars. During the Renaissance, most Europeans still lived by the law of primogeniture, in which the eldest son inherited the property. Many younger sons of the aristocracy continued to live the lives of aristocrats by becoming upper clergymen, a position of wealth and power. Although some of these clergymen faithfully served the church, many paid little attention to their clerical duties, and for this they were resented by many commoners.

Members of the Second Estate, the nobility, owned much of the land in Europe and held most of the important military and political positions. During the Renaissance, expectations for aristocrats changed; they were supposed to possess a classical education, have an interest in the arts, behave like gentlemen and ladies, and embrace the ideals of civic virtue. The Italian writer Baldassare Castiglione outlined the behavior expected of a Renaissance aristocrat in his book *The Courtier.*

The Third Estate—all those who did not make up the clergy or nobility—continued to diversify during the Renaissance, with peasant members of the Third Estate representing about 90 percent of the European population. In the Italian city-states and other trade centers, merchants and artisans gained considerable wealth and political influence, although many poor, often unemployed people also lived in those areas. At the bottom of the social structure were slaves. Western European slave markets had existed since the twelfth century, when Muslim slaves were sold by the Spanish to wealthy Italians. After the Black Death reduced the number of farm laborers, the demand for slaves soared and slaves of many different races were imported from Africa, the Balkans, Constantinople, Cyprus, Crete, and the lands surrounding the Black Sea, with the majority arriving from the Eastern Mediterranean and Black Sea regions. Italian law gave owners complete control over their slaves, but the slaves were often treated well because they were a considerable investment—an average healthy young slave cost about the equivalent of several years' wages for a free servant.

THE RENAISSANCE FAMILY

Marriages were arranged during the Renaissance, often as business deals designed to increase the wealth and status of families. In Italy, women typically married between ages 16 and 18, while most men married in their 30s or early 40s. Within the family, the man made all the legal and financial decisions and expected the woman to bear children and manage the home. For an aristocratic woman, this meant managing the servants, managing the estate while her husband was away, and hosting social gatherings. Aristocratic women typically used wet nurses and attempted to have as many children as possible so there would be a surviving heir despite the high mortality rate for children. Wives of merchants and farmers handled the home responsibilities and also helped their husbands in the shop or in the fields. Working-class women usually nursed their own children, so they did not conceive at the same rate as the wealthy. Sometimes young unmarried women made a living working as prostitutes in the cities.

AP® Tip

Remember that although Renaissance women had important roles in their families, most women did not have political rights and were considered lower in status than men. Unlike the Middle Ages, when women sometimes worked in shops and even served as masters in guilds, Renaissance women increasingly found themselves restricted from the guilds and without political and economic power. It is important to know about the changing roles played by women of the Renaissance era; facts like these can be useful when interpreting documents for a document-based question or writing a free-response thematic essay.

RENAISSANCE POLITICS

Two major forms of governance emerged during the Renaissance: the Italian city-states and National (New) Monarchies. In Italy, there were a number of small city-states and five dominant, wealthy, powerful city-states: Florence, the Papal States, Naples, Milan, and Venice. Florence, Milan, and Venice were all technically republics, although in practice they were governed by wealthy and powerful oligarchies directed by rich merchants and aristocratic families who often intermarried to increase their power. They rarely allowed true republican control and often excluded the common people of their territories from voting or even holding citizenship. Conflicts among the city-states prevented them from combining into a united Italy and often erupted into wars.

Diplomatic efforts and the Treaty of Lodi (1454), attempts to create a peaceful settlement and maintain an effective balance of power, fell victim to conflicts over familial land claims and papal elections. The competition among the states and their inability to cooperate with one another made them an inviting target for foreign invaders eager to gain control over their land and wealth. Eventually, rivalries between Spain and France and their ongoing battles in Italy led to the sacking of Rome in 1527 and the subsequent extension of Spanish power into

Italy. The inability of the states to band together to fight off foreign control ultimately delayed Italian unification and nationhood until 1870.

AP® Tip

The modern diplomatic system of resident ambassadors emerged in the Italian city-states during the Renaissance. Although temporary visiting ambassadors had been used during the Middle Ages, resident ambassadors first became widespread during this era. Their presence in the different states led to the development of protocols for the treatment of ambassadors and for conducting diplomatic business. This is a good example of one way that politics during the Renaissance differed from previous eras.

In Northern Europe, divided feudal kingdoms gradually gave way to National (New) Monarchies as growing towns began to form alliances with kings. This allowed the new monarchs to hire loyal merchants and townspeople for bureaucratic jobs, thus reducing the power of the nobles and weakening the bonds of feudal society. As a result of the Hundred Years' War and the Great Schism, the clergy and nobility were in decline and were less able to assert their power against the emerging monarchies. This allowed the emergence of sovereign states with centralized economic, military, and bureaucratic powers. The ability to create a standing national army with professional soldiers, and sometimes mercenaries, gave kings more power, but it also forced them to become creative fundraisers because they had to pay for their military and bureaucratic expenses without directly taxing the nobility. The most important National (New) Monarchies to emerge during the Renaissance were France, Spain, and England. England's defeat in the Hundred Years' War and the collapse of Burgundy allowed for the consolidation of the French monarchy. Following its defeat in the Hundred Years' War, England experienced a period of political upheaval. The War of the Roses, a civil war that began in the 1450s, ended in 1485, when Richard III was defeated by Henry Tudor, who as Henry VII consolidated the power of the English monarchy.

During the Middle Ages, Castile and Aragon emerged as the two strongest Christian kingdoms on the Iberian peninsula. The marriage of Isabella of Castile to Ferdinand of Aragon allowed for the creation of the Spanish monarchy; together, the two rulers could secure their borders, control the population, venture to the new world, and take control of religion in their realm through the institution of the Inquisition. Although both kingdoms maintained their own administrative institutions (such as their *Cortes* and courts), the royal council was composed mainly of middle-class bureaucrats instead of power-hungry noblemen, and it promoted the idea that the monarchs embodied state power, thus consolidating political power into their hands. Militarily, the development of a professional royal army by Ferdinand and Isabella to replace the feudal-style armies allowed the monarchs to effectively control their lands. By the beginning of the 1500s, the Spanish army, with its strong infantry force, had become the strongest in Europe, allowing Spain to expand its power to new territories. In terms of religion, the monarchs consolidated their control over church and religious matters in several ways. Ferdinand and Isabella gained control over the Spanish Church when they were granted the right to designate important Church officials. Likewise, the institution of the Inquisition in 1478 allowed them to expel Jews and Muslims and many converts suspected of not actually being fully converted, thus leading to uniformity of religious belief. The consolidation of Spanish power in the fifteenth century made Spain one of the most powerful nations in Europe by the sixteenth century.

The exception to this model of centralization was the Holy Roman Empire, the center of which later became modern Germany. By the thirteenth century, the Empire had grown into a collection of virtually independent principalities, free imperial city-states (self-governing cities), and ecclesiastical (church-owned and -governed) states, all nominally under the control of an elected Holy Roman Emperor. By allowing seven elector states to choose the emperor, the electoral process ensured weakness. Although the Habsburg family ruled the Empire continuously from 1452 on, emperors had to deal with internal disputes among the hundreds of individual German rulers and with external threats posed by the growing power of the Turks and the presence of the French in the Italian states.

The Renaissance witnessed the beginnings of a profound shift in political philosophy, as well as political organization. In *Education of a Christian Prince* (1516), the Dutch humanist Erasmus closely reflected medieval political views when he declared that a prince has moral obligations to his subjects. His contemporary Niccolo Machiavelli, who was active in Florentine politics and witness to the intrigue of Renaissance statecraft, wrote books and treatises on politics. The most famous is *The Prince*, written in 1513 but not published until 1532. He recommended a more practical approach to politics: to be successful, to accomplish his goals for the state, a prince should be guided not by moral conscience, but by expediency.

RENAISSANCE HUMANISM

Celebrating individualism and secularism, humanism was the defining intellectual movement of the Renaissance. The humanists, many of them writers and teachers, advocated the study of liberal arts and the examination of classical works. Humanism changed the way Europeans perceived the world and encouraged skepticism of traditional authorities, including the Catholic Church. Often called the father of humanism, the Italian writer known as Petrarch promoted the study of the classics and ancient Greece and Rome. The growth of humanism in Italy spawned a new interest in classical values, such as civic virtue, and a rising curiosity about classical writers and philosophers. Eager scholars, including Pico della Mirandola, even formed humanist societies—among them, the Neoplatonist organization known as the Florentine Platonic Academy, which enjoyed the patronage of Cosimo de' Medici.

The emergence of humanism and the growth of interest in intellectual pursuits among wealthy laymen led to the proliferation of humanist schools and tutors. Education was primarily for the elite, who believed it provided practical preparation for their participation in the lives of their communities. Renaissance humanists promoted the study of the humanities: grammar, rhetoric, poetry, ethics, and history. Basing their studies on the classical works of Greece and Rome, humanists began to free education and thinking from the tight grip of church authorities. With the development of the movable-type printing press in the mid-fifteenth century, the demand for printed materials and lay education grew rapidly.

Perhaps not surprisingly, the growth of the printing industry proved exceptionally profitable to printers. Demand for books created by the new, cheaper method of production created an explosion in printing. Intellectually, the expansion of a literate lay public and the growing number of schools and universities created an educated population that questioned the status quo and thirsted for new ideas. As a result, many types of printed materials became popular, including books on piety and religion, calendars and almanacs, works on philosophy, popular romances, and "how-to" books about subjects such as farming and child rearing. Movable-type printing allowed for the creation of standardized and definitive texts and facilitated cooperation among scholars in various regions of Europe, accelerating the tempo of learning and scientific discoveries. Printing also led to an explosion of religious materials, from Bibles and prayer books to biblical commentaries. Protestant reformers also used printing to distribute their new religious ideas, and both Protestants and Catholics put out propaganda about the Reformation. A literate lay public began to question the Church.

RENAISSANCE ART

The Renaissance is famously a period of creativity and innovation in art and architecture. Stimulus came from various quarters: the patronage of powerful and wealthy individuals and rulers, such as the Medici in Florence, financing for its projects from the Church, and investment by wealthy merchant groups, such as the Florentine cloth merchants.

Renaissance art differed from medieval art in several significant ways. Religious themes remained the subject of much Renaissance art, especially in Northern Europe, where many artists specialized in altarpieces and manuscripts. Classical and secular themes, however, also emerged—a result of the growing influence of humanism and the increasing interest in classical ideas and writings—and the renewed appreciation of human worth and individualism made portraiture popular. Advances in the study and application of mathematical and scientific principles were applied to Renaissance art; colors became more realistic, as did the portrayal of anatomy and the representation of perspective. Renaissance artists also depicted the first nudes since classical times. Renaissance sculpture and architecture changed as well, displaying classical influences and motifs in pieces such as Donatello's *David* and Brunelleschi's dome in the cathedral in Florence. As a result of these advances, most Renaissance artists considered the realistic portrayal of their subjects to be the primary goal of art.

The status of Renaissance artists also rose over the course of the Renaissance. Early Renaissance artists, still regarded as artisans, usually began their careers as apprentices in craft guilds. By the 1500s, artists were regarded as geniuses and held much higher status than a typical craftsman.

AP® Tip

Although there is an endless array of Renaissance artists, it is important to know the names and major works of some of the more famous ones. It is also important to be able to analyze the ways in which art of any time period is related to societal changes, using specific artists and their works as examples. You want to be prepared both to write intelligently about Renaissance art and to answer multiple-choice questions on the topic.

THE RENAISSANCE CHURCH

The power and credibility of the church were irreversibly damaged by the time of the Renaissance. During the 14th century, the Great Schism and calls for reform by religious leaders, such as John Hus and John Wyclif, provoked the questioning of Church teachings and attacks on its corruption and unbridled power. Despite the Church's efforts to stifle heretics, clean up abuses within itself, and resolve conflicts—for example, the papal crisis resolved by the Council of Constance—the erosion of confidence in the Church continued, furthered by the secular and political actions of some Renaissance popes. As a result, many humanist scholars no longer took the Church's admonitions concerning their intellectual activities as seriously as they once might have. The political, economic, religious, and social trends of the Renaissance combined with the breakdown of the Church eventually led to the Protestant Reformation.

Content Review Questions

1. The main goal of humanist education was to
   (A) create scholars who valued a life of learning and solitude.
   (B) create philosophers and historians.
   (C) provide education for the merchant class.
   (D) produce complete citizens who could participate in the civic life of their communities.

2. One of the important Renaissance changes that impacted artists was that
   (A) artists began to be treated as artistic geniuses rather than artisans.
   (B) artists began to paint with watercolors rather than oil paints.
   (C) artists began to paint in a fanciful style rather than stressing realism in their works.
   (D) artists began to be treated as artisans rather than artistic geniuses.

3. All of the following were effects of the invention of printing on European life EXCEPT that
   (A) Renaissance ideas and learning spread to even the poorest Europeans as education became more readily available.
   (B) with the greater availability of books, a greater desire for knowledge soon emerged.
   (C) printing led to the sharing of ideas among scholars and accelerated discoveries in fields such as the sciences.
   (D) printing led to the development of a greater lay reading public.

4. Which of the following aims was considered by many Northern Renaissance artists to be their primary goal?
   (A) The portrayal of important religious truths for the illiterate masses
   (B) The imitation of nature and the realistic portrayal of their subjects
   (C) The development of new types of paints
   (D) The portrayal of classical motifs

5. Which of the following was a major belief of John Wyclif?
   (A) The Church of England should break away from the Roman Catholic Church.
   (B) The Latin Vulgate Bible should be the only version in use, to avoid vernacular translations that might not accurately reflect the original text.
   (C) Popes should be stripped of their temporal authority and property.
   (D) The veneration of saints was important because it gave worshippers examples to follow.

6. Although slavery had largely disappeared in late medieval Europe, disasters such as the Black Death led to the reintroduction of slavery in Italy on a fairly large scale by the late fourteenth century. Where were Italian slaves primarily acquired?
   (A) Africa
   (B) Spain
   (C) The Eastern Mediterranean and Black Sea regions
   (D) Asia

7. Which of the following statements best describes Renaissance humanism?
   (A) It was promoted by the Church as a means to educate the population so that they could read the Bible.
   (B) It was an intellectual movement that rejected the ideals of the ancient Greeks and Romans.
   (C) It was rejected by Petrarch as detrimental to the advancement of society.
   (D) It was an intellectual movement that was based on the study of the classical works of the Greeks and Romans.

8. Which of the following originated in the Renaissance Italian city-states?
   (A) The concept of a social contract
   (B) The need for Christian moral principles as a guide for government leaders
   (C) The modern system of resident ambassadors and embassies
   (D) The use of the separation of powers

9. All of the following are true about Italian Renaissance humanism EXCEPT
   (A) humanists studied the liberal arts, based on the writings of ancient Greek and Roman authors.
   (B) humanism was the most important literary movement associated with the Renaissance.
   (C) Petrarch did more than anyone else to foster the development of humanism in the fourteenth century.
   (D) most humanists were members of the clergy rather than laymen.

10. All of the following were important characteristics that European nobles were expected to possess by c. 1500 EXCEPT
    (A) impeccable character, grace, talents, and birth into a worthy family.
    (B) achievements including military prowess, a classical education, and talent in the arts.
    (C) the ability to provide enough goods and services for local consumption to satisfy the needs of people in one's region.
    (D) good behavior and conduct, including the ability to show one's accomplishments but still remain modest and gracious.

Multiple-Choice Questions

Questions 1–3 refer to the following image.

Source: Interfoto/History/Alamy Stock Photo

1. One of the most important reasons for the formation of the Hanseatic League was
   (A) the protection of trade interests in the Netherlands.
   (B) the protection of new cottage industries in the German states.
   (C) the protection of trade interests along the Baltic and North Seas.
   (D) the protection of trade interests of Italian merchants in the Mediterranean region.

2. Lübeck was featured in the woodcut above because it was
   (A) primarily responsible for the foundation of the Hanseatic League.
   (B) the largest city on the Baltic sea.
   (C) the capital of the Hanseatic City-State.
   (D) the center of the Renaissance woolen industry.

3. The formation of the Hanseatic League represented which of the following trends?
   (A) The importance of textiles in the Renaissance economy
   (B) The growing importance of small Italian city-states in the European economy
   (C) The growing economic independence of the nobility from the national territorial states
   (D) The growing economic independence of merchants in the European economy

Questions 4–6 refer to the following quotation.

This leads us to a question that is in dispute: Is it better to be loved than feared, or vice versa? My reply is one ought to be both loved and feared; but, since it is difficult to accomplish both at the same time, I maintain it is much safer to be feared than loved, if you have to do without one of the two. For of men one can, in general, say this: They are ungrateful, fickle, deceptive and deceiving, avoiders of danger, eager to gain. As long as you serve their interests, they are devoted to you. They promise you their blood, their possessions, their lives, and their children, as I said before, so long as you seem to have no need of them. But as soon as you need help, they turn against you. Any ruler who relies simply on their promises and makes no other preparations, will be destroyed. For you will find that those whose support you buy, who do not rally to you because they admire your strength of character and nobility of soul, these are people you pay for, but they are never yours, and in the end you cannot get the benefit of your investment. Men are less nervous of offending someone who makes himself lovable, than someone who makes himself frightening. For love attaches men by ties of obligation, which, since men are wicked, they break whenever their interests are at stake. But fear restrains men because they are afraid of punishment, and this fear never leaves them. Still, a ruler should make himself feared in such a way that, if he does not inspire love, at least he does not provoke hatred.

Source: Machiavelli, *The Prince* (1513), trans. D. Wootton, (Indianapolis: Hackett Publishing Company, 1995), pp. 51–52.

4. Which of the following best describes a way in which the ideas of Machiavelli contradicted most late medieval theories of politics?
   (A) Machiavelli asserted that a ruler was justified in exercising his power only if it contributed to the common good of all the people he served.
   (B) Machiavelli asserted that a ruler ought to behave according to Christian moral principles.
   (C) Machiavelli asserted that the ethical side of a prince's activity was just as important as the practical results of his actions.
   (D) Machiavelli asserted that morality should not be the basis for political decisions.

5. Which of the following would most likely have contributed to Machiavelli's belief that it was "safer to be feared than loved"?
   (A) The Thirty Years War
   (B) Political unrest in Florence
   (C) Territorial challenges from the Ottoman Empire
   (D) The Great Schism

6. Machiavelli gave expression to which of the following preoccupations of Renaissance leaders?
   (A) The desire to gain political power
   (B) The desire to promote the arts
   (C) The desire to conquer lands in the New World
   (D) The desire to promote humanism

Short-Answer Questions

1. Compare the organization of medieval and Renaissance political structures and answer A, B, and C.
   A) Briefly explain ONE important difference between medieval and Renaissance political organization.
   B) Briefly explain ONE important difference between medieval and Renaissance social organization.
   C) Briefly analyze ONE factor that accounts for the difference you identified in B.

2. Answer A, B, and C by analyzing intellectual and artistic changes that occurred during the Renaissance.
   A) Briefly explain ONE important development that occurred in the visual arts during the Renaissance.
   B) Briefly explain ONE important intellectual development that emerged during the Renaissance.
   C) Briefly analyze ONE factor that accounts for the development you identified in A.

Long-Essay Questions

1. Analyze the economic, intellectual, and religious impacts of the development of the movable-type printing press in late fifteenth- and early sixteenth-century Europe. (Historical Thinking Skills: Causation)

2. Analyze the factors that contributed to the unification of Spain and the consolidation of Spanish power in the fifteenth century. (Historical Thinking Skills: Causation)

Answers

CONTENT REVIEW QUESTIONS

1. **(D)** Humanist schools drew elite, upper-class citizens and stressed a liberal arts curriculum as the key to freedom. Aiming to prepare citizens to serve their communities, they rejected the idea that the life of an intellectual was one of solitude (*Western Civilization*, 9th ed., pp. 344–49 / 10th ed., pp. 346–47; Historical Thinking Skills—Contextualization; Learning Objective OS-2; Key Concept 1.1).

2. **(A)** Answer A correctly describes a major change in attitude toward artists that occurred during the fifteenth century. At the beginning of the Renaissance, the medieval tradition of artists beginning their careers as apprentices to a craft guild master was commonplace. By the end of the fifteenth century, artists were viewed by society as creative geniuses who deserved great respect. Choices B, C, and D all

incorrectly describe trends in Renaissance art (*Western Civilization*, 9th ed., p. 355 / 10th ed., pp. 353–55; Historical Thinking Skills— Patterns of Continuity and Change Over Time; Learning Objective OS-5; Key Concept 1.1).

3. **(A)** Answers B, C, and D are all important impacts of the invention of movable-type printing in fifteenth-century Europe. Although the lay reading public did expand, Renaissance learning and ideas never did gain a broad base among the masses because education was still limited to nobles and those who could pay for an education (*Western Civilization*, 9th ed., p. 350 / 10th ed., p. 349; Historical Thinking Skills—Causation; Learning Objective OS-2; Key Concept 1.1).

4. **(B)** Northern Renaissance artists had a strong interest in realism and the imitation of nature. Choices A, C, and D all occurred during the Renaissance but were not the primary goals of the artists (*Western Civilization*, 9th ed., pp. 350–51 / 10th ed., p. 349–50; Historical Thinking Skills—Contextualization; Learning Objective OS-5; Key Concept 1.1).

5. **(C)** Wyclif rejected all claims not found directly in the Bible, and seeing no basis in scripture for their temporal claims, Wyclif believed that popes should be stripped of their authority and property. Although relatively revolutionary in his beliefs, Wyclif did not advocate a break from the Church. He favored the translation of the Bible into the vernacular so more people could read it and rejected pilgrimages and the worship of saints (*Western Civilization*, 9th ed., p. 362 / 10th ed., p. 361; Historical Thinking Skills—Contextualization; Learning Objective OS-11; Key Concept 1.3).

6. **(C)** The Eastern Mediterranean and the Black Sea regions were the largest sources of slaves for Italy until 1453, when the Ottoman Turks conquered the Byzantine Empire (*Western Civilization*, 9th ed., pp. 336–337 / 10th ed., pp. 335–36; Historical Thinking Skills—Contextualization; Learning Objective INT-7; Key Concept 1.4).

7. **(D)** Humanism was often seen as a threat to the power of the Church. Promoted by Petrarch and embraced by the elite, it was based on a study of the classics (*Western Civilization*, 9th ed., pp. 344–47 / 10th ed., pp. 343–46; Historical Thinking Skills—Patterns of Continuity and Change Over Time; Learning Objective OS-5; Key Concept 1.1).

8. **(C)** Answers A and D originated elsewhere. The use of resident ambassadors emerged during the Renaissance Italian wars and remains a feature of modern diplomacy (*Western Civilization*, 9th ed., pp. 343–44 / 10th ed., pp. 342–43; Historical Thinking Skills—Patterns of Continuity and Change Over Time; Learning Objective SP-1; Key Concept 1.2).

9. **(D)** Most humanists pursued secular occupations and were laymen, not members of the clergy (*Western Civilization*, 9th ed., pp. 344–47 / 10th ed., pp. 343–46; Historical Thinking Skills—Contextualization; Learning Objective OS-2; Key Concept 1.1).

10. **(C)** Although the nobility was beginning to diversify as a result of the growing wealth and power of the merchant class, expectations of proper behavior and the traditional characteristics of the nobility continued to define this social class (*Western Civilization*, 9th ed., pp. 335-36 / 10th ed., pp. 334-35; Historical Thinking Skills—Contextualization; Learning Objective IS-1; Key Concept 1.5).

MULTIPLE-CHOICE QUESTIONS

1. **(C)** The Hanseatic League was an alliance of Northern European trading cities located along the Baltic and North Seas (*Western Civilization*, 9th ed., pp. 334–35 / 10th ed., pp. 332–34; Historical Thinking Skills—Causation; Learning Objective PP-6; Key Concept 1.2).

2. **(A)** Lübeck was one of the leading cities in the formation of the Hanseatic League and became known as the "Queen of the Hansa" (*Western Civilization*, 9th ed., pp. 334–35 / 10th ed., pp. 332–34; Historical Thinking Skills—Causation; Learning Objective PP-6; Key Concept 1.2).

3. **(D)** The growth of the Hanseatic League represented the growing independence of merchants in the European economy and their ability to establish a monopoly over the trade of products such as timber, fish, and grains (*Western Civilization*, 9th ed., pp. 334–35 / 10th ed., pp. 332–34; Historical Thinking Skills—Contextualization; Learning Objective PP-1; Key Concept 1.4).

4. **(D)** Machiavelli disagreed with the traditional medieval view that morality and ethical concerns should provide the foundation of a prince's political actions. He believed that decisions should be based on a consideration of what will work best. Although choice A looks inviting, it is incorrect because, according to Machiavelli, what was best for the state might not be best for the common good of all the people served by a prince. Usually when an answer uses words like "all" or "none" it is incorrect, since most historical situations do not involve either all of the people or none of them (*Western Civilization*, 9th ed., pp. 343–45 / 10th ed., pp. 342–44; Historical Thinking Skills—Patterns of Continuity and Change Over Time; Learning Objective SP-1; Key Concept 1.1).

5. **(B)** In the years immediately preceding Machiavelli's writing of *The Prince*, Florence was torn apart by wars and political rivalries (*Western Civilization*, 9th ed., pp. 343–45 / 10th ed., pp. 342–44; Historical Thinking Skills—Contextualization; Learning Objective SP-1; Key Concept 1.1).

6. **(A)** Although some of the other answer choices might have been coincidental benefits enjoyed by Renaissance political leaders, the desire to gain and hold political power was crucial to ruling success. *The Prince* focused on how a ruler could gain political power (*Western Civilization*, 9th ed., pp. 343–45 / 10th ed., pp. 342–44; Historical Thinking Skills—Analyzing Evidence: Content and Sourcing, Contextualization; Learning Objective SP-1; Key Concept 1.1).

SHORT-ANSWER QUESTIONS

1. A) One difference that existed between medieval and Renaissance political organization was the decline of feudalism and the growth of National (New) Monarchies in Western Europe. Monarchies such as those found in Spain, France, and England no longer needed to depend on feudal structures to survive and, instead, began to dominate Europe politically and economically as they developed bureaucracies and standing armies and started to control global economic developments.

   B) One difference that existed between medieval and Renaissance social organization was the rise of the merchant class and the decline of the traditional nobility. Although nobles remained important and powerful in many places for many more centuries, in the National (New) Monarchies, their power began to erode, as the merchant class grew more powerful.

   C) One reason that the nobility began to lose power during the Renaissance was that the merchant class grew much more wealthy and powerful due to the growth of an international economy. When the merchants began to challenge and sometimes surpass the economic means of the landed nobility, the power of nobles began to decline. Likewise, as National (New) Monarchies formed national armies, no longer permitting nobles to control their own private standing armies, the nobles lost their hold on power.
   (*Western Civilization*, 9th ed., pp. 333–44 / 10th ed., pp. 334–343; Historical Thinking Skills—Comparison; Learning Objective SP-2; Key Concept 1.2)

2. A) One important change that occurred in the visual arts during the Renaissance was the creation of art that was more secular. During the middle ages, art was mostly created for the Catholic Church or for rich patrons who still commissioned religious works, hoping to bring the blessings of the church upon their kingdoms. During the Renaissance, art became more realistic and often portrayed realistic scenes and secular subjects. Renaissance art often showed the beauty in nature, including humans, and even depicted scenes from Greek and Roman mythology.

   B) One important intellectual development that occurred during the Renaissance was the emergence of humanism. Humanists studied the classical texts of the Greeks and Romans and applied their learning to the Renaissance world. Humanists stressed the genius of the human mind and the beauty of the human form and were not afraid to challenge traditional beliefs. Humanists hoped to perfect humankind and spread their learning through a liberal arts education, composed of poetry, grammar, rhetoric, history, and moral philosophy.

   C) One of the reasons for the growth of less religious and more secular subjects in the Renaissance visual arts was that there were more non-clerical patrons of the arts during the Renaissance than had been the case in previous centuries. The Church no longer possessed a monopoly on power in Renaissance society, so wealthy merchants and noblemen began to commission paintings that they enjoyed themselves, rather than feeling

the need to please the Church. As humanist education spread and the reintroduction of the classical works prompted an appreciation of ancient civilizations, humanist themes began to move into the visual arts.
(*Western Civilization*, 9th ed., pp. 344–56 / 10th ed., pp. 343–56; Historical Thinking Skills—Patterns of Continuity and Change Over Time; Learning Objective OS-1; Key Concept 1.1)

LONG-ESSAY QUESTIONS

1. Your essay should include a discussion of the economic, intellectual, and religious impacts of the printing press in the late fifteenth and early sixteenth centuries in Europe. Looking at the economic impact, the growth of the printing industry proved to be exceptionally profitable to printers. Demand for books skyrocketed. That, in turn, created greater demand for the new technology, which quickly spread to other parts of Europe.

    To discuss the intellectual impact, you should examine the growth of the new literate lay public and the expansion of schools and universities. This section of the essay should also discuss the types of printed materials that were popular, including scholarly works, which accelerated learning and scientific discoveries throughout Europe.

    As for the religious impact, discuss both the publishing of religious titles and the use of printing to distribute the new religious ideas of the Reformation. Because printing allowed the ideas to be spread to the lay public, the questioning of Church beliefs and authority began. Thus, printing affected the speed of the spread of the Reformation. Finally, this section should include a discussion of religious propaganda, which developed because the printing press made it easy to disseminate. In your conclusion, be sure to add a brief discussion (2–3 sentences) of synthesis. You could do this by adding another category of impacts, such as the political impact of printing. You could do so by comparing the printing press to another invention that had a profound impact on the world, such as the steam engine or the Internet. Be sure to make explicit connections between the topics covered in your essay and the impacts to which you are comparing them.
    (*Western Civilization*, 9th ed., p. 350 / 10th ed., p. 349; Historical Thinking Skills—Causation; Learning Objective IS-3; Key Concept 1.1)

2. This essay should include a discussion of the political, military, and religious factors that led to the unification of Spain in the fifteenth century. A good place to begin is with a discussion of the marriage of Ferdinand of Aragon to Isabella of Castile and the subsequent consolidation of political power in the hands of the monarchs. You should point out that although both kingdoms maintained their own administrative institutions (such as their *Cortes* and courts), the royal council was populated mainly by middle-class bureaucrats rather than power-hungry noblemen. It promoted the idea that the monarchs embodied state power.

The development of a professional royal army by Ferdinand and Isabella was an important factor. By the beginning of the 1500s, the Spanish army had become the strongest in Europe.

Religion was a valuable tool in Ferdinand and Isabella's consolidation of power. When they were granted the right to choose important Spanish Church officials, they gained control over the Spanish Church. Likewise, the institution of the Inquisition in 1478 allowed them to expel Jews and Muslims and many individuals who were suspected of not really being fully converted, thus leading to a uniformity of religious belief. To conclude your essay, be sure to add a brief (2–3 sentences) discussion of synthesis. In this case, you could either compare the consolidation of power in Spain to the consolidation of power elsewhere, such as the Bourbon consolidation of power in France following the French wars of religion, or you could contrast Spanish consolidation with the decentralization in the Holy Roman Empire in the sixteenth and seventeenth centuries.
(*Western Civilization*, 9th ed., pp. 359–60 / 10th ed., pp. 357–58; Historical Thinking Skills—Causation; Learning Objective SP-2; Key Concept 1.2)

2

The Reformation and Religious Wars: The 1500s–1648

Inspired by the writings of Christian humanists, troubled by the abuses that existed within the Roman Catholic Church, and increasingly concerned with church teachings concerning salvation, Martin Luther posted the Ninety-Five Theses in 1517, igniting a movement that split the Catholic Church and resulted in a century and a half of religious warfare. This movement, the Protestant Reformation, changed the face of Christianity and led to a series of political, economic, and social reforms that affected every sphere of life in Europe. From the breakdown of political authority in the Holy Roman Empire to the extension of education to more men and women in some areas in Europe and, finally, to the development of divergent styles of art, the Reformation sparked changes that significantly altered the religious, political, economic, and social organization of Europe.

Key Terms

Act of Supremacy
Anabaptists
Anglican Church
Catholic Counter-Reformation
Christian Humanism
Council of Trent
Diet of Worms
Edict of Nantes
Elizabethan Settlement
indulgences
Huguenots
Jesuits

justification
Lutheranism
Ninety-Five Theses
Peace of Augsburg
politiques
predestination
Puritans
reformation
religious pluralism
Schmalkaldic League
simony

Chapter Key Concepts

- The Reformation contributed to the outbreak of many civil wars that were sparked not only by religious differences but also by political and economic rivalries in regions such as the Holy Roman Empire.
- Although the Reformation was primarily a religious movement, it was a catalyst for social and economic changes that encouraged education so that men and women could read the Bible, and it secured limited rights for women within the family.
- Actions taken by Martin Luther splintered the Catholic Church and sparked the Reformation. Although Luther's message and actions inspired reformers, such as John Calvin, to split from the Catholic Church, most of these other religious revolutionaries did not entirely agree with Luther's theological ideas.
- The Catholic Reformation included the formation of reform orders, such as the Jesuits and the moral improvement of clerical practices, but it reaffirmed Catholic theological doctrine.

For a full discussion of the Reformation, see *Western Civilization*, 9th and 10th editions, Chapter 13.

Europe on the Eve of the Protestant Reformation

The Protestant Reformation officially began on October 31, 1517, the date that Martin Luther posted the Ninety-Five Theses at the Castle Church in Wittenberg, but it had taken root long before, when political, economic, intellectual, and religious factors led to the questioning of papal authority and Church practices.

Christian Humanism

The growth of Christian humanism, which quickly spread from Italy to Northern Europe through both trade and the new writings made available by the printing press, laid the groundwork for the Reformation. Like the Italian humanists, northern humanists focused on the classical works of Greece and Rome and on cultural and educational reform, but they also studied early Christian writings and the Bible. These "Christian humanists," yearning for the simple piety of the early Church, criticized some of the medieval traditions of the Catholic Church and called for its internal reform.

Often called the father of Christian humanism, Erasmus translated the New Testament from the early Greek manuscripts and advocated an educated approach to Christianity. Erasmus stressed a return to the simplicity of early Christianity and criticized many of the external trappings of the Catholic Church, such as the veneration of saints. He especially disapproved of the abuses by many churchmen of his time and satirized them in a book, *In Praise of Folly*.

AP® Tip

It is important to remember that the Christian humanists were critical of the corruption and abuses of the Catholic Church, but they did not advocate a split from it. Instead, they urged reform within the Church and looked for ways to combine classical and Christian values. Wyclif and Hus sometimes show up on AP® exams. They predated the reformers, but their ideas about justification by faith alone resemble Luther's.

Another prominent Christian humanist, Sir Thomas More, was a government official, English scholar, and author of the book *Utopia*, in which he outlined an ideal society much like a modern socialist model. More is remembered for both his devotion to the Roman Catholic religion and his execution for refusing to accept King Henry VIII's break with the Church.

CORRUPTION WITHIN THE CHURCH

Corruption within the Catholic Church also fueled the Protestant Reformation. The status and credibility of the Roman Catholic Church had been damaged by the Great Schism and by common clerical abuses, such as the fathering of illegitimate children, as well as by unethical business and financial dealings. Trying to increase its revenues, the Church sold leadership positions to wealthy nobles and businessmen. Known as simony, the practice sometimes led to pluralism, the holding of several Church positions by a wealthy Church leader, and often created absenteeism because it was impossible to work in more than one place at once. But the central issue that incited Martin Luther's criticism of the Roman Catholic Church was the selling of indulgences.

AP® Tip

Indulgences were partial remissions of temporal punishment for sin. One could purchase an indulgence for oneself or for one's relatives, alive or dead. It is important to remember that although indulgences exist within the Catholic Church today, their sale is no longer allowed.

MARTIN LUTHER AND THE PROTESTANT REFORMATION

Martin Luther, a Catholic monk, agonized over the question of salvation. He concluded that one could be saved not by good works or by indulgences, but only by faith in God, a belief that became central to his theology.

On October 31, 1517, Martin Luther posted his Ninety-Five Theses, an attack on the sale of indulgences. Copies were quickly printed up and distributed throughout the German states. Although initially the pope ignored them, Luther's ideas soon gained a popular audience. In 1519, the Church challenged Luther to a series of debates with Johann Eck, a Catholic churchman, in an effort to discredit him. Instead, the debates gave Luther a forum for his ideas.

Luther's theology diverged from the Roman Catholic Church's in several areas. Luther counted not seven sacraments, but two: baptism and the Lord's Supper, because they were the only ones described in the Bible. He rejected the idea of transubstantiation, the transformation of bread and wine into the physical body and blood of Christ during communion. Instead, he believed in consubstantiation, in which the bread and wine are not transformed but are filled with the spirit of Christ. Luther also rejected the hierarchical organization of the Catholic Church. He saw Christians as belonging to a "priesthood of all believers" who could interpret the Bible for themselves. And because scripture was the only source of religious truth, he said that Catholic traditions should not be the basis of religious belief. Luther also disagreed with the Church's demand for clerical celibacy and its insistence on Latin rather than the vernacular for services.

Luther then began to question the authority of the pope, which provoked the Church to condemn him. Moving toward a more permanent split with the Church, Luther wrote several more pamphlets laying out his beliefs, including "Address to the Christian Nobility of the German Nation," "The Babylonian Captivity," and "The Freedom of the Christian Man."

AP® Tip

Martin Luther was not the first to criticize the pope and Church practices, and he did not initially intend to start a new church. Since he was the first to actually split from the Roman Catholic Church and start a new church, he is often referred to as the Father of the Reformation.

Luther was excommunicated and called before the Diet of Worms, a council convened by Holy Roman Emperor Charles V in 1521. When Luther refused to recant, he was declared an outlaw and exiled. Frederick of Saxony intervened and kept Luther in hiding at Wartburg Castle, where he stayed for a year and wrote hymns and a translation of the New Testament. Pamphlets, woodcuts, and sermons by his followers also spread his ideas. Although many humanists had supported Luther's right to publish his ideas, many, such as Erasmus, believed that he had gone too far by breaking away from the Church, and criticized him for being too radical.

Luther had the support of many members of the nobility, who saw a chance to gain political independence from the Holy Roman Emperor. In addition, by supporting the German Reformed Church, or Lutheran Church, these princes freed themselves from papal dues owed to the Catholic Church. Eventually, they reaped more economic benefit when they forcibly acquired Church lands, convents, and monasteries. Needing the support and protection of the nobility, Luther supported the Knights' War, but he did not support the social discontent that emerged during the peasants' revolts, which he stingingly condemned in a pamphlet, "Against the Robbing and Murdering Hordes of Peasants."

Charles V was unhappy with the rebellion by Luther and the princes, but he was busy with military campaigns against the encroaching Ottoman Empire and the French until 1545. By then, the Lutheran princes posed a threat to the emperor's power. Both Charles and the Protestant Schmalkaldic League attracted international help, but after nearly a decade of war, they were stalemated. The ensuing Peace of Augsburg of 1555 established the principle *cuius regio, eius religio*, meaning "whose region, his religion." The princes could choose the religion—Catholicism or Lutheranism, but not Calvinism—of their respective states. A year later, Charles abdicated and became a monk, splitting his empire between his son Philip II, who gained the Spanish Empire, and his brother Ferdinand I, who gained the Holy Roman Empire.

AP® Tip

The Peace of Augsburg legalized Lutheranism but left the question of Calvinism unsettled. Keep in mind that although the princes could choose the religions of their individual states, this did not constitute freedom of religion for the general population, because residents were expected to follow the religion chosen by the prince.

THE PROTESTANT REFORMATION OUTSIDE OF GERMANY

By the mid-1500s, the Scandinavian countries, following the leads of their monarchs, had become strong Lutheran nations.

Switzerland's 13 cantons were split. Ulrich Zwingli, a humanist and Protestant reformer, preached a more radical Protestantism. Under Zwingli's leadership, the Zurich city council decreed Protestant reforms and created a state-run church. Artwork and music were banned from churches, and recognition of papal authority and the veneration of saints were rejected. An alliance with the Lutherans floundered on the issue of consubstantiation; Zwingli believed that the bread and wine were only symbols and did not contain the real spirit of Christ. By late 1531, civil war broke out between the Protestant and Catholic Swiss cantons, a war in which Zwingli died.

The even more radical Anabaptists, who often faced persecution by both Protestants and Catholics, usually lived apart, in their own communities. All members of the community were considered equals. Believing that membership in the Christian community should be an adult choice, they baptized only adults, and they read the Bible literally. Anabaptists adhered to a strict separation of church and state, and refused to hold public office, pay taxes that could be used for military purposes, or serve in the army. Most Anabaptist communities were pacifist. A shocking exception was the Anabaptist takeover of Munster in the 1534, followed by its fall in a siege by an army of Catholics and Lutherans.

Menno Simons, an important leader of the Dutch Anabaptists, reinvented and spread the religion. His followers, called Mennonites, carried it throughout Europe and eventually to North America.

CALVINISM

While Lutheranism dominated the first half of the sixteenth century, Calvinism dominated the latter half. Born and educated in France, John Calvin, a humanist scholar and lawyer, read smuggled works of Martin Luther and became convinced that the Catholic Church needed reformation. By the 1530s, French Protestants, known as Huguenots, faced persecution by the Crown, and Calvin fled to Geneva, a city that became the center of his brand of Protestantism. It was there that Calvin wrote *Institutes of the Christian Religion*, a summary of his beliefs, in 1536.

Calvin's theology resembled Luther's but differed in several respects. First, Calvin believed in predestination—that God determines before birth who will be saved and who will be damned. According to Calvin, a person could never know whether he or she was among the elect or the damned. Many of his followers in Geneva believed that they were among the chosen and so should legislate morality. They removed artwork from churches, banned dancing and singing, prohibited drinking and gambling, and punished what they considered heretical religious beliefs. Calvin's followers also promoted hard work and dignified labor—this is the origin of the "Puritan work ethic." Second, although Luther relied on the German princes to establish state-run churches and promote his beliefs, he believed in a degree of separation between church and state. Calvin, however, believed in theocracy; to that end, the Geneva city council established religious laws to govern the city.

Calvinism became the theological basis of the Puritan movements in Scotland, England, the Netherlands, and France and had an enormous impact worldwide, partially motivating the settlement of some of the North American colonies. Under the leadership of John Knox in Scotland, Calvinism emerged as the theological basis of the Presbyterian Church, which became the national church of Scotland, despite the fact that the monarchy under James V and Mary Queen of Scots was Roman Catholic.

THE ENGLISH REFORMATION

Unlike Martin Luther, who split from the Roman Catholic Church because of theological differences, King Henry VIII initiated the English Reformation because he wanted to divorce his wife. Henry and Catherine of Aragon had one child, Mary. In 1527, wanting a male heir and in the midst of an affair with Catherine's lady in waiting, Henry sent Cardinal Wolsey to request an annulment from the pope. Denied his request, Henry demanded an annulment from the English ecclesiastical court. Parliament took legal action to cut off papal authority, and in 1533, Thomas Cranmer, Archbishop of Canterbury, granted the king his annulment. He married a pregnant Anne Boleyn, who then gave birth to Elizabeth. In 1534, Parliament passed the Act of Supremacy, which made Henry the head of the English Church. Coupled with the Treason Act, which made it a capital crime to deny that the king was the head of the Church, this act completed the break with the Catholic Church. Henry had a total of six wives and fathered only one more heir, Edward, the son of Jane Seymour.

AP® Tip

Under Henry VIII, the theology of the Church of England changed very little, other than rejecting papal authority and closing monasteries. The *Book of Common Prayer* and the other theological changes that shaped the Church of England were introduced largely during the reign of his son, King Edward VI. This is an important point to remember when comparing and contrasting Reformation beliefs.

After Henry's death, in 1547, his son, Edward VI, became king. Under the guidance of Archbishop Cranmer and other Protestant leaders, Parliament enacted new laws that established a more Protestant theology and provided for clerical marriage and the elimination of artwork from Anglican churches. Following sickly Edward's death in 1553, his oldest sister, Mary Tudor, ascended to the throne and tried to re-Catholicize England. Nicknamed "Bloody Mary," she married Philip II of Spain, convinced Parliament to enact Catholic legislation, and instituted an English Inquisition, burning Protestant heretics at the stake. In 1558, after Mary's death, Elizabeth became queen, taking over a nation in religious chaos. During her rule, England experienced the Elizabethan Renaissance, became involved in overseas exploration, and grew into a world power.

Elizabeth I worked with Parliament to repeal the pro-Catholic legislation and to pass a new Act of Supremacy making her the head of both the government and the Church of England. This act, combined with the Act of Uniformity and the Thirty-nine Articles, comprised the Elizabethan Settlement, which revised the theology of the Church of England so that it was not as radical as the theology under Edward VI. For example, artwork was reinstated in the churches and some prayers that were more acceptable to former Catholics were reintroduced. Elizabeth was a *politique*, a political ruler who subordinated religious differences in favor of political unity. The settlement worked well except for a minority of radical Catholics and Puritans, who felt that the compromise betrayed true religion. Elizabeth cracked down on the radicals and, for the most part, religion was not a divisive issue during her reign.

Largely based on the power of the English navy, Elizabeth's foreign policy promoted the wealth and power of England. Elizabeth supported sea-dogs, such as Sir Francis Drake, and provided aid to Protestants who faced persecution in France and the Spanish Netherlands. As tensions between England and Spain mounted and personal animosity between Philip II and Elizabeth intensified,

Elizabeth agreed to the execution of Mary Stuart, known as Mary Queen of Scots, in 1587. This action became the final catalyst for the launching of the Spanish Armada; its defeat in 1588 started the decline of Spanish power and secured the power of Protestant England.

> ### AP® Tip
>
> Be sure that you do not confuse Mary Tudor with Mary Stuart. Mary Tudor was Queen Mary I of England. Mary Stuart was Mary Queen of Scots, a cousin of Elizabeth and Mary Tudor. Mary I was married to Philip II of Spain and ruled England from 1553 to 1558. Mary Stuart was finally executed after evidence revealed that she was involved in a plot with the Spanish to assassinate Queen Elizabeth and take over the English throne. Both Mary I and Mary Queen of Scots were Catholic.

REFORMATION POLITICS

Despite persecution, 40 to 50 percent of the nobility—as well as a number of subjects from other social classes—became Huguenots in an attempt to assert their power in France. A series of young, weak Valois kings and queen mother Catherine de' Medici saw France torn apart by rivalries among the three main families: the ultra-Catholic Guises, who were backed by Spain, and the Bourbons and Chatillons, both of whom were Huguenots. After the St. Bartholomew's Day Massacre in 1572, the War of the Three Henrys erupted, ending with the death of King Henry III of Navarre and the institution of the Bourbon monarchy. Henry of Navarre, who became King Henry IV of France, another *politique*, converted to Catholicism but issued the Edict of Nantes in 1598, giving Huguenots limited freedoms.

In Spain, the radical Catholic leadership of King Philip II led to an international crusade to promote Catholicism and eliminate Protestantism. Within his empire, he also sought to consolidate his own power and that of the Catholic Church by use of the inquisition. In the Netherlands, which was a mix of Catholics, Lutherans, Calvinists, and Anabaptists, Philip raised taxes to aid the ailing Spanish economy; the Dutch revolted. To punish them, Philip established the Council of Blood under the leadership of the Duke of Alba. The Catholic and Protestant Dutch united temporarily to oppose Philip, but after the sacking of Antwerp, the seven Dutch provinces in the north split from the Catholic provinces in the south. This created the modern division between the Netherlands and Belgium.

THE CATHOLIC COUNTER-REFORMATION

In response to the spread of Protestantism and growing demands for a purification of Church practices, the Catholic Church took action to defend itself. The Counter-Reformation consisted of several important actions that together led to the reinvigoration of the Catholic Church.

First, in 1535, the new pope, Paul III, called for an investigation of the problems of the Church; in response to the report, in 1545 he called the Council of Trent. Although Pope Paul III died before the Council concluded its work, he had put the Catholic Church on the road to recovery. Second, Pope Paul III officially recognized the Society of Jesus, also known as the Jesuits. This new religious order, founded by Ignatius of Loyola, promoted obedience to the Catholic Church and the Pope, advocated humanistic education in the vernacular, and supported missionary work, thus becoming an important tool in the Catholic Counter-Reformation. Finally, the Council of Trent, which met from 1545 to 1563, reaffirmed all of the theological beliefs of the Catholic Church and refused to make any compromises with the Protestants. The Council did, however, institute some practical reforms, such as prohibiting the sale of indulgences and improving the moral character of the clergy.

THE SOCIAL IMPACT OF THE REFORMATION

The Protestant Reformation created social changes, too. The family was highly valued by Protestants—who rejected clerical celibacy—and women were expected to bear children and instill in them Christian values. With the closing of nunneries, women had few alternatives to family life. Although limited basic education for women was encouraged so that they could read the Bible, higher education was not, and Protestant churches did not welcome women into church leadership. Protestant reformers did encourage education for a wider audience and, in some parts of the Holy Roman Empire, established publicly funded schools focusing on humanist ideas and Christian teachings.

AP® Tip

Protestant reformers such as Luther believed that education was necessary to allow followers—including women—to read the Bible. But these reformers continued to advocate the traditional role of wife and mother for women—reading the Bible was meant to make women better mothers. Be sure that you do not confuse religious reform with changes in traditional gender roles. Most reformers were actually quite traditional when it came to social issues.

CRISES OF THE EARLY SEVENTEENTH CENTURY

In the first half of the seventeenth century, the economies of Spain and the Mediterranean states faced recessions; imports of precious metals from the Americas had declined, and the center of trade had shifted away from the Italian states. In addition, that was a period of war, famine, and disease. As economic and social tensions festered, people found extreme explanations for these problems, including witches.

WITCHCRAFT HYSTERIA

Although not new to Europe, witchcraft trials and executions skyrocketed, causing Europeans to live in fear. Among the reasons for this outbreak of witchcraft hysteria were religious concerns, often exacerbated in areas still torn by the Reformation; a changing economic system in which communal values were disintegrating; and growing numbers of poor. As community charity became less available, many people, especially older women, began to sell herbs to survive and were subsequently accused of witchcraft. Because women were viewed as the weaker sex and more prone to temptation, the vast majority of witchcraft victims were women. Only when the Thirty Years' War was ending and a spirit of religious toleration was renewed did the witchcraft craze diminish.

WAR AND REBELLION

The Thirty Years' War (1618–1648) is often considered the last of the European religious wars. It erupted from both religious and political rivalries between the Protestant and Catholic Leagues over issues that had festered since 1555, when the Peace of Augsburg failed to recognize the legality of Calvinism. The war, mainly fought in the Holy Roman Empire, consisted of four major phases. It began with the Defenestration of Prague, when Bohemian princes rejected Archduke Ferdinand as their king and threw several of his representatives out of a castle window into a moat of manure. The nobles chose Frederick IV as their king, and Ferdinand (now the Holy Roman Emperor) declared war, using the imperial forces and those of Habsburg Spain to bring down the Protestant rebels, who got support from the Dutch.

In phase two, the Danish phase, Lutheran King Christian IV of Denmark made an anti-Habsburg alliance with England and the Dutch and marched in to help the Protestants in Germany, but lost to the Empire. Phase three, the Swedish phase, began when Swedish king Gustavus Adolphus marched into northern Germany to help the German Protestants and extend Swedish power. His death, however, crippled the Swedish effort. In 1635, wanting to halt the spread of Habsburg power, Catholic France arrived to help the Protestant Swedes and Germans, starting the Swedish-French phase. Largely a battle for supremacy between France and Spain, the war continued on German soil, devastating German lands. In 1659, the fighting between the two powers finally stopped, with France emerging as the dominant power in Europe.

Intended to end the war in 1648, the Peace of Westphalia reestablished the principle of *cuius regio, eius religio*, which gave to whoever controlled the land the right to choose the religion of that realm. This time, Calvinism could be chosen. France gained small amounts of Habsburg lands, and its growing power and prestige opened the door for the rise of Bourbon dominance under Louis XIV. Finally, the secularization of politics was confirmed when the pope was not even invited to the negotiation process. This devastating war weakened and splintered the German states but led to the rise of Prussia by the end of the century.

[handwritten margin note: 30 years war ended with Peace of Westphalia]

Between 1590 and 1640, much of continental Europe was also rocked by revolts. Peasants and artisans revolted mostly for economic reasons: Their taxes were high, there was a series of bad harvests in the late 1500s and early 1600s, and prices rose while wages fell. These revolts started in the Atlantic states, and spread to central Europe, the Italian states, and even parts of Russia. Noblemen in France, Sweden, Denmark, the Netherlands, and England also revolted, as they saw their traditional rights being diminished by the growing power of monarchs.

AP® Tip

The Treaty of Westphalia granted a large degree of independence to the Protestant princes and served notice that the Habsburgs could no longer tightly control their realm. German princes even substantially controlled their own foreign policy, further weakening the Habsburgs. The treaty was significant because it decentralized the German states, a situation that partially explains why German unification did not occur until 1871.

Content Review Questions

1. Which of the following is true about the Peace of Augsburg (1555)?
   (A) It ended the French wars of religion.
   (B) It declared that Calvinism, but not Lutheranism, was a legal religion.
   (C) It granted full freedom of religion in the Holy Roman Empire.
   (D) It established the right of German princes to decide between Lutheranism and Catholicism in their individual states.

2. Which of the following statements about Erasmus is true?
   (A) He was the most famous of the Italian humanists.
   (B) He was fully supportive of Martin Luther and the Protestant Reformation's split with the Roman Catholic Church.
   (C) He emphasized inner piety rather than the system of dogmatic beliefs and practices that the medieval Church stressed.
   (D) He believed that the Latin Vulgate was the Bible that should be used by true believers.

3. Both the Italian humanists and the Christian humanists called for
   (A) church reform.
   (B) a focus on the classics.
   (C) the application of the classics to government reform.
   (D) patronage of the arts.

4. All of the following were true of the Anabaptists EXCEPT
   (A) Anabaptists believed that only adults should be baptized.
   (B) Anabaptists were persecuted by both Catholics and Protestants.
   (C) Anabaptists refused to serve in the military because they did not believe in killing others.
   (D) Anabaptists often held local political positions in order to create more peaceful communities.

5. The primary cause of the English Reformation was
   (A) King Henry VIII's desire for an annulment.
   (B) King Henry VIII's belief in justification by faith alone.
   (C) the sale of indulgences.
   (D) the influence of Martin Luther's writings.

6. Which of the following was a major factor preventing the union of the Protestants led by Zwingli and Luther?
   (A) allowance of clerical marriages
   (B) closing of monasteries
   (C) interpretation of the Lord's Supper
   (D) the age of baptism

7. All of the following are reasons for the revolt against the Spanish in the Netherlands EXCEPT
   (A) the closing of Catholic churches in the Netherlands by Spain.
   (B) attempts by Philip II to strengthen his control over the Netherlands.
   (C) residents of the Netherlands realized that their taxes were being used for Spanish gain.
   (D) Philip II attempted to crack down on Calvinism in the Netherlands.

8. Which of the following did NOT contribute to the growth in support for the Protestant Reformation?
   (A) corruption within the Catholic Church
   (B) potential economic gain for nobles in Protestant regions
   (C) the printing press and its impact on the dissemination of new ideas
   (D) support for the new ideas by Charles V

9. The majority of Huguenots belonged to which of the following groups?
   (A) Scottish Presbyterian noblemen
   (B) French Catholic noblemen
   (C) French Calvinist noblemen
   (D) Scottish Presbyterian artisans

10. All of the following are significant reasons why the Thirty Years' War was a major turning point EXCEPT
    (A) the rise of France as a leading power in Europe.
    (B) the end of great religious wars in Europe.
    (C) the granting of religious freedom to Calvinists, as well as to Lutherans and Catholics.
    (D) the inclusion of the papacy in international diplomacy.

Multiple-Choice Questions

Questions 1–3 refer to the following quotation.

Martin Luther, *Against the Robbing and Murdering Hordes of Peasants*

The peasants have taken on themselves the burden of three terrible sins against God and man, by which they have abundantly merited death in body and soul. In the first place they have sworn to be true and faithful, submissive and obedient, to their rulers, as Christ commands ...

In the second place, they are starting a rebellion, and violently robbing and plundering monasteries and castles which are not theirs, by which they have a second time deserved death in body and soul, if only as highwaymen and murderers.... For rebellion is not simple murder, but is like a great fire, which attacks and lays waste a whole land....

In the third place, they cloak this terrible and horrible sin with the Gospel, call themselves "Christian brothers," receive oaths and homage, and compel people to hold with them to these abominations. Thus, they become the greatest of all blasphemers of God and slanderers of his holy Name ... It does not help the peasants, when they pretend that, according to Genesis I and II, all things were created free and common, and that all of us alike have been baptized.... For baptism does not make men free in body and property, but in soul; and the Gospel does not make goods common....

First, I will not oppose a ruler who, even though he does not tolerate the Gospel, will smite and punish these peasants without offering to submit the case to judgment. For he is within his rights, since the peasants are not contending any longer for the Gospel, but have become faithless, perjured, disobedient, rebellious murderers, robbers and blasphemers, whom even heathen rulers have the right and power to punish ...

Source: From *Martin Luther: Documents of Modern History* by E. G. Rupp and Benjamin Drewery. Palgrave Macmillan, 1970. Reproduced with permission of Palgrave Macmillan.

1. All of the following are reasons that Martin Luther condemned the actions of the peasants EXCEPT
   (A) the peasants were selling indulgences.
   (B) the peasants were not being obedient to their rulers.
   (C) the peasants were attacking the domains of nobles and clergymen.
   (D) the peasants were using religion as an excuse for their rebellion.

2. Which of the following played a significant role in Martin Luther's condemnation of the German Peasants' Revolt?
   (A) Martin Luther did not agree with any of the demands of the peasants.
   (B) Most peasants were Roman Catholics who were opposed to Luther's religious beliefs.
   (C) Martin Luther was dependent on the German princes for the protection and growth of his reformed church.
   (D) Most peasants were Calvinists who were opposed to Luther's religious beliefs.

3. Which of the following was a reason that the German peasants thought that Luther would support their revolt against the German princes?
   (A) They attended church every week and were loyal Lutherans.
   (B) Luther preached that people were equal in the eyes of God.
   (C) They had not benefited from the gradually improving economy of the early sixteenth century.
   (D) Many German princes harshly abused their peasants, demanding burdensome taxes and services from them.

Questions 4–6 refer to the following image.

Source: Musée Cantonal des Beaux-Arts, Lausanne/De Agostini Picture Library/ G. Dagli Orti/Bridgeman Images

4. During the French Wars of Religion, which of the following groups was massacred?
   (A) Roman Catholics
   (B) Lutherans
   (C) Anabaptists
   (D) Huguenots

5. Which of the following best explains the reasons for the crackdown against the Protestants during the French Wars of Religion?
   (A) King Charles IX feared that the growing strength of the Guise family threatened his political power.
   (B) The growing strength of the Roman Catholic forces in France caused King Charles IX to take action to protect his political power.
   (C) King Charles IX and his mother were convinced by the Guise family that the Huguenots were a dangerous threat to the monarchy.
   (D) The discovery of Spanish support for the Huguenots caused a serious threat to the French monarchy.

6. The St. Bartholomew's Day Massacre can be considered to be a turning point in French history because
   (A) it established the supremacy of Calvinist beliefs in France.
   (B) it led to a civil war that eventually established the Bourbon monarchy and led to a degree of religious tolerance.
   (C) it led to a civil war that clearly established the power of the Valois monarchy and led to the dominance of the Roman Catholic Church.
   (D) it established the supremacy of the Guise family and their control of the nation's religious beliefs.

Short-Answer Questions

1. Analyze the similarities and differences between Martin Luther and John Calvin and answer A, B, and C.
   A) Briefly explain one major similarity between the ideas of Martin Luther and those of John Calvin.
   B) Briefly explain one major difference between the ideas of Martin Luther and those of John Calvin.
   C) Briefly explain how the differences between the two men's ideas impacted the Protestant Reformation.

2. Answer A, B, and C by analyzing the impact of the changes created by the Council of Trent.
   A) Briefly explain one of the changes enacted by the Council of Trent.
   B) Briefly explain the way in which the Council of Trent dealt with demands for doctrinal changes.
   C) Briefly explain the ways in which the Council of Trent impacted the Reformation era.

Long-Essay Questions

1. Analyze the factors that prevented Charles V from crushing the Protestant Reformation. (Historical Thinking Skills: Causation)

2. Analyze the reasons for the deterioration of relations between England and Spain during the rule of Elizabeth I. (Historical Thinking Skills: Causation)

Answers

CONTENT REVIEW QUESTIONS

1. **(D)** The Peace of Augsburg established the principle of *cuius regio, eius religio,* giving the princes the right to pick the religions of their states (*Western Civilization,* 9th ed., pp. 378–79 / 10th ed., p. 377; Historical Thinking Skills—Causation; Learning Objective OS-2; Key Concept 1.3).

2. **(C)** A Christian humanist, Erasmus favored the simple piety of the early Christian church rather than the elaborate ceremonies and dogmatic beliefs of his time (*Western Civilization,* 9th ed., pp. 368–69 / 10th ed., pp. 366–68; Historical Thinking Skills—Comparison; Learning Objectives OS-2 and SP-1; Key Concept 1.1).

3. **(B)** Both Italian and Christian humanists valued their study of the classics and promoted education based on the classics (*Western Civilization,* 9th ed., p. 368 / 10th ed., p. 366; Historical Thinking Skills—Comparison; Learning Objective OS-11; Key Concepts 1.1 and 1.3).

4. **(D)** The Anabaptists did not believe in holding political office (*Western Civilization,* 9th ed., pp. 381–82 / 10th ed., pp. 379–80; Historical Thinking Skills—Comparison; Learning Objective OS-11; Key Concept 1.3).

5. **(A)** The pope's refusal to grant King Henry's request for an annulment of his marriage to Catherine of Aragon prompted Henry to break with the Catholic Church (*Western Civilization,* 9th ed., pp. 383–84 / 10th ed., pp. 380–81; Historical Thinking Skills—Causation; Learning Objective SP-2; Key Concept 1.3).

6. **(C)** Zwingli and Luther could not agree on the theology of the Lord's Supper (*Western Civilization,* 9th ed., pp. 380–82 / 10th ed., pp. 378–79; Historical Thinking Skills—Causation; Learning Objective OS-3; Key Concept 1.3).

7. **(A)** Philip II did not close Catholic churches in the Netherlands (*Western Civilization,* 9th ed., pp. 396–97 / 10th ed., pp. 392–94; Historical Thinking Skills—Causation; Learning Objective SP-11; Key Concept 1.3).

8. **(D)** Holy Roman Emperor Charles V, a staunch Catholic, opposed the Reformation (*Western Civilization,* 9th ed., pp. 368–71 / 10th ed., pp. 374-77; Historical Thinking Skills—Contextualization; Learning Objective SP-15; Key Concept 1.2).

9. **(C)** The majority of Huguenots were members of the French nobility. Although Huguenots made up only about 10 percent of the

French population, estimates place the number of aristocrats who were Huguenots at 40–50 percent (*Western Civilization*, 9th ed., p. 393 / 10th ed., pp. 390–91; Historical Thinking Skills—Contextualization; Learning Objective IS-1; Key Concept 1.5).

10. **(D)** The pope's exclusion from negotiations in Westphalia illustrates the increasing secularization of politics (*Western Civilization*, 9th ed., pp. 441–42 / 10th ed., p. 438; Historical Thinking Skills—Periodization; Learning Objectives SP-3 and SP-15; Key Concepts 1.2 and 1.3).

MULTIPLE-CHOICE QUESTIONS

1. **(A)** Although Martin Luther passionately condemned the sale of indulgences, it was the Roman Catholic Church, not the peasants, who were selling indulgences, so answer choice A is the correct answer. Answer choices B, C, and D all are reasons that Luther condemned the German Peasants' Revolts (*Western Civilization*, 9th ed., pp. 375–76 / 10th ed., pp. 373–74; Historical Thinking Skills—Causation; Learning Objective SP-11; Key Concept 1.3).

2. **(C)** Although Luther likely disagreed with the violence the peasants used against the German princes and probably was appalled when the peasants used Lutheran theology to justify their actions, he also was opposed to the revolts for a practical reason. The German princes had protected Luther from imperial ban by Charles V, so he was dependent upon them for the protection and growth of his reformed church, which was opposed by both the Pope and the Holy Roman Emperor (*Western Civilization*, 9th ed., pp. 375–76 / 10th ed., pp. 373–75; Historical Thinking Skills—Contextualization; Learning Objective SP-3; Key Concept 1.3).

3. **(B)** Answer choices C and D seem tempting, but these are reasons why the revolts occurred, rather than reasons that the peasants thought Luther would support their actions. Answer choice B is the best answer to this question, since it most directly explains why the peasants believed Luther would support them. Since Luther preached that men were equal in the eyes of God, peasants believed he would support their revolts as justified efforts to be treated more equally in this world (*Western Civilization*, 9th ed., pp. 375–76 / 10th ed., pp. 373–75; Historical Thinking Skills—Causation, Analyzing Evidence: Content and Sourcing; Learning Objective SP-2; Key Concept 1.3).

4. **(D)** The St. Bartholomew's Day Massacre occurred during the French Wars of Religion, when the Guise family convinced the French king and his mother that the Huguenots were a threat to the power of the monarchy. Thus, the Huguenots were targeted during the massacre (*Western Civilization*, 9th ed., pp. 375–76 / 10th ed., pp. 390–92; Historical Thinking Skills—Contextualization; Learning Objective OS-3; Key Concept 1.3).

5. **(C)** The Guise family engineered the St. Bartholomew's Day Massacre by convincing King Charles IX and his mother, Catherine de' Medici that the Huguenots posed a dangerous threat to the stability of the monarchy (*Western Civilization*, 9th ed., pp. 375–76 /

10th ed., pp. 390–92; Historical Thinking Skills—Causation; Learning Objective SP-3; Key Concept 1.2).

6. **(B)** The St. Bartholomew's Day Massacre ignited the War of the Three Henrys, a civil war that culminated in the death of the last Valois monarch, Henry III, and the ascendance of Henry of Navarre (King Henry IV), a Bourbon, to the throne. Wishing to promote stability and prosperity, King Henry IV issued the Edict of Nantes in 1598, allowing a degree of religious toleration for the Huguenots (*Western Civilization*, 9th ed., pp. 375–76 / 10th ed., pp. 390–92; Historical Thinking Skills—Periodization; Learning Objective SP-3; Key Concept 1.3).

Short-Answer Questions

1. A) Answers will vary, but might include the following: One major similarity between the ideas of Luther and Calvin was that they both rejected papal authority. The reformers did not recognize the authority of the Roman Catholic Church or the hierarchy of the church. Another similarity that could be included would be the rejection of indulgences or the rejection of the worship of saints.

   B) Answers will vary, but might include the following: One major difference between the two reformers was that Calvin believed in predestination while Luther did not, instead believing that one was justified by faith alone. Unlike Luther, Calvin believed that God chose some people, called the elect, to be saved and others, called the reprobate, to be damned. Luther disagreed with this idea, believing instead that all could be saved through their faith in God.

   C) One of the greatest impacts that occurred as a result of the differing ideas among the Protestant reformers was the splintering of the Reformation. Within the Holy Roman Empire, Lutherans fought against Catholics, Calvinists fought against Catholics, and Lutherans fought against Calvinists, weakening the Protestant movements in the German states.
   (*Western Civilization*, 9th ed., 71–77, 385–86 / 10th ed., pp. 377–83; Historical Thinking Skills—Comparison; Learning Objective OS-3 and OS-11; Key Concept 1.3)

2. A) Answers will vary but might include the following: Changes enacted by the Council of Trent included the prohibition of the sale of indulgences. Although the church still recognized the importance and efficacy of indulgences and allowed their continuation, the sale of indulgences was no longer allowed, taking away one of the biggest complaints leveled against the Roman Catholic Church by Protestant reformers such as Martin Luther.

   B) The Council of Trent dealt with challenges to church doctrine by making no changes at all to the beliefs of the church. Although the council tried to improve the moral character of the church, it did not make any alterations in the doctrine of the church.

C) The Council of Trent was the event that kicked off the Counter-Reformation, an era of reform in which the moral character and credibility of the Catholic Church were renewed. Due to the changes in church traditions imposed by the Council, many unpopular and unethical practices ceased and the church began to gain a renewed interest from the population.
(*Western Civilization*, 9th ed., pp. 392–93 / 10th ed., pp. 389–90; Historical Thinking Skills—Comparison; Learning Objective OS-2; Key Concept 1.3)

LONG-ESSAY QUESTIONS

1. Elected Holy Roman Emperor in 1519, Charles V disagreed with the Reformation and hoped to preserve the unity of the Catholic Church and the political integrity of his empire. He faced three major problems that prevented him from crushing the Protestant Reformation and forced him to compromise with the forces of division in the Peace of Augsburg. In your essay, be sure you do more than simply list or describe the causes; analyze the interaction of the factors and show how they combined to prevent Charles from halting the Reformation.

    The first, the threat from the French and the papacy, stemmed from a rivalry between Charles and the French king, Francis I, which resulted in a series of wars between 1521 and 1544. Fought over contested lands, these wars kept Charles from being able to unleash his armies against the Lutherans. The second problem was posed by the pope. Fearing Charles's growing power in Italy, Clement VII formed an alliance with Francis, prompting the sacking of Rome by Habsburg armies. At the same time, Charles faced threats from the Ottoman Empire, which advanced as far as Vienna in 1529, once again forcing Charles to use his armies for international threats. Although repelled from Vienna, the Turks continued to threaten Mediterranean lands and preoccupied the imperial forces.

    The Reformation was solidly entrenched by the time that Charles could use his army against the German princes. Many princes had discovered that support of the Protestant movement gave them more political and economic independence, for which they were willing to fight Charles. The French again complicated matters for Charles, this time by forming an alliance with the German Protestants. Charles was forced to accept a truce and conclude the Peace of Augsburg, a compromise that defeated his goals of Catholic and political unity. To conclude your essay, include a brief (2-3 sentences) discussion of synthesis. For this essay, your analysis could compare the reasons for Charles V's inability to stop the decentralization and the spread of reformation ideas with Mikhail Gorbachev's inability to stop the spread of democratic ideas in Eastern Europe and the USSR and the breakup of the Soviet bloc in the late 1980s.
    (*Western Civilization*, 9th ed., pp. 378–79 / 10th ed., pp. 374–77; Historical Thinking Skills—Causation, Synthesis; Learning Objective SP-2; Key Concept 1.3)

2. Your essay needs to identify the factors that led to problems between England and France in the sixteenth century and analyze how they led to the degeneration of relations. The factors that should be discussed include English support of Spanish enemies—including both the Netherlands and France—commercial and political rivalries, and the execution of Mary Queen of Scots following the revelation of her complicity in the Babington plot.

When Spain marched an army into the Netherlands in 1567, Elizabeth could no longer ignore the Spanish threat—Philip could use the Netherlands as a staging area for an invasion of England. English support for the Dutch heightened tensions between the two nations and intensified their commercial and political rivalries. With the approval of Queen Elizabeth, sea-dogs such as Francis Drake and John Hawkins harassed Spanish galleons, disrupting their trade with the Americas and infuriating King Philip. Following the impressive victory of the Spanish forces over the Turks at the Battle of Lepanto, Elizabeth concluded a mutual defense pact with France, a Spanish enemy. By providing English troops to the Netherlands and funds to Henry of Navarre's forces in France, Elizabeth convinced Philip that he could no longer risk having her on the English throne. Because Elizabeth would not marry him, Philip plotted to have Elizabeth killed and replaced with her cousin, Mary Queen of Scots. In 1587, the Babington Plot, linking the Spanish and Mary Stuart to an assassination plan, was uncovered. Elizabeth agreed to Mary Stuart's execution. This execution sparked the ire of Philip, who received papal support for an invasion of England. As Philip readied his navy, the sea-dogs harassed the Spanish. In 1588, Spain launched its armada in the fateful attack. Be sure you remember to include a brief (2-3 sentences) discussion of synthesis in your conclusion. For this essay, you might include a discussion of the deterioration of relations between the United States and the Soviet Union immediately after World War II, which eventually culminated in the Cold War, citing specific similarities and/or differences between the sixteenth century and twentieth century international relationships.
(*Western Civilization*, 9th ed., pp. 395–400 / 10th ed., pp. 392–97; Historical Thinking Skills—Causation; Learning Objective SP-15; Key Concepts 1.2 and 1.4)

3

EUROPEAN EXPANSION: 1500–1800

The sixteenth century marked the beginning of an age of exploration that introduced profound changes. Tempted by the promise of riches and luxuries and enchanted by the stories of Marco Polo, Europeans took an interest in traveling beyond European shores. As Europeans explored foreign lands, they encountered hitherto unknown peoples and cultures and established new political and economic relationships. While attempting to justify their actions by sending missionaries and government officials to Christianize and modernize these new acquisitions, Europeans plundered New World wealth and subjugated its peoples. By the beginning of the nineteenth century, Europeans had created a global trade network that brought wealth and power to the western powers and altered the balance of power in Europe and around the world.

KEY TERMS

astrolabe	indigenous peoples
Atlantic economy	joint-stock company
audiencias	mercantilism
Aztecs	Middle Passage
balance of trade	Mughal Empire
Columbian Exchange	*portolani*
commercial revolution	price revolution
conquistadors	Treaty of Tordesillas
encomienda	Triangular Trade
Incas	viceroy

CHAPTER KEY CONCEPTS

- Between 1500 and 1800, European powers moved into all parts of the world, establishing colonies and trade routes everywhere. Competition for the riches and political control of new lands led to heated rivalries among the great nations of the

Atlantic seaboard and dramatically affected the peoples of the colonial lands.

▨ European exploration and colonization of the New World transformed the world economy. Commercial capitalism developed during the sixteenth and seventeenth centuries as huge profits lured investors into joint-stock companies, and mercantilism developed as governments began to take control of economic affairs for their own gain.

▨ Known as the Columbian Exchange, the reciprocal importation and exportation of plants, animals, culture, microorganisms, and people that resulted from the Europeans' conquest of the New World revolutionized the world. Old and New World lifestyles changed, and Europeans gained a new understanding of geography and a new collective intellectual vision.

For a full discussion of European expansion in the New World, see *Western Civilization*, 9th and 10th editions, Chapter 14.

MOTIVES AND MEANS FOR EXPANSION

By the end of the 1500s, the center of European trade shifted from the Mediterranean to the Atlantic seaboard as Portugal, Spain, the Netherlands, England, and France set out to colonize the New World. Intellectual, economic, political, and religious motives drove their expansion.

Some Europeans were drawn to the new lands as a result of fantasy literature about the New World. But there were real riches, as medieval travelers to the Far East, such as Marco Polo, had described. After the Ottoman conquests and the collapse of the Mongol Empire reduced access to Asia by land, Europeans began to look for sea routes. Valuable Asian commodities and the prospect of bypassing Arab middlemen created a strong economic motive. Eager for political dominance, European nations vied for control of new lands. They were also intent on taking Christianity to New World natives. All in all, "God, gold, and glory" sums up the significant motives for exploring and colonizing the new world.

At the same time, the means of exploration were improving. The political and economic growth and consolidation of Europe's centralized monarchies created the financial means for voyages abroad. The caravel, a new, more mobile ship, and new navigational devices, including the compass and the astrolabe, were invented during this period. Maps improved dramatically by the end of the fifteenth century; Gerardus Mercator created a conformal projection map on which every line is a line of true direction. These, combined with a growing knowledge of geography and wind patterns, made sailing to the New World and around the continent of Africa much safer.

PORTUGUESE EXPLORATION

Prince Henry the Navigator had launched Portuguese exploration in the 1400s. Hoping to find more gold, he sent Portuguese ships south until they reached the Senegal River, in 1441, and established the slave trade, importing Africans for sale in Europe. They also traded in gold and ivory and eventually leased land from local African rulers to build defensive forts.

Searching for a sea route to India, the Portuguese kept venturing further south. By 1498, Vasco da Gama sailed around the Cape of Good Hope, stopped at several Muslim-controlled trading ports in modern-day Mozambique and Tanzania, and then traveled to the Port of Calicut, India, before returning to Portugal. The huge profits his investors reaped encouraged more commercial trips to India and eventually the establishment of a port at Goa (south of modern Mumbai). Increasing profits from the spice trade encouraged Portuguese merchants to sail further east, as they worked to destroy Arab traders. In 1511, the Portuguese seized the Muslim trading port of Malacca on the Malay peninsula, further consolidating their control of the spice trade. They then continued on to China and the Spice Islands, garnering a monopoly on the clove trade. Although they created trading posts in India and China, the Portuguese did not set up colonies in Asia. Their success was based mainly on their sailing and military technologies.

SPANISH EXPLORATION AND COLONIZATION

Aware that the world is a sphere but unaware of its size, the Spanish looked west for a route to the Spice Islands. Rejected by the Portuguese, Christopher Columbus asked Queen Isabella of Spain to finance a westward voyage. His first voyage, in 1492, took him to Cuba and Hispaniola. Believing he had reached Asia, Columbus convinced the Spanish to fund three more expeditions. In search of gold and opportunities to Christianize the natives, these voyages took him to many Caribbean islands and the coast of Central America.

Some realized that Columbus had not reached Asia, and eager to learn more about this new world and claim territory there, several European countries sponsored numerous voyages. Disputes over territory soon erupted. To settle them, in 1494 the pope divided the new world between Portugal and Spain in the Treaty of Tordesillas, with Spain gaining most of South America, except for modern-day Brazil.

Spanish conquistadors were privately funded, so they were authorized but not totally controlled by the Spanish crown. They were brutal, ravaging thriving native civilizations. In 1519, Hernán Cortés and his company marched into Tenochtitlan, where they were welcomed by the Aztec leader Moctezuma. The Spanish took Moctezuma hostage and pillaged the Aztec city. In 1520, the Aztecs managed to evict the Spanish, but they were already afflicted with smallpox, a European disease to which they had no immunity. Cortés, regaining his advantage, destroyed the Aztec empire. By the mid-sixteenth century, Spain had taken control of northern Mexico.

The great Inca Empire met a similar fate when Francisco Pizarro arrived with a force of nearly 200 men, in 1530. The Incas had already been weakened by smallpox, and the emperor's death set off a civil war between his two sons, clearing the way for Pizarro to destroy the empire and establish a Spanish capital in Lima, Peru.

Queen Isabella established the *encomienda*—in return for the right to govern the natives, using them for slave labor and collecting tributes, Spanish settlers were to care for their subjects, providing protection, paying them wages, and Christianizing them. In the main, the natives experienced terrible mistreatment, forced labor, disease, and starvation. An estimated 30 to 40 percent of the native population died. The protests of Dominican missionaries and writings by Bartolomé de Las Casas pressed the Spanish government to end the *encomienda* system in 1542, replacing it with the viceroy system. The pope granted the Spanish Crown great power over Church affairs in the New World, so Spanish missionaries converted many Indians to Catholicism.

DUTCH, FRENCH, AND ENGLISH COLONIZATION

During the seventeenth century, the Dutch, French, and English vied with the Spanish and Portuguese for control of the New World.

AFRICA AND THE SLAVE TRADE

While the Portuguese were the first to establish a foothold in Africa, other European nations soon wanted their own outposts along the route to the Spice Islands. Further, Africa itself offered profits.

As Europeans explored the coastal regions of Africa, the slave trade increased. Many slaves were sent to the Middle East and Europe, where they worked as household servants or farmhands. But the planting of sugar cane and the founding of plantations in the Caribbean and South America in the late fifteenth century greatly accelerated the need for labor, profoundly expanding the international slave trade. Direct delivery of slaves from Africa to the New World began in 1518, an arrangement that developed into "triangular trade."

> **AP® Tip**
>
> Triangular trade had three legs: European merchants shipped European-made items such as cloth and guns to Africa, where they traded them for slaves; the merchants then sailed to the New World, where they sold the slaves and purchased materials grown and manufactured in the Americas, such as molasses, rum, and tobacco; these items were then sold by the merchants when they returned to Europe, completing the triangle. It is important to be able to cite examples of items that were traded on each leg of the trading triangle.

Some ten million African slaves were sold in the Americas between the sixteenth and nineteenth centuries, about half of them transported and sold by the British. The high death rate among slaves en route to the Americas was caused by appalling conditions on the voyages. Once in the Americas, the death rate remained high because of New World diseases to which the slaves had no immunity, as well as malnutrition and overwork. It was commonly believed that Europeans controlled the slave trade; in fact, African slave traders obtained most slaves and set the terms of sale. While the slave trade boosted the economies of the European nations, it decimated many African societies. As villages were depopulated, European-manufactured items replaced goods made in African cottage industries, increasing poverty and the violence between tribes. Tribes that traded their neighbors for guns profited, and dominated Africa politically. Europeans largely accepted slavery. The French finally abolished it during the French Revolution, and the British in 1807.

SOUTHEAST ASIA

Portugal failed to gain control of Asia; the Portuguese empire was overextended, and its military could not dominate the region. This gave the Spanish, Dutch, and English an opening in Asia. The Spanish took over the Philippines and established a base from which to trade Asian goods with Mexico. During the early seventeenth century, the Dutch gradually took over Portuguese coastal forts along the Indian Ocean, forced the Portuguese out of the spice trade, and occupied Ceylon and Malacca. The Dutch also cut the British out of most of the spice trade. Consolidating its political and economic power in the region allowed the Dutch East India Company to establish lucrative pepper plantations, and the Dutch government gained control of most of the Indonesian islands. The European powers competed for trade and missionary privileges in continental Southeast Asia, but the Southeast Asian countries had political unity and so were able to resist European control.

INDIA

The Portuguese faced competition from the Dutch and the English in India by the end of the sixteenth century. By the mid-seventeenth century, the English had established a thriving trade, exchanging Indian-made textiles for spices in the East Indies and then selling the spices in England. The Dutch turned their attention away from India; the French had been forced out altogether by 1763. Having defeated the Mughal Empire, which had been in power for several centuries, the politically and militarily powerful British East India Company began to move inland.

CHINA AND JAPAN

Although the Portuguese arrived in China in 1514, serious pressure from the European nations did not occur until the late 1600s. The British East India Company founded a trading post in Canton in 1699 and developed a thriving trade in tea and silk. Fearing foreign domination, China restricted foreign traders to an island off the coast of Canton and allowed them to be there no more than six months a year. In the late eighteenth century, the British East India Company began to press for greater privileges.

The Portuguese, the first Europeans to land in Japan, developed a regional trade network among Japan, China, and Southeast Asia. The Japanese welcomed the European manufactured items, but in 1637, they forced European missionaries out of the country and soon after expelled most European traders. Only the Dutch managed to maintain limited trade relations with the Japanese.

THE AMERICAS

Portuguese and Spanish power declined in the Americas in the seventeenth century. The Armada's defeat and the ensuing loss of Spain's political and economic power decreased Spain's power in the Americas, inviting competition from the Dutch, English, and French.

The English and French developed numerous colonies in the West Indies, where, using slave labor, they established thriving sugar, tobacco, cotton, and coffee plantations. Especially important were Britain's sugar plantations in Jamaica and France's in Haiti.

At the beginning of the seventeenth century, the Dutch added to their commercial empire with the founding of New Netherlands, and the English added to their commercial empire with the founding of Jamestown. Throughout the seventeenth century, the English continued to expand their colonial empire in North America, founding other colonies, such as the Massachusetts Colony. By the latter half of the seventeenth century, however, competition for dominance in North America and for commercial supremacy led to the English seizure of New Netherlands, an action that expanded the North American holdings of England and put the Dutch West India Company out of business.

The English colonies in the West Indies and North America benefited the English economy; they were a source for raw materials for English manufacturers, then a market for English goods. The French founded Quebec in 1608 and began to acquire territory in modern Canada, where they profited from trade in fish, furs, timber, and leather. They also sent missionaries to this region: "Fish, fur, and faith" described their colonial motivations. In part because of tight regulation of its political and economic affairs, French North America was lightly populated. During the eighteenth century, France had to give away some North American possessions as a result of European wars, and in 1763, it lost its North American colonies to Britain in the Seven Years' War. Both nations, however, broke into Spanish and Portuguese markets, expanding their economies.

AP® Tip

Be sure that you know which European nations dominated the New World during which centuries. Spain and Portugal launched the age of exploration and were dominant in the sixteenth century. During the seventeenth century, Spanish and Portuguese power waned and the Dutch rose to prominence. The English and the French eclipsed the Dutch, becoming the chief powers for much of the eighteenth century. By the end of the 1700s, England had emerged as the paramount imperial power. It is also important to know the reasons that the different nations were dominant during different centuries.

THE IMPACT OF EXPANSION

THE CONQUERED

Conquered territories faced tremendous changes in their lifestyles and often suffered large population losses as a result of European warfare and diseases. In Africa, the slave trade devastated many coastal areas. In Asia, India began to experience dramatic changes as England gained greater control. Europeans devastated Native American populations by replacing their customs and institutions with European ones and introducing new crops and animals to the Americas. In Central and South America, the Latin American culture emerged when Spanish and Portuguese settlers mixed with native women. The children of these unions were known as *mestizos*; the children of European settlers and African slaves were called mulattoes. Thus, South and Central America became racially and culturally diverse.

Christian missionaries, mostly Catholics, went to the New World to spread religion and built villages, schools, hospitals, and orphanages; as a result, the Catholic Church gained great power in the Americas. Jesuit missionaries had some success in China and Japan, but the spread of Christianity eventually stalled because of conflicts between religious orders and Asian officials wary of threats to their power.

THE CONQUERORS

Many Europeans went to the New World to acquire wealth, gold and silver, land, and opportunities not available to them in Europe. The influx of precious metals from New World mines created staggering inflation that threatened the Spanish economy and social structure. The Potosi mines alone produced over 45,000 tons of silver for the Spanish between 1556 and 1783. The introduction of New World foods such as corn, potatoes, tomatoes, and chocolate diversified the European diet and economy and led to rapid population growth as potatoes became a staple. Coffee and tea houses opened in Europe, chocolate drinks grew in popularity, and Europeans sought Chinese luxury items, such as porcelain.

> ### AP® Tip
>
> The Columbian Exchange refers to the exchange of people, diseases, plants, and animals between Europe and the New World during the age of exploration. It is important to understand the exchanges. Some examples: Europeans took horses, cattle, chickens, apples, wheat, and turnips to the New World and brought tomatoes, potatoes, chocolate, turkeys, maize, squash, and tobacco back to Europe.

By the eighteenth century, growing rivalry over control of New World products and territories had led to bitter conflicts among European powers—some nations even advocated piracy as a means of gaining wealth and weakening their rivals.

ECONOMICS IN THE AGE OF EXPLORATION

With the growth of international trade, large population increases, the influx of precious metals into the European economy, and the creation of a world market in the fifteenth and sixteenth centuries, Europe experienced a "price revolution," a period of inflation during which wages fell behind the growing cost of food and other necessities. Workers and farmers who labored for a wage experienced a drop in the standard of living, but estate owners, who could raise rents, prospered, as did the commercial and industrial entrepreneurs, who benefited from increased trade and higher prices and decreased labor costs. Making matters worse for the lower classes, European governments, also suffering from the high inflation, borrowed money from bankers and passed the costs on to their subjects through higher taxes.

COMMERCIAL CAPITALISM

At the beginning of the sixteenth century, the Mediterranean, the Low Countries, Baltic ports, and the Rhine and Danube rivers were the centers of a flourishing European trade network. During the sixteenth century, an important shift occurred: nations on the Atlantic seaboard expanded to the New World, changing trade patterns and creating new world markets. By the seventeenth century, the Dutch had become the middlemen of European trade, dominating both European and Atlantic routes.

The expansion of trade and the cost of exploration gave rise to new commercial organizations. When family-owned banking firms could no longer supply the capital and services needed by overseas merchants, large commercial banks emerged. The Bank of Amsterdam provided traditional banking and also ran the Amsterdam Exchange, a stock exchange. The strength of Dutch shipping, combined with a superior banking system, fueled Dutch commercial expansion.

In addition, new forms of investment were created, the most important of which were joint-stock companies. Investors bought shares in a company, such as the Dutch East India Company, and received a cut of the profits. With large profits, these companies easily raised money for overseas commercial endeavors. Technologies that supported the overseas voyages, including shipbuilding and mining, also prospered. Bankers often made large loans to European governments in exchange for other rewards, such as land grants or mining rights on government lands, but sometimes these backfired. For example, the House of Fugger enjoyed mining privileges in Hapsburg lands, but it went bankrupt when the Hapsburgs could no longer repay the loans.

The commercial revolution created huge profits for those who had money to invest, but most Europeans—approximately 80 percent— were largely untouched by the commercial revolution and continued to depend on agriculture for their living. Although farmers in the west were generally free, most continued to owe feudal obligations to the nobility and lived traditional peasant lives. In Eastern Europe, conditions worsened for many farmers. For example, in Prussia and Russia, many lost their freedom and increasingly were tied to the land and the demands of the landowners.

MERCANTILISM

Mercantilism is an economic system based on the idea that there is a limited amount of bullion (gold and silver) in the world; it follows that the nation that controls the most wealth will be the nation that dominates the world economically and politically. To acquire more wealth, governments attempted to achieve a favorable balance of trade, often putting in protective tariffs, granting trade monopolies, encouraging investment in new domestic industries, and building roads and canals to further stimulate the national economy. Colonies provided cheap raw materials and a ready market for manufactured items, so European governments often heavily regulated colonial trade. By the seventeenth century, overseas trade was rapidly increasing, further globalizing the economy and encouraging emigration. The age of exploration had transformed European economic institutions and policies.

Content Review Questions

1. Which of the following is true about the commercial revolution in Europe?
   (A) Most of the money used for overseas commercial ventures came from European governments.
   (B) Joint-stock companies provided the means for individual investors to profit from overseas commercial ventures.
   (C) Private banking houses continued to be the standard financial institutions of the age of exploration.
   (D) Most nations saw a reduction in tariffs and trade restrictions during the commercial revolution.

2. Which of the following is the underlying premise of mercantilism?
   (A) Agriculture should be the backbone of the economy.
   (B) Government intervention in the economy is detrimental to its prosperity.
   (C) There is a limited amount of bullion in the world, and the nation that controls the most will dominate politically and economically.
   (D) Governments should work hard to prevent monopolies.

3. The nation that first established trading posts in India, launching the rapid expansion of the spice trade, was
   (A) Portugal.
   (B) Spain.
   (C) the Netherlands.
   (D) France.

4. The Columbian Exchange refers to the exchange between Europe and the New World of all of the following EXCEPT
    (A) native plants.
    (B) livestock.
    (C) diseases.
    (D) diamonds.

5. Which of the following is a true statement about the means of overseas expansion during the age of exploration?
    (A) The nations most heavily involved in overseas trade were those that had dominated trade during the medieval and Renaissance periods.
    (B) Ptolemy's world map quickly led explorers astray, and it was not until Mercator made his famous map that sailors were able to venture to the New World.
    (C) The invention of the quadrant allowed sailors to safely sail below the equator.
    (D) The growth of centralized monarchies during the Renaissance created governments that had the means to support overseas expansion.

6. Which region most effectively avoided European control?
    (A) China
    (B) The Americas
    (C) Southeast Asia
    (D) The East Indies

7. All of the following are true about the administration of the Spanish Empire in the New World EXCEPT
    (A) viceroys governed New World Spanish administrative districts beginning in the mid-sixteenth century.
    (B) there was no opposition to Spanish treatment of the Indians in the New World.
    (C) that although set up as a paternalistic system by Queen Isabella, conquering Spaniards often brutally used Indians for their own economic gain.
    (D) *audiencias* served as advisory groups and supreme judicial bodies in areas colonized by the Spanish.

8. All of the following were factors that motivated European exploration EXCEPT
    (A) desiring to spread their faith to non-Christian peoples.
    (B) wanting to visit fantastic new lands that they learned about by reading literature written by writers such as Marco Polo.
    (C) wishing to find a sea route to Asia.
    (D) wanting to enslave native peoples.

9. Which of the following best describes the experience of European explorers and traders in Japan?
   (A) The Japanese were appalled that Europeans tried to sell them firearms, and local lords fired on European ships.
   (B) The Japanese immediately rejected Christian missionaries and sent an army to expel them.
   (C) All Europeans except the Dutch were allowed to have limited trading rights in Japan.
   (D) The Japanese initially welcomed the Europeans and their goods but eventually expelled all but the Dutch.

10. Jesuit missionaries were successful in converting many Chinese to Christianity because
    (A) the Chinese had already been introduced to Christianity by the Portuguese and were curious about the Bible.
    (B) the Jesuits did not bring trade goods, such as clocks and other manufactured items to China.
    (C) the Jesuits pointed to similarities between Christian morality and Confucian ethics.
    (D) the Jesuits recruited Chinese men to become priests and used them to convert other Chinese.

Multiple-Choice Questions

Questions 1–3 refer to the following map.

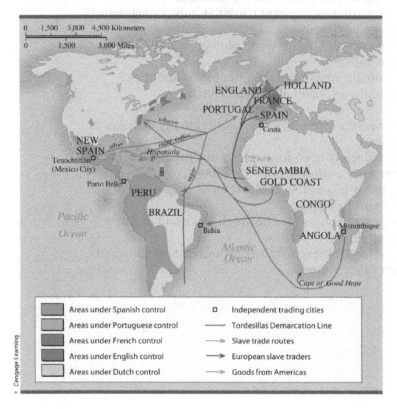

1. The map above shows a system of trade known as the
    (A) Columbian Exchange.
    (B) price revolution.
    (C) Triangular Trade.
    (D) *encomienda* system.

2. The turning point that prompted the importation of large numbers
    of slaves from West Africa to Brazil and the Caribbean was
    (A) the foundation of permanent colonies in North America by the
        British and the French.
    (B) the growth of cane sugar plantations in the New World.
    (C) the growth of tobacco plantations in the New World.
    (D) the foundation of the *encomienda* system.

3. The slave trade caused all of the following EXCEPT
    (A) great unity among Africans, as all wanted to avoid being
        captured by European slave traders.
    (B) increased warfare and violence among some African tribes.
    (C) the influx of European manufactured goods, which
        undermined the native system of production in many African
        communities.
    (D) the depopulation of some coastal regions of Africa.

Questions 4–6 refer to the following map.

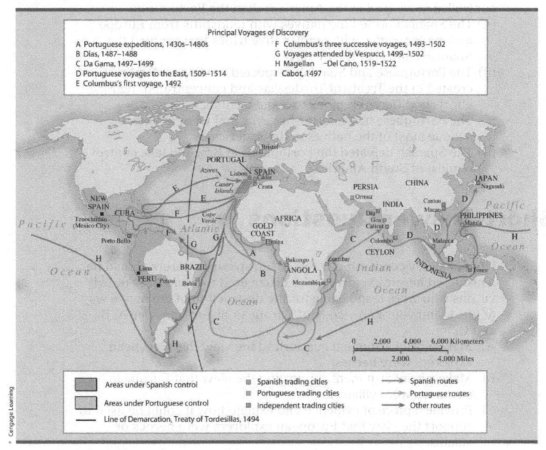

4. Portuguese exploration in the fifteenth and sixteenth centuries was aided by all of the following EXCEPT
   (A) Prince Henry the Navigator's sponsorship of explorers who traveled along the coast of Africa.
   (B) the search for gold and wealth.
   (C) the desire to spread Christianity and establish a friendly ally against the Muslims.
   (D) the desire to catch up with Spanish explorers who had gained an early advantage by being the first to launch voyages of exploration.

5. All of the following are important results of Spanish control of Potosi EXCEPT
   (A) the Portuguese began to extend their South American empire, quickly claiming large amounts of land in the center of the continent.
   (B) the influx of precious metals stimulated high inflation, contributing to the price revolution of the sixteenth century.
   (C) the mita was employed to draft native labor to work in the silver mines.
   (D) the Potosi mines provided large amounts of silver to the Spanish economy.

6. Which of the following was an important reason that the Spanish controlled more land in the Americas than the Portuguese?
    (A) The Spanish bribed the natives with foodstuffs from Europe and made treaties with many native tribes that granted the Spanish control of their lands.
    (B) The Portuguese and Spanish respected the line of demarcation created in the Treaty of Tordesillas and concentrated their efforts in different regions to avoid a conflict.
    (C) The Portuguese had inferior firearms and were unable to subdue most of the natives in the Americas.
    (D) The Spanish defeated the Portuguese in Brazil to take control of most of South America.

Short-Answer Questions

1. Opinions vary concerning whether European explorers should be considered heroic explorers who discovered the Americas or evil villains who were responsible for the destruction of the native way of life. Using your knowledge of European history, answer A, B, and C.
    A) Make a brief argument supporting the view that European explorers were heroes.
    B) Make a brief argument supporting the view that European explorers were villains.
    C) Provide a piece of evidence and explain how it could be used to support the view that European explorers were heroes or villains.

2. Analyzing the effects of the slave trade, answer A, B, and C.
    A) Briefly explain one economic effect of the slave trade.
    B) Briefly explain one political effect of the slave trade.
    C) Briefly explain one humanitarian effect of the slave trade.

Long-Essay Questions

1. Analyze the causes and effects of the price revolution of the sixteenth and early seventeenth centuries. (Historical Thinking Skills: Causation)

2. Analyze the motives for European expansion in the late fifteenth and sixteenth centuries. (Historical Thinking Skills: Causation)

Answers

CONTENT REVIEW QUESTIONS

1. **(B)** Joint-stock companies allowed individuals to invest in overseas ventures and make profits for themselves (*Western Civilization*, 9th ed., p. 432 / 10th ed., p. 428; Historical Thinking Skills—Contextualization; Learning Objectives INT-5, INT-6, PP-1, PP-6; Key Concepts 1.2, 1.4, and 1.5).

2. **(C)** The belief that there is a limited amount of wealth in the world and that the nation with the largest share of that wealth will dominate is central to the theory of mercantilism (*Western Civilization*, 9th ed., pp. 432–33 / 10th ed., p. 428; Historical Thinking Skills—Contextualization; Learning Objectives INT-5, INT-6, PP-1, PP-6; Key Concepts 1.2, 1.4, and 1.5).

3. **(A)** Portugal was the first to build trading posts in India; port facilities were set up in 1510 by Admiral Albuquerque in Goa (*Western Civilization*, 9th ed., p. 407 / 10th ed., pp. 403–04; Historical Thinking Skills—Contextualization; Learning Objectives INT-5, INT-6, PP-1, PP-6; Key Concepts 1.2, 1.4, and 1.5).

4. **(D)** Diamonds were not traded between Europe and the New World (*Western Civilization*, 9th ed., pp. 430–31 / 10th ed., pp. 425–26; Historical Thinking Skills—Contextualization; Learning Objective INT-5; Key Concept 1.4).

5. **(D)** A–C are incorrect—A, because trade shifted during the fifteenth and sixteenth centuries from the Mediterranean to the Atlantic. Only monarchies commanded the vast resources expansion required (*Western Civilization*, 9th ed., pp. 406–07 / 10th ed., p. 402; Historical Thinking Skills—Contextualization, Causation; Learning Objectives INT-5, INT-6, PP-1, PP-6; Key Concepts 1.2, 1.4, and 1.5).

6. **(C)** The Southeast Asian countries were most successful at avoiding European control (*Western Civilization*, 9th ed., pp. 419–20, 422 / 10th ed., pp. 415–18; Historical Thinking Skills—Comparison; Learning Objectives INT-5, INT-6, PP-1, PP-6; Key Concepts 1.2, 1.4, and 1.5).

7. **(B)** All of the choices are correct except for the fact that there was strong opposition to the brutal treatment of the Indians from people such as Bartolome de Las Casas, Anton Montecino, and other Dominican friars (*Western Civilization*, 9th ed., pp. 414–15 / 10th ed., p. 410; Historical Thinking Skills—Contextualization; Learning Objectives INT-3; Key Concepts 1.4).

8. **(D)** The desire to spread their faith, discover and visit new lands, find a sea route to the east, and gain wealth and prestige all motivated European exploration. As a result of exploration, many natives were enslaved, but this was not one of the main motives for exploration (*Western Civilization*, 9th ed., pp. 404–06 / 10th ed., pp. 400–01; Historical Thinking Skills—Causation; Learning Objectives INT-1; Key Concepts 1.4).

9. **(D)** Although the Japanese were at first interested in European manufactured items, they eventually expelled most missionaries and merchants when they feared that the missionaries were interfering in local affairs (*Western Civilization*, 9th ed., pp. 423–25 / 10th ed., pp. 420–21; Historical Thinking Skills—Contextualization; Learning Objectives INT-7, INT-11; Key Concepts 1.4).

10. **(C)** The Jesuits tried to gain converts to Christianity by pointing out similarities between Confucianism and Christianity (*Western Civilization*, 9th ed., p. 428 / 10th ed., p. 425; Historical Thinking Skills—Causation; Learning Objectives INT-1; Key Concepts 1.4).

Multiple-Choice Questions

1. **(C)** The Triangular Trade had three legs. Finished goods were sent from Europe to Africa (leg 1), where they were traded for slaves. Slaves were transported to the West Indies and the Americas (leg 2), where they were sold. Rum, tobacco, and other items found in the West Indies and the Americas were taken back to Europe (leg 3) and sold (*Western Civilization*, 9th ed., pp. 416–17 / 10th ed., pp. 412–14; Historical Thinking Skills—Contextualization; Learning Objectives INT-3, INT-5, PP-1; Key Concept 1.4).

2. **(B)** The widespread importation of West African slaves began when cane sugar plantations in the Caribbean and along the eastern coast of Brazil demanded more workers than the enslaved American Indian population could provide (*Western Civilization*, 9th ed., pp. 416–17 / 10th ed., p. 413; Historical Thinking Skills—Periodization; Learning Objectives INT-3, INT-5, INT-6, INT-7, INT-8, PP-1, IS-7; Key Concept 1.4).

3. **(A)** It was African slave traders who captured and sold other Africans into slavery (*Western Civilization*, 9th ed., pp. 416–17 / 10th ed., pp. 414–15; Historical Thinking Skills—Causation; Learning Objectives INT-3, INT-5, INT-6, INT-7, INT-8, PP-1, IS-7; Key Concept 1.4).

4. **(D)** Answer choices A, B, and C are all factors that aided Portuguese exploration. Although it might sound logical that the Portuguese would want to catch up with the Spanish explorers, it is not a factor, because the Portuguese launched their first voyages of exploration earlier than the Spanish (*Western Civilization*, 9th ed., pp. 407–09 / 10th ed., pp. 401–05; Historical Thinking Skills—Causation; Learning Objective INT-1; Key Concept 1.4).

5. **(A)** Portugal controlled land along the east coast of South America, but the Spanish control of the Potosi mines did not cause the Portuguese to expand into the interior of the continent (*Western Civilization*, 9th ed., pp. 407–09 / 10th ed., p. 425; Historical Thinking Skills—Causation; Learning Objectives INT-1, INT-5, INT-11, PP-1; Key Concept 1.4).

6. **(B)** When it became apparent that conflicts were emerging over control of New World territories, the Spanish and Portuguese monarchs negotiated a settlement that created a line of demarcation that divided the world into areas of Spanish and Portuguese influence. Sanctioned by the pope, this settlement granted Spain more land in the Americas

and Portugal more control of the Asian trade routes (*Western Civilization*, 9th ed., pp. 407–09 / 10th ed., p. 407; Historical Thinking Skills—Causation; Learning Objectives INT-3, INT-5, INT-6, INT-7, INT-8, PP-1, IS-7; Key Concept 1.4).

SHORT-ANSWER QUESTIONS

1. A) Answers will vary, but might include the following: Columbus can be considered a hero since he discovered America, a land with which Europeans were relatively unfamiliar in the late fifteenth century. The voyages of Columbus sparked other explorers to travel to the Americas, opening an era of great wealth and acquisition for the European nations on the Atlantic seaboard.

    B) Answers will vary, but might include the following: Columbus can be considered a villain since he traveled to the Americas and enslaved the native population of the areas he claimed. Besides this, diseases brought to the New World decimated the native populations, since natives had no immunity to European diseases such as smallpox.

    C) Answers will vary, but might include the following: One piece of evidence that could be used to support the argument that Columbus was a villain is that despite the fact that Queen Isabella decreed that the natives were to be treated humanely and not enslaved, Columbus shipped 500 Indians back to Spain as slaves and enslaved many more natives in the Americas, demanding tributes of gold.
    (*Western Civilization*, 9th ed., pp. 407–16 / 10th ed., pp. 403–12; Historical Thinking Skills—Argumentation; Learning Objectives INT-2, INT-3, INT-5, INT-6, INT-9, INT-11; Key Concept 1.4)

2. A) One important economic impact of the slave trade was the fact that the importation of cheap manufactured goods created by slave labor caused the decline of many local cottage industries, forcing many families into great poverty.

    B) One important political impact of the slave trade was the increase in violence and warfare among the African chiefs who were armed with weapons gained from the slave trade. As the demand for slaves grew, traditional African societies were decimated as the armed chiefs attacked their neighboring tribes in an attempt to take them captive and sell them to slave traders.

    C) One important humanitarian impact of the slave trade was the relocation of the slaves and the separation of many slaves from other family members. The capture and sale of slaves and the decimation of their communities created a tragic humanitarian impact on the lives of many Africans.
    (*Western Civilization*, 9th ed., pp. 426–29 / 10th ed., pp. 415–18; Historical Thinking Skills—Causation; Learning Objectives INT-2, INT-3, INT-5, INT-6, INT-9, INT-11, PP-1; Key Concept 1.4)

Long-Essay Questions

1. To answer this question successfully, you need to specifically discuss both the causes and the impacts of the price revolution. The price revolution of the sixteenth and early seventeenth centuries had several causes. One was the massive influx of precious metals from the New World that led to rapid inflation and quickly raised the price of food, land, and necessities. Other causes included a rapidly growing population and the increasing demand for food and land. The price revolution resulted in declining wages and consequently a declining standard of living for farmers and urban workers. Conversely, the landed aristocracy raised rents, increasing their wealth and power, and the merchant class prospered through their involvement in overseas trade. This money often was invested in the expansion of New World markets, continuing the inflationary cycle. Finally, governments raised taxes to pay back loans they had taken as a result of the increasing prices of goods and services, and the poor became further discontented. Be sure to add a brief (2-3 sentences) discussion of synthesis to your conclusion. For this essay, your synthesis could include a discussion of any period in history in which inflation had a significant impact on a nation or region. It could also include the discussion of any of the political or social impacts of the price revolution, such as the growing dissension between the aristocrats who had political power and social standing but lacked currency, and the merchants who had currency but who lacked political power and social standing.
    (*Western Civilization*, 9th ed., p. 432 / 10th ed., pp. 425–27; Historical Thinking Skills—Causation; Learning Objectives INT-7, INT-9, INT-11, PP-1, PP-6, PP-9; Key Concepts 1.2, 1.4, and 1.5)

2. Begin with a careful analysis of the reasons for the imperialism of the fifteenth and sixteenth centuries and a discussion of the political, economic, and religious motives for the expansion. Politically, exploration and expansion were possible because by the end of the 1400s, European monarchs on the Atlantic seaboard were increasing their power and resources and centralizing control over their nations. Going abroad allowed these nations to pursue more power, giving them political and military advantages over the nations that did not control overseas territories. Economically, nations pursued overseas expansion in an attempt to gain access to the wealth of the new lands. As the Ottoman Turks began to cut off the European overseas trade routes to the east, Europeans began to look for ways to reach the East Indies by sailing west. After Europeans reached the Americas, they began to acquire the wealth and precious metals found there and continued to look for ways to increase their material gain. Religious motives also drove expansion, with Europeans—especially the Spanish and Portuguese—eager to spread Christianity to the New World. During the 1500s, many Jesuit missionaries were sent to the Americas in an attempt to spread Catholicism to the new lands. To conclude your essay, be sure to add a brief (2-3 sentences) discussion of synthesis. For this essay, your synthesis could easily be accomplished by comparing European expansion in the fifteenth and sixteenth centuries

with the New Imperialism of the nineteenth century. Point out specific similarities and differences.
(*Western Civilization*, 9th ed., pp. 404–06 / 10th ed., pp. 400–03; Historical Thinking Skills—Causation; Learning Objectives INT-1, INT-2, INT-3, INT-4, PP-1, PP-6, PP-9; Key Concept 1.4)

Period 2: 1648–1815

Period 2 of the AP® European History framework examines the period from the Treaty of Westphalia through the Congress of Vienna. This period begins with a Europe tired from decades of religious war and political conflict and examines the rise of absolutism and constitutionalism. Searching for order, many Europeans turned to absolute monarchs to bring political stability and economic prosperity to their nations. In other areas of Europe, particularly in England, constitutionalism provided an alternative to absolutism, offering parliamentary oversight of the monarchy. By the eighteenth century, many European nations controlled large overseas empires, and rivalries on the continent and in the New World erupted into deadly wars that threatened the balance of power. The eighteenth century also witnessed continuing scientific discoveries and thriving intellectual inquiry, culminating in the Enlightenment, an era in which the tenets of absolutism were questioned by many philosophes who also suggested new, more liberal solutions to society's political, economic, and social problems. Requiring large investments of money, the eighteenth-century wars eventually contributed to the near bankruptcy of France, a situation that combined with political dissatisfaction and Enlightenment ideals to spark the French Revolution, a significant upheaval that overthrew the fabric of the old regime. Following several phases of revolution, Napoleon Bonaparte ascended into power, establishing a French Empire and eventually extending French control over much of Europe. Following his defeat, European leaders met in Vienna to redraw the map of Europe and reestablish order, eventually imposing conservatism over most of the continent. The following charts outline the learning objectives and topics from the content outline that fit into this era.

THEMATIC LEARNING OBJECTIVES FOR PERIOD 2

INTERACTION OF EUROPE AND THE WORLD

Learning Objectives—Students are able to…	Relevant Topics in the Concept Outline
INT-1: Assess the relative influence of economic, religious, and political motives in promoting exploration and colonization.	2.1.III—Rivalry between Britain and France 2.2.II—Worldwide economic network 2.2.III—Commercial rivalries
INT-3: Analyze how European states established and administered overseas commercial and territorial empires.	2.2.II—Mercantilism, slave labor system 2.2.III—Diplomacy and warfare
INT-5: Evaluate the impact of the Columbian Exchange—the global exchange of goods, plans, animals, and microbes—on Europe's economy, society, and culture.	2.2.II—Agricultural, industrial, and consumer revolutions in Europe; expansion of slave-labor system

Learning Objectives—Students are able to…	Relevant Topics in the Concept Outline
INT-6: Assess the role of overseas trade, labor, and technology in making Europe part of a global economic network and in encouraging the development of new economic theories and state policies.	2.2.II—European-dominated worldwide economic network; mercantilism 2.3.III—Commercial rivalries
INT-7: Analyze how contact with non-European peoples increased European social and cultural diversity and affected attitudes toward race.	2.1.IV—Slave revolt and independence of Haiti 2.2.II—Expansion of transatlantic slave-labor system 2.3.II—Increased exposure to representations of peoples outside Europe
INT-9: Assess the role of European contact on overseas territories through the introduction of disease, participation in the slave trade and slavery, effects on agricultural and manufacturing patterns, and global conflict.	2.2.II—Slave trade and new consumer goods
INT10: Explain the extent of and causes for non-Europeans' adoption of or resistance to European cultural, political, or economic values and institutions, and explain the causes of their reactions.	2.1.IV—Influence of French Revolution
INT-11: Explain how European expansion and colonization brought non-European societies into global economic, diplomatic, military, and cultural networks.	2.1.III—Colonial rivalry and warfare 2.1.IV—Revolution across the Atlantic 2.2.II—Slave trade 2.2.III—Diplomacy and colonial wars

POVERTY AND PROSPERITY

Learning Objectives—Students are able to…	Relevant Topics in the Concept Outline
PP-1: Explain how and why wealth generated from new trading, financial, and manufacturing practices and institutions created a market and then a consumer economy.	2.2.I—Market economy 2.2.II—European dominated worldwide economic network 2.3.III—New economic ideas espousing free trade and a free market 2.3.V—Art and literature reflected the values of commercial society
PP-2: Identify changes in agricultural production and evaluate their impact on economic growth and the standard of living in preindustrial Europe.	2.2.I—Agricultural Revolution 2.2.II—Importation of agricultural products from the Americas 2.4.I—Agricultural Revolution 2.4.V—Agricultural Revolution
PP-6: Analyze how expanding commerce and industrialization from the sixteenth through the nineteenth centuries led to the growth of cities and changes in the social structure, most notably a shift from a landed to a commercial elite.	2.4.IV—Increased migration to cities

Learning Objectives—Students are able to...	Relevant Topics in the Concept Outline
PP-7: Explain how environmental conditions, the Agricultural Revolution, and industrialization contributed to demographic changes, the organization of manufacturing, and alterations in the family economy.	2.2.I—The putting-out system 2.4.I—Agricultural Revolution and population growth 2.4.III—New demographic patterns; effects of Commercial Revolution
PP-9: Assess how peasants across Europe were affected by and responded to the policies of landlords, increased taxation, and the price revolution in the early modern period.	2.4.IV—Migration from rural areas to cities
PP-10: Explain the role of social inequality in contributing to and affecting the nature of the French Revolution and subsequent revolutions throughout the nineteenth and twentieth centuries.	2.1.IV—The French Revolution 2.1.V—Napoleon's domestic reforms 2.3.I—Challenge of rational and empirical thought to traditional values and ideas
PP-13: Analyze how cities and states have attempted to address the problems brought about by economic modernization, such as poverty and famine, through regulating morals, policing marginal populations, and improving public health.	2.4.IV—Policing of marginal groups

OBJECTIVE KNOWLEDGE AND SUBJECTIVE VISIONS

Learning Objectives—Students are able to...	Relevant Topics in the Concept Outline
OS-2: Analyze how religious reform in the sixteenth and seventeenth centuries, the expansion of printing, and the emergence of civic venues such as salons and coffeehouses challenged the control of the church over the creation and dissemination of knowledge.	2.3.III—New public venues and print media 2.3.IV—Natural religion; religious toleration
OS-3: Explain how political revolution and war from the seventeenth century on altered the role of the church in political and intellectual life and the response of religious authorities and intellectuals to such challenges.	2.1.IV—Nationalization of the Catholic Church; de-Christianization 2.3.IV—Toleration of Christian minorities and civil rights granted to Jews
OS-4: Explain how a worldview based on science and reason challenged and preserved social order and roles, especially the roles of women.	2.3.I—Arguments over exclusion of women from political life
OS-5: Analyze how the development of Renaissance humanism, the printing press, and the scientific method contributed to the emergence of a new theory of knowledge and conception of the universe.	2.3.I—Rational and empirical thought 2.3.II—New print media
OS-6: Explain how European exploration and colonization were facilitated by the development of the scientific method and led to a reexamination of cultural norms.	2.3.II—Representations of peoples outside Europe

Learning Objectives—Students are able to...	Relevant Topics in the Concept Outline
OS-7: Analyze how and to what extent the Enlightenment encouraged Europeans to understand human behavior, economic activity, and politics as governed by natural laws.	2.3.I—Challenge of rational and empirical thought 2.3.III—Challenge of new political and economic theories 2.3.IV—Revival of public sentiment and feeling
OS-8: Explain the emergence, spread, and questioning of scientific, technological, and positivist approaches to addressing social problems.	2.3.I—Application of principles of the Scientific Revolution to society and human institutions 2.3.II—New public venues and print media
OS-9: Explain how new theories of government and political ideologies attempted to provide a coherent explanation for human behavior and the extent to which they adhered to or diverged from traditional explanations based on religious beliefs.	2.1.I—Absolute monarchy 2.1.II—Alternatives to absolutism 2.1.IV—Liberal revolution; radical Jacobin republic 2.3.I—Political models of Locke and Rousseau 2.3.III—Political theories such as that of John Locke
OS-10: Analyze the means by which individualism, subjectivity, and emotion came to be considered a valid source of knowledge.	2.3.V—Emphasis on private life in the arts 2.3.VI—Revival of public sentiment and feeling
OS-11: Explain how and why religion increasingly shifted from a matter of public concern to one of private belief over the course of European history.	2.3.IV—Rational analysis of religious practices
OS-12: Analyze how artists used strong emotions to express individuality and political theorists encouraged emotional identification with the nation.	2.3.VI—Revival of public sentiment and feeling

STATES AND OTHER INSTITUTIONS OF POWER

Learning Objectives—Students are able to...	Relevant Topics in the Concept Outline
SP-1: Explain the emergence of civic humanism and new conceptions of political authority during the Renaissance, as well as subsequent theories and practices that stressed the political importance and rights of the individual.	2.1.II—Challenges to absolutism 2.1.IV—French Revolution 2.3.I—French Revolution 2.3.I—Enlightenment Principles 2.3.III—Social contract and capitalism 2.3.V—State patronage and new political ideals in art
SP-2: Explain the emergence of and theories behind the New Monarchies and absolutist monarchies, and evaluate the degree to which they were able to centralize power in their states.	2.1.I—Absolutism 2.1.II—English Civil War and Dutch Republic
SP-3: Trace the changing relationship between states and ecclesiastical authority and the emergence of the principle of religious toleration.	2.1.I—Absolutist religious policies 2.1.IV—French Revolution attack on religion 2.1.V—Napoleon and Concordat 2.3.IV—Religious toleration

Learning Objectives—Students are able to...	Relevant Topics in the Concept Outline
SP-4: Analyze how the new political and economic theories from the seventeenth century and the Enlightenment challenged absolutism and shaped the development of constitutional states, parliamentary governments, and the concept of individual rights.	2.1.IV—French Revolution 2.3.I—Enlightenment natural rights 2.3.III—Liberalism (Locke and Adam Smith)
SP-5: Assess the role of colonization, the Industrial Revolution, total warfare, and economic depressions in altering the government's relationship to the economy, both in overseeing economic activity and in addressing its social impact.	2.1.IV—French revolutionary equality and warfare 2.2.II—Commercial Revolution
SP-7: Explain the emergence of representative government as an alternative to absolutism.	2.1.II—Constitutionalism 2.1.IV—French Revolution 2.3.I—Enlightenment principles in politics 2.3.III—Social contract and capitalism
SP-9: Analyze how various movements for political and social equality—such as feminism, anti-colonialism, and campaigns for immigrants' rights—pressured governments and redefined citizenship.	2.1.IV—French Revolution—women and minorities 2.3.I—Natural rights 2.3.IV—Religious toleration (Jews)
SP-10: Trace the ways in which new technologies from the printing press to the Internet have shaped the development of civil society and enhanced the role of public opinion.	2.3.II—Civil society and literacy
SP-11: Analyze how religious and secular institutions and groups attempted to limit monarchical power by articulating theories of resistance to absolutism and by taking political action.	2.1.II—England and Dutch Republic 2.1.IV—French Revolution 2.3.I—Enlightenment ideals 2.3.III—Locke and Adam Smith
SP-12: Assess the role of civic institutions in shaping the development of representative and democratic forms of government.	2.3.II—Growth of civil society
SP-13: Evaluate how the emergence of new weapons, tactics, and methods of military organization changed the scale and cost of warfare, required the centralization of power, and shifted the balance of power.	2.1.IV—French revolutionary warfare 2.1.V—Napoleonic tactics and warfare
SP-15: Assess the impact of war, diplomacy, and overseas exploration and colonization on European diplomacy and balance of power until 1789.	2.1.III—Dynastic and colonial wars 2.1.IV—French revolutionary wars 2.2.III—Commercial rivalries and warfare
SP-16: Explain how the French Revolution and the revolutionary and Napoleonic wars shifted the European balance of power and encouraged the creation of a new diplomatic framework.	2.1.IV—French revolutionary warfare 2.1.V—Wars of Napoleon
SP-17: Explain the role of nationalism in altering the European balance of power, and explain attempts made to limit nationalism as a means to ensure continental stability.	2.1.IV—*Fraternité* and citizen armies 2.1.V—Napoleonic warfare

INDIVIDUAL AND SOCIETY

Learning Objectives—Students are able to...	Relevant Topics in the Concept Outline
IS-2: Explain how the growth of commerce and changes in manufacturing challenged the dominance of corporate groups and traditional estates.	2.2.I—Agricultural Revolution and cottage industry 2.4.IV—Urban migration and poverty
IS-3: Evaluate the role of technology, from the printing press to modern transportation and telecommunications, in forming and transforming society.	2.3.II—Civil society and publishing
IS-4: Analyze how and why the nature and role of the family has changed over time.	2.4.II—Consumerism and privacy in home 2.4.III—European marriage pattern and new concepts of childhood
IS-6: Evaluate the causes and consequences of persistent tensions between women's role and status in the private versus the public sphere.	2.1.IV—French Revolution 2.1.V—Napoleonic Code 2.3.I—Enlightenment and natural rights
IS-7: Evaluate how identities such as ethnicity, race, and class have defined the individual in relationship to society.	2.1.I—Nobles and absolutism 2.1.IV—French Revolution attack on feudalism/manorialism 2.1.V—Napoleon and "meritocracy" 2.2.II—Expansion of slave trade
IS-9: Assess the extent to which women participated in and benefited from the shifting values of European society from the fifteenth century onward.	2.1.IV—French Revolution 2.1.V—Napoleonic Era 2.3.I—Enlightenment 2.3.II—Salons 2.4.II—Consumerism and family life; privacy 2.4.III—Commercial Revolution
IS-10: Analyze how and why Europeans have marginalized certain populations (defined as "other") over the course of their history.	2.1.IV—Reign of Terror and counter-revolution 2.1.V—Napoleonic Empire

KEY CONCEPTS FROM THE COLLEGE BOARD

2.1 Different models of political sovereignty affected the relationship among states and between states and individuals.

2.2 The expansion of European commerce accelerated the growth of a worldwide economic network.

2.3 The popularization and dissemination of the Scientific Revolution and the application of its methods to political, social, and ethical issues led to an increased, although not unchallenged, emphasis on reason in European culture.

2.4 The experiences of everyday life were shaped by demographic, environmental, medical, and technological changes.

THE AGE OF ABSOLUTISM: THE 1600S

During the first half of the seventeenth century, Europe was racked by economic, social, and political crises from which emerged secular political systems that brought order to a population fearful of the ravages of war and internal rebellion. Although European states developed different political systems, aristocrats across the continent retained their power, and in many states, absolutism granted broad powers to monarchies. Divine Right monarchs attempted to control the political, economic, and social policies of their realms, often taking advantage of the lower classes to fund wars and building projects. In contrast to the system of absolutism that had developed on the European continent, by the end of the century constitutionalism was developing in England, and debates over political philosophy, characterized by the divergent theories of Thomas Hobbes and John Locke, began to be heard.

KEY TERMS

absolutism

Act of Toleration

balance of power

baroque

Battle of Lepanto

Bill of Rights

Bourbon dynasty

boyars

Defenestration of Prague

Divine-right monarchy

Dutch Realism

Fronde

gentry

Glorious Revolution

Habsburg dynasty

Hohenzollern dynasty

intendants

janissaries

junkers

mannerism

mercantilism

oligarchy

Parlements of France

Parliament of England

Peace of Westphalia

procurator

Romanov dynasty

sovereignty

Stuart monarchy

Treaty of Utrecht

urban gentry   War of Spanish Succession
Versailles   Westernization (Peter the Great)

Chapter Key Concepts

[handwritten: Search for stability after religious wars]

▪ In response to the religious wars and internal rebellions of the sixteenth and early seventeenth centuries, Europeans began to search for order and stability. Seemingly the key to political and economic security, absolutism became the dominant political system in most areas of Europe. England, on the other hand, turned to limited monarchy in response to the growing demands of Parliament.

▪ In much of Europe, social tensions brought on by war, famine, and disease escalated in the first half of the seventeenth century.

▪ Following the Renaissance, art and theater flourished in Europe. Art styles changed rapidly, moving from the mannerism of the mid-sixteenth century to the baroque style and Dutch realism of the first half of the seventeenth century and finally to French classicism by the end of the seventeenth century.

For a full discussion of state building and the search for order in the seventeenth century, see *Western Civilization*, 9th and 10th editions, Chapter 15.

ABSOLUTISM

A political system in which a divine-right monarch enjoys absolute power over all affairs of state, absolutism emerged in the seventeenth century. In theory, the monarch received this power from God and was responsible only to God for his actions—because God had ordained this ruler, no one had the right to question his authority. This theory of divine right was most prominently articulated by French bishop Jacques-Bénigne Bossuet. Although absolute monarchs wielded immense powers, they had to find ways to appease the nobles, who had the means to oppose them.

FRANCE

Catapulted into power in 1610, at age nine, Louis XIII struggled to maintain control of France. Cardinal Richelieu, his chief minister, orchestrated policies to control the growing power of the nobility and to strengthen the power of the king, even employing spies to root out and execute conspirators.

Louis XIV became king at age four and ruled until his death in 1715, just four days before his seventy-seventh birthday. Cardinal Mazarin, his chief minister, virtually ruled the state during Louis's minority and faced dangerous challenges to monarchial authority. Noblemen, upset at the continuing erosion of their power, sided with the Parlement of Paris, the nation's most significant court, to oppose Mazarin's tax increases. Although this revolt, the first Fronde, ended peacefully, a second Fronde led to violence when a different group of nobles again challenged royal power. Although both Frondes ended in a victory for Louis, he never forgot his experiences and worked to control the nobles' power-hungry tendencies.

AP® Tip

Cardinal Richelieu exercised great power. He centralized the monarchy by employing civil servants, called intendants, to carry out the king's orders, often at the expense of aristocratic authority. Although he tried to reform the French economy, he failed, and Louis XIV inherited a large debt when he succeeded to the throne in 1643. When considering the rule of absolute monarchs, also consider the influence of their advisors.

After Mazarin's death in 1661, Louis took personal control of the government and made France the envy of Europe. The epitome of an absolute monarch, Louis—known as the Sun King—still faced challenges from noblemen and towns and provinces that wanted to retain their own power. These challenges often shaped Louis's policies.

Although not truly absolute in his governing power, Louis exercised great control over the administration of France. He replaced high aristocrats on his royal council with lower ones and enticed the displaced nobles to move to Versailles, where they busied themselves with court life and were virtually powerless to affect regional or national policies or raise their own armies against the king. In control of his royal council, Louis was able to make most important foreign and domestic policy decisions.

Fearing that religious differences would breed political opposition, Louis sought to enforce the Bourbon motto: "One king, one law, one faith." To that end, he revoked the Edict of Nantes in 1685, removing the rights of French Huguenots to worship freely in their own cities, and he ordered the destruction of Protestant churches and schools, forcing several hundred thousand citizens to flee to the surrounding Protestant nations, where they created a large base of foreign opposition.

Economic stability was a crucial issue because of Louis's lavish spending and the debt passed on by his father. Jean-Baptiste Colbert, Louis's finance minister, pursued mercantilist policies in an attempt to maximize royal income and strengthen the French economy. To create a favorable balance of trade, he encouraged the expansion of domestic industries through special privileges and tax breaks and established a large free-trade zone called the Five Great Farms. Roads and canals were built or improved, and Versailles and the Louvre were remodeled. The tax burden for the nation, however, fell even more heavily on the peasant class.

Hungry for military glory, Louis created a standing professional army of some 100,000 men that swelled to about 400,000 during war. He initiated four significant wars during his reign, each time meeting resistance from an alliance of neighbors intent on controlling Bourbon expansion and protecting the balance of power. Louis gained little from his military endeavors. In 1702, he engineered the accession of his grandson to the Spanish throne, which led to the War of Spanish Succession. This, his final war, ended in 1713 with the Peace of

Utrecht, which allowed Philip V to accede to the throne of Spain but prevented a consolidation of France and Spain. The Habsburgs gained a few territories, as did Prussia, but England fared the best, gaining Gibraltar and territories in North America.

One cause of the French Revolution

> ### AP® Tip
>
> Louis's wars engaged France in almost constant military conflict and drained the French treasury. This debt eventually became one cause of the French Revolution.

Spain

Corruption

Outdated and inefficient administrative and military infrastructures; an overabundance of priests, monks, and privileged nobles who paid virtually no taxes; an economy crippled by recurring bankruptcy—all led to the decline of Spain in the early seventeenth century. Philip IV and his adviser the Count of Olivares failed to centralize government power and curtail the power of the nobility. Economic problems were exacerbated when Philip continued to fight France in the Thirty Years' War. Internal revolts resulting from its loss in the Thirty Years' War forced Spain to recognize Dutch independence and cede territory in the Spanish Netherlands to France.

Prussia

As the Thirty Years' War created a power vacuum in parts of central Europe, two major German states rose to power, one of which was Brandenburg-Prussia. The Hohenzollern family had long controlled Brandenburg, a minor duchy in northern Germany, and had added lands to the west, near the Rhine, and to the east, the province of East Prussia. During the Thirty Years' War, Hohenzollern leader Frederick William the Great Elector set up a large standing army to protect his noncontiguous territories. The army was overseen by the General War Commissariat, which raised taxes for its expenses. Soon this body was put in charge of political affairs, and Prussian aristocrats, the Junkers, quickly took on positions of power in the state. Frederick William gave the nobles almost complete power over the peasants and serfs on their estates, freedom from taxes, and positions of leadership in the army and the state. Many peasants lost their freedom, as the Junkers took over their land and made them serfs.

> ### AP® Tip
>
> Brandenburg–Prussia was just one of more than 300 German states in the Holy Roman Empire. This changed when Frederick III offered to help the Habsburgs in the War of Spanish Succession in return for the independence of Prussia and the title of Prussian king. Be sure you can discuss Prussia's origins.

AUSTRIA

Recognizing that they could no longer reunify and rule their former empire, the Habsburgs concentrated on consolidating their southern and eastern territories into the Austrian empire. A major threat to the Hapsburgs, the Ottomans challenged Austrian control of the regions east of Vienna and conducted the siege of Vienna in 1683. Despite their strength, the Ottomans eventually fell to a combined European army. This was a turning point for Austria: the Habsburg counterattack forced the Ottomans to accept the 1699 Treaty of Karlowitz, which granted large amounts of territory in Eastern Europe and the Balkans to Austria.

Spain had controlled most of the Italian states since 1556. The Treaty of Utrecht (1713) gave Austria control of the Spanish Netherlands and parts of Italy to check Bourbon power, but the growing multinational character made the empire hard to control and prevented the Habsburgs from forming a tightly administered empire like that of Prussia.

RUSSIA

Known as the Kingdom of Muscovy in the fifteenth century, Russia began to expand eastward under the leadership of Ivan IV "the Terrible" (1530–1584), the first ruler to use the title of tsar. Ivan expanded the power of the monarchy, brutally crushing the boyars—nobles—who challenged his control. Upon Ivan's death, the boyars fought one another in a brutal power struggle, the so-called Time of Troubles. In 1613, hoping to bring stability, the Zemsky Sobor, an advisory body of noblemen, chose as czar one of their own members, Michael Romanov, first in the last dynasty of Russia.

Seventeenth-century Russian society was highly stratified. At the top was a divine-right ruler aided by a Duma (legislature) and the Zemsky Sobor. As in Prussia, the boyars tightly controlled their peasants and expanded their power over the serfs. Farmers and merchants were bound to their cities, their businesses often controlled by the government. Peasants and merchants revolted but were crushed. Still, plagued by revolts, isolation from the west, and a split in the Russian Orthodox Church, Russia struggled.

Peter the Great became tsar in 1689 and set out to make Russia a great power by expanding his military and modernizing his nation. He established a 25-year draft, increased the standing army to about 210,000 men, and created a navy. He traveled to Western Europe to learn customs and technical skills, which he forced on Russia. Western art influenced the design of his crowning jewel, St. Petersburg. The Zemsky Sobor and the Duma were abolished, making way for a new bureaucratic system.

Peter reorganized the Russian Orthodox Church, creating the Holy Synod, an ecclesiastical body that ensured church loyalty. He even required nobles to cut their traditional beards and sleeves. Intransigent nobles lost their privileges. Although he tried to adopt Western customs and ideals, Peter enforced his will through violent means. His presence on the Baltic Sea created tension with Sweden, which Peter bested in the Great Northern War. When he died, Russia

Ivan IV the terrible l first Tsar

was stronger than ever militarily, economically, and politically, but many of his achievements dwindled quickly.

> **AP® Tip**
>
> Peter the Great created a Table of Ranks, a civil service system based on merit, by which he built a loyal aristocracy. Even commoners could rise to the rank of aristocrat. Keep this unique system in mind.

SCANDINAVIA

Rivalries for control of Baltic Sea trade led to problems between Denmark and Sweden. Denmark established a centralized administration controlled by the king, with noblemen the chief office holders. Sweden was weaker economically and politically than Denmark for much of the seventeenth century because the rulers succeeding Gustavus Adolphus were weak. Crowned in 1697, Charles XII, who declared himself responsible only to God, temporarily renewed the power of the monarchy.

THE OTTOMAN EMPIRE

Following the acquisition of Constantinople in 1453, the Ottoman Turks began an effort to take control of more Balkan territory. Despite setbacks, they advanced into Danube territories, conquering all the way to Vienna by 1529, where they were halted. The Turks were also advancing into the Mediterranean, but their power and control were reduced after the Battle of Lepanto in 1571, a decisive Spanish victory. By the seventeenth century, the Ottomans had trade and diplomatic relations with other European powers. Their strong, well-organized government was led by a sultan (a king) and grand viziers (prime ministers). Their military also was well organized, with Janissaries—Christian boys taken from their parents—loyal to the Sultan. In the second half of the seventeenth century, the Ottomans again attempted to expand into Habsburg lands, but a coalition of central and eastern European nations repulsed the siege of Vienna in 1683—the Turks' last serious threat to Europe.

> **AP® Tip**
>
> Although it was commonly thought that absolute rulers controlled every facet of their realm, new scholarship suggests that local rulers and institutions could have an impact. The landed nobility, holding most military and government positions, had real power. To exercise definitive control in his own nation, a king had to find ways either to work with the aristocracy or to manipulate them to his own advantage.

LIMITED MONARCHY AND REPUBLICS

While absolute monarchy dominated the continent in the seventeenth century, a few nations turned to a republican form of government or a limited monarchy. These included Poland, the Dutch Republic, and England.

POLAND

In 1569, Poland and Lithuania united, forming a strong state that ruled a vast amount of territory. The nobles elected the king and retained enormous power over the monarchy, the serfs, and the estates. After 1572, when the ruling Jagiello dynasty ended, the Polish noblemen decided to elect outsiders as kings; it would allow them to protect their powers and create the possibility of new foreign alliances. Weak kings had to share power with the Sejm, the assembly, which was dominated by the nobles. This led to weak government, which grew even weaker when the liberum veto, allowing a single member to stop the Sejm's proceedings, was agreed to in 1652.

THE DUTCH REPUBLIC

The Dutch gained great power in the seventeenth century because of their dominant role in Atlantic seaboard commerce. In 1648, the Treaty of Westphalia gave the seven northern provinces independence and recognition as the United Provinces of the Netherlands. Throughout the seventeenth century, leaders who favored a republican form of government struggled with the house of Orange, which wanted more power to strengthen the monarchy. The republican faction and the States General, a representative legislature, ruled for most of the century. In 1672, fearing foreign threats, the States General invited William III of Orange to assume power. After his death, however, the States General took back control.

The financial dominance of Amsterdam fueled the sixteenth-century success of the Dutch Republic. Between 1570 and 1610, the city's population of 30,000 doubled, in part because of the influx of religious refugees from the Spanish Netherlands. In response, Dutch leaders built more canals and housing and encouraged expansion of business—military equipment, for one. By 1660, the city had grown to 200,000 and thrived as the commercial center of Europe. Its ambitious merchants had large fleets to service the North Sea herring industry and transport goods of other nations and of the Dutch East India and West India trading companies. Profits from trade were used to establish the Bank of Amsterdam and the Amsterdam Stock Exchange, which promoted more financial growth. However, the rise of English power, continued warfare, and challenges to Dutch shipping led to serious economic problems by the beginning of the eighteenth century.

ENGLAND IN THE SEVENTEENTH CENTURY

JAMES I

James I (James VI of Scotland), cousin of Queen Elizabeth I, assumed the English throne in 1603 and founded the Stuart dynasty. Having helped Queen Elizabeth rule, Parliament immediately clashed with James because he claimed the divine right of kings. James also had difficult dealings with Puritan leaders, many of whom served in the House of Commons or held other important government jobs.

> ### AP® Tip
>
> The ongoing struggle between Stuart monarchs and Parliament led to a constitutional system by the end of the seventeenth century. Be sure you can contrast English constitutionalism with French absolutism in the seventeenth century.

CHARLES I

Charles I became king in 1625, continuing the conflicts with Parliament. Parliament forced Charles to accept the Petition of Right in 1628, designed to limit royal power. Unwilling to abide by it, Charles ruled without Parliament from 1629 to 1640. Like his father, he clashed with his subjects over the collection of extralegal taxes and religious policies. When Charles tried to force the Scottish Presbyterian Church to use the Anglican Book of Common Prayer, Scotland declared war on England. Charles was forced to call Parliament and ask for funds, but the "Long Parliament" (1640–1660) granted funds only in return for new restrictions on the king's power. By 1641, Parliament was split over religious policy; some members were happy with the Anglican Church, while some Puritans wanted to eliminate the bishops. Charles hoped to use this split to regain control, but when he sent troops to arrest some members at a meeting of Parliament, the Parliamentary forces united against the king and civil war broke out.

The civil war saw Cavaliers, supporters of the king, facing Roundheads, supporters of Parliament. The Parliamentary forces, allied with Scotland and trained in the latest military tactics by Oliver Cromwell, captured the king in 1646. But the Parliamentary forces split; the Presbyterian majority, who wanted to restore Charles and establish a Presbyterian state church, was pitted against the army and more radical Independents, Puritans who hated the king and were loyal to Cromwell. The radicals prevailed. They purged Parliament, creating a body known as the Rump Parliament, which then tried Charles for treason. He was convicted and beheaded.

OLIVER CROMWELL

After Charles's execution, Parliament declared England a Commonwealth. Cromwell used his army to brutally suppress a Catholic rebellion in Ireland and uprisings in Scotland. There was opposition at home, too. The Levellers, a radical group of reformers, advocated extreme democracy and equality, and the Rump Parliament was difficult to work with. Cromwell crushed the Levellers, sent the Rump Parliament home, then set himself up as Lord Protector in 1653, using his army to stay in power. Cromwell died in 1658 and was succeeded by his son. Parliament deemed army rule unworkable and so restored the Stuart monarchy. Charles II was crowned in 1660.

CHARLES II

Charles ruled with Parliament, giving it great power over taxation. Parliament made the Anglican Church once again the state church and passed laws against Puritans and Catholics. Believing these laws unjust, and in order to protect his Catholic brother, James, Charles suspended the laws with the Declaration of Indulgence. Infuriated, Parliament passed the Test Act to bar Catholics from holding public office and to ban James from becoming king. Charles eventually disbanded Parliament. By the Treaty of Dover, he got financial help from the French in exchange for abandoning his alliance with the Dutch and vague promises to become a Catholic.

JAMES II

Charles II was succeeded by his brother in 1685. Openly Catholic, James II angered Parliament by appointing Catholics to government positions. Hoping he would soon die and be succeeded by one of his Protestant daughters, Parliament allowed James to remain king but ousted him when his second wife, a Catholic, bore a son in 1688, threatening a Catholic hereditary monarchy.

AP® Tip

It is important to understand the differences between Tories and Whigs. Tories disliked James II but wanted to retain the traditional system of succession; Whigs wanted to exclude him from the throne. These differences simmered until the birth of James's Catholic son. Between 1688 (Glorious Revolution) and 1832 (Great Reform Bill), most Tories supported royal power and the Church of England, while most Whigs supported parliamentary power and constitutional monarchy and freedom for all Protestants. Whigs were more open to reform, but neither party disrupted the traditional power of the nobility.

THE GLORIOUS REVOLUTION

Fearing a Catholic dynasty, Tory leaders joined with the Whigs to invite William of Orange, husband of James's Protestant daughter Mary, to rule England. William and Mary raised an army and sailed to England in 1689 to fight for the throne, but James and his family fled to France. This "Glorious Revolution" brought to power two monarchs who agreed to recognize Parliament as the source of their power and to accept the Bill of Rights as the basis for a constitutional monarchy. Further settling old wounds, William and Mary and Parliament agreed to the Toleration Act, which granted Puritans (but not Catholics) the right to public worship.

POLITICAL PHILOSOPHY AND REVOLUTION

England's many political crises of the seventeenth century prompted the development of two models of political philosophy known as social contract theory, one by Thomas Hobbes (1588–1679), the other by John Locke (1632–1704). Both began with a "state of nature," without civil laws or authorities that at some point gave way to civil society. From there, Hobbes and Locke, holding vastly different views of human nature and the state of nature, arrived at starkly different models of the proper organization of government. Their political philosophies are still used today.

- Hobbes believed that the state of nature resembled a state of chaos in which humans acted selfishly, having no respect for other people or for natural law. In *Leviathan* (1651), Hobbes asserts that self-preservation drives people to do anything—no matter how cruel or immoral—and that only a government that grants all power to an absolute ruler and forbids rebellion can provide security.

- In *Two Treatises of Government* (1689), Locke held that people are born free and equal, with the inalienable rights of "life, liberty and property." He believed that humans would live relatively peacefully in the state of nature but that conflicts over these rights could arise. To settle differences, people would create a government based on a social contract: individuals would empower a government to protect their rights. Government would act as an umpire. Unlike Hobbes, Locke believed that the people had the right to overthrow a government that did not carry out its obligations and protect the inalienable rights of its citizens.

EUROPEAN CULTURE

The enormous artistic energy unleashed by the Renaissance continued throughout Europe in the sixteenth and seventeenth centuries. By the 1520s, the art of the high Renaissance had given way to Mannerism, a style characterized by proportions and figures distorted to reflect the suffering and uncertainty of the times. One famous Mannerist painter was El Greco. The enormous artistic energy unleashed by the Renaissance continued throughout Europe in the sixteenth and seventeenth centuries. By the 1520s, the art of the high Renaissance had given way to Mannerism, a style characterized by proportions and figures distorted to reflect the suffering and uncertainty of the times. One famous Mannerist painter was El Greco.

Replacing Mannerism in the late sixteenth century, the Baroque style was the art of the Catholic Counter-Reformation. It used dramatic movement, color, and lighting effects to evoke intense emotion and spiritual awe. Among the most famous baroque artists were Rubens, Bernini, and Artemisia Gentileschi, a female artist best known for her series of Old Testament heroines, particularly *Judith Slaying Holofernes*.

French Classicism, more subdued than the baroque, emerged in the second half of the seventeenth century. A reaction to the baroque style, which was thought to be too showy, French Classicism reflected the classical values of the Renaissance. Nicholas Poussin was one of the most famous French Classicist artists.

Differing significantly was Dutch Realism. Unlike baroque artists, who often depicted religious themes, the Dutch masters painted landscapes, still-lifes, townscapes, and portraits of wealthy merchants and leaders of Dutch society. Dutch Calvinism forbade artwork in churches, so artists painted secular scenes that would appeal to a lay clientele. The Dutch realists included Judith Leyster, a prominent female artist. The stars were Rembrandt van Rijn and Johannes Vermeer.

English and Spanish literature also flourished, as did theater. The Elizabethan Renaissance included William Shakespeare, Christopher Marlowe, John Donne, and Edmund Spenser. The Spanish Golden Age saw the founding of theaters in most major Spanish cities, including Mexico City. The most notable Spanish playwright was Lope de Vega. While English and Spanish playwrights wrote for a broad audience, French dramatists wrote for the elite. With patronage from French nobles and the court of Louis XIV, French theater became popular in the second half of the seventeenth century; famous playwrights included Molière and Racine.

The seventeenth century saw a divergence in political structure that profoundly affected all of Europe. Both absolutism and constitutionalism attempted to bring order to a world wracked by war and religious conflict. By the end of the century, England and France had emerged as the dominant European powers. Both pursued the same goals, but each was governed differently.

Content Review Questions

1. Which of the following institutions was most responsible for the rise of Prussia?
   (A) The army
   (B) The monarchy
   (C) The organized civil service system
   (D) The States General

2. Which of the following is the most important reason for the English Civil War?
   (A) The relative levels of poverty in England
   (B) Conflicts between Puritans and Catholics
   (C) Conflicts between Parliament and the king
   (D) The king's attempt to impose the Anglican *Book of Common Prayer* on Scotland

3. All of the following statements are true about the reign of Peter the Great of Russia EXCEPT
   (A) Westernization benefited Russians from every social class and reduced the financial burdens on the Russian masses.
   (B) women benefited greatly from Peter's cultural reforms.
   (C) Peter instituted the Table of Ranks to create opportunities for non-nobles to serve the state and join the nobility.
   (D) to obtain money for the army and navy, Peter adopted Western mercantilistic policies to stimulate economic growth.

Source: National Gallery of Art, Washington, DC//Superstock

4. The painting above is representative of Mannerism because
   (A) the painting reflects the classical focus on the human body.
   (B) the subject of the work is a classical scene.
   (C) the subject of the work is a religious figure.
   (D) the painting uses elongated bodies and skewed proportions to reflect anxiety and suffering.

5. The most important reason Louis XIV built the palace of Versailles was that he wanted to
   (A) make his court the envy of Europe.
   (B) enjoy a lavish life for himself and his family.
   (C) create a museum to house French works of art and literature.
   (D) limit the authority of the nobility and prevent them from gaining enough power to threaten his control of the country.

6. During the seventeenth century, Austria
   (A) built a strong navy to fight off the Ottoman Turks and defeated them at the Battle of Lepanto.
   (B) was never able to form a strongly centralized state because of the many nationalities that co-existed within its borders.
   (C) was ruled by the Hohenzollern family, which built a strong military state dominated by the king and the Junkers.
   (D) lost control of the Italian states and was forced to cede them to Spain at the beginning of the eighteenth century.

7. Which of the following explains the significance of the 1683 Siege on Vienna?
   (A) The defeat of the Ottomans at Vienna ended any significant threat to Europe from the Turks.
   (B) It showed that the Europeans would never be safe from Ottoman aggression.
   (C) It proved that rifts between European nations were too deep for them to unite against a common enemy.
   (D) The defeat of the Ottomans at Vienna led to the collapse of the Ottoman Empire.

8. All of the following resulted from the Glorious Revolution EXCEPT
   (A) James II was replaced by William and Mary.
   (B) limited religious toleration was extended to the Catholics.
   (C) Parliament's authority was reaffirmed.
   (D) a Bill of Rights was adopted and limited the power of the monarchy.

9. The most important contribution made by Bishop Jacques Bossuet was
   (A) publishing a scripture-based justification for divine-right monarchy.
   (B) serving as the tutor for the only surviving legitimate son of Louis XIV.
   (C) delivering the funeral oration for Queen Henrietta Maria, widow of Charles I.
   (D) writing an anti-papal treatise at the bidding of Louis XIV.

10. The Roman Catholic Church, along with monarchies and city-states often commissioned works to be done in the baroque style in an attempt to do which of the following?
   (A) Celebrate the wealth and power of the commercial elites
   (B) Realistically portray the true images of church leaders and government officials
   (C) Use dramatic and oversized images to promote their stature and power
   (D) Use classical styles and geometric perspective to compare church leaders and government officials to classical rulers

Multiple-Choice Questions

Questions 1–3 refer to the following quotation.

The Bill of Rights

And thereupon the said lords spiritual and temporal and Commons ... declare:

1. That the pretended power of suspending laws, or the execution of laws, by regal authority, without consent of parliament is illegal.

2. That the pretended power of dispensing with the laws, or the execution of law by regal authority, as it has been assumed and exercised of late, is illegal....

4. That levying money for or to the use of the crown by pretense of prerogative, without grant of parliament, for longer time or in other manner than the same is or shall be granted, is illegal.

5. That it is the right of the subjects to petition the king, and all commitments and prosecutions for such petitioning are illegal.

6. That the raising or keeping a standing army within the kingdom in time of peace, unless it be with consent of parliament, is against law.

7. That the subjects which are Protestants may have arms for their defense suitable to their conditions, and as allowed by law.

8. That election of members of parliament ought to be free.

9. That the freedom of speech, and debates or proceedings in parliament, ought not to be impeached or questioned in any court or place out of parliament.

10. That excessive bail ought not to be required, nor excessive fines imposed, nor cruel and unusual punishments inflicted.

11. That jurors ought to be duly impaneled and returned, and jurors which pass upon men in trials for high treason ought to be freeholders.

12. That all grants and promises of fines and forfeitures of particular persons before conviction are illegal and void.

13. And that for redress of all grievances, and for the amending, strengthening, and preserving of the laws, parliament ought to be held frequently.

Source: From *The Statutes: Revised Edition* (London: Eyre and Spottiswoode, 1871), Vol. 2, pp. 10–12.

1. Which of the following is true about the impact of the English Bill of Rights?
   (A) It established the basis of absolutism in England.
   (B) It established the basis of constitutionalism in England.
   (C) It established the principle that the monarch would possess the ability to suspend laws.
   (D) It established the principle that the monarch had the right to overturn parliamentary elections.

2. All of the following were reasons that Parliament insisted upon monarchial agreement to the Bill of Rights EXCEPT
   (A) Parliament wanted to prevent the abuse of monarchial power.
   (B) Parliament wanted to assert its control over the monarchy.
   (C) Parliament feared that William and Mary would continue the oppressive style of governing that they had established in the Netherlands.
   (D) they wanted to institutionalize the parliamentary powers they had established as a result of the Glorious Revolution.

3. Who among the following would most likely have agreed with the political ideals embodied in the Bill of Rights?
   (A) John Locke
   (B) Thomas Hobbes
   (C) Niccolo Machiavelli
   (D) Jean Bodin

Questions 4–6 refer to the following map.

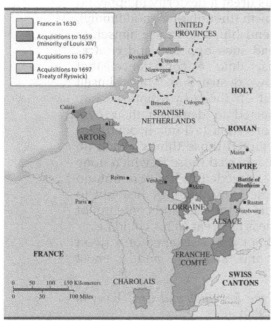

© Cengage Learning

4. All of the following were causes of the wars of Louis XIV EXCEPT
   (A) a desire for military glory.
   (B) the pursuit of royal power.
   (C) the desire to ensure the domination of the Bourbon dynasty over European affairs.
   (D) the desire to extend Bourbon dominance by controlling the monarchy of the Holy Roman Empire.

5. Louis XIV made most of his territorial acquisitions at the expense of which monarchy?
   (A) Hapsburgs
   (B) Bourbons
   (C) Hohenzollerns
   (D) Hanoverians

6. The Treaty of Utrecht can be considered to be an important turning point in European History because
    (A) it marked the culmination of the French colonial wars.
    (B) it signaled the rise of France as the strongest European power.
    (C) it signaled the rise of the English empire.
    (D) it marked the culmination of Spanish expansion.

Short-Answer Questions

Lord Clarendon, *The History of the Rebellion and Civil Wars in England*

He was one of those men, ... whom his very enemies could not condemn without commending him at the same time: for he could never have done half that mischief without great parts of courage, industry, and judgment. He must have had a wonderful understanding in the natures and humors of men, and as great a dexterity in applying them; who, from a private and obscure birth (though of a good family), without interest or estate, alliance or friendship, could raise himself to such a height, and compound and knead such opposite and contradictory tempers, humors, and interests into a consistence, that contributed to his designs, and to their own destruction; whilst himself grew insensibly powerful enough to cut off those by whom he had climbed, in the instant that they projected to demolish their own building. What [a Roman writer] said of Cinna [a Roman politician] may very justly be said of him: he attempted those things which no good man dared have ventured on; and achieved those in which none but a valiant and great man could have succeeded. Without doubt, no man with more wickedness ever attempted any thing, or brought to pass what he desired more wickedly, more in the face and contempt of religion, and moral honesty; yet wickedness as great as his could never have accomplished those trophies, without the assistance of a great spirit, an admirable circumspection and sagacity, and a most magnanimous resolution.

Source: Lord Clarendon, *The History of the Rebellion and Civil Wars in England*, vol. 6 (Oxford University Press, 1839).

1. Using the excerpt above, answer A, B, and C by analyzing the character of Oliver Cromwell.
    A) Briefly explain Lord Clarendon's argument concerning the assessment of Oliver Cromwell's character.
    B) Provide one piece of evidence that would support the argument made by Lord Clarendon.
    C) Provide one piece of evidence that would undermine the argument made by Lord Clarendon.

2. Answer A, B, and C by analyzing the factors that strengthened and limited absolutism.
   A) Briefly explain the factors that strengthened the rule of absolute monarchs.
   B) Briefly explain one factor that limited absolutism.
   C) Provide one example that illustrates the way in which Louis XIV strengthened his absolute power in France.

Long-Essay Questions

1. Analyze the reasons for the emergence of Amsterdam as the commercial and financial center of Europe in the seventeenth century. (Historical Thinking Skills: Causation)

2. Analyze the factors that led to the rise of one absolute power in Europe in the seventeenth century. (Historical Thinking Skills: Causation)

Answers

CONTENT REVIEW QUESTIONS

1. **(A)** Even though the monarchy under Frederick William the Great Elector was important, it was the army and its General War Commissariat that allowed for Prussia's rise (*Western Civilization*, 9th ed., pp. 451–52 / 10th ed., pp. 448–49; Historical Thinking Skills—Contextualization; Learning Objective SP-15; Key Concept 2.1).

2. **(C)** The most important reason for the war was the conflict between the king and Parliament over which had ultimate governing authority (*Western Civilization*, 9th ed., pp. 462–63 / 10th ed., pp. 458–59; Historical Thinking Skills—Causation; Learning Objective SP-11, SP-4; Key Concept 2.1, 2.3).

3. **(A)** The reforms of Peter the Great might seem to have benefited all social classes in Russia, but, in fact, his reforms greatly benefited the upper classes at the expense of the lower classes. The majority of Russians did not benefit from the reforms (*Western Civilization*, 9th ed., pp. 453–56, 470 / 10th ed., pp. 450–53; Historical Thinking Skills—Contextualization; Learning Objectives SP-1, IS-6, IS-7, IS-9; Key Concept 2.1, 2.3).

4. **(D)** Mannerist artists skewed proportions and purposely eliminated balance and harmony to portray suffering, doom, and anxiety (*Western Civilization*, 9th ed., pp. 468–69 / 10th ed., p. 464; Historical Thinking Skills—Analyzing Evidence: Content and Sourcing; Learning Objective OS-3; Key Concept 2.1).

5. **(D)** Although A **looks** promising—the court at Versailles was the envy of Europe—it is not the most important. Versailles was a place to coop up the nobility so they could not threaten his power (*Western Civilization*, 9th ed., pp. 445–48 / 10th ed., pp. 441–44; Historical Thinking Skills—Causation; Learning Objective SP-2; Key Concept 2.1).

6. **(B)** The multinational composition of Austria made it difficult to build a centralized empire (*Western Civilization*, 9th ed., pp. 452–53 / 10th ed., p. 449; Historical Thinking Skills—Contextualization; Learning Objective SP-2; Key Concept 2.1).

7. **(A)** Following the retreat of the Ottoman Turks at Vienna, the Turks kept most of their empire, but they never again seriously threatened the other Europeans (*Western Civilization*, 9th ed., p. 458 / 10th ed., pp. 454–55; Historical Thinking Skills—Contextualization; Learning Objective SP-15; Key Concept 2.1).

8. **(B)** The Toleration Act granted the right to public worship to Puritans but not to Catholics (*Western Civilization*, 9th ed., p. 466 / 10th ed., pp. 462–63; Historical Thinking Skills—Causation; Learning Objective SP-2, SP-7; Key Concept 2.1).

9. **(A)** In *Politics Drawn from the Very Words of Holy Scripture*, Bishop Bossuet wrote a compelling justification of divine right (*Western Civilization*, 9th ed., p. 444 / 10th ed., p. 440; Historical Thinking Skills—Contextualization; Learning Objective SP-2; Key Concept 2.1).

10. **(B)** The Roman Catholic church, monarchies, and leaders of city-states all commissioned baroque art to increase their power and impress a largely illiterate audience with their importance. The dramatic style was used to enhance their images in the eyes of many Europeans (*Western Civilization*, 9th ed., pp. 468– 71 / 10th ed., pp. 464–66; Historical Thinking Skills—Causation; Learning Objective SP-1; Key Concept 1.3).

Multiple-Choice Questions

1. **(B)** Limitations on the power of the monarchs required by the English Bill of Rights established the principle of constitutionalism (*Western Civilization*, 9th ed., pp. 466–67 / 10th ed., pp. 462–63; Historical Thinking Skills—Patterns of Continuity and Change Over Time; Learning Objectives SP-2, SP-7; Key Concept 2.1).

2. **(C)** Parliament invited William and Mary to assume the throne of England in the Glorious Revolution, because they wanted to limit the power of the monarchy. William did not have an oppressive reputation in the Netherlands (*Western Civilization*, 9th ed., pp. 466–67 / 10th ed., pp. 462–63; Historical Thinking Skills—Causation; Learning Objectives SP-2, SP-7; Key Concept 2.1).

3. **(A)** John Locke argued for the rule of law, the protection of rights, and constitutional government, thus supporting the ideas found in the Bill of Rights (*Western Civilization*, 9th ed., pp. 466–67 / 10th ed., pp. 462–63; Historical Thinking Skills—Argumentation; Learning Objectives SP-4, SP-7, OS-9; Key Concepts 2.1, 2.3).

4. **(D)** The fourth war of Louis XIV, the War of Spanish Succession, began over the efforts of Louis to put his grandson on the Spanish throne and did not involve an attempt by King Louis to control the monarchy of the Holy Roman Empire (*Western Civilization*, 9th ed., pp. 459–61 / 10th ed., pp. 446–47; Historical Thinking Skills—Causation; Learning Objective SP-2; Key Concept 2.1).

5. **(A)** The majority of land taken over by Louis XIV as a result of his wars was previously possessed by the Hapsburg family (*Western Civilization*, 9th ed., pp. 459–61 / 10th ed., pp. 446–47; Historical Thinking Skills—Contextualization; Learning Objectives SP-13, SP-15; Key Concepts 2.1, 2.2).

6. **(C)** The Treaty of Utrecht, ending the War of Spanish Succession, ended French efforts to gain more territory and forced French recognition of the legitimacy of the Hanoverian monarchy in England. Gaining control of Gibraltar and important territories in North America, England emerged as a great power (*Western Civilization*, 9th ed., pp. 459–61 / 10th ed., p. 538; Historical Thinking Skills—Periodization; Learning Objective SP-15; Key Concept 2.1).

SHORT-ANSWER QUESTIONS

1. A) In the excerpt by Lord Clarendon, he argues that Oliver Cromwell was both a wise man with a great spirit and a wicked man who was willing to act with dishonesty and take sacrilegious actions when he needed to in order to achieve his goals. Although he admired the achievements of Cromwell, Lord Clarendon also saw the sometimes unscrupulous nature of his character.

   B) One piece of evidence that supports the assessment by Lord Clarendon is Cromwell's conquest of Ireland. Cromwell's New Model Army defeated the Irish confederates who were allied with the royalists in England and brutally took over their lands. As a result of anti-Catholic laws passed by Cromwell and his allies, Cromwell managed to mercilessly suppress the majority of the Irish population and indirectly cause a famine that wiped out about 50% of the Irish people.

   C) One piece of evidence that undermines the argument made by Lord Clarendon is that Oliver Cromwell was responsible for readmitting the Jews to England. Despite the opposition of some English clergymen and merchants, Cromwell eventually worked out a deal that allowed Jewish people to enter England. This action was taken to benefit the English economy and weaken the Dutch.
   (*Western Civilization*, 9th ed. pp. 462–65 / 10th ed., pp. 458–61; Historical Thinking Skills—Interpretation, Argumentation; Learning Objectives SP-2, SP-4, SP-7, SP-9, SP-11; Key Concepts 2.1, 2.3)

2. A) One factor that strengthened the rule of absolute monarchs was their ability to curtail the power of the nobility. By reducing the economic and political power of the nobles and prohibiting their ability to raise their own private armies, monarchs strengthened their own power and the power of the state. To reduce the power of the nobility, many absolute monarchs not only limited aristocratic military power, but they also built stronger bureaucracies and larger national armies. Absolute monarchs also used the theory of divine right to support their rule.

B) One factor that limited absolutism was the power of local and regional institutions that were often controlled by members of the nobility. Local laws and privileges often limited the extent to which absolute monarchs could impose their will upon the people, placing great governing power in the hands of nobles who served as military officers, judges, and administrators.

C) One way that Louis XIV strengthened his absolute power in France was the relocation of many nobles to the Palace of Versailles and the corresponding development of an intendant system in which qualified members of the third estate (usually members of the upper middle class) served in bureaucratic positions in the provinces. These loyal civil servants carried out the will of the king while the nobles were entertained at Versailles, essentially giving up their ability to challenge Louis' power.
(*Western Civilization*, 9th ed., pp. 462–65 / 10th ed., pp. 440–43, 455–56, 462–63; Historical Thinking Skills—Causation, Argumentation; Learning Objective SP-2; Key Concept 2.1)

LONG-ESSAY QUESTIONS

1. There are numerous reasons for Amsterdam's success in the seventeenth century. The political stability provided by the leadership of the prosperous merchants and burghers in the city government of Amsterdam and the Dutch States General set the stage. Dutch businessmen used their huge fleets of ships not only for domestic trade but also for overseas trade, making the Dutch the "middlemen" of Europe. The economic prosperity of the Dutch East and West Indian companies and the founding of the Exchange Bank of Amsterdam and the Amsterdam Stock Exchange were also important.

   The wealthy citizens of Amsterdam, Calvinists, lived frugally and valued hard work, characteristics that helped them create prosperous business endeavors. Serving in many high positions in government, the Amsterdam merchants and owners supported improvement of the city's canal system, housing, and business facilities. Population growth fed the expansion of business. The financial success of the Dutch East India and West India companies and the profits acquired from the sale of firearms, a local industry, created the capital needed for financial dominance and the foundation of new financial institutions, eventually making Amsterdam the commercial and banking center of Europe. In your conclusion, remember to add a brief (2-3 sentences) discussion of synthesis. For this essay, your discussion could include a comparison of the

rise of Amsterdam with the rise of a different commercial center in a different era, such as the financial rise of London during the Industrial Revolution or Florence or Venice during the Renaissance.
(*Western Civilization*, 9th ed., pp. 432–33 / 10th ed., pp. 456–57; Historical Thinking Skills—Causation; Learning Objectives PP-1, PP-3, PP-6; Key Concepts 2.2, 2.4)

2. Answers will vary but might include: The Thirty Years' War tore apart the Holy Roman Empire, leaving over 300 states and principalities. Prussia's evolution from an insignificant state to one of the leading empires in Europe was the result of the leadership of Frederick William, the Great Elector, the development of a strong army, the creation of an efficient bureaucratic system, and the support of the Prussian Junkers. Frederick William, the Great Elector, was the Duke of Prussia and the Elector of Brandenburg, as well as the ruler of some land near the Rhine Valley. A staunch Calvinist, Frederick William supported religious toleration during and after the Thirty Years' War. He had the support of most factions of his population, and by encouraging displaced Huguenots to settle in his war-ravaged lands, he brought in skilled artisans, strengthening his nation. The development of a 40,000-man standing army by 1678 further strengthened the growing Prussian state; the creation of the General War Commissariat, which levied taxes for the army and oversaw its training, created a strong military base for the new nation. The War Commissariat soon turned into the institution of civil government, giving military leaders great power in the Prussian state and creating a military tradition that continued even into the twentieth century. Finally, the tacit deal between Frederick William and the Junkers, who agreed to support the Hohenzollerns in return for nearly unlimited power over their peasants and an exemption from taxes, ensured domestic tranquility. By his personal leadership, Frederick William, the Great Elector, laid the foundation for the rise of Prussia in the seventeenth century. To conclude this essay, be sure to add a brief (2-3 sentences) discussion of synthesis. Because this essay asks you to discuss the rise of any of the seventeenth century European absolute monarchies, your synthesis could include comparison discussion of the rise of Louis XIV of France.
(*Western Civilization*, 9th ed., pp. 452–53 / 10th ed., pp. 448–49; Historical Thinking Skills—Causation; Learning Objectives SP-2, SP-15; Key Concept 2.1)

5

THE SCIENTIFIC REVOLUTION: THE 1600S

As the Renaissance encouraged scholars to think for themselves, explorers expanded geographical and cultural views of the world, astronomers observed phenomena that did not fit conventional models, and the authority of the Catholic Church suffered from the splintering of the Reformation. Europeans began to think about their world in new ways, eventually adopting a scientific and mathematical view of the universe. This marked the beginning of a more modern intellectual mindset that manifested itself not only in new discoveries and inventions but also in the intellectual revolution that led to a more secular view of the world.

KEY TERMS

alchemy
Aristotelian philosophy
astrology
Cartesian dualism
cosmology
deductive method
empiricism
geocentric (Ptolemaic) conception of the universe
heliocentric conception of the universe
Hermeticism

inductive method
natural laws
natural philosophers
Principia Mathematica
querelles des femmes
rationalism
Royal Academy of the Sciences
Royal Society
scholasticism
scientific method
Scientific Revolution
world machine

CHAPTER KEY CONCEPTS

▦ Scientific societies promoted the new scientific concept of the natural world, attracting the attention—and patronage—of governments that hoped to use this new knowledge.

▦ Science became a part of the high culture of Europe during the seventeenth century, with Europe's wealthy, educated elites eager to exploit the practical applications of science to their own advantage in trade and industry.

▦ The transition to a new world view proved to be a difficult process for some to accept. Threatened by scientific discoveries that contradicted centuries-old church teachings, Protestant and Catholic church leaders tried unsuccessfully to silence the spread of new scientific ideas, as the trial of Galileo demonstrates.

▦ The Scientific Revolution ushered in a transformation in intellectual thought that revolutionized the concept of the universe and the place of humans in it, challenging traditional religious views of the world and marking a fundamental break with the old intellectual order.

For a full discussion of the Scientific Revolution, see *Western Civilization,* 9th and 10th editions, Chapter 16.

ORIGINS OF THE SCIENTIFIC REVOLUTION

Although medieval scholars had studied the natural world and employed mathematical and scientific thinking in many ways, the Catholic Church forced them to stay within the boundaries of the old order, the conception of the world laid out by thinkers such as Aristotle, Galen, and Ptolemy. Several factors led sixteenth- and seventeenth-century thinkers to challenge accepted beliefs and eventually spurred them to embrace a more modern scientific model.

First, Renaissance scholars read more of the classical works in the original Greek and realized that even during classical times, other scholars and writers had challenged the great authorities of the old order. Building on the intellectual curiosity of the Renaissance, humanist scholars put away their fear of retribution from Church authorities and asked questions about the world. They were particularly influenced by Plato's insistence that an understanding of mathematics is essential for an understanding of the universe, as well as by the rediscovery of the mathematical works of ancient scholars.

AP® Tip

Remember that the Scientific Revolution had far-reaching consequences. For example, Renaissance artists applied the principles of science and mathematics to their art, even dissecting bodies to understand anatomy, a practice deemed unacceptable by the Church.

Second, the age of exploration had created a demand for new technology, so explorers and merchants began to turn to science to solve practical problems and design equipment, such as better navigational tools. With the invention of the printing press around 1450, the scientific community in Europe began to come together; having read the same published works, scientists—for example, Galileo and Kepler—often corresponded with one another. As a result, scientists began to build on each other's observations and theories, and the speed of scientific advancement accelerated.

Finally, Renaissance Hermeticism held that the universe was the embodiment of God's creation and that humans, as creations of God, could understand the universe's direct nature for beneficial purposes. Hermeticism combined alchemy and astrology and used mathematical magic to unlock the secrets of the universe, so most believed that only an intellectual elite could use it. It was not the magic, but Hermeticism's interest in controlling nature, that was significant. For famous scientists, such as Copernicus, Kepler, Galileo, and Newton, Hermetic magic served as an intellectual springboard.

ADVANCES IN ASTRONOMY

Many notable achievements of the Scientific Revolution came in the field of astronomy. Traditionally accepted views of the universe were based on the geocentric model, in which Earth, made up of earth, air, fire, and water, was the fixed center of the universe, surrounded by revolving concentric spheres.

AP® Tip

The traditional model of the universe based its assumptions on the ideas of Ptolemy and Aristotle, promoting Ptolemy's geocentric belief and Aristotle's concept that circular motion was perfectly shaped and appropriate for heavenly bodies.

The Church clung tightly to this view because it implied that man was the center of God's universe. However, sixteenth-century astronomers realized that their observations did not fit this model; they tried to modify it to make it both acceptable to the Church and consistent with the physical evidence they witnessed.

COPERNICUS

In 1543, Polish astronomer and mathematician Nicolaus Copernicus's book *On the Revolutions of the Heavenly Spheres* was published—it rocked the scientific community. Advancing a heliocentric, or sun-centered, model of the universe, it challenged Aristotle's work and the Church's view of man's place in the universe and man's relationship to God. At first the Catholic Church ignored his theory, but Protestant reformers quickly denounced it. As Copernicus's ideas gained more attention from astronomers, the Catholic Church joined in the denunciations.

BRAHE

Tycho Brahe, a Danish astronomer and the imperial mathematician for Holy Roman Emperor Rudolf II, gathered detailed records of observations over some twenty years. He rejected the geocentric model, but he did not fully agree with the Copernican model, either. Brahe advocated a two-part model: all heavenly bodies revolve around the sun except for Earth and its moon, and the sun and all of its planetary bodies revolve around Earth.

KEPLER

Johannes Kepler, a German astrologer, astronomer, and mathematician, worked with Brahe and eventually succeeded him as an imperial mathematician to Rudolf II. Inheriting Brahe's observational data allowed Kepler to apply the data to his emerging ideas and eventually publish three laws of planetary motion. He proved mathematically that the sun is the center of the universe; that the planets have elliptical orbits and that the orbital speeds of planets vary depending on the distance of each planet from the sun; and that planets with smaller orbits revolve more slowly than those with larger orbits. Collectively, these affirmed heliocentrism and further refined the details of Copernican theory.

GALILEO

Galileo, a scientist and mathematician from Pisa, built an improved telescope and turned it to the heavens, discovering craters on the moon, the four largest moons of Jupiter, the existence of stars in the Milky Way, and sunspots. In his book *Starry Messenger* (1610), Galileo firmly advocated the Copernican model, which had been condemned by the Catholic Inquisition in Rome. In 1616, Galileo attracted his own attention from the Inquisition, which prohibited him from declaring Copernicanism fact. His book *Dialogue on the Two Chief World Systems: Ptolemaic and Copernican*, published in 1632, unequivocally supported Copernican theory and was immediately put on the Catholic Index of Prohibited Books. The Inquisition put Galileo on trial in 1633, found him guilty of violating his 1616 sentence, and put him under house arrest. Galileo spent his final years studying mechanics and motion and making discoveries about acceleration and inertia. His experience with the Catholic Church discouraged Italian scientists; soon after, England, France, and the Dutch Republic became the forefront for scientific innovation.

NEWTON

Sir Isaac Newton, English mathematician, alchemist, and scientist, invented calculus as a method for explaining infinitesimal changes in motion. He also discovered the three laws of motion, laid out in his most famous work, the *Principia Mathematica* (1687). Explaining the motion of the universe and demonstrating that the universe operated according to set principles that could be discovered through the use of human reason, Newton presented a mechanistic model of the universe, one in which the world was like a machine that operated according to natural scientific laws. A religious man, Newton believed that God created universal laws of motion and moved the heavenly bodies according to those laws; many later thinkers used his model to discount the need for divine intervention. Newton's worldview—the accepted worldview until Einstein's theory of relativity shattered it—suggested that if human reason could discover natural laws governing the physical universe, human reason might also discover natural laws governing fields such as politics and society. In stimulating investigation in those fields, Newton's worldview led to the Enlightenment.

ADVANCES IN MEDICINE AND CHEMISTRY

Like astronomy, medicine underwent revolutionary change in the sixteenth and seventeenth centuries. Medieval medicine had been based on the ideas of Galen, a second-century A.D. Greek physician who dissected animals to investigate human anatomy. His inaccurate model of human anatomy, paired with his inaccurate model of human physiology, critically impeded an understanding of disease, which Galen attributed to an imbalance of the four humors (blood, yellow bile, phlegm, and black bile). The commonplace practice of blood-letting is a product of Galen's postulation that treating the imbalance would cure the disease.

Leading the revolution in medicine, Paracelsus began with the premise that just as chemical reactions occur in the universe, they also occur within the human body. Paracelsus posited that disease results from chemical imbalances and can be cured by correcting the imbalances with chemical remedies. Vesalius concentrated on anatomy. Having dissected human bodies as a professor of surgery at the University of Padua, he assembled an illustrated handbook of human anatomy, *On the Fabric of the Human Body* (1543). Although he corrected many of Galen's anatomical errors, he still did not correctly explain the circulatory system. That fell to William Harvey, whose book *On the Motion of the Heart and Blood* (1628) showed the heart as the center of the circulatory system, pumping blood through a circuit of arteries and veins.

Chemistry emerged as a new field of study in the seventeenth century. Robert Boyle, among the first to use controlled experiments, theorized that pressure affects the volume of gases. Boyle also hypothesized that matter is composed of atoms. A century later, Antoine Lavoisier built on Boyle's model and formulated a modern system of naming elements.

WOMEN IN THE SCIENCES

Prior to the Renaissance, the view that the proper role of a woman was to be a daughter, wife, and mother was so prevalent that women rarely received higher education unless they became nuns. However, Renaissance humanism permitted the education of some elite women.

Scientific education for women, unlike humanist education, came mostly from informal sources. Noblewomen learned of the sciences from their husbands, fathers, and brothers. Occasionally, they attended meetings of scientific societies with their male relatives or sat in as listeners at scientific discussions. A few privileged women made names for themselves in the sciences, but scientific societies in

England and France did not admit any women as members until the twentieth century.

One such noblewoman was Margaret Cavendish, Duchess of Newcastle. In addition to poetry, essays, plays, popular fiction—even an early example of science fiction—she wrote six books on natural philosophy in which she criticized both rationalism and empiricism and questioned the scientific method.

French and English women in the sciences mainly came from aristocratic families. In Germany, the majority of women in the sciences had a craft production background. For example, Maria Merian was trained in illustration in her father's workshop. A serious entomologist, she traveled to Surinam in 1699 to study insects and plants. Her book, *Metamorphosis of the Insects of Surinam*, is notable for both her close observation and her excellent illustrations of the insect life.

Maria Winkelmann learned astronomy in a family observatory, trained by her father, her uncle, and a neighbor. She married Gottfried Kirch, a renowned German astronomer, and was his assistant at the Berlin Academy of Science observatory, where she discovered a comet. Although well qualified, she was denied the position of assistant astronomer at the observatory after her husband's death.

> ### AP® Tip
>
> It is important to remember that only elite, privileged women received humanist learning. Most women in Europe were unaffected by Renaissance humanism and the Scientific Revolution.

In the age-old debate on the inherent nature of women, the traditional male view held that women were weak, irrational, and easily corruptible, and therefore not fit for higher education. In the sixteenth and seventeenth centuries, that view was challenged. Women argued that they possessed rational minds and should be allowed to participate in the scientific and intellectual revolutions of their age but that they needed an education—that education was the key to a broader understanding of the world and valuable participation in society. By the eighteenth century, however, women had lost ground in many traditionally female fields—for example, midwifery—when the occupations first were considered professions and then came to be dominated by men. Although a handful of women did have roles in the sciences, the Scientific Revolution generally promoted traditional beliefs about women. Some men, such as Benedict de Spinoza, even used the new sciences to further promote male superiority, claiming that women were naturally inferior beings.

THE SCIENTIFIC METHOD

As the accepted view of the universe changed and science became popularized, the Scientific Revolution spurred thinkers to question the very process of scientific inquiry and ask about the nature of man and how one could discover truth. Two of the most important such thinkers were Francis Bacon and René Descartes.

Bacon (1561–1626), an English jurist and amateur scientist, proposed a revolutionary reorganization of the scientific process. In his book *Novum Organum*, Bacon asserted that misunderstandings—he called them idols—clouded human knowledge and needed to be eliminated in order to achieve intellectual certainty; scientists should reject the assumptions of previous thought and use the inductive method rather than the deductive method—in other words, gather evidence through observation, then proceed to make general hypotheses and axioms. Unlike Descartes, Bacon trusted his senses and believed that all human knowledge entered the mind through the perception of the senses. This made Bacon an empiricist, because he rejected as uncertain any assertion that could not be proven through experiments and observations.

Descartes (1596–1650), a French philosopher and mathematician, founded modern rationalism, the belief that the basis of knowledge is human reason, not physical observation or experience. Descartes built his philosophy with the process of systematic doubt—he doubted everything, from the existence of the world around him to his own existence. An extreme rationalist, he concluded that he could not trust his senses and so discounted all knowledge he perceived with them. Eventually, he decided that the only thing he knew for sure was that he existed—doubting was the affirmation of his thinking and his existence. This led to his declaration "I think, therefore I am" in *Discourse on Method.* Descartes then postulated the existence of God as the creator of thinking things and of the world around him. He argued that the mind uses mathematics to help explain the world and could be trusted, while the senses could not. Descartes favored deductive thinking: using rational thought, one proceeds from general principles and axioms to specific and complex truths. A related principle, Cartesian dualism, holds that the mind and body are separate—the mind being a spiritual entity and the body a physical one. Thus, a mechanistic model of humanity emerged.

AP® Tip

It is important to understand how thinkers built on one another's ideas. Newton eventually defined the modern scientific method, building on the ideas of both Bacon and Descartes. He combined the empiricism and inductive thinking of Bacon with the rationalism and deductive thinking of Descartes to create a method that began with observations and experiments, proceeded to general axioms, prompted new deductions based on the general concepts, and then tested the new deductions through more experimentation.

THE SPREAD OF SCIENTIFIC KNOWLEDGE

Several vehicles for the dissemination of scientific ideas emerged during the seventeenth century. Scientific journals and societies dedicated to the study and advancement of science helped create a community of scientists. The public was interested, too.

Although the first scientific societies originated in Italy, the English Royal Society (founded in 1662) and the French Academy of the Sciences (1666) proved more important in the advancement of scientific research and ideas. Both grew from informal gatherings of scientists and received royal support—at first for investigating practical applications of science to industry and technology, but soon after for concentrating theoretical work. During the wars of Louis XIV, however, the French Academy worked with the Marquis de Louvois, the war minister, because the French government provided the Academy's members with generous monetary support and salaries. German states, copying the English and French models, also supported small scientific societies.

The publication of scientific journals further encouraged cooperation among scientists, allowing them to read the results of one another's experiments and build on shared ideas. In France, journals aimed at both practicing scientists and the educated public had a wider circulation than comparable English journals, which were generally only distributed to Royal Society members and other active scientists.

Several important factors led to the rapid acceptance of the usefulness of science. In the larger society, literate merchants and aristocrats saw that scientific applications could provide them with ways to make greater profits. Some political leaders used science to create stability in their nations. While some Puritan leaders wanted to pursue radical scientific changes, most aristocrats and political leaders pursued the application of science to the improvement of conditions in their nations, such as increasing crop yields or making trade more efficient. In using science to improve nations, the governing elite enhanced its own political power.

SCIENCE AND RELIGION

As scientists began to make discoveries that called into question the traditional theological claims about the world and the universe, conflicts arose between science and religion. Galileo, whose ideas were victims of such disagreements, believed that such conflict was not inevitable; the Church should refrain from making decisions about the nature of the universe based on Biblical texts that could be interpreted in many different ways. The Church, however, clung to the traditional cosmology of the universe. The split between science and religion widened, even though many scientists were deeply religious and feared the effects would lead people to a rejection of their faith.

Two thinkers tried to bridge the divide:

▪ Benedict de Spinoza (1632–1677), a Dutch lens grinder and philosopher, advocated rationalism as a means to understanding. He believed that understanding of universal truths cannot be discovered adequately and completely by sense perceptions alone. Although he rejected Cartesian dualism, Spinoza agreed with many of the mathematical ideas of Descartes and read most of his works. A Jew excommunicated from his synagogue at the age of twenty-four and ostracized by Christian churches, Spinoza believed that God and nature are inseparable—that God is the universe. This philosophy, pantheism, is the subject of *Ethics Demonstrated in the Geometrical Manner*.

▪ Blaise Pascal (1623–1662) was a French mathematician and scientist. In *Pensées*, Pascal asserted that Christianity did not contradict reason and, in an explanation known as Pascal's wager, that the most reasonable action was to bet that God exists: if one were correct, he would go to heaven; if incorrect, he had lost nothing. According to Pascal, finite human reason cannot adequately comprehend an infinite universe and God, so only faith can bring a person close to God. Pascal hoped to bring together religion and science, but like many other seventeenth-century thinkers, his efforts failed, and philosophers became more secular in their thinking on the eve of the Enlightenment.

The Scientific Revolution of the sixteenth and seventeenth centuries turned medieval cosmology upside down and radically changed human perceptions concerning man, the universe, and God. The new science prompted a variety of reactions, ranging from outright hostility on the part of many organized churches to eager acceptance by scientists and those educated people who realized that science could be used to bring profits, stability, and practical improvements to the human condition. Most important, Newton's discovery of natural laws that govern the physical world prompted philosophers to search for natural laws that govern many aspects of society and politics, a trend that created great optimism and hope for the future and ushered in the Enlightenment.

Content Review Questions

1. All of the following thinkers fully accepted the heliocentric model EXCEPT
   (A) Copernicus.
   (B) Brahe.
   (C) Kepler.
   (D) Galileo.

2. The major reason that the Catholic Church did not immediately reject the writings of Copernicus was because most church leaders
   (A) believed he was right.
   (B) welcomed his theory as a chance to prove the truth of the Ptolemaic system.
   (C) believed that his theory would not attract much following and thought it best not to call attention to it.
   (D) ignored it because many Protestant leaders had denounced it— the Catholic leaders did not want to be like the Protestants in any way.

3. Which of the following pairs of thinkers had the greatest impact on the development of the scientific method?
   (A) Copernicus and Galileo
   (B) Copernicus and Kepler
   (C) Bacon and Descartes
   (D) Bacon and Galileo

4. Which of the following pairs of thinkers had the greatest impact on science prior to the Scientific Revolution?
   (A) Plato and Aristotle
   (B) Ptolemy and Aristotle
   (C) Ptolemy and Plato
   (D) Galen and Pythagoras

5. Which of the following is true of women during the Scientific Revolution?
   (A) Society expected women to be a good daughters, wives, and mothers.
   (B) Male scientists often welcomed the participation of women in their scientific societies.
   (C) In Germany, large numbers of women were allowed to participate in the sciences.
   (D) The participation of women in the sciences quickly led to the transfer of greater political rights to women.

6. All of the following are true of Hermetic magic EXCEPT
   (A) Europe's intellectual elite practiced Hermetic magic during the Renaissance.
   (B) many famous scientists, including Kepler and Galileo, practiced Hermetic magic.
   (C) Hermetic magic combined mathematics and alchemy.
   (D) Hermetic magic discouraged actual scientific progress.

7. All of the following are true of the relationship between religion and science during the sixteenth and seventeenth centuries EXCEPT
   (A) almost all scientists rejected religious beliefs.
   (B) Galileo believed religion and science should not be pitted against each other.
   (C) the growing split between religion and science emerged largely because churches clung to medieval beliefs about the universe and the world.
   (D) Pascal tried to unite Christianity and science by showing that science rests on a basis of order and reason, and religion on faith.

8. Vesalius challenged the ideas of Galen by
   (A) asserting that diseases originated from chemical imbalances.
   (B) publishing an illustrated thesis that outlined the structure of the body and the organs, correcting Galen's misconceptions about human anatomy.
   (C) affirming that the same blood in the body flows in both the veins and the arteries; Galen thought there were two systems.
   (D) stating that diseases could be cured with chemical treatments.

9. Which of the following scientists laid the foundation for modern physiology by discovering the circulation of blood?
   (A) Paracelsus
   (B) Vesalius
   (C) Galen
   (D) Harvey

10. Johannes Kepler's most significant accomplishment was
    (A) discovering sunspots.
    (B) proving mathematically that planetary orbits are elliptical.
    (C) advocating a heliocentric model.
    (D) discovering Jupiter's moons.

Multiple-Choice Questions

Questions 1–3 refer to the following quotation.

René Descartes, *Discourse on Method*

I came to believe that the four following rules would be found sufficient, always provided I took the firm and unswerving resolve never in a single instance to fail in observing them.

The first was to accept nothing as true which I did not evidently know to be such ... to include nothing additional to what had presented itself to my mind so clearly and so distinctly that I could have no occasion for doubting it.

The second, to divide each of the difficulties I examined into as many parts as may be required for its adequate solution.

The third, to arrange my thoughts in order, beginning with things the simplest and easiest to know, so that I may then ascend little by little, as it were step by step, to the knowledge of the more complex ...

And the last, in all cases to make enumerations so complete, and reviews so general, that I should be assured of omitting nothing.

Those long chains of reasonings, each step simple and easy ... have led me to surmise that all the things we human beings are competent to know are interconnected in the same manner, and that none are so remote as to be beyond our reach or so hidden that we cannot discover them—that is, provided we abstain from accepting as true what is not thus related, i.e., keep always to the order required for their deduction one from another. And I had no great difficulty in determining what the objects are with which I should begin, for that I already knew, namely, that it was with the simplest and easiest.

Source: N. K. Smith, *Descartes' Philosophical Writings*, (London: Palgrave Macmillan, 1958).

1. The quotation above reflects which of the following ideas?
   (A) Empiricism
   (B) Rationalism
   (C) Hermeticism
   (D) Scholasticism

2. Which of the following would most likely have disagreed with the statement above?
   (A) Bacon
   (B) Spinoza
   (C) Descartes
   (D) Leibnitz

3. All of the following are important intellectual contributions of René Descartes's EXCEPT
   (A) development of analytical geometry.
   (B) development of the coordinate system.
   (C) popularization of the ideas of rationalism.
   (D) popularization of the use of empirical evidence for proving hypotheses.

Questions 4–6 refer to the following image.

Source: RMN-Grand Palais/Art Resource, NY

4. The painting above illustrates which of the following statements about the scientific revolution?
   (A) Political leaders such as Louis XIV often interfered with scientific societies because they feared their power.
   (B) Political leaders such as Louis XIV often funded scientific societies in hopes of achieving practical benefits for their nations.
   (C) Scientists often faced trials for contradicting traditional scientific beliefs.
   (D) Political leaders such as Louis XIV often forced members of the nobility to listen to scientific lectures.

5. Which of the following statements is true about the comparison between the French Royal Academy of the Sciences and the Royal Society of England?
   (A) The English Royal Society emphasized theoretical research while the French Royal Academy concentrated on the practical value of research.
   (B) The English Royal Society focused its efforts on medical research, paying little attention to industry, while the French Royal Academy collected tools and machines.
   (C) The English Royal Society and the French Royal Academy were bitter rivals, rarely cooperating or sharing their research with one another.
   (D) The English Royal Society received little encouragement, while the French Royal academy received abundant state support with members being appointed and paid by the government.

6. All of the following are reasons for the rapid acceptance of new scientific ideas in the seventeenth century EXCEPT
   (A) literate merchants and propertied elites believed that science offered new ways to exploit resources for a profit.
   (B) lower-class members of society believed that science would open new doors for them, creating new jobs to improve their standard of living.
   (C) political interests used the new scientific conception of the natural world to bolster social stability by making changes that increased the food supply and commerce.
   (D) princes and kings recognized the military applications of the mathematical sciences.

Short-Answer Questions

1. Answer A, B, and C by analyzing the role of women in the origins of modern science.
   A) Briefly describe the accomplishments of ONE woman who played a role in the sciences in the seventeenth century.
   B) Briefly describe the problems faced by ONE woman who met with opposition to her role in the sciences.
   C) Briefly explain the reasons that some people opposed the participation of women in the sciences.

2. Answer A, B, and C by analyzing the way in which sixteenth- and seventeenth-century scientists contributed to a changing view of medicine.
   A) Briefly explain how Paracelsus changed traditional views and practices in the medical field.
   B) Briefly explain how Vesalius changed traditional views on anatomy.
   C) Briefly explain how William Harvey changed traditional medical knowledge.

Long-Essay Questions

1. Compare and contrast the ideas of Francis Bacon and René Descartes. (Historical Thinking Skills: Comparison)

2. Analyze the contributions of Copernicus, Kepler, Galileo, and Newton to the changing model of the universe in the sixteenth and seventeenth centuries. (Historical Thinking Skills: Patterns of Continuity and Change Over Time)

Answers

CONTENT REVIEW QUESTIONS

1. **(B)** Brahe postulated a system in which all planetary bodies except Earth and its moon revolve around the sun and the sun and its orbiting planets in turn revolve around Earth (*Western Civilization*, 9th ed., p. 481 / 10th ed., p. 477; Historical Thinking Skills—Comparison; Learning Objective OS-5; Key Concept 2.3).

2. **(C)** Because Copernicus conservatively presented his ideas as only a theory and retained the circular orbits of Aristotle, the Church largely ignored his work until it began to gain a greater following (*Western Civilization*, 9th ed., pp. 480–81 / 10th ed., pp. 475–76; Historical Thinking Skills—Causation; Learning Objectives OS-2, OS-5; Key Concept 2.3).

3. **(C)** Bacon and Descartes were the two thinkers who had the greatest impact on the development of the scientific method. Both rejected unproven scientific assumptions and their methods of scientific inquiry were crucial to the work of other scientists (Western Civilization, 9th ed., pp. 494–95 / 10th ed., pp. 490–91; Historical Thinking Skills—Causation; Learning Objectives OS-2, OS-5; Key Concept 2.3).

4. **(B)** Ptolemy and Aristotle had the greatest impact because together their ideas defined the model of the universe that was accepted until the sixteenth and seventeenth centuries (*Western Civilization*, 9th ed., pp. 478–79 / 10th ed., pp. 474–75; Historical Thinking Skills—Causation; Learning Objectives OS-2, OS-5; Key Concept 2.3).

5. **(A)** Although a few elite women did participate in the sciences in the sixteenth and seventeenth centuries, the traditional attitude that a woman's role was in the home as a good daughter, wife, and mother dominated society. Although choice D might look tempting, women did not receive more rights, and some thinkers, such as Spinoza, actually used the sciences to argue for women's inferiority (*Western Civilization*, 9th ed., pp. 490–92 / 10th ed., pp. 486–88; Historical Thinking Skills—Contextualization; Learning Objectives OS-4, OS-7; Key Concept 2.3).

6. **(D)** Many scholars believe that Hermetic magic encouraged the study of science because the desire to control nature served as one of the motivating factors of the Scientific Revolution (*Western Civilization*, 9th ed., p. 478 / 10th ed., p. 474; Historical Thinking Skills—Causation; Learning Objective OS-1; Key Concept 1.1).

7. **(A)** Although both Protestant and Catholic church leaders condemned many of the ideas of leading scientists, many scientists saw the problem not as an inherent conflict between science and religion, but as a conflict between scientific discoveries and outdated interpretations of the Bible. Many scientists had faith in God and believed in a God who had created the well-ordered universe (*Western Civilization*, 9th ed., pp. 497–98 / 10th ed., pp. 493–96; Historical Thinking Skills—Contextualization; Learning Objective OS-8; Key Concept 2.3).

8. **(B)** Vesalius personally dissected bodies and created an illustrated book to more accurately describe human anatomy (*Western Civilization*, 9th ed., pp. 488–90 / 10th ed., pp. 485–88; Historical Thinking Skills—Contextualization; Learning Objective OS-7; Key Concept 2.3).

9. **(D)** Harvey discovered that the heart was the starting point for the circulation of the blood and demonstrated that it flowed in veins and arteries, making a complete circuit before returning to the heart. This discovery overturned the ideas of Galen and laid the foundation for modern physiology (*Western Civilization*, 9th ed., p. 489 / 10th ed., pp. 485–86; Historical Thinking Skills—Causation, Contextualization; Learning Objective OS-7; Key Concept 2.3).

10. **(B)** Choice C might look tempting, because Kepler did advocate the heliocentric model, but the question asks for his most significant contribution, which was his mathematical explanation of the elliptical shape of planetary orbits (*Western Civilization*, 9th ed., pp. 481–82 / 10th ed., pp. 477–78; Historical Thinking Skills—Comparison, Contextualization; Learning Objective OS-5; Key Concept 2.3).

MULTIPLE-CHOICE QUESTIONS

1. **(B)** Rationalism is the system of thought based on the belief that human reason and experience are the main sources of knowledge. Descartes concluded that the only thing he knew with certainty was his existence, which he discovered through the process of thinking, rather than through his physical senses (*Western Civilization*, 9th ed., pp. 493–94 / 10th ed., pp. 448–90; Historical Thinking Skills—Analyzing Evidence: Content and Sourcing; Learning Objectives OS-2, OS-5, OS-6; Key Concept 2.3).

2. **(A)** The quote was written by René Descartes, a rationalist, who distrusted his senses, preferring to base his ideas on a rationalist epistemology. Bacon was an empiricist who wanted concrete, sensory proof (*Western Civilization*, 9th ed., pp. 494–95 / 10th ed., pp. 489–90; Historical Thinking Skills—Comparison; Learning Objectives OS-2, OS-5, OS-6; Key Concept 2.3).

3. **(D)** Descartes was a rationalist who demanded arguments be proven using self-evident truths rather than empirical evidence (*Western Civilization*, 9th ed., pp. 494–95 / 10th ed., pp. 488–91; Historical Thinking Skills—Comparison; Learning Objectives OS-2, OS-5, OS-6; Key Concept 2.3).

4. **(B)** The painting shows Louis XIV and controller general Colbert meeting with the Academy of Sciences. Colbert's presence suggests a practical reason for Louis's visit and illustrates the fact that many political leaders funded the royal societies in the hopes of achieving benefits for their nations (*Western Civilization*, 9th ed., pp. 495–96 / 10th ed., pp. 491–93; Historical Thinking Skills—Causation; Learning Objectives OS-2, SP-2; Key Concepts 2.1, 2.3).

5. **(D)** The French Royal Academy was under government control and received abundant support from the crown, while the English Royal Society evolved out of informal gatherings of scientists and received little government support (*Western Civilization*, 9th ed., pp. 495–96 / 10th ed., pp. 491–93; Historical Thinking Skills—Comparison; Learning Objectives OS-2, OS-5, OS-7; Key Concepts 2.1, 2.3).

6. **(B)** Although educated citizens and rulers perceived the benefits of the new science, most members of the lower class were untouched by scientific knowledge and discoveries (Western Civilization, 9th ed., pp. 495–96 / 10th ed., pp. 491–93; Historical Thinking Skills—Contextualization; Learning Objectives OS-2, OS-4, OS-5, OS-7; Key Concepts 2.1, 2.3).

SHORT-ANSWER QUESTIONS

1. A) One woman who successfully played a role in the sciences in the seventeenth century was Maria Merian, a famous entomologist. She learned the art of illustration in her father's workshop and used this skill to create accurate drawings of insects and plants. She took a scientific journey to Surinam, using the information she recorded to produce Metamorphosis of the Insects of Surinam in which she drew 60 pictures of the developmental cycles of insect life.

   B) One woman who met with opposition to her role in the sciences was Maria Winkelmann. She was an educated woman who worked with her husband as an astronomer, even discovering a comet. After the death of her husband, however, she was refused a job as an assistant astronomer by the Berlin Academy. Claiming that "mouths would gape" if they hired a woman for the position, they instead hired a man.

   C) Some seventeenth-century people opposed the participation of women in the sciences, believing that the sciences were the domain of educated men. The standard expected of a woman in that day was to perform domestic duties, such as taking care of the household and raising children, being a good daughter, wife, and mother. Although some women did succeed in the sciences, few enjoyed that opportunity. New opportunities emerged for elite women during the late Renaissance period, but even these women were only expected to pursue a humanist education, studying classical and Christian works. Only those who participated in the informal scientific networks of their male relatives had any chance to learn about the sciences.
   (*Western Civilization*, 9th ed., pp. 490–91 / 10th ed., pp. 486–88; Historical Thinking Skills—Comparison, Causation; Learning Objectives OS-4, OS-8, IS-10; Key Concepts 2.1, 2.3)

2. A) Paracelsus changed traditional views and practices in the medical field in several ways. He rejected Galen's belief that since disease was based on an imbalance of the four humors— blood, yellow bile, phlegm, and black bile— treatment should consist of bleeding and purging to remove the imbalance. Instead, Paracelsus introduced the idea that diseases were caused by chemical imbalances and could be cured with chemical treatment, sometimes using toxic substances to treat medical problems.

   B) Andreas Vesalius changed traditional views on anatomy by correcting many of the inaccuracies found in Galen's book, *On Anatomical Procedures*. Unlike Galen, who based his observations on animal research, Vesalius based his book on the careful examination of human bodies that he dissected. This first-hand knowledge gave Vesalius a much more accurate anatomical model.

   C) William Harvey not only changed traditional medical knowledge, but he also corrected the errors of near-contemporaries, such as Vesalius. Harvey is responsible for leading modern medicine to completely turn against the erroneous assertions of Galen and instead promoting an accurate model of the circulatory system. Harvey most famously discovered that the heart was the starting point of circulation and that it worked like a pump, circulating blood in a system that involved both the veins and arteries. This discovery directly contradicted Galen's idea that the liver was the beginning of the circulatory system and Vesalius's idea that there were two kinds of blood in the veins and arteries. Harvey set the stage for the modern field of physiology.
   (*Western Civilization*, 9th ed., pp. 488– 89 / 10th ed., pp. 484–86; Historical Thinking Skills—Patterns of Continuity and Change Over Time; Learning Objective OS-5; Key Concept 2.3)

LONG-ESSAY QUESTIONS

1. Although these two thinkers differed greatly in their approaches to scientific inquiry, Bacon and Descartes had several important similarities: both wanted proof for knowledge and both rejected the authority of the thinkers and scientists who came before them. Be sure to talk about both the similarities and the differences between the two men. Several significant differences define the philosophies of Descartes and Bacon. Although both criticized their predecessors for jumping to conclusions and accepting ideas on the authority of the Church and the ancients, their methods of obtaining scientific proof differed. Bacon, an empiricist, demanded evidence that could be derived through the senses and through experimentation. He advocated the inductive method, in which scientists begin with evidence obtained from experiments and use that evidence to arrive at hypotheses that can be tested upon further experimentation. Bacon believed that assertions based only on the authority of previous scientists or on mathematical reasoning could not be accepted because they lacked physical evidence of their truth.

Descartes, on the other hand, was a rationalist and a deductive thinker who believed that the senses could not be trusted. Instead, he demanded truth derived from reason and saw mathematical proof as the highest form of evidence that could be obtained to ascertain the veracity of an axiom. He advocated suspending belief in all statements that did not appear in the mind as completely certain and without doubt. From that point, he asserted that one must break down a problem or scientific question into smaller parts and then deduce one solution from the next until eventually one arrived at a solution that could be considered true. Although the two men's methods differed greatly, their ultimate goal of rejecting questionable truths and finding proof for assertions was the same. To conclude your essay, be sure to include a brief (2-3 sentences) discussion of synthesis. For this essay, you could include a discussion of the impact of Bacon and Descartes on the Enlightenment thinkers in non-scientific fields, such as politics and economics.
(*Western Civilization*, 9th ed., pp. 494–95 / 10th ed., pp. 490–91; Historical Thinking Skills—Comparison; Learning Objectives OS-2, OS-5, OS-6; Key Concept 2.3)

2. When Copernicus first cast his eyes on the heavens, the accepted worldview was based on the Ptolemaic–Aristotelian model, in which the hand of God placed mankind in the center of a universe in which all of the heavenly bodies revolved in perfect circles around the earth. This cosmology pleased the Catholic Church, since it gave a special spot to mankind as the center of God's attention.

By the sixteenth century, astronomers began to question this traditional system, and many tried to find a way to reconcile their observations with the geocentric model. Finally, Copernicus, a Polish astronomer and mathematician, dared to publish his heliocentric conception of the universe, prompting a century of debate over the true nature of the heavens. Copernicus, however, acted conservatively and sought to reconcile his heliocentric observations with the Aristotelian belief in the perfection of circular motion. His system, while heliocentric, still posed a model of the universe in which the planets followed circular orbits. Kepler, Galileo, and Newton all made adjustments to the system introduced by Copernicus until a completely new, mechanistic model dominated Western thinking by the late seventeenth century. A student and colleague of Brahe, Kepler inherited all of Brahe's observational data and used it to prove his three laws of planetary motion, the most significant of which stated mathematically that the planets followed elliptical orbits.

Galileo built a better telescope and began to decisively and openly support the Copernican model, prompting the Catholic Church to take action against him. By this point, the Church clung to traditional beliefs and literal interpretations of Biblical verses, fearing what would happen if their whole concept of man and the heavens fell apart. Even though the Roman Inquisition condemned him, he still continued his work on force and motion, helping to explain the motion of the planets.

Finally, Newton discovered the universal law of gravitation and the universal laws of motion, which he published in his famous work *Principia Mathematica*. Newton's discovery of these laws and their application to planetary motion transformed the developing Copernican model into a mechanistic model in which the universe operates like a machine according to unchanging natural laws. Together, Newton and his predecessors gradually discredited the medieval cosmology, ushering in a more rational and secular view of the world. In order to conclude your essay, you will need to write a brief (2–3 sentences) analysis of synthesis. For this essay, this discussion could compare the ways in which these astronomers challenged traditional beliefs to show that the world operated according to natural laws, with ways in which the Enlightenment thinkers challenged traditional political beliefs while proposing new political systems based on their perception of the perceived natural political laws that govern the universe. (*Western Civilization*, 9th ed., pp. 479–89 / 10th ed., pp. 474–84; Historical Thinking Skills—Patterns of Continuity and Change Over Time; Learning Objectives OS-7; Key Concept 2.3)

6

THE ENLIGHTENMENT: THE 1700s

With roots in both the Scientific Revolution and the seventeenth-century beliefs of the English philosopher John Locke, the Enlightenment offered new ideas about how to change the world. The application of scientific method and rational, empirical thought processes to politics, the economy, society, and religion led the intellectuals of the movement, called philosophes, to call for change in government, economic policy, human behavior, and religion. Women, political officials, economists, and educators were also eager to encourage responsible government, expanded education, and rational human interaction. Others, however, challenged this emphasis on reason in European culture and particularly the expanded role for women.

KEY TERMS

atheism	original state of nature
Deism	philosophe
Encyclopedia	physiocrat
feminism	Pietism
general will	rationalism
laissez-faire	Rococo
natural law	salon
natural rights	separation of powers
neoclassicism	skepticism
mercantilism	*tabula rasa*
Methodism	the social contract
old order	

187

CHAPTER KEY CONCEPTS

- Thinking about the ideal society, the philosophes studied a variety of government systems. They were especially concerned with the problems created by absolutism.
- A broad education with a focus on literacy became important to the upper and middle classes as people tried to understand and improve their world. New public venues, such as coffeehouses and lending libraries, along with expanded print media, popularized enlightened ideas in spite of censorship by the government and the Church.
- Physiocrats like Adam Smith rejected mercantilism in favor of laissez-faire capitalism.
- Women gained recognition during the Enlightenment as they hosted salons and wrote about their concerns.
- The rational study of religious practices and beliefs led to the demand for religious toleration and the development of Deism. Partly in reaction to Deism, Christianity changed as Europeans strove for more religious devotion.
- Changes in art and music during this time reflected both the interests of the aristocracy and the desire to emulate the logic and reason of ancient Rome.
- Enlightenment values were challenged by the Romantic revival of public sentiment and feeling. Rousseau emphasized the role of emotion rather than logic in the improvement of society and advocated traditional roles for women.

For a full discussion of the Enlightenment, see *Western Civilization*, 9th and 10th editions, Chapter 17.

LIFE UNDER THE OLD ORDER

Despite the spread of Reformation ideas and English parliamentary reforms, the world of early eighteenth-century Europe was one that was still predominantly controlled by government and religious figures. In particular, the Roman Catholic Church and monarchies that existed in Catholic regions, such as France and Austria, stressed the importance of the past and tradition. But based on ideas that had emerged in the seventeenth century, political and religious powers would soon be shaken to their foundations.

The Scientific Revolution, encouraged especially by Charles II in England and Louis XIV in France, had offered a new view of the world beginning in the late seventeenth century. In analyzing the physical world, scientists laid the groundwork for analyzing other topics, such as politics and human behavior. For example, Isaac Newton believed that the universe was created according to natural laws, laws that could be understood by careful study. His mathematical calculations in the studies of motion, gravity, and light, and his prominence as a leader of England's scientific community, encouraged others to look for patterns in a wide range of areas, such as government authority

John Locke, the great pre-Enlightenment thinker, had provided a foundation for the philosophes. His belief in the *tabula rasa*—the blank slate, the mind without mental content at birth—emphasized the importance of education and experience. A reasonable, orderly study of the world, he believed, would lead to the creation of better human beings and, thus, a better society.

AP® Tip

An essential historical thinking skill is the analysis of Patterns of Continuity and Change Over Time. Look back at Chapter 1 and think about the ideals of the Renaissance. To what extent do the ideals of the Enlightenment represent a break with old beliefs? To what extent do they represent an extension of those old beliefs?

COMMON INTERESTS AND BELIEFS

Although the Enlightenment was centered in France, the philosophes were spread across Europe. They were interested in numerous topics and held a wide variety of beliefs, but they shared several underlying assumptions.

First, they believed that the Old Order, referred to by the French term *ancien régime*, was repressive and that political and religious authorities used brute force and tradition to sustain an autocracy that perpetuated despotism, social and legal inequality, religious intolerance, and ignorance. For there to be progress, the philosophes believed, the traditional power of church and state had to be challenged.

Second, they believed that it was possible to change the political and social orders. Drawing on classical philosophy, especially that of Aristotle, Renaissance humanism, and Locke's writings, the philosophes held that every human being possessed natural rights, rights that cannot be usurped by any government. The Lockean rights of life, liberty, and property could be safeguarded only when human institutions conformed to logic and reason. To ensure these rights, the philosophes called for an end to the Old Order and the creation of a new world of progress and hope.

AP® Tip

It is essential that you understand the importance of Causation. The impact of the Scientific Revolution and the work of John Locke on the Enlightenment form an important area of European history, one that frequently appears on the AP® exam. You should be able to analyze—break into parts and discuss the interaction of the parts—the causes of the Enlightenment, especially its roots in seventeenth-century England and its response to autocratic methods of control by both state and Church.

MAJOR PHILOSOPHES

To build a new world, the philosophes proposed a number of reforms. Some—for example, the Baron de Montesquieu and Voltaire—suggested political reforms, while social reforms were laid out by Rousseau and Wollstonecraft.

THE BARON DE MONTESQUIEU

Charles-Louis de Secondat, Baron de Montesquieu, was a French noble who studied forms of government, looking at how they responded to natural rights. Author of *The Spirit of the Laws* (1748), Montesquieu believed that men were born equal but that they lost that equality under oppressive government and social systems. Therefore, protection by law was key to a reasonable form of government. He especially appreciated the English parliamentary system, deriving from it the political theory for which he is most known, the separation of powers. The separating of powers into executive, legislative, and judicial branches led to another theory for which Montesquieu is well known, the system of checks and balances.

VOLTAIRE

Another French philosophe who admired the British system of government was François-Marie Arouet, known as Voltaire. The well-educated son of a middle-class family, he showed his intelligence early when, after studying law, he gained widespread fame as a writer of philosophy. His fiery temper and ardent fight against the religious intolerance of the Catholic Church and the absolutist French government frequently got him in trouble. After a quarrel with a French nobleman, he fled to England, where his passion and wit made him popular among the British nobility. During his more than two years there, he came to appreciate much about the English political system, writing *Philosophic Letters on the English* (1734, 1778), in which he praised England's religious toleration and constitutional monarchy.

JEAN-JACQUES ROUSSEAU

The Swiss-born Rousseau continued the search for the best governmental system. His conclusion, laid out in *The Social Contract* (1762), was quite different from Montesquieu's and Voltaire's. Coming from a difficult family background, Rousseau had a vision of the ideal society and government that rested on the premise that people had natural rights and were happy in their original, natural states. However, as inequalities arose, people entered into a social contract with one another, surrendering their rights to the community and submitting to the "general will," or will of the group. If their government failed in its purpose, the people had the right to overthrow and replace it.

Rousseau patterned his basic ideas of natural rights on John Locke's, but there were differences. Locke was more concerned with individual rights and limiting government. Rousseau, on the other hand, held that the individual's rights should be subordinated to the interests of the community, emphasizing the general will as supreme in creating true freedom.

Rousseau also delved into social issues, such as education and women's role in society. In his book *Emile* (1762), Rousseau expounded his belief that people were born good but that society corrupted them, and that people were happiest when they balanced reason and emotion. The purpose of education, then, was to bring a person back to his true moral state. On the other hand, Locke believed that because people had no inherent morality (*tabula rasa*), education actually defined a person. Rousseau also included in *Emile* his thoughts on women: they could be educated in certain areas but were at their best when they were submissive to men, which, he believed, was their natural role.

DAVID HUME

A Scottish philosophe, Hume believed, as other Enlightenment intellectuals did, that society could be improved. His theories, like Rousseau's, included some ideas that would become popular with nineteenth-century Romantics. As Rousseau emphasized the balance of reason and emotion, Hume also looked at how to blend the two. In his *Treatise on Human Nature* (1739–1740), Hume discussed his "science of man," a framework that could be used to study human beings. He wrote that reason alone could not be the basis of the analysis of any facet of life; people needed faith to balance how they understood their world. Like Locke, Hume believed that people have natural rights and should have some influence on their government. But unlike Locke, Hume held that authority and liberty should work together to make the best political system, that authority per se was not bad unless it was extremely tyrannical.

DENIS DIDEROT

Diderot, a French philosophe and writer, brought together the writings of many philosophes in his twenty-eight-volume *Encyclopedia* (1751–1765), which included works that decried autocracy and religious superstition and supported natural law and toleration. Because the *Encyclopedia* included many entries critical of the old order, Diderot faced governmental censorship. Yet, because of the work, the belief in toleration and natural rights, especially the right to education, grew widespread during the Enlightenment.

ADAM SMITH

Smith, another Scotsman, also contributed to the new approach to thinking during the Enlightenment, but in a very different way. Smith believed—as did the French physiocrats—that the best economic system was not the old order mercantilism but a new way of trading, free trade. Led by François Quesnay, the physiocrats held that just as there were natural political and social laws, there were also natural economic laws. One economic law was laissez-faire, an economic system in which the "invisible hand" of the market, the law of demand and supply, would rule. With laissez-faire, there would be no external control by the government of the economy as there had been with mercantilism, and social and economic order would result. Smith codified and amplified the physiocrats' theories in *The Wealth of Nations* (1776), not only emphasizing the importance of a free market but also declaring that the true wealth of a nation was in the work of its people, not in the gold and silver bullion so important to the countries dependent on mercantilism. Like so many other enlightened thinkers, Smith believed in the freedom of the individual to make choices.

Until this point there has been no mention of the impact of women thinkers. Interestingly, although women had a role in the salon culture and the promulgation of Enlightenment ideals (discussed in the section titled "Eighteenth Century Society"), there were few women actually involved in writing during the Enlightenment.

Mary Wollstonecraft

An Englishwoman, Wollstonecraft was an outstanding proponent of enlightened ideals, especially focusing on the roles and rights of women. During this period, some men held that women had only certain rights or were capable of only some learning. But Wollstonecraft took on the issue headlong. Because of financial problems in her family, Wollstonecraft's education had been haphazard. Yet she read widely, so once she was ready to espouse her beliefs, she had a vast literary foundation from which to draw. Her concerns about the rights of women were developed over that same lifetime of blessings and difficulties. In *Thoughts on the Education of Daughters* (1787), she wrote, as had Hume and Rousseau, that reason should be balanced with instinct. Therefore, the purpose of educating girls was to encourage in them a personal strength and the ability to be independent of men. In *A Vindication of the Rights of Woman* (1792), Wollstonecraft continued her argument about the importance of education, along with another main theme—that God had made women equal to men in abilities and rights. Interestingly, although both she and Rousseau believed in natural rights, including various freedoms, Wollstonecraft's belief that women were equal to men and had the right to independence was in direct contrast to Rousseau's view of women in *Emile*.

AP® Tip

As you study any time period, continually compare and contrast the variations within it. To best understand the Enlightenment, make a chart in which you list information on the philosophes, their writings, and their beliefs. Also, make note of ways in which they were both similar and different. This will give you a better grasp of each person, which will help you in answering multiple-choice questions, as well as provide the specifics necessary for a well-crafted essay.

EIGHTEENTH-CENTURY SOCIETY

Society during the Enlightenment changed in many ways. One development directly linked to the Enlightenment was the growth of salons. Gatherings of philosophes and those interested in discussing how to create a better world, salons were an integral factor in the spread of enlightened ideas. Held in upper-class homes, they were generally hosted by women, such as Madame Geoffrin, who gained recognition and more social influence through them.

Another change during this time was an interest—encouraged by many philosophes—in improving laws and making punishments more fairly fit crimes. Cesare Beccaria led a movement to press for the use of prisons for rehabilitation, not just punishment.

The lives of common people changed little. They still worked hard in much the same type of agrarian work as they had for several hundred years, looking forward to the holy days and feasts that had always been their outlet. Yet some differences were gradually developing. Medical care was improving as doctors and surgeons received better training, although hospitals remained dangerous places where diseases spread rapidly from patient to patient. There were also greater opportunities to receive an education. Although university education was generally out of their reach, the lower classes could get a basic education, especially from their parish churches. With some education and access to the many new periodicals and broadsheets spurred by the greater literacy, the common people expanded their understanding of the world.

Probably the greatest social change came in the area of religion. Many philosophes espoused Deism, which describes God as a great watchmaker who created the universe, then left it on its own, allowing it total self-determination. Philosophes also often encouraged religious toleration, especially by the monarchs who came to them for advice—the enlightened despots. But this religious toleration was not widespread and generally did not extend to Jews.

However, other religions moved decisively away from logic and reason. The Roman Catholic Church still held to its doctrines and belief in an all-powerful God. Within the Protestant faiths, two popular movements arose. Pietism, which began in the Germanic states, encouraged a personal relationship with God. Along that same line, John and Charles Wesley led a revival in England, beginning what would become known as Methodism. The heart of this new faith was the importance of having a deep relationship with God. Thus, religion during the Enlightenment saw movements both toward and away from logic.

EIGHTEENTH-CENTURY CULTURE

From literature and music to art, eighteenth-century culture developed alongside and in response to the ideas of the Enlightenment. Logic, faith, and new views of the world were shown through the work of great writers, composers, and artists.

LITERATURE

Writers did much to expand literature. Encouraged by, and encouraging the growth of, literacy, more periodicals were founded. Historians looked to the past for lessons that could lead to a better world. A new form of story-telling—novels—appeared, initially in England. Interestingly, novels provided women not only the stories they wanted to read, but also the opportunity to write them.

MUSIC

The focus of music during the eighteenth century was both religious and secular. New forms of music, such as the opera and the symphony, were created in Italy, England, Austria, and the German states. Johann Sebastian Bach, the epitome—and virtually the end—of Baroque music, focused on religious compositions. German-born George Frederick Handel, famous for *Messiah*, found enormous success in England, where he was patronized by the courts of George I and George II. Probably the greatest composer of this time was Wolfgang Amadeus Mozart. A child prodigy who played for the court of Maria Theresa, Mozart mastered many musical forms.

ART

Art most dramatically represented the changing views of the eighteenth century. The death of Louis XIV in 1715 marks the beginning of the Rococo style, a reaction by the nobility to the classical baroque of the palace at Versailles. As the Enlightenment highlighted reason, Neoclassicism emphasized the values of ancient Greece and Rome. It was the dominant artistic style of the last quarter of the century.

Developed during the reign of Louis XV, Rococo focused on the idealized life of the French nobility, with its power and fashion centered at Palais-Royal, the court of Louis's regent, Philippe d'Orléans. Love, fantasy, and domestic life were the subjects of its major artists. Jean-Antoine Watteau's *Departure from Cythera* is a great example of a fantastical image of the carefree lives of aristocracy. One of the most widely recognized Rococo paintings is *The Swing*, by Jean-Honoré Fragonard, showing a young woman and her lover caught up in the frivolity of the time. Fragonard also documented the increase in literacy in *Young Girl Reading*. The growing influence of women was shown in the work of Élisabeth-Louise Vigée-Le Brun, who painted portraits of eminent women of the time. The favorite artist of Marie Antoinette, Louis XVI's wife, she painted some thirty portraits of the queen.

Neoclassicism directly reflected Enlightenment ideals by linking the logic and reason of the classical world to late-eighteenth century events. Spurred by excavations in Italy, the publication of such works as *Decline and Fall of the Roman Empire*, and the revolutionary movements in America and France, young artists from across Europe traveled to Italy to study. Preeminent among these young painters was Jacques-Louis David. After returning to France, he painted his seminal work, *Oath of the Horatii*, emphasizing the importance of loyalty and morality. David later painted in support of the French Revolution, most famously a work meant to garner support for the revolution, *The Death of Marat.*

AP® Tip

Art appears on the AP® European History exam in both multiple-choice and essay questions. When studying it, focus less on the artistic components such as color and shape, and more on how each artist and artistic work reflected the period of time and the culture in which he or she worked. The works of David, for example, are influenced by the Enlightenment in the artist's choice of classical Roman subject matter in the case of *Oath of the Horatii*, and his espousal of revolutionary ideals as seen in *The Death of Marat*. The historical thinking skills of Periodization, Contextualization, and Analyzing Evidence: Content and Sourcing are all used when analyzing works of art.

THE IMPACT OF THE ENLIGHTENMENT

The Enlightenment had a significant impact on governments around the world. Several monarchs, the so-called enlightened despots, gained many of their ideas for reform directly from the philosophes. The American and French revolutions drew from the work of the philosophes both their inspiration and some facets of their eventual governmental structures.

Content Review Questions

1. During the eighteenth century, Pietism and Methodism stressed
   (A) a personal experience with God.
   (B) a religion of the head more than the heart.
   (C) the belief in a God who created the universe and then left it alone.
   (D) the basic doctrines of the Anglican Church.

2. Where did the work of Wolfgang Amadeus Mozart and other composers move the musical center of Europe?
   (A) From France to Germany and Russia
   (B) From the Austrian Empire to England
   (C) From Germany and Italy to the Austrian Empire
   (D) From Italy and England to Germany

3. Montesquieu's political theory of the separation of powers is inextricably tied to
   (A) Deism.
   (B) the physiocrats.
   (C) his theory of human development.
   (D) checks and balances.

4. In what area was eighteenth-century medicine especially threatening to the lives of patients?
   (A) Training of doctors
   (B) Cleanliness of hospitals
   (C) Midwives delivering babies
   (D) The licensing of surgeons

5. Which of the following books supported the basic tenets of the physiocrats?
   (A) Voltaire's *Philosophic Letters*
   (B) Adam Smith's *The Wealth of Nations*
   (C) Denis Diderot's *Encyclopedia*
   (D) Jean-Jacques Rousseau's *The Social Contract*

6. All of the following statements about Mary Wollstonecraft are true EXCEPT
   (A) a strong advocate for women's education, Wollstonecraft argued that women should focus on learning how to care for a household.
   (B) a belief in natural rights was central to her philosophies.
   (C) Wollstonecraft held that women were equal to men, not subservient to them.
   (D) Wollstonecraft, an Englishwoman, wrote *Thoughts on the Education of Daughters*, in which she argued for reason balanced with instinct.

7. Unlike Rococo art, Neoclassical art
   (A) focused on the revolutionary movement in America.
   (B) emphasized the importance of reason and morality.
   (C) showed a love of literature.
   (D) offered images of royalty, including Louis XIV and Louis XV.

8. Literature during this period saw all of the following EXCEPT
   (A) the development of the novel.
   (B) a growing interest in Catholic literature.
   (C) the startup of daily newspapers in many towns.
   (D) the founding of magazines on a wide variety of topics, from politics to family life.

9. Like Montesquieu, Voltaire admired the political system in
   (A) England.
   (B) France.
   (C) Russia.
   (D) Italy.

10. David Hume believed
    (A) Locke's theory on natural rights was incorrect.
    (B) reason and faith could not coexist.
    (C) society was in such disarray that little could be done to improve it.
    (D) emotion was more important than reason.

Multiple-Choice Questions

Questions 1–3 refer to the following image.

Source: Archivio di Stato, Bologna//Alinari/Art Resource, NY

1. The above painting could be used as evidence of all of the
   following EXCEPT
   (A) the roots of the Enlightenment in sixteenth-century science.
   (B) the importance of scientific academies for the advancement of
   enlightened ideals.
   (C) women were allowed to join scientific societies alongside men.
   (D) improvements in the military made scientific ideas more
   palatable to rulers of the period.

2. All of the following helped lead to the Enlightenment EXCEPT
   (A) scientists' study of the physical world.
   (B) the widespread impact of Rousseau's theory of general will.
   (C) Isaac Newton's mechanized view of the universe.
   (D) European monarchs' support of scientific societies.

3. The influence of the scientific revolution on religion is seen in
   (A) the Deist view of God as the mechanic who had created
   the universe but had no direct involvement in the
   world he had created
   (B) the emphasis on a mystical relationship with God through
   worship of the saints.
   (C) the increased power of the Jesuit order.
   (D) a rise in persecution of Jews and other religious minorities.

Questions 4–6 refer to the following quotation.

But I say, there is scarce any city or borough in Europe, where blood has not been spilt for religious quarrels; I say, that the human species has been perceptibly diminished, because women and girls were massacred as well as men; I say, that Europe would have had a third larger population, if there had been no theological disputes. In fine, I say, that so far from forgetting these abominable times, we should frequently take a view of them, to inspire an eternal horror for them; and that it is for our age to make reparation by toleration, for this long collection of crimes, which has taken place through the want of toleration, during sixteen barbarous centuries.

Source: Voltaire, *The Ignorant Philosopher* and *Candide*, in J. Butt, trans., Candide or Optimism (London: Penguin Classics, 1947).

4. The above quote can be seen as evidence of Voltaire's argument
   (A) for religious toleration and peace.
   (B) that Europe would be overcrowded if not for deaths during the religious wars.
   (C) that there were no theological disputes in Europe for sixteen centuries.
   (D) that women and girls should have the right to serve in the military along with men.

5. The above writing by Voltaire would have been most influenced by
   (A) the Great Northern War.
   (B) the Thirty Years' War.
   (C) the English Civil War.
   (D) the American Revolution.

6. Voltaire's satirical writing included enlightened ideals even as he argued against the power of
   (A) the English Parliament and King.
   (B) the factory owners over their workers.
   (C) the French church and state.
   (D) landowners over the peasantry.

Short-Answer Questions

1. Many historians argue that the Scientific Revolution is the most important cause of the Enlightenment. Answer A, B, and C.
   A) Briefly explain one reason that historians place such importance on the rise of science as an historical cause.
   B) Choose one piece of evidence and explain how it shows the importance of the scientific revolution to the development of Enlightenment thought.
   C) Briefly explain one cause other than the Scientific Revolution for the rise of the Enlightenment.

2. Historians often debate the importance of various enlightened figures and their impact on the world.
   A) Choose one philosophe and briefly explain TWO effects his or her ideas had on Europe or the world.
   B) Choose another philosophe and briefly explain why his or her ideas are less important.

Long-Essay Questions

1. To what extent did Enlightenment ideals challenge absolutist government and the Catholic Church? (Historical Thinking Skills: Patterns of Continuity and Change Over Time)

2. Discuss the roles women played in the Enlightenment as both participants and subjects of discussion. (Historical Thinking Skills: Contextualization)

Answers

CONTENT REVIEW QUESTIONS

1. **(A)** Both Pietism and Methodism taught the importance of having a personal religious experience with God. They were in direct opposetion to the religious ideas stemming from the Enlightenment, including Deism. They also disagreed with the stricter practices of the Catholic and Anglican churches (*Western Civilization*, 9th ed., pp. 527–28 /10th ed., pp. 523–24; Historical Thinking Skills—Comparison; Learning Objective OS-11; Key Concept 2.3).

2. **(C)** There were great composers across Europe during the first half of the eighteenth century, especially in Germany and Italy, but the last half of the century was led by Mozart and other great composers in the Austrian Empire (*Western Civilization*, 9th ed., pp. 527–28 /10th ed., pp. 514–16; Historical Thinking Skills—Patterns of Continuity and Change Over Time, Periodization; Learning Objective OS-12; Key Concept 3.6).

3. **(D)** Montesquieu's theory of the separation of powers was dependent on checks and balances to limit and control each branch of government (*Western Civilization*, 9th ed., pp. 505–06 / 10th ed., pp. 502–03; Historical Thinking Skills—Causation, Contextualization; Learning Objective OS-7; Key Concept 2.3).

4. **(B)** With increased training and careful licensure, doctors and surgeons were better able to help their patients, and pharmacists and midwives continued to help patients who could not afford to go to doctors and surgeons. But in the days before antiseptics, hospitals tended to spread as many diseases as they cured (*Western Civilization*, 9th ed., pp. 533–34 / 10th ed., pp. 518–19; Historical Thinking Skills—Comparison, Patterns of Continuity and Change Over Time; Learning Objective OS-5, OS-7; Key Concept 1.1, 2.3).

5. **(B)** The physiocrats rejected mercantilism and favored, instead, laissez-faire and natural economic laws. In *The Wealth of Nations*, Adam Smith codified laissez-faire, emphasizing the individual's economic freedom (*Western Civilization*, 8th ed., pp. 9th ed., pp. 521–22 / 10th ed., p. 507; Historical Thinking Skills—Comparison, Contextualization, Patterns of Continuity and Change Over Time; Learning Objective OS-7; Key Concept 2.3).

6. **(A)** Wollstonecraft argued for the rights of women in many areas, especially education. She did not believe that women's education should focus on learning how to manage a household (*Western Civilization*, 9th ed., p. 513 / 10th ed., pp. 510–11; Historical Thinking Skills—Patterns of Continuity and Change Over Time; Learning Objective OS-4; Key Concept 2.3).

7. **(B)** Neoclassicism reflected the classical ideals of reason, loyalty, and morality (*Western Civilization*, 9th ed., pp. 517–18 / 10th ed., pp. 513–14; Historical Thinking Skills—Periodization, Contextualization; Learning Objective OS-10; Key Concept 2.3).

8. **(B)** The publishing of novels, history, newspapers, and magazines grew during the eighteenth century as more people became literate and the philosophes looked to a variety of methods to spread their ideas (*Western Civilization*, 9th ed., pp. 519–21 / 10th ed., pp. 516–17; Historical Thinking Skills—Patterns of Continuity and Change Over Time, Causation, Contextualization; Learning Objective OS-8; Key Concept 2.3).

9. **(A)** Montesquieu's analysis of the English political system and Voltaire's years of living in England led them both to appreciate various facets of English political life (*Western Civilization*, 9th ed., pp. 505–08 / 10th ed., pp. 502–06; Historical Thinking Skills—Causation, Contextualization; Learning Objective OS-7; Key Concept 2.3).

10. **(D)** Believing society could be improved through both reason and faith, Hume's focus was the study of man and his emotions (*Western Civilization*, 9th ed., pp. 508–09 / 10th ed., p. 507; Historical Thinking Skills—Patterns of Continuity and Change Over Time, Contextualization; Learning Objective OS-10, OS-12; Key Concept 2.3, 3.6).

MULTIPLE-CHOICE QUESTIONS

1. **(C)** There are no women in the painting since women would not have been allowed to join scientific academies (*Western Civilization*, 9th ed., pp. 512–14 / 10th ed., pp. 509–12; Historical Thinking Skills—Periodization, Analyzing Evidence: Content and Sourcing; Learning Objective OS-4, OS-8; Key Concept 2.3).

2. **(B)** Rousseau rejected many of the logical, scientific ideas of the Enlightenment, preferring to rely on emotion (*Western Civilization*, 9th ed., pp. 511–12 / 10th ed., pp. 508–10; Historical Thinking Skills—Causation; Learning Objective OS-10; Key Concept 2.3).

3. **(A)** Enlightenment thinkers saw the world as created in a logical way in accord with natural law. They thought of God as the creator of a mechanical universe, but they did not think he was directly involved in the world (*Western Civilization*, 9th ed., pp. 507–08 10th ed., p. 506; Historical Thinking Skills—Periodization, Contextualization; Learning Objective OS-5, OS-11; Key Concept 2.3).

4. **(A)** Voltaire saw religious persecution and particularly religious war as being the major problem of his time (*Western Civilization*, 9th ed., pp. 507–09 / 10th ed., pp. 503–06; Historical Thinking Skills—Analyzing Evidence: Content and Sourcing; Learning Objective OS-8; Key Concept 2.3).

5. **(B)** The Thirty Years' War, which ended about 50 years before Voltaire's birth, was known for its religious persecution and incredible atrocities (*Western Civilization*, 9th ed., pp. 507–09 / 10th ed., pp. 503–06; Historical Thinking Skills—Causation, Periodization, Analyzing Evidence: Content and Sourcing; Learning Objective SP-3; Key Concept 2.1, 2.3).

6. **(C)** Voltaire turned his satirical pen most often against the Catholic church and the French government (*Western Civilization*, 9th ed., pp. 507–09 / 10th ed., pp. 503–06; Historical Thinking Skills—Analyzing Evidence: Content and Sourcing, Synthesis; Learning Objective OS-7, OS-9; Key Concept 2.3).

SHORT-ANSWER QUESTIONS

1. Science definitely played a large role in the rise of the Enlightenment. Thinkers like John Locke and philosophes like Montesquieu placed great importance on the use of logic and reason, searching for universal laws that governed society just as natural laws explained natural phenomena. In The Spirit of Laws, for example, Montesquieu argues for a logical government that contains three branches, each of which has powers that logically check the powers of the other branches, thus preventing any group from gaining too much power. Science was not the only important cause of the enlightenment, though. As middle-class people became wealthy, more literate, and more aware of the power that their absolutist monarchs held over them, a wish for equality and a say in their government became more important to them. Rousseau, for example, argued that if a government was not upholding its part of the social contract, the people could validly rise up against it.
(*Western Civilization*, 9th ed., pp. 504–07 / 10th ed., pp. 500–02; Historical Thinking Skills—Comparison, Argumentation, Causation, Contextualization; Learning Objective OS-7; Key Concept 2.3)

2. Although philosophes such as Voltaire and Diderot argued for religious toleration and political equality, Rousseau was the most influential of all of them. His ideas of natural child-rearing, as expressed in *Emile* and *Julie: or, the New Eloise*, took literate Europe by storm. Women began nursing their own babies instead of sending them off to wet-nurses. Swaddling became a thing of the past and people began to treat their children with more kindness and less abuse. Voltaire's ideas of religious toleration were not new.

Others had been arguing for it since the time of the religious wars (Henry IV and the Edict of Nantes, for example) and many people were calling for more equality in the government. Rousseau's ideas, however, were groundbreaking, and they affected children all over Europe and America.
(*Western Civilization*, 9th ed., pp. 507–13 / 10th ed., pp. 502–10; Historical Thinking Skills—Comparison, Argumentation, Causation; Learning Objective OS-4, OS-7, OS-8; Key Concept 2.3)

Long-Essay Questions

1. This question uses the thinking skills of Causation and Patterns of Continuity and Change Over Time, asking you to synthesize an answer on two topics (state and church) and to "analyze the extent" of the Causation. A good place to begin is with a discussion of the types of governments in place in Europe at the opening of the eighteenth century. Joseph II, the Holy Roman Emperor, and Louis XIV of France are good examples of monarchs who used both religion and a noble class to maintain the power and authority of state. You should also discuss the organization of the Catholic Church, especially its focus on followers having an unswerving faith in the correctness of its dogma. As you finish that part of your essay, a summary commentary on similarities and differences in the methods used by both state and church would establish a nice foundation for your analysis of how the Enlightenment contradicted previous eras. Offer examples of countries that did not follow this same method of control, such as England and the Netherlands. Then you can get into the heart of your argument by talking about several enlightened thinkers and how each reacted to various facets of absolutist control. You should mention in your argument that these philosophes often looked to parliamentary governments, such as England's, for examples of enlightened government. This, then, could temper an argument that the Enlightenment was a direct reaction to state and religious absolutism, because it was also influenced by govern-ments that tried somewhat to reflect the needs of their people. It is important to add this last part since the questions asks "to what extent." You must find another cause other than the Enlightenment to mention. To conclude your essay, remember to include a brief (2-3 sentences) discussion of synthesis. In this essay, your synthesis could compare methods used by Enlightenment thinkers to challenge the control of absolute monarchs and the eighteenth century church to methods used by people in Eastern Europe and the USSR to oppose totalitarian control in the last decades of the twentieth century.
(*Western Civilization*, 9th ed., pp. 507– 08, 524–28 / 10th ed., pp. 502–09, 521–24; Historical Thinking Skills—Patterns of Continuity and Change Over Time; Learning Objective OS-7, OS-9, OS-11; Key Concept 2.3)

2. It is important to look at the structure of this question and make sure you answer both parts of it—women as both participants in and subjects of Enlightenment ideas. You may think that you do

not have enough examples of women to do a good job writing this essay, but remember that you can and should use examples of male writers and artists who wrote ABOUT or depicted women in their works along with examples of women themselves. At least two body paragraphs are needed to organize this essay, but three would be even better. Some women participated in the Enlightenment as hostesses at salons and occasionally as writers themselves. They also participated by reading the works of philosophes and discussing them. Some philosophes advocated more education for women, causing Rousseau to write vehemently against the idea. In response to Rousseau's ideas of traditional gender roles for women, Mary Wollstonecraft wrote a *Vindication of the Rights of Women*, calling for education and equality for both sexes. This discussion of the interplay of new ideas and old gender norms causes a gradual change over time, which is one of the historical thinking skills necessary for a high level essay. In your conclusion, remember to add a brief (2-3 sentences) discussion of synthesis. You could successfully accomplish this by comparing the roles women played in the Enlightenment as both participants and as subjects of discussion with the roles women played during the Renaissance or the Victorian Era as both participants and subjects of discussion. Point out some specific similarities and/or differences.

(*Western Civilization*, 9th ed., pp. 502, 512–15 / 10th ed., pp. 500, 509–12; Historical Thinking Skills—Contextualization; Learning Objective OS-4; Key Concept 2.3)

7

POLITICAL AND SOCIAL DYNAMICS IN THE 1700s

As Enlightenment ideals spread across Europe, monarchs became interested in implementing aspects of some of them, specifically religious toleration and the abolition of serfdom. In particular, during the latter half of the eighteenth century, three rulers in Eastern Europe—Joseph II of Austria, Catherine II of Russia, and Frederick II of Prussia—came to power eager to reform their respective countries. At the same time, war persisted. Most wars were fought primarily for territorial expansion and economic gain rather than for religious or ideological reasons. The century also saw the beginnings of the Industrial Revolution, during which the upper classes grew in wealth and the divide between rich and poor widened.

KEY TERMS

Agricultural Revolution	Junkers
balance of power	market economy
consumer revolution	mercantilism
cottage industry	primogeniture
enclosure acts	putting-out system
enlightened absolutism	reason of state
estates	Seven Years' War
Glorious Revolution	slave labor system
Grand Tour	War of Austrian Succession
infanticide	War of Spanish Succession

CHAPTER KEY CONCEPTS

- Politically, there were some changes during the eighteenth century. Although absolutism remained the predominant form of government across all of Europe except England, the Netherlands, and Switzerland, several monarchs in Eastern

205

and Central Europe experimented with enlightened despotism by offering some rights to their people. The inability of the Polish monarchy to consolidate its power over the nobles led to the Partitions of Poland by Russia, Prussia, and Austria, effectively erasing Poland from existence.

- Eighteenth-century monarchs also waged larger, more encompassing wars in an attempt to build bigger, stronger states. Commercial rivalries influenced diplomacy and warfare as European sea powers vied for control of trade routes and colonies.

- Mercantilism remained the preferred economic system of the absolutists. However, revolutions in agriculture and industry had a substantial impact on Europe, especially in the west, leading to the growth of capitalism. These economic changes directly affected the highly structured levels in society, opening up opportunities for the lower classes to improve their economic condition. The rising demand for raw materials and products from the New World led to an expansion of the slave trade.

- During the latter half of the eighteenth century, rulers in Russia, Prussia, and Austria put in place policies that reflected the ideals of the enlightened philosophes, but they did not enact any policies that in any way endangered their own power.

For a full discussion of Europe in the 1700s, see *Western Civilization*, 9th and 10th editions, Chapter 18.

Eighteenth-Century Politics

Over the course of the eighteenth century, five major powers arose. In Western Europe, France and England grew to have great political and economic might. Their main rivals, Spain and the Netherlands, no longer had the strength to hold them at bay. In Eastern Europe, Prussia and Russia set out to rival the still-great Austria, mostly through the conquest of strategic tracts of land.

In the west, France began the century under the reign of Louis XIV, marking the height of European absolutism. At Louis XIV's death in 1715, his great-grandson, Louis XV, became king. Although he reigned until 1774, Louis XV never gained the same level of control as his grandfather. That was in part because he began his reign as a five-year-old and in part because of France's enormous economic problems, a result of its tax policies and almost constant wars under Louis XIV. After Louis XV's death, his grandson came to power. He, too, was unable to exercise the same centralized power as had Louis XIV. Although still a major European power, France was weaker by the end of the century and ripe for revolution.

England, on the other hand, had seen great gains in representative government during the seventeenth century and began the new century with Parliament working side by side with the Stuart monarchy. When Queen Anne died childless in 1714, England looked for leadership from Stuart cousins in Hanover, a German state. The Hanoverians, especially George I and George II had little feel for the

British political system. As a consequence, they depended heavily on their chief ministers, giving Parliament even more influence than it had gained with such difficulty during the 1600s. Eighteenth-century prime ministers—especially Robert Walpole, the first to have that title, and William Pitt the Elder—helped craft major policies during the reign of George II, including many English economic and military policies.

To the east of England and France, absolutism characterized the eighteenth century. Three monarchs in Eastern Europe are generally referred to as enlightened absolutists, or enlightened despots: Frederick II of Prussia, Catherine II of Russia, and Joseph II of Austria. Although other monarchs had tried various enlightened reforms in their countries, Catherine, Frederick, and Joseph justified their absolutism by encouraging reforms. In the end, however, they did not succeed in creating much long-term change.

In Prussia, the Hohenzollerns encouraged the growth of a highly structured society and the building of a strong, militaristic state. Continuing a policy begun by Frederick William the Great Elector, Frederick William I gave the Junkers, the Prussian noble class, the highest positions in the military. This maintained the strong link between military virtue, based on loyalty, and the role of nobles in his state, and was key to the efficient bureaucracy he created to run the Prussian government.

Despite his father's disapproval of his intellectual interests, Frederick II (the Great) was interested in Enlightenment ideals, and he implemented several political reforms, including the establishment of a single law code, religious toleration, and equal legal treatment for his people. Frederick also made social and cultural improvements in the areas of religious freedom, education, literature, music, science, and agriculture. To improve agriculture, Frederick ordered the cultivation of potatoes as a hedge against rising bread prices and possible famine and ordered that they be made a part of his soldiers' diet.

Catherine II (the Great), wife of Tsar Peter III, took over as autocrat of Russia after the murder of her husband in 1762. German by birth, she never remarried, and ruled alone for over thirty years. She corresponded with several philosophes, most notably Voltaire. Through this long-term exchange of letters, Catherine came to believe in many of the ideals of the Enlightenment and subsequently attempted to introduce them to the people of Russia. She offered greater local self-government and legal reforms and encouraged the expansion of education, the arts, and science. However, in time, Catherine was forced to choose between providing Enlightenment policies for her people and strengthening her state. To maintain and build Russia, Catherine set out to conquer lands to the south and west. Further, in quelling Pugachev's Rebellion, an anti-government revolt that included peasants, Catherine wound up extending serfdom. In attempting to strengthen Russia, she put herself at odds with the very enlightenment ideals she had espoused and weakened her ability to effect change because of her indebtedness to the nobles who had helped her.

In the Austrian Empire, Joseph II, son of Maria Theresa, continued the long history of Austrian Habsburg rule. Like Frederick the Great and Catherine the Great, he sought to put in place enlightened policies. A man of deep convictions, Joseph introduced religious toleration, tax reform, and educational improvements. To reform the Austrian legal system, he offered equal legal treatment for all people, and ended torture and the death penalty. Although he was considered by many historians the most enlightened of the enlightened despots, most of Joseph's reforms did not last beyond his death in 1790.

AP® Tip

The response to Enlightenment ideals by absolute monarchs such as Frederick II, Catherine II, and Joseph II is a frequent theme on the AP® European History exam. Focus your study on several policies for each ruler and how those policies reflected the Enlightenment. Think about the extent to which they truly embodied enlightened ideals—did they enact any policies that lessened their own power?

EIGHTEENTH-CENTURY WARS

Dabblers in Enlightenment ideals, these enlightened despots and other leaders across Europe were deeply engaged in devastating wars during the eighteenth century. Religion was displaced by concerns over the continental balance of power as the major cause of European wars.

Rulers during this period also began to shift from making decisions aimed at extending their dynasty to making decisions based on reason of state—the strength of their country considered in a longer timeframe. As a consequence, European countries began competing to become major powers as leaders put the longevity of their own states over virtually all else.

WAR OF THE SPANISH SUCCESSION

A good example of this is the War of the Spanish Succession, the last of the many wars Louis XIV waged over the course of his long reign. When the last Habsburg ruler of Spain died in 1700, Louis was eager to see his grandson Philip become king. Concerned about the continued growth of France, several countries, including England, the Holy Roman Empire, and the Netherlands, went to war to stop Louis. The Treaty of Utrecht, ending a war that had dragged on for more than a decade, allowed Philip to take the Spanish throne but guaranteed that the French and Spanish monarchies would never unite. This war began a century of warfare in which nations attempted to achieve balance of power (allowing no one country to dominate others) as they strove to become major European powers.

WAR OF THE AUSTRIAN SUCCESSION

The War of the Austrian Succession, beginning in 1740, was led by Frederick II (the Great) of Prussia. His goal was to seize Austrian Silesia and thwart the rise of Maria Theresa, whom he assumed would be weak. England joined in support of Austria, thus leading France, England's traditional enemy, to join with Prussia. The war ended with the signing of the Treaty of Aix-la-Chapelle, which returned Europe to its status quo with one exception: Prussia refused to give up Silesia and had begun its climb to become a major European power.

THE SEVEN YEARS' WAR

Austria's loss of Silesia set the stage for another war, which broke out in 1756. The Seven Years' War grew out of two major conflicts. The first was a clash between England and France in the New World, beginning in North America and what is now known as the French and Indian War. The second was the attack on Saxony by Frederick II of Prussia, part of his plan to build a greater Prussia. But there was a drastic changing of alliances. As the war progressed, England joined its old enemy, Prussia, and some small German states against Austria, which allied with its old enemy, France, and Russia. This so-called Diplomatic Revolution demonstrated the growing desire for balance of power in Europe.

The victory of Prussia and England, both in Europe and in colonies around the world, led to dramatic changes in that balance of power. With the Treaty of Hubertusburg and the Treaty of Paris in 1763, Prussia became a truly major European state, England solidified its position as a major colonial power, and France and Austria were greatly weakened.

EIGHTEENTH-CENTURY SOCIETY

As the eighteenth century progressed, life expectancy increased for many reasons, including better foods and fewer devastating diseases. Also, the general structure of the family began to change. Although the father was still the head of the household, families tended to build stronger bonds, with the upper and middle classes tending to focus more on the development of their children.

Additionally, as society changed and the ideals of the Enlightenment spread, the laws and customs of primogeniture began to change. The eldest son was still considered by many to be the prime inheritor of family estates, but this was no longer automatically presumed; in England in particular, the upper classes began to look at all of their children as deserving of equal attention.

Society continued to be divided into classes—an upper class, a middle class, a working class (including small farmers), and the poor. In Western Europe these classes—or estates, as they were called in France—had been entrenched for hundreds of years, so the upper class was solidly in power. The wealthy continued to own large tracts of land on which multitudes of peasants worked. As towns grew and the expanding middle class developed trade and, especially in Britain, early cottage industries, the city working class and poor increased in number. The gap between the lives of the upper and middle classes in the cities and the peasants in the countryside was tremendous.

An important custom of the upper class—especially the English—was the Grand Tour. Reflecting the ideals of the Enlightenment, the Grand Tour gave young, prosperous European men the opportunity to learn about life as they traveled across the continent. They frequently went to France to learn about refined culture and to Italy to learn about ancient Rome and art, spending some time along the way on less than educational pursuits.

At the other end of the socioeconomic spectrum, peasants lived hard lives. In England, because of the continued enclosure of land and agricultural methods that made more efficient use of the land, many who had owned and worked small plots were forced out. Working others' land, they could survive only at the subsistence level. This pushed them toward the growing towns for work, where they might end up as beggars—before the development of the factory system, there was little for them in the towns. Although in earlier centuries beggars had been aided by charity, by the eighteenth century town authorities looked to other options, such as incarceration and public works projects, in dealing with the poor.

EIGHTEENTH-CENTURY ECONOMICS

During the eighteenth century, there were several economic changes. For more than a century, rulers had relied on mercantilism to build empires. An empire provides economic gain by requiring its colonies to trade only with the mother country. Mercantilism was the economic system preferred by many seventeenth-century absolutists, such as Louis XIV, but as absolutism waned, so did mercantilism, especially with the growth of the more economically productive cottage industries and early factories. The physiocrats, led by François Quesnay, also spoke out against mercantilism, encouraging governments to allow the development of free enterprise. By the end of the century, capitalism was on the rise in Europe.

With the growth of industry, beginning in England, the more static agrarian and mercantilistic economies gave way to dynamic profit-oriented ones. Early manufacturers were unable to meet the growing demand for goods, so cottage industry, free of guild restrictions and done in homes, offered greater productivity and, therefore, increased profits. During the latter half of the eighteenth century, the cottage industry system was supplanted by the early factory system. Bringing workers together in one building and using machines powered by water, the latter proved much more profitable than the former. Aiding this economic growth were the Agricultural Revolution and the expansion of banking, which provided the loans and letters of credit underlying it. Agriculture's transition from primitive to modern production methods—for example, the replacement of the wooden plow by the iron plow—increased the production capacity of land. Improved farming methods led to greater productivity, and as a result of this greater access to food, the population grew. Further, fewer farm workers were needed to produce that food. At the same time, there was a rising need for industrial workers. All in all, increased agricultural productivity fueled industrial growth by providing the food supplies needed by the growing urban populations.

These economic changes, especially dramatic in England, led to greater international trade and, in turn, to Europe's growing economic presence in the world. Colonies, essential to mercantilism, were just as important to the growth of capitalism in Europe. The factory system depended on increasing quantities of raw materials and markets, both of which could be supplied by colonies. The increased demand for raw materials and New World products led to an expansion of the slave labor system.

AP® Tip

Socioeconomic history is an important component of the AP® exam. Look for ways to connect economic trends to contemporaneous social developments. This type of synthesis is one of your Historical Thinking Skills.

BEYOND ENLIGHTENED DESPOTS

During the eighteenth century, while rulers fought to build their states into major European powers, Enlightenment thought was leading many to hope for a better world. But as the social gaps between the classes widened, the desire of enlightened despots to bring progress to their countries was insufficient to the task. Thus, in 1789, this widening socioeconomic division, along with impending bankruptcy in France, exploded into revolution.

Content Review Questions

1. Joseph II of Austria instituted all of the following Enlightenment policies EXCEPT
   (A) ending the death penalty.
   (B) offering equal legal treatment.
   (C) introducing religious toleration.
   (D) providing a constitutional monarchy.

2. Another enlightened despot, Frederick the Great brought all of the following enlightenment policies to Prussia EXCEPT
   (A) offering equal legal treatment for his people.
   (B) ending serfdom in all of Prussia.
   (C) providing a single legal code.
   (D) granting religious toleration.

3. To what extent did the European class system change during the eighteenth century?
   (A) With the development of cottage industries and a growing middle class, the gap between the upper and lower classes grew.
   (B) Because of Enlightenment ideals, the gap between rich and poor was lessened and virtually disappeared.
   (C) The development of estates replaced the old class system.
   (D) Because of their ability to move to towns where they could find work, the poor were more willingly accepted by the upper class.

4. What was the first step in the transition from agrarian and mercantilistic economies to industrialization?
   (A) The manufacture of products through cottage industries
   (B) Guilds creating more structure for the production of quality products
   (C) Adam Smith's writing of *The Wealth of Nations*
   (D) The growing profits from mercantilism as gold and silver flowed into state treasuries

5. What was the backbone of the Prussian military state?
   (A) The Hohenzollerns depended on their parliament to maintain their strong position in central Europe.
   (B) At the core of the Prussian state was an absolutist king, William III, who made all major decisions.
   (C) The Prussian military, based on the hiring of mercenaries from a neighboring German state, Hesse, provided the needed strength to make the Hohenzollerns the most powerful royal family on the continent.
   (D) The Hohenzollern rulers worked closely with the Junkers to build a strong military.

6. Which of the following was an outcome of the War of Austrian Succession and the Seven Years' War?
   (A) Alliances remained strong during and after each war.
   (B) The borders of European nations remained the same.
   (C) Prussia became a major European power as a result of the two wars.
   (D) Each war led to a major French victory in the New World, especially during the French and Indian War.

7. After the death of Louis XIV, to what extent did France maintain the same degree of absolutism?
   (A) Although France lost many wars after Louis's death, absolutism remained strong in France for the rest of the eighteenth century.
   (B) The kings who followed Louis XIV tried to maintain the same level of power but were unable to do so.
   (C) The kings who followed Louis XIV held absolute power over both France and the territories it gained during eighteenth-century wars.
   (D) After the French loss in the War of Austrian Succession, French absolutism would never be as strong as under Louis XIV.

8. To what extent did the Agricultural Revolution support the Industrial Revolution?
   (A) The Agricultural Revolution provided the food supplies for the increasing city populace, most of whom worked in the factories.
   (B) The Industrial Revolution processed most of the foodstuffs grown because of the Agricultural Revolution.
   (C) Because the Agricultural Revolution occurred after the Industrial Revolution, it did not support the development of industry at all.
   (D) With the demand for more workers in the countryside, the Agricultural Revolution actually slowed the progress of the Industrial Revolution.

9. Catherine the Great's attempts at enlightened rule were thwarted by
   (A) Pugachev's Rebellion, which swept away her power.
   (B) a weak nobility that was pro-reform but afraid of the serfs.
   (C) the great power to her west, Poland.
   (D) the need to appease powerful nobles and keep serfs under control.

10. After the death of Queen Anne and the succession of George I of Hanover, England's government
   (A) came more under control of power German princes.
   (B) was ruled by a more powerful Parliament and Prime Minister.
   (C) gave all men the right to vote.
   (D) was in disarray due to hatred of Hanoverian policies.

Multiple-Choice Questions

Questions 1–3 refer to the following image.

Source: Franz Stephan I (1708–65) with his wife Marie-Therese (1717–80) and their children (oil on canvas), Mytens or Meytens, Martin II (1695–1770) (school of) / Château de Versailles, France/Bridgeman Images

1. What assumption about Maria Theresa is best supported by the painting above?
   (A) The Austrian Empire controlled by Maria Theresa was vast and powerful.
   (B) Maria Theresa, as queen, was subservient to her husband, the king.
   (C) Several of Maria Theresa's children died in infancy.
   (D) Maria Theresa was proud of her large family.

2. The reign of Maria Theresa (1717–1780) and other absolute rulers of the eighteenth century would have been most influenced by
   (A) her alliance with the Prussians.
   (B) her strict adherence to the principles of enlightened despotism.
   (C) her reliance on powerful nobles.
   (D) her wish to consolidate her power and lands.

3. The son of Maria Theresa, Holy Roman Emperor Joseph II, showed his belief in enlightened despotism by doing all of the following EXCEPT
   (A) freeing the serfs.
   (B) granting universal male suffrage.
   (C) promoting modern agricultural practices.
   (D) building schools and hospitals.

Questions 4–6 refer to the following quotation.

David Davies, *The Case of Labourers in Husbandry Stated and Considered*

The depriving of all landed property has beggared multitudes. It is plainly agreeable to sound policy, that as many individuals as possible in a state should possess an interest in the soil; because this attaches them strongly to the country and its constitution, and makes them zealous and resolute in defending them. But the gentry of this kingdom seem to have lost sight of this wise and salutary policy. Instead of giving to labouring people a valuable stake in the soil, the opposite measure has so long prevailed, that but few cottages, comparatively, have now any land about them. Formerly many of the lower sort of people [had land on which] they raised for themselves a considerable part of their subsistence.... But since these small parcels of ground have been swallowed up in the contiguous farms and enclosures, and the cottages themselves have been pulled down, the families which used to occupy them are crowded together in decayed farmhouses, with hardly ground enough about them for a cabbage garden; and being thus reduced to be mere hirelings, they are of course very liable to come to want....

Thus an amazing number of people have been reduced from a comfortable state of partial independence to the precarious condition of hirelings, who, when out of work, must immediately come to their parish [for welfare]. And the great plenty of working hands always to be had when wanted, having kept down the price of labour below its proper level, the consequence is universally felt in the increased number of dependent poor.

Source: From David Davies, *The Case of Labourers in Husbandry Stated and Considered* (London, 1795), pp. 55–56.

4. The above quotation laments the problems of
    (A) landowners who must enclose their property to keep out the animals kept by peasant farmers.
    (B) entrepreneurs who make money from cottage industry.
    (C) peasants driven off their lands by the Enclosure Movement.
    (D) parish priests who must take care of those who have lost their jobs.

5. According to author David Davies, what is the benefit of having as many peasants as possible to work the land?
    (A) Working on the land makes a bond between the people and their country.
    (B) Peasants who have work and food are less likely to rebel.
    (C) It takes the pressure off the churches, which are relied on for charity.
    (D) It is more beneficial to the enclosure movement and cottage industry.

6. A significant facet of the lives of the poor in the eighteenth century was that
   (A) they were well supported by the Roman Catholic Church.
   (B) they finally had the opportunity to own their own land instead of having to work for others.
   (C) local governments found that rather than allowing them to beg, it was better to put them in jail or make work for them.
   (D) towns set up charities to help support them financially.

Short-Answer Questions

1. Choose two wars fought in the eighteenth century and answer A, B, and C.
   A) Briefly explain ONE important similarity between the two wars you have chosen.
   B) Briefly explain ONE important difference between the two wars you have chosen.
   C) Briefly analyze ONE factor that accounts for the difference you identified in Part B.

2. Answer A, B, and C.
   A) Briefly explain the concept of mercantilism as practiced by Louis XIV and other rulers of the period.
   B) Briefly explain the concept of laissez-faire economics as discussed by Adam Smith.
   C) Briefly explain ONE reason that mercantilist policies in favor of laissez-faire policies began to be used less by the end of the eighteenth century.

Long-Essay Questions

1. Compare the enlightened policies of any two European monarchs during the eighteenth century or any two enlightened despots. (Historical Thinking Skills: Comparison)

2. Starting with a discussion of the images on the next page, compare and contrast the lives of the upper and working classes in eighteenth-century Europe. (Historical Thinking Skills: Comparison)

Source: Yale Center for British Art///Paul Mellon Collection/The Bridgeman Art Library

Source: Cottage Industry, 1791 (engraving)/Hincks, William (1752-97)/British Library, London, UK/Bridgeman Images

Answers

CONTENT REVIEW QUESTIONS

1. **(D)** Although Joseph II offered many Enlightenment policies to his people, he did not create a constitutional monarchy (*Western Civilization*, 9th ed., pp. 549–50 / 10th ed., pp. 539–40; Historical Thinking Skills—Synthesis; Learning Objective SP-1, SP-4; Key Concept 2.1).

2. **(B)** In spite of his enlightened leanings and Voltaire's admonitions to do so, Frederick II of Prussia did not free the serfs (*Western Civilization*, 9th ed., pp. 537–41 / 10th ed., pp. 532–34; Historical Thinking Skills—Patterns of Continuity and Change Over Time; Learning Objective SP-1, SP-4; Key Concept 2.1).

3. **(A)** The money generated by increased trade, a result of a growing middle class and the beginnings of a revolution in industry, caused the gap between the upper and middle classes and the lower class to widen during the eighteenth century (*Western Civilization*, 9th ed., pp. 558–59 / 10th ed., pp. 550–56; Historical Thinking Skills—Causation; Learning Objective PP-1; Key Concept 2.2).

4. **(A)** To make products more efficiently and for greater profit, production moved from individual homes to cottage industries (*Western Civilization*, 9th ed., pp. 552–53 / 10th ed., pp. 548–49; Historical Thinking Skills—Causation; Learning Objective PP-2, IS-2; Key Concept 2.2).

5. **(D)** The Hohenzollerns depended on the Junkers, the Prussian noble class, to build a strong military, which eventually developed an efficient bureaucracy for managing the state (*Western Civilization*, 9th ed., pp. 537–38 / 10th ed., pp. 532–34; Historical Thinking Skills—Causation; Learning Objective SP-2; Key Concept 2.1).

6. **(C)** Both wars combined to make Prussia a major European power (*Western Civilization*, 9th ed., pp. 543–45 / 10th ed., pp. 540–42; Historical Thinking Skills—Causation, Patterns of Continuity and Change Over Time; Learning Objective SP-2; Key Concept 2.1 and 2.2).

7. **(B)** Louis XV and Louis XVI did not have the personal abilities of Louis XIV, and French absolutism weakened during their reigns (*Western Civilization*, 9th ed., p. 533 / 10th ed., p. 530; Historical Thinking Skills—Causation; Learning Objective SP-2; Key Concept 2.1).

8. **(A)** Because the Agricultural Revolution supplied greater quantities of food, the urban populations could continue to grow (*Western Civilization*, 9th ed., pp. 550–51, 558–59 / 10th ed., pp. 543–48; Historical Thinking Skills—Causation; Learning Objective PP-2, IS-2; Key Concept 2.4).

9. **(D)** Pugachev's Rebellion made Catherine II realize that the serfs could too easily gain power if freed. In addition, she needed the powerful nobles on her side, and they did not wish to free the serfs. As a result, the Charter of Nobility actually took more rights away from serfs and gave more to the nobles (*Western Civilization*, 9th ed., p. 541 / 10th ed., p. 537; Historical Thinking Skills—Causation, Patterns of Continuity and Change Over Time; Learning Objective SP-4; Key Concept 2.1).

10. **(B)** Queen Anne, although she did not have any children, appointed as her heir the ruler of Hanover, George I. Since he (and his son after him) were German, they allowed Parliament and the prime minister much power to run the government (*Western Civilization*, 9th ed., p. 534 / 10th ed., p. 531; Historical Thinking Skills—Causation, Patterns of Continuity and Change Over Time; Learning Objective SP-2; Key Concept 2.1).

MULTIPLE-CHOICE QUESTIONS

1. **(D)** The fact that Maria Theresa had herself painted with her children shows how important they were to her. She ruled the Holy Roman Empire herself and was not subservient to her husband (*Western Civilization*, 9th ed., pp. 538–39, 544 / 10th ed., pp. 534–35, 540; Historical Thinking Skills—Argumentation, Synthesis; Learning Objective SP-2, IS-4; Key Concept 2.1).

2. **(D)** Maria Theresa's right to rule the Holy Roman Empire was challenged by Frederick II of Prussia. While known as an enlightened despot, she made minor reforms and did not strictly adhere to the principles explained by Voltaire and other philosophes (*Western Civilization*, 9th ed., pp. 538–39, 544 / 10th ed., pp. 534–35, 540; Historical Thinking Skills—Causation, Synthesis; Learning Objective SP-2; Key Concept 2.2).

3. **(B)** There was no legislature in the Holy Roman Empire and no thought of universal male suffrage yet (*Western Civilization*, 9th ed., pp. 538–39, 544 / 10th ed., pp. 534–35, 540; Historical Thinking Skills—Synthesis; Learning Objective SP-2; Key Concept 2.2).

4. **(C)** Peasant farmers were driven off their lands by wealthy landowners who wished to raise livestock (*Western Civilization*, 9th ed., pp. 550–51 / 10th ed., pp. 547–48; Historical Thinking Skills—Causation, Contextualization; Learning Objective PP-2; Key Concept 2.2).

5. **(A)** Davies points to the bond for the land itself, formed by farmers who work their own land (*Western Civilization*, 9th ed., pp. 550–51 / 10th ed., pp. 547–48; Historical Thinking Skills—Contextualization, Analyzing Evidence: Content and Sourcing; Learning Objective PP-2, IS-2; Key Concept 2.2).

6. **(B)** Land-owning peasants were a significant part of the labor force in the eighteenth century (*Western Civilization*, 9th ed., pp. 550–51 / 10th ed., pp. 547–48; Historical Thinking Skills—Contextualization, Analyzing Evidence: Content and Sourcing; Learning Objective PP-2; Key Concept 2.2).

SHORT-ANSWER QUESTIONS

1. You might use the War of Spanish Succession and the War of Austrian succession for this essay or other wars fought in this period. Both of these wars began because of succession issues, but writing this as an answer will NOT get you the point. You must go into more detail. Both occurred because of the wish for power by an absolute monarch, and both of those monarchs were concerned with weakening the power of the Hapsburgs. However, Louis XIV wanted to take control of the traditional French enemy, Spain, while Frederick II of Prussia wanted to assert his growing power by taking the title of Holy Roman Emperor from Maria Theresa of Austria. Both wars occurred both in Europe and in colonies controlled by the European nations. After the War of Spanish Succession, France and Spain became allies, while after the War of Austrian Succession, Austria and Prussia became enemies. One

thing that accounts for the differences seen in the wars is that the alliances formed in the Spanish war affected who fought with whom in the Austrian conflict. The fact that England was ruled by a German monarch after 1715 also made a difference.
(*Western Civilization*, 9th ed., pp. 543–45 / 10th ed., pp. 539–43; Historical Thinking Skills—Causation, Patterns of Continuity and Change Over Time; Learning Objective SP-2; Key Concept 2.1 and 2.2)

2. Mercantilism as practiced by Louis XIV and his finance minister Colbert, along with many other nations of the seventeenth and eighteenth century was an attempt to keep as much gold within one's own country as possible. To do this, a country needed to export more goods than it imported, and colonies were a big help in doing this. Colonies provided raw materials and markets for finished goods made in the mother country, so mercantilist laws requiring colonies to trade with only the mother country and tariffs on foreign goods were among the mercantilist laws passed. Adam Smith, however, proposed that there was a natural law of supply and demand that caused the economy to move up and down. It needed to be left alone to do what it would naturally do (laissez-faire in French). As the agricultural revolution and the use of cottage industry began to affect Europe, and the Early Industrial Revolution began in Great Britain, mercantilist policies were less and less effective. Huge economic swings, such as the bubble economies of Louisiana and the South Sea Companies, further seemed to prove that Smith was correct. France's loss of colonies in the eighteenth-century wars meant their policies had to change as well.
(*Western Civilization*, 9th ed., pp. 432–33, 509–13 / 10th ed., pp. 443–44, 507, 532, 549–50; Historical Thinking Skills—Patterns of Continuity and Change Over Time; Learning Objective PP-2; Key Concept 2.2)

Long-Essay Questions

1. This essay is a combination of a causation question and a comparison question. You are asked to look at how much influence the ideals of the Enlightenment had on the rulers of the period and to evaluate the extent to which they actually followed those ideals. You must also craft a historical argument and bring in evidence to support your claim. You might begin your essay by outlining some of the fundamental values of the Enlightenment, such as natural law, reason, and progress. Then deal with specific beliefs of the philosophes—for example, freedom from censorship, the importance of education, religious toleration, denunciation of slavery, and the value of constitutional government. After you have laid that foundation, describe how each monarch did or did not embody those fundamental values and specific beliefs and implement Enlightenment policies. As you discuss each ruler, make sure that you evaluate not only how much he or she wanted to implement enlightened policies, but also how well the policies were actually carried out based on the constraints that each ruler had to take into consideration when contemplating the implementation of Enlightenment policies. Be sure to add a brief (2–3 sentences) synthesis discussion to your essay. For this essay, you could

compare the rulers you discussed to another enlightened despot, such as Napoleon.
(*Western Civilization*, 9th ed., pp. 537–41 / 10th ed., pp. 530–37 Historical Thinking Skills—Comparison; Learning Objective SP-2, SP-4; Key Concept 2.1)

2. This compare/contrast question asks you to craft a historical argument using the evidence you are given and your own knowledge. The first image shows an upper-class family. Begin with a discussion of the room, including its size and furnishings, and then talk about the people, their clothing, how they are seated in relationship to each other, and what they are doing. Next, discuss the second image, which shows a working-class family. Talk about the same points that you discussed in relation to the first image. After you describe the images, use them to compare the lives of the people in them. Discuss how each shows a family together in the home, each person dressed in a similar manner and contributing in various ways to the family's goal.

   Note also the differences. The upper-class family is spread across the room, with the children dressed as miniature adults. This family clearly wants to display its wealth, with its home's high ceilings, beautiful paintings, expansive fireplace, and exquisitely designed rug. The family also wants to demonstrate its emphasis on education with such items as a globe and telescope prominently placed. In addition, the older children are pursuing educational interactions with their parents, while the younger children are playing.

   From the second image you should draw a very different conclusion. Rather than showing education or recreation, the clear focus in this image is that the working-class family uses its home to provide for its welfare. The family members work closely together, each with a role in the production of cloth, which the father is weaving on the right. The windows and walls are plain, and the floor is bare, though it is noteworthy that a dog is lying on it. The image of the dog, usually reserved to paintings of wealthy families, offers a bit of irony in the life of this working-class family. Be sure to add a brief (2-3 sentences) synthesis discussion to your conclusion. For example, for this essay, you could discuss the differences in the lives of the rich and the poor during a different century.
   (*Western Civilization*, 9th ed., pp. 547–50, 553–60 / 10th ed., pp. 550–56; Historical Thinking Skills—Comparison; Learning Objective PP-2, PP-4, IS-2, IS-4; Key Concept 2.2)

8

REVOLUTION: 1763–1815

Toward the end of the eighteenth century, several factors combined to trigger a revolution in France: Enlightenment ideals that questioned the rigid class system of the old order, the loss of colonies, government overspending in the Colonial Wars and the American Revolution, and resistance to reform by the king and nobility. Transforming France from a monarchy to a republic and then to an empire, the French Revolution increased nationalistic impulses in countries across Europe.

KEY TERMS

Bastille
cahiers de doléances
Civil Constitution of the Clergy
Code Napoleon
Committee of Public Safety
Concordat of 1801
Congress of Vienna
Constituent Assembly
Constitution of 1791
consulate
Continental System
Declaration of the Rights of
    Man and the Citizen
Declaration of the Rights of
    Woman and the Female
    Citizen
De-Christianization
directory estates (first, second,
    and third)

Estates-General
Great Fear
Haitian Slave Revolt
Jacobin Republic
Louis XVI
Napoleon Bonaparte
National Assembly
nationalism
old order
Reign of Terror
Republic of Virtue
Robespierre
sans-culottes
Society for Revolutionary
    Republican Women
Tennis Court Oath
Thermidorean Reaction
Toussaint L'Ouverture
Women's March on Versaille

CHAPTER KEY CONCEPTS

▓ Many longstanding social grievances led to the Revolution, especially the lack of any real power for the Third Estate, the largest of the estates and made up of commoners. The Revolution was sparked by a wheat famine, which pushed up

223

the price of bread and amplified long-smoldering resentment of high taxes and exorbitant government debt.

▪ Political developments drove the French Revolution. From the initial reactions against the rule of Louis XVI to the Constitutional Monarchy of the Liberal Phase, through the execution of Louis XVI and the Reign of Terror, political ineptitude, corruption, and crisis caused many to want to change the government in France.

▪ The French Revolution was fed by the Enlightenment ideal that government should address the needs of its people. Although the new French Republic paid little attention to Enlightenment ideals, revolutionary armies, raised by a national draft, and later Napoleon's new military tactics spread the Enlightenment to much of the European continent.

▪ Economic and social reforms instituted by the Jacobin Republic included fixed prices and wages, a policy of de-Christianization, and an emphasis on equality and human rights. While women participated actively in the revolution and many hoped to gain rights as well, the improvement in the legal status of women did not last long.

▪ Napoleon Bonaparte made many lasting domestic reforms, even as he curtailed rights within France and expanded the French Empire and influence. This control inspired nationalistic responses throughout Europe, which eventually led to his defeat by a coalition of European powers.

▪ Some, such as Toussaint L'Ouverture, inspired by enlightened ideals, led a slave revolt in Saint Domingue. The overthrow of French rule led to the establishment of Haiti as a sovereign nation, while others condemned its violence and overthrow of traditional authority.

▪ Supporters of the Revolution, and later Napoleon, used the arts, especially painting and architecture, as propaganda.

For a full discussion of the French Revolution and the Napoleonic era, see *Western Civilization*, 9th and 10th editions, Chapter 19.

CAUSES OF THE FRENCH REVOLUTION

PROBLEMS OF THE OLD ORDER

In France, there were long- and short-term causes stemming from the problems of the old order. One major issue was the rigid system of estates. The First Estate was composed of Catholic clergy, a minuscule 0.5 percent of the population owning about 10 percent of the land and exempt from feudal dues and other taxes. The Second Estate, the nobility, accounted for some 1.5 percent of the population and owned between 25 and 30 percent of the land. Also exempt from such taxes as the taille, nobles dominated the government. Both of these estates were divided, however, with some members aligned with the king. Many of those who were not sympathized with the Third Estate, which comprised some 98 percent of the population yet had very little power. The Third Estate had various groups, from the growing bourgeoisie to the peasants, who made up 75 to 80 percent of the population. Each

Third Estate barely any power [handwritten margin note]

group had ~~grievances against~~ the government, ranging from economic concerns, such as taxes, rents, and the prices of goods to political concerns, such as a desire for a more liberal government.

SHORT-TERM CAUSES

Several short-term causes kindled the revolt against the French government. One was the Enlightenment and its ideals. Enlightenment belief in the value of education and the questioning of traditional sources of authority were used to justify ending the old system in France. Another short-term cause was the severe financial crisis, a result of debts for foreign wars and the court's lavish spending on both its privileged lifestyle and its rigid control of the government. That was caused by the fact that the First and Second Estates would not allow any input from the Third Estate. Furthermore, the bureaucracy of the government was housed at Versailles, so it was physically distanced from the Third Estate; there were tremendous costs associated with living and working at the palace. A wheat famine triggered bread riots, amplifying an already strained economic situation. A third short-term cause was Louis XVI's unresponsiveness. When confronted with the severity of the social, political, and economic situations, Louis refused to listen to his advisers, such as Maupeou and Calonne, who urged reform. Instead, he worked to maintain the old order.

THE AMERICAN EXPERIENCE

There were many causes of the French Revolution, some of which were the events in Britain's North American colonies. Looking for new revenues after the Seven Years' War (known in North America as the French and Indian War), the British believed that the Americans should help pay for the war. Many colonists balked. Well-versed in Enlightenment ideals and used to years of benign neglect by Britain, they were ready for independence. During the American Revolution, the colonists were split in their loyalties. France, however, smarting from defeats by Britain in previous wars in the colonies and on the continent, supported the Americans from the start through to the war's end, in 1781.

The American Revolution had a profound impact on Europe and around the world. In France, support for the Americans had weakened French coffers, contributing to the state's financial problems. But many took note of the fact that colonies could win independence from a major European power. Finally, the new United States government, drawing on Enlightenment ideals, had shown their practical application.

> ### AP® Tip
>
> To discuss the French Revolution, you need to be able to describe the intellectual, social, economic, and political factors leading up to it. This is a common question on the AP® exam. Another is the connection between the Enlightenment and the French Revolution.

THE FRENCH REVOLUTION

THE FIRST OR LIBERAL PHASE

In 1789, when Louis XVI was desperately in need of funds and called the Estates-General to find some, he unintentionally gave the Third Estate an opportunity to air its grievances. A meeting of representatives from all three estates, the Estates-General, was held at Versailles. Each estate had only one vote, putting the representatives of the Third Estate in an impossible situation: the first two estates could combine their votes to thwart the third.

The Third Estate presented the king with *cahiers de doléances* (petitions) requesting a variety of changes in France. Although Louis did not respond favorably to their concerns, some members of the clergy and the nobility spoke out in favor of the Third Estate. Because the number of Third Estate representatives was equal to the number of representatives for the other two estates combined, the support of those clergymen and nobles was significant when the Third Estate proposed voting by head (by person) rather than by order.

Garnering the support of clergymen, such as Abbé Sieyès, a member of the First Estate who wrote in favor of the Third Estate in *What Is the Third Estate?*, and thwarted by the First Estate's refusal to allow voting by head, the Third Estate declared itself the National Assembly. Locked out of their meeting room by Louis, members of the Third Estate moved to the palace tennis court, vowing to stay there until they had created a new constitution for France. This set them on a direct path of conflict with Louis, who threatened to dissolve the entire Estates-General.

AP® Tip

Two important historical thinking skills are periodization and interpretation. These two skills combine in the French Revolutionary era because different historians interpret the events differently. While one historian might make the case for the revolution beginning with the fall of the Bastille, another might cite the Tennis Court Oath or the bankruptcy of the French government as the start of the Revolution. Now add the skill of Causation to the mix. Some historians look at the political causes of the Revolution as being the more important ones, while Marxist historians see economic factors as mattering more. And finally, when does the revolution end—in 1799 when Napoleon takes over or in 1815 when he is defeated and a Bourbon king returns to the throne? Being able to explain the differing interpretations of historical events is a necessary skill of the AP® exam.

From that point, events across France pushed the Revolution forward. Incensed by the king's actions at Versailles and by the increasing military presence in France, Parisians stormed and seized the Bastille, a prison, and armory in Paris, on July 14, 1789. In the countryside, peasants, encouraged by the fall of the Bastille, attacked their lords and stole and burned records of their feudal obligations in what is known as the Great Fear.

The National Assembly (later known as the Constituent Assembly) drew up the *Declaration of the Rights of Man and the Citizen*, which was based on the ideals of the philosophes and the American Declaration of Independence. On October 5, 1789, thousands of women from Paris marched on Versailles demanding bread for their children. They returned to Paris the next day with Louis XVI, his wife Marie Antoinette, and their son.

Two important documents followed, in 1790 and 1791. The Civil Constitution of the Clergy required that the Catholic clergy swear allegiance to the new constitution and be elected by and paid by the French people. The National Assembly drew up a new constitution creating a limited monarchy and ending absolutism in France.

During the course of 1791, the bourgeoisie gained more political power. The Jacobins, a political group composed mainly of wealthy members of the bourgeoisie, rose to a position of dominance as they spread the more radical ideas. Although many in the bourgeoisie supported Louis as a constitutional, or limited, monarch, he undercut their support when he and his family attempted to flee France.

Foreign powers, especially Austria and Prussia, worried about political changes in France and the possible overthrow of a monarch and his Austrian-born queen. France had declared war on Austria in April 1792. When an attack on the Austrian Netherlands failed and an Austrian-Prussian invasion seemed likely, Parisian mobs took the palace and the assembly, effectively ending the French monarchy. Political power passed to the new Paris Commune, which was made up of more radical Frenchmen, including the sans-culottes.

THE JACOBIN REPUBLIC AND THE REIGN OF TERROR

The revolution then took a bloody turn. Led by the brilliant attorney Maximilien Robespierre, the radical Jacobins were intent on maintaining the purity of their revolution. As a result, thousands of their supposed enemies were arrested and guillotined. At the same time, the National Convention tried Louis, found him guilty of treason, and sent him to the guillotine.

By 1793, the revolutionary factions were turning on one another. Compounding this, a foreign threat was posed by a large coalition of European nations. To protect France and the Revolution, the Committee of Public Safety was charged with drafting thousands of men for an army able to push the invaders out of France.

To protect the Revolution from its supposed enemies within France, the committee ordered the Reign of Terror. Thousands more were sent to the guillotine, including Louis's wife, Marie Antoinette; Olympe de Gouges, a former revolutionary Girondin and advocate for women's political rights; and simple peasants. In ridding itself of its enemies, the committee believed that it was setting in place a Republic of Virtue, one in which a belief in virtue would replace a belief in Christianity and one that only true enemies need fear, while loyal citizens feared nothing.

In addition to all the violence, bureaucratic efforts were aimed at creating and reinforcing the idea of a new order. To separate itself from the old order and the power of the Catholic Church, the National Convention instituted a policy of de-Christianization—for example, churches were closed, priests were encouraged to marry, and Notre Dame Cathedral was renamed the Temple of Reason. In addition, the calendar was completely remade. These efforts were not well received by the people, whose Catholic faith was strong.

CLOSING STAGES

As the Revolution continued to attack those it perceived to be disloyal, infighting grew. France had defeated its foreign enemies, so domestically things should have been calmer. Robespierre pushed to continue the guillotining. By doing so, he made himself a target, and was himself guillotined on July 28, 1794. Robespierre's death marked the beginning of the so-called Thermidorean Reaction, an end to the chaos and violence.

In August 1795, a new constitution was written. It created a Directory run by five directors who relied on the military to help restore order. Under the Directory, the middle class was the big winner both economically and politically. The sans-culottes did not fare so well. The Directory was assailed by the right, especially monarchists, and by the left, the radical republicans, primarily the Jacobin remnant. It could not stand. By 1799 it was ripe for the coup d'état led by Napoleon.

AP® Tip

Chronology is important when you are looking for causes and effects in history. To understand the French Revolution, develop a good timeline of the events from 1789 to 1815. One approach is to periodize the revolution by government or according to the degree of radicalism. You should be able to make a logical argument as to the beginning, stages, and ending of the French Revolution, and you need to be able to prove or defend that argument with evidence. The skills of Argumentation and Analyzing Evidence: Content and Sourcing are imperative to do well on the exam.

NAPOLEON

NAPOLEON'S RISE

Born on the French island of Corsica, as a youth Napoleon Bonaparte moved with his family to mainland France, where he was given an outstanding military education. He rose quickly through the ranks of the army, winning amazing victories for the French against the European enemies of the revolution.

Napoleon's rise was based not only on his remarkable military prowess, but also on his personality. His strength of character, his concern for his troops, his intelligence, his ability to quickly assess situations, and his dogged determination made him a person who could win the heart of a country as well as its military victories.

In 1799, in its desire to find peace at the end of the revolution, France chose Napoleon to be the leader of her new republic, the Consulate, which succeeded the fallen Directory. He became the First Consul, eventually making his position good for life. In 1804, the French allowed Napoleon to crown himself emperor.

In stabilizing France after the devastation of the revolution, Napoleon put into place many changes. A great military leader, Napoleon built a large empire over most of western and central Europe and installed his family members on the thrones of various territories. His Grand Empire, at its peak in 1810, reached from Spain in the west to Poland (Grand Duchy of Warsaw), deep in the east. Forcing alliances with Russia, Prussia, and Austria, he reduced them to minor states. One of the first nations to try to stop the French Revolution and a major European power for centuries, Austria was a particularly important ally for him. Napoleon divorced his beloved first wife, the childless Josephine, to marry Marie of Austria, daughter of Austria's emperor. This marriage provided both a direct link to France's old enemy and a son.

DOMESTIC GAINS

Napoleon carried out many reforms, although several were made as Napoleon's despotism grew. Politically, he strengthened and centralized the French government. His law code, the Code Napoleon, guaranteed equal legal treatment, religious toleration, trial by jury, and an end to serfdom and the vestiges of feudalism. It also did away with primogeniture and allowed women equal inheritance rights. Although it also took away some rights, the code generally set in place many of the ideals espoused by the philosophes just decades earlier. Napoleon would later go against some of those ideals—for example, by censoring speech and the press and by ordering arbitrary arrest and imprisonment.

Napoleon did much to bring France back to its feet economically. He pleased the bourgeoisie by encouraging the growth of business, collecting taxes fairly and efficiently, and creating the Bank of France to oversee all of it. Government debts were paid promptly so that France could be seen as an economically stable nation.

Napoleon began rebuilding France with an eye to both efficiency and beauty. He built roads, bridges, and canals, infrastructure for France's developing economy. He dredged harbors to give France a base for both a worldwide economy and a powerful navy. Paris, devastated by the Revolution, needed help. Beautification of Paris would serve two purposes: glorification of France and glorification of Napoleon.

New schools provided more uniform standards and required courses that extolled France and its emperor. They grew at the expense of church schools, which had controlled French education for centuries.

The Catholic Church in France took the hardest hit. Besides losing control of education, the Church was forced by the Concordat of 1801 to abandon all claims to lands confiscated during the Revolution. The state could choose bishops, although the pope could still remove them, and the state would pay the salaries of all clergy, both Catholic and Protestant. The pope was forced to accept that Catholicism would not be reestablished as France's state religion—it would be recognized only as the majority religion. Later, in 1809, as part of his foreign policy, Napoleon annexed the Papal States and took the pope prisoner, making Napoleon the true enemy of the church, from which he was excommunicated.

Napoleon's Fall

Having subdued virtually the entire continent, Napoleon was left with only one major enemy, Britain. Along with the growth of nationalism across the continent, France's ill-conceived war against Russia, and his overreaching ambition, led to Napoleon's downfall.

Napoleon set out to defeat France's enemy, England, through economic warfare beginning after Trafalgar, in 1806. But the Continental System, his blockade of Britain from the continent, only made his position worse: Britain could still trade with the rest of the world, and nations across Europe resented French meddling with their trade. Further, in response to Napoleon's blockade, Britain blockaded the continent from any external trade, angering the nations under French control even more.

This economic warfare amplified rising nationalism in Napoleon's empire. Countries that, for various reasons, had accepted French control rose against France. Italian and German states saw the growth of nationalism, a sense of unity built on shared language, ethnicity, and religion. Inspired by the French Revolution, people across Europe saw that they could apply Enlightenment ideals, especially self-determination, without Napoleonic control. Napoleon had made enemies of entire countries, not just their leaders.

The breaking point was Napoleon's war against Russia. Tsar Alexander I had been Napoleon's chief ally on the east. But Russia suffered economically under the Continental System, so in 1812 it resumed trade with Britain. Angered by this breach, Napoleon invaded. This disastrous attack devastated his army. It also shone a bright light on his weaknesses, especially his rash, ego-driven decision making. Russia used a variety of ploys, such as poisoning wells and destroying crops and animals, to outwait Napoleon. He and his troops were trapped by an early, hard winter, and only a remnant of his once aptly named Grand Army escaped Russia.

Within two years, after European nations rallied to fight him and win a decisive battle at Waterloo, in Belgium, Napoleon was banished to the island of Elba. Within a year he gathered forces and came back to France and removed the new king, Louis XVIII, from power. But European nations allied again, and in a decisive victory at Waterloo, defeated Napoleon. He was again removed and exiled, this time to St. Helena, where he died in 1821.

AP® Tip

Another common AP® exam topic is the link between Napoleon and the French Revolution and its predecessor, the Enlightenment. As you read, note the ways in which Napoleon reflected and rejected the ideals of the Enlightenment and the goals and actions of the French Revolution.

THE LEGACY OF THE FRENCH REVOLUTION AND NAPOLEON

The French Revolution and Napoleon brought about considerable social change. Although women had influenced the Enlightenment through its salon culture, they did not play a major role during the French Revolution. They did take part in early spontaneous protests, and with a powerful spokesperson in Olympe de Gouges, who wrote the *Declaration of the Rights of Woman and the Female Citizen*, gained a few rights, such as more freedom in managing their children. Later, during the more radical phases, women were not allowed to join many of the clubs and political groups, and could not run for elected office. In response, they formed their own political clubs, most notably the Society for Revolutionary Republican Women. Men shut them down, however, believing, like Rousseau, that women's focus should be home and children. Later, under the Code Napoleon, women lost the few rights they had gained during the Revolution. One injustice that was addressed was slavery. During the Revolution, the government wavered on the issue, but in the end it abolished slavery in France and throughout the empire.

There was considerable political change, too. Most important was the emphasis on democracy. Beginning with the National Convention, the French spoke of liberty, equality, and fraternity, democratic principles based on Enlightenment ideals. These were the basis for such changes as the prohibition of primogeniture, the end of imprisonment for debt, a planned education system, and enactment of a republican constitution and codified law.

Napoleon's law code has had an enduring impact—it is the basis of current law not only in France, but in countries around the world. The streamlining of the national government and the de-emphasizing of local control led France to its unitary system of government, which is still in place. Finally, the nationalism that bloomed during the Revolution and under Napoleon remains vibrant; along with the French, people around the world celebrate Bastille Day and sing "La Marseillaise."

This period also brought geopolitical changes. The major development occurred when Napoleon gained control of most of Europe. He ended the Austrian-dominated Holy Roman Empire and put in its place the Confederation of the Rhine (under Napoleon) and its successor, the German Confederation (after 1815). Napoleon had transformed an empire that had been one of the Austrian Habsburgs' important territorial holdings, involving hundreds of small German states, into a union of thirty-nine larger states. The formation of these larger states, thus breaking the control of hundreds of local German princes, set the stage for further German unification and the creation of the state of Germany in 1871.

AP® Tip

As you study various eras in European history, note the lives of women in different social and economic classes. Here, compare women's lives during the French Revolution and the Napoleonic era with women's lives during other eras, especially those of conflict and revolution.

The French Revolution and the Napoleonic era were followed by a period of reaction. Conservative governments across Europe were alarmed by France's tumultuous quarter-century, and they sought to end revolutions and restore the old order. In response to both the Revolution and the conservative reaction to it, strong feelings of nationalism took hold in Europe and led to the creation of new countries and the dissolution of old ones.

Content Review Questions

1. How did Napoleon rise to power in France?
    (A) After a great victory against the British in Egypt, he claimed the throne of France.
    (B) Born in Paris during the heart of the Enlightenment, Napoleon claimed he could put Enlightenment ideals into place.
    (C) Napoleon's charismatic personality and great military leadership encouraged people to support him as he led a coup d'état.
    (D) Thanks to his close association with the Jacobins, Napoleon rose through the support of the political clubs in France.

2. With a background of hosting Enlightenment salons, who was exiled to the German states for writing novels and political works denouncing Napoleon?
    (A) Therese de Geoffrin
    (B) Rousseau
    (C) Voltaire
    (D) Germaine de Stael

3. As the French Revolution began, what countries became its most vocal enemies?
    (A) Spain and Austria
    (B) Prussia and Italy
    (C) Italy and Spain
    (D) Austria and Prussia

4. All of the following statements about the Code of Napoleon are true EXCEPT?
   (A) divorce was legal.
   (B) it recognized the principle of equality of all citizens before the law.
   (C) women had total control over their property.
   (D) serfdom and feudalism were abolished.

5. Which of the following is true of the policies of Robespierre and Napoleon?
   (A) Both Robespierre and Napoleon supported the continuation of slavery in Haiti.
   (B) Both Robespierre and Napoleon advocated Enlightenment ideals while possessing great power over the French population.
   (C) Both Robespierre and Napoleon pursued the de-Christianization of France.
   (D) Both Robespierre and Napoleon were eventually defeated by other European powers after greatly overextending their military forces.

6. The Reign of Terror involved all of the following EXCEPT
   (A) the Republic trying to remove its enemies.
   (B) thousands being sent to the guillotine.
   (C) lords attacking peaceful peasants.
   (D) a belief in creating a Republic of Virtue.

7. Napoleon's popularity with the French people can be seen through which of the following?
   (A) His acceptance at the beginning of the Hundred Days
   (B) The economic benefits of the Continental System
   (C) The celebration at his victory over Russia
   (D) The overwhelming acceptance of his initial Reign of Terror

8. The final act that led Louis XVI to threaten to dissolve the Estates-General was
   (A) the Estates-General's vote to disband Louis's government and to institute a more liberal form of government.
   (B) the Third Estate's creation of the National Assembly and its pledge to draw up a new constitution for France.
   (C) his fear of the impact of the American War for Independence.
   (D) the enlightened ideals of the philosophes, especially those who advocated violent revolution against the old order.

9. What was the role of women in the French Revolution?
   (A) Because women could read, they were allowed to join the various radical parties.
   (B) Women were not involved in the Revolution, but were given a role in church, where they read from the gospel and collected money.
   (C) Women were allowed to vote as long as they voted in specially designated areas.
   (D) Women could not join men's political clubs, but they did form their own.

10. Who or which of the following would have supported the *cahiers de doléances* sent to Louis XVI asking for a fair voting system in the Estates-General?
    (A) the First Estate
    (B) the Second Estate
    (C) the Third Estate
    (D) Louis XVI

Multiple-Choice Questions

Questions 1–3 refer to the following quotation.

Historians have long assumed that the modern history of Europe began with two major transformations—the French Revolution and the Industrial Revolution. Accordingly, the French Revolution has been portrayed as the major turning point in European political and social history, when the institutions of the "old regime" were destroyed and a new order was created based on individual rights, representative institutions, and a concept of loyalty to the nation rather than the monarch. This perspective does have certain limitations, however.

France was only one of a number of areas in the Western world where the assumptions of the old order were challenged. Although some historians have called the upheavals of the eighteenth and early nineteenth centuries a "democratic revolution," it is probably more appropriate to speak of a liberal movement to extend political rights and power to the bourgeoisie in possession of capital— citizens besides the aristocracy who were literate and had become wealthy through capitalist enterprises in trade, industry, and finance. The years preceding and accompanying the French Revolution included attempts at reform and revolt in the North American colonies, Britain, the Dutch Republic, some Swiss cities, and the Austrian Netherlands. The success of the American and French Revolutions makes them the center of attention for this chapter.

Not all of the decadent privileges that characterized the old European regime were destroyed in 1789, however. The revolutionary upheaval of the era, especially in France, did create new liberal and national political ideals, summarized in the French revolutionary slogan, "Liberty, Equality, Fraternity," that transformed France and were then spread to other European countries through the conquests of Napoleon. After Napoleon's defeat, however, the forces of reaction did their best to restore the old order and resist pressures for reform.

Source: From *Western Civilization*, 10th ed. by Jackson Spielvogel, pp. 559–60. Stamford, CT: Cengage Learning, 2018.

1. According to Jackson Spielvogel, the French Revolution was
   (A) one of the two movements that define the beginning of the Modern Era.
   (B) more important than the Industrial Revolution, which only affected the economy.
   (C) a liberal movement that extended rights to the wealthy middle class.
   (D) a radical movement that brought liberty, equality, and fraternity to all Frenchmen.

2. The author of the above passage would most likely agree with which of the following historical interpretations of the French Revolution?
   (A) Marxist view of historical events that emphasized the importance of economics above all other factors
   (B) A religious interpretation that emphasized Jacobin de-Christianization policies
   (C) A purely political interpretation that highlighted lack of rights of the middle class
   (D) A combination of political, social and economic factors led to marked but not total change in France

3. The success of the American Revolution
   (A) had little impact on the French Revolution, since the United States was formed ten years later.
   (B) showed French revolutionaries that enlightened ideals could be put into practice.
   (C) frightened Louis XVI into making much-needed reforms in France.
   (D) angered Napoleon and led to the War of 1812.

Questions 4–6 refer to the following image.

Source: © Bettmann/Corbis

4. The man being ridden in the above cartoon symbolizes
   (A) the horrors of the slave trade.
   (B) the common man or Third Estate.
   (C) the need for horses as transportation.
   (D) the power of the Third Estate in the Estates-General.

5. The author of the above cartoon would most likely agree with all of
   the following EXCEPT
   (A) the abolition of the privileges of the nobility and the clergy.
   (B) the signing of the *Declaration of the Rights of Man and the
       Citizen.*
   (C) the writing of the *Declaration of the Rights of Woman and the
       Female Citizen.*
   (D) the storming of the Bastille.

6. All of the following are accurate statements concerning the
   Estates-General EXCEPT
   (A) the Third Estate made up about 50 percent of the French
       population.
   (B) the First Estate was the clergy.
   (C) the Estates-General met at Versailles starting in 1789.
   (D) the First and Second Estates each had about 300 delegates.

Short-Answer Questions

Source: RMN-Grand Palais/Art Resource, NY

Source: Erich Lessing/Art Resource, NY

1. Referring to the above images of Napoleon, answer A, B, and C, thinking about the extent propaganda crafted the image that Napoleon wanted portrayed.
   A) Choose one aspect of the first image and briefly explain how it portrays Napoleon's vision of his rule.
   B) Choose one aspect of the second image and briefly explain how it portrays Napoleon's vision of his rule.
   C) Briefly explain ONE reason for a difference between the two paintings.

2. Answer A, B, and C referring to the ways the French Revolution and Napoleon affected the lives of French women.
   A) Briefly give ONE example of women's participation in the French Revolution.
   B) Briefly explain ONE right granted to women during the French Revolution.
   C) Briefly explain the effect of the Code Napoleon on women's rights.

Long-Essay Questions

1. Analyze the relative importance of the long-term social and political causes of the French Revolution. (Historical Thinking Skills: Causation)

2. To what extent did Napoleon adhere to the enlightened ideals of the French Revolution? (Historical Thinking Skills: Patterns of Continuity and Change Over Time)

Answers

CONTENT REVIEW QUESTIONS

1. **(C)** Napoleon's charismatic personality and great military leadership made him the type of leader people would want to follow. Thus, when he returned from a campaign in Egypt, Napoleon was able to lead a successful coup d'état (*Western Civilization*, 9th ed., pp. 586–87 / 10th ed., p. 583; Historical Thinking Skills—Causation; Learning Objective SP-7; Key Concept 2.1).

2. **(D)** Germaine de Stael, known for her wit and strong opinions, was a vocal opponent of Napoleon's despotism (Western Civilization, 9th ed., p. 590 / 10th ed., p. 586; Historical Thinking Skills—Causation, Patterns of Continuity and Change Over Time; Learning Objective SP-6; Key Concept 2.1).

3. **(D)** Austria and Prussia were afraid of a successful revolution against a monarchy (*Western Civilization*, 9th ed., p. 577 / 10th ed., p. 573; Historical Thinking Skills—Causation, Contextualization; Learning Objective SP-7, SP-16; Key Concept 2.1).

4. **(C)** Napoleon embraced many Enlightenment ideals, but he agreed with Rousseau that women had different roles than men (*Western Civilization*, 9th ed., pp. 588–89 / 10th ed., p. 585; Historical Thinking Skills—Patterns of Continuity and Change Over Time; Learning Objective IS-6, IS-9; Key Concept 2.1).

5. **(B)** Both Robespierre and Napoleon took actions to promote Enlightenment ideals, such as equality and the abolition of feudal privileges, but each controlled virtually dictatorial powers over France (*Western Civilization*, 9th ed., pp. 577-91 / 10th ed., pp. 573–88; Historical Thinking Skills—Comparison; Learning Objective PP-10; Key Concept 2.1).

6. **(C)** Peasants attacked their lords in a panic known as The Great Fear, taking over manor houses and destroying tax records (*Western Civilization*, 9th ed., pp. 577–81 / 10th ed., pp. 567, 573–81; Historical Thinking Skills—Causation, Patterns of Continuity and Change Over Time, Periodization; Learning Objective PP-10; Key Concept 2.1).

7. **(A)** After his escape from Elba, Napoleon was welcomed by French troops and commoners alike (*Western Civilization*, 9th ed., p. 593 / 10th ed., p. 589; Historical Thinking Skills—Causation, Patterns of Continuity and Change Over Time, Periodization; Learning Objective PP-10, SP-16; Key Concept 2.1).

8. **(B)** Louis XVI was resistant to political change. He threatened to end the Estates-General when the Third Estate voted to make itself the National Assembly and write a new constitution (*Western Civilization*, 9th ed., p. 581 / 10th ed., p. 577; Historical Thinking Skills—Causation; Learning Objective SP-4, SP-7; Key Concept 2.1).

9. **(D)** Women were excluded from political clubs, so they created their own, usually in the face of opposition from men (*Western Civilization*, 9th ed., pp. 581–83 / 10th ed., pp. 578–79; Historical Thinking Skills—Patterns of Continuity and Change Over Time; Learning Objective IS-9; Key Concept 2.1).

10. **(C)** The Third Estate created and supported the cahiers, which were its requests for change (*Western Civilization*, 9th ed., p. 571 / 10th ed., p. 566; Historical Thinking Skills—Causation, Periodization; Learning Objective SP-7; Key Concept 2.1).

MULTIPLE-CHOICE QUESTIONS

1. **(C)** Spielvogel does not see the French Revolution as extending rights to all, but only to the wealthy bourgeoisie who ended up in control of the government. Other similar political movements and the Industrial Revolution were happening at the same time and causing as much, if not more lasting change (*Western Civilization*, 9th ed., pp. 563–64 / 10th ed., pp. 570–71; Historical Thinking Skills—Argumentation, Interpretation; Learning Objective SP-4, SP-7, IS-5, PP-10; Key Concept 2.1).

2. **(D)** Spielvogel emphasizes that there were political rights gained, economic factors and social issues involved, not simply one factor or the other (*Western Civilization*, 9th ed., pp. 563–64 / 10th ed., pp. 563–67; Historical Thinking Skills—Causation, Argumentation, Interpretation; Learning Objective SP-4, SP-7, IS-5, PP-10; Key Concept 2.1).

3. **(B)** The American Revolution, which occurred 10 years before the French, showed the French people that enlightened reforms could work. Louis XVI's lack of reforms was one of the causes of the revolution, as was the bankruptcy of the French government, partially caused by the help they had given the Americans against the British (*Western Civilization*, 9th ed., pp. 564–70 / 10th ed., p. 563; Historical Thinking Skills—Causation; Learning Objective SP-4, SP-7; Key Concept 2.1).

4. **(B)** The cartoon symbolizes the unfair distribution of wealth and power in the Estates-General. Each Estate got one vote in the legislature. By showing the clergy (First Estate) and nobles (Second Estate) riding on and benefiting from the common man (Third Estate), the cartoonist is satirizing the French Old Regime government (*Western Civilization*, 9th ed., pp. 566–70 / 10th ed., pp. 563–66; Historical Thinking Skills—Analyzing Evidence: Content and Sourcing; Learning Objective SP-4, SP-7; Key Concept 2.1).

5. **(C)** Abolition of noble and clergy privileges would be number one on our cartoonist's list of things to do. Giving rights to the common man would come a close second and the storming of the Bastille would probably be something close to his heart. Most men of the period did not agree with the idea that women and men should be equal, so he most likely would not agree with the writing of the Declaration of the Rights of Women (*Western Civilization*, 9th ed., pp. 571–73 / 10th ed., pp. 568–71; Historical Thinking Skills—Analyzing Evidence: Content and Sourcing, Synthesis; Learning Objective SP-4; Key Concept 2.1).

6. **(A)** The Estates-General began to meet at Versailles in May of 1789 with the First Estate (clergy) and the Second Estate (nobility) each having about 30 delegates. Ninety of the 282 representatives were young and interested in enlightened ideals. The Third Estate, however, which made up 97 percent of the French population, only had one-third of the members of the Estates-General (*Western Civilization*, 9th ed., p. 571 / 10th ed., pp. 563–66; Historical Thinking Skills—Analyzing Evidence: Concept and Sourcing, Synthesis; Learning Objective SP-4, SP-7; Key Concept 2.1).

SHORT-ANSWER QUESTIONS

1. Begin your analysis of the images as propaganda by pointing out that each painting shows a different facet of Napoleon's character and leadership abilities. Gros painted Napoleon as the great young military leader—charismatic, confident, strong. A highly idealized view, this Napoleon was worthy of leading French troops and the French nation. In the second painting, Napoleon is again shown in a good light, although he was older by the time David painted him. In this image, Napoleon was still a confident, charismatic leader. He was now a political leader, however, crowning himself emperor and his wife, Josephine, empress, with extensive regalia and the evident approval of the pope. In addition, although Napoleon is not shown in military garb, representatives of the military are among the central figures, making clear his continued control of the military. Here David created the penultimate image of political power to set Napoleon's role as emperor.
(*Western Civilization*, 9th ed., pp. 586–90 / 10th ed., pp. 582–86; Historical Thinking Skills—Patterns of Continuity and Change Over Time, Argumentation, Analyzing Evidence: Content and Sourcing; Learning Objective SP-3, SP-4; Key Concept 2.1)

2. Women participated in the French Revolution by forming their own versions of the political clubs that men had formed but not allowed the women to join. Some women, such as Olympe de Gouges in her *Declaration of the Rights of Woman and the Female Citizen*, called

for equal rights with men. Women also participated in the bread riots, protesting the high cost of or lack of bread. The best example of this would be the Women's March on Versailles. During the Revolution women were granted some rights, namely the right to own property, initiate divorce, and take cases before the courts. These rights did not last long, however. The women's political clubs were closed down during the reign of terror; Olympe de Gouges was guillotined; and the Code Napoleon subordinated women to their husbands, taking away all the rights they had gained.
(*Western Civilization*, 9th ed., pp. 573–75 / 10th ed., pp. 568-71, 578-79; Historical Thinking Skills—Causation, Patterns of Continuity and Change Over Time, Argumentation; Learning Objective IS-6, SP-9; Key Concept 2.1)

LONG-ESSAY QUESTIONS

1. Causation and Argumentation are two of the main historical thinking skills required on the AP® Exam. The relative importance of the various causes of the French Revolution is a standard AP®-type question and has been a source of argument for historians since the Revolution began. You must take a stand in your essay about which of the causes, political or social, is the more important one—and use evidence to prove your point. This question DOES NOT ask you to look at economic causes, so the unfair tax burden on the poor and the economic collapse of the French Government are not topics for discussion in the body of your essay. Instead, the political backwardness of the Old Regime and the social issues of equality brought forward by the Enlightenment are your subjects in this essay. Anger at the power and rights possessed by the French Catholic Church could also be a part of your paper. A paragraph on the makeup and voting patterns of the Estates-General, a paragraph on the influence of enlightened ideals, and a paragraph on the power of the Church would be good organization for your essay. Remember in the conclusion to come back to your main point, telling the reader which of the causes of the revolution was more important than the other. Also, make sure that you add a brief (2-3 sentences) discussion of synthesis to the conclusion of your essay, by comparing/contrasting the causes of the French Revolution to another revolution, or by focusing on a different category of causes for revolution, such as a brief discussion of economic causes.
    (*Western Civilization*, 9th ed., pp. 567–70 / 10th ed., p. 583; Historical Thinking Skills—Causation, Argumentation, Synthesis; Learning Objective SP-4, SP-7, SP-11; Key Concept 2.1)

2. In this essay, you are asked to make a judgment about Napoleon and his reign. You must synthesize your knowledge of the Enlightenment, the French Revolution, and of Napoleon into a historical argument, using evidence to prove your points. One way to come at this topic would be to start off with a discussion of the enlightened ideals of the Revolution. Then discuss Napoleon. You might want to divide his reign into the earlier, more reforming part and the later Empire. Make sure to discuss specific reforms, such as the Code Napoleon and specific actions such as the

Concordat of 1801. Another possible way to look at this question would be to write about the specific ideals and how Napoleon embodied or did not embody each one, each in its own separate paragraph. Remember at the end to come back to the question itself and make a judgment about Napoleon. Was he truly enlightened or not? Was he enlightened during part of his reign? Was he enlightened in some ways and not in others? Be sure to add a short (2-3 sentences) discussion of synthesis to your conclusion, comparing Napoleon to an enlightened despot, such as Frederick the Great. Your synthesis discussion must specifically compare/contrast aspects of ruling in which the two leaders were or were not enlightened.
(*Western Civilization*, 9th ed., pp. 587–90 / 10th ed., pp. 584–86; Historical Thinking Skills—Argumentation, Patterns of Continuity and Change Over Time, Synthesis; Learning Objective SP-7, SP-13, SP-17, IS-6, IS-7; Key Concept 2.1)

Period 3: 1815–1914

Period 3 of the AP® European History framework examines the developments that occurred between the defeat of Napoleon and the outbreak of World War I. This time period begins with the reemergence of conservatism, imposed on many regions by the Congress of Vienna, examines the reactions to the conservative settlement that culminated in the revolutions of 1848, continues through the age of nationalism and imperialism, and culminates in the events that ignited the First World War. Industrialization quickly spread throughout parts of the European continent following the end of the Napoleonic Wars, bringing significant demographic, economic, political, and ideological changes. Finally, this era marked a turning point in the history of Europe and its relationship with the non-European world, as well. Similar to the fifteenth and sixteenth centuries, Europeans exploited technological advances that allowed them to venture further into the interior of Africa and gain control of an ever-growing global economy. The following charts outline the learning objectives and topics from the content outline that fit into this era.

THEMATIC LEARNING OBJECTIVES FOR PERIOD 3

INTERACTION OF EUROPE AND THE WORLD

Learning Objectives—Students are able to…	Relevant Topics in the Concept Outline
INT-1: Assess the relative influence of economic, religious, and political motives in promoting exploration and colonization.	3.5.I—National rivalries; raw materials and markets
INT-2: Analyze the cultural beliefs that justified European conquest of overseas territories and how they changed over time.	3.5.I—Cultural and racial superiority 3.6.II—Social Darwinism
INT-3: Analyze how European states established and administered overseas commercial and territorial empires.	3.5.II—Industrial and technological developments
INT-4: Explain how scientific and intellectual advances—resulting in more effective navigational, cartographic, and military technology—facilitated European interaction with other parts of the world.	3.1.III; 3.5.II—Communication and transportation technologies associated with industrialization
INT-6: Assess the role of overseas trade, labor, and technology in making Europe part of a global economic network and in encouraging the development of new economic theories and state policies.	3.1.III—New means of communication and transportation 3.5.I—Search for raw materials and markets
INT-7: Analyze how contact with non-European peoples increased European social and cultural diversity and affected attitudes toward race.	3.5.I—Ideology of cultural and racial superiority 3.5.III—Imperial encounters with non-European peoples

243

Learning Objectives—Students are able to...	Relevant Topics in the Concept Outline
INT-9: Assess the role of European contact on overseas territories through the introduction of disease, participation in the slave trade and slavery, effects on agricultural and manufacturing patterns, and global conflict.	3.5.III—Imperial conflicts and alliances
INT10: Explain the extent of and causes for non-Europeans' adoption of or resistance to European cultural, political, or economic values and institutions, and explain the causes of their reactions.	3.5.I—Latin American revolutions 3.5.III—Responses to imperialism
INT-11: Explain how European expansion and colonization brought non-European societies into global economic, diplomatic, military, and cultural networks.	3.5.I—Imperialist motives, Racial Darwinism 3.5.III—Responses and resistance to imperialism

POVERTY AND PROSPERITY

Learning Objectives—Students are able to...	Relevant Topics in the Concept Outline
PP-1: Explain how and why wealth generated from new trading, financial, and manufacturing practices and institutions created a market and then a consumer economy.	3.1.I—Great Britain's industrial dominance 3.1.II—Industrialization of Continental Europe 3.1.III—The Second Industrial Revolution
PP-3: Explain how geographic, economic, social, and political factors affected the pace, nature, and timing of industrialization in Western and Eastern Europe.	3.1.I—Industrial dominance of Great Britain 3.1.II—Industrialization of Continental Europe. 3.1.III—Second Industrial Revolution 3.2.V—Some areas lagged in industrialization
PP-4: Explain how the development of new technologies and industries—as well as new means of communication, marketing, and transportation—contributed to expansion of consumerism and increased standards of living and quality of life in the nineteenth and twentieth centuries.	3.1.III—New technologies and means of communication 3.2.IV—Mass marketing, efficient methods of transportation, new industries
PP-6: Analyze how expanding commerce and industrialization from the sixteenth through the nineteenth centuries led to the growth of cities and changes in the social structure, most notably a shift from a landed to a commercial elite.	3.2.I—Development of new classes 3.2.II—Migration from rural to urban areas 3.3.II—Government reforms of cities
PP-7: Explain how environmental conditions, the Agricultural Revolution, and industrialization contributed to demographic changes, the organization of manufacturing, and alterations in the family economy.	3.1.III—Mechanization and the factory system 3.2.II—Rapid population growth 3.2.III—Altered family structure and relations
PP-8: Analyze socialist, communist, and fascist efforts to develop responses to capitalism and why these efforts gained support during times of economic crisis.	3.3.I—Evolution of socialist ideology 3.3.III—Labor unions

Learning Objectives—Students are able to…	Relevant Topics in the Concept Outline
PP-10: Explain the role of social inequality in contributing to and affecting the nature of the French Revolution and subsequent revolutions throughout the nineteenth and twentieth centuries.	3.3.I—Development of ideologies 3.4.I The Concert of Europe; political revolts and revolutions 3.4.II—National unification and liberal reforms 3.6.II—Marx's critique of capitalism
PP-13: Analyze how cities and states have attempted to address the problems brought about by economic modernization, such as poverty and famine, through regulating morals, policing marginal populations, and improving public health.	3.2.II—Overcrowding in cities 3.3.II—Government reform of cities
PP-14: Explain how industrialization elicited critiques from artists, socialists, worker's movements, and feminist organizations.	3.3.I—Socialist critiques of capitalism 3.3.III—Political movements and social organizations 3.6.I—Romantic writers' response to the Industrial Revolution 3.6.II—Marx's critique of capitalism; realist and materialist themes in art and literature
PP-15: Analyze efforts of government and nongovernmental reform movements to respond to poverty and other social problems in the nineteenth and twentieth centuries..	3.2.III—Labor laws and social welfare programs 3.3.II—Government expansion of functions 3.3.III—Response of political movements and social organizations

OBJECTIVE KNOWLEDGE AND SUBJECTIVE VISIONS

Learning Objectives—Students are able to…	Relevant Topics in the Concept Outline
OS-3: Explain how political revolution and war from the seventeenth century on altered the role of the church in political and intellectual life and the response of religious authorities and intellectuals to such challenges.	3.4.I—Conservative attempts to strengthen adherence to religious authorities
OS-4: Explain how a worldview based on science and reason challenged and preserved social order and roles, especially the roles of women.	3.2.III—Cult of domesticity 3.3.I—Radical and republican advocates of suffrage and citizenship 3.3.III—Feminists and feminist movements
OS-6: Explain how European exploration and colonization were facilitated by the development of the scientific method and led to a reexamination of cultural norms.	3.5.II—Industrial and technological developments 3.5.III—Imperial encounters with non-European peoples
OS-8: Explain the emergence, spread, and questioning of scientific, technological, and positivist approaches to addressing social problems.	3.3.I—Liberal, radical and republican, and socialist ideologies 3.3.II—Government responses to industrialization 3.3.III—Responses of political movements and social organizations 3.6.II—Turn toward a realist and materialist worldview

Learning Objectives—Students are able to…	Relevant Topics in the Concept Outline
OS-9: Explain how new theories of government and political ideologies attempted to provide a coherent explanation for human behavior and the extent to which they adhered to or diverged from traditional explanations based on religious beliefs.	3.3.I—Ideologies 3.4.I—Political revolts and revolutions
OS-10: Analyze the means by which individualism, subjectivity, and emotion came to be considered a valid source of knowledge.	3.3.I—Liberal, radical and republican emphasis on individual rights 3.6.I—Romanticism's emphasis on intuition and emotion 3.6.III—Relativism in values and emphasis on subjective sources of knowledge
OS-12: Analyze how artists used strong emotions to express individuality and political theorists encouraged emotional identification with the nation.	3.3.I—Nationalism 3.4.II—National unification and liberal reform 3.6.I—Romanticism 3.6.III—Freudian psychology and modern art
OS-13: Explain how and why modern artists began to move away from realism and toward abstraction and the non-rational, rejecting traditional aesthetics.	3.6.I—Romantic break with neoclassical forms and rationalism 3.6.III—Shift to subjective, abstract, and expressive in the arts

STATES AND OTHER INSTITUTIONS OF POWER

Learning Objectives—Students are able to…	Relevant Topics in the Concept Outline
SP-1: Explain the emergence of civic humanism and new conceptions of political authority during the Renaissance, as well as subsequent theories and practices that stressed the political importance and rights of the individual.	3.3.I—Political ideologies 3.3.II—Growth of regulatory state 3.3.III—Political movements and parties
SP-3: Trace the changing relationship between states and ecclesiastical authority and the emergence of the principle of religious toleration.	3.3.I—Political ideologies and religion 3.4.I—Conservatism
SP-4: Analyze how the new political and economic theories from the seventeenth century and the Enlightenment challenged absolutism and shaped the development of constitutional states, parliamentary governments, and the concept of individual rights.	3.3.I—Ideologies of change 3.3.III —Mass political movements and reform 3.4.I—Post-1815 revolutions 3.4.II—National unification and nation-building
SP-5: Assess the role of colonization, the Industrial Revolution, total warfare, and economic depressions in altering the government's relationship to the economy, both in overseeing economic activity and in addressing its social impact.	3.1.I—British industrialization 3.1.II—Continental industrialization 3.1.III—Second Industrial Revolution 3.3.II—Government regulation and reform

Learning Objectives—Students are able to...	Relevant Topics in the Concept Outline
SP-7: Explain the emergence of representative government as an alternative to absolutism.	3.3.I—Ideologies of liberation 3.3.III—Mass movements and reform 3.4.I—Revolutions from 1815–1848 3.4.II—Nationalism and unification
SP-9: Analyze how various movements for political and social equality—such as feminism, anti-colonialism, and campaigns for immigrants' rights—pressured governments and redefined citizenship.	3.3.III—Workers, feminists and reform 3.5.III—Responses to imperialism (nationalism)
SP-10: Trace the ways in which new technologies from the printing press to the Internet have shaped the development of civil society and enhanced the role of public opinion.	3.1.III—Second Industrial Revolution—transportation and communication
SP-11: Analyze how religious and secular institutions and groups attempted to limit monarchical power by articulating theories of resistance to absolutism and by taking political action.	3.3.I—Ideologies of change 3.4.I—Post–1815 revolutions
SP-12: Assess the role of civic institutions in shaping the development of representative and democratic forms of government.	3.3.III—Mass political movements and parties
SP-13: Evaluate how the emergence of new weapons, tactics, and methods of military organization changed the scale and cost of warfare, required the centralization of power, and shifted the balance of power.	3.4. III—Industrialization of warfare 3.5.II—Second Industrial Revolution and imperialism
SP-14: Analyze the role of warfare in remaking the political map of Europe and in shifting the global balance of power in the nineteenth and twentieth centuries.	3.4.III—Congress of Vienna and Concert of Europe 3.4.II—Crimean War 3.4.III— Unification of Italy and Germany
SP-16: Explain how the French Revolution and the revolutionary and Napoleonic wars shifted the European balance of power and encouraged the creation of a new diplomatic framework.	3.4.I—Congress of Vienna settlement
SP-17: Explain the role of nationalism in altering the European balance of power, and explain attempts made to limit nationalism as a means to ensure continental stability.	3.4.I—Congress of Vienna and Metternich 3.4.II—Conservative Realpolitik 3.4.III—Unification of Italy and Germany 3.5.I—Nationalism as a motive for imperialism 3.5.III—Imperial conflicts and colonial nationalism
SP-18: Evaluate how overseas competition and changes in the alliance system upset the Concert of Europe and set the stage for World War I.	3.4.II—Crimean war and conservative nationalism 3.4.III—Unification of Italy and Germany 3.5.I—Imperialism 3.5.III—Imperial rivalries and conflicts

INDIVIDUAL AND SOCIETY

Learning Objectives—Students are able to…	Relevant Topics in the Concept Outline
IS-2: Explain how the growth of commerce and changes in manufacturing challenged the dominance of corporate groups and traditional estates.	3.2.I—Industrialization and bourgeoisie
IS-3: Evaluate the role of technology, from the printing press to modern transportation and telecommunications, in forming and transforming society.	3.1.II—Industrialization 3.1.III—Second Industrial Revolution and mass production 3.2.IV—Transportation and consumerism 3.3.II—Governmental reform of infrastructure 3.5.II—Industry and empire
IS-4: Analyze how and why the nature and role of the family has changed over time.	13.2.III—Companionate marriage and domesticity
IS-5: Explain why and how class emerged as a basis for identity and led to conflict in the nineteenth and twentieth centuries.	3.2.I—New industrial classes 3.2.III—Proactive legislation and leisure 3.3.I—Socialism and anarchism 3.3.III—Worker movements and reformers 3.4.I—Post-1815 revolutions
IS-6: Evaluate the causes and consequences of persistent tensions between women's role and status in the private versus the public sphere.	3.2.III—Companionate marriage and domesticity 3.3.I—Radicalism and feminism 3.3.III—Feminism and women in reform movements
IS-7: Evaluate how identities such as ethnicity, race, and class have defined the individual in relationship to society.	3.2.I—Industrialization and class 3.2.III—Middle and working class families 3.3.I—Post–1815 ideologies 3.3.III—Mass political movements and governmental reform 3.5.III—Interaction with and responses by colonies 3.6.II—Social Darwinism and Marxism
IS-9: Assess the extent to which women participated in and benefited from the shifting values of European society from the fifteenth century onward.	3.2.III—Industrialization, proactive legislation, and leisure 3.3.I—Post–1815 ideologies of change 3.3.III—Mass political movements and feminism
IS-10: Analyze how and why Europeans have marginalized certain populations (defined as "other") over the course of their history.	3.2.V—Persistence of serfdom and feudalism 3.3.I—Nationalism, anti-Semitism, and chauvinism 3.5.I—Racial Darwinism and White Man's Burden 3.5.III—Imperial-influenced art and colonial independence movements 3.6.I—Social Darwinism

KEY CONCEPTS FROM THE COLLEGE BOARD

3.1 The Industrial Revolution spread from Great Britain to the Continent, where the state played a greater role in promoting industry.

3.2 The experiences of everyday life were shaped by industrialization, depending on the level of industrial development in a particular location.

3.3 The problems of industrialization provoked a range of ideological, governmental, and collective responses.

3.4 European states struggled to maintain international stability in an age of nationalism and revolutions.

3.5 A variety of motives and methods led to the intensification of European global control and increased tensions among the Great Powers.

3.6 European ideas and culture expressed a tension between objectivity and scientific realism on one hand, and subjectivity and individual expression on the other.

9

THE INDUSTRIAL REVOLUTION: 1750–1870

Before the French Revolution and Napoleonic Wars shook Europe, Britain had a foretaste of the tremendous economic changes that would dramatically change the world. In the late eighteenth and early nineteenth centuries, several factors aligned that led to the creation of factories. Urban centers swelled as people left their rural homes and fields to make their livelihoods in cities.

KEY TERMS

Anti-Corn Law League	Industrial Revolution
Bessemer Process	Jeremy Bentham
bourgeoisie	John Stuart Mill
capital	joint-stock investment bank
capitalism	Luddites
Chartist movement	mass production
Crystal Palace	Mines Act of 1842
entrepreneur	Proletariat
Factory Act of 1833	tariff
Flora Tristan	Ten Hours Act of 1847
Great Exhibition of 1851	trade union

CHAPTER KEY CONCEPTS

- Great Britain was able to dominate the industrial economy by mechanizing the production of textiles, iron, and steel. Its supply of iron, coal, and other raw materials, its large work force, stable political climate, and forward-thinking political class served as a solid foundation for the Industrial Revolution.
- Economic growth during the Industrial Revolution both resulted from and supported the revolution. The creation of new technology required large amounts of capital (money or

251

property). The handsome profits from that new technology made for strong economies that fueled the development of dynamic urban centers.

▨ The Industrial Revolution took place in ~~France~~, ~~Prussia~~, and ~~other nations~~ of Western Europe, often with state sponsorship, while Eastern and Southern Europe were held back by various factors, including geography, lack of resources, powerful traditional nobility, and the persistence of serfdom.

▨ New classes, the bourgeoisie and the proletariat, developed in industrializing areas due to socioeconomic changes that created new divisions of labor.

▨ ~~Europe experienced~~ rapid population growth and urbanization, which led to overcrowded cities and rural depopulation.

▨ ~~Liberals~~, ~~radicals~~, and ~~conservatives~~ developed ideologies as a response to industrial and political revolutions.

For a full discussion of the Industrial Revolution, see *Western Civilization*, 9th and 10th editions, Chapter 20.

FACTORY PRODUCTION

Mass production of goods in factories in the nineteenth century had three highly interdependent aspects: it used materials and labor efficiently, it exploited natural energy sources well, and it generously rewarded economic investment.

First, production was concentrated in one location. Materials and labor were brought to the factory to maximize the effectiveness of both. Factory owners got more out of their workers' time, especially in comparison with the cottage system. More goods could be produced in a factory than by the same number of workers in cottages.

Mass production depended on a division of labor and standardization of parts for the efficiencies that boost output. Division of labor involves one worker performing only one operation—the model in previous centuries had called for a craftsman with apprentices, each taking a product from inception to completion. Along with the division of labor, standardization of parts affected output. Factories specified a set size and shape for parts so they could be used interchangeably in the goods the factory produced. This increased productivity also made for a more economical use of raw materials as there was less waste in such a planned, standardized system.

A second aspect of mass production was the location of factories near sources of power. Early in the Industrial Revolution, work was often situated near a concentration of either labor or markets. As the revolution progressed, machinery driven by water power—for example, looms—required factories to be near rivers or streams. When the steam engine was invented in the 1760s, factories were built near the mines that provided the coal or coke for it. The steam engine would revolutionize factory production, greatly amplifying productivity. Because of this increased productivity, more workers were needed in factories. As a result, cities grew tremendously.

Finally, the backbone of factory production was great capital investment. The people who invested in industry gained impressive personal profit from their investments, which they reinvested in their businesses to buy the expensive factory buildings and machines. Without this large influx of capital, the Industrial Revolution could not have taken place.

These entrepreneurs led the development of a robust system of laissez-faire capitalism. Based on the economic theories expounded by Adam Smith a century earlier, it comprised five fundamental components: private ownership, free enterprise, profit motive, competition, and market economy.

THE INDUSTRIAL REVOLUTION IN GREAT BRITAIN

WHY BRITAIN?

The greater productivity of the eighteenth-century cottage system and Agricultural Revolution put Great Britain in a position to lead Europe into a new age of rapid industrial growth. Agricultural changes—for example, new techniques such as crop rotation—led to the need for new tools, which encouraged early industrialists to create better farming implements. As new techniques and tools made the land more productive and enclosure of that land continued, fewer farm workers were needed. These displaced workers often moved from the countryside to towns in search of work. The increased productivity on farms provided the food necessary to support this rapid urban growth.

Britons supported the Industrial Revolution. The enclosure movement—the consolidation by large landowners of small, privately held lands—and the loss of commons had left a large number of people in need of new work. Britain had a group of skilled workers with the experience to design the machines that filled British factories. Britain also had entrepreneurs who were willing to take financial risks to start new businesses.

These entrepreneurs felt secure investing in Britain's industrial growth because of its strong economic state. Britain's mercantilist relationship with its colonies had given rise to a wealthy class of merchants who helped bankroll the factory system. The British trading network, strong and extensive, quickly located markets for the new factory-produced goods. Finally, Britain's well-organized, sound national banking system provided credit and economic stability, both of which were essential for ensuring the capital needed to buy the expensive machines mass production required.

A unified country with a stable, competent government, Great Britain provided the Industrial Revolution with a secure foundation. The parliamentary system gave greater voice to British subjects than many other European countries gave their citizens. The British government had also developed a solid infrastructure, especially good roads, which became part of the efficient British transportation system of the late eighteenth and early nineteenth centuries.

Finally, Great Britain had many geographic advantages. First, as an island it was exempt from many Continental disputes. Britain also had a number of great harbors that supported its worldwide trading network and numerous navigable rivers for transporting goods from inland factories to coastal harbors. In addition, the country was rich in mineral resources, including iron ore for machines and coal and coke to generate steam to power the machines.

> ## AP® Tip
>
> Causation is one of the most important thinking skills tested on the AP® Exam. The reasons for the growth of the Industrial Revolution in Britain is a major theme in European history. Be sure you know the reasons why and conditions under which the Industrial Revolution began in Britain rather than elsewhere.

BRITISH TECHNOLOGY

With excellent sources of raw cotton in India and the American South, Great Britain became a major producer of the world's woven cotton cloth, moving the textile industry from homes to factories. The spinning jenny, invented by James Hargreaves in 1764, the water-frame spinning machine patented by Richard Arkwright in 1768, and various machine-driven looms, coupled with the placing of factories by rivers as sources of power, greatly increased the output of workers. This increase eventually ended the cottage industry system.

The invention of the steam engine further transformed the production of textiles. With the steam engine as a source of power, factories no longer had to be situated near a river, and they could produce cotton cloth much faster than ever before. This created more demand for cotton, including more imported from India and the American South, and led to the sale of British textiles around the world.

The development of the iron industry also spurred industrial development in Britain. Not only was it used to manufacture the machines that were essential to factories, it was an industry in its own right, growing tremendously during the nineteenth century.

BRITISH TRANSPORTATION

To move raw materials and finished products, new types of transportation were needed. Rivers had provided an effective way to move goods, but with the rapid growth of production and with factories no longer needing to be next to rivers for power, canals and railroads were constructed to provide more transportation connections.

By the end of the eighteenth century, canals linked factories to rivers, greatly facilitating trade. Goods could be moved more quickly and safely on canals than on roads. Canals also provided a more reliable method of moving materials across the country, because the transport of goods along roads could be slowed by bad weather.

The biggest revolution in transportation, however, was the railroad. By the beginning of the nineteenth century, railroads in Britain were powered by steam engines and could carry large loads faster and more cheaply than boats in canals. The railroad eventually took on the major role of transporting goods in Britain.

This growth of British industrial might was clearly on display at the Great Exhibition of 1851. Held in London in the Crystal Palace, a huge glass and iron building set in Hyde Park, it brought together in one place many of the great machines of the day. There, along with the wonders of exotic lands around the world, the public could see the tremendous industrial power of the growing British factory system.

THE SPREAD OF INDUSTRIALIZATION

The factory system that became so entrenched in Britain grew more slowly on the Continent. After the French Revolution and the Napoleonic Wars, most of the Continent was physically and economically devastated. Countries struggled just to rebuild their governments, financial systems, and manpower.

There were other obstacles on the Continent. Initially, there was little capital available to build the machines necessary to compete with Britain in a global market. In addition, guilds were stronger there than in Britain, and they worked against the development of industry; with industrialization, the guilds would lose their ability to monitor the quality of goods, a role that they had had for centuries. The Continental nations also did not have the network of good roads and ease of river transportation that supported the Industrial Revolution in Britain.

Finally, the British, eager to protect their edge, did not allow machines, skilled workers, or even plans for machines to leave the country. As industry developed in Britain, little of it moved to the Continent.

But as the nineteenth century progressed, France and Belgium began to grow as centers of industry. British factory workers who escaped their country's regulation of industry took plans for factories and machines with them, to the benefit of nations nearby. The French and Belgian governments put in place protectionist policies to help their fledgling industries grow. They set very high tariffs, taxes on imports, to keep out foreign manufactured goods, and provided the infrastructure—especially railroads—needed to carry both raw materials to factories and finished products to markets. The development of joint-stock banks also encouraged industrial growth in Continental Europe by providing the required capital. With the discovery of major concentrations of coal in Belgium and the German states, they eventually took the lead in manufacturing on the Continent. In fact, Prussia became the leading German state as her industrial strength grew.

Like Continental Europe, the United States was slow to begin industrializing, but by the mid-nineteenth century, it had embarked on a period of great industrial growth. With help from emigrating Britons, who brought their plans and their know-how, the United States built the workforce and infrastructure for an American Industrial Revolution that rivaled Europe's and England's by the end of the century.

The failure to industrialize in Eastern and Southern Europe was due to various factors, such as geography and lack of resources, the continuation of serfdom and powerful landed political elites, and the lack of substantial government support as in Western European countries. As in the United States, where the North industrialized and the South stayed more agriculturally based with a system of slave labor doing the work on large plantations, Russian nobles kept serfdom and an agriculturally based economy alive until the 1860s.

THE SOCIAL IMPACT OF INDUSTRIALIZATION

As industrialization spread across Europe, society changed in many ways. The interaction among the Enclosure Movement, the Agricultural Revolution, and the Industrial Revolution led to a tremendous population increase. Along with this came a growth of cities, as factories drew thousands of workers. Rapidly growing cities, such as Manchester, England, could not keep up with the demand for housing and infrastructure, including roads, sewage disposal, and police. With the overcrowding of workers came those who took advantage of them through a wide variety of crimes. Thus, these squalid living conditions led many reformers to push for public health improvements and public safety.

City life was substantially different from rural life. The old class of tradesmen that had flourished under the guild system no longer had the power it once held. As factories hired more and more workers, the importance of artisans diminished. Factory workers performed monotonous, repetitious, sometimes dangerous tasks. Women and children were employed in mines, as well as factories—indeed, prior to the Factory Act of 1833, women and children made up the majority of workers in British textile factories. This was a far cry from the old system of families working side by side on farms or in cottage industries.

Factory workers often went home to packed, unsanitary tenements. Soot from the factories blackened the buildings and filled the air. Diseases such as typhoid and cholera swept through crowded cities, killing thousands. Those who survived were generally less healthy than those who worked in the countryside.

> ### AP® Tip
>
> Social history is an important thread through all of European history. Be prepared to discuss the impact of the Industrial Revolution on society as a part of a continuum of how major social issues reflect their eras.

RESPONSES TO PROBLEMS OF INDUSTRIALIZATION

New ideologies competed with old ways of thinking about the problems of industrialization and what to do about them. Liberals tended to support the extension of the right to vote to factory owners and called for the right to run factories without government interference. Radicals in Great Britain, called republicans on the Continent, demanded universal male suffrage. Some argued that equal rights should be extended to women as well.

Throughout the nineteenth century, many people stepped forward to help workers. Fighting poor working conditions and technological unemployment (the loss of a job because a machine could perform the task), trade unions formed to protect both the quality of goods produced and the lives of the workers who produced them. Luddites, a group of skilled craftsmen, directly attacked and disabled the machines that brought factory workers not only unemployment but also boring, dangerous working conditions. The British Parliament passed several acts, including the Factory Acts of 1833 and 1847, that lowered the number of working hours allowed and raised the minimum working age. It also directly addressed the lives of working children, not only cutting the number of hours children could work but also requiring education for them. The Mines Act of 1842 took women and children out of the underground mining operations, although they still worked above ground.

Individuals and groups also tried to improve the lives of workers. Edwin Chadwick's three-year investigation into the living conditions of the working classes was published as the *Report on the Condition of the Labouring Population of Great Britain* (1842). It was the basis for his recommendation for building an adequate sewage system. *London: A Pilgrimage* (1872) brought together 180 engravings by Gustave Doré, a French artist. Many disliked the book because so many of the compelling images showed the grim world of the urban poor. Help for workers came in a different form with the Chartist movement, begun in 1838. Its goal was to help workers in their lives outside the factories. To that end, it pushed for universal male suffrage and the removal of property qualifications for members of Parliament as a way to provide social and economic improvements in Britain.

AP® Tip

Don't think about just one class of people when you are studying for the exam. It is equally important to look at the impact of the industrial revolution on the wealthy elites as it is to concentrate on the poor working class. Factory owners could become enormously wealthy, rivaling and often surpassing the nobles, buying up land and building lavish homes in the country. They filled their city homes and country estates with the products they made and with things imported from all over the world. They had time for leisure activities and relationships within the family changed. However, some felt that if they did not run their businesses ruthlessly, they could go bankrupt and lose everything.

As factories ran more efficiently—often around the clock—there was greater demand for raw materials and a wider mass market. Responding to the accelerated demand, European nations were engaged in a fierce competition for colonies, especially in Africa and Asia, by the end of the nineteenth century. At the same time, a new philosophy developed: socialism. It offered a variety of ideas for building a new society able to deal with the problems of industrialization.

Content Review Questions

1. All of the following are true statements about steam power EXCEPT
   (A) James Watt adapted Thomas Newcomen's steam engine, which pumped water from mines, so that it could be used in factories.
   (B) steam engines were used in textile factories.
   (C) steam power required factories to be located near rivers.
   (D) steam engines were powered by coal.

2. Industry developed in nations outside Britain because
   (A) in the United States, slavery was so extensive there were plenty of workers for factories.
   (B) in France, high tariffs protected growing industries.
   (C) in India, the cotton industry was big enough that Indians built their own large textile industry.
   (D) the German states, through direct trade with Britain, gained unprecedented access to the most modern equipment.

3. How did the Agricultural Revolution lead to the Industrial Revolution?
   (A) The Agriculture Revolution's emphasis on use of heavy equipment caused a rise in the factory production of farm machinery.
   (B) The Agricultural Revolution caused the growth of industry because most of the wealth that supported the building of factories came from the large land-owning farmers.
   (C) The most successful machines of the Industrial Revolution were invented by workers who had gained their ideas from what they had witnessed during the Agricultural Revolution.
   (D) With the greater productivity of farms, many unemployed workers moved to cities to take jobs in factories, and the cities in turn had the food necessary to support the additional population.

4. One of the major economic causes for British industrial success was
   (A) a sound banking system that provided necessary credit.
   (B) the creation of the pound as a separate currency from the euro in use on the Continent.
   (C) that the British government did not get involved in the country's economy.
   (D) that her economy was already strong from a powerful trade among guilds.

5. Which of the following describes the difference between the Luddites and the Chartists?
   (A) The Chartists used illegal means; the Luddites used legal means.
   (B) The Luddites were violent whereas the Chartists were nonviolent.
   (C) The Luddites worked on providing workers the right to vote; the Chartists focused on getting the vote for women.
   (D) The Chartists fought to minimize working hours for children; the Luddites focused on improving working conditions for adults.

   Chartists ↳ nonviolent

6. One of the main reasons the Industrial Revolution began in Great Britain was that
   (A) Parliament placed high taxes on merchants, which it used to build canals and railroads.
   (B) rivers could provide needed transportation.
   (C) Britain had a stable government that encouraged a strong economy.
   (D) Britain did not have to fight Napoleon, so it could focus on improving the lives of the people.

7. Which of the following statements about transportation is most accurate?
   (A) Steam-powered railroads provided fast, cheap transportation of people and industrial goods.
   (B) By the beginning of the nineteenth century, railroad lines crisscrossed England, providing much-needed transportation of goods.
   (C) With the rise of railroads, more goods were transported by canal and river.
   (D) Until the first tunnels and chasm-spanning bridges were built in the twentieth century, railroads did not achieve their full potential.

8. All of the following were true of entrepreneurs during the Industrial Revolution EXCEPT
   (A) they worked hard in the factories, providing the needed labor.
   (B) they were the financial backbone of factory production.
   (C) they made great profits and put them back into their businesses to continue to build wealth.
   (D) they offered an enormous capital investment.

9. A major component in the efficient use of factories, mass production was
   (A) the use of railroads.
   (B) the building of factories where the workers were most easily available.
   (C) the importance of having workers perform the same task repeatedly.
   (D) government support of all phases of production.

10. What attributes of laissez-faire capitalism were key to the development of the Industrial Revolution?
   (A) Private ownership, free enterprise, profit motive, competition, and market economy
   (B) Group ownership, free enterprise, profit motive, competition, and domestic economy
   (C) Group ownership, free enterprise, profit motive, monopolies, and market economy
   (D) Private ownership, free enterprise, profit motive, competition, and domestic economy

Multiple-Choice Questions

Questions 1–3 refer to the following images.

Source: V&A Images, London/Art Resource, NY

Source: © ARPL/HIP/The Image Works

1. The two works on the previous page best illustrate
   (A) the massive social and economic gulf between the elites in British society and the working classes.
   (B) the equality of women in both upper and lower classes.
   (C) that emphasis put on fancy clothing by the upper classes in Great Britain caused textile workers to be forced to work overtime.
   (D) that all classes of people worked hard and were rewarded for it with exhibitions and shows.

2. Using your knowledge of the Industrial Revolution and the above illustration of the Great Exhibition of 1851, all of the following are true EXCEPT
   (A) the Crystal Palace was made of iron and glass to show the power of the newly developed materials.
   (B) Prince Albert used the Great Exhibition to promote British industrial might.
   (C) Prince Albert was attempting to catch up with France's industrial dominance and earlier industrial exhibitions.
   (D) It had many visitors from both Great Britain and abroad.

   Prince Albert was trying to show off

3. The lives of urban factory workers were quite difficult for all of the following reasons EXCEPT
   (A) they lived in crowded, unsanitary tenements.
   (B) diseases could spread quickly and devastate large numbers of people.
   (C) men and women—but not their children—worked in dangerous situations.
   (D) urban sanitation was poor.

Questions 4–6 refer to the following map.

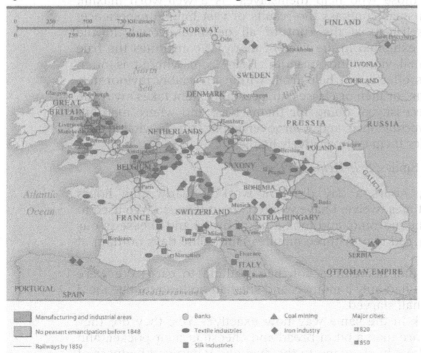

4. The map on the previous page shows the spread of
   (A) railways after 1850.
   (B) textile and mining centers in Europe.
   (C) famines and epidemics due to industrial pollution.
   (D) industrial areas in southern and eastern Europe.

5. One of the main reasons that the Industrial Revolution grew at a
   slower pace on the Continent than in Great Britain was that
   (A) Belgian-manufactured goods were of lower quality than
       French goods.
   (B) the British sent examples only of their lower-quality machines
       to the Continent.
   (C) European countries' roads and river transportation were not
       as good as Britain's.
   (D) the guilds, which were very unpopular on the Continent, threw
       their support behind the development of industry in Belgium.

6. The spread of the Industrial Revolution to Eastern Europe was
   hampered by
   (A) their tradition of not allowing child labor.
   (B) their abundance of ports, rivers, and canals.
   (C) a powerful landed nobility that relied on serfdom for
       agricultural labor.
   (D) the prevalence of socialist and communist beliefs among the
       workers.

Short-Answer Questions

"Heaven helps those who help themselves" is a well-worn maxim,
embodying in a small compass the results of vast human experience.
The spirit of self-help is the root of all genuine growth in the
individual; and, exhibited in the lives of many, it constitutes the true
source of national vigor and strength. Help from without is often
enfeebling in its effects, but help from within invariably invigorates.
Whatever is done for men or classes, to a certain extent takes away the
stimulus and necessity of doing for themselves; and where men are
subjected to overguidance and overgovernment, the inevitable tendency is to render them comparatively helpless....

Source: Samuel Smiles, *Self-Help*, 1859.

For how many hours a day did you work?—Nearly nine hours
regularly; sometimes twelve; I have worked about thirteen. We used to
go in at six in the morning, and took a bit of bread and cheese in our
pocket, and stopped two or three minutes; and some days nothing at
all to eat.

How was it that sometimes you had nothing to eat?—We were
over-burdened. I had only a mother, and she had nothing to give me. I
was sometimes half starved....

Do they work in the same way now exactly?—Yes, they do; they
have nothing more than a bit of bread and cheese in their pocket, and
sometimes can't eat it all, owing to the dust and damp and badness of

air; and sometimes it is as hot as an oven; sometimes I have seen it so hot as to melt a candle.

What are the usual wages of a boy of eight?—They used to get 3d or 4d a day.

Source: E. R. Pike, *Human Documents of the Industrial Revolution in Britain* (London: Unwin & Hyman, 1966).

1. Answer A, B, and C.
   A) Briefly explain the point of view of Samuel Smiles in the first excerpt.
   B) Briefly explain the point of view of the person testifying in the second excerpt.
   C) Briefly explain ONE important social or economic difference between the two.

2. Briefly answer A and B.
   A) Explain TWO important advantages of Great Britain that allowed it to industrialize before the rest of the continent of Europe.
   B) Explain ONE disadvantage that Eastern Europe had that caused it to industrialize later.

Long-Essay Questions

1. Analyze the reasons why industrialization began in Britain rather than on the Continent. (Historical Thinking Skills: Causation, Periodization, Comparison)

2. In what ways and to what extent did governments and reformers respond to the problems of industrialization between 1815 and 1914? (Historical Thinking Skills: Change and Continuity Over Time, Causation, Periodization)

Answers

CONTENT REVIEW QUESTIONS

1. **(C)** During the early phase of the Industrial Revolution, factories were water-powered, so were situated by rivers or streams. When Watt developed the steam engine powered by coal, the Industrial Revolution's success was ensured, allowing factories to be situated away from rivers (*Western Civilization*, 9th ed., p. 599 / 10th ed., pp. 595–96; Historical Thinking Skills—Causation, Patterns of Continuity and Change Over Time, Periodization; Learning Objective PP-3; Key Concept 3.1).

2. **(B)** France gave protection to their growing industries through high tariffs on imported goods (*Western Civilization*, 9th ed., pp. 605–08 / 10th ed., pp. 601–05; Historical Thinking Skills—Causation, Patterns of Continuity and Change Over Time, Periodization; Learning Objective PP-3; Key Concept 3.1).

3. **(D)** With improvements in agriculture that allowed fewer workers to raise more food, rural workers moved to the factory cities looking for work. Because the Agricultural Revolution led to a tremendous growth in production, there was enough food to feed the growing urban population (*Western Civilization*, 9th ed., p. 597 / 10th ed., p. 593; Historical Thinking Skills—Causation, Periodization, Synthesis; Learning Objective PP-7, IS-2; Key Concept 2.2).

4. **(A)** Britain's sound banking system provided flexible credit to support the growth of industry (*Western Civilization*, 9th ed., p. 597 / 10th ed., p. 593; Historical Thinking Skills—Causation; Learning Objective PP-1; Key Concept 3.1).

5. **(B)** The Luddites used illegal, violent actions—for example, smashing machines in factories—while the Chartists used more nonviolent legal means to bring the vote to men and provide better parliamentary representation for workers (*Western Civilization*, 9th ed., p. 620 / 10th ed., p. 616; Historical Thinking Skills—Comparison, Synthesis; Learning Objective PP-2, PP-3, PP-4; Key Concept 3.2, 3.3).

6. **(C)** A stable political climate and laws protecting private property made Britain a good place for the Industrial Revolution to grow. Great Britain did fight in the Napoleonic Wars, although it did not suffer as much as the Continental nations (Western Civilization, 9th ed., pp. 597–99 / 10th ed., p. 593; Historical Thinking Skills—Causation; Learning Objective PP-3; Key Concept 2.2, 3.1).

7. **(A)** Steam-powered railroads were the fastest, cheapest mode of transporting goods in nineteenth-century Britain (*Western Civilization*, 9th ed., pp. 600–01 / 10th ed., pp. 596–98; Historical Thinking Skills—Causation, Interpretation; Learning Objective PP-4; Key Concept 3.2).

8. **(A)** Entrepreneurs financed the Industrial Revolution. They did not work in the factories (*Western Civilization*, 9th ed., p. 597 / 10th ed., p. 593; Historical Thinking Skills—Comparison, Synthesis; Learning Objective PP-1; Key Concept 3.1).

9. **(C)** Mass production called for workers to do one task over and over in as efficient a manner as possible (*Western Civilization*, 9th ed., pp. 601–02 / 10th ed., pp. 598–99; Historical Thinking Skills—Synthesis; Learning Objective PP-4, IS-3; Key Concept 3.1).

10. **(A)** The Industrial Revolution **depended** on strong individuals who owned their businesses and traded in a competitive market economy to earn profits (*Western Civilization*, 9th ed., p. 597 / 10th ed., pp. 593–94; Historical Thinking Skills—Interpretation, Synthesis; Learning Objective PP-3, IS-3; Key Concept 3.1).

MULTIPLE-CHOICE QUESTIONS

1. **(A)** While the first image of Queen Victoria and her family shows upper and middle class people, all incredibly well dressed and with the leisure time to attend such an exhibition, the second image of workers in a factory setting shows the hard work of attending to the machines (*Western Civilization*, 9th ed., pp. 602–04 / 10th ed., pp. 598–601; Historical Thinking Skills—Comparison, Analyzing Evidence: Content and Sourcing, Synthesis; Learning Objective IS-3, IS-5, IS-7; Key Concept 3.1, 3.2).

2. **(C)** The Great Exhibition was commissioned by Prince Albert to show off Britain's industrial might in being the leading industrial nation, far and above countries on the continent. The Crystal Palace was made of steel and glass, materials that could not be made in large quantities before this period, and was visited by over six million people from both Britain and foreign countries. (*Western Civilization*, 9th ed., pp. 602–04 / 10th ed., pp. 599–601; Historical Thinking Skills—Periodization, Contextualization, Analyzing Evidence: Content and Sourcing Synthesis; Learning Objective PP-1, PP-4; Key Concept 3.1).

3. **(C)** Children did work—and sometimes died doing it—in factories (*Western Civilization*, 9th ed., pp. 617–19 / 10th ed., pp. 612–14; Historical Thinking Skills—Periodization, Analyzing Evidence: Content and Sourcing Learning Objective IS-5, IS-7; Key Concept 3.2).

4. **(B)** The map shows textile and mining centers. It also shows the places where serfdom continued after 1848 (*Western Civilization*, 9th ed., p. 606 / 10th ed., p. 602; Historical Thinking Skills— Periodization, Analyzing Evidence: Content and Sourcing; Learning Objective PP-3; Key Concept 3.1).

5. **(C)** The Continental nations did not have the network of good rivers and roads that Britain had, and so could not move raw materials and finished goods as effectively as they were moved in Britain (*Western Civilization*, 9th ed., p. 605 / 10th ed., p. 601; Historical Thinking Skills—Causation, Periodization, Analyzing Evidence: Content and Sourcing Learning Objective PP-3; Key Concept 3.1).

6. **(C)** There definitely was a tradition of child labor in Eastern Europe, but there was a lack of ports, canals, and roads. Socialism and communism spread to Eastern Europe much later. A strong nobility that was invested in keeping the status quo of landownership and rights over an enslaved peasantry was a major reason for lack of industrialization (*Western Civilization*, 9th ed., pp. 605–06 / 10th ed., p. 604; Historical Thinking Skills—Causation, Periodization, Analyzing Evidence: Content and Sourcing; Learning Objective PP-3; Key Concept 3.1).

SHORT-ANSWER QUESTIONS

1. A) As an industrialist, Samuel Smiles believed in liberalism. He wanted the government to leave him alone and allow him to run his factory so that it made the maximum profit. He worked hard to get to where he was and believed in the value of hard work for others. He might have also believed in a social

Darwinist idea that the upper and middle classes were more evolved than the lower classes.

B) The person testifying to the government committee in the second excerpt is obviously a lower class child who works in a mine. As a lower-class person being questioned by people of a higher class, it is amazing that he answers as forthrightly and truthfully as he does, although he could be making things look worse in order to get help for him and his fellow workers.

C) These two excerpts show the extreme poverty and the abuse of the workers by factory and mine owners. They show the extreme divide between the classes that was developing during the industrial revolution. They also show that neither side understood what the other's problems were and had little sympathy for them.
(*Western Civilization*, 9th ed., pp. 602–04, 615–19 / 10th ed., pp. 598–99, 607–14; Historical Thinking Skills—Comparison, Analyzing Evidence: Content and Sourcing, Interpretation, Synthesis; Learning Objective IS-5; Key Concept 3.1, 3.2)

2. Great Britain had many advantages over the rest of Europe when it came to industrialization. It had iron and coal mines on its own soil as well as many raw materials. It had many colonies from which to obtain more raw materials and which acted as markets for finished goods. It had a good transportation system, many rivers and canals, and a thriving shipping industry. It had an overabundance of working-class people who needed jobs, and it had a government that allowed free rein to its entrepreneurs and inventors and a good banking system to provide capital. Eastern Europe, on the other hand, was hampered by its lack of colonies and transportation systems. It was also controlled by a land-owning noble class that had kept the serfs in bondage to work on large farms.
(*Western Civilization*, 9th ed., pp. 597–99, 605–07 / 10th ed., pp. 608–10, 616–18; Historical Thinking Skills—Causation, Comparison; Learning Objective PP-1, PP-3, PP-4; Key Concept 3.1)

LONG-ESSAY QUESTIONS

1. This is a good example of a Causation question that also throws in some Comparison analysis. A good way to respond to this prompt is to organize your essay around the various areas in which Great Britain was strong—politics, economics, population, and geography. As you work your way through each area, discuss the situation on the Continent and how it differed from Britain.

Britain's strength was based on its stable political state, so make sure that you describe it as an important foundation. Compare Britain's peaceful representative government, dating back to the 1600s, with those of France and its neighbors, all caught up to one degree or another with the French Revolution. Point out that Britain had the luxury to focus on political and economic ascendency while the Continental countries had to focus on rebuilding their governments, cities, infrastructure, and population. Also look at Britain's economic policies in encouraging trade and in supporting the building of an excellent infrastructure of roads, canals, and railroads. Britain's economic situation was strong. Mercantilism had provided a good economic base, and the great banking system offered the credit necessary to finance the transition from the cottage industry to industrialization. Compare this with the economic toll the Napoleonic Wars took on the Continent and the shortage of both government and private funding for industrial growth.

Britons played an important role in building the country's industrial strength. Talk about the three main groups necessary to drive industrial growth: entrepreneurs willing to risk their money to fund it, skilled workers to design the machines, and workers to make the products. Point out the relationship between the Agricultural Revolution and the Industrial Revolution in providing factory workers. Discuss the guild restrictions and aversion to risk that were common on the Continent.

Britain's geography, also important, can be discussed in a number of ways. Make sure that you point out that as an island, Britain was isolated from many Continental conflicts. It was also blessed with many deep harbors that served as excellent ports. The internal geography is important too, so mention the rivers that served as thoroughfares to the sea and the natural resources, such as coal and iron ore. In contrast, the Continent's geographic limitations included the many conflicts spilling over from country to country and, for several nations, little or no access to year-round sea trade. Be sure to add a brief (2-3 sentences) synthesis discussion to your essay. For this essay, you could compare Britain's early industrialization with its role in the Second Industrial Revolution.
(*Western Civilization*, 9th ed., pp. 597–99 / 10th ed., pp. 593–601; Historical Thinking Skills—Causation, Periodization, Comparison; Learning Objective PP-1, PP-3, PP-4; Key Concept 3.1)

2. Begin your essay with a discussion of the problems of industrialization but do not spend too much time on this. Describe the rapid growth of cities and the lack of services, such as sewage disposal, that could have provided healthier living conditions. Be sure to deal with the struggles of everyday life with such things as overcrowding in filthy tenements and widespread crime.

There's a lot to include about the workplace but again, your focus should be more on the reforms or lack thereof, so don't go off on a long tangent here. Mention, for example, the monotonous, dangerous working conditions that led to many injuries and deaths, and the long, hard hours women and children worked in both factories and mines. Be sure to discuss the move away from creativity and toward conformity as the importance of the guilds and craftsmanship gave way to mass production and industrial growth.

Once you have described the problems of industrialization, analyze the governmental and private responses to those problems. It is important to include the fact that many middle-class factory owners saw little reason to change. Conservatives argued that things should stay the same, while Liberals argued for more rights for the *owners* of the factories, not for the workers. Nevertheless, Parliament passed a number of acts to address problems, such as long working hours, child labor, and poor

working conditions. You can discuss any of the many private, nongovernmental efforts to address industrial-era problems: trade unions pushing for better working conditions and benefits; groups, such as the Chartists and Luddites, that had their own ideas and methods for trying to improve not only the working lives but also the rights of the industrial workers; and individuals who were moved to action by the plight of urban factory workers. Be sure to add a brief (2–3 sentences) synthesis discussion to your essay. For this essay, you could compare the responses to the problems of industrialization at this time with the solutions offered during the twentieth century.
(*Western Civilization*, 9th ed., pp. 602–04, 615–19 / 10th ed., pp. 598–99, 611–15; Historical Thinking Skills—Continuity and Change Over Time, Causation, Periodization; Learning Objective IS-5; Key Concept 3.1, 3.2, 3.3)

10

REVOLTS AGAINST THE OLD ORDER: 1815–1850

In reaction to the French Revolution and Napoleon, European royalty led a conservative movement to return Europe to life under the old order. Movements for liberalism and nationalism combined with social and economic unrest brought about by the Industrial Revolution, however, overwhelmed the continent throughout the first half of the nineteenth century.

KEY TERMS

bourgeoisie
Concert of Europe
Congress of Vienna
conservatism
Decembrist Revolt
Friedrich Engels
Charles Fourier
Frankfurt Assembly
Greek revolt
Grossdeutsch
July Revolution
Kleindeutsch
liberalism
Karl Marx

nationalism
Robert Owen
Peterloo Massacre
principle of intervention
principle of legitimacy
proletariat
Quadruple Alliance
Reform Act of 1832
Revolutions of 1848
risorgimento
Romanticism
Saint Simon
socialism
utopian socialists

CHAPTER KEY CONCEPTS

▪ A series of revolts, provoked by nationalist and liberal senti-ments, swept Europe. Revolutions against the conservative order of the Congress of Vienna and the Concert of Europe kept most of Europe in turmoil during the first half of the century.

- In response to the Industrial Revolution, ideas such as socialism and anarchism were offered to improve the lives of Europeans.
- During the first half of the nineteenth century, Romanticism, which influenced art, literature, and music, was the prominent cultural movement.

For a full discussion of the period 1815–1850, see *Western Civilization*, 9th and 10th editions, Chapter 21.

NEW IDEOLOGIES: LIBERALISM AND NATIONALISM

During the nineteenth century, new ideologies developed as Europe went through great economic and political changes set in motion by the Industrial Revolution and by the French Revolution and Napoleon. Liberalism begins with the belief that people should be able to make their own choices. It took two forms during the nineteenth century: economic liberalism and political liberalism.

Economic liberalism, or classical economics, espoused the belief that not only should people have the right to own businesses, but governments should also allow businesses to function free of government interference. The case for laissez-faire was made most forcefully by Thomas Malthus and David Ricardo, economists who set the issue in the context of population increases. Malthus believed that the population could expand only so much before outrunning the food supply. Building on that idea, Ricardo's "iron law of wages" held that as wages rose, people had more children, which eventually led to lower wages because of an increased number of workers.

Political liberalism, rooted in the thinking of John Locke and the philosophes of the Enlightenment, focused on people's basic rights, including the rights to freedom of speech and equality before the law. Those who advocated these rights encouraged the development of constitutional governments; legislative assemblies; and the extension of suffrage, the right to vote.

The nineteenth century also saw the flowering of nationalism, the unity that comes of shared traditions, languages, customs, religions, and ethnicities. Nationalism fed desires for independence from imperial control and unification with others of a shared nationality to form a nation-state. Nationalism was especially strong in Germany, Italy, and the Austrian Empire.

THE CONGRESS OF VIENNA

With the defeat of Napoleon, the Quadruple Alliance—Great Britain, Prussia, Russia, and Austria, the four major European powers—met to arrange a peace settlement; the Congress of Vienna was led by Austrian foreign minister Klemens von Metternich, the very symbol of nineteenth-century reactionary politics. His goal was to return Europe to the stability of the old order and check the spread of liberalism and nationalism. The issues to be dealt with included who should rule France, the balance of power, security, territorial concerns, and the place of France in Europe. The four great powers reached four settlements. However, in the 1820s, as Britain became concerned with Spanish and Portuguese moves to squelch Latin American revolts, it gradually shifted away from the more conservative nature of the alliance.

One settlement, the principle of legitimacy, was crucial to those who wanted to restore order: legitimate monarchs needed to return to their thrones. Louis XVIII, the brother of Louis XVI, had been put on France's throne after Napoleon's initial defeat. Monarchs in Spain and the Italian states were also returned to power.

Another settlement dealt with the principle of compensation: the victorious nations were rewarded with land. Russia gained some Polish lands, Prussia got part of Saxony, and Austria gained control of parts of Italy. Territorial changes were designed to balance power so that never again could one nation dominate Europe. Of special concern was the prevention of any growth of French hegemony, the authority exercised by one power over others. To that end, France's borders were put back to their pre-revolutionary boundaries, and the country had to pay compensation, as well as accept an occupying army.

Two other settlements that had deep repercussions during the first half of the nineteenth century were the denial of democracy and the denial of nationalism. The primary mechanisms for that were wars, led especially by Austria and France, in which foreign forces invaded a neighbor to squelch liberal and national movements. Under Metternich's leadership, the Quadruple Alliance sought to deny any voice to the people in selecting their rulers or governments. Concerned about the nationalism that grew up in response to the Napoleonic Wars, they also worked to deny nationalist groups both independence and unification with others of the same nationality.

The Quadruple Alliance, also known as the Concert of Europe, was the backbone of the conservative reaction, and lasted until Metternich fled Austria in 1848. It had two purposes: to enforce the Vienna settlements and to suppress revolutions. By 1818, with the solidifycation of the Bourbon French government, France joined the Concert.

Believing that conservatism—the maintenance of order using traditional sources of power—would help Europe remain free of revolution, the Concert supported hereditary powers and refused the call of liberalism. Indeed, the Concert asserted its right to intervene in any country to quell revolts that threatened order.

Revolts tended to be based on liberalism and nationalism. Liberals believed in some sort of representative government, allowing for participation by the middle class, if not the working class. Nationalist forces usually helped groups fight for independence from the powers that controlled them.

> ## AP® Tip
>
> Be sure you understand the Congress of Vienna—why it was called, who called it, who attended, and the decisions made there. Be able to compare it to other major treaties—the Peace of Westphalia (1648) for example or the Versailles Treaty after WWI. Another way to think about these treaties is as "turning points" of history. To what extent did the Congress of Vienna mark a major change in the history of Europe? Was the treaty a success or did more problems arise because of it? Were things totally different afterward or were there things that stayed the same? These questions of Periodization, Causation, and Patterns of Continuity and Change Over Time are all historical thinking skills that are tested on the AP® Exam.

EARLY NINETEENTH-CENTURY REVOLTS

ITALY AND SPAIN

Among the first revolts that the Concert of Europe faced erupted in Italy and Spain. The Concert sent Austrian troops to Italy to suppress a revolt in the Kingdom of the Two Sicilies for a limited constitutional monarchy. In Spain, an attempt to force King Ferdinand VII to accept a limited constitutional monarchy was thwarted in 1823 by a Quadruple Alliance–backed French army sent into Spain.

LATIN AMERICA

Many successful nationalistic revolutions occurred in Latin America. With roots in Spanish and Portuguese mercantilism and slavery, these revolutions began when European control weakened during the Napoleonic Wars. Beginning in Argentina in 1810, the movement against Continental powers freed most South and Central American nations from European control.

Having succeeded in Italy and Spain, the Concert was eager to reach across the Atlantic and help Spain and Portugal hold onto their colonies. But the British opposed the idea and, further, joined with the United States to protect the growing revolutionary movements and fledgling nations. These new nations provided Britain with both raw materials for its growing factory system and markets for the goods it was producing.

GREECE

The Greeks led one of the few successful European nationalistic revolts during the nineteenth century, in large measure because the great powers supported it. Ottoman Turks had controlled a large part of southeastern Europe, including Greece, for hundreds of years; the British, French, and Russians, eager to see the removal of the Muslim Turks, gave military and moral support to the Greeks. By 1832, the Greeks had their independence and a new Greek monarchy.

RUSSIA

After the death of Alexander I in 1825, a struggle ensued for his throne. Although Alexander had attempted to enact some Enlightenment reforms, he had become reactionary, wanting to move Russia back to stricter control. He was succeeded by his conservative brother Nicholas. Many Russian liberals had assumed that Alexander's other brother, the more liberal Constantine, would become tsar. The Decembrist Revolt, their attempt to install a more liberal government, was squelched. It pushed Nicholas toward a more reactionary stance.

REVOLTS IN THE 1830S

Revolts, led by both liberals and nationalists, continued in the 1830s, but the conservatives, opposed to change, began to lose their grip on Europe.

In 1824, upon the death of Louis XVIII, his brother Charles X, a conservative, ascended the French throne. Liberals disturbed by Charles's policies revolted in 1830. The July Revolution brought to the throne Louis Philippe, Charles's cousin, and a constitutional government. It also inspired three other revolutions.

The Congress of Vienna had united the Belgians and the Dutch after the fall of Napoleon. The Catholic Belgians, however, wanted to be independent of the Protestant Dutch, so they fought the Dutch, and in 1830, with the support of the major powers, gained independence under a constitutional monarch, Leopold of Saxe-Coburg.

Still, some revolts failed. Poland wanted to be free of Russian control, but a nationalist revolt was crushed by Russian troops in 1831. An attempt by three northern Italian states to overthrow Austrian control failed when Austria sent in troops. But the revolt saw the birth of the *risorgimento* (resurgence), a movement led by Giuseppe Mazzini that was a strong force in the eventual unification of Italy.

THE REVOLUTIONS OF 1848

A major turning point came in 1848, when a revolution in France sparked revolts for liberalism and nationalism across much of Europe. Unable to deal with the rising liberal movement, and with his government mired in economic and political corruption, Louis Philippe abdicated the French throne in February 1848. A provisional government took over, and after a battle between moderates and radicals, a constitution was drawn up calling for an elected presidency. The French elected Louis Napoleon, a nephew of Napoleon Bonaparte.

Pressure for liberal reforms also ignited revolutions in the German states. As some of the reforms were enacted, a call was made for a new constitution, to be drawn up by the newly formed Frankfurt Assembly. It was immediately problematic because it attempted to make government decisions for all of the German states. But its biggest problem was deciding what should make up the new German state—all German states (*Grossdeutsch* or Big German) or all except the province of Austria (*Kleindeutsch* or Little German). When the Austrians chose to stay out, the Prussian king, Frederick William IV, was offered the throne of a united Germany. However, he refused it; with no leader, the movement fell apart.

As nationalism swept across Europe, the Austrian Empire could no longer maintain control of the many nationalities it had long held together. The Hungarians, especially, wanted more recognition in the Austrian government. As revolts grew, Metternich, the architect of this period of reactionary politics, was dismissed and fled Austria. In settling the variety of disputes across the empire, Austria eventually allowed the Magyars in Hungary a measure of self-governance. Soon after, other nationalities, among them the Czechs and Croats, began to clamor for self-rule. The revolts in Austria itself were calls for liberal reforms, but neither the nationalists nor the liberals were successful.

In Italy, the liberal movements that had developed in the 1830s gained strength. Across northern Italy, revolutionaries fought to remove Austrian control and set up constitutional governments. But only in Piedmont were they successful.

Both the successes and the failures of the revolutions of 1848 were significant. The successes—the removal of Metternich, the recognition of Hungarian authority in the Austrian Empire, and the creation of constitutional governments in France and Piedmont—provided foundations for the continued liberalization of European governments. The failures of 1848 were often the result of the lack of coordination among nationalities or various liberal groups. Achievement of their goals of independence and constitutionalism would be delayed until late in the nineteenth and early in the twentieth centuries.

AP® Tip

For a solid understanding of the growth of liberalism and nationalism in response to Metternich's reactionary leadership, make a chart comparing the various nineteenth-century revolts. Include each revolt's year(s); whether it was for liberalism, nationalism, or both; the overall goals; and the outcome. A requirement of the newly redesigned AP® exam is a more extensive knowledge of two or three revolts. Be able to compare and contrast some of the revolts, their causes, the details of what happened and how successful they were. The Greek War for Independence, the Decembrist Revolt, and the recurring Italian revolts would be good ones to know in more detail.

INDUSTRIALIZATION AND REFORM

As the Industrial Revolution spread across Europe during the nineteenth century, governments and reformers responded to the concerns of the factory owners and workers. This was particularly true in Great Britain, where the Industrial Revolution began.

As Britain's urban populations grew, the middle and lower classes sought fair representation in Parliament. The middle class, in particular, wanted political strength that reflected its economic might. As a result, it began to support the Whigs over the Tories, who tended to represent the landed classes. Despite rising discontent, the Tories remained in power until 1830, even after the Peterloo Massacre of 1819, when troops in Manchester attacked 60,000 protestors, including both workers and members of the middle class, killing eleven.

After the 1830 revolution in France, and with memories of the Peterloo Massacre in mind, the Whigs realized that it was important to offer reforms. The Reform Act of 1832 finally permitted representation in urban centers and loosened the property qualifications to vote. Many reforms were enacted to help the poor. Poorhouses were set up to provide them with a place to live and to force them to find work, an approach followed by other countries. Some organizations offered education, especially in trades, to help the poor find jobs. Religious institutions gave religious instruction to them, hoping especially to help children resist the vices that were developing in the growing cities.

As urban areas developed, so did crime and, thus, the need to provide for the safety of urban dwellers. British police, unpaid men who worked to keep order, were replaced by paid forces with professional officers. The same happened in France and Germany. The punishing of criminals also changed, with reformers urging imprisonment and rehabilitation of criminals rather than capital punishment.

SOCIALISM

Another group offered a different solution to the problems of industrialization. Socialists favored sharing resources, rather than competing for them. Socialism holds that the shared ownership and operation of the methods of production offer hope for better lives for the working classes.

The earliest type of socialism was utopian socialism, which advocated the voluntary end of capitalism based on the merits of socialism. Utopian socialism appeared in many forms, primarily in Britain and France.

Socialists such as Louis Blanc and Charles Fourier believed that organizing workers into groups would lead to thriving societies. Blanc advocated the organization of workers into workshops or cooperatives, while Fourier taught the creation of model societies through the analysis of personality types and rotation of work.

Other socialists, including Robert Owen and the Comte de Saint-Simon, thought that compassion and Christian principles would flower in socialist communities. Owen worked toward that goal by creating communities for workers in Scotland and the United States.

ROMANTICISM

During the nineteenth century, art, music, literature, and religion were dominated by Romanticism. An intellectual movement in direct opposition to the logic and linear nature of the Scientific Revolution and the Enlightenment, Romanticism emphasized emotion, faith, love, nature, melancholy, exoticism, and the past.

In style and subject matter, Romantic artists were quite different from the Neoclassicist artists. Painters such as Caspar David Friedrich and J.M.W. Turner used their art to show the glories of nature. Others, such as Eugene Delacroix and Theodore Géricault, painted the exotic and the scandalous.

Romantic writers, such as William Wordsworth, also focused on the beauty of nature, whether calm or dramatic. They also aligned the love of God with the love of nature, a religious focus in direct conflict with the logic of the Enlightenment and the deist belief in the uninvolved watchmaker view of God.

Romanticism also found expression in music—for example, Ludwig van Beethoven's driving, emotional pieces. Others, such as Hector Berlioz, showed the powerful nature of love.

Romanticism also left its mark on religion, both Catholicism and Protestantism. Especially through the work of François de Chateaubriand, Catholicism was linked to God through nature rather than doctrines and mandated beliefs. Protestantism also looked to a natural connection to God, one based on finding emotional intensity in everyday experiences.

Powerful forces behind the events during the first half of the nineteenth century, nationalism and liberalism continued to fuel political change during the second half. This was especially the case with unification in Germany and Italy and the continued fragmenting of the Austrian Empire. Socialism, begun by the utopian socialists, was further developed by the scientific socialists Karl Marx and Friedrich Engels, who adapted it to fit their analysis of the repercussions of the Industrial Revolution.

Content Review Questions

1. All of the following statements about the causes of the early nineteenth century revolutions are true EXCEPT
   (A) many of the ideologies of liberalism had their roots in the Enlightenment and were tied to middle-class men.
   (B) nationalism brought people together with ties of language, traditions, and customs.
   (C) conservatism encouraged people to revolt against Austria because they wanted to join the Metternich System.
   (D) the revolutionaries wanted to become their own state.

2. Which of the following statements about the Quadruple Alliance is true?
   (A) A major purpose of the Quadruple Alliance was to enforce liberal economic policies across Europe.
   (B) The Quadruple Alliance was also known as the Concert of Europe.
   (C) In reaction to the formation of the Quadruple Alliance, Napoleon abdicated as emperor of France.
   (D) The Quadruple Alliance ended with the meeting of the Congress of Vienna.

3. The importance of the principle of legitimacy to conservatives is shown in all of the following statements EXCEPT
   (A) the Decembrist Revolt put Alexander I on the Russian throne.
   (B) a Bourbon was returned to the French throne.
   (C) after the removal of Napoleon, the rightful king of Spain was returned to his throne.
   (D) Austria forced the return of monarchs to Italy.

4. Although the Quadruple Alliance was concerned with revolutions occurring across Europe, its members did support the Greek revolt during the 1830s because
   (A) Greece was fighting the Russians, who were quite powerful in Eastern Europe and thus a major threat to the alliance.
   (B) the Quadruple Alliance was more concerned with removing a foreign power from Europe than worrying about the success of a European revolt.
   (C) the Greeks were no threat to the other European powers and they could easily be made a part of the Austrian Empire.
   (D) Greece was a colony of Italy, one of the members of the alliance.

5. The conflict in the Frankfurt Assembly between those who favored a policy of *Grossdeutsch* and those who favored *Kleindeutsch* was settled when
   (A) Metternich freed the Prussian state.
   (B) the Austrians did not join the move to create a united Germany.
   (C) the Russians invaded Prussia, removing the Prussian king.
   (D) a constitution was established and created a balance between both sides.

6. Three of the major revolts in the 1830s, in Italy, Poland, and Belgium, had which fact or outcome in common?
   (A) All three countries lost a bid to create a constitutional government.
   (B) Each of the three countries had just been taken over by one of the German states; they were fighting against those states.
   (C) These three western European countries were fighting against Eastern European powers.
   (D) Italy, Poland, and Belgium all fought for independence from a neighboring power.

7. Utopian socialists advocated all of the following EXCEPT
   (A) overthrowing the owners of factories.
   (B) following Christian principles to create an ideal socialist society.
   (C) organizing workers into workshops.
   (D) building communities for workers where work was decided by personality type and rotated to keep it more interesting.

8. All of the following describe nineteenth-century liberalism EXCEPT
   (A) liberalism focused on the basic rights of people.
   (B) businesses should be free of any government interference.
   (C) the feeling of unity that came from liberalism had its roots in common languages.
   (D) liberals generally supported constitutional governments.

9. All of the following statements about the July Revolution are true EXCEPT
   (A) Charles X was overthrown.
   (B) revolutionaries used barricades to protect themselves from government forces.
   (C) Louis-Phillippe came to power because of the support of the upper middle class.
   (D) the revolution took place in France against Louis XVI.

10. In response to the first revolts against the Concert of Europe during the 1820s,
   (A) Austrian and French troops quelled the revolts.
   (B) the Concert of Europe decided not to waste its time or resources in stopping them and, thus, they were successful.
   (C) the Concert did very little and therefore the Italian revolt was successful; however, the Spanish revolt was not.
   (D) Britain sent troops, including a large naval force, to stop a large German revolt.

Multiple-Choice Questions

Questions 1–3 refer to the following image.

Source: Erich Lessing/Art Resource, NY

1. Which statement best describes the painting?
   (A) It is clearly Romantic because it shows the power of God.
   (B) As a Gothic painting, it refers back to the Middle Ages.
   (C) It is a weak representation of Romanticisim in that it shows neither love nor reference to emotion.
   (D) Through its clear reference to an exotic scene from the past, it is Romantic.

2. Romantic style art often can be seen as
   (A) a reaction against the logic and reason of the Neoclassical art of the Enlightenment Period.
   (B) a celebration of the progress made by the Industrial Revolution.
   (C) anger at revolts and revolutions.
   (D) a reaction against the Catholic Church.

3. The artist who painted the work pictured on the previous page would most likely agree with the philosophy of
   (A) Chateaubriand's nature poetry.
   (B) supernatural works like Mary Shelley's Frankenstein.
   (C) depictions of nationalistic fervor and exotic foreign lands by Lord Byron.
   (D) scientific progress such as that made by Sir Isaac Newton.

Questions 4–6 refer to the following map.

Source: © Cengage Learning

4. According to the map shown on the previous page
    (A) the majority of the revolts of 1848 occurred in France and Italy.
    (B) the Austrian Empire suffered more from revolts than all the rest of Europe combined.
    (C) revolts were common in England, Spain, and Russia.
    (D) the German Confederation was a hotbed of revolt and revolution.

5. A major reason for the trend identified in the map is
    (A) political freedom made it easy for people to rebel.
    (B) the desire of Germanic people to have more of a say in their governments.
    (C) France, as it had done before under Napoleon, ruled much of Europe.
    (D) due to the Enlightenment ideal of equality, serfs rebelled in Eastern and Central Europe.

6. All of the following were immediate repercussions of the revolutions of 1848 EXCEPT
    (A) the failure of some revolts because of a lack of coordination among the revolutionary groups.
    (B) Italian states gained total independence from the control of Austria.
    (C) suffrage was extended to the working classes of France.
    (D) the Czechs and other nationalities in the Austrian Empire were squashed by not only Austrian armies but also the intervention of Russia.

Short-Answer Questions

Source: © The Art Gallery Collection/Alamy   Source: © National Gallery, London/Art Resource, NY

1. Referring to the paintings on the previous page, answer A, B, and C.
   A) Briefly explain TWO aspects of Romantic style seen in Friedrich's *The Wanderer Above the Sea of Fog* and Turner's *Rain, Steam, and Speed—the Great Western Railway.*
   B) Briefly explain a third aspect of Romantic style that is NOT seen in the paintings.
   C) Briefly explain how the paintings differed from the artistic style that preceded them, the Neoclassical style.

2. Answer A, B, and C based on the following excerpt.

   Those who share in this spirit have then quite another tendency in their student life, Love of Fatherland is their guiding principle. Their purpose is to make a better future for the Fatherland, each as best he can, to spread national consciousness, or to use the much ridiculed and maligned Germanic expression, more folkishness, and to work for better constitutions....

   We want more sense of community among the several states of Germany, greater unity in their policies and in their principles of government; no separate policy for each state, but the nearest possible relations with one another; above all, we want Germany to be considered one land and the German people one people. In the forms of our student comradeship we show how we want to approach this as nearly as possible in the real world. Regional fraternities are forbidden, and we live in a German comradeship, one people in spirit, as we want it for all Germany in reality. We give ourselves the freest of constitutions, just as we should like Germany to have the freest possible one, insofar as that is suitable for the German people. We want a constitution for the people that fits in with the spirit of the times and with the people's own level of enlightenment, rather than what each prince gives his people according to what he likes and what serves his private interest. Above all, we want the princes to understand and to follow the principle that they exist for the country and not the country for them. In fact, the prevailing view is that the constitution should not come from the individual states at all. The main principles of the German constitution should apply to all states in common, and should be expressed by the German federal assembly. This constitution should deal not only with the absolute necessities, like fiscal administration and justice, general administration and church and military affairs and so on; this constitution ought to be extended to the education of the young, at least at the upper age levels, and to many other such things.

   Source: M. Walker, ed., *Metternich's Europe* (London: Walker & Co, 1968).

   A) Briefly explain TWO demands being made by the German students' unions.
   B) In what way does this excerpt highlight an aspect of nationalism?
   C) What is von Gagern's point of view, and how does it contribute to his reason for writing this excerpt?

Long-Essay Questions

1. In what ways did Romantic artists and composers break from classical artistic forms? What were the main influences on their works? (Historical Thinking Skills: Patterns of Continuity and Change Over Time, Causation)

2. Analyze the causes of two revolts in the first half of the nineteenth century. To what extent were they a result of the Concert of Europe? (Historical Thinking Skills: Causation)

Answers

Content Review Questions

1. **(C)** Systems were motivated by liberalism and nationalism, especially as many peoples wanted to create their own state. Those who were conservative, such as those who followed the ideas of Metternich, wished to keep the status quo and so would reject revolution (*Western Civilization*, 9th ed., pp. 634–35 / 10th ed., pp. 630–32; Historical Thinking Skills—Causation, Synthesis; Learning Objective SP-1, SP-4, SP-16, SP-17; Key Concept 3.4).

2. **(B)** The Quadruple Alliance, reaffirmed at the Congress of Vienna, was also known as the Concert of Europe. Its members—Britain, Russia, Austria, and Prussia—were concerned with stopping revolutions (*Western Civilization*, 9th ed., pp. 627–28 / 10th ed., p. 623; Historical Thinking Skills—Patterns of Continuity and Change Over Time; Learning Objective SP-1, SP-4, SP-16, SP-17; Key Concept 2.1, 3.4).

3. **(A)** The Decembrist Revolt occurred after the death of Alexander I (*Western Civilization*, 9th ed., pp. 625, 633–34 / 10th ed., pp. 621, 629–30; Historical Thinking Skills—Patterns of Continuity and Change Over Time, Periodization; Learning Objective SP-16, SP-17; Key Concept 3.4).

4. **(B)** The European powers were more concerned with removing a foreign power, the Ottoman Turks, from Europe than they were with stopping a revolt against that foreign power (*Western Civilization*, 9th ed., pp. 630–31 / 10th ed., pp. 625–27; Historical Thinking Skills—Causation, Analyzing Evidence: Content and Sourcing; Learning Objective SP-16, SP-17; Key Concept 3.4).

5. **(B)** The fight between those who **wanted** Austria to join a united German state and those who didn't ended when Austria chose not to join the movement (*Western Civilization*, 9th ed., p. 644 / 10th ed., p. 640; Historical Thinking Skills—Causation, Contextualization, Synthesis; Learning Objective SP-1, SP-4, SP-16, SP-17; Key Concept 3.4).

6. **(D)** Each of these countries fought for independence from a neighboring country in the 1830s: Italy from Austria, Poland from Russia, and Belgium from the Netherlands (*Western Civilization*, 9th ed., p. 639 / 10th ed., p. 635; Historical Thinking Skills—Causation, Comparison; Learning Objective SP-16, SP-17; Key Concept 3.4).

7. **(A)** The utopian socialists offered a wide variety of solutions to the problems of industrialization. However, they did not advocate the use of force (*Western Civilization*, 9th ed., p. 635 / 10th ed., p. 632; Historical Thinking Skills—Causation, Interpretation; Learning Objective SP-1, SP-4; Key Concept 3.1).

8. **(C)** Political liberals focused on the rights of all people. Economic liberals believed government should not be involved in the free flow of an economy. Answer C pertains to nationalism, not liberalism (*Western Civilization*, 9th ed., pp. 634–36 / 10th ed., pp. 630–32; Historical Thinking Skills—Analyzing Evidence: Content and Sourcing; Learning Objective SP-1, SP-4; Key Concept 3.3).

9. **(D)** The July Revolution took place in France in 1830. Charles X was replaced by his cousin Louis Philippe (*Western Civilization*, 9th ed., pp. 638–39 / 10th ed., pp. 634–35; Historical Thinking Skills—Causation; Learning Objective SP-1, SP-4; Key Concept 3.4).

10. **(A)** The first revolts against the Concert of Europe in Italy and Spain were stopped by troops from neighboring Austria and France (*Western Civilization*, 9th ed., pp. 627–28 / 10th ed., pp. 623–24; Historical Thinking Skills—Causation, Patterns of Continuity and Change Over Time; Learning Objective SP-16, SP-17; Key Concept 3.4).

MULTIPLE-CHOICE QUESTIONS

1. **(D)** As an exotic scene from the past based on a poem by the Romantic poet Lord Byron, this painting, *The Death of Sardanapalus*, by Delacroix, is a prime example of Romanticism (*Western Civilization*, 9th ed., pp. 652–53 / 10th ed., pp. 646–48; Historical Thinking Skills—Causation, Analyzing Evidence: Content and Sourcing; Learning Objective OS-10, OS-12; Key Concept 3.6).

2. **(A)** The Romantic style of Art was a reaction against the Enlightenment and Neoclassical art, which called for logic and reason, symmetry, and a reliance on Greek and Roman themes. Romantic style celebrated nature, not the mechanistic progress of the Industrial Revolution with its accompanying pollution. Romanticism also celebrated the nationalism of the revolts and revolutions of the 1820s through 1848, and it was part of a revival of Catholicism and other religious belief (*Western Civilization*, 9th ed., pp. 652–53 / 10th ed., pp. 646–48; Historical Thinking Skills—Causation, Contextualization, Analyzing Evidence: Content and Sourcing; Learning Objective OS-10, OS-12; Key Concept 3.6).

3. **(C)** This painting, *The Death of Sardanapalus* by Delacroix, depicts events of the Greek War for Independence and is based on a poem by Lord Byron who fought and died in that war (*Western Civilization*, 9th ed., pp. 652–53 / 10th ed., pp. 646–48; Historical Thinking Skills—Periodization, Contextualization, Analyzing Evidence: Content and Sourcing; Learning Objective OS-10, OS-12; Key Concept 3.6).

4. **(D)** The map shows the majority of revolutions occurring in the German Confederation. There were no revolts in England, Russia, or Spain in 1848 and only one in France (*Western Civilization*, 9th ed., pp. 641–46 / 10th ed., pp. 637–41; Historical Thinking Skills—Analyzing Evidence: Content and Sourcing; Learning Objective SP-4, SP-7, SP-11; Key Concept 3.4).

5. **(B)** Germans were concerned with the conservative nature of their governments and pushed for more liberalism, such as having a voice through more liberal constitutions, a free press, etc. (*Western Civilization*, 9th ed., pp. 641–46 / 10th ed., p. 640; Historical Thinking Skills—Causation, Contextualization, Analyzing Evidence: Content and Sourcing, Analyzing Evidence: Content and Sourcing; Learning Objective SP-4, SP-7, SP-11; Key Concept 3.4).

6. **(B)** Italian states were somewhat successful in pushing back against Austrian influence, but eventually Italian revolts were ended by Austria and the French support of the pope (*Western Civilization*, 9th ed., pp. 641–46 / 10th ed., pp. 637–41; Historical Thinking Skills—Causation, Contextualization; Learning Objective SP-4, SP-7, SP-11; Key Concept 3.4).

SHORT-ANSWER QUESTIONS

1. Part A of the question asks you to look at two Romantic-style paintings and explain what aspects of Romanticism are seen in them. You could mention the overwhelming power of nature seen in *The Wanderer* or the impact of industrialization in *Rain, Steam, and Speed*. Both paintings are also asymmetrical and show much emotion.

   Part B: One aspect of Romanticism NOT seen in these paintings is nationalism. Part C: The Neoclassical style, as opposed to the style of above paintings, lacked emotion, was rigidly symmetrical, often showed Greek or Roman themes, and was influenced by the logic and reason of the Enlightenment.
   (*Western Civilization*, 9th ed., pp. 651–53 / 10th ed., pp. 646–48; Historical Thinking Skills—Patterns of Continuity and Change Over Time, Historical Argumentation, Analyzing Evidence: Con-tent and Sourcing; Analyzing Evidence: Content and Sourcing, Synthesis; Learning Objective OS-10, OS-12; Key Concept 3.6)

2. The German student unions, as discussed in the excerpt by Von Gagern, wanted a constitution for a unified Germany. They wanted education policies as well as monetary, religious, and military policy to be overseen by this new unified government. One of the prime beliefs of nationalists was in unifying lands where people were of the same ethnic group, in this case all Germans. As a student, Von Gagern's point of view would be influenced by his wish to have a

good education. He wrote this letter to his father to explain his reasons for joining this student group. Presumably, his father is paying for his schooling and therefore he needs to stay in his father's good graces for continued financial support.
(*Western Civilization*, 9th ed., pp. 632–33 / 10th ed., pp. 628–29; Historical Thinking Skills—Historical Argumentation, Analyzing Evidence: Content and Sourcing; Synthesis; Learning Objective SP-11, SP-17; Key Concept 3.4)

LONG-ESSAY QUESTIONS

1. You should begin your essay with a quick overview of the Neo-classical style of art that came before this time period, explaining how it was influenced by the Scientific Revolution and Enlightenment. You could bring in an example or two to illustrate your point (David's *Death of Marat or The Oath of the Horatii*). Your next paragraph should be about the ideals of the Romantic period, showing how they differed from the Neoclassical—emphasis on religion, nationalism, nature, and emotion—with specific examples of each. Discussion of the influence of the nationalistic revolts of the 1820s, 1830s, and 1848, of the Industrial Revolution, and the rebellion against the logic of the preceding period could be written in a separate paragraph or embedded within your discussion of the artworks themselves. Be sure to add a brief (2-3 sentences) synthesis discussion to your essay. For this essay, you could compare Romantic artists with Baroque artists in their break from classical art forms.
   (*Western Civilization*, 9th ed., pp. 651–53 / 10th ed., pp. 646–49; Historical Thinking Skills—Patterns of Continuity and Change Over Time, Causation; Learning Objective OS-8, OS-10, OS-11, OS-12, OS-13; Key Concept 3.6)

2. Begin by giving some brief background on the precedent set by the French Revolution of 1789 and the takeover of much of Europe by Napoleon in encouraging revolutions in the nineteenth century. A paragraph on the Congress of Vienna Treaty and its goals is a must. To talk about the revolts, organize your essay in chrono-logical order, emphasizing Causation, liberalism, and nationalism as you write. Remember that you need to talk about only TWO revolts, but you need to bring in as much detail as possible about them and link them back to the Concert of Europe. Be sure to add a brief (2-3 sentences) synthesis discussion to your essay. For this essay, you could compare the early nineteenth century revolts to the revolts against Soviet control in the late twentieth century.
   (*Western Civilization*, 9th ed., pp. 625–46 / 10th ed., pp. 621–42; Historical Thinking Skill—Causation Causation; Learning Objective SP-16, SP-17; Key Concept 3.4)

11

THE AGE OF REALISM: 1850–1871

The failure of the popular revolts of 1848 prompted authoritarian governments across Europe to engage in a pragmatic form of decision making called *Realpolitik*. Between 1850 and 1871, new leaders used a realistic approach to nation building, which included the acceptance of differing degrees of liberal reform. Realism was also evident in the world of science as scientific knowledge was used to solve social problems. The fields of art and literature were also influenced by Realism; in their works, painters and novelists examined the everyday life of ordinary people.

KEY TERMS

Ausgleich	organic evolution
Austro-Prussian War	pasteurization
Austro-Sardinian War	populism
bourgeoisie	proletariat
The Communist Manifesto	Realism
Crimean War	*Realpolitik*
dual monarchy	Red Shirts
Franco-Prussian War	Reform Act of 1867
joint-stock investment bank	Second Empire
materialism	Victorian Age
mir	*zemstvos*
natural selection	*Zollverein*

CHAPTER KEY CONCEPTS

- After putting down the revolutions of 1848, authoritarian forces reasserted themselves across Europe, engaging in nation building and liberal reform on their own terms.

287

- The industrial innovations first introduced in Britain in the early nineteenth century now spread across the Continent, increasing industrial output and economic prosperity.
- In response to the long hours and poor working conditions that emerged as a result of industrialization, workers organized. Significant change did not occur, however, until socialist parties and socialist trade unions, based upon the ideas of Karl Marx, appeared after 1870.
- Realism dominated the worlds of art and literature as proponents rejected Romanticism in favor of depictions of everyday life and ordinary people.

For a full discussion of this period, see *Western Civilization*, 9th and 10th editions, Chapter 22.

NATION BUILDING AND REFORM

New conservative leaders including Otto von Bismarck and Count Camillo di Cavour came to power after 1850, marking the beginning of a period of authoritarian rule. Yet many of these leaders used liberalism to secure power. In addition, the balance of power across Europe was dramatically transformed as new nations emerged during the second half of the nineteenth century.

FRANCE AND THE SECOND EMPIRE

The events of 1848 led to the election of Louis Napoleon as president of the Second French Republic. Louis Napoleon wanted to dominate the French government, so in 1851 he seized control of the National Assembly, and then asked the French people to allow him to serve in office for a ten-year term. His overwhelming victory in 1851 influenced his decision to create a new French empire. Again the French people approved, and in 1852 Louis Napoleon became Napoleon III. The Second Empire was born.

As emperor of France, Napoleon III served as a model for other authoritarian rulers at that time. Although he maintained control over the vital functions of the government, the French people acceded to that, because he also introduced many domestic policies that were beneficial to the economic and social welfare of the nation. During the early part of his rule, he helped industrialize France, bringing great prosperity to the nation. One of his major achievements was the redesign of Paris, and with the guidance of Baron Haussmann, he oversaw the creation of a modern infrastructure that advanced public health, thwarted insurrections, and improved aesthetics.

THE END OF THE CONCERT OF EUROPE

Napoleon III was eager to reestablish France as the dominant force in Europe. By mid-century it had become apparent that the Ottoman Empire was disintegrating. The question then became which European nation would benefit the most from the decline of the Ottomans. All of the European powers—but especially Russia and Austria—had interests in the territories. France and Britain were afraid of Russian advances in southeastern Europe, so they supported the Ottoman Empire after it declared war on Russia in 1853.

The ensuing Crimean War was a military disaster, with substantial losses for all sides. More than 250,000 soldiers died, with over 60 percent of the soldiers succumbing to disease; the only positive outcome of the conflict was the recognition of professional nurses under the leadership of Florence Nightingale. Combined French and British forces laid siege to the Russian fortress at Sevastopol, which fell in 1855. The Treaty of Paris, signed in 1856, served to bring an end to the Concert of Europe as Austria and Russia, former allies, now became enemies. Russia's defeat led to its retreat from European affairs and altered the balance of power.

ITALIAN UNIFICATION

Attempts at revolution had been made in the Italian states since the 1830s; all met with defeat. Italian nationalists under the leadership of Mazzini and his *risorgimento* had gained support but failed to overthrow the influence of Austria and France. The tide began to change with the appointment of Count Cavour as prime minister of Piedmont. Cavour was a wealthy nobleman who advocated a constitutional government. In 1859, he struck a deal with Napoleon III, gaining French military support in order to drive the Austrians out of Italy, in return for granting the French Nice and Savoy. The French fought two battles with the Austrians, then bowed out of the war. Although Cavour did not gain all the territory he sought, the fighting gave rise to nationalist movements throughout northern Italy. These eventually came together under the leadership of Piedmont and Count Cavour.

In southern Italy, Giuseppe Garibaldi led his Red Shirts against the Bourbon king of the Two Sicilies. Fighting against great odds, Garibaldi's bold leadership proved victorious. As the Red Shirts prepared to march up the Italian peninsula, Count Cavour intervened so as to prevent war with France, which had been protecting Rome since the failed revolution of 1848. The Piedmontese army invaded the Papal States and Naples, prompting a confrontation with Garibaldi and his Red Shirts. Garibaldi accepted the rule of the Piedmontese under the leadership of King Victor Emmanuel II, and the kingdom of Italy was declared in 1861. With help from Prussia, Italy was able to finalize its territorial conquest by gaining Venetia from Austria and Rome from France. Thus, in 1870, a new united Italian state was complete.

GERMAN UNIFICATION

After the failure of the Frankfort Assembly in 1848, Prussia used economic tactics to help establish German unity. By 1853, all of the German states other than Austria had joined a customs union called the *Zollverein*. Economic progress was achieved by eliminating tolls on trade routes between member states. A growing middle class was given more voice in the Prussian constitution, yet power remained firmly in the hands of the king. When middle-class liberals challenged the growing influence of the Prussian military, King William I appointed Otto von Bismarck chancellor in hopes of containing liberal dissent.

Bismarck's reign as chancellor proved vitally important to the fate of not only Germany but Europe as well. A dominating force, Bismarck practiced *Realpolitik*, in which political decisions are based on everyday realities—such as the growing political power of the labor movement—rather than ethics or morality. In practice, this meant allowing his enemies certain victories as long as the overall political advantage remained on the side of Prussia. Bismarck chose to launch an aggressive foreign policy as a way to distract liberals upset with the military's involvement in domestic affairs.

Under Bismarck's leadership, Prussia was involved in three wars that eventually led to a unified Germany. Prussia's victory over Denmark (1864) served as a precursor to the Austro-Prussian War (1866). Prussian military superiority brought victory to Bismarck, allowing him to negotiate Prussian dominance over German affairs. Bismarck's military victories gained him liberal support and created a sense of nationalism that furthered his plans for a new German government controlled by Prussia.

THE FRANCO-PRUSSIAN WAR

The growth of Prussia as a European power inevitably led to conflict with France. Napoleon III grew wary of Prussian maneuvering in Germany and saw a confrontation as a way to bolster his sagging popularity at home. Meanwhile, Bismarck cleverly edited a diplomatic telegram, the "Ems Dispatch," to make it especially insulting to the French, thus goading Napoleon III into declaring war against Prussia in July 1870.

The French army proved no match for the very well trained Prussian armies. The French army, including Napoleon III, was captured at the Battle of Sedan. The Second French Empire subsequently fell, while the Prussian army laid siege to Paris. After four months, Paris surrendered, and a peace treaty was signed. France was forced to pay an indemnity and relinquish Alsace and Lorraine to the new German state.

By the end of the war, the southern German states agreed to join the North German Confederation. This was confirmed by the proclamation of William I as emperor of the Second German Empire. Military victory brought German unification under Prussian leaders, who espoused militarism alongside authoritarian rule. Nationalism had won out over liberalism.

AP® Tip

The Franco-Prussian War had long-term implications for Europe. Not only did the war give rise to a new German state, but France's humiliation would prove a potent reason for the French people's dislike of Germany and contribute to France's overwhelming need for revenge. Also remember that the French removal of its troops from Rome during this war was the final step in Italian unification, making Rome the Italian capital.

THE AUSTRIAN EMPIRE

As was true elsewhere in Europe, industrialization brought not only economic change, but social change as well. In Austria, the rise of an urban proletariat served to challenge the autocratic rule of the

Habsburgs. Military defeat in Italy and, later, Prussia forced great changes on the Austrian empire. The Compromise of 1867 created the Dual Monarchy of Austria–Hungary, with each part of the empire receiving its own constitutional government under a single monarch, Francis Joseph. The compromise did very little to satisfy the desires of the ethnic nationalities whose members remained under the power of the ethnic Germans and Magyars.

IMPERIAL RUSSIA

Russia's defeat in the Crimean War highlighted the need for greater reform—it was obvious to the tsar and the conservative leadership that Russia was falling drastically behind the western European powers. Tsar Alexander II attempted to address the deficiencies of the Russian system. One of the first reforms was the abolition of serfdom in 1861. Later, in 1864, Alexander II created local assemblies called *zemstvos*, which allowed for limited self-government.

Reformers in Russia demanded further change as the number of radical groups increased in number. Violence against Russian officials grew more frequent, culminating in the assassination of Alexander II by members of the People's Will. Convinced Alexander's death resulted from reform measures he had made, his son and successor, Alexander III, turned back to the repressive rule associated with autocratic Russia.

VICTORIAN ENGLAND

Great Britain did not face the same degree of social and political turbulence as much of continental Europe. In part this was a result of the Reform Act of 1832, which gave political representation to the middle class. The Victorian Age was noted for its middle-class prosperity, which ushered in a period of national pride associated with the reign of Queen Victoria. Not every social group expressed satisfaction with the political situation, however; members of the working class demanded the franchise for themselves, too. This goal was achieved through the Reform Act of 1867, which extended voting rights to urban working-class males.

During much of the Victorian era, British politics were dominated by two politicians: Liberal Party Prime Minister William Gladstone and his Conservative Party counterpart, Benjamin Disraeli. Both parties used reform to attract new voters. Disraeli was responsible for the Reform Act of 1867, while Gladstone and the Liberal Party took credit for policies that opened the doors to civil service employment.

[Handwritten margin notes: Reform act of 1832 — political representation to ~~working~~ middleclass; Reform act of 1867 — voting rights to urban working-class males]

INDUSTRIALIZATION AND ITS CRITICS

As industrialization spread across Europe, many nations experienced considerable economic growth. Great Britain's growth began with its textile industry; the Continent's growth began with railroads. The rail industry, in turn, stimulated growth in iron and coal. Governments also helped encourage economic growth by eliminating trade barriers and promoting financial institutions that could provide the necessary capital for industrial growth.

the Communist manifesto

MARX AND ENGELS

As industrialization swept across Europe, critics of capitalism became more vocal. None were more influential than Karl Marx and Friedrich Engels. Marx, a journalist, was forced to leave Germany after his newspaper was suppressed. While in Paris he met Engels, the son of a wealthy cotton manufacturer and author of *The Conditions of the Working Class in England,* an exposé of industrial life. Marx and Engels collaborated on a treatise to promote a radical working-class movement. *The Communist Manifesto* was intended to stir workers into unified action. The proletariat, they wrote, would engage in a class struggle with bourgeois society in which the workers would prevail and form a classless society. Unlike socialists, communists did not believe that social change was possible within the framework of a democratic capitalist state.

THE FIRST INTERNATIONAL

After the publication of the *Communist Manifesto* in 1848, Marx devoted the rest of his life to developing his ideas concerning history and society. *Das Kapital* examined the foundations of modern political economy. But many of his ideas never found a large audience because his all-consuming efforts to organize the working class left little time for writing. In 1864, he helped establish the International Working Men's Association, or "First International," which promoted the interests of the leading working-class organizations of the time. Dissension among member groups proved the undoing of the First International, and soon Marx's ideas were taken up by national socialist political parties across Europe that advocated planned economies rather than working-class revolution.

SCIENCE AND CULTURE

Science and the arts underwent significant transformations between the years 1850 and 1871. Rapid changes in the world of science led to a great expansion of scientific knowledge and a challenge to accepted Western worldviews. In the world of art, Romanticism gave way to Realism, as writers and artists set out to show ordinary life in the world around them.

SCIENTIFIC ADVANCES

Scientific knowledge had been growing since the advent of the Scientific Revolution. Those discoveries, however, remained in the realm of the scientific community and of little practical consequence to the general public. By the mid-nineteenth century, however, the general public was more aware of the expansion of scientific knowledge, as discoveries with more practical applications were made. Advances in thermodynamics influenced inventions such as the electric generator, while discoveries by Louis Pasteur led to advances in public health. Indeed, scientific progress led some to believe that all truth lay in the realm of science and the natural world rather than the spiritual world. The influence of scientists and intellectuals gave rise to a secularization of European society that was reflected in the acceptance of materialism as the overarching worldview of the period. Truth was to be found in the concrete material existence of human beings rather than the spirituality of the church or the emotionalism of the Romantics.

CHARLES DARWIN AND THE THEORY OF EVOLUTION

Scion of an upper-class British family, Charles Darwin was interested in geology and biology. In 1831, he joined a Royal Navy expedition as a naturalist. Over the five years the H.M.S. *Beagle* sailed around the world, Darwin studied plant and animal life on islands that had not been touched by humans. His observations led to his theory of evolution through the principle of natural selection, which he laid out in *On the Origin of Species by Means of Natural Selection* (1859).

Darwin's research while traveling in South America and the South Pacific gave him evidence that plants and animals evolve over a period of time from simpler life forms. Darwin was influenced by the thinking of Thomas Malthus, who held that all species were engaged in a struggle for existence, the result of the population's growing faster than the food supply. Darwin expanded on that notion, believing that individuals can succeed in the struggle for existence only by adapting to their environment through chance variants, in a process called natural selection. Initially, Darwin's ideas were concerned with plant and animal species, but with the publication of *The Descent of Man* in 1871, his arguments dealt with the animal origins of human beings. That unleashed tremendous controversy within European society. Many were troubled by Darwin's direct challenge to the Bible's creation story and the implication that humans are ordinary products of nature rather than exalted beings.

AP® Tip

The AP® exam often features questions concerning the repercussions of Darwin's ideas. Although many people were distraught over the implications of Darwin's theories, some, such as Herbert Spencer, created their own theories based on Darwin's notions of natural selection. Spencer's ideas gave rise to Social Darwinism, which used Darwin's theories—incorrectly—to justify a range of political, social, and economic policies. In particular, the phrase "survival of the fittest" was well suited to the growing aggressiveness of the modern industrial economy.

HEALTH CARE

Breakthroughs in the natural sciences during the nineteenth century significantly influenced advances in health care during the period. Perhaps the most important work was performed by French chemist Louis Pasteur, who by 1857 was able to prove the link between microorganisms and disease. Like many of the scientific discoveries made at that time, this one spurred practical applications put into effect by governments and industry. For instance, the wine industry first used pasteurization to keep its wine from spoiling. Later, Pasteur's experiments with microorganisms led to the common acceptance of many types of vaccinations.

SOCIOLOGY

As the role of science grew in importance during the nineteenth century, researchers began to apply scientific principles to other fields. One such area was the study of society. French researcher Auguste Comte examined society through the use of scientific methods and discovered general laws pertaining to social interaction. His ideas eventually gave birth to the field of sociology, which would gain widespread popularity by the end of the century.

LITERATURE

By mid-century, the literary world embraced the concept of materialism, which had also influenced the scientific community. Novelists turned to the realities of everyday life as subject matter for their works. Romanticism was rejected by authors who sought to find truth through accurate depictions of the common man rather than a romantic hero. Novelists of the Realist movement avoided the ornate and flowery language popularized by the Romantics in favor of representative dialects. For example, French author Gustave Flaubert accurately depicted small-town France in *Madame Bovary* (1857). British Realists William Thackeray and Charles Dickens likewise attempted to distance themselves from the Romantic style, offering true-to-life depictions of the middle and lower classes.

Show what real life is like

ART

As was the trend in the literary world, by the mid-nineteenth century many visual artists had rejected Romanticism in favor of the gritty motifs of Realism. French painters Gustave Courbet and Jean-François Millet showed people engaged in everyday activities. This represented a radical departure from the accepted subject matter of traditional art. Courbet depicted the dreary existence of workers and rural peasants as they engaged in mundane activities. Millet's most famous work, *The Gleaners*, depicts three peasant women gathering grain. Showing the connection between humans and nature, Millet was criticized for his crude subject matter. Taking cues from the Realists, later artists continued to challenge artistic norms, leading the world of art to entirely new directions.

The period between 1850 and 1871 witnessed the spread of industrialization across much of Europe, bringing prosperity to many Europeans for the first time. The failure of the revolutions of 1848 brought to power a new breed of conservative leaders who practiced *Realpolitik* to achieve their goals. In addition, scientific and technological breakthroughs provided Europeans with an unwavering faith in progress. National pride accompanied this sense of optimism, continuing to influence European behavior into the next century.

Content Review Questions

1. All of the following statements about the Crimean War are true EXCEPT
   (A) war broke out when Russia demanded the right to protect Christian shrines in Palestine.
   (B) France and Britain declared war on Russia in order to protect the balance of power in Europe.
   (C) Russia allied with the Ottoman Empire in order to prevent French and British control of the Dardanelles.
   (D) a majority of the deaths came from disease rather than the battlefield.

2. Which of the following accurately represents the "Eastern Question"?
   (A) Why is Eastern Europe less modernized than Western Europe?
   (B) Who would benefit most from the industrialization of Eastern Europe?
   (C) Who would benefit most from the disintegration of the Ottoman Empire?
   (D) Which European nation will be able to establish the most lucrative spheres of influence in China?

3. What was Garibaldi's reaction to Cavour's invasion of Naples?
   (A) Garibaldi ordered his Red Shirts to lay down their arms rather than engage in civil war.
   (B) Garibaldi quickly formed an alliance with France and attacked Cavour's forces.
   (C) Garibaldi turned to Bismarck and the Prussians for assistance.
   (D) Garibaldi surrendered on the condition that he become the prime minister of a united Italy.

4. How did the Reform Act of 1867 influence the Liberal and Conservative parties of Great Britain?
   (A) Both political parties went after the women's vote.
   (B) Both political parties were forced to organize more effectively.
   (C) Both political parties sought the support of the monarchy.
   (D) Both political parties embraced socialism.

5. All of the following were outcomes of the Franco-Prussian War EXCEPT
   (A) the Second French Empire collapsed.
   (B) King William I became emperor of the Second German Empire.
   (C) leadership of the Second German Empire was dominated by the southern German states of Bavaria and Württemberg.
   (D) France gave up the provinces of Alsace and Lorraine.

6. As a result of the assassination of Alexander II
   (A) Russian serfs received their emancipation.
   (B) local assemblies called zemstvos were created.
   (C) Russia declared war on Austria.
   (D) Russia repressed all opposition to autocratic rule.

7. According to Karl Marx, the ultimate goal of society was
   (A) the creation of a permanent dictatorship to rule over the people.
   (B) the creation of a classless society.
   (C) the creation of labor unions to promote the welfare of the working class.
   (D) the creation of a society in which the government would encourage private charity for the poor through churches and other religious organizations.

8. Charles Darwin's theories of evolution and natural selection were controversial because
   (A) they directly contradicted the ideas of Karl Marx.
   (B) they were viewed as promoting political revolution.
   (C) the theories suggested that human beings evolved from earlier and simpler forms of life.
   (D) the theories directly criticized organized religion.

9. As a result of the Compromise of 1867, Austria and Hungary
   (A) had a shared monarchy.
   (B) had a shared capital.
   (C) had separate armies.
   (D) had a shared constitution.

10. All of the following were important changes and discoveries in the field of medicine in the mid to late nineteenth century EXCEPT
    (A) the development of vaccines for rabies, diphtheria, typhoid fever, cholera, and plague.
    (B) bacterial discoveries that led to greater emphasis on preventive measures such as improved purification of water supplies.
    (C) the development disinfectants to eliminate infections during surgery.
    (D) the discovery of the use of antibiotics to treat bacterial infections.

Multiple-Choice Questions

Questions 1–3 refer to the following image.

Source: Erich Lessing/Art Resource, NY

1. The painting above represents which of the following movements?
   (A) Romanticism
   (B) Impressionism
   (C) Realism
   (D) Post-Impressionism

2. Based on the picture above, all of the following would be characteristics of Realism EXCEPT
   (A) a desire to depict the everyday life of ordinary people.
   (B) an emphasis on imagination and emotion.
   (C) an attempt at photographic imitation.
   (D) an interest in the natural environment.

3. The emergence of Realism stemmed largely from which of the following?
   (A) The materialistic outlook of mid-nineteenth-century society
   (B) The desire of artists to compete with the new field of photography that was just emerging
   (C) The romantic outlook of mid-nineteenth-century society
   (D) The desire to portray heroic figures in their art

Questions 4–6 refer to the following map.

Source: © Cengage Learning

4. Which of the following events indirectly led to the completion of Italian unification?
   (A) The Crimean War
   (B) The Greek Revolt
   (C) The foundation of the Second French Empire
   (D) The wars of German unification

5. By 1850, which of the following had played a significant role in unifying the Italian peninsula?
   (A) Metternich
   (B) Napoleon
   (C) Mazzini
   (D) Wilhelm I

6. All of the following contributed to the Kingdom of Piedmont's leading role in Italian unification EXCEPT
   (A) its entry into the Crimean War on the side of the allies.
   (B) King Victor Emmanuel II's appointment of Cavour as prime minister.
   (C) its alliance with Austria.
   (D) its economic and industrial expansion.

Short-Answer Questions

1. Answer A, B, and C by analyzing the revolution in health care that occurred in the second half of the nineteenth century.
   A) Briefly explain ONE discovery that significantly impacted the medical field in the late nineteenth century.
   B) Provide an explanation of ONE medical practice that was related to the discovery in A.
   C) Briefly explain ONE way that new medical knowledge spread in the late nineteenth century.

2. Compare and contrast the policies of Benjamin Disraeli and William Gladstone, then answer A, B, and C.
   A) Briefly explain one policy supported by Prime Minister Benjamin Disraeli.
   B) Briefly explain one policy supported by Prime Minster William Gladstone.
   C) Briefly compare the overall impact of the policies of Disraeli and Gladstone.

Long-Essay Questions

1. Compare and contrast the unification processes of nineteenth-century Italy and Germany. (Historical Thinking Skills: Comparison)

2. Analyze the concept of *Realpolitik* as it was practiced in Europe between 1850 and 1871. (Historical Thinking Skills: Contextualization, Comparison)

Answers

CONTENT REVIEW QUESTIONS

1. **(C)** Russia fought against the combined forces of France, Britain, and the Ottoman Empire (*Western Civilization*, 9th ed., pp. 661–62 / 10th ed., pp. 656–58; Historical Thinking Skills—Causation; Learning Objectives SP-13, SP-14, SP-17; Key Concept 3.3, 3.5, 3.6.

2. **(C)** The Eastern Question addressed the issue of the consequences of the weakness of the Ottoman Empire, asking who would benefit most from the disintegration of the empire. Rivalries created by the Eastern Question contributed to the outbreak of World War I. None of the other choices have anything to do with the Eastern Question (*Western Civilization*, 9th ed., pp. 660–61 / 10th ed., p. 656; Historical Thinking Skills—Contextualization; Learning Objectives SP-13, SP-14, SP-17; Key Concept 3.3, 3.5, 3.6).

3. **(A)** Garibaldi yielded to the forces from Piedmont, thus leading to the eventual unification of Italy (*Western Civilization*, 9th ed., pp. 664–65 / 10th ed., pp. 660–61; Historical Thinking Skills—Causation; Learning Objectives OS-12, SP-4, SP-7, SP-15, SP-17, SP-18; Key Concept 3.3, 3.4, 3.6).

4. **(B)** The Reform Act of 1867 increased the number of voters in Britain, which forced the leading political parties to organize more effectively in order to win support (*Western Civilization*, 9th ed., pp. 674–75 / 10th ed., p. 670; Historical Thinking Skills—Causation; Learning Objectives SP-7; Key Concept 3.3).

5. **(C)** The new German empire was dominated by Prussia and Otto von Bismarck (*Western Civilization*, 9th ed., pp. 668–69 / 10th ed., p. 664–65; Historical Thinking Skills—Causation; Learning Objectives OS-8; Key Concept 3.3).

6. **(D)** Alexander III viewed the reform efforts of his father, Alexander II, as a failure and a threat to Russian stability (*Western Civilization*, 9th ed., p. 673 / 10th ed., pp. 667–69; Historical Thinking Skills—Contextualization; Learning Objectives PP-12, OS-12, SP-4, SP-7, SP-15, SP-17, SP-18; Key Concept 3.3, 3.4, 3.6).

7. **(B)** Although choice A might look tempting, it is incorrect because Marx envisioned the creation of the dictatorship of the proletariat as a temporary means to reorganize production and redistribute wealth. After its job was done, Marx believed that this state would wither away and a classless society would emerge. Thus the emergence of a classless society is the correct answer (*Western Civilization*, 9th ed., pp. 679–80 / 10th ed., pp. 673–75; Historical Thinking Skills—Contextualization; Learning Objectives PP-12, OS-12, SP-4, SP-7, SP-15, SP-17, SP-18; Key Concept 3.3, 3.4, 3.6).

8. **(C)** Darwin's ideas pointed to a link between humans and other animals (*Western Civilization*, 9th ed., pp. 680–82 / 10th ed., pp. 676–77; Historical Thinking Skills—Causation; Learning Objectives OS-8; Key Concept 3.3).

9. **(A)** The Ausgleich, or Compromise of 1867, called for a shared monarchy, foreign policy, and army. Francis Joseph was emperor of Austria and king of Hungary (*Western Civilization*, 9th ed., p. 671 / 10th ed., p. 666; Historical Thinking Skills—Causation; Learning Objectives SP-7; Key Concept 3.4).

10. **(D)** All of the medical advances listed in choices A–C played a role in the modernization of medical treatment in the nineteenth century. Antibiotics were not discovered for medical use until the late 1920s (*Western Civilization*, 9th ed., pp. 682–84 / 10th ed., pp. 677–79; Historical Thinking Skills—Causation; Learning Objectives OS-8; Key Concept 3.3).

MULTIPLE-CHOICE QUESTIONS

1. **(C)** The work of Jean-Francois Millet represented the Realist artistic movement, with its depiction of the lives of ordinary people in everyday settings (*Western Civilization*, 9th ed., pp. 686–87 / 10th ed., pp. 680–82; Historical Thinking Skills—Contextualization; Learning Objectives OS-8; Key Concept 3.6).

2. **(B)** All of the choices are characteristics of Realism except the emphasis on imagination and emotion, which are attributes of Romanticism (*Western Civilization*, 9th ed., pp. 684–87 / 10th ed., pp. 680–82; Historical Thinking Skills—Contextualization; Learning Objectives OS-8; Key Concept 3.6).

3. **(A)** As materialism gained a following in nineteenth-century society, many artists desired to portray realistic subjects that actually existed, rather than spiritual figures that materialists believed did not even exist. The growing popularity of science and materialism in the mid-nineteenth-century in Europe shifted artists' attention from Romanticism to Realism (*Western Civilization*, 9th ed., pp. 684–87 / 10th ed., p. 680; Historical Thinking Skills—Contextualization; Learning Objectives OS-8; Key Concept 3.6).

4. **(D)** Although Italy was almost entirely unified by 1860, Venetia and Rome remained in foreign hands. Italy was an ally of Prussia. As a result of the Prussian victory in the Austro-Prussian War of 1866, Austria was forced to evacuate Venetia, and Prussia gave it to Italy. Rome was taken by Italy when the French were forced to pull their troops from Rome to help defend France during the Franco-Prussian war. Thus, the wars of German unification indirectly completed Italian unification (*Western Civilization*, 9th ed., pp. 663–70 / 10th ed., pp. 658–65; Historical Thinking Skills—Causation; Learning Objectives OS-8; Key Concept 3.3).

5. **(C)** Mazzini was one of the early leaders of Italian unification; Napoleon and Metternich opposed Italian unification, while Wilhelm I did not come to power in Prussia until after the unification of Italy (*Western Civilization*, 9th ed., pp. 663–65 / 10th ed., pp. 640–41, 660; Historical Thinking Skills—Contextualization; Learning Objectives PP-12, OS-12, SP-4, SP-7, SP-15, SP-17, SP-18; Key Concept 3.3, 3.4, 3.6).

6. **(C)** The economic and industrial expansion of the Kingdom of Piedmont allowed Cavour to use the increasing revenues to equip a large army that he used to pursue unification. The kingdom's entry into the Crimean War helped prove to other European nations that it was an emerging national power, and it encouraged the French to form an alliance with Cavour, thus aiding the process of Italian unification under the Kingdom of Piedmont (*Western Civilization*, 9th ed., pp. 663–65 / 10th ed., pp. 659–61; Historical Thinking Skills—Contextualization; Learning Objectives PP-12, OS-12, SP-4, SP-7, SP-15, SP-17, SP-18; Key Concept 3.3, 3.4, 3.6).

SHORT-ANSWER QUESTIONS

1. A) One discovery that significantly impacted the medical field in the late nineteenth century was the germ theory of disease. Researchers including Pasteur and Koch discovered that specific microorganisms caused specific diseases, creating the field of study known as bacteriology. Pasteur first focused his efforts on organisms that cause food to spoil and then changed his focus to human medical inquiry, eventually developing a rabies vaccine. Koch discovered anthrax and tuberculosis bacteria and eventually matched 21 different bacteria to their diseases.

   B) As a result of the discovery of the role of bacteria in causing disease, new surgical practices were developed. Joseph Lister discovered that if a surgical room and instruments were treated with carbolic acid, germs that would otherwise have complicated surgeries by causing infections such as gangrene could be eliminated. This led other surgeons and scientists to continue investigating more ways to improve the cleanliness of surgery.

   C) One way that new medical knowledge spread in the late nineteenth century was through the institution of many new medical schools. These schools provided training for doctors and encouraged Europeans to pursue careers in the health care profession. Although standard curriculum requirements among the various medical schools did not exist for many decades, by the end of the nineteenth century a more standardized body of knowledge had begun to emerge and European and American doctors began to be better prepared to deal with medical problems faced by the public.
   (*Western Civilization*, 9th ed., pp. 682–84 / 10th ed., pp. 677–79; Historical Thinking Skills—Contextualization; Learning Objectives SP-10, IS-3; Key Concept 3.1)

2. A) One policy supported by Prime Minister Benjamin Disraeli was the extension of the vote to a greater number of British men. Although the Great Reform Bill of 1832 had increased the number of voting men in England, the vast majority of the population did not have a voice in government. As a conservative, Disraeli believed that reducing the monetary requirements for voting would provide support for conservative legislation, so he opened the vote to many male urban workers.

   B) One policy supported by Prime Minster William Gladstone was civil service legislation that opened government jobs only to those who passed competitive exams. This policy change virtually eliminated the spoils system and made government more transparent. The drive to make government more honest also involved the introduction of secret ballots for voting and the abolition of the practice of selling military commissions.

   C) The overall impact of the policies of Disraeli and Gladstone was to extend democratic participation to a greater number of men in England and make government more accountable to the people. Although Disraeli was a conservative and Gladstone

was a liberal, both Victorian prime ministers led England on a path to reform and modernized the British government.
(*Western Civilization*, 9th ed., pp. 673–75 / 10th ed., p. 670; Historical Thinking Skills—Comparison; Learning Objectives SP-4, SP-7, SP-9; Key Concept 3.3, 3.4)

LONG-ESSAY QUESTIONS

1. This is a straightforward analysis of German and Italian unification. With compare-and-contrast questions, it is necessary to look at similarities and differences. Nationalism, of course, played an important role in both unification movements. Both Bismarck of Prussia and Cavour of Piedmont exploited strong feelings of nationalism to rally support for unification under the domination of their respective regions. In both unification movements, regional differences had to be overcome. Bismarck achieved his goals by waging war against lesser opponents, such as Denmark and Austria. Prussian victory encouraged other German states to give their support to the Prussian leadership. Likewise, Count Cavour played a similar role in convincing other Italian states to support the kingdom of Piedmont. Both unification movements relied on strong personalities that overshadowed the monarchs. The differences between the unification movements include the fact that in Italy there was another dominant figure, Giuseppe Garibaldi. Unlike in Germany, in Italy the threat of civil war was a reality. Only the patriotism of Garibaldi kept Italian unification from falling apart. Another difference was that Prussia fought three major conflicts, including the Franco-Prussian War. Although Italy engaged in conflict against Austria, the unification movement relied greatly on the military assistance of France and Prussia. The unification of Italy did not influence Europe's balance of power in the same way German unification did. Although France was interested in Italy, it did not share the same concern with its own unification as it did with Germany's. This is reflected in the outbreak of the Franco-Prussian War. Be sure to add a brief (2–3 sentences) synthesis discussion to your essay. For this essay, you could compare German and Italian unification with the creation of the European Union.
(*Western Civilization*, 9th ed., pp. 663–69 / 10th ed., pp. 655, 658–65; Historical Thinking Skills—Comparison; Learning Objectives SP-7; Key Concept 3.4)

2. First it is necessary to define the term *Realpolitik*, which refers to the making of political decisions based on practical realities rather than theories or ethics. Many mid-nineteenth-century leaders practiced *Realpolitik* for various reasons. For leaders like Napoleon III of France or Otto von Bismarck of Germany, one of the most important reasons was the influence of liberalism on national politics. Revolutions that had occurred during the 1840s had been put down. Authoritarian leaders dominated many states in Europe. The new leaders, however, recognized the importance of running a government that was responsive to the needs of the population. Although initially reluctant to relinquish any power to an elected legislative body, Napoleon III nonetheless acted to help improve

the lives of the working class through the construction of hospitals and better housing. As the number of industrial workers grew, Napoleon III recognized the need to engage in further liberal reform.

Bismarck is considered the foremost practitioner of nineteenth-century Realpolitik. Most apparent was his keen understanding of the necessities regarding military conflict. He befriended whoever he thought would be useful in achieving his aims. For example, during the Danish War, Bismarck arranged to fight alongside Austria, with the intention of removing Austria from German affairs. Austria was forced to recognize Prussia as an equal, and soon faced Bismarck's forces on the battlefield, during the Austro-Prussian War. Finally, seizing the opportunity to achieve military victory over Prussia's great rival, Bismarck forced France into war against Prussia. The resounding success of the Prussian forces led to the unification of Germany under the leadership of Prussian King William I.

Other discussion items might include the actions of Tsar Alexander II of Russia. Although he maintained the autocratic tradition of imperial Russia, he also saw the practical advantages to emancipating the serfs and establishing the *zemstvos*. Even in Great Britain, both political parties understood the practical advantages of expanding voting rights through the Reform Act of 1867. Be sure to add a brief (2–3 sentences) synthesis discussion to your essay. For this essay, you could compare the Realpolitik of Napoleon III and Bismarck with Machiavelli's political thought in *The Prince*.

(*Western Civilization*, 9th ed., pp. 663–69 / 10th ed., pp. 654–58, 661–65; Historical Thinking Skills—Contextualization, Comparison; Learning Objectives SP-7; Key Concept 3.4)

12

THE "AGE OF PROGRESS": 1871–1894

In the second half of the nineteenth century, European society was transformed by the Second Industrial Revolution, which brought material prosperity that created a sense of optimism. Many believed that advances in science and technology would cure the problems that had plagued Europe for centuries. Along with the Second Industrial Revolution came the growth of mass society, and with that came mass politics. Many governments became responsive to the ideas of liberalism, including extending political democracy and suffrage to a greater number of adult males. Governments also became more involved in the lives of their citizens; this fostered the concept of national identity, which would play an important role in the following century.

KEY TERMS

anarchism	mass society
cartels	nationalities
depression	problem
emigration	Paris Commune
evolutionary socialism	plutocracy
Georges-Eugene Haussmann	revisionism
home rule	Second Industrial Revolution
Kulturkampf	Social Democratic Party (Germany)
Marxism	tariffs
mass education	Third Republic
mass leisure	tariffs
mass politics	the "Woman Question"

CHAPTER KEY CONCEPTS

- Political reforms led to the expansion of political democracy, with voting rights given to men throughout much of Europe. However, some European rulers resisted liberalism in order to maintain their power.
- Economic progress reached new heights during the Second Industrial Revolution. Breakthroughs in science and technology promoted new prosperity and an improved standard of living.
- The Age of Progress led to the emergence of mass society. Europeans witnessed transformations in social structures, gender roles, education, and leisure-time activities.

For a full discussion of the Second Industrial Revolution and the Age of Progress, see *Western Civilization*, 9th and 10th editions, Chapter 23.

INDUSTRIAL PROSPERITY

INDUSTRIAL GROWTH AND NEW PRODUCTS

The Second Industrial Revolution saw the invention of products that transformed not only industrial production, but also the world in which people lived. With the introduction of the Bessemer process in the 1860s, steel production increased tremendously. Soon steel was used in a variety of ways that influenced manufacturing. Transportation was also affected by the increased use of steel as shipping and railroad industries incorporated steel in designing improved products. Advances in electricity were also revolutionary. By the end of the century, European cities enjoyed the benefits and convenience of electricity, which served as the primary source of energy used in lighting, transportation, and factory work.

New technology led to increased industrial production, forcing manufacturers to look for new markets. As overseas markets became saturated, nations turned to consumers at home. A dramatic rise in population, coupled with an increase in national incomes, provided businesses with domestic markets for their goods. Prices on goods declined as businesses incorporated improved technology along with cheaper transportation costs. Through various methods, manufacturers stimulated consumer desire to own new products. The modern consumer economy was born.

Key to a strong national economy was the handling of foreign competition. Reliance on domestic markets led governments to enact protective tariffs that limited foreign competition. Furthermore, major industries formed cartels to control the perceived chaos associated with unbridled competition. In many countries, the steel, coal, and chemical industries worked together to stabilize the market by eliminating the competition.

By 1870, Germany had surpassed Great Britain as the leading industrial power of Europe. German industrialists were more open to innovation, and the German government encouraged the advancement of science and technology, fields that were vital to industry. British leaders, on the other hand, clung to the Victorian ideal of the amateur scientist. Not all of Europe experienced industrialization.

Some nations continued to have agriculturally based economies. However, technological advances encouraged overproduction, which led to falling prices. This situation benefited large farmers at the expense of the smaller farmers, who could not keep up with the advances in science and technology.

THE SECOND INDUSTRIAL REVOLUTION AND WOMEN

Changes associated with the Second Industrial Revolution created job opportunities for women. Prior to the 1870s, most women who sought employment performed piecework in sweatshops. After 1870, however, white-collar jobs became available to them. As they expanded, industry and government needed secretaries and salesclerks, jobs that were appealing because they allowed women to escape the drudgery of the sweatshops. Prostitution proliferated when rural working-class girls and women who settled in urban areas faced uncertain job prospects.

THE WORKING CLASSES

Trade unions emerged during the first half of the nineteenth century to help unemployed workers. In the second half of that century, industrial workers formed political parties and labor unions. In Germany, the German Social Democratic Party organized around the revolutionary ideals of Karl Marx, and by the eve of World War I, it was the largest party in Germany. Other European nations also had socialist political parties. Forming a loose association called the Second International, socialists all over Europe worked together for international action.

Progress was impeded by divisions among groups. Orthodox Marxists remained strictly tied to the ideals of Karl Marx, but evolutionary socialists pursued a policy of revisionism, believing that Marxist thought needed to evolve with the times. Further, socialists had to contend with the rise of nationalism, which was widespread by the end of the nineteenth century. The conflict between the Marxist desire for international cooperation and fervent nationalism would come to a head at the outbreak of World War I, with nationalism becoming the clear choice of the masses.

During this period, radicals drifted away from Marxist socialism to the far more revolutionary anarchist movement. Led by extremists from across Europe, anarchists believed that traditional socialism was ill-suited to confront the capitalist system. They felt that only a movement dedicated to abolishing government could achieve a truly revolutionary society. As the century came to a close, anarchists turned to assassination as a tool to achieve their goals; despite the many prominent figures killed, revolution never materialized.

THE BIRTH OF MASS SOCIETY

Fueled by an increase in population and the overall prosperity of the Second Industrial Revolution, a new mass society emerged after 1870. In the process, social behavior changed dramatically. Once insular and focused only on local matters, Europeans began to take an interest in regional and national affairs.

Demographics

Europe's population nearly doubled between 1850 and 1910. Initially this increase was the result of a rise in the birth rate, but toward the end of the century, it was caused by a decline in the death rate. Medical breakthroughs played an important role in enhancing overall health, and as Europe grew more urbanized, gains came through such improvements in public health as safe water supplies and sewage disposal.

Industrial growth during the Second Industrial Revolution could not sustain the increased European population. Many rural poor migrated to urban centers seeking employment, but industrialized regions could accommodate only limited numbers. Those who could not find work looked across the Atlantic to North America, where there was a booming economy hungry for laborers. At the turn of the century, over one million Europeans left Europe annually. Many left to find work, but many—oppressed minorities—left expressly to flee Europe. Russian Jews constituted almost 12 percent of the total emigration to the United States during the early decades of the twentieth century.

The mass exodus of the rural population to Europe's urban centers is one of the most important phenomena of the nineteenth century. Cities across Europe grew at astronomic rates as people sought the opportunities modern industry afforded. Municipal governments redesigned the layouts of cities, tearing down medieval walls and alleyways and replacing them with parks and boulevards. Because working-class housing was overcrowded, unsanitary, and dangerous, municipal governments had to regulate housing, build working-class housing, and improve infrastructure to prevent the spread of disease.

> ### AP® Tip
>
> Breakthroughs in transportation influenced all facets of mass society. People no longer had to live next to their places of employment, thus setting the stage for future suburbs. New forms of transportation also gave rise to new mass leisure activities as urban residents could now travel to other sections of town (or even abroad) with little effort.

Social Structure

Middle Class became more wealthy

The prosperity associated with the Second Industrial Revolution drove change within European society. The landed aristocracy and the powerful industrialists merged to form a new elite. A plutocracy of wealthy businessmen exerted its influence on the lives of most Europeans, including the aristocracy. By the end of the nineteenth century, wealth had shifted from the landed aristocracy to the upper middle class as income from the landed estates continued to decline. This led to an intermingling of the aristocracy and wealthy industrialists, including intermarriage.

The middle class was diverse, consisting of professionals and white-collar workers such as sales representatives and department store clerks. Because this social stratum was so large, the middle class was extremely influential, and its values, including the importance of hard work, dominated European society. Intent on improving their social status, members of the middle class were sticklers for proper social behavior.

Middle-class women in the late nineteenth century exerted great influence over gender relations. The Industrial Revolution gave rise to a clear separation of gender roles: men worked outside the home, leaving women in charge of many domestic matters. Most middle-class households employed domestic servants, giving middle-class women time to focus on childcare or engage in leisure activities. Working-class women often had to work, even after marriage. By the turn of the century, however, wages earned by husbands and grown children allowed many working-class women to follow the same domestic paths as their middle-class counterparts.

Mass education made a big difference in the lives of many Europeans. In the early nineteenth century, education had been mostly for the elite, with wealthy sons going off to universities to study Greek and Latin. As the century progressed, the role of education in European society evolved tremendously. Western governments wanted an educated population to serve the needs of the modern state. As the franchise was granted to more adult males, it was necessary to make them educated voters. In addition, mass education fed the rise of nationalism by providing a unifying force that promoted national values. Increased literacy rates gave rise to newspapers, which used sensationalism to attract readers. In many European nations, adult illiteracy had been virtually eliminated by the turn of the century.

Economic prosperity, combined with new technology, opened a new era of mass leisure. Workers had the time and money to enjoy activities outside the home. Improved urban transportation allowed people to travel from their neighborhoods to athletic events, amusement parks, and dance halls. Trains ferried people to beaches beyond city limits. Organized athletics emerged toward the end of the nineteenth century, with associations forming to create rules and arrange competition. Professional sports became popular among urbanites who sought new loyalties amid an ever-changing urban environment. Tourism became an industry as more people could afford to travel abroad.

THE NATIONAL STATE AND MASS POLITICS

GREAT BRITAIN

During the second half of the nineteenth century, efforts were made to put liberalism into practice. This required expanding political democracy by extending voting rights for men and creating political parties. These efforts produced mass politics as more people were allowed to take part in the political process.

Great Britain led the way. By the 1870s, Britain had a thriving two-party system that encouraged reformers to push for the expansion of suffrage, and by 1884 nearly all adult males had the right to vote.

Women, however, did not receive suffrage rights until the twentieth century. The Redistribution Act made political representation more egalitarian by eliminating the outmoded political districts, and salaries for members of the House of Commons meant those of lesser means could hold public office. The British government's reform attempts did not extend to Ireland. Irish leaders began to call for home rule, but conservatives in Britain believed that granting Ireland any concessions would lead only to violence. Home rule for Ireland would not take place until the end of World War I.

AP® Tip

Strained relations between Ireland and Great Britain date back to the 1600s. The "Irish Question" refers to the dilemma the British government faced in granting the Irish political independence. Foremost was the situation in Ulster, where a significant proportion of the population was Protestant and wished to remain part of Great Britain. This issue would continue to plague Britain throughout the twentieth century.

FRANCE

France struggled to establish a republican government. After its defeat in the Franco-Prussian War in 1870, a provisional republican government was established, only to be dismissed by popular vote. Radical republicans responded by creating an independent government in Paris, the Commune, with support from many working-class men and women. The National Assembly refused to relinquish power and attacked the Commune and massacred thousands of Commune supporters. For decades, tensions would persist between the radical working class and the conservative middle class. Although a majority of the National Assembly favored a return to monarchy, their inability to agree on a king led to the solidification of the republic. The Constitution of 1875 marked the beginning of the Third Republic, which would last for the next sixty-five years.

GERMANY

Like France, the old order in Germany wanted to maintain control of political institutions. Although Germany achieved unification, its society remained extremely divided. The German constitution provided for representation based on universal male suffrage; in reality, most political power remained in the hands of the chancellor and the emperor. As with France, the military had tremendous influence, acting as defender of the monarchy and the aristocracy. Beginning in 1871, Otto von Bismarck was the most important figure in German politics, until his forced resignation in 1890. As chancellor, Bismarck accepted many liberal reforms in the name of centralization of German laws. He even aligned with liberal reformers to attack the Catholic Church through his program of *Kulturkampf*. By the end of the 1870s, however, Bismarck had abandoned liberal reforms in light of the perceived threat from a growing socialist movement. To attract workers from the socialist party, Bismarck initiated social-welfare legislation such as disability benefits and old-age pensions. His measures failed to diminish public desire for a socialist agenda. The new emperor, William II, replaced Bismarck in 1890, but the gulf between the German government and the socialists continued to widen.

AUSTRIA-HUNGARY

With the creation of the Dual Monarchy in 1867, Austria instituted a parliamentary system of government. As with Germany, the Austrian emperor, Francis Joseph, ignored parliament and continued to appoint and dismiss his own ministers. The many nationalities were a growing problem for the empire. Unable to please both the ethnic Germans and the national minorities, Francis Joseph tried to keep the empire together by emphasizing loyalty to the Catholic Church and expanding the imperial bureaucracy.

RUSSIA

In Russia, the mere thought of liberal reform was dismissed as dangerous and harmful to imperial rule. The limited reforms that had been initiated by Alexander II were quickly overhauled after his assassination in 1881. His son, Alexander III, viewed his father's reforms as a mistake and worked to return power to the tsar. Both social reformers and revolutionaries were persecuted, and the powers of the local assemblies curtailed. Alexander initiated a program of Russification that banned all languages except Russian in schools. Alexander's many repressive measures alienated national groups. In 1894, Alexander III was succeeded by his son, Nicholas II, who continued his father's absolutist policies.

[handwritten margin note: doesn't want reform]

> ### AP® Tip
>
> One theme that runs throughout Russian history is the repression of dissenters. Dating back to the earliest tsars and continuing through the Soviet era, those who spoke out against the government often faced reprisal. Many dissenters were forced to go underground, where they plotted more radical actions.

As Europe entered the twentieth century, the social dynamics associated with the mass society joined with the politics of the new national states to create a growing sense of nationalism. This combination would sow the seeds for a rivalry among nations that would eventually lead to war.

Content Review Questions

1. All of the following were associated with the Second Industrial Revolution EXCEPT
   (A) petroleum.
   (B) chemicals.
   (C) steel.
   (D) textiles.

2. Despite the prosperity of the late nineteenth century, Europeans experienced a series of economic crises between 1873 and 1895. All of the following contributed to European economic uncertainty EXCEPT
   (A) agricultural overproduction.
   (B) severe rural overpopulation.
   (C) competition from newly established Russian industries.
   (D) slumps in domestic and international business cycles.

3. The goals of evolutionary socialism were
   (A) to promote radical revolution among the proletariat.
   (B) to organize political parties and work through democratic channels.
   (C) to embrace global anarchism.
   (D) to cooperate with the bourgeoisie in building nationalism.

4. All of the following statements are true about the demographic structure of Europe between 1870 and 1914 EXCEPT
   (A) the population of Europe nearly doubled, but the birth rate dropped significantly.
   (B) the wealthy elite constituted about 5 percent of the population and controlled 30 to 40 percent of the wealth.
   (C) the number of wealthy, landed aristocrats remained stable throughout the period.
   (D) literacy rates rose dramatically and adult illiteracy nearly disappeared in western Europe.

5. By 1900, which of the following had cornered 90 percent of the market for dyestuffs and also led in the development of photographic plates and film?
   (A) Belgium
   (B) France
   (C) England
   (D) Germany

6. Which statement best reflects the tsarist policies of Russia during the late nineteenth century?
   (A) The Russian tsar became a strong advocate for reform.
   (B) Political power was gradually transferred from the tsar to the zemstvos.
   (C) Russification allowed all adult males the right to vote.
   (D) Reformers were persecuted and tsarist power remained absolute.

7. During the late nineteenth century, nearly 80 percent of Europeans belonged to which social stratum?
   (A) Lower class
   (B) Middle class
   (C) Upper middle class
   (D) Aristocracy

8. All of the following statements about late nineteenth-century European society are true EXCEPT
   (A) as the nineteenth century progressed, marriage rates increased and illegitimacy rates decreased.
   (B) as the nineteenth century progressed, working-class children were increasingly viewed as potential wage earners.
   (C) as the nineteenth century progressed, birth rates declined.
   (D) as the nineteenth century progressed, working-class parents devoted more attention to their children.

9. Reform measures in Great Britain between 1860 and 1914 accomplished all of the following EXCEPT
   (A) they gave women the right to vote.
   (B) they extended the franchise to nearly all adult males.
   (C) they eliminated "rotten" boroughs.
   (D) they provided salaries to members of the House of Commons.

10. All of the following statements regarding the *Kulturkampf* are true EXCEPT
    (A) Bismarck abandoned the *Kulturkampf* in order to gain support from the Socialist Democratic Party.
    (B) during the *Kulturkampf*, Bismarck received support from the liberals.
    (C) Bismarck distrusted Catholic loyalty to the new Germany.
    (D) Bismarck abandoned the *Kulturkampf* in order to concentrate on attacking the socialists.

Multiple-Choice Questions

Questions 1–3 refer to the following map.

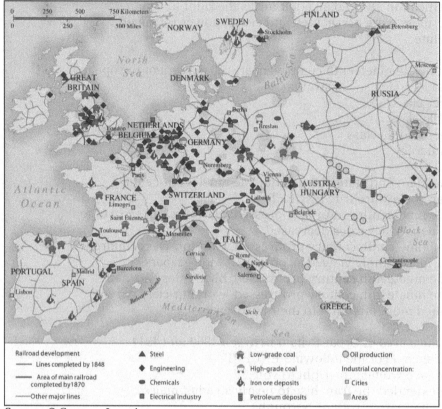

Source: © Cengage Learning

1. All of the following are true of the European economic zones of the late nineteenth century EXCEPT
    (A) Western Europe was more industrialized than Eastern Europe by 1900.
    (B) by the end of the nineteenth century, steel production, electricity, petroleum, and chemicals were the leading industries in Western Europe.
    (C) during the Second Industrial Revolution, Germany surpassed England as the industrial leader in Europe.
    (D) steel production surpassed agriculture as the most important economic activity in Eastern Europe.

2. Which of the following is true about the new patterns for European agriculture in late nineteenth-century Europe?
   (A) Grain prices rose due to the scarcity of grain production caused by the exodus of farmers to urban jobs.
   (B) The cost of purchasing newly invented equipment and chemical fertilizers led to the emergence of farm cooperatives.
   (C) Due to the rising cost of food products, many nations subsidized the cost of food for poor citizens.
   (D) When Western Europeans witnessed the rising costs of food, many workers left the factories to raise pigs, olives, and prunes.

3. Which of the following is the most significant reason that the late nineteenth century was known as *la belle époque*?
   (A) The final decades of the nineteenth century experienced an economic explosion that created great prosperity in many nations.
   (B) Railroad deaths decreased in the final decades of the nineteenth century due to the invention of better safety equipment on train engines.
   (C) Grain prices rose, giving Eastern European farmers the ability to improve their standard of living.
   (D) The final decades of the nineteenth century experienced a growth of democracy in nearly every nation of Europe, creating governments that provided protection of individual rights.

Questions 4–6 refer to the following image.

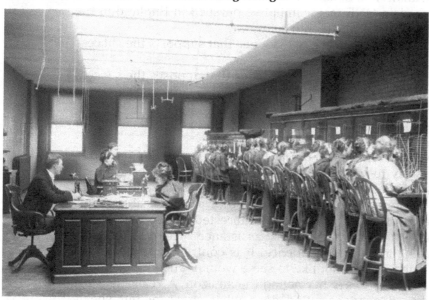

Source: Museum of the City of New York/The Art Archive at Art Resource, NY

4. All of the following were considered new job opportunities for women during the Second Industrial Revolution EXCEPT
   (A) pieceworkers.
   (B) salesclerks.
   (C) telephone operators.
   (D) teachers.

5. Most of the new white-collar jobs available to women were pursued by which of the following groups?
   - (A) Working-class men
   - (B) Middle-class women
   - (C) Aristocratic women
   - (D) Working-class women

6. All of the following are true about employment for women in the late nineteenth century EXCEPT
   - (A) fewer manufacturing jobs were available to women in the late nineteenth century due to the growth of new industries in the Second Industrial Revolution.
   - (B) the expansion of government services created a large number of white-collar jobs.
   - (C) since middle-class women began to receive an education equivalent to men by the late nineteenth century, job opportunities available to them were nearly unlimited.
   - (D) increased demand for white-collar jobs at relatively low wages and a shortage of male workers led to the hiring of more women workers.

Short-Answer Questions

1. Analyze the impact of British reform initiatives in the late nineteenth century and answer A, B, and C.
   - A) Briefly explain ONE major initiative pursued in England in the second half of the nineteenth century.
   - B) Briefly explain ONE piece of evidence that supports the success of that initiative.
   - C) Briefly explain ONE piece of evidence that opposes the success of that initiative.

Question 2 refers to the following excerpts.

Elizabeth Poole Sanford, *Woman in Her Social and Domestic Character*
Nothing is so likely to conciliate the affections of the other sex as a feeling that woman looks to them for support and guidance. In proportion as men are themselves superior, they are accessible to this appeal. On the contrary, they never feel interested in one who seems disposed rather to offer than to ask assistance. There is, indeed, something unfeminine in independence. It is contrary to nature, and therefore it offends. We do not like to see a woman affecting tremors, but still less do we like to see her acting the amazon. A really sensible woman feels her dependence. She does what she can; but she is conscious of inferiority, and therefore grateful for support. She knows that she is the weaker vessel, and that as such she should receive honor. In this view, her weakness is an attraction, not a blemish.

In every thing, therefore, that women attempt, they should show their consciousness of dependence. If they are learners, let them evince a teachable spirit; if they give an opinion, let them do it in an unassuming manner. There is something so unpleasant in female self-sufficiency that it not unfrequently deters instead of persuading, and prevents the adoption of advice which the judgment even approves.

Henrik Ibsen, *A Doll's House*

NORA: I must try to gain experience, Torvald.

HELMER: Forsake your home, your husband, your children! And you don't consider what the world will say.

NORA: I can't pay attention to that. I only know that I must do it.

HELMER: This is monstrous! Can you forsake your holiest duties?

NORA: What do you consider my holiest duties?

HELMER: Need I tell you that? Your duties to your husband and children.

NORA: I have other duties equally sacred.

HELMER: Impossible! What do you mean?

NORA: My duties toward myself.

HELMER: Before all else you are a wife and a mother.

NORA: That I no longer believe. Before all else I believe I am a human being just as much as you are—or at least that I should try to become one. I know that most people agree with you, Torvald, and that they say so in books. But I can no longer be satisfied with what most people say and what is in books. I must think things out for myself and try to get clear about them.

Sources: Elizabeth Poole Sanford, *Woman in Her Social and Domestic Character* (Boston: Otis, Broaders & Co., 1842), pp. 5–7, 15–16; Henrik Ibsen, *A Doll's House*, in W. D. Camp, *Roots of Western Civilization* (New York: Wiley, 1983).

2. Compare the two views of women portrayed in the excerpts above and answer A, B, and C.
   A) Briefly describe the proper role and behavior of women expressed by Elizabeth Poole Sanford in the first excerpt.
   B) Briefly describe the contrasting view of women depicted in the Ibsen excerpt.
   C) To what extent did the attitudes reflected in the first excerpt affect the middle-class family of the late nineteenth century?

Long-Essay Questions

1. Choose TWO nations in Europe during the nineteenth century and compare and contrast their efforts to establish liberal reform. (Historical Thinking Skills: Comparison)

2. Analyze the main characteristics of mass society as it emerged during the second half of the nineteenth century. (Historical Thinking Skills: Contextualization)

Answers

CONTENT REVIEW QUESTIONS

1. **(D)** Textile production was more closely associated with the First Industrial Revolution (*Western Civilization*, 9th ed., p. 691 / 10th ed., p. 687; Historical Thinking Skills—Contextualization; Learning Objectives PP-1, PP-4; Key Concept 3.1, 3.2).

2. **(C)** Although Russia was beginning to develop industrially by the late nineteenth century, competition from the new Russian industries was not one of the causes of the long depression. More important causes involved the falling agricultural prices and the fluctuations in the business cycle partially caused by the American Panic of 1873 (*Western Civilization*, 9th ed., p. 694 / 10th ed., pp. 689–90; Historical Thinking Skills—Causation; Learning Objectives PP-1, PP-3, PP-4; Key Concept 3.1, 3.2).

3. **(B)** Evolutionary socialism worked for social change by democratic means rather than by revolution (*Western Civilization*, 9th ed., p. 699 / 10th ed., p. 695; Historical Thinking Skills—Contextualization; Learning Objectives PP-14, PP-15, OS-8, OS-9, SP-1, SP-4; Key Concept 3.3).

4. **(C)** As aristocrats whose income came from landed estates declined, many invested in the new industries of the second industrial revolution. In Great Britain, landed aristocrats constituted 73 percent of the millionaires in 1850 and only 27 percent by 1914 (*Western Civilization*, 9th ed., pp. 706–713 / 10th ed., pp. 702–08; Historical Thinking Skills—Contextualization; Learning Objectives PP-1, PP-4, IS-2, IS-3, IS-5; Key Concept 3.1, 3.2).

5. **(D)** By the turn of the twentieth century, Germany had begun to surpass Great Britain in the chemical industry as well as in the production of steel (*Western Civilization*, 9th ed., p. 691 / 10th ed., p. 687; Historical Thinking Skills—Contextualization; Learning Objectives PP-1, PP-3, PP-4; Key Concept 3.1, 3.2).

6. **(D)** Both Alexander III and his son, Nicholas II, worked to uphold the autocratic rule of tsarist Russia (*Western Civilization*, 9th ed., p. 720 / 10th ed., p. 716; Historical Thinking Skills—Contextualization; Learning Objectives SP-3, SP-11; Key Concept 3.4).

7. **(A)** The lower class consisted of rural peasants and the urban working class. The composition of the lower classes varied greatly from region to region (*Western Civilization*, 9th ed., p. 707 / 10th ed., p. 703; Historical Thinking Skills—Causation; Learning Objectives PP-6, IS-2, IS-3; Key Concept 3.1, 3.2).

8. **(C)** Between 1850 and 1910 the birthrate grew while families began to focus more attention on their children. (*Western Civilization*, 9th ed., pp. 710–12 / 10th ed., pp. 703–08; Historical Thinking Skills—Contextualization; Learning Objectives OS-4, IS-4, IS-7; Key Concept 3.2, 3.3).

9. **(A)** Reform measures affected much of society, but British women did not gain suffrage until 1918 (*Western Civilization*, 9th ed., p. 716 / 10th ed., p. 712; Historical Thinking Skills—Causation; Learning Objectives OS-4, SP-9, IS-6; Key Concept 3.3).

10. **(A)** After losing public support, Bismarck abandoned the *Kulturkampf* in favor of persecuting the German socialists (*Western Civilization*, 9th ed., p. 718 / 10th ed., p. 714; Historical Thinking Skills—Causation; Learning Objectives SP-3, IS-7, IS-10; Key Concept 3.3, 3.4).

MULTIPLE-CHOICE QUESTIONS

1. **(D)** By 1900, Europe was divided into two distinct economic zones, with the nations of Western Europe being industrialized while those in Eastern Europe depended largely on agriculture for their economic security. Agriculture remained the dominant economic activity in Eastern Europe (*Western Civilization*, 9th ed., pp. 694–96 / 10th ed., pp. 690–91; Historical Thinking Skills—Contextualization; Learning Objectives PP-1, PP-3, PP-4, IS-3; Key Concept 3.1, 3.3).

2. **(B)** Since the cost of farm equipment and chemical fertilizers were very expensive, only the large estate owners could afford to buy them. Consequently, individual farmers joined together to form farm cooperatives that provided capital for purchasing the new agricultural technologies (*Western Civilization*, 9th ed., pp. 694–96 / 10th ed., pp. 690–91; Historical Thinking Skills—Contextualization; Learning Objectives PP-1, PP-3, PP-4, IS-3; Key Concept 3.1, 3.3).

3. **(A)** The prosperity and inventions created by the Second Industrial Revolution and the economic boom that led many western nations out of the depressions that they faced in the 1870s and 1880s led to an era of optimism and material comfort that was unparalleled in Europe. This new era of prosperity prompted the era to be called *la belle époque* (*Western Civilization*, 9th ed., pp. 694–96 / 10th ed., pp. 690–92; Historical Thinking Skills—Contextualization; Learning Objectives PP-1, PP-3, PP-4, IS-3; Key Concept 3.1, 3.3).

4. **(A)** The new job opportunities associated with the Second Industrial Revolution meant that women had other options besides performing piecework at home (*Western Civilization*, 9th ed., pp. 696–97 / 10th ed., pp. 692–93; Historical Thinking Skills—Contextualization; Learning Objectives PP-7, OS-4, IS-4, IS-6, IS-9; Key Concept 3.2, 3.3).

5. **(D)** Many white-collar jobs were claimed by working class women who saw a white-collar job as an opportunity to escape from the lower class (*Western Civilization*, 9th ed., pp. 696–97 / 10th ed., pp. 692–93; Historical Thinking Skills—Contextualization; Learning Objectives PP-7, OS-4, IS-4, IS-6, IS-9; Key Concept 3.2, 3.3).

6. **(C)** Middle-class women in the late nineteenth century did not receive an education equivalent to a man's education, so their job opportunities remained limited (*Western Civilization*, 9th ed., pp. 696–97 / 10th ed., pp. 692–93; Historical Thinking Skills—Contextualization; Learning Objectives PP-7, OS-4, IS-4, IS-6, IS-9; Key Concept 3.2, 3.3).

SHORT-ANSWER QUESTIONS

1. You may choose to pick a different initiative, so answers could be different. One possible answer for each part is listed below.

A) One major initiative pursued in England in the second half of the nineteenth century was the expansion of suffrage. At mid-century, many British men did not have the right to vote, despite the passage of the Great Reform Bill of 1832, and no British women could vote. Efforts by the working class to achieve industrial reform included gaining the right to vote, so that they could choose representatives to Parliament who would promote their interests. They expressed these demands in the Chartist movement in hopes of changing their situation.

B) One piece of evidence that supports the success of that initiative was the passage of the Reform Act of 1867 and the Reform Act of 1884. The Reform Act of 1867 granted suffrage to many working-class voters, but some men were still excluded. The Reform Act of 1884 gave the right to vote to all men who paid regular rents or taxes, thus including the majority of British farmers and adding about two million more male voters to the electorate.

C) One piece of evidence that opposes the success of that initiative was the fact that women were not given the right to vote. Although many women had demanded the right to vote and had supported the Chartist movement by marching in rallies and even becoming lecturers for the cause, Parliament did not grant women the right to vote in either the Reform Act of 1867 or the Reform Act of 1884. As a result, the National Union of Women's Suffrage Societies began to actively demand women's voting rights.
(*Western Civilization*, 9th ed., p. 716 / 10th ed., p. 712; Historical Thinking Skills—Causation; Learning Objectives PP-15, OS-4, OS-8, SP-1, SP-4, SP-7, SP-9, SP-11, SP-12, IS-5, IS-6, IS-7, IS-9; Key Concepts 3.2, 3.3)

2. A) In the first excerpt, Elizabeth Poole Sanford defines the proper role and behavior of women according to traditional gender-based social roles. According to Sanford, women were inferior to men. Men provided for their families by working outside the home while proper women stayed at home where they provided for the needs of their husbands and children. Many women accepted this traditional domestic role, since women remained legally inferior and economically dependent, giving them few other choices.

B) In contrast, in *A Doll's House*, Ibsen suggested that the domestic role limited women's options. He insinuated that women should no longer be dominated by their fathers and husbands but instead should fight for their rights and take a more active part in the world. Rather than being tied to a traditional domestic role, a growing number of people believed that the nineteenth-century middle-class woman should be able to be more independent and free from her husband's authority.

C) The new cult of middle-class domesticity advanced an ideal of togetherness that changed family life. Women were educated in singing and crafts and learned how to provide for a happy family atmosphere. Mothers now protected their children from the dangers of the world and spent more time playing games with their kids. The domestic role celebrated in the first excerpt created women who nurtured their husbands and children. (*Western Civilization*, 9th ed., pp. 707–11 / 10th ed., pp. 703–08; Historical Thinking Skills—Analyzing Evidence: Content and Sourcing, Comparison; Learning Objectives PP-7, OS-4, SP-9, IS-4, IS-6; Key Concepts 3.2, 3.3)

LONG-ESSAY QUESTIONS

1. Much of nineteenth-century European political history involved a struggle between the forces of liberal reform and the forces of the old order. This struggle varied greatly from state to state.

   The most successful at achieving reform was Great Britain. Parliament enacted reform measures expanding suffrage to almost all adult males. Although women were excluded from political participation, farm workers were given voting rights for the first time. Reform legislation also reconfigured the local political districts to give the fast-growing urban industrial centers representation equal to that of the far less populated rural districts.

   In comparison, most other European nations had more difficulty in instituting liberal reform. In France, reform took hold only after the radical Paris Commune was put down. Monarchists in the National Assembly wanted to return to a strong monarchy, but when no suitable candidate emerged, a constitution was put forth and a republican form of government emerged. Like Britain, France had a bicameral legislature; unlike Britain, France's national government was dominated by forces opposed to republican government.

   The situation was much more confusing in Germany. That nation had a parliamentary government and universal male suffrage, but powerful authoritarian forces and conservative social groups maintained control. Real political power remained in the hands of the chancellor, who answered only to the emperor. The military exerted tremendous influence in Germany—so as long as the emperor controlled the military, he controlled the nation. Keep in mind that Bismarck instituted liberal reform measures in an attempt to lure workers away from the socialist party.

   Russian attempts at liberal reform were met with great resistance as the nineteenth century progressed. After the 1881 assassination of Tsar Alexander II, his son, Alexander III, claimed that previous reform had been a mistake and that absolutist rule had to be protected. Liberals were persecuted by the secret police, and the powers of the *zemstvos* were curtailed. In addition, the tsar attempted to control the numerous minority groups within Russia by establishing the radical Russification program. Alexander III's son, Nicholas II, continued his father's policies, which eventually led to greater conflict in the twentieth century.

   In Austria-Hungary, any attempts at liberal reform were met with problems regarding national minorities. Although Austria had a parliamentary form of government, Emperor Francis Joseph maintained almost total control over government affairs. Any

liberal measures enacted only served to destroy the nation's fragile bonds. Be sure to add a brief (2-3 sentences) synthesis discussion to your essay. For this essay, you could compare nineteenth century liberal reforms with the liberal reforms offered by the enlightened absolutists.
(*Western Civilization*, 9th ed., pp. 690–721 / 10th ed., pp. 686–717; Historical Thinking Skills—Comparison; Learning Objectives PP-10, PP-15, OS-8, SP-4, SP-5, SP-9, SP-12, IS-3, IS-7; Key Concept 3.3, 3.4, 3.5)

2. A successful answer to this question will examine multiple aspects of mass society, including population growth, urbanization, the changing social structure, education, leisure, and women's suffrage. Population growth in Europe during the second half of the nineteenth century greatly influenced European society. At the same time, Europeans migrated in significant numbers from the countryside to the cities, forcing governments to take an active role in urban planning and public health. Entire urban centers were redesigned to accommodate the needs of the modern industrialized city.

   The social structure of mass society was also changing. The dominance of the landed aristocracy was severely tested by the rise of a new elite: wealthy businessmen. As this new elite grew in size, it gradually fused with the aristocracy to form a new upper class. Mass society also affected the role of women in European society; the rising economy allowed many women to work less and spend more time raising their children.

   The needs of mass society required an expanded public education system. Many countries made elementary education compulsory and looked to education as a way to both serve the vocational needs of local industry and encourage a growing sense of nationalism. As literacy grew, so did the demand for mass-circulated newspapers. Tabloids, especially, had a huge reader-ship. As Europe became more prosperous, leisure activities grew in demand. Professional sports, music and dance halls, and amusement parks all vied for public attendance. The new mass leisure time marked a departure from previous popular culture, which was primarily community based. The new leisure activities were large-scale operations that turned amusement into big business. Be sure to add a brief (2–3 sentences) synthesis discussion to your essay. For this essay, you could compare late nineteenth century mass society with late twentieth century mass society.
(*Western Civilization*, 9th ed., pp. 690–721 / 10th ed., pp. 686–717; Historical Thinking Skills—Contextualization; Learning Objectives PP-10, PP-15, OS-8, SP-4, SP-5, SP-9, SP-12, IS-3, IS-5, IS-7; Key Concept 3.2, 3.3, 3.4, 3.5)

13

MODERNITY AND WAR: 1894–1914

Belief in human progress was a cornerstone of modern society at the turn of the twentieth century. Advances in science and technology influenced all facets of life—in industry and in the home. But that progress also gave rise to destructive forces. European powers used advances in human thought and technology to gain control over rival nations and people, which led to protests and eventual war as Europe exploded in a frenzy of hatred. 1914 witnessed the outbreak of World War I, a war that would end the optimism of the late nineteenth century and set the stage for a half-century of turmoil and destruction.

KEY TERMS

abstract art
anticlericalism
anti-Semitism
cubism
genocide
Impressionism
militarism
mobilization
Modernism
nationalization
pogroms
Post-Impressionism

psychoanalysis
relativity theory
reparations
revolutionary
Scramble for Africa
self-determination
socialism
Social Darwinism
suffragists
transformismo
Volkish thought
Zionism

CHAPTER KEY CONCEPTS

▪ Global powers used growing nationalism to justify imperialism, which in turn led to political rivalries and eventual war that, in the end, reshaped the political landscape of Europe.

- Tremendous economic growth across Europe at the turn of the century fostered competition for resources and markets, leading to imperialism and an arms race.
- In the era leading to World War I, new ideas regarding science and philosophy challenged the notions of progress associated with Enlightenment thought.

For a full discussion of the period between 1894 and the outbreak of World War I, see *Western Civilization*, 9th and 10th editions, Chapter 24.

MODERN SCIENTIFIC AND ARTISTIC THOUGHT

Scientific progress throughout the nineteenth century had suggested that the world is rational and orderly and that all problems could be solved through the application of scientific research. But new discoveries at the end of the century shook the foundations of science. Marie Curie's discovery of radium in 1902 and Max Planck's quantum theory in 1900 challenged Isaac Newton's longstanding theories. The work of Albert Einstein was a further complication for Newtonian physics. Published in 1915, Einstein's theory of relativity held that space and time are relative to the observer, rather than absolute. His theory would open an age in physics of new discoveries and greater uncertainty.

In the field of philosophy, the usefulness—even the possibility—of rational thought was questioned. Friedrich Nietzsche held that society's embrace of the rational had stunted human potential. By abandoning Christianity and giving free rein to emotion and instinct, one could become a superhuman.

Another important figure was Sigmund Freud, who developed his ideas on the human mind into a type of research called psychoanalysis. He theorized that human behavior is controlled by repressed experiences that can be resolved only through the analysis of subconscious memories.

As Darwin's theory of evolution became widely understood, it was soon applied in other fields. Herbert Spencer argued that social progress was a result of the "struggle for survival"; the fittest prospered at the expense of the weak. Soon extremists would use Spencer's ideas to justify nationalist and racist agendas.

These ideas found their way into the literature of the day. Many novelists incorporated Darwinian theory into their own work. This was especially true of the French novelist Émile Zola, the leading proponent of the literary movement called Naturalism, which portrayed characters caught up in social forces beyond their control. The earlier optimistic realism was gone.

A transformation in art had begun in the 1870s. The Impressionist movement, which originated in France, rejected the goal, set during the Renaissance, of rendering reality. Instead, the Impressionists embraced nature and worked to capture the appearance of changing light and fleeting moments. Claude Monet, one of the best-known Impressionists, spent a lifetime painting the same haystacks and seacoast and water lilies in different light.

In the 1880s, French artists including Paul Cézanne and Vincent Van Gogh formed a new movement, Post-Impressionism. They used color and line to express inner feelings and portray subjective reality. Modern art had begun.

At the turn of the century art broke with realism, pushed by the rise in popularity of photography. The philosophical and psychological milieus encouraged experimentation. Pablo Picasso created a unique form of art known as Cubism, in which reality is viewed from various vantage points and rendered in geometric design forms. Soon, with the advent of abstract art, reality was abandoned altogether and gave way to pure shapes and color.

NEW DIRECTIONS IN POLITICS

Anxiety arose throughout Europe late in the nineteenth century. The mass politics that had emerged earlier created turmoil that disturbed even liberals. Previously silent voices clamored for representation. The working class turned to socialism to represent its needs, while right-wing nationalists turned to racism.

With the rise of liberalism in Europe, women sought rights and privileges previously granted only to men. Foremost among these was the right to vote. Feminists in Britain began to push for voting rights as early as the 1840s. As the century progressed, feminists such as Emmeline Pankhurst turned to more radical methods.

> ### AP® Tip
>
> Women's history has often been the topic—directly or indirectly—of essay questions on social history. Make sure that you have a good understanding of the changes and continuities in the lives of women throughout European history, especially noting the changes in women's rights during the twentieth century.

Anti-Semitism grew at the end of the century, as Social Darwinism encouraged efforts to deny Jews rights. Extreme nationalism, especially in Germany and Austria, gave rise to political groups that exploited anti-Semitism. Jews in Eastern Europe faced pogroms (organized massacres), in which residents of entire villages were slaughtered. Many Eastern European Jews emigrated to the United States, Canada, and Palestine. In Palestine, Theodor Herzl led a nationalist movement, Zionism, to establish a Jewish state in the Middle East.

Mass politics benefited many Europeans, but also led to conflict. For example, the rising influence of the British working class forced the Liberal Party to enact legislation that addressed the needs of labor. To gain the workers' support, Liberal leaders pushed through Parliament a social welfare program radically opposed to the liberal concept of laissez-faire.

In France, there was resistance to the republican desire for a more democratic society by the army, royalists, and the church. The Dreyfus Affair, which gripped the nation in the late 1890s, brought the conflict to a head. Alfred Dreyfus, a Jewish army officer, was accused of selling army secrets, and in 1895 was found guilty and sentenced to life imprisonment. Soon after, evidence emerged proving his innocence. Radical republicans used the Dreyfus Affair to force the elimination of many of the privileges traditionally granted to the old order.

In Russia, the minister of finance, Sergei Witte, worked to improve weak industrial production. Tremendous industrial growth, based primarily on the expansion of railroads, was unleashed, and by 1900, Russia was the world's fourth largest producer of steel. The growth of factories led a radical working class to embrace socialism. Government repression forced it underground, where the socialists began advocating for terrorism.

In 1904, Russia went to war against Japan over territorial expansion in the Far East. Much to the surprise of most European leaders, the Japanese won. Political and social discontent in Russia increased as both the middle class and workers pushed for greater reform. In St. Petersburg in January 1905, workers marched to the Winter Palace to present the tsar with a list of grievances. Soldiers opened fire on the peaceful marchers, sparking a revolt throughout Russia by workers, peasants, and the middle class. After months of disturbance, Tsar Nicholas II issued the October Manifesto, granting civil liberties and increasing the political franchise. Reform was short-lived, however, as Nicholas later curtailed many of the very reforms he had granted.

New Imperialism

In the 1880s, European powers began a new search for foreign territory in Asia and Africa. Intense rivalries drove the extraordinary expansion of colonial empires. Governments had two main desires: military logistics and prestige. Britain, for example, needed fueling stations for its navy and territorial outposts that were vital to protecting overseas interests. National pride was also a central factor. As domestic turmoil increased during the late nineteenth century, governments used imperialist gains to distract attention from the unrest at home.

Other forces contributing to this "new imperialism" included Social Darwinism, religion, and economics. The "white man's burden," a racist justification of imperialism, held that the white man had a moral duty to take his superior culture to the inferior native. Economic motives also played a role, as European industrialists continued to seek out natural resources in regions abroad.

The Scramble for Africa

European states had little control over the African continent before the 1880s, limiting themselves to a few long-established trading outposts. The British then began increasing their presence in South Africa, where they confronted not only native Zulus but also Dutch colonists called Boers, with whom they went to war in 1899. The Boer War ended in a British victory and allowed for the formation of the Union of South Africa.

By 1890, other European nations had joined the "Scramble for Africa." Portugal, France, Italy, and Belgium all claimed territory. Europeans used their superior military force to overwhelm and slaughter the defenseless Africans, and by the end of the century had partitioned the entire continent, with the exceptions of Liberia and Ethiopia.

NEW IMPERIALISM IN ASIA

As with Africa, European states had had a presence in the Far East since the sixteenth century. Famous trading entities, such as the British East India Company, had dominated large territorial areas for many years.

Subjugation posed problems, however, as the British discovered in India. In 1857, the British East India Company faced a revolt by native Indian soldiers serving with the British army. On hearing rumors about the use of animal fat on British rifle cartridges, these sepoys killed over 200 English women and children, sparking a reprisal that led to the destruction of Indian villages. In the wake of the rebellion, control of India was transferred from the East India Company to the British government, and Queen Victoria became empress of India.

Elsewhere, the French were in Southeast Asia, the Dutch were in Indonesia, the Germans were in some of the South Pacific islands, and the Americans were in the Philippines. Except for American trade privileges, Japan managed to avoid being colonized, but became a colonial power when it annexed Korea in 1910.

China's decline during the nineteenth century presented opportunities for Western nations. The British gained Hong Kong in 1842 and soon acquired trading rights in many other Chinese cities. Other Western states were eager for influence there too. The rivalry prevented a complete conquest of China. Instead, the territory was divided into spheres of influence with an "open-door" trade policy.

China resented Western dominance. Beginning in 1900, the Boxer Rebellion was an attempt to force all foreigners out of China. After a number of Western government officials, businessmen, and missionaries were killed, an army of British, French, German, Russian, American, and Japanese troops put down the revolt and demanded further concessions from the weakened Chinese rulers. Soon after, the Manchu dynasty was overthrown by Chinese revolutionaries, who created the Republic of China in 1912.

SETTING THE STAGE FOR WAR

In the fifty years before World War I, Europe had remained remarkably peaceful, primarily because of the diplomacy of Germany's Otto von Bismarck. But after his removal from office, changes were made that threatened the stability and eventually brought about war.

The decline of the Ottoman Empire upset the balance of power throughout Europe. Russia and Austria were especially interested in controlling Ottoman territory in Eastern Europe. Bismarck worked to reduce Russian influence while negotiating the Triple Alliance (1882), which committed Germany, Austria, and Italy to maintaining the European status quo. Emperor William II negated a great deal of Bismarck's efforts to keep Europe from war when he dismissed Bismarck in 1890. To give Germany its "place in the sun," he embraced confrontation. The Kaiser severed ties with Russia, which then entered an alliance with France, and he threatened Britain, which then formed the Triple Entente with France and Russia.

[handwritten margin note: removal of Otto von Bismarck]

The rise of nationalism in the nineteenth century was especially problematic for Austria, which sought control over its Slavic-speaking territories. In 1908, when Austria annexed Bosnia and Herzegovina to prevent the formation of a larger Serbian kingdom, Russia encouraged the Serbs to go to war. Only after William II interceded—even threatening war against Russia—did Serbia back down. Still, the Serbs pushed for greater power in the Balkans. Sides were drawn as Germany continued to back Austrian efforts, while Russia lent increasing support to the Serbian cause. By 1914, this was a point of national pride: Austria was fixed on crushing Serbian desires, while Russia was set on promoting them.

Content Review Questions

1. Near the end of the nineteenth century, a dramatic change in the realm of ideas and culture challenged human faith in progress and reason. All of the following were among those challenges EXCEPT
   (A) a new view of the physical universe.
   (B) mass consumption motivated by increased advertising.
   (C) alternative views of human nature.
   (D) radically innovative forms of literary and artistic expression.

2. Friedrich Nietzsche believed that Western bourgeois society was incapable of cultural creativity because
   (A) excessive emphasis was placed on the rational faculty at the expense of emotions.
   (B) middle-class Europeans lacked spirituality.
   (C) popular culture influenced a growing number of Europeans.
   (D) revolutionary socialism failed to advance one's emotional well-being.

3. The goal of psychoanalysis is to
   (A) determine a patient's pleasure principle.
   (B) undermine a patient's Oedipus complex.
   (C) resolve a patient's psychic conflict.
   (D) enhance a patient's reality principle.

4. The philosopher Herbert Spencer believed all of the following EXCEPT
   (A) societies are organisms that evolve over time.
   (B) in society, the strong advance while the weak decline.
   (C) it is vital for the state to take part in social reform.
   (D) death of the weak and feeble is a natural process that makes society stronger.

5. The painting on the next page reflects which style of art?
   (A) Impressionism
   (B) Abstract
   (C) Cubism
   (D) Post-Impressionism

Source: Digital Images © The Museum of Modern Art/Licensed by Scala/Art Resource, NY

6. The Zionist Movement was influenced by all of the following EXCEPT
   (A) nationalist movements in Italy, Ireland, and Greece.
   (B) the Ottoman tradition of promoting cultural diversity.
   (C) anti-Semitism in Austria and Germany.
   (D) the quota systems of many European universities.

7. The Dreyfus Affair resulted in all of the following EXCEPT
   (A) moderate and conservative republicans gained more power over radical factions.
   (B) most Catholic religious orders that controlled many French schools were forced out of France.
   (C) the church and state were officially separated.
   (D) the government seized church property.

8. The Russian Revolution of 1905 was inspired by all of the following EXCEPT
   (A) massive food shortages in Russian cities.
   (B) dissatisfied nationalities in regions dominated by minority ethnic Russians.
   (C) the peasants' desire for land.
   (D) government reform of religious institutions.

9. All of the following are causes of the New Imperialism EXCEPT which of the following?
   (A) Marxist ideologies
   (B) Social Darwinism
   (C) Religious motives
   (D) The search for raw materials

10. Italian leader Giovanni Giolitti used which of the following methods to consolidate his power in the years preceding World War I?
(A) Military enforcement of his policies
(B) *Transformismo*
(C) Risorgimento
(D) Gaining the support of the pope who endorsed his government

Multiple-Choice Questions

Questions 1–3 refer to the following image.

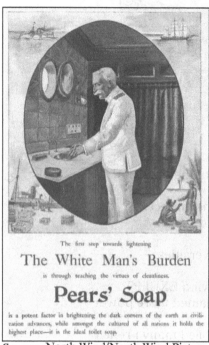

1. Which of the following motives for New Imperialism is reflected in this advertisement?
(A) Economic gain due to the exploitation of native labor
(B) Economic gain due to the availability of cheap raw materials
(C) Political gain due to the acquisition of a larger empire
(D) Social duty to spread European civilization to the natives

2. All of the following were used to justify New Imperialism EXCEPT
(A) Social Darwinism.
(B) Humanitarian concerns known as "the white man's burden."
(C) Darwinism.
(D) Religious zeal.

3. Which of the following would have been least likely to have supported New Imperialism?
(A) A Marxist
(B) A Whig member of the British Parliament
(C) A Catholic priest
(D) A French businessman

Questions 4–6 refer to the following map.

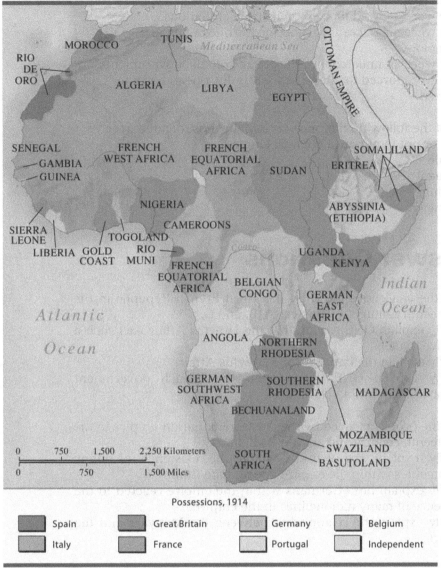

Possessions, 1914

Spain	Great Britain	Germany	Belgium
Italy	France	Portugal	Independent

Source: © Cengage Learning

4. As seen in this map, how did nineteenth century imperialism differ from earlier forms of interaction between Europe and Africa?
   (A) Fewer European nations were involved in African colonization.
   (B) Europeans employed their military strength and industrial technology to control new territories rather than controlling the regional trade networks by establishing a few trading posts.
   (C) Europeans claimed colonies, but did not try to explore and settle in the interior regions, since too many Europeans had died in previous decades because of disease and confrontation with the natives.
   (D) Europeans used locally trained military to carry out the oppression of local populations in previous decades but abandoned that practice by the end of the century.

5. Which of the following is true of the Africans who resisted European rule?
   (A) They were allowed to keep their tribal affiliations.
   (B) They were massacred by superior European military technology.
   (C) They were assimilated into European colonial governments.
   (D) They were forced to attend schools in Europe to become civilized.

6. Which of the following nations was initially most divided over whether or not to pursue a colonial empire?
   (A) Britain
   (B) Portugal
   (C) Belgium
   (D) Germany

Short-Answer Questions

1. Analyze the challenges faced by the Third French Republic in the late nineteenth century and answer A, B, and C.
   A) Briefly explain ONE reason that the Dreyfus Affair was such a divisive issue.
   B) Briefly explain the impact of the Dreyfus Affair.
   C) Briefly explain ONE reason that the French government alienated the working class.

2. Analyze the problems faced by the Austro-Hungarian Empire in the late nineteenth century and answer A, B, and C.
   A) Briefly explain the way in which the existence of many nationalities within the empire affected the Empire.
   B) Briefly explain how Germans within the empire reacted to the existence of many nationalities in the empire.
   C) Briefly explain the relationship between the Magyars and the empire.

Long-Essay Questions

1. Analyze the methods and goals of European suffragists in the late nineteenth and early twentieth centuries. (Historical Thinking Skills: Contextualization)

2. Explain how the intellectual and cultural developments of the late nineteenth and early twentieth centuries shaped modern consciousness. (Historical Thinking Skills: Contextualization)

Answers

CONTENT REVIEW QUESTIONS

1. **(B)** Mass consumption emerged during the second industrial revolution as an outgrowth of the prosperity and progress of the era. All of the other choices shattered old beliefs and opened the way to modern consciousness (*Western Civilization*, 9th ed., pp. 714–16, 724 / 10th ed., pp. 720–22; Historical Thinking Skills—Contextualization; Learning Objective OS-6, OS-8, OS-9, OS-10, OS-13; Key Concept 3.3, 3.5, 3.6).

2. **(A)** Friedrich Nietzsche believed that humans are driven more by irrational forces than by reason and that the emphasis on reason and rational thought had prevented Western society from achieving cultural creativity (*Western Civilization*, 9th ed., p. 725 / 10th ed., p. 721; Historical Thinking Skills—Causation; Learning Objective OS-6, OS-8, OS-9, OS-10, OS-13; Key Concept 3.3, 3.5, 3.6).

3. **(C)** Sigmund Freud believed that the unconscious shapes human behavior. He attempted to help patients resolve psychic conflicts by unlocking repressed thoughts (*Western Civilization*, 9th ed., pp. 726–27 / 10th ed., pp. 722–23; Historical Thinking Skills—Causation; Learning Objective OS-6, OS-8, OS-9, OS-10, OS-13; Key Concept 3.3, 3.5, 3.6).

4. **(C)** Social Darwinists such as Herbert Spencer believed that the state should not help the downtrodden because that goes against the natural process of human existence (*Western Civilization*, 9th ed., p. 727 / 10th ed., pp. 722–24; Historical Thinking Skills—Causation; Learning Objective OS-6, OS-8, OS-9, OS-10, OS-13, IS-7, IS-10; Key Concept 3.3, 3.5, 3.6).

5. **(D)** This work by Vincent van Gogh is Post-Impressionist. Post-Impressionists used shape, color, and pattern to express their feelings (*Western Civilization*, 9th ed., pp. 732–33 / 10th ed., pp. 728–29; Historical Thinking Skills—Contextualization; Learning Objective OS-6, OS-8, OS-9, OS-10, OS-13; Key Concept 3.3, 3.5, 3.6).

6. **(B)** The Ottoman authorities opposed Jewish immigration to Palestine, which took place despite that opposition (*Western Civilization*, 9th ed., p. 738 / 10th ed., pp. 735–36; Historical Thinking Skills—Causation; Learning Objective IS-10; Key Concept 3.3).

7. **(A)** The radical republicans gained more power in the aftermath of the Dreyfus Affair, leading to reprisals against anti-republicans and the church (*Western Civilization*, 9th ed., p. 741 / 10th ed., p. 737; Historical Thinking Skills—Causation; Learning Objective IS-10; Key Concept 3.3).

8. **(D)** The Russian Revolution of 1905 was influenced by working-class and peasant dissatisfaction. The royal family had no intention of reforming the church (*Western Civilization*, 9th ed., p. 743 / 10th ed., pp. 738–39; Historical Thinking Skills—Causation; Learning Objective PP-10, SP-4, SP-11; Key Concept 3.4).

9. **(A)** Socialist ideology did not support imperialism. Instead, Marxists condemned imperialism as an evil outgrowth of capitalism (*Western Civilization*, 9th ed., pp. 745–47 / 10th ed., pp. 741–42; Historical Thinking Skills—Causation; Learning Objective INT-1, INT-2, INT-3, INT-4, INT-6, PP-10; Key Concept 3.1, 3.5, 3.6).

10. **(B)** Giolitti used the process of *transformismo* to gain support for his policies, meaning that he transformed his old political rivals into supporters by political and economic bribery (*Western Civilization*, 9th ed., pp. 740–41 / 10th ed., p. 737; Historical Thinking Skills—Causation; Learning Objective SP-7; Key Concept 3.3).

MULTIPLE-CHOICE QUESTIONS

1. **(D)** The ad suggests that the soap will help to brighten the darkness of native civilizations, implying that one motive for New Imperialism is the extension of European civilization to areas that the colonizers believed were not as civilized as they were (*Western Civilization*, 9th ed., pp. 745–47 / 10th ed., pp. 741–44; Historical Thinking Skills—Causation; Learning Objectives INT-1, INT-2, INT-11, IS-10; Key Concepts 3.5, 3.6).

2. **(C)** Darwinism, itself, was not a cause of New Imperialism. Intellectuals, such as Herbert Spencer, took Darwin's ideas and applied them to society, believing that the fittest in society would survive and the rest could be exploited by the imperialists (*Western Civilization*, 9th ed., pp. 745–47 / 10th ed., pp. 741–44; Historical Thinking Skills—Causation, Argumentation; Learning Objectives INT-1, INT-2, INT-11, IS-10; Key Concepts 3.5, 3.6).

3. **(A)** A Marxist would not have supported New Imperialism because Marxists associated imperialism with economic greed. Marxists saw imperialism as the end stages of capitalism because it concentrated wealth in fewer and fewer hands and exploited the majority of people (*Western Civilization*, 9th ed., pp. 745–47 / 10th ed., pp. 741–44; Historical Thinking Skills—Causation; Learning Objectives INT-1, INT-2, INT-11, IS-10; Key Concepts 3.5, 3.6).

4. **(B)** All of the major European nations participated in the scramble for Africa in the last two decades of the nineteenth century. They employed European military strength and industrial technology to dominate the natives, who were no match for the new weapons and techniques of the Europeans. Unlike previous decades, the Europeans settled whole colonies, rather than primarily only establishing trading posts (*Western Civilization*, 9th ed., pp. 747–49 / 10th ed., pp. 742–46; Historical Thinking Skills—Patterns of Continuity and Change Over Time; Learning Objectives INT-1, INT-3, INT-4, INT-5; Key Concepts 3.1, 3.5).

5. **(B)** Due to the fact that the Europeans wanted the African colonies and their riches and also due to their belief that Europeans were a superior race, the nations of Europe used devastating force to destroy African opposition (*Western Civilization*, 9th ed., pp. 747–49 / 10th ed., pp. 742–46; Historical Thinking Skills—Contextualization; Learning Objectives INT-2, INT-3, INT-7, INT-10, INT-11, IS-10; Key Concepts 3.5, 3.6).

6. **(D)** Chancellor Bismarck was at first opposed to using German resources to obtain a colonial empire, believing it was more important to secure its position in Europe. Eventually, Bismarck and other German officials changed their minds and began to secure colonies, realizing that it was necessary to build an overseas empire, if they were going to stay in power (*Western Civilization*, 9th ed., pp. 745–46 / 10th ed., pp. 742–46; Historical Thinking Skills—Patterns of Continuity and Change Over Time; Learning Objectives INT-6; Key Concepts 3.5).

SHORT-ANSWER QUESTIONS

1. A) One reason that the Dreyfus Affair was such a divisive issue in the Third French Republic was that it pitted the conservative and anti-Semitic government against the radical republicans who wanted to break the power of the Catholic Church and the army and promote a more democratic society. The affair polarized society, with some right-wing journalists using it as an excuse to publish their anti-Semitic views while other writers, such as Zola, actively opposed the government and called them out for being anti-Semitic. The Dreyfus Affair provided proof to the less conservative French citizens of the corruption that existed in the government and the need for change.

   B) The Dreyfus Affair led to the formation of a new government under the radical republicans, who proceeded to try to reduce the power of the Catholic Church and the army. High-ranking army officers were fired, and many French religious orders who had been active in education were exiled. By 1905, the Dreyfus Affair led to the complete separation of church and state, with government acquisition of church property.

   C) One reason that the French government alienated the working class was that the working conditions of the French workers were horrible and the government had failed to enact reforms to improve their situation. The government was slow to act and didn't believe that the workers' conditions were a major concern, since only about one-quarter of the French population worked in industry. The French workers, however, began to call strikes and demonstrations to call public attention to their plight. In response to the strikes, the government brutally suppressed the workers, alienating them in the process.
   (*Western Civilization*, 9th ed., p. 741 / 10th ed., p. 737; Historical Thinking Skills—Causation; Learning Objective SP-3, SP-4, IS-7, IS-10; Key Concept 3.3)

2. A) The existence of many nationalities within the empire affected the Austro-Hungarian Empire by making it very difficult for the government to accomplish its goals. The empire was in decline by the end of the nineteenth century due to the granting of universal suffrage to all people in the empire in 1907. This situation gave small ethnic minorities who had never had a significant role in government members within the imperial parliament. Once they had members in parliament, they began to call for autonomy, forcing the prime ministers to

rule by decree. This situation led to more and more tensions within the empire in the years preceding World War I.

B) Germans within the empire reacted to the existence of many nationalities in the empire by developing a potent and dangerous German nationalism. Germans felt threatened by the rising presence of the smaller minorities in the parliament, since they had traditionally one of the most dominant minority groups within the empire. To preserve their position, they began to form radical political parties that supported unification with Germany. Some German radicals also joined the Christian Socialist party, an anti-Semitic party that was very nationalistic.

C) The Magyars began to clamor for independence at the turn of the twentieth century, hoping to gain complete separation from Austria. After demanding the right to have their own army, the Magyars faced considerable opposition from the Emperor and other Austrian officials who threatened to impose universal male suffrage on Hungary. Fearing a loss of their power, the Magyars rescinded their demands and cooperated with the empire, knowing that they needed to be on good terms with Austria to keep their power.

(*Western Civilization*, 9th ed., p. 742 / 10th ed., p. 738; Historical Thinking Skills—Contextualization; Learning Objective OS-12, SP-17, IS-7, IS-10; Key Concepts 3.3, 3.5, 3.6)

Long-Essay Questions

1. For this question, be sure to address both the methods and goals of European suffragists. Women had been calling for suffrage and other legal rights since the mid-nineteenth century, but after the Reform Bills of 1867 and 1884, which gave most men the right to vote, women began to agitate more actively for their rights. Tied to the desire for equal political rights was the right to vote. Women believed that if they had the right to vote, then they would also be able to gain other rights, such as more equity in marriage and divorce laws and laws concerning the custody of children. Two women spearheaded competing women's suffrage movements in England, and they used contrasting methods. Millicent Fawcett, a moderate liberal, formed the National Union of Women's Suffrage Societies, a group that believed that they must act responsibly if they hoped to get Parliament to grant them the right to vote. Emmeline Pankhurst founded the Women's Social and Political Union (WSPU), a much more violent organization that was willing to take any actions necessary to gain the right to vote for women. Methods used by Pankhurst's organization included publicity stunts and use of the media to put forth their demands. WSPU members also went on hunger strikes, chained themselves to lamp-posts, burned railroad cars, and broke the windows of department stores. Although women did not gain the right to vote in most nations until after World War I, the efforts of the suffragists to gain the right to vote and other legal rights were pursued with a variety of methods, from peaceful to violent, in the years preceding the war. Be sure to add a brief (2–3 sentences) synthesis discussion to your essay. For this essay, you could compare this period of

focusing on women's rights with the focus on women's rights in the late twentieth century.
(*Western Civilization*, 9th ed., pp. 735–38 / 10th ed., pp. 731–34; Historical Thinking Skills—Contextualization; Learning Objectives OS-4, SP-9, IS-6, IS-9; Key Concept 3.3)

2. For this question, be sure to address both intellectual and cultural aspects of European thought and explain how these developments influenced modern consciousness at the turn of the century. Tremendous change took place across Europe toward the end of the nineteenth century. New ways of thinking broke with the accepted ideas. Most nineteenth-century Europeans believed in progress. Advances in science confirmed the limitless power of rational thought, and evidence of human advancement was everywhere. At the turn of the century, however, advances in science, coupled with new intellectual beliefs, gave rise to a new modern consciousness. The work of scientists such as Marie Curie, Max Planck, and Albert Einstein represented a radical departure from previous notions and opened a new frontier in physics. Other intellectual developments also challenged previously held notions of human reality. Looking at all of the irrational forces that made up human existence, philosopher Friedrich Nietzsche questioned the influence reason played in shaping mankind. Likewise, the work of Sigmund Freud pointed to the human unconscious as the key factor in determining human behavior.

All of these advances in human thought challenged European society and shook the optimism associated with the Enlightenment. In the world of art and literature, great changes that corresponded with the intellectual developments in science and thought were taking place. European novelists broke away from the relative optimism of the earlier Realist movement, writing instead about overwhelming forces beyond the control of everyday people. Writers such as Émile Zola emphasized mankind's struggle for survival and the impacts of heredity and environment on one's fate. Painters, too, broke with traditional cultural norms. Impressionist and Post-Impressionist works contrasted starkly with the Realist paintings of the early nineteenth century. Reality became much more subjective in works by artists such as Paul Cézanne and Vincent van Gogh. As Europe entered the twentieth century, the transformation of ideas of reality by such artists as Pablo Picasso and Wassily Kandinsky led to abstract painting, which abandoned visual representation altogether. The uncertainties that emerged from turn-of-the-century thought would become important elements of post-war Europe during the 1920s and beyond. Be sure to add a brief (2-3 sentences) synthesis discussion to your essay. For this essay, you could compare these intellectual and cultural developments with those in the Renaissance and how they shaped modern Europe.
(*Western Civilization*, 9th ed., pp. 724–35 / 10th ed., pp. 720–31; Historical Thinking Skills—Contextualization; Learning Objectives OS-10, OS-12, OS-13; Key Concept 3.6)

Period 4: 1914 to the Present

Period 4 of the AP® European History framework examines the developments that occurred between the outbreak of World War I and the present. World War I disrupted the fragile balance of power that had prevented a general war in Europe in the late nineteenth century and demonstrated the degree of destruction that new technologies could inflict. Europeans, confused and distraught over the conditions that they faced after the war, began to question the rationality of the world. The Versailles conference and League of Nations attempted to create a lasting peace in the postwar years, but extremism threatened the peace, allowing for the rise of communism in Russia and fascism in Italy and Germany. With the growing aggression of the Nazi state, the economic problems stemming from the Great Depression, and the growth of Stalinism, peace proved elusive and soon Europe degenerated into World War II. Following this war, uneasy alliances soon faltered and Europeans found themselves living in a bipolar world with the United States economically and politically controlling the western bloc and the USSR creating satellite states in the east. As the gap between the East and West grew during the Cold War years, discontent began to destabilize the Eastern bloc and the West began to practice more economic cooperation through the development of the European Coal and Steel Community and the European Economic Community. The accession of Mikhail Gorbachev in 1985 marked the beginning of a new period in Soviet history. His policies of *glasnost* and *perestroika* significantly changed Soviet responses to the growing democratization movements in Eastern Europe, culminating in the revolutions of 1989 and the collapse of the Soviet Union. By the 1990s, Europe was in a state of change, as ethnic nationalism began to transform the map through war and secession. The ongoing movement for cooperation expanded with the formal creation of the European Union in 1993 and the adoption of the euro at the end of the millennium. Globalization, new technologies, and continually evolving international relationships continue to alter the course of Europe's political and economic future.

The following charts outline the learning objectives and topics from the content outline that fit into this era.

THEMATIC LEARNING OBJECTIVES FOR PERIOD 4

INTERACTION OF EUROPE AND THE WORLD

Learning Objectives—Students are able to...	Relevant Topics in the Concept Outline
INT-1: Assess the relative influence of economic, religious, and political motives in promoting exploration and colonization.	4.1.VII—Post-WWI mandate system
INT-2: Analyze the cultural beliefs that justified European conquest of overseas territories and how they changed over time.	4.1.VII—Principle of national self-determination

339

Learning Objectives—Students are able to…	Relevant Topics in the Concept Outline
INT-3: Analyze how European states established and administered overseas commercial and territorial empires.	4.1.VII—Mandate system
INT-6: Assess the role of overseas trade, labor, and technology in making Europe part of a global economic network and in encouraging the development of new economic theories and state policies.	4.2.IV—Post-war reconstruction of industry and infrastructure; consumerism 4.4.I—New communication and transportation technologies
INT-7: Analyze how contact with non-European peoples increased European social and cultural diversity and affected attitudes toward race.	4.1.VII—National self-determination 4.2.III—Increased immigration into Europe 4.4.III—Anti-immigrant agitation and extreme nationalist political parties
INT-8: Evaluate the United States' economic and cultural influence on Europe and responses to this influence in Europe.	4.1.I—Emergence of United States as a world power. 4.1.II—Wilsonian idealism 4.1.IV—Cold War; world monetary and trade systems and geopolitical alliances 4.2.III—1929 stock market crash 4.2.IV—Marshall Plan 4.3.IV—United States' influence on elite and popular culture 4.4.III—Green parties; revolt of 1968
INT-9: Assess the role of European contact on overseas territories through the introduction of disease, participation in the slave trade and slavery, effects on agricultural and manufacturing patterns, and global conflict.	4.1.I—Cause of First World War 4.1.IV—Cold War outside Europe 4.1.VII—Decolonization
INT-10: Explain the extent of and causes for non-Europeans' adoption of or resistance to European cultural, political, or economic values and institutions, and explain the causes of their reactions.	4.1.VII—Independence movements and mandates
INT-11: Explain how European expansion and colonization brought non-European societies into global economic, diplomatic, military, and cultural networks.	4.1.I—World War I outside Europe 4.1.IV—Cold War outside Europe 4.3.III—Colonial emigration to Europe 4.4.III—Guest workers

POVERTY AND PROSPERITY

Learning Objectives—Students are able to…	Relevant Topics in the Concept Outline
PP-1: Explain how and why wealth generated from new trading, financial, and manufacturing practices and institutions created a market and then a consumer economy.	4.2.IV—Post-war economic growth 4.3.IV—Increased imports of United States technology and popular culture 4.4.I—Mass production, new food technologies and industrial efficiency

Learning Objectives—Students are able to…	Relevant Topics in the Concept Outline
PP-3: Explain how geographic, economic, social, and political factors affected the pace, nature, and timing of industrialization in Western and Eastern Europe.	4.2.I—Russia's incomplete industrialization
PP-4: Explain how the development of new technologies and industries—as well as new means of communication, marketing, and transportation—contributed to expansion of consumerism and increased standards of living and quality of life in the nineteenth and twentieth centuries.	4.3.II—Medical technologies 4.4.I—Mass productions, food technologies, industrial efficiency, communication and transportation technologies 4.4.II—New modes of reproduction
PP-5: Analyze the origins, characteristics, and effects of the post-World War II "economic miracle" and the economic integration (the euro zone).	4.1.IV—World monetary and trade systems 4.1. V—European economic and political integration 4.2.IV—Post-war economic growth and welfare benefits 4.4.I—Creation of a consumer culture 4.4.II—Professional careers for women; the baby boom 4.4.III—Increased immigration to Europe
PP-8: Analyze socialist, communist, and fascist efforts to develop responses to capitalism and why these efforts gained support during times of economic crisis.	4.2.I—The Russian Revolution 4.2.II—The ideology of fascism 4.2.III—The Great Depression
PP-10: Explain the role of social inequality in contributing to and affecting the nature of the French Revolution and subsequent revolutions throughout the nineteenth and twentieth centuries.	4.2.I—The Russian Revolution
PP-11: Analyze the social and economic causes and consequences of the Great Depression in Europe.	4.2.II—Increased popularity of fascist ideology 4.2.III—The Great Depression 4.3.I—Belief in progress breaks down
PP-12: Evaluate how the expansion of a global consumer economy after World War II served as a catalyst to opposition movements in Eastern and Western Europe.	4.2.V—Collapse of the Soviet Union 4.3.IV—Criticism of United States' technology and popular culture 4.4.III—Green parties; revolts of 1968
PP-13: Analyze how cities and states have attempted to address the problems brought about by economic modernization, such as poverty and famine, through regulating morals, policing marginal populations, and improving public health.	4.2.IV—Expansion of social welfare programs
PP-14: Explain how industrialization elicited critiques from artists, socialists, worker's movements, and feminist organizations.	4.3.I—Belief in progress breaks down 4.3.IV—Criticism of United States' technology and popular culture

Learning Objectives—Students are able to…	Relevant Topics in the Concept Outline
PP-15: Analyze efforts of government and nongovernmental reform movements to respond to poverty and other social problems in the nineteenth and twentieth centuries.	4.2.I—The Russian Revolution 4.2.IV—Expansion of social welfare programs 4.2.V—Social welfare programs in Central and Eastern Europe; *perestroika*
PP-16: Analyze how democratic, authoritarian, and totalitarian governments of the left and right attempted to overcome the financial crises of the 1920s and 1930s.	4.2.I—Lenin's New Economic Policy; Stalin's economic modernization 4.2.III—Dependence on American investment capital; attempts to rethink economic policies

OBJECTIVE KNOWLEDGE AND SUBJECTIVE VISIONS

Learning Objectives—Students are able to…	Relevant Topics in the Concept Outline
OS-3: Explain how political revolution and war from the seventeenth century on altered the role of the church in political and intellectual life and the response of religious authorities and intellectuals to such challenges.	4.3.III—Continued role of organized religion
OS-4: Explain how a worldview based on science and reason challenged and preserved social order and roles, especially the roles of women.	4.4.II—Family responsibilities; economic changes and feminism 4.4.III—Gay and lesbian movements
OS-8: Explain the emergence, spread, and questioning of scientific, technological, and positivist approaches to addressing social problems.	4.3.I—Challenges to the belief in progress 4.3.III—Benefits and challenges of science and technology
OS-9: Explain how new theories of government and political ideologies attempted to provide a coherent explanation for human behavior and the extent to which they adhered to or diverged from traditional explanations based on religious beliefs.	4.2.II—Fascist rejection of democracy, glorification of war, and nationalism
OS-10: Analyze the means by which individualism, subjectivity, and emotion came to be considered a valid source of knowledge.	4.3.I—Challenge to confidence in science and human reason 4.3.IV—Self-expression and subjectivity in the arts
OS-11: Explain how and why religion increasingly shifted from a matter of public concern to one of private belief over the course of European history.	4.3.III—Continued role of organized religion
OS-12: Analyze how artists used strong emotions to express individuality and political theorists encouraged emotional identification with the nation.	4.2.II—Fascist nationalism
OS-13: Explain how and why modern artists began to move away from realism and toward abstraction and the non-rational, rejecting traditional aesthetics.	4.3.IV—Experimentation, self-expression, and subjectivity in the arts

STATES AND OTHER INSTITUTIONS OF POWER

Learning Objectives—Students are able to...	Relevant Topics in the Concept Outline
SP-1: Explain the emergence of civic humanism and new conceptions of political authority during the Renaissance, as well as subsequent theories and practices that stressed the political importance and rights of the individual.	4.3.II—Industrialized warfare 4.4.II—Women's rights 4.4.III—Dissenting groups in politics
SP-3: Trace the changing relationship between states and ecclesiastical authority and the emergence of the principle of religious toleration.	4.1.IV—Post-World War II religious conflicts 4.3.III—Second Vatican Council and immigration
SP-5: Assess the role of colonization, the Industrial Revolution, total warfare, and economic depressions in altering the government's relationship to the economy, both in overseeing economic activity and in addressing its social impact.	4.1.V—Post-1945 European unity 4.2.I—Russian Revolution 4.2.III—Great Depression 4.2.IV—Economic miracle and welfare state 4.2.V—Planned economies in Eastern Europe
SP-6: Explain how new ideas of political authority and the failure of diplomacy led to world wars, political revolutions, and the establishment of totalitarian regimes in the twentieth century.	4.1.I—Causes of World War I 4.1.II—Versailles settlement 4.1.III—Appeasement and World War II 4.2.I—Bolshevik Revolution and Stalin 4.2.II—Fascism
SP-8: Explain how and why various groups, including communists and fascists, undermined parliamentary democracy through the establishment of regimes that maintained dictatorial control while manipulating democratic forms.	4.1.III—Nazi aggression and *Blitzkrieg* 4.2.I—Bolshevik Revolution and Stalin 4.2.II—Rise of Fascism
SP-9: Analyze how various movements for political and social equality—such as feminism, anti-colonialism, and campaigns for immigrants' rights—pressured governments and redefined citizenship.	4.1.VII—Decolonization 4.2.V—Collapse of communism 4.4.II—Feminism 4.4.III—Post-1945 critics and dissenters
SP-10: Trace the ways in which new technologies from the printing press to the Internet have shaped the development of civil society and enhanced the role of public opinion.	4.2.II—Mass media and propaganda 4.4.I—Total war and higher standard of living
SP-12: Assess the role of civic institutions in shaping the development of representative and democratic forms of government.	4.4.II—Women and feminism 4.4.III—Post-1945 dissenting groups
SP-13: Evaluate how the emergence of new weapons, tactics, and methods of military organization changed the scale and cost of warfare, required the centralization of power, and shifted the balance of power.	4.1.I—Total warfare, 1914–1918 4.1.III—World War II 4.1.IV—Nuclear weapons and Cold War 4.1.VI—Post-1945 nationalist/separatist movements and guerilla warfare 4.3.II—Genocide and nuclear war

Learning Objectives—Students are able to…	Relevant Topics in the Concept Outline
SP-14: Analyze the role of warfare in remaking the political map of Europe and in shifting the global balance of power in the nineteenth and twentieth centuries.	4.1.I—World War I 4.1.II—Versailles settlement 4.1.III—World War II 4.1.IV—Cold War 4.1.VII—Decolonization 4.2.II—Fascist aggressions 4.2.V—Ethnic cleansing in the Balkans
SP-17: Explain the role of nationalism in altering the European balance of power, and explain attempts made to limit nationalism as a means to ensure continental stability.	4.1.1—Nationalism as a cause of World War I 4.1.II—National self-determination and League of Nations 4.1.III—Fascism and "new racial order" 4.1.IV—Cold War and collapse of communism 4.1.V—European unity 4.1.VI—Colonial independence movements 4.2.II—Fascism and extreme nationalism 4.2.V—Eastern European resistance to communism and Balkan conflicts 4.4.III—Immigration and anti-immigrant groups
SP-18: Evaluate how overseas competition and changes in the alliance system upset the Concert of Europe and set the stage for World War I.	4.1.I—Causes of World War I
SP-19: Explain the ways in which the Common Market and collapse of the Soviet Empire changed the political balance of power, the status of the nation-state, and global political alliances.	4.1.IV—Cold War and collapse of communism 4.1.V—European unity 4.2.V—Collapse of communism and Balkan conflicts

INDIVIDUAL AND SOCIETY

Learning Objectives—Students are able to…	Relevant Topics in the Concept Outline
IS-3: Evaluate the role of technology, from the printing press to modern transportation and telecommunications, in forming and transforming society.	4.4.I—Technology as destructive and improving standard of living
IS-4: Analyze how and why the nature and role of the family has changed over time.	4.4.II—Women in workforce, feminism, and baby boom 4.4.III—Feminism and gay/lesbian movements
IS-5: Explain why and how class emerged as a basis for identity and led to conflict in the nineteenth and twentieth centuries.	4.2.I—Russian and Bolshevik revolutions
IS-6: Evaluate the causes and consequences of persistent tensions between women's role and status in the private versus the public sphere.	4.4.II—Total war, post-1945 feminism, and political opportunities

Learning Objectives—Students are able to...	Relevant Topics in the Concept Outline
IS-7: Evaluate how identities such as ethnicity, race, and class have defined the individual in relationship to society.	4.1.III—Nazi racism and the Holocaust 4.1.VI—Post-1945 nationalist and separatist movements 4.4.I—Total war and genocide 4.4.III—Youth, gay/lesbian, immigrant dissenters
IS-8: Evaluate how the impact of war on civilians has affected loyalty to and respect for the nation-state.	4.1.I—World War I and total war on the home front 4.2.I—Russian Revolution and Civil War 4.2.II—Spanish Civil War and World War II 4.3.I—Destructive effects of technology 4.4.I—Total war and genocide
IS-9: Assess the extent to which women participated in and benefited from the shifting values of European society from the fifteenth century onward.	4.4.II—Military production, economic recovery, and post-1945 feminism
IS-10: Analyze how and why Europeans have marginalized certain populations (defined as "other") over the course of their history.	4.1.III—Fascist racism and genocide 4.1.VI—Post-1945 nationalist and separatist movements 4.1.VII—Mandates and decolonization 4.2.I—Kulaks and Great Purges 4.2.II—Fascist propaganda 4.2.V—Balkan conflicts and wars 4.3.III—Guest workers and immigration 4.4.I—Total war and genocide 4.4.III—Post-1945 dissenting groups

KEY CONCEPTS FROM THE COLLEGE BOARD

4.1 Total war and political instability in the first half of the twentieth century gave way to a polarized state order during the Cold War, and eventually to efforts at transnational union.

4.2 The stresses of economic collapse and total war engendered internal conflicts within European States and created conflicting conceptions of the relationship between the individual and the state, as demonstrated in the ideological battle among liberal democracy, communism, and fascism.

4.3 During the twentieth century, diverse intellectual and cultural movements questioned the existence of objective knowledge, the ability of reason to arrive at truth, and the role of religion in determining moral standards.

4.4 Demographic changes, economic growth, total war, disruptions of traditional social patterns, and competing definitions of freedom and justice altered the experiences of everyday life.

14

TURMOIL AND WAR: 1914–1945

World War I drastically altered the economic, social, and political order and left disillusionment in its wake. At the end of World War I, many problems remained unresolved, which led to extended conflict among the nations of Europe. Complicating matters was the fact that revolution in Russia had brought into power a Marxist government that western powers perceived as a major threat to European stability. Any shred of optimism disintegrated with the Great Depression, a global economic collapse. Fascist governments grew stronger in nations afflicted by great turmoil: Italy, Spain, and Germany. Civil war in Spain foreshadowed the full-scale conflict that would emerge at the end of the 1930s. Efforts by France and Great Britain to avoid another European war were thwarted by the aggressive intent of Nazi Germany. Only through the combined efforts of Great Britain, the United States, and the Soviet Union was Germany defeated and peace restored to Europe, but by then, millions were dead and Europe was once again divided.

KEY TERMS

Allied powers
appeasement
authoritarian state
Axis powers
blitzkrieg
Bolsheviks
Cold War
collectivization
conscription
Dadaism
Dawes Plan
fascism

final solution
fuhrerprinzip
general strike
Great Depression
Hiroshima
League of Nations
lebensraum
mandates
National Socialist
German Workers' Party (Nazis)
New Economic Policy (NEP)
Normandy invasion

Nuremberg laws
propaganda
Schlieffen Plan
Soviets
Spanish Civil War
Holocaust
Stalingrad
Surrealism
totalitarianism
total war

Treaty of Brest–Litovsk
Treaty of Locarno
Treaty of Versailles
trench warfare
unconditional surrender
war communism
War Guilt Clause
Weimar Germany
Yalta

CHAPTER KEY CONCEPTS

▧ Unprepared for war, Russia collapsed into revolution in 1917—first against the tsar and then against the provisional government—and finally a bitter civil war erupted. By 1921, Lenin ruled the USSR using a communist system, the first nation in the world to adopt communism as its national ideology.

▧ Modernism in the arts reflected the anxiety present in society, and artists no longer intended to realistically depict the world around them. As individual consciousness became the source of meaning in the world, artists hoped to capture their inner feelings and their own vision of reality in their works.

▧ At the end of World War I, communism had taken root in the Soviet Union, Germany was infuriated by the terms of the Treaty of Versailles, and aggressive fascist governments were undermining peace. European leaders failed to prevent another catastrophic conflict, and Europe plunged into World War II. Even more destructive than World War I, it left Europe divided between a pro-democratic West and a Soviet-backed East.

▧ The years 1919–1945 were marked by both optimism and great disillusionment. Europeans made economic progress during the 1920s, only to see it obliterated by the Great Depression. Authoritarian states appealed to many searching for hope and order in a bleak world. World War II brought substantial hardship, but European economies rebounded and went on to reach new economic heights following the war.

▧ Artists and intellectuals reflected the despair of the interwar years. German expressionists focused on the suffering of, and damages to, humanity caused by the First World War, Dadaists expressed a contempt for Western traditions, and surrealists portrayed an illogical and disturbing world in which objects were divorced from their normal context and the irrational became tangible. Traditional codes of behavior were also overturned, as women and youth sought greater freedom.

For a full discussion of the period 1914–1945, see *Western Civilization*, 9th and 10th editions, Chapters 25–27.

THE OUTBREAK OF WAR

In the summer of 1914, myriad factors came together to unleash one of the great tragedies in world history.

A byproduct of nineteenth-century liberalism, nationalism fed intense rivalries in Europe. National honor was a high priority of European leaders, most of whom were influenced by bombastic military leaders, and diplomacy was based on the principles of nationalism.

Many historians argue that European leaders used warfare to remedy domestic social problems, such as the push by minority groups—including the Serbs, Irish, and Poles—for political independence, and the socialist labor movement across Europe.

So dependent on the military, European powers created some of the largest armies known to mankind. Advances in transportation, communication, and public health allowed for armies of nearly one million troops. With such substantial forces, some European nations used conscription to force men to join, and governments depended on military leadership to make political decisions.

On June 28, 1914, Austrian Archduke Francis Ferdinand and his wife, Sophia, were assassinated in Sarajevo by a Bosnian nationalist. The Austrian government wanted to use the act to punish all Serbian nationalists. Emperor William II gave Austria a "blank check"—Germany's "full support" for any reprisal against Serbia. Austria then sent an ultimatum so extreme that Serbia had no choice but to reject it. Austria declared war on Serbia, trusting that the conflict would be limited in scope and duration.

Mobilization was complex, demanding detailed planning and precise execution. Russia had the largest army in Europe and mobilization plans for war against both Germany and Austria. When Tsar Nicholas II called for a partial mobilization against Austria, he was told that would be impossible. The resulting full mobilization provoked Germany to declare war on Russia.

With the formation of the Triple Entente, Germany faced the probability of a two-front war. Its strategy for such a scenario was the Schlieffen Plan, which called for the German army to strike quickly against the French, taking Paris and forcing the French to surrender, and then turning quickly to the east and defeating the Russian army before it had a chance to fully mobilize. With the Schlieffen Plan, Germany was forced to declare war on France, which led Great Britain to declare war on Germany because Belgian neutrality had been violated by the German march toward Paris. In a matter of days, the great powers of Europe were at war. Across the continent, news of the war prompted enthusiasm. Nationalists welcomed it—even diehard socialists favored war.

THE GREAT WAR

Eager troops marched off, sure they would be home for Christmas. But both the British and the Russians mobilized quickly. On the outskirts of Paris, the German advance was halted. The machine gun completely changed warfare. Its deadly efficiency spurred the digging of massive trench systems that would eventually stretch across much of Western Europe. The defining feature of World War I would be trench warfare.

In Eastern Europe, the Germans scored an early victory over the Russians, and then joined forces with the Austrians to push Russia back. With over two million soldiers dead, Russia was no longer a serious problem to the Central Powers. Germany turned back to the west. Both sides found that frontal assaults to break through enemy lines were fruitless as wave after wave of soldiers was mowed down.

As the war turned into a stalemate, new allies were sought. When the Ottoman Empire joined the Central Powers, the Allied forces suffered a disastrous defeat in an attempt to establish a front near Constantinople. The British, led by Lawrence of Arabia, encouraged Arab leaders to revolt against the Ottomans, and by 1918, the Ottoman Empire was finished. The Allies also attacked German colonial holdings in Africa and Asia.

In 1917, the United States joined the war, abandoning neutrality when the Germans resumed unrestricted submarine warfare.

War on such a massive scale makes extraordinary demands on a nation. Governments centralized their powers, manipulated their economies, used propaganda to hold public support, and enlisted the citizenry to produce goods for the war effort. As a result, society changed in many ways during World War I. For example, labor unions gained more power because a satisfied workforce is needed to keep the war machine rolling; in addition, governments curtailed civil liberties, announcing that anyone speaking out against the war would face charges of treason.

Women also were significantly affected by the war. Wartime contingencies forced them to take jobs usually held by men in both offices and heavy industry. They also gained the right to vote. Many Europeans were persuaded that granting women suffrage would lend a moral dimension to national politics and perhaps prevent another war.

REVOLUTION

The war brought misery to everyone, at home and on the front lines. As the death toll mounted, angry citizens openly challenged the status quo. In Russia the discontent led to full-scale revolution.

Russian dissatisfaction with tsarist rule had been felt long before World War I. But the war proved a catastrophe for Russia, whose huge army had been ineffective, as had Nicholas II and his wife, Alexandra, who ruled while Nicholas was at the front. Led by resentful top government officials, disenchantment with the monarchy grew. With working-class mothers leading the way, tens of thousands marched through Petrograd protesting the war and the near-starvation that many Russians faced. The army refused to put down the protest. On March 15, 1917, Nicholas II abdicated.

A liberal provisional government was established but was challenged at the outset by councils of workers and soldiers, divided between two factions: the moderate Mensheviks and more radical Bolsheviks. The Bolsheviks, led by Vladimir Lenin, called for the complete destruction of the capitalist system.

During the summer of 1917, the provisional government decided to remain in the war, launching an offensive that failed significantly. The Bolsheviks seized power and made good on their earlier promises: land was given to the peasants, factories were turned over to the workers, and civil rights were accorded to women. The Treaty of Brest–Litovsk ended Russia's involvement in the war.

AP® Tip

The Russian Revolution is often paired with the French and American Revolutions in Comparison questions in the AP® exam. Be sure you understand how the fear and distrust that grew out of the rivalry between Russia and the West emerged during this time period. These attitudes shaped much of twentieth-century history.

Success did not come easily for the Communists (as the Bolsheviks were soon called), as various groups challenged Soviet rule. This culminated in a bloody three-year civil war. Across Russia, the Red Army fought against fragmented anti-Communist forces unable to effectively unite (the White Army). Strongly united behind a common purpose that allowed for coherent military strategy, the Communist forces won.

The Communists also had success with a policy of "war communism" that allowed them to nationalize industry, control agricultural production, and centralize government. A secret police force, the Cheka, was called on to eliminate all opposition. Thousands were executed, including the entire royal family.

THE WAR ENDS

When Russia withdrew from the war, the Germans launched a massive offensive on the western front. At first the German gamble appeared to be successful, but with the arrival of fresh troops from America, the German advance was halted. As more American troops entered the battlefields, German leaders realized that victory was impossible. William II abdicated, and on November 11, 1918, a new German government signed an armistice.

The war devastated Europe. Some 9 million soldiers died; 22 million were wounded. The social fabric of European society was torn apart. Germany and Austria–Hungary experienced political upheaval. In Germany, radical socialists vying for political supremacy lost when leaders of the moderates instructed the army to kill the radicals' leaders. The senselessness of the war led many Europeans to search for peace. They found a voice in U.S. president Woodrow Wilson, who drew up an outline for lasting peace, the Fourteen Points. Key provisions were the elimination of secret diplomacy, the right of self-determination, and a "general association of nations" to help ensure democracy around the world.

THE TREATY OF VERSAILLES

Wilson's popularity throughout Europe did not soften the ambitions of the victors. Meeting in Paris in early 1919, David Lloyd George of Britain and Georges Clemenceau of France agreed that Germany should be held responsible for the war and pay harsh reparations. The British aimed to secure their overseas empire, while the French wanted to protect themselves from future German aggression. After much compromise, they agreed to Wilson's League of Nations. On June 28, 1919, the Treaty of Versailles was signed. The Germans were outraged by the terms, particularly Article 231, the so-called War Guilt Clause.

Eastern Europe was also reconfigured. New nation-states were created to satisfy ethnic nationalism and serve as potential allies to France and Britain. Austria–Hungary was dismantled; Austria, Hungary, and Czechoslovakia emerged as new nations, while the Balkans were reshaped to provide land for Romania and Serbia. The Ottoman Empire was dissolved into new Arab states; however, Britain and France controlled them as mandates on behalf of the newly created League of Nations.

The peace process put into place a structure that might have prevented future world wars. But protecting peace would require a vigorous effort by the global powers, and when the U.S. Senate refused to ratify the Treaty of Versailles, it was doomed. When the United States retreated into isolationism, Britain followed suit, and France found itself alone to face the wrath of Germany.

A PRECARIOUS PEACE

One of the most difficult post-war situations involved Germany and France. In the name of national security, France insisted that Germany make reparations for World War I. After an initial payment, Germany realized that reparations were not economically or politically feasible. To force Germany to pay, France occupied the Ruhr valley, precipitating a German economic disaster. The Deutsche Mark became worthless, and German extremists grew in popularity.

To address the situation, an international commission proposed the Dawes Plan, calling for a reduction in reparations and U.S. loans for German economic recovery. The Dawes Plan relied on foreign investment, primarily from the United States. Although Germany's economy improved in the short run, the dependency on foreign economies proved detrimental at the onset of the Great Depression. France and Germany kept up momentum with further diplomacy, resulting in the Treaty of Locarno (1925), which established Germany's western borders. The agreement produced great optimism, later reinforced by the Kellogg-Briand Pact, which was designed to outlaw war as an "instrument of national policy." These diplomatic measures, however, were unenforceable.

AP® Tip

Be sure you understand the weaknesses of post-war Germany and the Weimar Republic. Especially important is the growth of extremism in response to the economic and political instability of the 1920s and 1930s. These factors are key to understanding the rise of Nazi Germany.

THE GREAT DEPRESSION

Economies in the United States and much of Europe flourished during the 1920s, giving many government leaders the impression that the market economy was impervious to decline. This was utterly disproved when the American stock market crashed in 1929. American investors pulled their money from European banks, forcing major European financial institutions to fail. As governments raised tariffs to protect home industry, the global market came to a standstill and nations around the world suffered.

Unemployment rapidly set upon nations, most severely in Germany. Long bread lines became a common sight, as Europeans took the brunt of the international economic crisis. Governments that had sung the praises of the free market now were reluctant to provide aid for citizens in dire circumstances. Demagogues who aroused the emotions and prejudices of the people offered simplistic explanations to the disastrous problems in many nations and attracted many new followers.

THE RETREAT FROM DEMOCRACY

The myriad problems in the 1920s gave rise to stark social divisions that threatened national cohesion and democratic forms of governance. Many European countries embraced totalitarianism, establishing dictatorships that controlled the political, economic, and social spheres. Propaganda was one of the most important methods of taking control. Techniques of manipulation that had been developed during the war were adopted by extremists to convince a desperate public that only with a single leader and a single party could a nation's destiny be achieved. Democracy was derided as ineffective—even unhelpful.

Fascism took root in nations that had suffered humiliation and economic deprivation. Fascist leaders blended the principles of totalitarian rule with extreme nationalism to produce a form of government that denied individual freedoms in favor of the collective will of the masses or, in the cases of Italy and Germany, for the good of the state or the nation.

FASCIST ITALY

Italy suffered greatly during World War I. When the country's demands for new territory after the war were rejected, extremists made the case that Italy had been cheated. In addition, high unemployment among returning soldiers set the stage for the rise of a fascist government.

Benito Mussolini led the fascist movement in Italy. Having been expelled from the Socialist Party, Mussolini formed the Fascio di Combattimento (League of Combat) in 1919 and took advantage of rising anticommunism to gain the support of middle-class industrialists. His supporters soon resorted to armed violence. Large numbers of war veterans formed black-shirted paramilitary groups that set out to intimidate political opposition.

Emboldened, the Fascists marched to Rome to seize power in 1922. The gamble was successful, and Mussolini was named prime minister of Italy. Within three years, Mussolini had established a fascist dictatorship. The Fascists, however, never achieved total domination. For example, the mass media was not completely cooperative, and Italian youth rebelled against forced militarization. Even the Church, through the Lateran Accords, demanded recognition as the "sole religion of the state" in return for the Vatican's support of the Fascists.

NAZI GERMANY

Among the many problems faced by the democratic Weimar Republic, established in Germany after the war, were weak leadership and severe economic problems exacerbated by the Great Depression. These difficulties provided an opening for the Nazi party, led by Adolf Hitler. A failed Austrian artist, Hitler had served in World War I and then moved to Munich to get involved in politics. He organized the National Socialist German Workers' Party—or Nazis—in 1921; it grew quickly in strength.

Confident of their popular support, Hitler and his followers staged an uprising at a Munich beer hall in 1923. The uprising failed, and Hitler was arrested and sentenced to prison, where he wrote *Mein Kampf*, an autobiographical account of the Nazi party and its underlying ideology. Hitler stressed German nationalism, anti-Semitism, anti-communism, and *Lebensraum*, the notion that superior nations have the right to expand their borders.

To further his goals, Hitler appealed to Germany's youth. As the economy continued to plummet during the 1930s and the Nazis gained seats in the Reichstag, members of Germany's elite were eager to cooperate with them. Wealthy industrialists and landed aristocrats envisioned Hitler as a pawn in their efforts to thwart the communists. Within months, however, the Nazis had used the German parliament to secure a dictatorship. By 1934, Hitler had become sole ruler of Germany and leader of the Third Reich.

> ### AP® Tip
>
> The Nazis succeeded for many reasons—discontent with the Weimar government; anger over the Treaty of Versailles; and economic factors, including the dramatic increase in German employment rates, a result of efforts to rearm. In addition, the German military elite agreed with Hitler's plan for expanding the country's borders. Finally, strong anticommunist factions across Western Europe, especially in France and Britain, supported Hitler's foreign policy.

Totalitarianism in Germany was based on Aryan racial superiority, and the German people would lead a global movement to assert Aryan dominance. The Nazis skillfully used public demonstrations to suggest mass support, and as in fascist Italy, women and children played an important role in advancing totalitarianism. Virulent anti-Semitism quickly became official government policy. The rights of Jews were limited by the Nuremberg Laws, which called for the political, social, and legal separation of Germany's Jewish population from Aryan Germany. By the end of the 1930s, German Jews were being sent to concentration camps.

THE SOVIET UNION

The communist victory in the Russian Civil War brought totalitarian government. The war's devastation forced communist leader Vladimir Lenin to institute his New Economic Policy in 1921, allowing for small-scale capitalism. In 1922, the Communists created the Union of Soviet Socialist Republics, the Soviet Union. Lenin's death in 1924 set off a power struggle for Soviet leadership. Two camps formed within the Communist Party; the Left, led by Leon Trotsky, called for international revolution, while the Right called for "socialism at home." Joseph Stalin, party general secretary, used his position to gain control of the party, and Trotsky was soon expelled from it.

Stalin instituted radical measures to transform the Soviet Union into a modern industrial state. Five-year Plans outlined production goals, emphasizing heavy industry at the expense of agriculture. Propaganda campaigns were used to inspire workers, whose wages and working conditions declined throughout the period. Peasants were forced onto collective farms, and all private property was eliminated. Those who fought this policy met with severe retribution—the government even forced famines in recalcitrant regions such as the Ukraine. Those who openly disagreed with Soviet policy—be they military leaders or peasants—were sent to forced labor camps.

THE SPANISH CIVIL WAR

The Great Depression gave rise to political instability in Spain until 1936, when the Popular Front, a coalition of antifascist parties including democrats and radical socialists, took control. The Spanish military rebelled, however, and launched a three-year civil war.

Led by General Francisco Franco, the right-wing rebels were aided by the fascist regimes of Italy and Germany. Hitler, in particular, saw the civil war as an opportunity to test military weapons and strategy. The Popular Front requested assistance from other European nations, but because it counted socialists among its members, only the Soviet Union would lend support.

Franco's forces overwhelmed the republican army. Many civilians died as a result of indiscriminate aerial bombing raids—the subject matter of Pablo Picasso's *Guernica*. With victory, Franco became dictator of Spain, a position he would hold until his death in 1975.

CULTURE DURING THE INTERWAR YEARS

Two factors greatly changed European society during the interwar years: the advent of the eight-hour workday gave Europeans time to participate in leisure activities, once the exclusive domain of the wealthy; and the development of innovations, such as radio and motion pictures. Radio broadcasts became a familiar feature in much of Europe during the 1920s, and by the 1930s, going to the movies on a weekly basis was a common activity.

Authoritarian governments grasped the significance of this new technology and quickly used it to control the masses. Radio broadcasts or motion pictures were ideal media for fascist propaganda. The 1934 documentary by German director Leni Riefenstahl, *Triumph of the Will*, presented a Nazi political rally in Nuremberg in a sympathetic light meant to exploit viewer emotions.

Artists working in the postwar years were inspired by the war's destruction. Abstract art was embraced, and Dadaism and Surrealism emerged. Dadaists set out to create "anti-art," to reflect what they perceived as the insanity of life. Surrealists including Salvador Dali explored irrational thought and the world of the subconscious.

Literature was influenced by Sigmund Freud's theories, many of which became part of the cultural landscape during the 1920s. Writers such as James Joyce and Virginia Woolf used "stream of consciousness" to capture their fictional characters' thoughts through inner dialogues. Joyce's *Ulysses*, published in 1922, follows a day in the life of an ordinary Dubliner, through inner dialogues that underscore the complexity of human existence.

THE ROAD TO WAR

In the long run, Hitler was determined to conquer Russia and its perceived inferior Slavic peoples. In Hitler's mind, the Russian Revolution had brought forth a weak government controlled by Jews. By invading Russia, Hitler could provide the German people with needed land (and oil) and use the Slavic people as slave labor. But first Hitler had to embark on a "diplomatic revolution" that would break Germany free from the confines of the Versailles Treaty and allow it to gain valuable territory in Eastern Europe.

The British especially turned to appeasement. When Hitler reoccupied the Rhineland, in violation of the Treaty of Versailles, he met with no military opposition from the French, who refused to confront Germany without first gaining the support of the British. By the end of 1936, Hitler had scrapped the Treaty of Versailles and formed military alliances with Italy and Japan. Neville Chamberlain, an ardent appeaser elected British Prime Minister in 1937, believed that the success of the British empire depended on German cooperation. Emboldened, Hitler carried out the *Anschluss*—the annexing of Austria—with no interference.

In 1938, British and French leaders met with Hitler in Munich to discuss Hitler's demand to annex the Sudetenland region of Czechoslovakia. Agreeing to all of Hitler's desires, Chamberlain declared that he had achieved "peace in our time." Recognizing Western democracies' lack of will, Hitler took all of Czechoslovakia.

Next on Hitler's list was Poland. To invade Poland, he had to contend with the Soviet Union. In August of 1939, Hitler and Stalin signed the Nazi-Soviet Nonaggression Pact, which divided Eastern Europe into spheres of influence, and included the separation of Poland. On September 1, 1939, German forces invaded Poland. Two days later, Britain and France declared war on Germany. World War II had begun.

WAR

In preparing for war, the Germans developed a new form of military warfare called Blitzkrieg, or "lightning war." The idea was to knock out the enemy quickly through coordinated air strikes and mechanized infantry attacks. Air and ground assaults were launched with great success across Western Europe. The Germans conquered Poland within a month and divided it with the Soviets, who themselves had overtaken eastern Poland. After a period of inactivity, known as the "phony war," the Germans resumed attacks on Western Europe in the spring. German troops quickly conquered Northern Europe, while the French surrendered three-fifths of their own nation to the Germans and placed the remaining territory under the authoritarian rule of Marshal Pétain in the town of Vichy.

Once the war began, the SS started imposing Hitler's Final Solution—the complete annihilation of the Jewish people of Europe. Many European Jews were sent to ghettos, and special strike forces exterminated entire Jewish villages in Eastern Europe. Before long, Hitler would call for the creation of death camps where Jews—along with Gypsies, Slavs, homosexuals, and the infirm—could be annihilated systematically.

British dissatisfaction forced Chamberlain to resign. Winston Churchill, the next British prime minister, despised Hitler and refused to capitulate. Hitler would have to invade. A successful amphibious assault would require control of the air, so the Germans launched a massive air campaign. At the start, British military bases and communication centers were targeted, but Hitler changed tactics: to destroy morale, he ordered the bombing of cities. In fact, however, morale subsequently soared. Churchill convinced Britons to "never surrender."

Thwarted in Britain, Hitler turned elsewhere, sending German troops to North Africa to aid the Italian army. But his true ambition was to conquer the Soviet Union, and he was confident that his superb army could defeat the ill-trained, poorly led Soviet forces. Germany attacked the Soviet Union in June 1941, but the Soviets resisted, and by December, the Germans were bogged down at the start of an unusually harsh winter.

PEARL HARBOR

Since the beginning of the twentieth century, Japan had worked to become a world power through industrialization. The Great Depression and ensuing economic crisis gave more influence to the Japanese military, which encouraged a policy of expansion in the Pacific Rim.

In 1931, Japan invaded Manchuria and began an encroachment that led to full-scale war with the Chinese in 1937. Interested in Soviet-controlled Siberia, Japan formed an alliance with Hitler, and then turned its attention to European holdings to the south. This led to reprisals from the United States, which, in turn, prompted the Japanese surprise attack on the American naval fleet housed at Pearl Harbor, Hawaii, on December 7, 1941. The next day, the United States declared war on Japan. Three days later, Hitler declared war on the United States, bringing America into the European conflict.

TURNING POINTS

The U.S. entry into the war resulted in the Grand Alliance among the United States, Britain, and the Soviet Union. Although suspicious of one another, Roosevelt, Churchill, and Stalin recognized that they had to unite to defeat Germany. Agreeing to secure an unconditional surrender from the Axis powers, they ensured a unified front and made an approach of divide and conquer challenging for Hitler.

World War II demanded even more from the home front than World War I. Every facet of society was influenced by the needs of the military. Large numbers of workers were given jobs in factories and on farms. In Britain, the United States, and the Soviet Union, women were recruited for the industrial workforce. Only in Germany did the female workforce not increase substantially, because conquered regions had become a source of forced labor there.

In the spring of 1942, the Axis nations were at their zenith of power: Japan controlled much of the Pacific, while Germany controlled most of Europe and North Africa. But the tide soon began to change. In North Africa, combined British and American forces defeated Erwin Rommel's Afrika Korps. In the Pacific, U.S. forces knocked out four Japanese aircraft carriers at the Battle of Midway, crippling Japan's offensive capability. A key victory came in Stalingrad, the focus of both Hitler and Stalin. Both men had ordered their forces to achieve victory at all costs. By winter, Soviet reserves had reached Stalingrad and surrounded German troops, forcing their surrender in February 1943. By the spring, German forces were on the defensive as the Red Army pushed toward Germany.

THE CONCLUSION

When Germany invaded the Soviet Union, Stalin had been eager for British and American forces to open a western front as soon as possible. On June 6, 1944, Allied forces landed on the beaches of Normandy, catching the Germans by surprise. Within months, the Allies liberated Paris, and then turned their sights on Berlin. Desperate attempts by the Germans to regain the advantage—the Battle of the Bulge on the western front and the Battle of Kursk on the eastern front—proved unsuccessful. Allied victories continued during the winter of 1944–1945, and German defeat was only a matter of time. As the Red Army closed in, Hitler took his own life. The German high command surrendered a week later, on May 7, 1945.

The Allies turned their attention to Asia. After the victory at Midway, American forces had been slowly working their way across the Pacific, clearing one small island after another before closing in on the Japanese mainland. Convinced that an amphibious assault would lead to massive American casualties, President Harry Truman instead ordered a newly created atomic bomb dropped on Hiroshima. Three days later, on August 9, 1945, a second bomb was dropped on Nagasaki, and the Japanese surrendered, ending the most destructive war in history.

AFTERMATH

The war's final death toll—both civilian and military—was over 60 million people, a large number of those in China and the Soviet Union. The economic devastation was hard to fathom; cities were in ruins, and all of Europe's infrastructure was severely damaged.

Victory came with many political challenges, starting with the Grand Alliance of Britain, the United States, and the Soviet Union. Churchill, Roosevelt, and Stalin met throughout the war. The 1945 Yalta Conference set the stage for the Cold War: in return for Soviet military assistance against the Japanese, Roosevelt agreed to Soviet demands for both territory in East Asia and a role of influence in Eastern and Central Europe.

After Germany's surrender, the Grand Alliance deteriorated quickly. At their final meeting, in Potsdam in July 1945, Truman confronted Stalin on free elections in Eastern Europe, a point that Stalin was unwilling to concede. A few months later, Churchill publicly warned of an "iron curtain" across a divided Europe.

Content Review Questions

1. All of the following were underlying factors of the outbreak of World War I EXCEPT
   (A) rivalries over colonial and commercial interests.
   (B) overwhelming discontent with Europe's royal families.
   (C) national aspirations of ethnic minority groups.
   (D) the growth of socialist labor movements.

2. The concept of total war that emerged during World War I included all of the following EXCEPT
   (A) expansion of civil liberties.
   (B) mass conscription.
   (C) planned economies.
   (D) centralization of government powers.

3. In general, which of the following is most true of trade unions during World War I?
   (A) Trade unions saw membership decrease.
   (B) Trade unions were mostly ignored by government authorities.
   (C) Trade unions did not cooperate with government authorities.
   (D) Trade unions gained prestige and increased membership.

4. All of the following factors contributed to the Bolshevik victory in the Russian Civil War EXCEPT
   (A) the organizational talents of Leon Trotsky.
   (B) the inability of the Whites to agree on a common goal.
   (C) the Red army's advantage of holding the interior line of defense.
   (D) the military prowess of Admiral Alexander Kolchak.

5. The Lateran Accords of 1929 pertained to
   (A) German rearmament.
   (B) French political discord.
   (C) Spanish nationalism.
   (D) Italian fascism.

6. With the Treaty of Locarno,
   (A) borders between France and Germany were agreed on, thus assuring future peace.
   (B) reparations between Germany and France were set at a level that promoted German economic stability.
   (C) Germany was allowed to rearm at levels acceptable to League of Nation members.
   (D) it was agreed that diplomatic controversies would be resolved by the League of Nations.

7. All of the following were characteristics of the totalitarian states of the 1930s EXCEPT
   (A) rule by a single leader or party.
   (B) promotion of individual freedoms.
   (C) use of modern mass propaganda techniques.
   (D) control of the intellectual and cultural life of the nation.

8. All the following were reasons that the Nazi party was able to seize power in Germany EXCEPT
   (A) Germany was experiencing serious economic problems during the period of the Weimar Republic.
   (B) the Nazi party appealed to young Germans.
   (C) Hitler opted to allow Catholic and Protestant churches to remain free of Nazi influence.
   (D) the effective use of propaganda created a strong image of a new Germany.

9. Which of the following resulted from Stalin's Five-year Plans?
   (A) Peasants were allowed to sell their produce for a profit in local markets.
   (B) Retail stores that employed fewer than 20 people could operate under private ownership.
   (C) Hunger led to an untold number of deaths in the countryside.
   (D) Rapid industrialization and collectivization of farms occurred at tremendous human cost.

10. Which of the following would be considered turning points in World War II?
   (A) Allied victories at Midway and Stalingrad
   (B) Allied victories at London and North Africa
   (C) German victories at Paris and Antwerp
   (D) The Japanese bombing of Pearl Harbor and German victories in North Africa

Multiple-Choice Questions

Questions 1–3 refer to the following image.

Source: Staatliche Kunstsammlungen, Dresden. © Artists Rights Society (ARS), New York/VG Bild-Kunst, Bonn//Digital image Erich Lessing/Art Resource, NY

1. The painting above best represents which artistic style?
   (A) Impressionism
   (B) German Expressionism
   (C) Dadaism
   (D) Surrealism

2. Which of the following was a main focus of German Expressionist artists after World War I?
   (A) An optimistic view of the great potential of the German population
   (B) A realistic portrayal of the human form
   (C) Great pride in the German nationalistic tradition
   (D) The suffering and shattered lives caused by the war

3. Who among the following would have best understood and most appreciated the work of the German Expressionists?
   (A) Salvador Dali
   (B) Claude Monet
   (C) Pierre-Auguste Renoir
   (D) Gustave Courbet

Questions 4–6 refer to the following image.

Source: Harlingue/Roger Viollet/Getty Images

4. This image exemplifies the struggles of the depression in Europe by showing
   (A) American investors withdrawing money from European banks.
   (B) overproduction of agricultural goods thus allowing more access to food.
   (C) people waiting in line for goods because of increasing factory production.
   (D) the need to depend on handouts and government support.

5. Although this was not the first depression in European history, the Great Depression was different because
   (A) it was much worse than previous depressions.
   (B) it only impacted Europeans.
   (C) it did not impact the French, but the Germans suffered greatly.
   (D) it was not nearly as severe as the depression of 1873.

6. Which of the following was the most significant result of the Great Depression in Europe?
   (A) Increased loyalty to national governments that enacted social welfare programs to help the poor
   (B) Growing extremism, as fascism and communism seemed to offer a better alternative to economic distress than existing governments
   (C) Adoption of strong laissez-faire policies to address economic woes
   (D) Rejection of Marxism

TURMOIL AND WAR: 1914–1945 ❖ **363**

Short-Answer Questions

1. Analyze the reasons for the rise of the Nazis in Germany during the interwar years and answer A, B, and C.
   A) Briefly explain ONE political reason for the consolidation of Nazi power.
   B) Briefly explain ONE economic reason for the consolidation of Nazi power.
   C) Briefly explain ONE other reason for the consolidation of Nazi power.

2. Analyze the impact of World War II on the civilian population of the USSR and answer A, B, and C.
   A) Briefly explain the emergency mobilization measures that affected the Soviet civilian population.
   B) Briefly explain the role of Soviet women in the war effort.
   C) Briefly explain the role of the Soviet peasants in the war effort.

Long-Essay Questions

1. Identify and explain the causes for both optimism and anxiety in Europe during the 1920s. (Historical Thinking Skills: Causation, Contextualization)

2. Describe and analyze how Nazi racial views influenced German foreign policy before and during World War II. (Historical Thinking Skills: Causation, Contextualization)

Answers

CONTENT REVIEW QUESTIONS

1. **(B)** At the outbreak of the war, most Europeans viewed their own royal families favorably. By the end of the war, this support had often turned to anger, which influenced the collapse of several monarchies (*Western Civilization*, 9th ed., p. 762 / 10th ed., pp. 758–59; Historical Thinking Skills—Causation; Learning Objectives INT-9, SP-6, SP-18; Key Concept 4.1).

2. **(A)** To quell dissent and boost morale, all of the major belligerents suppressed civil liberties (*Western Civilization*, 9th ed., pp. 773–781 / 10th ed., pp. 772–77; Historical Thinking Skills—Causation; Learning Objectives SP-1, IS-8; Key Concept 4.1, 4.4).

3. **(D)** Trade unions gained widespread acceptance during the war because of the dire need for workers (*Western Civilization*, 9th ed., p. 778 / 10th ed., p. 774; Historical Thinking Skills—Contextualization; Learning Objectives PP-13, PP-15, IS-8; Key Concept 4.1, 4.2).

4. **(D)** Admiral Alexander Kolchak did not help the Red Army; instead, he led the first serious White threat to the Bolsheviks, pushing westward from Siberia and advancing almost all the way to the Volga River (*Western Civilization*, 9th ed., pp. 786–87 / 10th ed., pp. 782–83; Historical Thinking Skills—Causation; Learning Objectives PP-8, SP-5; Key Concept 4.2).

5. **(D)** With the Lateran Accords, the Catholic Church agreed to support the fascist government in return for recognition as the sole religion of Italy, as well as the political independence of Vatican City (*Western Civilization*, 9th ed., p. 809 / 10th ed., p. 805; Historical Thinking Skills—Contextualization; Learning Objectives OS-3, SP-3; Key Concept 4.1, 4.3).

6. **(A)** Riding a wave of cooperation, French and German diplomats settled the border issue, thus prompting great optimism in the two countries (*Western Civilization*, 9th ed., pp. 799–800 / 10th ed., p. 795; Historical Thinking Skills—Causation; Learning Objectives SP-6; Key Concept 4.1).

7. **(B)** Totalitarian states subordinated individual freedoms to the collective will of the masses (*Western Civilization*, 9th ed., pp. 805–06 / 10th ed., pp. 801–02; Historical Thinking Skills—Contextualization; Learning Objectives OS-9, OS-12, SP-6, SP-8, SP-17; Key Concepts 4.1, 4.2).

8. **(C)** As happened with schools and universities, Catholic and Protestant churches were brought under Nazi control (*Western Civilization*, 9th ed., p. 815 / 10th ed., p. 808; Historical Thinking Skills—Causation; Learning Objectives PP-11, SP-8, IS-10; Key Concept 4.2).

9. **(D)** Choices A and B were established principles of Lenin's New Economic Policy and were reversed by Stalin's Five-year Plans. Choice D is correct, because the Five-year Plans resulted in an increase in steel production from 4 to 18 million tons per year, hard coal output went from 36 to 128 million tons, and 26 million family farms were collectivized into 250,000 units. Peasants who did not want to give up their land were starved to death to force them into submission (*Western Civilization*, 9th ed., pp. 816–18 / 10th ed., pp. 812–14; Historical Thinking Skills—Causation; Learning Objectives PP-15, PP-16, SP-5, SP-8; Key Concept 4.2).

10. **(A)** Allied victories at Midway and Stalingrad changed the course of the war and set the stage for victory over the Axis powers (*Western Civilization*, 9th ed., pp. 845–47 / 10th ed., pp. 839–42; Historical Thinking Skills—Periodization; Learning Objectives SP-13, SP-14; Key Concept 4.1).

MULTIPLE-CHOICE QUESTIONS

1. **(B)** Otto Dix served in World War I and experienced first-hand the horrors of war. Dix was a German Expressionist (*Western Civilization*, 9th ed., pp. 825–26 / 10th ed., pp. 820–21; Historical Thinking Skills—Analyzing Evidence: Content and Sourcing; Learning Objectives PP-14, OS-10, OS-13; Key Concept 4.3).

2. **(D)** Otto Dix and other German Expressionists focused on the devastating effects of World War I and the horrible suffering it caused many Germans (*Western Civilization*, 9th ed., pp. 825–26 / 10th ed., p. 820–21; Historical Thinking Skills—Interpretation; Learning Objectives PP-14, OS-10, OS-13; Key Concept 4.3).

3. **(A)** Salvador Dali, as a Surrealist, would have understood Dix's desire to deeply analyze the issues of his time (*Western Civilization*, 9th ed., pp. 825–26 / 10th ed., p. 820–21; Historical Thinking Skills—Comparison; Learning Objectives PP-14, OS-10, OS-13; Key Concept 4.3).

4. **(C)** Industrial production plummeted throughout most of the world, causing severe unemployment (*Western Civilization*, 9th ed., pp. 800–02 / 10th ed., pp. 796–97; Historical Thinking Skills—Causation; Learning Objectives INT-8, PP-11, SP-5; Key Concept 4.1, 4.2).

5. **(A)** The depth of the Great Depression was much more devastating than previous economic downturns. By 1932, 25 percent of the British workforce and 40 percent of German workers were unemployed (*Western Civilization*, 9th ed., pp. 800–02 / 10th ed., pp. 796–97; Historical Thinking Skills—Patterns of Continuity and Change Over Time; Learning Objectives INT-8, PP-11, SP-5; Key Concept 4.1, 4.2).

6. **(B)** As existing governments seemed incapable of solving the economic crisis, both left-wing and right-wing extremists seemed to offer an alternative to the disastrous predicament in which many Europeans found themselves (*Western Civilization*, 9th ed., pp. 800–02 / 10th ed., pp. 796–97; Historical Thinking Skills—Patterns of Continuity and Change Over Time; Learning Objectives INT-8, PP-11, SP-5, SP-6; Key Concept 4.1, 4.2).

SHORT-ANSWER QUESTIONS

1. A) One political reason for the consolidation of Nazi power was the rejection of the Versailles settlement and the corresponding growth of nationalism in Germany. Hitler and the Nazis rejected the punitive treaty and promoted national pride, national honor, and traditional militarism. Although they never won a majority of votes in the Reichstag, the growth of the Nazi party and its electoral gains advanced the political career of Hitler. Once in power as German Chancellor, Hitler systematically dismantled the existing republic by enacting the Enabling Act, outlawing other political parties, and purging the civil service of Jews and democratic elements.

   B) One economic reason for the consolidation of Nazi power was the Great Depression. As unemployment rose dramatically between 1929 and 1932 (eventually reaching 40 percent of the workforce), the suffering of the German people made them desperate and willing to accept any leader, no matter how extreme, who seemed to offer a solution to the crisis. Once in power, the Nazis initiated public works projects with grants to private firms to build projects such as the autobahn and put Germans back to work. Rearmament and defense spending eventually brought Germany out of the Great Depression.

C) One social reason for the consolidation of Nazi power was the use of rallies, festivals, and Nazi propaganda to build nationalism and create unity among the people who began to feel like they were part of a greater German fellowship. Rallies such as the Nuremburg rally each September and festivals such as the Harvest festival held each October appealed to a population that wanted to belong. The emphasis on the greatness of the Aryan race also promoted social unity. The creation of organizations such as the Hitler Youth also indoctrinated people into the Nazi system while they felt like they were enjoying entertainment and camaraderie. Finally, the use of propaganda to promote the greatness of the German people and the Nazi regime also created a bond among the people and between the people and the new regime.
(*Western Civilization*, 9th ed., p. 815 / 10th ed., pp. 805–811; Historical Thinking Skills—Causation; Learning Objectives PP-11, SP-8, IS-10; Key Concept 4.2)

2. A) World War II greatly impacted the USSR, with two of every five persons killed in the war being Soviet citizens. As a result, the entire population was needed to mobilize for the war. The emergency mobilization measures that affected the Soviet civilian population included the dismantling of Soviet factories in the western parts of the nation and their reconstruction in somewhat safer areas to the east. Soviet citizens were expected to help with the effort to relocate the factories and to work in the factories to produce as much military equipment as they could in order to hold off the Nazi invasion. Since 55 percent of the Soviet national income went for war materials, as compared with 15 percent before the war broke out, Soviet citizens experienced severe shortages of food, housing, and other consumer goods. As an example, civilian food consumption fell by 40 percent during the war and many factory workers lived in run down temporary facilities.

B) During World War II, Soviet women played a significant role in the war effort. Women of all ages, including young girls worked in factories, on railroads, and in mines to support the troops. During the war, the number of women working in war production increased by nearly 60 percent. Women also worked in the fields, harvesting food and they helped the war effort by serving as air-raid wardens and by constructing defenses against the enemy. Some women also served in the military, supporting the troops as snipers and pilots who carried out night raids on enemy troops.

C) Soviet peasants supported the war effort by serving in the military and providing food for the Soviet army and civilians. Since 47 percent of the existing farmland was lost to enemy troops in the first few months of the war, severe food shortages plagued the nation. To help make up for the shortfall, Soviet peasants were moved to new lands in the Urals, Siberia, and Soviet Asia where they literally plowed the land by hand, since most of their tractors and other mechanized farm implements were recommissioned for military use. Peasants

also served in the military, making up about 60 percent of the soldiers.
(*Western Civilization*, 9th ed., pp. 856–57 / 10th ed., pp. 850–51; Historical Thinking Skills—Contextualization; Learning Objectives SP-10, SP-13, IS-4, IS-6, IS-7, IS-8, IS-9; Key Concept 4.4)

LONG-ESSAY QUESTIONS

1. This essay calls for an examination of two seemingly divergent emotions experienced by Europeans in the aftermath of World War I. The 1920s have been dubbed the Age of Anxiety for the unease that permeated European society. First and foremost were the economic problems. The Weimar Republic faced constant turmoil as severe inflation was set off by Germany's problems with reparation payments. Changes in Russia also added to the sense of anxiety; the Russian Revolution caused pro-capitalist forces in the West to take on a sense of panic. Culturally, European artists and writers commented on the alienation and hopelessness associated with the war's destruction.

   There were, however, reasons to be optimistic. After the initial problems associated with the end of fighting, many Europeans were cautiously optimistic about their future. Britain, France, and Germany had new leaders who saw the advantages of conciliation rather than confrontation. Germany demonstrated a good-faith adherence to the abhorrent Treaty of Versailles, which prompted an international committee to draw up the Dawes Plan in August 1924. It called for a reduction in German reparations, but more importantly, it allowed for American loans to pour into Germany, a boost to European economies. In 1925, European diplomats concluded the Treaty of Locarno, which settled questions regarding the western borders of Germany, and soon after, Germany entered the League of Nations. Two years later, nations that signed the Kellogg-Briand Pact agreed to renounce war as a form of international diplomacy. Western European nations also began to recognize the Soviet Union, helping forge communication with the new Soviet state. Taken together, the spirit of cooperation and Europe's improving economic health created a sense of hope. Be sure to add a brief (2-3 sentences) synthesis discussion to your essay. For this essay, you could compare this time of optimism and anxiety with the optimism and anxiety of the 1960s.
   (*Western Civilization*, 9th ed., pp. 856–57 / 10th ed., pp. 793–808, 812, 814–15, 817–21, 823–24; Historical Thinking Skills—Causation, Contextualization; Learning Objectives SP-10, SP-13, IS-4, IS-6, IS-7, IS-8, IS-9; Key Concept 4.4)

2. Begin this essay by linking the idea of Aryan racial superiority with social Darwinism. Hitler believed Aryans deserved certain privileges, including *Lebensraum*, and looked down on what he saw as "lesser" races, such as people of Slavic origin. Hitler's obsession with *Lebensraum* led him to look eastward. He acquired Austria first, and then Czechoslovakia. With his invasion of Poland, World War II began. Because of their acts of appeasement, Hitler viewed France and England as weak and unwilling to engage Germany in a full-scale war. Therefore, he launched the

Blitzkrieg to quickly knock out the weak democracies of Western Europe so he could then conquer the Soviet Union.

In the end, Hitler's racist views helped undermine German success. The German military underestimated the fighting power of the Red Army, and Hitler's intransigence toward the "inferior" Soviets led to his defeat at Stalingrad. In addition, Hitler underestimated the democracies of Great Britain and the United States and their willingness to fight. Be sure to add a brief (2-3 sentences) synthesis discussion to your essay. For this essay, you could compare the influence of Nazi racial views on foreign policy with the influence of late twentieth century European racial views on foreign policy.

(*Western Civilization*, 9th ed., pp. 850–55 / 10th ed., pp. 843–48; Historical Thinking Skills—Causation, Contextualization; Learning Objectives SP-14, SP-17, IS-7, IS-8, IS-10; Key Concept 4.1, 4.2, 4.4)

15

THE COLD WAR AND AFTER: 1945 TO THE PRESENT

After World War II, there were many changes in Europe. Great Britain, France, and Germany saw their influence diminish as the Soviet Union and the United States became global superpowers. Europe was divided between Soviet-dominated Eastern Europe and U.S.-influenced democratic Western Europe, as the Cold War raged across the world. This division, often referred to as the Iron Curtain, persisted for nearly fifty years, until the Soviet Union collapsed in the early 1990s. Eastern European revolutions in 1989 and the disintegration of Yugoslavia in the 1990s changed the face of Europe and introduced an era of change on the European continent. The fall of the Soviet Union accelerated Europe's drive toward unity and cooperation, making the growth of the European Union in the twenty-first century possible.

KEY TERMS

abstract	ethnic cleansing
Expressionism	Eurocommunism
Berlin Air Lift	European Economic Community
Berlin Wall	European Union
Brezhnev Doctrine	existentialism
containment	feminism
Cuban Missile Crisis	*glasnost*
decolonization	globalization
denazification	guest workers
de-Stalinization	iron curtain
détente	Korean War
domino theory	Manhattan Project

369

Marshall Plan
multiculturalism
mutual deterrence
nationalization
North Atlantic Treaty
   Organization (NATO)
perestroika

Postmodernism
Stalinization
socialized medicine
Truman Doctrine
Warsaw Pact
welfare state

CHAPTER KEY CONCEPTS

- After World War II, Eastern and Western Europe were separated by a global rivalry between the United States and the Soviet Union that continued until the Soviet Union collapsed in the early 1990s.

- After the war, the economies of Western Europe rebounded. Governments embraced various forms of social welfare policy at home while confronting decolonization abroad.

- The aftermath of war led many artists and intellectuals to question the meaning of traditional society, while advances in technology influenced the rise of popular culture.

- Increasing globalization in the international community has led to new economic and social challenges as well as hopes for a brighter future.

For a full discussion of Europe from 1945 to the present, see *Western Civilization*, 9th and 10th editions, Chapters 28–30.

COLD WAR BEGINNINGS

Most historians agree that a post-war rivalry between the United States and the Soviet Union was unavoidable. Their biggest conflict centered on the fate of Eastern Europe. The Soviet Union wanted a buffer zone against potential military threats from the West; the United States saw Soviet domination as a threat to the democratic freedom of the liberated nations in Eastern Europe. When conflict emerged in Greece and Turkey, the United States issued the Truman Doctrine, which promised financial support to nations threatened by communist expansion.

Of all the U.S. efforts to assist Europeans after the war, one of the most important was the Marshall Plan, which provided massive financial aid to promote economic recovery and foster political stability. The plan helped Europe rebuild, but also led to further conflict with the Soviet Union. Mutual suspicions led to a long-term rivalry and forced the United States to remain active in foreign affairs. To respond to Soviet aggression around the world, American diplomat George Kennan designed a policy that called for "long-term, patient but firm and vigilant containment of Russian expansive tendencies."

Cold War tensions erupted in post-war Germany in 1948. When the Western powers set out to unify their zones, the Soviets blockaded West Berlin, necessitating a dramatic airlift. The Soviets eventually ended the blockade but set up a communist East Germany.

That Churchill and Truman had not told Stalin about the Manhattan Project accounts for much of the tension between the United States and the Soviet Union. The Manhattan Project was a research and development project that produced the first nuclear weapons during World War II. When the Soviet Union detonated its first atomic bomb in 1949, the United States worked to produce larger and more lethal nuclear weapons, sparking the arms race. The concept of mutual deterrence was used to prevent nuclear annihilation.

Military alliances were also used as a means to European security. In 1949, nine Western European nations, the United States, and Canada formed the North Atlantic Treaty Organization (NATO), agreeing to provide military assistance in the event of an attack. In 1955, the Soviet Union responded by forming its own military alliance, the Warsaw Pact, with seven East European countries.

EUROPE AND THE WORLD

Cold War tensions quickly spread beyond Europe, especially after the Chinese communists defeated the American-backed nationalists in 1949. In 1950, when North Korea invaded South Korea, United Nations forces—mostly Americans—were sent to turn back the invasion. Mao Zedong sent Chinese troops into North Korea, leading to more fighting and eventually a stalemate. China had officially entered the Cold War.

European powers found that they could no longer continue colonial rule. The cost was prohibitive, and indigenous peoples were rebelling. The success of decolonization varied according to location. In Africa, the process was typically nonviolent, often led by Western-educated intellectuals such as Kwame Nkrumah, who guided Ghana to independence in 1957. But only after the Mau Mau uprising proved an unsustainable drain on Britain's resources did Britain grant Kenya independence, in 1963. Where a substantial European population existed, the transition to independence was more complicated. The French experienced great difficulties in North Africa, especially in Algeria, where nationalists fought a guerilla war for many years, until they won independence in 1962.

In the Middle East, Turkey, Saudi Arabia, Iran, and Iraq achieved independence at the end of World War I. After World War II, Jordan, Syria, and Lebanon became independent states. They formed the Arab League to promote Arab unity, but were unified on only one issue: the settlement of Palestine. Britain had taken control of the area after World War I, but the Zionist movement and increased Jewish settlement caused friction, and the pressure for an independent Jewish state in Palestine was powerful. Although Jews were a clear minority in Palestine, the United Nations divided Palestine into two states; the state of Israel was created in 1948. Tensions with its neighbors continue to this day.

In 1956, two years after taking control of Egypt, Gamal Abdel Nasser nationalized the Suez Canal Company, threatening British and French ships' passage to the Indian Ocean. Israel joined with Britain and France to attack Egypt. The United States and the Soviet Union forced a withdrawal, arguing that the invasion was a return to colonialism. Nasser emerged as the leading figure in the Pan-Arab movement.

In Asia, British worries that massive bloodshed would accompany Indian independence were justified; the partitioning of India proved deadly, as millions of Hindus and Muslims shifted across the India-Pakistan border. Unwilling to leave Southeast Asia, French forces fought a bloody guerilla war, led by the Communist Ho Chi Minh. Vietnam was divided between the communist north and the pro-Western south, and would remain divided until the mid-1970s. But its experience with the Vietnamese nationalists forced France to grant independence to Laos and Cambodia.

Cold War politics hung over decolonization. As the European powers relinquished control over their territories, the superpowers supplied military and financial support to emerging states in an effort to thwart rival expansion. This often led to armed conflict—as in Vietnam, starting in the mid-sixties. Some newly independent nations, however, chose to remain nonaligned, frustrating the superpowers, which were unable to exert direct influence.

THE SOVIET UNION

Despite being a global superpower, the Soviet Union nonetheless faced tremendous hardships at home. With the USSR's economic infrastructure destroyed by the war, Stalin used drastic measures to spur economic renewal. Soon after, the country witnessed unimaginable industrial growth, thanks largely to the astounding efforts of the Soviet workers. The Soviets also had great success in science, highlighted by the launching of Sputnik in 1957. But consumer goods and adequate housing were scarce, and political terror continued unabated, as dissent was put down.

The Soviet Union continued to dominate Eastern Europe except in Yugoslavia, where Josip Broz Tito, exploiting Yugoslavian nationalism, insisted on an independent communist state free from Soviet influence. Upon Stalin's death in 1953, Nikita Khrushchev took over and initiated a process of de-Stalinization. Many people in Eastern Europe used this opportunity to press for political freedom. In 1956, first Poland and then Hungary attempted to gain independence. Poland was given some independence after pledging to remain in the Warsaw Pact. In Hungary, the ruling Stalinist party was ousted in favor of the reform-minded leader Imry Nagy. Soon after, the Red Army removed Nagy from office and put down all dissension. Hungary's experience dimmed prospects for revolts in Eastern Europe.

Another problem bedeviling the Soviets was the city of Berlin. West Berlin, an affluent island in destitute East Germany, was an embarrassment to Communist leaders as many East Germans escaped into West Berlin. In 1961, Khrushchev ordered the construction of a wall around West Berlin, which became a bleak symbol of a divided Europe.

Meanwhile, Khrushchev and the United States had a confrontation over the deployment of Soviet missiles in the Caribbean. In 1959, Cuban revolutionary Fidel Castro set up a government modeled on Soviet communism. Unwilling to have a communist country so close to the homeland, the United States attempted to overthrow Castro. An invasion by U.S.-backed Cuban exiles was an embarrassing failure. The so-called Bay of Pigs invasion encouraged Castro to form closer ties with the Soviet Union.

On the pretext of preventing American attacks, Khrushchev set out to build nuclear missiles sites on Cuban soil, a plan that the United States firmly rejected. In response, Khrushchev pointed out that American missiles were located in Turkey, on the Soviet border. The United States ordered the Soviets to halt all missile-laden Soviet ships sailing to Cuba and blockaded Cuba to prevent their arrival. After many tense hours, Khrushchev agreed to turn the fleet around, on the condition that the United States promise not to invade Cuba and to remove its missiles from Turkey. To avoid another close call, both superpowers made genuine efforts to improve communication.

Khrushchev's popularity among Soviet leaders declined, and in 1964, the Soviet Politburo forced him into retirement. His successor was Leonid Brezhnev, whose nearly two decades of leadership were marked by a more relaxed atmosphere within the Soviet Union. The superpowers entered a period of reduced tensions called détente, signified by the Antiballistic Missile Treaty of 1972 and the Helsinki Agreement of 1975. Détente came to an end with the Soviet invasion of Afghanistan in 1979 and the election of Ronald Reagan in 1980. Reagan increased the tension by providing military aid to Afghan rebels.

AP® Tip

During the period of détente, the United States set out to improve relations with Communist China. By the end of the 1970s, the two nations had created a "strategic relationship" to counter Soviet influence in Asia. Although the People's Republic of China was a communist nation, both China and the U.S. shared the common goal of preventing Soviet expansion.

When Brezhnev died in 1982, the Soviet Union was involved in an unpopular military engagement in Afghanistan that drained resources from needed economic development. Further, the Soviet political structure had become ossified, as the political elite dismissed any attempts at reform. The Soviet economy was faltering because workers had little incentive to increase productivity. Innovation lagged behind the West's, and alcoholism soared. Brezhnev's successor, Yuri Andropov, began reform. One step was the appointment of Mikhail Gorbachev as party secretary in 1985.

Gorbachev, who had come of age during Khrushchev's rule and understood the value of reform, saw the necessity of radical change. He first called for perestroika, or restructuring, to energize the flagging Soviet economy with a limited free market and ownership of private property. Next he initiated a policy of glasnost, or openness, to encourage discussion of the country's problems by both citizens and officials. These reforms released enormous pent-up frustrations that were felt everywhere, from newspaper editorials to rock concerts. Coupled with reforms that took political authority away from the Communist Party, the Soviet Union was primed for a massive change, and ethnic groups within the country began to push for greater independence.

By 1991, the Soviet Union had ceased to exist. Soviet hardliners initiated a coup against Gorbachev, but it failed when Gorbachev refused to cooperate with the hardliners and a large resistance movement led by Russian president Boris Yeltsin emerged. Gorbachev resigned, turning leadership over to Yeltsin. Under Yeltsin, Russia implemented a free-market economy and a democratic form of government but experienced many problems, including widespread corruption and the rise of organized crime.

TRANSITION IN EASTERN EUROPE

In 1968, more than ten years after Hungary had attempted to free itself from Soviet domination, a reform movement sprang up in Czechoslovakia. Alexander Dubcek sought to create "communism with a human face," but the Soviet military, invoking the Brezhnev Doctrine, crushed this "Prague Spring." In 1980, Polish workers formed an independent labor movement, Solidarity. Led by Lech Walesa, it earned the support of many Poles, including intellectuals and the Catholic clergy. The Polish Communist government attempted to stifle Solidarity, but unrest increased, leading to free elections. Gorbachev stood on the sidelines as Walesa was elected president in 1990.

As more reform movements emerged throughout Eastern Europe, East Germans began streaming to neighboring Hungary, and millions of people took to the streets. In November 1989, the East German government opened all of its borders with the West, and the Berlin Wall, the long-time symbol of the Cold War, was the scene of celebration as delirious people took it down with sledgehammers. By October 1990, East and West Germany reunified.

The fall of communism brought tragic consequences in Yugoslavia, which broke apart in the late 1980s. Volatile separatist movements fought each other for territory and soon began a genocidal rampage referred to as "ethnic cleansing." All told, nearly 250,000 Bosnians were killed and another two million left homeless. NATO forces halted Serbian attacks against ethnic Albanians in Kosovo, but only through a concerted bombing campaign did the Yugoslav forces relent.

THE REVIVAL OF WESTERN EUROPE

Western Europe's remarkable recovery after World War II shaped the political landscape for many nations. Although communism had an influence early on, Western Europe embraced moderate democracy with an emphasis on social welfare.

In the post-war years, France was dominated by Charles de Gaulle. The former resistance leader helped establish a French provisional government after the war, and then became president in 1958, launching the Fifth Republic. De Gaulle built a strong military and established France as a nuclear superpower. Throughout the 1960s, the French economy grew steadily, but the nationalization of industry and resulting overwhelming deficits were a problem. As the government attempted to deal with rising costs, student protests and labor strikes brought an end to the de Gaulle presidency in 1969. During the 1970s and 1980s, France shifted to the left as socialist

François Mitterrand enacted reform measures favoring workers. Continued economic troubles led to the election of conservative Jacques Chirac in 1995. Faced with high unemployment, many French began speaking out against the large number of immigrants who had recently settled in the country. This led to rising tensions within France—still a significant issue in the twenty-first century.

With the creation of the Federal Republic of Germany in 1949, West Germany began a stunning renewal. Its leader, Christian Democratic Konrad Adenauer, established close ties with other Western European nations and the United States. West Germany dealt harshly with former Nazi officials, most notably during the famous Nuremburg trials, and a healthy economy allowed it to pay reparations to Holocaust victims. The threat of a communist invasion led it to re-arm and join NATO in 1955.

In the following decades, West Germany moved from center-right politics to the center-left politics of the Social Democrats. Chancellor Willy Brandt initiated a policy of *Ostpolitik* to improve contact with East Germany, but most of his successors concentrated on improving the West German economy. As unemployment fell and wages skyrocketed, West Germany experienced a severe labor shortage and turned to foreign "guest workers" to fill key jobs. These workers, essential to the economy, still have not been fully accepted, socially or politically.

In 1945, the British people voted Churchill's Conservative Party out of office. The Labour Party, led by Clement Attlee, created the modern welfare state. Major industries and the Bank of England were nationalized, and health care was socialized as the government required doctors and dentists to participate in the national plan.

With the high cost of the welfare state, the British economy struggled through the '50s, '60s, and '70s, with government leadership alternating between the Labour and Conservative parties. In 1979, Britons elected the first female prime minister, Margaret Thatcher. A Conservative, the "Iron Lady" attempted to restructure the social welfare state by reducing taxes and government bureaucracy. The economy improved, but Thatcher's policies led to some social unrest.

WESTERN EUROPEAN UNITY

Europe's process of unification began with NATO. In 1951, the European Coal and Steel Community (ECSC) was set up to create a common market for coal and steel products. In 1957, the Rome Treaty created the European Economic Community (EEC), known as the Common Market. This alliance became the world's largest exporter and purchaser of raw materials, rivaled only by the United States in steel production.

In 1973, Great Britain, Ireland, and Denmark joined the European Economic Community to form the European Community (EC), renamed the European Union (EU) in 1994. A primary EU goal was to create a common currency called the euro. By 2007, the euro had officially replaced thirteen national currencies. The establishment of a common agricultural policy, in which subsidies are provided for European farmers in order to allow them to successfully compete in the world agricultural market, has also helped the European economy.

Subsidies for job training, education, and modernization, as well as greater flexibility in travel among member nations, has caused many Europeans to support membership in the EU. Moving into the twenty-first century, the EU began incorporating the nations of eastern and southeastern Europe into the union. This new alliance became the world's largest exporter of raw materials and was rivaled only by the United States in steel production.

In the last few years, the EU has suffered several crises. Beginning in 2009, Greece struggled to repay international debts as a worldwide recession coupled with poor government policies led other nations to doubt Greece's financial stability. To receive a financial bailout, as of 2016 Greece was working on an austerity package with the International Monetary Fund and the European Union.

In 2015 with growing violence in the Middle East, especially Syria, over one million immigrants entered Europe looking for refuge. Because of concerns over how they entered and because of growing nationalism across Europe, tensions built as countries sought the best solutions to the repercussions of the flood of immigrants.

In 2016 the solidity of the EU was tested as the people of the United Kingdom passed a referendum to leave the union. Because of the passage of Brexit (Britain exit), David Cameron, the British Prime Minister, resigned as the UK struggled to maintain its member states and create a new government.

SOCIETY AND CULTURE

Post-war economic prosperity greatly helped the working class. Increased wages unleashed consumerism, particularly in the auto industry. Through Western Europe's implementation of the welfare state, members of the working class received expanded health care and old-age pensions. Likewise, access to higher education was made available to them.

At first, women saw few gains. In Britain and West Germany, women were discouraged from working, but as birth rates began to decline in the late 1950s, women had more opportunities to enter the workforce. They still faced discrimination, as seen by the large disparity between men's and women's salaries. Influenced by the French feminist Simone de Beauvoir, women in both Europe and the United States began to assert themselves as a political and social movement advocating for liberation from traditional gender roles. In the 1960s, feminism took the form of the women's liberation movement, which advocated for true equality with men, both economically and socially.

> ### AP® Tip
>
> Europeans witnessed challenges to traditional morals and manners after both world wars. Two areas that saw significant change were sexuality and women's rights. With the introduction of the birth control pill in the 1960s, women enjoyed a newfound freedom that influenced many facets of European life.

Artists continued to reject notions of traditional art as they grappled with the destruction of World War II and the despair of the modern world. During the war, many important artists fled Europe for the United States, shifting the center of the artistic world to New York City. American painters such as Jackson Pollack and Andy Warhol were at the forefront of the artistic movements known as Abstract Expressionism and Pop Art. Disillusionment also influenced literature, as seen in the works of Samuel Beckett, whose play *Waiting for Godot* belongs to the literary movement called Theater of the Absurd. The absurdists were greatly influenced by existentialism. Two of the leading voices of existentialism, Frenchmen Albert Camus and Jean-Paul Sartre, argued that man, alone in the world and without any preordained destiny, must rely on himself to find hope in an absurd and depersonalized world.

Technology was transforming. Communication over great distances became instantaneous, making the world more interconnected than ever before. Europeans saw themselves as members of a global, interdependent community. Large multinational corporations spanned continents, directly influencing the lives of people far removed from their headquarters. Technological advances dramatically improved life in the developed world, but not in developing nations, presenting a new challenge to the nations of Europe.

Content Review Questions

1. The policies of British Prime Minister Margaret Thatcher can best be described as
   (A) a decrease in government social welfare spending and taxation.
   (B) a return to pre-war colonialism.
   (C) an attempt to cooperate more closely with trade unions.
   (D) an increase in government involvement in social welfare programs.

2. The Brezhnev Doctrine called for
   (A) Soviet intervention in any threatened socialist state.
   (B) a Soviet boycott of all Western consumer goods.
   (C) Soviet missile deployment in East Germany.
   (D) a Soviet boycott of the 1984 Los Angeles Olympics.

3. All of the following statements describe the modern welfare state EXCEPT
   (A) the state has a duty to provide for the basic social needs of its people.
   (B) the state should engage in the privatization of major industries.
   (C) the state should raise taxes so as to be able to provide inexpensive housing and free medical care.
   (D) the state should cooperate with trade unions to promote the welfare of the labor movement.

4. All of the following statements are true about the student revolts of 1968 EXCEPT
   (A) new attitudes toward sex and the use of drugs were two manifestations of a growing youth movement in the 1960s.
   (B) following World War II, universities grew quickly, leading to crowded classrooms, professors who paid little attention to the students, and students who believed that their education was not relevant.
   (C) student protesters in Paris were joined by over half of the French workforce before the French government instituted wage hikes in May 1968.
   (D) student protesters in Czechoslovakia forced the liberalization of communist policies in the Prague Spring.

5. All of the following contributed to the collapse of the Soviet Union EXCEPT
   (A) the radical reforms of Mikhail Gorbachev.
   (B) the rise of nationalist movements within the Soviet Union.
   (C) the creation of a new Soviet parliament.
   (D) the appointment of Boris Yeltsin as head of the Soviet Union.

6. All of the following were social trends in the post-war Western nations EXCEPT a(n)
   (A) increase in the number of women in the workforce.
   (B) increase in the number of white-collar personnel.
   (C) decline in the number of industrial jobs.
   (D) increase in average family size.

7. All of the following prompted reforms initiated by Mikhail Gorbachev EXCEPT
   (A) severe economic problems in the Soviet Union, including a downturn in the standard of living.
   (B) an ideological rivalry with the People's Republic of China.
   (C) rising costs of military action in central Asia.
   (D) problems associated with the rigid structure of Soviet bureaucracy.

8. *Piazza d'Italia* (shown on the next page), by Charles Moore, is representative of a style that mixes past tradition with Modernist innovation. This style which was popular during the mid to late twentieth century is known as
   (A) Pop Art.
   (B) Art Brut.
   (C) Expressionism.
   (D) Postmodernism.

Source: © Robert Holmes/Corbis

9. "What peculiarly signalizes the situation of woman is that she …
finds herself living in a world where men compel her to assume the
status of the Other."
To whom is the above quotation attributed?
(A) Jean-Paul Sartre
(B) Simone de Beauvoir
(C) Margaret Thatcher
(D) Charles de Gaulle

10. "Man is nothing else but what he makes of himself."
The above quotation is an example of which of the following
philosophies?
(A) Deconstructionism
(B) Abstract Expressionism
(C) Existentialism
(D) Transcendentalism

Multiple-Choice Questions

Questions 1–3 refer to the following image.

Source: © Marc Riboud/Magnum Photos

1. All of the following are reasons that decolonization accelerated following 1945 EXCEPT
   (A) colonial subjugation was at odds with the goals pursued by the allies in overthrowing the dictatorships in Germany and Italy.
   (B) European nations, weakened by years of war, provided an easy target for indigenous peoples who were ready to fight for their freedom.
   (C) European colonies knew they could defeat their overlords, because they had military support from the United States.
   (D) colonial residents knew that Europeans in World War II fought for national self-determination and wanted to determine the fate of their own nations.

2. Why did the French attempt to maintain control of Algeria, rather than grant independence to the colony as it had done in Morocco and Tunisia?
   (A) The French wanted to maintain control of the natural resources found in Algeria.
   (B) Over two million French settlers lived in Algeria and the French wanted to keep them in the empire.
   (C) The Algerians had refused to fight for the French in World War II, so French leaders wanted to punish them by keeping them subjugated.
   (D) The French feared that the Algerian Muslims would practice terrorism against France if they were granted independence.

3. All of the following nations found themselves embroiled in Cold War politics in the process of decolonization EXCEPT
   (A) Vietnam.
   (B) India.
   (C) Indonesia.
   (D) Morocco.

Questions 4–6 refer to the following map.

Source: © Cengage Learning

4. Which of the following ethnic groups was responsible for the ethnic cleansing in Yugoslavia?
   (A) Serbs
   (B) Albanians
   (C) Bosnians
   (D) Croats

5. All of the following are true of the conflict in Kosovo EXCEPT
   (A) Kosovo had been an autonomous province in Yugoslavia since 1974.
   (B) The Kosovo Liberation Army (KLA) refused to allow NATO forces into its territory, since it wanted to crush the Albanians without foreign help.
   (C) NATO and the United States started a bombing campaign when Slobodan Milosevic refused to sign a peace plan that would have given ethnic Albanians in Kosovo autonomy.
   (D) Most inhabitants of Kosovo were ethnic Albanians, but the Serb minority that considered Kosovo sacred territory refused to recognize the independence of Kosovo.

6. All of the following are true of the complicated situation that degenerated into the Yugoslavian crises of the 1990s EXCEPT
   (A) the nation of Yugoslavia, created after World War I, was an artificial creation that combined Serbs, Croats, and Slovenes into one nation, despite their ethnic differences.
   (B) Bosnia faced especially serious problems, due to the large number of Serbs who lived within its borders.
   (C) under the leadership of Marshal Tito, ethnic difference were kept in check.
   (D) Bosnia was the first of the six republics to declare its independence in June 1991.

Short-Answer Questions

1. Answer A, B, and C by identifying the goals of European unity in the years following World War II, and discuss attitudes toward the European Union.
   A) Briefly explain ONE goal of European efforts at unity following World War II.
   B) Briefly explain ONE argument for supporting the European Union.
   C) Briefly explain ONE argument for opposing the European Union.

2. Analyze the reasons for the increase in European immigration and the impact of the influx of people on European society and answer A, B, and C.
   A) Briefly explain the reasons for the migration of people into European nations since World War II.
   B) Briefly explain ONE problem created in Europe from the large influx of immigrants.
   C) Briefly explain ONE reaction to the influx of immigrants that is common to many European nations.

Long-Essay Questions

1. Compare and contrast the process of decolonization as it related to post-war Britain and France. (Historical Thinking Skills: Comparison)

2. During the Cold War, Soviet authority was challenged throughout Eastern Europe on several occasions. Analyze the efforts made by TWO Eastern European nations to resist Soviet domination between the years 1945 and 1991. (Historical Thinking Skills: Comparison)

Answers

CONTENT REVIEW QUESTIONS

1. **(A)** Thatcher strongly opposed increasing the welfare state. Like Ronald Reagan, she lowered taxes and government spending on social programs, which led to economic stability but much social dissension (*Western Civilization*, 9th ed., pp. 911–12 / 10th ed., pp. 905–06; Historical Thinking Skills—Contextualization; Learning Objectives PP-15, PP-16; Key Concept 4.2).

2. **(A)** The Brezhnev Doctrine stated that the Soviet Union reserved the right to use military force to challenge any effort by reform movements to overthrow pro-Soviet leadership in Soviet satellite countries. The Soviet military entered the Czechoslovakian capital of Prague in 1968 to restore a pro-Soviet government (*Western Civilization*, 9th ed., pp. 907–08 / 10th ed., pp. 901–02; Historical Thinking Skills—Causation; Learning Objectives SP-1, SP-5, SP-9, SP-12, SP-13, SP-17; Key Concept 4.2, 4.4).

3. **(B)** The modern welfare state, as practiced in Great Britain, emphasized government control over primary industry, as well as health care. Therefore, under the modern welfare state, the government strove to nationalize, not privatize, industry (*Western Civilization*, 9th ed., pp. 892–94 / 10th ed., pp. 882–85, 888–89; Historical Thinking Skills—Contextualization; Learning Objectives PP-15, PP-16; Key Concept 4.2).

4. **(D)** Although the Prague Spring attempted to liberalize communist policies, it was unsuccessful in achieving its goals, as Soviet troops invaded Prague (*Western Civilization*, 9th ed., pp. 901–05; 908–10 / 10th ed., pp. 897–900, 903–05; Historical Thinking Skills—Causation; Learning Objectives SP-1, SP-5, SP-9, SP-12, SP-13, SP-17; Key Concept 4.2, 4.4).

5. **(D)** Boris Yeltsin played a vital role in the destruction of the Soviet Union as president of the Russian Republic, but not as leader of the Communist Party. Mikhail Gorbachev served as the final general secretary until becoming president of the Soviet Union (*Western Civilization*, 9th ed., pp. 928–31 / 10th ed., pp. 921–23; Historical Thinking Skills—Causation; Learning Objectives PP-12, PP-15, SP-9, SP-19; Key Concept 4.2).

6. **(D)** Family size decreased, which in turn brought about many social changes throughout Europe, in particular an increase in the number of women in the workforce (*Western Civilization*, 9th ed., pp. 894–95 / 10th ed., pp. 889–90; Historical Thinking Skills—Contextualization; Learning Objectives PP-1, PP-4, PP-5, PP-12, PP-13, PP-14, PP-15, SP-1, SP-5, SP-9, IS-4, IS-6, IS-9 ; Key Concept 4.2, 4.3, 4.4).

7. **(B)** Although at times the Soviet Union and the People's Republic of China had disagreements and viewed each other with suspicion, the Soviet relationship with China had little to do with Gorbachev's reforms (*Western Civilization*, 9th ed., pp. 930–31 / 10th ed., pp. 921–23; Historical Thinking Skills—Causation; Learning Objectives PP-15, SP-1, SP-19; Key Concept 4.2, 4.4).

8. **(D)** *Piazza d'Italia* by Charles Moore is representative of Post-modernism. It is an outdoor plaza that combines Roman columns with stainless steel and neon lights. The mixing of modern-day materials with historical reference is characteristic of the Postmodernist style (Western Civilization, 9th ed., pp. 921–22 / 10th ed., pp. 914–16; Historical Thinking Skills—Contextualization; Learning Objectives PP-14, OS-13; Key Concept 4.3).

9. **(B)** In her 1949 work, *The Second Sex*, Beauvoir argued that despite gains European women had made during the twentieth century, they still faced limits that men did not, and therefore that women, still defined by their differences from men, had second-class status (*Western Civilization*, 9th ed., pp. 894–95 / 10th ed., pp. 889–90; Historical Thinking Skills—Causation; Learning Objectives PP-14, OS-4, SP-1, SP-9, IS-4, IS-9; Key Concept 4.3, 4.4).

10. **(C)** The quotation is by Jean-Paul Sartre, a French intellectual and leading existentialist. He held that the world is absurd and without meaning, yet not without hope, because humans are capable of giving their lives meaning by taking responsibility for their own actions (*Western Civilization*, 9th ed., p. 897 / 10th ed., pp. 891–92; Historical Thinking Skills—Contextualization; Learning Objectives OS-8, OS-10, OS-13; Key Concept 4.3).

Multiple-Choice Questions

1. **(C)** Although they were fighting for their freedom, the colonies did not receive any military aid from the United States (*Western Civilization*, 9th ed., pp. 876–81 / 10th ed., pp. 870–71; Historical Thinking Skills—Causation; Learning Objectives INT-7, INT-9, SP-9, SP-14; Key Concept 4.1).

2. **(B)** Over two million French settlers lived in Algeria, and the French government feared for their safety if Algeria won its independence (*Western Civilization*, 9th ed., pp. 876–81 10th ed., p. 872; Historical Thinking Skills—Periodization, Contextualization; Learning INT-7, INT-9, SP-9, SP-14; Key Concept 4.1).

3. **(D)** Of the nations listed in the answer choices, Morocco was the only one that did not either become involved in direct military conflict or diplomatic and economic crises as a result of Cold War rivalries (*Western Civilization*, 9th ed., pp. 876–81 / 10th ed., p. 875; Historical Thinking Skills—Causation; Learning Objectives INT-7, INT-9, SP-9, SP-14; Key Concept 4.1).

4. **(A)** Serbs, led by Slobodan Milosevic, attempted to take control of territory within the newly created republics of the former Yugoslavia. Bosnian Muslims suffered great losses at the hands of the Serbs (*Western Civilization*, 9th ed., pp. 935–36 / 10th ed., pp. 928–29; Learning Objectives INT-7, SP-1, IS-7, IS-10; Key Concept 4.1, 4.2, 4.4).

5. **(B)** Kosovo's inhabitants welcomed the protection of NATO during the Kosovo crisis (Western *Civilization*, 9th ed., pp. 876–81 / 10th ed., pp. 928–29; Historical Thinking Skills—Causation; Learning Objectives INT-7, INT-9, SP-9, SP-14; Key Concept 4.1).

6. **(D)** Croatia and Slovenia were the first of the six republics to declare their independence in June 1991 (*Western Civilization*, 9th ed., pp. 876–81 / 10th ed., pp. 928–29; Historical Thinking Skills—Causation; Learning Objectives INT-7, INT-9, SP-9, SP-14; Key Concept 4.1).

SHORT-ANSWER QUESTIONS

1. A) One goal of European efforts at unity following World War II was to encourage prosperity following the war. Beginning with the European Coal and Steel Community and quickly evolving into the European Economic Community, Western European member nations eliminated tariffs within the community and concentrated on the production of goods in which they had a competitive advantage. The goal of these early organizations revolved around the belief that a European free trade zone with common economic policies would bring prosperity to nations still recovering from World War II.

    B) One argument for supporting the European Union (EU) is that the use of a single European currency and adherence to common economic policies contributes to the prosperity of member nations. For example, the formulation of common agricultural policies with subsidies for farmers enables EU farmers to successfully compete on the world market. Likewise, aid to the EU's poorest regions, as well as subsidies for job training, education, and modernization, has improved the economic power and prosperity of European Union members. Since the European Union is the world's largest single trading entity and handles one-quarter of the world's commerce, supporters believe that the EU as a whole is a much more effective economic organization than each nation could be individually.

    C) One argument for opposing the European Union is that the official representatives of the European Union are not democratically responsible to the people. Some nations and European citizens worry that representatives who make policies concerning the European Central Bank or European parliament could mandate actions that violate the best interests of individual nations, thus reducing their political and economic sovereignty.
    (*Western Civilization*, 9th ed., p. 940 / 10th ed., pp. 932–33; Historical Thinking Skills—Argumentation; Learning Objectives SP-17, SP-19; Key Concept 4.1)

2. A) Severe labor shortages caused by World War II and a declining birthrate in the 1950s and 1960s forced many European nations to rely on immigrants and guest workers in order to staff essential jobs. As a result of decolonization, millions immigrated to Europe from former colonies, looking for safety and jobs. By the 1980s and 1990s, many people arrived in Europe as refugees from Africa, Asia, and the Middle East, and Eastern Europeans also migrated to Western European nations due to genocide and persecution.

   B) One problem created in Europe from the large influx of immigrants was that the growing number of people strained educational and social welfare services of European nations. By 1998, one-third of inner-city children in London did not speak English as their first language. Calls for the passage of laws restricting immigration emerged as many European citizens had to pay higher taxes to support social welfare systems that threatened to bankrupt their nations.

   C) One reaction to the influx of immigrants that is common to many European nations is the growth of anti-foreign sentiment and right-wing political parties that promote restricting the rights of immigrants. For example, the National Front in France and the Republican Party in Germany both advocated policies to promote nationalism and villainize foreigners. Even some moderate governments have recently aimed legislation at immigrants, such as the requirement that a person must pass a Dutch language and culture test before being accepted into the Netherlands.
   (*Western Civilization*, 9th ed., pp. 946–47 / 10th ed., pp. 940–41; Historical Thinking Skills—Argumentation; Learning Objectives INT-7, INT-11, SP-17, IS-7, IS-10; Key Concept 4.3, 4.4)

LONG-ESSAY QUESTIONS

1. For this question you should begin by defining decolonization as the process when the European powers relinquished control of their colonies. A proper thesis will address the point that at the end of World War II, it was clear that for both political and economic reasons, both France and Great Britain needed to engage in decolonization, but that they achieved their goals through different means and with varied success. Independence movements had been present in most of the colonies since the end of World War I. As was the case in India, the independence movements often agreed to postpone their actions until the war was concluded. Once that happened, the independence movements resumed their activities, forcing the French and British governments to respond. With pressing needs at home, many French and British citizens expressed little enthusiasm for maintaining their colonial empires.

   The two countries had different outcomes from the decolonization process, with the French engaging in armed conflict that brought unfortunate results. Led mostly by intellectuals, the colonial independence movements proceeded mostly without bloodshed. In Africa, the British met some resistance in Kenya, but oversaw a peaceful transition in most of its former colonies. The French had more difficulty in Africa, especially in Algeria, because of the large number of French citizens residing in that region. Guerrilla warfare ensued as the French government refused to grant Algerian independence. Only after the creation of the Fifth French Republic did Algeria eventually gain its freedom.

The biggest challenge to British decolonization was the division of India. Under the leadership of Mahatma Gandhi and Jawaharlal Nehru, the Indian colony was divided into Muslim Pakistan and Hindu India. In East Asia, France attempted to retain control of Indochina, one of its colonies. The independence movement that emerged led to a successful guerrilla war against the French, eventually leading to French recognition of a Vietnamese nation. Be sure to add a brief (2–3 sentences) synthesis discussion to your essay. For this essay, you could compare late twentieth century British and French decolonization with American decolonization.
(*Western Civilization*, 9th ed., pp. 876–81 / 10th ed., pp. 870–75; Historical Thinking Skills—Comparison; Learning Objectives INT-7, INT-9, SP-9, SP-14; Key Concept 4.1)

2. Soviet influence was challenged to various degrees throughout the Cold War. Indeed, the post-war history of Soviet hegemony was that of resistance and repression. Although several Eastern European nations rebelled against Soviet authority, none were completely successful. Early on, the Soviets faced dissent in countries including Czechoslovakia and Yugoslavia. In Czechoslovakia, a tradition of democratic institutions provided a challenge to Communist leaders. When it appeared that the Communist Party would have to share power with non-Communist factions, the Communists seized control of the government and dissolved the rival parties. In Yugoslavia, Communist leader Marshal Tito linked Yugoslav independence to the cause of national freedom and refused to capitulate to Soviet attempts to control the Yugoslav government. After nearly a decade, Soviet leaders conceded Yugoslavia's right to its own style of communism.

After Stalin's death in 1953, Poland and Hungary tested Soviet domination. The Soviets pressured the reform efforts of both. In the case of Hungary in 1956, they invaded and overthrew the Hungarian leadership. Although Soviet force prevented full-scale reform in Hungary and elsewhere, by the late 1950s Moscow conceded some control over Eastern European domestic policies in an effort to prevent further rebellion. In 1968, however, new leadership in Czechoslovakia attempted dramatic reform of the existing communist power structure, only to face an invasion by the Red Army, which crushed the reform movement during the Prague Spring. Soviet actions reflected the Brezhnev Doctrine, which called for the use of force wherever socialist regimes were threatened.

Another nation you might examine is Poland, where Soviet domination was challenged by labor leader Lech Walesa and the Solidarity labor movement. By the late 1980s, new Soviet leadership under Mikhail Gorbachev refused to intervene in Polish elections, thus paving the way for Walesa's election as Polish president. Other Eastern European nations also took advantage of Gorbachev's policies and pushed for political freedom. Communist regimes fell in Hungary, Czechoslovakia, Romania, and East Germany. For the most part the transition was peaceful; however, in some cases—for example, Romania—the communist response led to bloodshed. Be sure to add a brief (2-3 sentences) synthesis discussion to your essay. For this essay, you could compare efforts to resist Soviet domination with efforts to resist the Spanish imperialism during the sixteenth and seventeenth centuries. (*Western Civilization*, 9th ed., pp. 906–10 / 10th ed., pp. 877–80, 902–04; Historical Thinking Skills—Comparison; Learning Objectives SP-1, SP-5, SP-9, SP-12, SP-13, SP-17; Key Concept 4.2, 4.4)

Part III

Practice Tests

PRACTICE TEST 1

AP® EUROPEAN HISTORY EXAMINATION
Section I
Part A: Multiple-Choice Questions
Time: 55 minutes
Number of questions: 55
Percent of examination score: 40%

DIRECTIONS: The multiple-choice section consists of question sets organized around a stimulus material—a primary or secondary source, a historian's argument, or a historical problem. For each question, select the best response.

Questions 1–3 refer to the following map.

Source: © Cengage Learning

1. At its largest, Napoleon's Grand Empire—lands under his control and allies—included all of the following countries EXCEPT
   (A) England.
   (B) Russia.
   (C) Austria.
   (D) Spain.

2. Which of the following countries were allied to France but not under French control?
   (A) Spain and Italy
   (B) Westphalia and Saxony
   (C) Great Britain and the Ottoman Empire
   (D) Austria and Russia

GO ON TO NEXT PAGE

3. Napoleon's relationship with the Catholic Church included all of the following EXCEPT
   (A) making the Catholic Church the official state religion.
   (B) enacting the Concordat of 1801.
   (C) requiring the church to give up claims to land confiscated during the Revolution.
   (D) annexing the Papal States.

Questions 4–7 refer to the following image.

Source: Portrait of Peter I or Peter the Great, 1717, Nattier, Jean-Marc (1685–1766)/State Hermitage Museum, St. Petersburg, Russia/Bridgeman Images

4. The victory of Peter the Great in the Great Northern War led to which of the following outcomes?
   (A) Russia, Prussia, and Austria partitioned Sweden, causing its complete dissolution.
   (B) Russia established a strong Baltic presence and Sweden became a second-rate power.
   (C) Russia forced the surrender of Poland, giving Russia control over Estonia, Latvia, and Lithuania.
   (D) Russia and Prussia shared control of the Baltic, which was patrolled by the Russian navy.

5. All of the following are true of Peter the Great's policies concerning women EXCEPT
   (A) Peter allowed women to marry of their own free will.
   (B) Peter demanded that upper-class Russian women remove their veils.
   (C) Peter demanded that noble women participate in the social gatherings that he required the nobles of St. Petersburg to host.
   (D) Peter allowed noble women to vote in provincial elections.

6. Which of the following had the greatest impact on the structure of Russian society?
   (A) The introduction of the Table of Ranks
   (B) The enslavement of Russian merchants who traded on the Baltic Sea
   (C) The decrease in taxes on the peasantry
   (D) The formation of the Russian navy

7. Which of the following characteristics of the monarchy of Peter the Great is represented in the image?
   (A) Peter the Great pursued a policy of westernization in Russia.
   (B) Peter the Great believed that he ruled by divine right.
   (C) Peter the Great believed that the development of a strong army and navy was important.
   (D) Peter the Great spent little on war, urging peace to help the Russian economy.

Questions 8–10 refer to the following map.

Source: © Cengage Learning

8. In the map above, it is clear that
    (A) the Spanish Empire's lands were vastly more extensive than England's or France's.
    (B) most of the fighting in the Seven Years' War was on French and British territory.
    (C) Russia did not participate at all in the war.
    (D) Sweden, Poland, and Hungary were the main combatants.

9. Debts incurred from the Seven Years' War and other wars of the eighteenth century?
    (A) were paid off quickly from stock speculation gains.
    (B) were negligible and had little effect on the countries involved.
    (C) led the English to tax their colonists more, causing unrest.
    (D) were not a problem for France, which gained colonies when the war ended.

10. A drastic change in political alliances that occurred during the Seven Years' War did all of the following EXCEPT
    (A) break the traditional friendship of the German States and Austria.
    (B) ally former enemies England and Prussia.
    (C) bring England and France together to better control their territories in the Americas.
    (D) make enemies of Saxony and Prussia.

GO ON TO NEXT PAGE

Questions 11–13 refer to the following map.

Source: © Cengage Learning

11. As a result of the Munich Conference (September 28–29, 1938),
    (A) Germany declared war on France.
    (B) the Soviet Union invaded Austria.
    (C) Japan bombed Pearl Harbor.
    (D) Germany took control of the Sudetenland.

12. Who among the following was the strongest proponent of appeasement?
    (A) Winston Churchill
    (B) Neville Chamberlain
    (C) Charles De Gaulle
    (D) Joseph Stalin

13. Why was Hitler's invasion of Prague a turning point in international diplomacy?
    (A) It convinced Britain and France that Hitler could not be trusted and led to their promise to protect Poland, in the event of an attack by Germany.
    (B) It was the first act of appeasement carried out by Britain and France and led to a decade of attempts to avoid a general war against Germany.
    (C) It was the first time that Hitler had taken over a nation that belonged to another European empire.
    (D) It convinced Britain and France that diplomacy was the only way to avoid a war against Hitler.

Questions 14–16 refer to the following image.

Source: © Yale Center for British Art///Paul Mellon Collection/The Bridgeman Art Library

14. The painting above shows evidence of
   (A) the middle- and upper-class ideal of the nuclear family.
   (B) the use of birth control to limit family size.
   (C) the total control fathers had over their wives and children.
   (D) the importance of hard work and simple lifestyles in Protestant homes.

15. Background elements in the painting above show which of the following about the people pictured?
   (A) The family was very religious.
   (B) Learning and science were important to them.
   (C) The children were sent off to work in factories at an early age.
   (D) They had little time for leisure activities.

16. In comparison to the family depicted above, a lower-class family of the period would have had to deal with all of the following issues EXCEPT
   (A) the possible enclosure of their farm.
   (B) the making of extra money by participating in cottage industry.
   (C) crop failures and famine.
   (D) the cost of sending their children to school.

GO ON TO NEXT PAGE

Questions 17–20 refer to the following quotation.

Concerning the matter of a wife [for you], it appears to me that if Francesco di Messer Tanagli wishes to give his daughter, that it would be a fine marriage.... Francesco Tanagli has a good reputation, and he has held office... You may ask: "Why should he give her to someone in exile?" There are three reasons. First, there aren't many young men of good family who have both virtue and property. Second, she has only a small dowry... Third, I believe that he will give her away, because he has a large family and he will need help to settle them....

[July 26, 1465] ... Francesco is a good friend of Marco [Parenti, Alessandra's son-in-law] and he trusts him. On S. Jacopo's day, he spoke to him discreetly and persuasively, saying ... that when we had made up our minds, she will come to us willingly. [He said that] you were a worthy man, but that he had only a small dowry to give her, and so he would prefer to send her out of Florence to someone of worth, rather than to give her to someone here, from among those who were available, with little money.... We have information that she is affable and competent. She is responsible for a large family (there are twelve children, six boys and six girls) ...

[August 31, 1465] ... I have recently received some very favorable information [about the Tanagli girl] from two individuals.... They are in agreement that whoever gets her will be content.... Concerning her beauty, they told me what I had already seen, that she is attractive and well-proportioned.... She reads quite well ... and she can dance and sing....

[Filippo Strozzi eventually married Fiametta di Donato Adimari in 1466.]

Source: G. Brucker, ed., *The Society of Renaissance Florence* (Toronto: University of Toronto Press, 1971).

17. As suggested by the quotation to the left, all of the following were possible reasons that marriages were arranged during the Renaissance EXCEPT
    (A) marriages were often arranged to seal business and family connections with other respectable families.
    (B) marriages were often arranged to seal political alliances.
    (C) marriages were often arranged to improve social status.
    (D) marriages were often arranged to keep children from making poor decisions concerning a marriage partner.

18. Which of the following best describes the status of Renaissance women?
    (A) Women were allowed to marry for love.
    (B) Women were forbidden from becoming prostitutes.
    (C) Women managed their households and had a certain degree of autonomy in their daily lives.
    (D) Women married at relatively late ages compared with their male counterparts.

19. Which of the following is true of Italian Renaissance families?
    (A) Renaissance women married at a very young age, and their husbands were generally older.
    (B) Most upper-class Renaissance parents had few children because their education and upbringing were expensive.
    (C) Lower-class women had more children than upper-class women in order to have more family members to help support the family financially.
    (D) About 20 percent of Florentine children in the merchant class died before age 20.

20. All of the following were important considerations in marriage negotiations EXCEPT
    (A) family reputation.
    (B) love.
    (C) size of the dowry.
    (D) beauty and competence of the future wife.

Questions 21–23 refer to the following image.

Source: Trades Union Congress, London/The
Bridgeman Art Library

21. This image was created to
    (A) show the importance of British
        shipping in carrying products to a
        worldwide market.
    (B) illustrate ancient sea gods and
        goddesses as symbols of maritime
        power in the nineteenth century.
    (C) advertise a shipwright company and
        the various ways it could ship goods.
    (D) show the various facets and benefits
        of a trade union.

22. The importance of shipping to the
    British Empire can be seen in all of the
    following EXCEPT
    (A) the prominence given to sailing
        vessels in the image above.
    (B) the transportation of raw materials
        to factories and finished products to
        markets.
    (C) the discovery of new lands and the
        expansion of the Empire.
    (D) the high wages and prestige given to
        sailors.

23. Trade unions worked for the betterment
    of
    (A) workers' wages and hours.
    (B) owners' rights over their workers.
    (C) the expansion of child labor.
    (D) consumer safety when using
        products.

GO ON TO NEXT PAGE

Questions 24–27 refer to the following map.

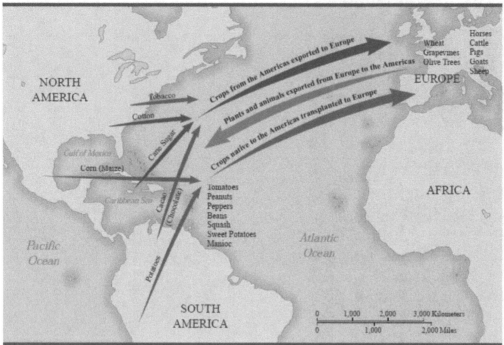

Source: © Cengage Learning

24. Which food, introduced as a result of the Columbian Exchange, became a dietary staple for many Europeans?
    (A) wheat
    (B) olives
    (C) pigs (pork)
    (D) potatoes

25. Which of the following was an important impact that the Columbian Exchange had on Europe?
    (A) Population levels declined as new plants brought from the new world poisoned many people.
    (B) Coffeehouses became popular in Europe, providing a place for wealthier Europeans to meet and discuss political and social ideas.
    (C) Europeans began to believe that natives from the Americas were near equals, after eating the foods brought over from the New World.
    (D) Europeans died in large numbers of smallpox, a disease introduced to Europe from the Americas.

26. Which of the following animals, introduced to the Americas from Europe, revolutionized the lives of Native Americans?
    (A) horses
    (B) alpacas
    (C) llamas
    (D) sheep

27. All of the following were important social, economic, and political effects of European expansion in the New World EXCEPT
    (A) many ordinary European women found marriage opportunities in the New World due to a lack of white women in the Americas.
    (B) importation of New World gold and silver brought wealth into Western European economies, contributing to the price revolution.
    (C) conflicts over trade led increased economic and political cooperation among the Spanish, English, Dutch, and French.
    (D) demand for plantation crops, such as tobacco and sugar, led to the expansion of the slave trade.

Questions 28–30 refer to the following image.

Source: © Bettmann/Corbis

28. As suggested by the cartoon above, all of the following were reasons true political democracy failed to develop in Germany in the years prior to World War I EXCEPT
   (A) the German army was dominated by the old Prussian Junkers and supported conservative forces, such as the monarchy, in society, essentially preventing reform.
   (B) Chancellor Bismarck prevented the growth of democratic institutions and favored conservatism over socialism when he undertook repressive measures against the Social Democrats.
   (C) average citizens in Germany were not educated enough to participate in a meaningful way in a participatory democracy.
   (D) the German constitution made the ministers of government, including the chancellor, responsible to the emperor, rather than the popularly elected parliament, so public opinion and parliamentary demands had little impact on policy.

29. The dismissal of Bismarck by William II led to which of the following?
   (A) An immediate end to the Kultur-kampf was initiated by William II.
   (B) William II convinced the Reichstag to pass a series of harsh laws against German socialists.
   (C) William II concluded a series of alliances that created a universal peace that lasted for over 50 years.
   (D) William II's increasingly aggressive foreign policy heightened tensions in Europe and eventually contributed to the outbreak of World War I.

30. The woman personifying Germany in the background of the image is concerned for which of the following reasons?
   (A) The resignation of Bismarck increased the possibility for war.
   (B) Germans feared the imminent death of Bismarck, who was very ill.
   (C) The resignation of Bismarck left Germany open to attack from France.
   (D) Germans feared that William II would greatly persecute the socialists.

GO ON TO NEXT PAGE

Questions 31–33 refer to the following quotation.

Nikita Khrushchev, Address to the Twentieth Party Congress, February 1956

Comrades, ... quite a lot has been said about the cult of the individual and about its harmful consequences.... The cult of the person of Stalin ... became at a certain specific stage the source of a whole series of exceedingly serious and grave perversions of Party principles, of Party democracy, of revolutionary legality.

Stalin abandoned the method of ideological struggle for that of administrative violence, mass repressions and terror.... Mass arrests and deportations of many thousands of people, execution without trial and without normal investigation created conditions of insecurity, fear and even desperation.

Stalin showed in a whole series of cases his intolerance, his brutality and his abuse of power...

Many Party, Soviet and economic activists who were branded in 1937–8 as "enemies" were actually never enemies, spies, wreckers and so on, but were always honest communists;

This was the result of the abuse of power by Stalin, who began to use mass terror against the Party cadres...

Stalin was a very distrustful man, sickly suspicious.... Everywhere and in everything he saw "enemies," "twofacers," and "spies." Possessing unlimited power, he indulged in great willfulness and choked a person morally and physically. A situation was created where one could not express one's own will. When Stalin said that one or another would be arrested, it was necessary to accept on faith that he was an "enemy of the people." What proofs were offered? The confession of the arrested.... How is it possible that a person confesses to crimes that he had not committed? Only in one way—because of application of physical methods of pressuring him,

tortures, ... taking away of his human dignity.

Source: Reprinted from the Congressional Record, 84th Congress, 2nd Session (Washington, D.C.: U.S. Government Printing Office), Vol. 102, Part 7, pp. 9389–9402.

31. Why did Khrushchev condemn Stalin in his 1956 speech to the Twentieth Party Congress?
    (A) He believed that Stalin had cheated on his wife and was an immoral man.
    (B) He believed that Stalin was a traitor who had sold secrets to Hitler during World War II.
    (C) He believed that Stalin's use of terror, administrative violence, and mass repression was a crime against the Soviet people.
    (D) He believed that Stalin's creation of Soviet satellite nations in Eastern Europe was a crime against the people of the Eastern European nations.

32. De-Stalinization involved all of the following EXCEPT
    (A) closing some of the Siberian prison camps.
    (B) supporting the democratization of Eastern European satellite nations.
    (C) reducing some of the powers of the secret police.
    (D) granting a slight bit of intellectual freedom to writers and artists.

33. Which of the following was a characteristic of Khrushchev's economic policies?
    (A) He placed the greatest emphasis on further development of heavy industry.
    (B) He attempted to increase agricultural output by having farmers raise more livestock.
    (C) He decreased military spending while maintaining the Soviet nuclear arsenal.
    (D) His emphasis on light industry and production of more consumer goods led to a sharp decline in the industrial growth rate.

Questions 34–37 refer to the following map.

Source: © Cengage Learning

34. The map above shows the countries of Europe
    (A) during the reign of Napoleon I.
    (B) during the French Revolution.
    (C) after the Congress of Vienna.
    (D) after the Peace of Westphalia.

35. During the time period shown above
    (A) Germany was united into a single country.
    (B) legitimate monarchs were restored to the thrones of Spain and France.
    (C) Napoleon returned to rule France for 10 more years.
    (D) Tsar Alexander stepped down as ruler of Russia.

36. One of the most important problems faced by Europe at this point in time was
    (A) rivalries over the control of the divided German states.
    (B) the growing power of the Ottoman Empire.
    (C) the expanding power of the Hapsburg family.
    (D) rivalries over the control of the Kingdom of Poland.

37. The fact that Austria benefited greatly from the outcome of the Napoleonic Wars may be attributed to
    (A) the strong friendship between Napoleon and Metternich.
    (B) a secret alliance between Metternich and Tsar Alexander I.
    (C) Metternich's tactic of staying out of the war and focusing on industrialization instead.
    (D) Metternich's conservative agenda and control over the Congress of Vienna meetings.

GO ON TO NEXT PAGE

Questions 38–41 refer to the following quotation.

Galileo Galilei, The Starry Messenger

About ten months ago a report reached my ears that a certain Fleming had constructed a spyglass by means of which visible objects, though very distant from the eye of the observer, were distinctly seen as if nearby... A few days later the report was confirmed to me in a letter from a noble Frenchman at Paris, Jacques Badovere, which caused me to apply myself wholeheartedly to inquire into the means by which I might arrive at the invention of a similar instrument. This I did shortly afterwards ... Finally, sparing neither labor nor expense, I succeeded in constructing for myself so excellent an instrument that objects seen by means of it appeared nearly one thousand times larger and over thirty times closer than when regarded without natural vision.

Now let us review the observations made during the past two months, once more inviting the attention of all who are eager for true philosophy to the first steps of such important contemplations. Let us speak first of that surface of the moon which faces us. For greater clarity I distinguish two parts of this surface, a lighter and a darker; the lighter part seems to surround and to pervade the whole hemisphere, while the darker part discolors the moon's surface like a kind of cloud, and makes it appear covered with spots.... From observation of these spots repeated many times I have been led to the opinion and conviction that the surface of the moon is not smooth, uniform, and precisely spherical as a great number of philosophers believe it (and the other heavenly bodies) to be, but is uneven, rough, and full of cavities and prominences, being not unlike the face of the earth, relieved by chains of mountains and deep valleys.

Source: E. S. Carlo, *The Sidereal Messenger of Galileo Galilei: And a Part of the Preface to Kepler's Dioptrics Containing the Original Account of Galileo's Astronomical Discoveries* (London: Rivingtons, 1880), pp. 10–11, 14–15.

38. Which of the following was a significant achievement of Galileo?
    (A) He invented the telescope.
    (B) He improved the technology of the telescope.
    (C) He promoted the geocentric model of the universe.
    (D) He was the first to mathematically prove that planets had elliptical orbits.

39. Which of the following best describes the significance of Galileo's observations?
    (A) He confirmed the geocentric model.
    (B) He proved that the Copernican system was an inadequate explanation of the universe.
    (C) He confirmed the heliocentric model.
    (D) He proved that the planets had elliptical orbits.

40. All of the following were reasons why the Roman Catholic Church condemned Galileo EXCEPT
    (A) his observations threatened holy scripture and no longer placed humans at the center of God's universe.
    (B) he refused to refrain from teaching that the Copernican system was not a fact and only a mathematical supposition.
    (C) he refused to reject his belief in the Copernican model.
    (D) his observations threatened popular belief in the Copernican system.

41. Which of the following best describes the impact of Galileo's condemnation by the Inquisition?
    (A) It hampered further scientific work in Italy, passing leadership in science to the northern countries.
    (B) It hampered further scientific work in Italy, passing leadership in science to Russia.
    (C) It shifted the focus of scientific work from astronomy to anatomy.
    (D) It increased the popularity of the Roman Catholic Church, since people realized the church was protecting them from heretical ideas.

Questions 42–45 refer to the following map.

Source: © Cengage Learning

42. Why did Austria-Hungary disagree with Serbia's desire to create a large Serbian kingdom in the beginning of the twentieth century?
(A) The Austrians thought that an independent Serbia would threaten the unity of their empire.
(B) The Austrians thought that an independent Serbia would be easily taken over by Russia.
(C) The Austrians thought that an independent Serbia would immediately declare war on Bosnia.
(D) The Austrians thought that an independent Serbia would become an ally of the Ottoman Empire.

43. What was the most important result of the First and Second Balkan Wars?
(A) Austria lost control of most of its Balkan territories.
(B) Inhabitants of the Balkans were angry about the settlements, and more tension was building among the great powers.
(C) Bulgaria gained a great deal of territory and became a strong Balkan nation.
(D) The Ottoman Empire gained control of most of the Balkan peninsula, renewing its strength in the region.

44. What was the primary reason that Serbia wanted to acquire Albanian territory?
(A) The Albanians and Serbians shared a common language and common ethnic heritage.
(B) Taking Albanian territory would have given Serbia an advantage over the Ottoman Empire.
(C) Serbia wanted to gain a port on the Adriatic Sea.
(D) Serbia's alliance with Germany would have been more effective if the German navy could have used a Serbian port on the Adriatic Sea to aid Serbian military efforts.

45. All of the following statements accurately describe the region seen in the map EXCEPT
(A) the presence of three great empires in the region created serious tensions.
(B) the presence of many nationalities in the region led to ethnic nationalism.
(C) Ottoman control of the Black Sea, following the Crimean War, led to a series of diplomatic agreements that allowed the Russians to use the Bosphorus and Dardanelles.
(D) Ottoman control of the Bosphorus and Dardanelles impacted Russian diplomatic and economic policy significantly in the first two decades of the twentieth century.

GO ON TO NEXT PAGE

Questions 46–48 refer to the following image.

Source: © RMN-Grand Palais (Art Resource, NY)

46. The above painting, *The Oath of the Horatii* by Jacques-Louis David, is a good example of Neoclassical art because of
    (A) the religious nature of the subject matter.
    (B) the inclusion of women in the background of the painting.
    (C) the use of geometric perspective.
    (D) the classical Roman story it tells.

47. David's paintings were often used by the French Republic and Napoleon
    (A) to push their agenda to take over Rome.
    (B) as entertainment to keep the poor happy.
    (C) to showcase their enlightened ideals and their power.
    (D) to highlight their beliefs about women's participation in government.

48. The Neoclassical painting above can be compared to Renaissance art in all of the following ways EXCEPT
    (A) it includes Roman-style architecture and themes.
    (B) it is secular in nature rather than religious.
    (C) it was painted for a patron.
    (D) its use of patriotism as an element.

Questions 49–52 refer to the following map.

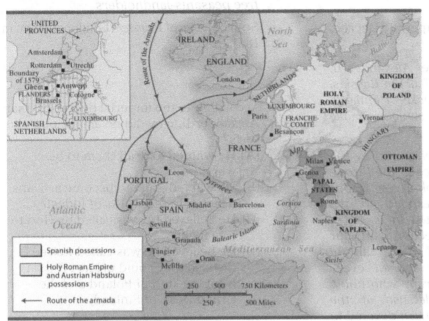

Source: © Cengage Learning

49. England was threatened by Spanish territory in the Netherlands for all of the following reasons EXCEPT
   (A) the Netherlands could be used as a launching area for a Spanish attack, due to its close proximity to England.
   (B) Spanish control of the sea lanes around the Netherlands could threaten English trade routes.
   (C) the English feared that growing Spanish power could threaten the Elizabethan religious settlement.
   (D) an increasingly powerful Spain would threaten England's control of its North American colonies.

50. The expansion of the Hapsburg family threatened which of the following principles during the late sixteenth century?
   (A) Balance of power
   (B) Monarchial centralization
   (C) United Christendom
   (D) Military superiority

51. The defeat of the Spanish Armada in 1588 was a turning point in Spanish history because
   (A) it marked the growth of French naval power.
   (B) it led to a nearly permanent decline in Spanish power.
   (C) it forced the Spanish monarchy to invest more money in the modernization of the Spanish navy.
   (D) it led to a political revolution that established a constitutional monarchy in Spain.

52. All of the following were reasons why Spain launched its attack on England in 1588 EXCEPT
   (A) Spain wanted to gain control of English trade routes.
   (B) England had been aiding the Dutch Protestants in their fight against the Spanish.
   (C) Spain wanted to overthrow Queen Elizabeth I and make England a Protestant nation.
   (D) England had been taking over Spanish settlements in the Americas and Spain wanted to stop the English from stealing Spanish lands.

GO ON TO NEXT PAGE

Questions 53–55 refer to the following quotation.

Tsar Alexander II, Imperial Decree, March 3, 1861

By the grace of God, we, Alexander II, Emperor and Autocrat of all the Russias, King of Poland, Grand Duke of Finland, etc., to all our faithful subjects, make known:

Called by Divine Providence and by the sacred right of inheritance to the throne of our ancestors, we took a vow in our inner-most heart to respond to the mission which is intrusted to us as to surround with our affection and our Imperial solicitude all our faithful subjects of every rank and of every condition, from the warrior, who nobly bears arms for the defense of the country to the humble artisan devoted to the works of industry; from the official in the career of the high offices of the State to the laborer whose plow furrows the soil....

We thus came to the conviction that the work of a serious improvement of the condi-tion of the peasants was a sacred inheritance bequeathed to us by our ancestors, a mission which, in the course of events, Divine provi-dence called upon us to fulfill....

In virtue of the new dispositions above men-tioned, the peasants attached to the soil will be invested within a term fixed by the law with all the rights of free cultivators....

At the same time, they are granted the right of purchasing their close, and, with the consent of the proprietors, they may acquire in full property the arable lands and other appurtenances which are allotted to them as a permanent holding. By the acquisition in full property of the quantity of land fixed, the peasants are free from their obligations toward the proprietors for land thus purchased, and they enter definitely into the condition of free peasants-landholders.

Source: *Annual Register* (London: Longman, 1861) p. 207.

53. According to the imperial decree by Tsar Alexander II, why did he emancipate the serfs?
    (A) He wanted to draft them to be warriors.
    (B) He wanted them to become artisans devoted to the works of industry.
    (C) He believed he was called by God to free them.
    (D) He believed he was called to free them so they could protect Russia from the king of Poland and the Grand Duke of Finland.

54. Which of the following statements best describes the condition of the peasants in the years following emancipation?
    (A) The peasants were free and enjoyed the use of land provided to them free of cost from the government.
    (B) The peasants were free landowners, and many joined the village mirs that provided free use of community farming tools and seeds.
    (C) The peasants were prosperous, since they were given some of the best farmland by the government.
    (D) The peasants were hindered by primitive agriculture practices and a lack of real land reform.

55. Which of the following is a true statement about nineteenth-century Russian rulers, such as Alexander II?

(A) Russian rulers, such as Alexander II, pushed through a program of reform and modernization. This gave rise to revolutionary movements that culminated in the Revolution of 1905.

(B) Russian rulers, such as Alexander II, eliminated all aristocratic privileges in an attempt to appease the dissatisfied lower classes.

(C) Russian rulers, such as Alexander II, refused to enact any reforms, in fear of giving up too much power.

(D) Russian rulers, such as Alexander II, pushed through a program of reform and modernization which satisfied the lower classes, preventing revolutionary movements.

STOP
END OF SECTION I, PART A

IF YOU FINISH BEFORE TIME IS CALLED, YOU MAY CHECK YOUR WORK ON THIS SECTION. DO NOT GO ON TO SECTION I PART B UNTIL YOU ARE TOLD TO DO SO.

AP® EUROPEAN HISTORY EXAMINATION
Section I
Part B: Short-Answer Questions
Time: 50 minutes
Number of questions: 4
Percent of examination score: 20%

DIRECTIONS: Part B of the examination contains four questions. You will have 50 minutes to respond to all questions. You are not required to develop and support a thesis statement in your response. Rather, focus on directly answering each question using evidence from your study of history.

Machiavelli, *The Prince* (1513)

> *This leads us to a question that is in dispute: Is it better to be loved than feared, or vice versa? My reply is one ought to be both loved and feared; but, since it is difficult to accomplish both at the same time, I maintain it is much safer to be feared than loved, if you have to do without one of the two. For of men one can, in general, say this: They are ungrateful, fickle, deceptive and deceiving, avoiders of danger, eager to gain. As long as you serve their interests, they are devoted to you. They promise you their blood, their possessions, their lives, and their children, as I said before, so long as you seem to have no need of them. But as soon as you need help, they turn against you. Any ruler who relies simply on their promises and makes no other preparations, will be destroyed. For you will find that those whose support you buy, who do not rally to you because they admire your strength of character and nobility of soul, these are people you pay for, but they are never yours, and in the end you cannot get the benefit of your investment. Men are less nervous of offending someone who makes himself lovable, than someone who makes himself frightening. For love attaches men by ties of obligation, which, since men are wicked, they break whenever their interests are at stake. But fear restrains men because they are afraid of punishment, and this fear never leaves them. Still, a ruler should make himself feared in such a way that, if he does not inspire love, at least he does not provoke hatred. For it is perfectly possible to be feared and not hated. You will only be hated if you seize the property or the women of your subjects and citizens.*

Erasmus, *Education of a Christian Prince* (1516)

> *A good prince ... is a living likeness of God, who is at once good and powerful. His goodness makes him want to help all; his power makes him able to do so. On the other hand, an evil prince, who is like a plague to his country, is the incarnation of the devil, who has great power joined with his wickedness. All his resources to the very last, he uses for the undoing of the human race....*
>
> *[A good prince is one] who holds the life of each individual dearer than his own; who works and strives night and day for just one end—to be the best he can for everyone; with whom rewards are ready for all good men ... for so much does he want to be of real help to his people, without thought of recompense, that if necessary he would not hesitate to look out for their welfare at great risk to himself; who considers his wealth to lie in the advantage of his country; who is ever on the watch so that everyone else may sleep deeply; who grants no leisure to himself so that he may spend his life in the peace of his country; who worries himself with continual cares so that his subjects may have peace and quiet.... He does everything and allows everything that will bring everlasting peace to his country, for he realizes that war is the source of all misfortunes to the state.*

Sources: Machiavelli, *The Prince* (1513), trans. D. Wootton (Indianapolis: Hackett Publishing Company, 1995), pp. 51–52; Erasmus, *Education of a Christian Prince* (1516), trans. L. K. Born (New York: Columbia University Press, 1936).

1. Compare the views of Machiavelli and Erasmus from the quotations above and answer A, B, and C.
   A) Briefly explain Machiavelli's views concerning the characteristics of a good ruler.
   B) Briefly explain Erasmus's views concerning the characteristics of a good ruler.
   C) Briefly explain one reason that Machiavelli's views are more cutthroat than those of Erasmus.

2. Answer A, B, and C by analyzing the motives for the development of mass education in state-run systems.
   A) Briefly explain ONE social reason for the development of mass education.
   B) Briefly explain ONE economic reason for the development of mass education.
   C) Briefly explain ONE political reason for the development of mass education.

3. Analyze the impact of the Protestant Reformation on society in the sixteenth century. Answer A, B, and C.
   A) Briefly explain one impact of the Protestant Reformation on education.
   B) Briefly explain one impact of the Protestant Reformation on the family.
   C) Briefly explain one impact of the Protestant Reformation on women.

4. Analyze the process and impact of the unification of Germany and answer A, B, and C.
   A) Briefly explain ONE way in which Bismarck used warfare to unify Germany.
   B) Briefly explain ONE example of how Chancellor Otto von Bismarck used *Realpolitik* in the unification of Germany.
   C) Briefly analyze the impact of the unification of Germany on European affairs.

STOP
END OF SECTION I

IF YOU FINISH BEFORE TIME IS CALLED, YOU MAY CHECK YOUR WORK ON THIS SECTION. DO NOT GO ON TO SECTION II UNTIL YOU ARE TOLD TO DO SO.

AP® EUROPEAN HISTORY EXAMINATION
Section II: Free-Response Essays
Part A: Document-Based Question (DBQ)
Suggested writing time: 55 minutes
Percent of examination score: 25%

DIRECTIONS: The following question is based on the accompanying Documents 1–7. The documents have been edited for the purposes of this exercise. This question is designed to test your ability to apply several historical thinking skills simultaneously, including historical argumentation, appropriate use of relevant historical evidence, contextualization, and synthesis. Your response should be based on your analysis of the documents and your knowledge of the topic.

Write a well-integrated essay that does the following:

- States an appropriate thesis that directly addresses *all parts* of the question.
- Supports the thesis or an appropriate argument with evidence from all or all but one of the documents AND knowledge of European history beyond/outside the documents.
- Analyzes a majority of the documents in terms of such features as their intended audience, purpose, point of view, format, argument, limitations, and/or social context as appropriate to the argument.
- Places the argument in the context of the broader regional, national, or global process.

QUESTION 1. Evaluate the responsibility of various nations for the Cold War.

Document 1

Source: Map of the New European Alliance Systems in the 1950s and 1960s.

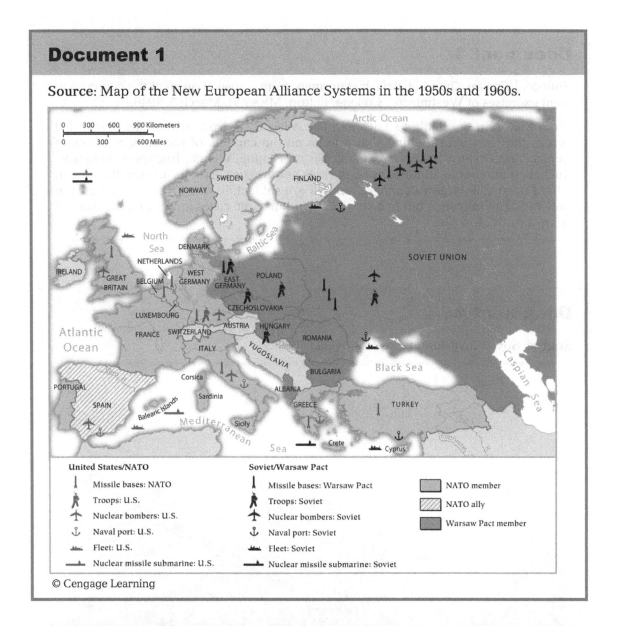

© Cengage Learning

Document 2

Source: George Kennan, American diplomat, from *The Long Telegram*, February 22, 1946.

At the bottom of [the Soviet] neurotic view of world affairs is a traditional and instinctive Russian sense of insecurity.... We have here a political force committed fanatically to the belief that with the United States there can be no permanent modus vivendi, that it is desirable and necessary the internal harmony of our society be disrupted, our traditional way of life be destroyed, the international authority of our state be broken, if Soviet power is to be secure.... This is admittedly not a pleasant picture....

GO ON TO NEXT PAGE

Document 3

Source: Winston Churchill, British statesman, from a speech given at the commencement exercises of Westminster College, Fulton, Missouri, March 5, 1946.

From Stettin in the Baltic to Trieste in the Adriatic an iron curtain has descended across the Continent. Behind that line lie all the capitals of the ancient states of Central and Eastern Europe. Warsaw, Berlin, Prague, Vienna, Budapest, Belgrade, Bucharest and Sofia; all these famous cities and the populations around them lie in what I must call the Soviet sphere, and all are subject, in one form or another, not only to Soviet influence but to a very high and in some cases increasing measure of control from Moscow.

Document 4

Source: Soviet Invasion of Czechoslovakia, 1968.

© CTK/Alamy

Document 5

Source: Joseph Stalin, General Secretary of the Central Committee of the Soviet Communist Party, reply to Winston Churchill, March 14, 1946.

In substance, Mr. Churchill now stands in the position of a firebrand of war. And Mr. Churchill is not alone here. He has friends not only in England but also in the United States of America.

In this respect, one is reminded remarkably of Hitler and his friends. Hitler began to set war loose by announcing his racial theory.... Mr. Churchill begins to set war loose, also by a racial theory, maintaining that only nations speaking the English language are fully valuable nations, called upon to decide the destinies of the entire world.

Document 6

Source: Nikolai Novikov, Soviet diplomat, telegram to Soviet Foreign Minister Vyacheslav Molotov, September 27, 1946.

Obvious indications of the U.S. effort to establish world dominance are also to be found in the increase in military potential in peacetime....

Careful note should be taken of the fact that the preparation by the United States for a future war is being conducted with the prospect of war against the Soviet Union, which in the eyes of American imperialists is the main obstacle in the path of the United States to world domination.

Document 7

Source: Imre Nagy, Hungarian Prime Minister, Last Message, November 4, 1956.

This fight is the fight for freedom by the Hungarian people against the Russian intervention, and it is possible that I shall only be able to stay at my post for one or two hours. The whole world will see how the Russian armed forces, contrary to all treaties and conventions, are crushing the resistance of the Hungarian people. They will also see how they are kidnapping the Prime Minister of a country which is a Member of the United Nations, taking him from the capital, and therefore it cannot be doubted at all that this is the most brutal form of intervention.... [T]oday it is Hungary and tomorrow, or the day after tomorrow, it will be the turn of other countries because the imperialism of Moscow does not know borders, and is only trying to play for time.

END OF DOCUMENTS FOR PART A.
GO ON TO THE NEXT PAGE.

AP® EUROPEAN HISTORY EXAMINATION
Section II: Free-Response Essays
Part B: Long-Essay Questions
Suggested planning and writing time: 35 minutes
Percent of examination score: 15%

DIRECTIONS: You are to choose ONE question from the two questions below. Make your selection carefully, choosing the question that you are best prepared to answer thoroughly in the time permitted. You should spend 5 minutes organizing or outlining your answer. Write your answer to the question on the lined pages of the Section II free-response booklet, making sure to indicate the question you are answering by writing the appropriate question number on the top of each page.

Write an essay that:

- has a relevant thesis.
- addresses all parts of the question.
- supports your thesis with specific evidence.
- is well organized.

QUESTION 1. Compare German Nazism under Hitler with Soviet Communism under Stalin. (Historical Thinking Skills: Comparison).

QUESTION 2. Compare the ideas expressed by Jean-Baptiste Colbert (1619–1683) and Adam Smith (1723–1790) about methods for increasing a nation's wealth. (Historical Thinking Skills: Comparison)

END OF EXAMINATION

ANSWERS FOR SECTION I, PART A: MULTIPLE-CHOICE QUESTIONS

ANSWER KEY FOR PART A: MULTIPLE-CHOICE QUESTIONS

1. B	12. B	23. A	34. C	45. C
2. D	13. A	24. D	35. B	46. D
3. A	14. A	25. B	36. A	47. C
4. B	15. B	26. A	37. D	48. D
5. D	16. D	27. C	38. B	49. D
6. A	17. D	28. C	39. C	50. A
7. C	18. C	29. D	40. D	51. B
8. B	19. A	30. A	41. A	52. D
9. C	20. B	31. C	42. A	53. C
10. C	21. D	32. B	43. B	54. D
11. D	22. D	33. D	44. C	55. A

EXPLANATIONS FOR PART A: MULTIPLE-CHOICE ANSWERS

1. **(B)** Napoleon was never able to conquer England, although he was able to take almost all of the Continent either as truly conquered or as allied states (*Western Civilization*, 9th ed., pp. 590–91 / 10th ed., pp. 586–88; Historical Thinking Skills—Periodization, Analyzing Evidence: Content and Sourcing; Learning Objective SP13, SP 17; Key Concept 2.1).

2. **(D)** Austria and Russia signed alliances with the French but the Austrian Empire and the Russian Empire were not under his control (Western Civilization, 9th ed., pp. 590–91 / 10th ed., pp. 586–88; Historical Thinking Skills—Analyzing Evidence: Content and Sourcing, Contextualization; Learning Objective SP-13, SP-17; Key Concept 2.1).

3. **(A)** Napoleon did not make Catholicism the official state religion, but allowed it to be acknowledged as the religion of the majority (*Western Civilization*, 9th ed., pp. 587–88 / 10th ed., p. 584; Historical Thinking Skills—Causation, Patterns of Continuity and Change Over Time; Learning Objective SP-3; Key Concept 2.1).

4. **(B)** With the Russian victory over Sweden in the Great Northern War, Russia became a great European power and Sweden fell to second-rate status (*Western Civilization*, 9th ed., pp. 453–56 / 10th ed., pp. 451–53; Historical Thinking Skills—Periodization; Learning Objectives SP-13, SP-15; Key Concept 2.1).

5. **(D)** Women benefited greatly under the rule of Peter the Great, gaining many freedoms enjoyed by Western European women. Peter, like the rulers in other European states, did not allow women to vote (*Western Civilization*, 9th ed., pp. 453–56 / 10th ed., p. 451; Historical Thinking Skills—Contextualization; Learning Objectives IS-6, IS-9; Key Concept 2.3, 2.4).

6. (**A**) Peter the Great's introduction of the Table of Ranks was designed to create a new nobility based on merit instead of birth and gave non-nobles the ability to serve the state and join the nobility, significantly changing the structure of Russian society (*Western Civilization*, 9th ed., pp. 453–56 / 10th ed., pp. 450–51; Historical Thinking Skills—Contextualization; Learning Objectives IS-7; Key Concept 2.1).

7. (**C**) Peter the Great developed the first Russian navy and created a large, well-equipped army to protect his nation, making Russia a strong military power by the time he died in 1725 (*Western Civilization*, 9th ed., pp. 453–56 / 10th ed., pp. 450–53; Historical Thinking Skills—Contextualization; Learning Objectives SP-13, SP-15; Key Concept 2.1).

8. (**B**) Most of the areas of conflict are shown on French and British territory (*Western Civilization*, 9th ed., pp. 543–46 / 10th ed., pp. 540–43; Historical Thinking Skills—Analyzing Evidence: Content and Sourcing; Learning Objective SP-2; Key Concept 2.1).

9. (**C**) While England was able to raise taxes on its nobles and colonies, which caused unrest in America, France was not able to raise taxes on the nobles at all, heading it toward eventual bankruptcy (*Western Civilization*, 9th ed., pp. 543–46 / 10th ed., pp. 540–43; Historical Thinking Skills—Causation, Patterns of Continuity and Change Over Time; Learning Objective SP-2, SP-5; Key Concept 2.1).

10. (**C**) England and France continued to fight through the American Revolution and the War of 1812. Austria and Prussia fought on opposing sides in this war, while Prussia took over Saxony (*Western Civilization*, 9th ed., pp. 543–46 / 10th ed., pp. 540–42; Historical Thinking Skills—Causation, Patterns of Continuity and Change over Time; Learning Objective SP-2; Key Concept 2.2).

11. (**D**) The Munich Conference, the high point of Western appeasement, led to German advances in Czechoslovakia (*Western Civilization*, 9th ed., p. 836 / 10th ed., p. 831; Historical Thinking Skills—Causation; Learning Objectives SP-6, SP-8, SP-17, SP-18; Key Concept 4.1, 4.2).

12. (**B**) Neville Chamberlain, British prime minister in the 1930s, believed that war should be avoided at all costs. Trying to avoid another devastating crisis like World War I, he was willing to appease Hitler in hopes that Hitler's demands could be satisfied diplomatically (*Western Civilization*, 9th ed., p. 836 / 10th ed., p. 831; Historical Thinking Skills—Comparison; Learning Objectives SP-6, SP-8, SP-17, SP-18; Key Concept 4.1, 4.2).

13. **(A)** When he invaded Prague, Hitler broke the Munich Agreement, convincing the British and the French that he could not be trusted. This led to their protection of Poland in September, 1939 and the outbreak of World War II (*Western Civilization*, 9th ed., p. 836 / 10th ed., p. 831; Historical Thinking Skills—Periodization; Learning Objectives SP-6, SP-8, SP-17, SP-18; Key Concept 4.1, 4.2).

14. **(A)** This is a fairly large family with five children but the portrait shows no other relative. Although the father is holding a stick, he seems to be playing with his son, not controlling him. The children are playing games rather than working hard. Leisure time is obviously something this family values (*Western Civilization*, 9th ed., pp. 547–50 / 10th ed., pp. 543–46; Historical Thinking Skills—Patterns of Continuity and Change Over Time, Analyzing Evidence: Content and Sourcing; Learning Objective IS-4; Key Concept 2.4).

15. **(B)** The background of the painting shows scientific equipment, not religious items. The people are obviously wealthy enough to enjoy leisure time and would not need to send children off to work (*Western Civilization*, 9th ed., pp. 547–50 / 10th ed., pp. 543–46; Historical Thinking Skills—Argumentation, Analyzing Evidence: Content and Sourcing; Learning Objective IS-4; Key Concept 2.4).

16. **(D)** Only wealthy families sent their children to school or paid for tutors for them. A lower-class child would not get an education at this time (*Western Civilization*, 9th ed., pp. 547–50 / 10th ed., pp. 543–46; Historical Thinking Skills—Periodization, Comparison, Analyzing Evidence: Content and Sourcing, Synthesis; Learning Objective IS-4; Key Concept 2.4).

17. **(D)** Marriages were often arranged like business deals and were often used to seal political, family, and business agreements. Parents often tried to slightly improve their social status by marrying their children to a family of higher standing (*Western Civilization*, 9th ed., pp. 337–40 / 10th ed., pp. 336–38; Historical Thinking Skills—Analyzing Evidence: Content and Sourcing; Learning Objective IS-4; Key Concept 1.5).

18. **(C)** Within their households, Renaissance women had a certain degree of control over their daily lives. Renaissance men made all of the legal decisions for their families and controlled the lives of their children. Marriages were arranged to increase the status of the family, not for love. Since men married at an older age than women, their use of prostitutes was considered acceptable (*Western Civilization*, 9th ed., pp. 337–40 / 10th ed., pp. 336–38; Historical Thinking Skills—Analyzing Evidence: Content and Sourcing; Learning Objective IS-6; Key Concept 1.5).

19. **(A)** Renaissance women married at a very young age, and their husbands were generally considerably older. Most upper-class families had more children than lower-class families did. About 50 percent of Florentine merchant-class children died before the age of 20. There was no legal age at which children legally became adults (*Western Civilization,* 9th ed., pp. 337–40 / 10th ed., pp. 336–38; Historical Thinking Skills—Contextualization; Learning Objective IS-4; Key Concept 1.5).

20. **(B)** During the Renaissance, marriages were essentially a business deal. Children of the upper classes were not allowed to marry for love (*Western Civilization,* 9th ed., pp. 337–40 / 10th ed., pp. 336–38; Historical Thinking Skills—Contextualization; Learning Objective IS-4; Key Concept 1.5).

21. **(D)** The Associated Shipwright's Society was a trade union created to help shipbuilders achieve better working conditions and wages. The bottom panel shows some of the benefits it provided (*Western Civilization,* 9th ed., p. 620 / 10th ed., pp. 615–16; Historical Thinking Skills—Analyzing Evidence: Content and Sourcing, Synthesis; Learning Objective OS-9, PP-8; Key Concept 3.2).

22. **(D)** Sailors did not make high wages for their difficult and hazardous work (*Western Civilization,* 9th ed., p. 620 / 10th ed., pp. 615–16; Historical Thinking Skills—Causation, Contextualization, Analyzing Evidence: Content and Sourcing; Learning Objective OS-9, PP-8; Key Concept 3.2).

23. **(A)** Trade unions worked for the betterment of the worker, calling for higher wages, shorter hours, safer conditions, and less child labor (*Western Civilization,* 9th ed., p. 620 / 10th ed., pp. 615–16; Historical Thinking Skills—Patterns of Continuity and Change Over Time, Contextualization, Analyzing Evidence: Content and Sourcing; Learning Objective OS-9, PP-8; Key Concept 3.2).

24. **(D)** Potatoes were introduced to Europe when they were brought back by European explorers as part of the Columbian Exchange. Potatoes provided an important addition to the European diet, especially in parts of Northern Europe (like Ireland), resulting in booming population growth (*Western Civilization,* 9th ed., pp. 429–31 / 10th ed., pp. 425–26; Historical Thinking Skills—Contextualization; Learning Objective INT-5; Key Concept 1.4).

25. **(B)** Besides the introduction of new foods, new beverages were also introduced, including coffee and chocolate. Coffeehouses developed into meeting places where educated Europeans discussed political, social, and intellectual ideas (*Western Civilization,* 9th ed., pp. 429–31 / 10th ed., pp. 425–46; Historical Thinking Skills—Contextualization; Learning Objectives INT-5, OS-2; Key Concept 1.1, 1.4).

26. **(A)** Alpacas and llamas were domesticated by natives in the New World prior to European contact. Although sheep made an important contribution to life in the Americas, the animal introduced from Europe that made the greatest impact on life in America was the horse (*Western Civilization*, 9th ed., pp. 429–31 / 10th ed., pp. 423–26; Historical Thinking Skills—Contextualization; Learning Objective INT-5; Key Concept 1.4).

27. **(C)** Conflicts over trade led to bitter rivalries and wars over trade routes and New World claims (*Western Civilization*, 9th ed., pp. 429–31 / 10th ed., pp. 403–05, 423–28; Historical Thinking Skills— Contextualization; Learning Objectives INT-5, INT-6; Key Concept 1.4).

28. **(C)** The German population was educated enough to participate in elections and participate in a democratic government. The development of real political democracy, however, was prevented by the other factors presented in the answer choices (*Western Civilization*, 9th ed., pp. 717–19 / 10th ed., pp. 713–16; Historical Thinking Skills—Causation; Learning Objectives SP-3, SP-17; Key Concept 3.1, 3.4).

29. **(D)** William II became emperor in 1888. In 1890, William II fired Bismarck in order to pursue his own policies. Aggressive actions by William II, such as his intervention in the Moroccan Crisis, pushed the English, French, and Russians closer and created tensions that eventually contributed to the outbreak of World War I (*Western Civilization*, 9th ed., pp. 717–19 / 10th ed., pp. 713–16; Historical Thinking Skills—Causation; Learning Objectives SP-3, SP-17; Key Concept 3.1, 3.4).

30. **(A)** Following German unification, Bismarck manipulated foreign alliances to isolate France and avoid a continental war. The resignation of Bismarck presented the possibility that William II could pursue a more aggressive foreign policy, as represented by the fact that he is sitting on a throne of cannonballs in the cartoon (*Western Civilization*, 9th ed., pp. 717–19 / 10th ed., pp. 713–16; Historical Thinking Skills— Causation; Learning Objectives SP-3, SP-17; Key Concept 3.1, 3.4).

31. **(C)** Khrushchev believed that Stalin's use of terror, administrative violence, and mass repression was a crime against the Soviet people and took steps to curtail some of the activities of the secret police (*Western Civilization*, 9th ed., pp. 841–43 / 10th ed., pp. 877–78; Historical Thinking Skills—Causation; Learning Objectives SP-8, SP-13; Key Concept 4.1, 4.2).

32. **(B)** Although Khrushchev granted a small degree of reform to citizens in the USSR, he crushed revolts in Hungary and other Eastern bloc nations (*Western Civilization*, 9th ed., pp. 841–43 / 10th ed., pp. 877–78; Historical Thinking Skills—Contextualization; Learning Objectives SP-8, SP-13; Key Concept 4.1, 4.2).

33. **(D)** Khrushchev's attempt to increase agricultural output by having farmers grow corn in the region east of the Urals, combined with his emphasis on the consumer economy, led to a sharp downturn in industrial production (*Western Civilization*, 9th ed., pp. 841–43 / 10th ed., pp. 877–79; Historical Thinking Skills—Causation; Learning Objectives PP-3, SP-13; Key Concept 4.1, 4.2).

34. **(C)** The Congress of Vienna Treaty after the second defeat and exile of Napoleon radically changed the map of Europe (*Western Civilization*, 9th ed., p. 626 / 10th ed., pp. 621–22; Historical Thinking Skills—Causation, Periodization, Analyzing Evidence: Content and Sourcing; Learning Objective SP-14; Key Concept 3.4).

35. **(B)** One of the main principles of the Congress of Vienna Treaty was the idea of legitimacy. Germany did not become a united country until 1871 and a tsar remained in control of Russia until 1917. While Napoleon returned once from exile in 1814 and ruled for 100 days, he was exiled again to St. Helena where he lived until his death (*Western Civilization*, 9th ed., p. 625 / 10th ed., pp. 621–22; Historical Thinking Skills—Periodization, Synthesis; Learning Objective SP-14; Key Concept 3.4).

36. **(A)** One of the most important diplomatic issues of the early nineteenth century was the fate of the divided German states and the rivalry between Austria and Prussia over control of the Germans (*Western Civilization*, 9th ed., p. 625 / 10th ed., pp. 621–22; Historical Thinking Skills—Periodization, Synthesis; Learning Objective SP-14; Key Concept 3.4).

37. **(D)** Since Metternich hosted the other leaders in Vienna to make the treaty after the Napoleonic Wars, he set the conservative agenda for the Congress and was able to make sure Austria and the Holy Roman Empire, of which he was the prime minister, gained land and power from the treaty (*Western Civilization*, 9th ed., p. 627 / 10th ed., pp. 622–23; Historical Thinking Skills—Periodization, Synthesis; Learning Objective SP-14; Key Concept 3.4).

38. **(B)** Although Galileo did not actually invent the telescope, he improved the technology of the telescope, making it possible to see clearly heavenly objects that had not been visible to earlier astronomers (*Western Civilization*, 9th ed., pp. 483–86 / 10th ed., pp. 478–82; Historical Thinking Skills—Patterns of Continuity and Change Over Time; Learning Objectives OS-5; Key Concept 2.3).

39. **(C)** Galileo's observations provided empirical proof of the heliocentric model of the universe, confirming the Copernican system (*Western Civilization*, 9th ed., pp. 483–86 / 10th ed., pp. 478–82; Historical Thinking Skills—Contextualization; Learning Objectives OS-5; Key Concept 2.3).

40. **(D)** Galileo supported the Copernican model of the universe, unlike the Roman Catholic Church, which endorsed the Ptolemaic system, which placed the earth in the center of the universe (*Western Civilization*, 9th ed., pp. 483–86 / 10th ed., pp. 478–82; Historical Thinking Skills—Causation; Learning Objectives OS-2, OS-5; Key Concept 2.3).

41. **(A)** After the condemnation and house arrest of Galileo, it became dangerous to publish and pursue innovative scientific ideas in Italy. As a result, leadership in scientific research shifted north to England, the Dutch Republic, and France (*Western Civilization*, 9th ed., pp. 486–88 / 10th ed., pp. 478–79; Historical Thinking Skills—Periodization; Learning Objectives OS-5; Key Concept 2.3).

42. **(A)** The Austrian Empire was plagued by nationalist sentiments among their many ethnic minorities. Granting independence to Serbia might threaten the unity of the Austrian empire, as other ethnic minorities might also demand their independence (*Western Civilization*, 9th ed., pp. 756–57 / 10th ed., p. 738; Historical Thinking Skills—Causation; Learning Objectives SP-7, SP-17; Key Concept 3.4).

43. **(B)** As a result of the First and Second Balkan Wars, the various nations with interests in the Balkans turned against one another and ended the wars with a lot of anger. The great powers also grew angry with one another, since they all had designs on the future of the Balkans. These wars increased tensions in the region, rather than bringing about a resolution to their differences (*Western Civilization*, 9th ed., pp. 756–57 / 10th ed., pp. 752–53; Historical Thinking Skills—Causation; Learning Objectives SP-7, SP-17; Key Concept 3.4).

44. **(C)** One of the primary goals of Serbia was to gain a port on the Adriatic Sea, since Serbia was a landlocked nation (*Western Civilization*, 9th ed., pp. 756–57 / 10th ed., pp. 752–53; Historical Thinking Skills—Causation; Learning Objectives SP-7, SP-17; Key Concept 3.4).

45. **(C)** Following the Crimean War, the Treaty of Paris made the Black Sea a neutral body of water and allowed the Ottoman Empire to retain control of the straits. The control of the Bosphorus and Dardanelles by the Ottoman Empire impacted Russian trade and led Russia to try to obtain control of the straits in the decades before World War I (*Western Civilization*, 8th ed., pp. 711–14 / 9th ed., pp. 756–57 / 10th ed., pp. 656–58; Historical Thinking Skills—Contextualization; Learning Objectives SP-7, SP-17; Key Concept 3.4).

46. **(D)** *The Oath of the Horatii* by David is a Neoclassical painting because of its reliance on a classical Roman storyline. Other evidence would be the use of Roman architectural elements, stylized Roman garments and weapons (*Western Civilization*, 9th ed., pp. 159–60 / 10th ed., pp. 514–15; Historical Thinking Skills—Periodization, Contextualization, Analyzing Evidence: Content and Sourcing; Learning Objective OS-10; Key Concept 2.3).

47. (**C**) David painted for the French Republican Government and later for Napoleon, emphasizing the ideals of the time. His *Death of Marat* is a masterpiece of political propaganda, as is his portrait, *Napoleon Crossing the Alps* (*Western Civilization*, 9th ed., pp. 159–60 / 10th ed., pp. 514–15, 567, 585; Historical Thinking Skills—Analyzing Evidence: Content and Sourcing, Contextualization; Learning Objective OS-10; Key Concept 2.3).

48. (**D**) Both Renaissance and Neoclassical art often contained classical Greek or Roman themes, were painted for a specific patron, and were secular in nature. However, while Renaissance art did sometimes highlight civic humanism, the duty of a person to his city, Neoclassical art can be seen as promoting patriotism (*Western Civilization*, 9th ed., pp. 74, 159–60 / 10th ed., pp. 349–53, 514–15, 567, 585; Historical Thinking Skills—Periodization, Comparison, Synthesis; Learning Objective OS-10; Key Concept 2.3).

49. (**D**) Since Philip II was strongly Catholic and wished to enforce the Catholic faith in every place that he was able to conquer, England had good reason to fear that a Spanish takeover of the Netherlands could not only threaten England economically and militarily but also religiously. D is the correct answer choice, since the British did not establish permanent colonies in North America until the seventeenth century (*Western Civilization*, 9th ed., pp. 395–400 / 10th ed., pp. 392–97; Historical Thinking Skills—Analyzing Evidence: Content and Sourcing, Causation; Learning Objective SP-15; Key Concept 1.2).

50. (**A**) Hapsburg control of Spain, the Netherlands, and the Holy Roman Empire threatened the European balance of power, causing other nations to fear the family's expansion (*Western Civilization*, 9th ed., pp. 395–400 / 10th ed., pp. 392, 394–95, 397; Historical Thinking Skills—Patterns of Continuity and Change Over Time; Learning Objective SP-13; Key Concept 1.2).

51. (**B**) Although some of the other answers might seem tempting, the defeat of the Spanish Armada did not lead to political revolution and did not lead to greater spending on the Spanish navy. Answer choice B is correct, since the defeat of the armada led to a virtually permanent decline in Spanish power (*Western Civilization*, 9th ed., pp. 395–400 / 10th ed., pp. 392–97; Historical Thinking Skills—Periodization; Learning Objective SP-13; Key Concept 1.2).

52. (**D**) England was a Protestant nation, and Spain wanted to make it Catholic. The English were not acquiring Spanish lands in the Americas (*Western Civilization*, 9th ed., pp. 395–400 / 10th ed., pp. 392–97; Historical Thinking Skills—Analyzing Evidence: Content and Sourcing, Causation; Learning Objective SP-15; Key Concept 1.2).

53. (**C**) Tsar Alexander II made it clear that he was chosen by divine right and believed that it was his sacred duty to free the serfs (*Western Civilization*, 9th ed., pp. 671–73 / 10th ed., pp. 666–69; Historical Thinking Skills—Analyzing Evidence: Content and Sourcing, Causation; Learning Objectives SP-5, SP-9, IS-5; Key Concept 3.2, 3.3).

54. (**D**) Since landowners sold only their worst lands to the government to distribute to the newly freed peasants, the peasants were land-starved and many found it difficult to grow enough food to survive. Since the government expected the village mirs to reimburse it for the land, the peasants were indebted to the mirs (*Western Civilization*, 9th ed., pp. 671–73 / 10th ed., pp. 666–69; Historical Thinking Skills—Causation; Learning Objectives SP-5, SP-9, IS-5; Key Concept 3.2, 3.3).

55. (**A**) During the nineteenth century, Russian tsars such as Alexander II began to modernize and provide some degrees of reform to the Russian nation. Reforms such as the emancipation of the serfs and the creation of a system of zemstvos that provided a taste of local government eventually gave rise to revolutionary movements, as many Russians hoped for more substantial change (*Western Civilization*, 9th ed., pp. 671–73 / 10th ed., pp. 666–69; Historical Thinking Skills—Causation, Analyzing Evidence: Content and Sourcing; Learning Objectives SP-5, SP-9, IS-5; Key Concept 3.2, 3.3).

ANSWERS FOR SECTION I, PART B: SHORT-ANSWER QUESTIONS

QUESTION 1

A) Machiavelli believed that a good ruler was one who could seize political power without the fetters of morality. For Machiavelli, a good ruler was one who was feared by the people, and was willing to take any actions necessary to keep his power. Although this ruler must appear to be a noble, Christian man, he only needed to keep order and maintain control, fooling and tricking the people when necessary to preserve his power.

B) Erasmus believed that a good ruler was one who based his decisions and actions on his moral obligations to his subjects. Erasmus, a Christian humanist, believed that a ruler should follow Christian principles and treat his subjects with respect, truly doing his best to meet their needs. For Erasmus, a good ruler must do everything he can to bring peace to his nation and must truly care for his people, sacrificing everything for their welfare.

C) Machiavelli's personal experiences in Florence help explain the reasons that Machiavelli is more concerned about maintaining the power of the prince than promoting the general welfare of the individuals in the nation. Machiavelli lived through war and political upheaval in Florence and realized that a good prince was one who could keep factions from destroying the state. In his opinion, a prince would rule over a prosperous kingdom and have a successful reign, if the prince could secure his own political power.

(*Western Civilization*, 9th ed., p. 345 / 10th ed., p. 344; Historical Thinking Skills—Comparison; Learning Objective SP-1; Key Concept 1.1)

Question 2

A) One social reason for the development of mass education was that liberals believed that education was imperative for personal and social improvement. Liberals hoped to replace Catholic schools with secular public schools and hoped that through education, all people, including working-class residents, would learn social discipline and have their minds elevated. Hoping that education would bring out the goodness in people, liberals hoped that education would decrease the crime rate and improve the standard of living in the cities.

B) One economic reason for the development of mass education stemmed from industrialization. Many jobs available during the second industrial revolution required more skills than the factory jobs of the first industrial revolution. People who had an education could move up the social ladder and hold jobs that provided better pay, such as teaching, nursing, banking, and working in other white-collar jobs such as post office and subway station clerks. Having an education gave workers hope for a brighter future, and industrialists benefited from the development of an educated work force.

C) One political reason for the development of mass education was that extension of voting rights required an educated electorate. State-funded schools also promoted nationalism and patriotism and national unity. Governments benefited from the common curriculum taught in schools around the nation, since they were able to use the schools to indoctrinate students in national values and behaviors desired by the state.

(*Western Civilization*, 9th ed., pp. 725–27 / 10th ed., pp. 708–09; Historical Thinking Skills—Causation; Learning Objectives PP-15, OS-8, OS-12, SP-7; Key Concept 3.3, 3.4)

Question 3

A) Many Protestant reformers emphasized the need for people to read and understand the Bible for themselves. Consequently, Protestant regions tended to support the opening of schools designed to create a semiliterate congregation of believers who could take an active part in the life of the church. Protestant schools used humanist methods and emphasized classical learning, while attempting to provide the new churches with good ministers and their societies with good citizens.

B) Since Protestant reformers abandoned the Roman Catholic idea of the holiness of celibacy, they also promoted the idea that the family was the center of life and that marriage was a partnership between men and women. Although the men and women had traditional roles within the family, there was a new emphasis on the idea of marrying for love and for sharing the responsibility of the family.

C) Although Protestant reformers preached that all people were equal in the eyes of God, when it came to daily living women were still expected to be subordinate to their husbands. Women were expected to do as their husbands asked and to bear children. Most common women did have access to basic education, as they were expected to read the Bible and help their children learn to read. Women lost the ability to become nuns, and higher education was not promoted for women, since their expected vocation was to be a wife and mother.

(*Western Civilization*, 9th ed., pp. 387–88 / 10th ed., pp. 383–86; Historical Thinking Skills—Patterns of Continuity and Change Over Time; Learning Objective IS-9; Key Concept 1.5)

QUESTION 4

A) One way in which Bismarck used warfare to unify Germany was through his declaration of war on Denmark. Bismarck declared war on Denmark because Denmark had recently taken action to incorporate Schleswig and Holstein into Denmark. This action was in violation of international treaty agreements, giving Bismarck legal authority to oppose the annexation. Besides this, the two states had large German populations, making German nationalists outraged at the Danish actions. By declaring war on Denmark and engineering the collaboration with Austria, Bismarck established Prussia as the leading power in German unification.

B) One example of how Chancellor Otto von Bismarck used *Realpolitik* in the unification of Germany was his use of the Ems telegram to set the stage for the Franco-Prussian War. Following a dispute concerning the candidacy of Prince Leopold of Hohenzollern, a cousin of the Prussian Kaiser, to the Spanish throne, the French ambassador demanded an apology and a promise to never support Prince Leopold's candidacy again. To inform him of the situation, the Kaiser sent the Ems telegram to Bismarck. Seeing an opportunity to insult Napoleon III and get him to declare war on Prussia, Bismarck edited the telegram and sent it to France. As expected, the French declared war, a war that became the final step in German unification. This is an example of *Realpolitik*, since Bismarck clearly took it upon himself to manipulatively edit the telegram and send it off, an action that was neither honest nor ethical. Bismarck, throughout the process of unification, was willing to take any action necessary to achieve his goals.

C) German unification impacted Europe by shifting the balance of power to the advantage of Germany. The unification of Germany under the leadership and military power of Prussia established a strong, conservative nation in central Europe. The powerful military and extensive industrial development of Germany made Germany the most powerful nation in Europe

426 ❖ Practice Test 1

and set the stage for the growing role of Germany in world politics in the decades to come.

(*Western Civilization*, 9th ed., pp. 665–69 / 10th ed., pp. 655, 661–65; Historical Thinking Skills—Contextualization, Causation; Learning Objectives SP-4, SP-14, SP-17, SP-18; Key Concept 3.4)

<u>Answer for Section II, Part A: Document-Based Question (DBQ)</u>

The Documents

Below are short analyses of the documents. The italicized words suggest what your margin notes might include:

Document 1 Map of the Cold War alliances—NATO and the Warsaw Pact—and the military capabilities of each side. *Both sides had a large buildup of troops and allies.*

Document 2 Kennan states that Soviet insecurity has created a situation in which the Soviet Union will not feel safe or ease up on its aggressiveness until it has destroyed America domestically and internationally. *Is he referring to capitalism when he refers to "our traditional way of life"? The document shows the American belief in the aggressiveness of the Soviet Union. Is he biased?*

Document 3 In this speech, Churchill coins the term "iron curtain" and observes that the Soviet Union is encroaching on Eastern Europe, establishing a sphere of influence in the region. *Similar to doc 2—it shows the aggressiveness of the Soviet Union and reflects concern that the Soviet Union is expanding into Europe. As a British ex-prime minister, is he biased?*

Document 4 This photograph of the Soviet invasion of Czechoslovakia, in 1968, was one of many taken of Soviet efforts to crush the reform movement in led by Alexander Dubcek. Photographs like this one were used by the west to illustrate the brutality of Soviet communism and justify American intervention in Western Europe and the escalation of the arms race. *Similar to docs 2 & 3, it shows the aggression of the USSR. Does it have a western bloc bias?*

Document 5 Stalin's reply clearly blames Churchill and the United States for the growing tensions between East and West. By comparing Churchill to Hitler, he makes the West seem even more warlike. *Did Churchill's speech intensify the tensions and cement the divide? Is this reply biased?*

Document 6 A Soviet telegram that blames the Cold War on the American desire to dominate the world—the exact opposite of Kennan's telegram, Document 2. *This is similar to doc 5, blaming the West for the division. Is he biased?*

DOCUMENT 7 In this message, Imre Nagy blames the Soviet Union for interfering in Hungarian politics and warns other nations of its aggression. *Is he biased because he's facing the wrath of the Soviet Union? As an Eastern European source, does it seem to support the claims of Churchill and Truman?*

YOUR ESSAY FOR THE DOCUMENT-BASED QUESTION

Given that this question addresses the skill of causation, your thesis should focus on the degree to which the Soviet Union and the United States caused the Cold War. A possible thesis for this DBQ would argue that there are three points of view concerning responsibility for the Cold War. You might say something like this: "Among the many points of view concerning the assignment of responsibility for the Cold War are those that charge the Soviet Union with causing the tensions and those that attribute the blame to the United States and her western allies." This is an example of a sophisticated thesis. Your thesis does not have to sound like this word for word, but it should communicate these basic ideas. You need to be sure your thesis makes an argument that clearly answers the prompt and addresses all parts of the question, and it must be based on an analysis of the documents as well as outside evidence. By extending your thesis beyond assigning blame solely to either the Soviet Union or the West, you are also completing one of the tasks that can help you earn the point for synthesis.

You are then ready to prove your thesis, using the documents and outside information to address the question and provide evidence in the context of your arguments. Remember that in order to earn the top score, you need to use all or all but one of the documents to support your thesis and also provide evidence from outside of the documents to further support your claims. In this case, it means you will need to provide analysis of six or seven documents in your essay. Be sure that you use the documents correctly and that you utilize them to prove your thesis.

Next, think about how you will analyze the purpose, intended audience, historical context, or point of view of each document that you use. To analyze point of view, you can illustrate the perspective or bias of the documents. Remember that to earn credit for point of view, you must not only explain the point of view or bias of the author, you should also explain the reasons that that author holds that position. For example, you could write: "Nagy's view of the Soviet Union as an imperialistic power is understandable because as the Hungarian prime minister, he was destined to be removed from office." You could also write: "The veracity of Stalin's view must be questioned, since as the Soviet general secretary, he would obviously hold anti-Western views." Besides analysis of point of view, you can also get credit for analyzing the intended audience, purpose, or historical context of each document. For example, you might explain that Nagy is writing in response to the Soviet condemnation of his attempts to democratize elections in Hungary, or you might explain that Churchill is giving his speech to an American audience in hopes of warning Americans of the growing

Soviet threat and also in hopes of encouraging America to take action to protect Europe from further Soviet aggression.

A good response must also include outside information to support your thesis. In this case, you might bring in evidence from the early 1980s to show that the Soviet Union not only invaded Budapest when the Hungarians tried to gain a little bit of autonomy and invaded Prague a decade later, but they also pressured the puppet government in Poland to suppress the Solidarity movement in an attempt to maintain control over Eastern Europe. To further expand your outside information you could bring in evidence to show that the United States placed nuclear weapons in Western Europe, escalating the arms race.

A good response must demonstrate an understanding of the broader context of the question. For example, in this case, you could mention that many modern historians assign responsibility for intensification of the discord to both parties. You could also discuss the impact of this conflict on Eastern and Western Europe.

Finally, a good response will include a brief (2-3 sentences) discussion of synthesis. For this essay, you could compare the division of Europe during the Cold War with the division of Europe during the age of religious wars. You could compare the ways in which religion divided Europe in the sixteenth and seventeenth centuries with the ways in which ideological differences divided Europe in the twentieth century.

SCORING In You earn 1 point for thesis; 1 point for making a solid argument, 1 point for using at least six of the documents to support the thesis or a relevant argument, 1 point for analyzing the intended audience, purpose, historical context, and/or author's point of view for at least four of the documents you use; 1 point for including analysis of evidence beyond/outside the documents to support the thesis or a relevant argument; 1 point for connecting the historical phenomena relevant to your arguments to a broader historical context (contextualization); and 1 point for synthesis: either extending or modifying the argument by comparing/contrasting the argument with another place or time, another discipline, or another course theme. Thus, if you earn a perfect score, you will earn 7 points on your essay.

The DBQ essay counts for one-quarter of the examination grade, so it pays to do a good job on this part of the exam.

ANSWERS FOR SECTION II, PART B: LONG-ESSAY QUESTIONS

QUESTION 1

This prompt asks you to apply the historical thinking skill of comparison. To fully answer the question, you must compare German Nazism with Soviet communism. To do that, you must draw a distinction between the differing economic theories of the two systems and the practical implementation of their programs. In any "compare and contrast" question, be sure that you discuss both similarities *and* differences.

Your thesis must address ways that the two systems were both similar and different. For example, you might write: "Although diametrically opposed in theory, German Nazism and Soviet communism used similar methods to enforce the implementation of their ideals. Socially, the Nazis believed that not all men were created equal and actively sought to categorize people, while the Soviets believed in the equality of all mankind. Economically, the Nazis believed in the protection of private property and business and promoted a type of capitalism, while the Soviets condemned private property and actively forced collectivization on the nation. Politically, however, the two systems were very similar in practice, with both creating one-party totalitarian states and both using terror, propaganda, and constriction of civil liberties to enforce their will."

The body of your essay should then discuss the similarities and differences between the two regimes as outlined in your thesis. Beginning with the social differences, point out that whereas Hitler had his hierarchy of races and wanted to promote the Aryan race while eliminating many others, Stalin preached the equality of citizens and tried to enforce this new standard, often using violence. The next paragraph should discuss the economic differences between Nazism and communism, specifically contrasting Hitler's protection of private property with Stalin's collectivization campaign and his purge of the kulaks and wealthy Russians.

To earn the synthesis point, you need to do one of the tasks listed in the final bullet in the long essay directions. Your synthesis discussion should be 2-3 sentences that fully explain your extension to the argument. For example, in your conclusion you might discuss how, despite these differences, the two were quite similar, with both using propaganda, violence, the media, terror, and the restriction of civil liberties to promote their aims. To support your expanded argument, you could specifically show how Stalin's rewriting of history and glorification of himself was similar to Hitler's use of propaganda—such as the "Hitler over Germany" campaign and his use of the media, as in the creation of such films as *The Triumph of the Will*.

QUESTION 2

This question requires you to demonstrate the historical skill of comparison. Your thesis should comment on how both Colbert and Smith were interested in achieving the same goal, but approached it from very different perspectives. Colbert extolled the virtues of mercantilism, while Smith propounded the necessity of the free market. Colbert looked to increase the wealth of France through a policy of mercantilism, which called for government regulation of economic activities to benefit the state. The most important piece of mercantilist policy was a favorable balance of trade, achieved by decreasing imports and increasing exports. A key tool is high tariffs on foreign goods, which Colbert used to decrease imports, especially textiles from England and the Dutch Republic. Colbert assisted with the development of the French manufacturing sector. He invited skilled artisans from abroad to teach French workers the skills needed to create luxury goods, and he promoted French industry through a series of economic measures, including tax exemptions and subsidies. To improve transportation, he oversaw the construction of roads and canals. Colbert also created the French merchant marine in order to carry French goods abroad. Ironically, all of Colbert's hard work was for naught, because King Louis XIV continued spending lavishly on personal expenditures as well as on military causes.

Among the Enlightenment thinkers who applied methods developed in the Scientific Revolution to analyze society were the physiocrats. They were a group of economists who believed that the wealth of a nation derived from the value of its land and that wealth itself could only be increased by agriculture. Although the movement first emerged in France, it was the Scottish philosopher Adam Smith who popularized the field of economics and the arguments of the physiocrats. Smith rejected mercantilism, saying that wealth is best derived through the natural economic forces of supply and demand. Unlike mercantilists, physiocrats argued that the state should not be involved in regulation of the economy; rather, it should leave the economy alone. This policy became known as laissez-faire. In *The Wealth of Nations,* Smith condemns the mercantilists' use of tariffs to protect home industry. When one country can supply another country with a product more cheaply than if the second country produced the item itself, it is better for the second country to purchase from the first country than to manufacture the product itself. Smith differed from the physiocrats in his belief that a nation's wealth stemmed not from its soil, but from its labor. Finally, he believed that government should limit itself to three main functions: military, police, and infrastructure, including roads and canals.

To earn the synthesis point, you need to do one of the tasks listed in the final bullet in the long essay directions. Remember that your synthesis discussion should be 2–3 sentences that fully explain the extension to your argument. For example, in your conclusion, you might point out that application of the ideas of Adam Smith was not limited to the eighteenth century. To further extend the argument, you might explain that Smith's ideas proved extremely influential and lay at the foundation of economic liberalism, which would shape economic policy throughout the nineteenth century and beyond.

PRACTICE TEST 2

AP® EUROPEAN HISTORY EXAMINATION
Section I
Part A: Multiple-Choice Questions
Time: 55 minutes
Number of questions: 55
Percent of examination score: 40%

DIRECTIONS: The multiple-choice section consists of question sets organized around a stimulus material—a primary or secondary source, a historian's argument, or a historical problem. For each question, select the best response.

Questions 1-4 refer to the following quotation:

A Letter to Czechoslovakia

To the Central Committee of the Communist Party of Czechoslovakia

Warsaw, July 15, 1968

Dear comrades!
On behalf of the Central Committees of the Communist and Workers' Parties of Bulgaria, Hungary, the German Democratic Republic, Poland, and the Soviet Union, we address ourselves to you with this letter, prompted by a feeling of sincere friendship based on the principles of Marxism-Leninism and proletarian internationalism and by the concern of our common affairs for strengthening the positions of socialism and the security of the socialist community of nations.

The development of events in your country evokes in us deep anxiety. It is our firm conviction that the offensive of the reactionary forces, backed by imperialists, against your Party ... , threatens to push your country off the road of socialism and that consequently it jeopardizes the interests of the entire socialist system....

We neither had nor have any intention of interfering in such affairs as are strictly the internal business of your Party and your state, nor of violating the principles of respect, independence, and equality in the relations among the Communist Parties and socialist countries....

At the same time we cannot agree to have hostile forces push your country from the road of socialism and create a threat of severing Czechoslovakia from the socialist community.... This is the common cause of our countries, which have joined in the Warsaw Treaty to ensure independence, peace, and security in Europe, and to set up an insurmountable barrier against aggression and revenge...

That is why we believe that a decisive rebuff of the anticommunist forces, and decisive efforts for the preservation of the socialist system in Czechoslovakia are not only your task but ours as well....

Source: "A Letter to Czechoslovakia," *Moscow News*, supplement to no. 30917 (1968), pp. 3–6.

1. The USSR responded to the "Prague Spring" by
   (A) initiating a blockade of West Berlin to prevent further defections.
   (B) sending troops into Czechoslovakia.
   (C) invading Budapest in order to overthrow the Nagy regime.
   (D) cutting off trade routes between East Germany and Czechoslovakia.

GO ON TO NEXT PAGE

2. The Soviet policy expressed in the letter to Czechoslovakia became the basis of which of the following policies?
   (A) Warsaw Pact
   (B) peaceful coexistence
   (C) Brezhnev Doctrine
   (D) Perestroika

3. All of the following are true of Soviet repression in post-war Europe EXCEPT
   (A) after 1968, it was justified by the Brezhnev Doctrine.
   (B) although the Solidarity movement seemed to successfully gain a few concessions when it was first formed, its freedom vanished in 1981 with the arrest of its leaders.
   (C) Romania enjoyed more civil liberties than any other Soviet bloc nation.
   (D) the East German government had strong ties to the USSR and the Stasi used repressive methods to control the population.

4. All of the following were reasons that some Eastern European nations began to resist Soviet control EXCEPT
   (A) many Eastern Europeans resented the censorship and lack of freedom they experienced.
   (B) some Eastern Europeans hoped that reforms created by de-Stalinization would allow them to gain more freedom
   (C) many Eastern Europeans resented Russian control of the economy and the poor economic conditions they were forced to endure.
   (D) many Eastern Europeans hated the Soviet detente policy.

Questions 5–7 refer to the following image.

Source: RMN-Grand Palais/Art Resource, NY

5. The above gathering in eighteenth-century Paris is most likely to be
   (A) a salon hosted by a noblewoman.
   (B) a meeting of the Royal Society.
   (C) an Anabaptist church service.
   (D) a performance for King Louis XV.

6. Evidence of the social status of the owner of the home shown above can be inferred from
   (A) the simplicity of the clothing worn by the group.
   (B) the appearance of servants and slaves.
   (C) the artwork on the walls, carpets on the floors, and comfortable armchairs.
   (D) the entertainers and singers.

7. A historian wishing to learn more about the sort of gathering seen in the painting above might look for evidence in
   (A) parish church records.
   (B) official French government documents.
   (C) diaries and letters written by the participants.
   (D) the published works of scientists and philosophes.

Questions 8–11 refer to the following quotation.

The Industrial Revolution caused a quantum leap in industrial production. New sources of energy and power, especially coal and steam, replaced wind and water to run machines that significantly decreased the use of human and animal labor and at the same time increased productivity. This in turn called for new ways of organizing human labor to maximize the benefits and profits from the new machines; factories replaced workshops and home work-rooms. Many early factories were dreadful places with difficult working conditions. Reformers, appalled at these conditions, were especially critical of the treatment of married women. One reported, "We have repeatedly seen married females, in the last stage of pregnancy, slaving from morning to night beside these never-tiring machines, and when ... they were obliged to sit down to take a moment's ease, and being seen by the manager, were fined for the offense." But there were also examples of well-run factories. William Cobbett described one in Manchester in 1830: "In this room, which is lighted in the most convenient and beautiful manner, there were five hundred pairs of looms at work, and five hundred persons attending those looms; and, owing to the goodness of the masters, the whole looking healthy and well-dressed."

Jackson Spielvogel, *Western Civilization*, 10th ed., p. 592.

8. According to historian Jackson Spielvogel, the Industrial Revolution
   (A) caused some change in European society and culture but was not revolutionary.
   (B) was a terrible time of history with little good to show for it.
   (C) was a time of revolutionary change in almost all aspects of society.
   (D) occurred only in Great Britain and the United States.

9. In what way was the organization of labor changed by industrialization, according to the quotation to the left?
   (A) People moved from cities to farms in order to provide more raw materials for factories.
   (B) Hundreds of people crowded into one room to work to maximize the benefits for the factory owner.
   (C) Human labor was replaced by that of animals.
   (D) Pregnant women were allowed to work while sitting.

10. An example of the poor conditions in factories cited in the quotation to the left is
    (A) pregnant women were forced to stand while working and were fined if they sat down.
    (B) married women could not work alongside their husbands.
    (C) five hundred people were crammed into one room in terrible conditions.
    (D) workers were kept in dark conditions so no one could see how ill they were.

11. In the view of William Cobbett, quoted in the quotation to the left, factories were clean, well-lit, safe places to work. It is most likely that Cobbett is a
    (A) factory worker.
    (B) Luddite.
    (C) Chartist.
    (D) factory owner or large commercial farmer.

GO ON TO NEXT PAGE

Questions 12–15 refer to the following image.

Source: Private Collection/Photo©Tarker/Bridgeman Images

12. The engraving above shows
(A) Revolutionary forces preparing to execute King Louis XVI by the guillotine.
(B) French soldiers committing atrocities in Spain during the Napoleonic wars.
(C) the power of the nobility and clergy over the Third Estate.
(D) a mob of British Redcoats taking French King Louis XVI hostage.

13. This engraving would most likely have been produced for
(A) a private patron to put on the wall of his home.
(B) the Catholic Church.
(C) a radical newspaper.
(D) Diderot's *Encyclopedie*.

14. A later event that could have been influenced by the one depicted above is
(A) the slave revolt in Haiti led by Toussaint L'Ouverture in 1804.
(B) the American Revolution.
(C) Napoleon's coup d'état against the Revolutionary government of France.
(D) the writing of *Declaration of the Rights of Women and the Female Citizen*.

15. The Reign of Terror involved all of the following EXCEPT
(A) the Republic trying to remove its enemies.
(B) thousands being sent to the guillotine.
(C) an attempt to rid France of supporters of the monarchy.
(D) the women's march on Versailles.

Questions 16–18 refer to the following image.

Source: RMN-Grand Palais/Art Resource, NY

16. All of the following are true of the Palace of Versailles EXCEPT
    (A) many powerful subjects came to Versailles to find favor and offices for themselves from the king.
    (B) it was the personal household of the king.
    (C) it was the location of central governmental machinery in France.
    (D) it was built entirely with private funds from the king and did not impact the national debt.

17. To offset the spending of King Louis XIV, Jean-Baptiste Colbert instituted all of the following policies EXCEPT
    (A) forced private industrialists to build canals and roads to increase internal trade.
    (B) invited Venetian glassmakers and Flemish clothmakers to France.
    (C) granted special privileges, including tax exemptions to people who started new industries in France.
    (D) established new luxury industries, such as a royal tapestry works.

18. Which of the following statements best describes life at the court of Versailles?
    (A) Ordinary French citizens brought their grievances before the court for the king's decision.
    (B) King Louis XIV lived and reigned in great privacy, only taking part in court ceremonies when absolutely necessary.
    (C) Great nobles and churchmen participated in lavish court ceremonies to gain offices, titles, and pensions granted by King Louis XIV.
    (D) Nobles often visited the palace to speak with the king about financial and political policies before going back to govern their provinces.

GO ON TO NEXT PAGE

Questions 19–21 refer to the following maps.

Source: © Cengage Learning

19. According to the map above, which country gained the most from the first Partition of Poland?
    (A) Prussia
    (B) Russia
    (C) Poland itself
    (D) Austria

20. Which of the following was an effect of the continued expansion of Prussia through the Partitions of Poland?
    (A) A drop in trade due to the Russian annexation of ports along the Baltic Sea.
    (B) Continuous animosity and war with Russia over territory in Lithuania.
    (C) An increase in Prussian economic and political strength due to land gains that united once scattered Hohenzollern land holdings.
    (D) Nationalist rebellions in East Prussia and Lithuania.

21. What was a major cause of the War of the Austrian Succession?
    (A) Poland's weakness, brought on by elected monarchs
    (B) Prussia's newfound alliance with France, Austria's traditional enemy
    (C) England's concern about the growing threat of Austria in Eastern Europe
    (D) the death of Charles VI of Austria and the ascension of Maria Theresa to the throne

Questions 22–24 refer to the following map.

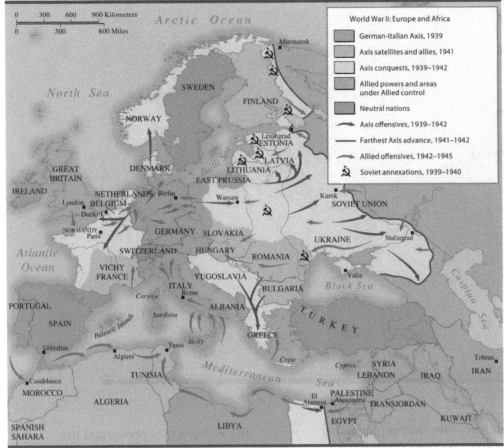

Source: © Cengage Learning

22. Which of the following was a primary objective that Hitler failed to achieve on the Eastern Front of World War II?
(A) Axis conquest of the Ukraine
(B) Axis conquest of the Baltic States
(C) Axis conquest of much of Poland
(D) Elimination of the Soviet army and the subsequent collapse of the USSR

23. The German decision to invade the Soviet Union was based on all of the following EXCEPT
(A) the German belief that if the Soviet Union was defeated, the British would surrender.
(B) the German hope that a decisive victory over the Soviet Union would lead to France's surrender.
(C) the German belief that the Soviet military leadership was weak and ineffective.
(D) Hitler's anti-Semitism and hatred of the Slavic people.

24. By the time World War II was over, which nation had annexed the most territory?
(A) Germany
(B) Italy
(C) the USSR
(D) France

GO ON TO NEXT PAGE

Questions 25–27 refer to the following map.

Source: © Cengage Learning

25. Which of the following best explains the shift in economic and political power from the Mediterranean to the Atlantic seaboard during the fifteenth and sixteenth centuries?
    (A) The lack of trading partners in North Africa
    (B) The growth of large national monarchies in Western Europe
    (C) The absence of cities on the Baltic Sea
    (D) Control of North Africa by the Ottoman Empire

26. Which of the following factors played a role in the maintenance of a more feudal society in Eastern Europe?
    (A) Convenient access to Middle Eastern trade routes made exploration unnecessary.
    (B) Industrial technology emerged first in Eastern Europe, causing serfs to be used as a cheap labor force in eastern factories.

    (C) Fewer cities prevented the development of a strong merchant class that could challenge political authorities.
    (D) Smaller nation-states found it easier to control their populations through feudalism.

27. Which of the following factors helps explain the reason for animosity between France and the Holy Roman Empire?
    (A) The Holy Roman Empire had better access to the sea and threatened French trade routes.
    (B) France and England were in an alliance against the Holy Roman Empire.
    (C) The Holy Roman Empire controlled more land and was a strong united military opponent.
    (D) The Holy Roman Empire and France shared a long border and wanted to keep one another from expanding.

Questions 28–30 refer to the following image.

Source: RMN-Grand Palais/Art Resource, NY

28. After opening trade relations with Japan, Portuguese ships most often participated in which of the following?
(A) Regional trade between Japan, China, and Southeast Asia
(B) Direct trade between Europe and Japan
(C) Shipbuilding, using Japanese techniques
(D) Direct trade between Japan and the Americas

29. All of the following were important commodities sold by Europeans in Asia EXCEPT
(A) firearms.
(B) lumber.
(C) clocks.
(D) eyeglasses.

30. Which of the following led some native inhabitants, such as the Japanese, to expel most Europeans from their lands?
(A) European merchants often cheated native inhabitants out of a great deal of money, using unethical business practices.
(B) European merchants took control of native harbors and would not leave.
(C) European missionaries refused to minister to native inhabitants.
(D) European missionaries, often very successful in converting the native inhabitants, interfered in local politics.

GO ON TO NEXT PAGE

Questions 31–33 refer to the following images.

Source: Underwood & Underwood/Corbis

31. One of the most important changes in the urban centers of Europe in the late nineteenth century was that
(A) underground subway systems were constructed.
(B) underground sewer systems were constructed.
(C) better roads were constructed that linked urban and rural areas.
(D) new bridges were constructed to link different sectors of large cities.

32. All of the following were reasons that urban populations grew quickly in the nineteenth century EXCEPT
(A) migration from rural areas to cities was enticing because of job opportunities in factories and service trades.
(B) health and living conditions in cities were improving in the late nineteenth century.
(C) poverty and the inability to acquire adequate amounts of land drove people out of rural areas.
(D) movie theaters and other exciting entertainment encouraged migration to the cities.

33. As suggested by the photographs to the left, all of the following are true of nineteenth-century urban improvements EXCEPT
(A) the construction of streetcar and commuter train lines connected the cities where people worked to the suburbs where they lived.
(B) many of the improvements found in the cities catered to the middle classes.
(C) old residential districts in cities like Paris were remodeled and modernized to provide good quality housing for the working class.
(D) public parks were created in many large cities to provide residents with a place to enjoy fresh air and sunshine.

Questions 34–37 refer to the following image of children in the community of New Lanark, Scotland.

Source: Eileen Tweedy/The Art Archive at Art Resource, NY

34. The town pictured above was revolutionary in that
    (A) children of workers went to school and learned to dance rather than working in the factories.
    (B) children of workers were taken away from their families and taught to be more socially elite.
    (C) men, women, and children were all paid equally.
    (D) the children of noble and middle-class families interacted with children of the workers.

35. The town of New Lanark is an example of
    (A) a Marxist style government in action.
    (B) a utopian socialist community.
    (C) a pre-industrial society.
    (D) a small farming village.

36. Which of the following philosophers would most agree with the way Robert Owen ran New Lanark?
    (A) Jeremy Bentham and John Stuart Mill
    (B) Friedrich Engels and Karl Marx
    (C) Metternich and Alexander I
    (D) Henri de Saint Simon and Charles Fourier

37. Which problems faced by the workers would NOT have been solved by Owen's society?
    (A) Child labor in the factories
    (B) Long hours and low pay
    (C) Workers' lack of ownership of the product they made
    (D) The boring tediousness of doing the same job over and over again

GO ON TO NEXT PAGE

Questions 38–40 refer to the following quotation.

Margaret Cavendish, "The Philosophical and Physical Opinions"

But to answer those objections that are made against me, as first how should I come by so much experience as I have expressed in my several books to have? I answer: I have had by relation the long and much experience of my lord, who hath lived to see and be in many changes of fortune and to converse with many men of sundry nations, ages, qualities, tempers, capacities, abilities, wits, humours, fashions and customs.

And as many others, especially wives, go from church to church, from ball to ball, ... gossiping from house to house, so when my lord admits me to his company I listen with attention to his edifying discourse and I govern myself by his doctrine: I dance a measure with the muses, feast with sciences, or sit and discourse with the arts.

The second is that, since I am no scholar, I cannot know the names and terms of art and the divers and several opinions of several authors. I answer: that I must have been a natural fool if I had not known and learnt them, for they are customarily taught all children from the nurse's breast, being ordinarily discoursed of in every family that is of quality, and the family from whence I sprung are neither natural idiots or ignorant fools, but the contrary, for they were rational, learned, understanding and witty....

But as I have said my head was so full of my own natural fantasies, as it had not room for strangers to board therein, and certainly natural reason is a better tutor than education. For though education doth help natural reason to a more sudden maturity, yet natural reason was the first educator: for natural reason did first compose commonwealths, invented arts and science, and if natural reason hath composed, invented and discovered, I know no reason but natural reason may find out what natural reason hath composed, invented and discovered with the help of education....

Source: From Kate Aughterson, *Renaissance Woman: A Sourcebook* (London and New York: Routledge, 1995); pp. 286–288.

38. Margaret Cavendish claimed that she had obtained her intellectual knowledge from which of the following sources?
    (A) The influence of her family and her studies at Oxford
    (B) The influence of her family and participation in discussions and with her husband
    (C) Participation in discussions with her husband and her studies at Oxford
    (D) Participation in discussions with her husband and participation in the English Royal Society

39. Which of the following is a major difference between women who participated in the sciences in France and those who participated in the sciences in Germany?
    (A) French women in the sciences were usually from aristocratic backgrounds while German women in the sciences usually became involved in the sciences from craft production.
    (B) French women participated in the sciences much more often than women in Germany.
    (C) German women in the sciences were usually from aristocratic backgrounds while French women in the sciences usually became involved in the sciences from craft production.
    (D) Most women astronomers came from France.

40. All of the following are true of women in the sciences in the sixteenth and seventeenth centuries EXCEPT
    (A) women were not generally allowed in the royal scientific societies.
    (B) many women involved in the sciences faced discrimination and obstacles in their careers.
    (C) women often became involved in the sciences when they participated in scientific studies with their husbands and fathers.
    (D) many women involved in the sciences found acceptance in royal societies where their contributions were greatly valued.

Questions 41–44 refer to the following map.

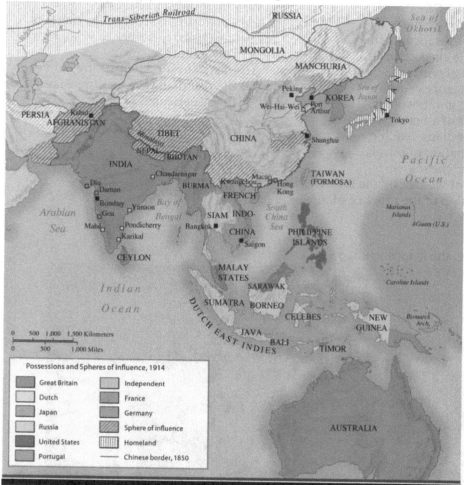

Source: © Cengage Learning

41. What is one major way that New Imperialism in Africa differed from New Imperialism in China?
    (A) In Africa, the European nations established directly occupied colonies, but in China, they established spheres of influence while allowing China to remain nominally free.
    (B) In Africa, the European nations practiced economic imperialism, but in China, they established direct occupation and deposed the Chinese emperor.
    (C) In China, fewer nations practiced imperialism than in Africa.
    (D) The United States took a more active role in African imperialism than they did in China.

42. Which of the following led to allied attacks against the Chinese imperial government that weakened it so much that it eventually was overthrown by Sun Yat-sen?
    (A) The Sepoy Rebellion
    (B) The Opium War
    (C) The Boer War
    (D) The Boxer Rebellion

GO ON TO NEXT PAGE

43. All of the following were results of British rule in India EXCEPT
    (A) the introduction of western-style schools and colleges for Indian upper and middle class children.
    (B) the introduction of western technological advances such as railroads, banks, and hospitals.
    (C) the development of a better standard of living for all Indians, leading to the virtual elimination of poverty among the lower classes.
    (D) the recognition of women by the law and the elimination of the practice of sati.

44. All of the following were motives for new imperialism EXCEPT
    (A) the desire to secure new markets.
    (B) the desire to secure new sources of raw materials.
    (C) the desire to "civilize" the natives.
    (D) the desire to take over new lands in the Americas.

Questions 45–47 refer to the following image.

Source: British Museum, London//UIG via Getty Images

45. The painting on the previous page showing an eighteenth-century English coffeehouse could best be used by a historian
    (A) to explain the sharing of ideas that occurred in new venues at that period.
    (B) to explain Adam Smith's theories of laissez-faire economics.
    (C) to analyze the clothing styles of the middle and upper classes.
    (D) to compare eighteenth-century drinking establishments to those of earlier times.

46. Aside from coffeehouses, another example of the spread of literacy in eighteenth-century Europe could be
    (A) the development of scientific societies such as the Royal Society of Charles II.
    (B) the development of the rotary press.
    (C) the spread of public elementary school education.
    (D) the writing of Diderot's Encyclopedia and the development of lending libraries.

47. King Charles II of England actually banned coffeehouses for a time because
    (A) it was believed that coffee was bad for the health.
    (B) women were not allowed in coffeehouses.
    (C) he saw the spread of ideas in coffeehouses as possibly dangerous to his power.
    (D) he disliked the ideas of the scientific revolution that were discussed there.

Questions 48–51 refer to the following quotation.

Queen Elizabeth I, "The Golden Speech"

My loving people, we have been persuaded by some, that are careful of our safety, to take heed how we commit ourselves to armed multitudes, for fear of treachery; but I assure you, I do not desire to live to distrust my faithful and loving people. Let tyrants fear; I have always so behaved myself that, under God, I have placed my chiefest strength and safeguard in the loyal hearts and good will of my subjects. And therefore I am come amongst you at this time, not as

for my recreation or sport, but being resolved, in the midst and heat of the battle, to live or die amongst you all; to lay down, for my God, and for my kingdom, and for my people, my honor and my blood, even in the dust. I know I have but the body of a weak and feeble woman; but I have the heart of a king, and of a king of England, too; and think foul scorn that Parma or Spain, or any prince of Europe, should dare to invade the borders of my realm: to which, rather than any dishonor should grow by me, I myself will take up arms; I myself will be your general, judge, and rewarder of every one of your virtues in the field. I know already, by your forwardness, that you have deserved rewards and crowns; and we do assure you, on the word of a prince, they shall be duly paid you. In the mean my lieutenant general shall be in my stead, than whom never prince commanded a more noble and worthy subject; not doubting by your obedience to my general, by your concord in the camp and by your valor in the field, we shall shortly have a famous victory over the enemies of my God, of my kingdom, and of my people.

Source: From Elizabeth I's Speech at Tilbury in 1588.

48. This speech, given by Elizabeth I, served which of the following purposes?
    (A) It rallied the troops to oppose Catholic heretics who threatened Elizabeth's reign.
    (B) It rallied the troops to fight against the imminent attack of the Spanish armada.
    (C) It rallied the troops to protect the queen from traitors who wished to free Mary Queen of Scots and place her on the throne of England.
    (D) It rallied the troops to fight against the imminent attack of the French navy.

49. The speech by Queen Elizabeth was most likely addressed to which of the following groups?
    (A) Members of the British Parliament
    (B) Members of the British military forces
    (C) Members of the upper classes
    (D) British Catholics

GO ON TO NEXT PAGE

50. The speech by Queen Elizabeth I contradicted the traditional, accepted role of a sixteenth-century woman in all of the following ways EXCEPT
    (A) Queen Elizabeth was very well educated, as seen in her speech.
    (B) Queen Elizabeth took an active interest in the political and military affairs of her nation.
    (C) Queen Elizabeth portrayed the typical image of a woman, asserting she had a weak and feeble body.
    (D) Queen Elizabeth served in a position of authority in her nation.

51. Queen Elizabeth I is known as a *politique* for which of the following reasons?
    (A) She supported her nation, rallying the troops when foreign dangers threatened English safety.
    (B) She implemented a harsh policy of religious persecution of Puritans, believing they threatened the stability of her nation.
    (C) She supported the arts, initiating a strong interest in theater.
    (D) She implemented a religious settlement that put political unity ahead of theological differences.

Questions 52–55 refer to the following quotation.

Karl Marx and Friedrich Engels, The Communist Manifesto

We have seen ... that the first step in the revolution by the working class is to raise the proletariat to the position of ruling class.... The proletariat will use its political supremacy to wrest, by degrees, all capital from the bourgeoisie, to centralize all instruments of production in the hands of the State, . . and to increase the total of productive forces as rapidly as possible...

Nevertheless, in the most advanced countries, the following will be pretty generally applicable:

1. Abolition of property in land and application of all rents of land to public purposes....

When, in the course of development, class distinctions have disappeared, and all production has been concentrated in the whole nation, the public power will lose its political character. Political power ... is merely the organized power of one class for oppressing another. If the proletariat during its contest with the bourgeoisie is compelled, by the force of circumstances, to organize itself as a class, if, by means of a revolution, it makes itself the ruling class, and ... sweeps away by force the old conditions of production, then it will ... have swept away the conditions for the existence of class antagonisms ... and will thereby have abolished its own supremacy as a class.

In place of the old bourgeois society, with its classes and class antagonisms, we shall have an association, in which the free development of each is the condition for the free development of all.

Source: From *The Communist Manifesto* by Karl Marx and Frederick Engels, trans. Samuel Moore, 1888.

52. All of the following influenced the ideas of Marx EXCEPT
    (A) French utopian socialism.
    (B) the First International.
    (C) observation of industrial conditions in England.
    (D) German philosophers such as Hegel.

53. Which of the following best explains the ideas of Marx?
    (A) It was possible to establish a Marxist society through either reform or revolution.
    (B) In the final stage of the development of a Marxist society, a direct democracy would be elected to rule the nation.
    (C) In industrial societies, the proletariat consistently exploited the bourgeoisie.
    (D) The ultimate goal of Marxism was the creation of a classless society.

54. All of the following are true of the First International Working Men's Association EXCEPT
(A) it was formed by British and French trade unionists.
(B) it served as an umbrella organization for working class interests.
(C) its members were all members of the proletariat who worked together peacefully to advance communist goals.
(D) Karl Marx served on its General Council.

55. All of the following are true of Marxism EXCEPT
(A) Marxism asserted that a communist society could only be established though violent revolution.
(B) Marxism asserted that class struggles were the defining characteristic of all previous societies.
(C) Marxism asserted that political rivalries were the defining characteristic of all previous societies.
(D) Marxism asserted that the abolition of private property was necessary to create a communist society.

STOP
END OF SECTION I, PART A

IF YOU FINISH BEFORE TIME IS CALLED, YOU MAY CHECK YOUR WORK ON THIS SECTION. DO NOT GO ON TO SECTION I PART B UNTIL YOU ARE TOLD TO DO SO.

AP® EUROPEAN HISTORY EXAMINATION
Section II
Part B: Short-Answer Questions
Time: 50 minutes
Number of questions: 4
Percent of examination score: 20%

DIRECTIONS: Part B of the examination contains four questions. You will have 50 minutes to respond to all questions. You are not required to develop and support a thesis statement in your response. Rather, focus on directly answering each question using evidence from your study of history.

1. Analyzing the factors that made fifteenth and sixteenth century European expansion possible, answer A, B, and C.
   A) Briefly explain one technological development that contributed to the success of overseas expansion.
   B) Briefly explain one economic factor that contributed to the success of overseas expansion.
   C) Briefly explain one intellectual development that contributed to the success of overseas expansion.

George Kennan, The Long Telegram, February 1946

In summary, we have here a political force committed fanatically to the belief that with the United State there can be no permanent modus vivendi, that it is desirable and necessary the internal harmony of our society be disrupted, our traditional way of life be destroyed, the international authority of our state be broken, if Soviet power is to be secure.... In addition it has an elaborate and far-flung apparatus for exertion of its influence in other countries, an apparatus of amazing flexibility and versatility, managed by people whose experience and skill in underground methods are presumably without parallel in history. Finally, it is seemingly inaccessible to considerations of reality in its basic reactions.... This is admittedly not a pleasant picture.... But I would like to record my conviction that the problem is within our power to solve—and that without recourse to any general conflict.... I think we may approach calmly and with good heart the problem of how to deal with Russia ... [but] we must have the courage and self-confidence to cling to our own methods and conceptions of human society. After all, the greatest danger that can befall us in coping with this problem of Soviet communism is that we shall allow ourselves to become like those with whom we are coping.

Nikolai Novikov, Telegram, September 27, 1946

One of the stages in the achievement of dominance over the world by the United States is its understanding with England concerning the partial division of the world on the basis of mutual concessions. The basic lines of the secret agreement between the United States and England regarding the division of the world consist, as shown by facts, in their agreement on the inclusion of Japan and China in the sphere of influence of the United States in the Far East.... The American policy in China is striving for the complete economic and political submission of China to the control of American monopolistic capital....

Obvious indications of the U.S. effort to establish world dominance are also to be found in the increase in military potential in peacetime and in the establishment of a large number of naval and air bases both in the United States and beyond its borders....

Careful note should be taken of the fact that the preparation by the United States for a future war is being conducted with the prospect of war against the Soviet Union, which in the eyes of American imperialists is the main obstacle in the path of the United States to world domination. This is indicated by facts such as the tactical training of the American army for war with the Soviet Union as the future opponent, the placing of American strategic bases in regions from which it is possible to launch strikes on Soviet territory, intensified training and strengthening of Arctic regions as close approaches to the USSR, and attempts to prepare Germany and Japan to use those countries in a war against the USSR.

Source: *Origins of the Cold War: The Novikov, Kennan, and Roberts 'Long' Telegrams of 1946.* (Kenneth M. Jensen, editor) Washington, DC: Endowment of the United States Institute of Peace, 1993. pp. 20–21, 28–31, 8, 16. Reprinted with permission.

2. Analyze the causes that contributed to the development of the Cold War, as perceived by the United States and the Soviet Union, and answer A, B, and C.
   A) Briefly explain why Eastern Europe became a cause of dispute between the superpowers.
   B) Briefly explain ONE piece of evidence used by the Soviet Union to show that the United States was responsible for the initial development of the Cold War.
   C) Briefly explain ONE piece of evidence used by the United States to show that the Soviet Union was responsible for the initial development of the Cold War.

3. Analyze differing views on the debate over the nature of women in the seventeenth century.
   A) Briefly explain ONE argument rejecting the traditional view of women in the seventeenth century.
   B) Briefly explain ONE argument supporting the traditional view of women in the seventeenth century.
   C) Explain one piece of evidence used to support the argument in part B.

4. Answer A, B, and C by analyzing the way in which the policies of the Liberals in England were transformed in the years immediately preceding World War I.
   A) Briefly explain ONE demand advocated by British trade unions at the turn of the twentieth century.
   B) Briefly explain ONE demand advocated by British Socialists.
   C) Briefly describe the changes made by the British Liberals in response to the demands of the trade unions and the Socialists.

STOP
END OF SECTION I

IF YOU FINISH BEFORE TIME IS CALLED, YOU MAY CHECK YOUR WORK ON THIS SECTION. DO NOT GO ON TO SECTION II UNTIL YOU ARE TOLD TO DO SO.

AP® EUROPEAN HISTORY EXAMINATION
Section II: Free-Response Essays
Part A: Document-Based Question (DBQ)
Suggested writing time: 55 minutes
Percent of examination score: 25%

DIRECTIONS: The following question is based on the accompanying Documents 1–7. The documents have been edited for the purposes of this exercise. This question is designed to test your ability to apply several historical thinking skills simultaneously, including historical argumentation, appropriate use of relevant historical evidence, contextualization, and synthesis. Your response should be based on your analysis of the documents and your knowledge of the topic.

Write a well-integrated essay that does the following:

- States an appropriate thesis that directly addresses *all parts* of the question.
- Supports the thesis or an appropriate argument with evidence from all or all but one of the documents AND knowledge of European history beyond/outside the documents.
- Analyzes a majority of the documents in terms of such features as their intended audience, purpose, point of view, format, argument, limitations, and/or social context as appropriate to the argument.
- Places the argument in the context of the broader regional, national, or global process.

QUESTION 1. Compare and contrast various British reactions to the rise of Nazi Germany and the foreign policy decisions of German Chancellor Adolf Hitler during the period 1933–1939.

Document 1

Source: Editorial written by Lord Rothermere, publisher of the *Daily Mail*, July 10, 1933.

I urge all British young men and women to study closely the progress of the Nazi regime in Germany. They must not be misled by the misrepresentations of its opponents. The most spiteful distracters of the Nazis are to be found in precisely the same sections of the British public and press as are most vehement in their praises of the Soviet regime in Russia. They have started a clamorous campaign of denunciation against what they call "Nazi atrocities," which, as anyone who visits Germany quickly discovers for himself, consists merely of a few isolated acts of violence such as are inevitable among a nation half as big again as ours, but which have been generalized, multiplied and exaggerated to give the impression that Nazi rule is a bloodthirsty tyranny.

Document 2

Source: Letter to the editor written by a leading pacifist, the Rev. H. R. Sheppard, *Manchester Guardian*, October 16, 1934.

The main reason for this letter, addressed primarily to men, is the urgency of the present international situation, and the almost universally acknowledged lunacy of the manner in which nations are pursuing peace.... [I]t seems essential to discover whether or not it be true, as we are told, that the majority of thoughtful men in this country are convinced that war of any kind or for any cause, is not only a denial of Christianity, but a crime against humanity which is not to be permitted by civilised people.

Document 3

Source: Report by Anthony Eden, British Foreign Secretary, regarding meeting with representatives from the French, Belgian, and Italian governments, March 11, 1936.

The Prime Minister thought at some stage it would be necessary to point out to the French that the action they proposed would result only in letting loose another great war in Europe. They might succeed in crushing Germany with the aid of Russia, but it would probably only result in Germany going Bolshevik....

In addition, public opinion was strongly opposed to any military action against the Germans in the demilitarized zone. In particular, the ex-Service men were very anti-French. Moreover, many people, perhaps most people were saying openly that they did not see why the Germans should not re-occupy the Rhineland. In these circumstances, it was generally accepted that it was worth taking almost any risk in order to escape from that situation....

GO ON TO NEXT PAGE

Document 4

Source: Sir Oswald Mosley, leader of the British Union of Fascists, October 4, 1936.

Credit: Getty Images / Central Press

Document 5

Source: "Fascist march stopped after disorderly scenes," *Manchester Guardian*, October 5, 1936.

The Fascists marched in London yesterday—but away from the East End, not through it. Their proposed procession through the heart of the Jewish quarter—which had caused strong protests to be made to the Home Secretary and had created a tense situation in the East End—was stopped by the police when it was on the point of setting out and it went, instead, along the Embankment.

There were extraordinary scenes in the East End long before the procession was due to start. Tremendous crowds gathered along the whole route of the proposed procession, and there were frequent clashes, in which the police had to draw their truncheons, shop windows were broken, many people suffered injury, and many arrests were made.

The excitement in the East End continued long after the Fascist procession had been abandoned, and both the Communists and the Fascists held meeting last night.

The Communists … had arranged a counter-demonstration at Aldgate and Cable Street. So great were the crowds that had assembled for this purpose … that all the traffic was held up. Every time a bus or tram load of policemen arrived they were greeted with ironical cheering, booing and the Communist salute.

Document 6

Source: Public Order Act of 1936, His Majesty's Government, Great Britain and the United Kingdom.

An Act to prohibit the wearing of uniforms in connection with political objects and the maintenance by private persons of associations of military or similar character; and to make further provision of public order on the occasion of public processions and meetings in public places.

1. Prohibition of uniforms in connection with political objects

Subject as hereinafter provided, any person who in any public place or at any public meeting wears uniform signifying his association with any political organisation or with the promotion of any political object shall be guilty of an offence.

2. Prohibition of quasimilitary organisations

If the members or adherents of any association of persons, whether incorporated or not, are a organised or trained or equipped for the purpose of enabling them to be employed in usurping the functions of the police or of the armed forces of the Crown ... shall be guilty of an offence.....

Document 7

Source: Winston Churchill, Conservative member of Parliament, speech to the House of Commons, October 5, 1938.

We are in the presence of a disaster of the first magnitude which has befallen Great Britain and France. Do not let us blind ourselves to that....

And do not suppose that this is the end. This is only the beginning of the reckoning. This is only the first sip, the first foretaste of a bitter cup which will be proffered to us year by year unless by a supreme recovery of moral health and martial vigor, we arise again and take our stand for freedom as in the olden time.

END OF DOCUMENTS FOR PART A.
GO ON TO THE NEXT PAGE.

AP® EUROPEAN HISTORY EXAMINATION
Section II: Free-Response Essays
Part B: Long-Essay Questions
Suggested planning and writing time: 35 minutes
Percent of examination score: 15%

Directions: You are to choose ONE question from the two questions below. Make your selection carefully, choosing the question that you are best prepared to answer thoroughly in the time permitted. You should spend 5 minutes organizing or outlining your answer. Write your answer to the question on the lined pages of the Section II free-response booklet, making sure to indicate the question you are answering by writing the appropriate question number on the top of each page.

Write an essay that:

- has a relevant thesis.
- addresses all parts of the question.
- supports your thesis with specific evidence.
- is well organized.

Question 1. Analyze the major factors that led to the rise and fall of the Spanish empire from the Age of Exploration to the Age of Absolutism (1490–1650). (Historical Thinking Skills: Causation)

Question 2. Analyze the factors that caused Continental Europe to industrialize much later than Great Britain. (Historical Thinking Skills: Causation)

END OF EXAMINATION

ANSWERS FOR SECTION I, PART A: MULTIPLE-CHOICE QUESTIONS

ANSWER KEY FOR PART A: MULTIPLE-CHOICE QUESTIONS

1. B	12. A	23. B	34. A	45. A
2. C	13. C	24. C	35. B	46. D
3. C	14. A	25. B	36. D	47. C
4. D	15. D	26. C	37. C	48. B
5. A	16. D	27. D	38. B	49. B
6. C	17. A	28. A	39. A	50. C
7. C	18. C	29. B	40. D	51. D
8. C	19. B	30. D	41. A	52. B
9. B	20. C	31. B	42. D	53. D
10. A	21. D	32. D	43. C	54. C
11. D	22. D	33. C	44. D	55. C

EXPLANATIONS FOR PART A: MULTIPLE-CHOICE ANSWERS

1. **(B)** The Soviet Union sent troops to Prague in 1968 to put down reform efforts. This sent a clear message that Soviet leadership would not tolerate any challenge to its domination in Eastern Europe (*Western Civilization*, 9th ed., pp. 908–10 /10th ed., pp. 903–04; Historical Thinking Skills—Causation; Learning Objectives PP-3, SP-13, SP-14; Key Concept 4.1, 4.2).

2. **(C)** The letter to Czechoslovakia outlined the basis of the Brezhnev Doctrine, a policy that allowed Soviet troops to intervene in any nation that was threatened by western capitalist powers. This doctrine justified the invasion of Prague and later actions in Afghanistan and Nicaragua (*Western Civilization*, 9th ed., pp. 908–10 / 10th ed., p. 904; Historical Thinking Skills—Causation; Learning Objectives PP-3, SP-13, SP-14; Key Concept 4.1, 4.2).

3. **(C)** Romania did not enjoy civil liberties and was under the strict communist control of its dictator Nicolae Ceausescu (*Western Civilization*, 9th ed., pp. 908–10 / 10th ed., pp. 903–04; Historical Thinking Skills—Causation; Learning Objectives PP-3, SP-13, SP-14; Key Concept 4.1, 4.2).

4. **(D)** The detente policy of the early 1960s actually encouraged some Eastern Europeans to call for more freedom. As relations improved slightly with the west, Eastern Europeans hoped that the USSR would be less likely to oppose their demands for greater autonomy (*Western Civilization*, 9th ed., pp. 908–10 / 10th ed., pp. 876, 879, 902–03; Historical Thinking Skills—Causation; Learning Objectives PP-3, SP-13, SP-14; Key Concept 4.1, 4.2).

5. **(A)** The painting is set in a wealthy person's living room or salon, a party to which hostesses invited members of the nobility to hear and discuss enlightened ideas. The people are too well dressed to be Quakers and there is no evidence of a religious setting. There is also no evidence of anything scientific in the room and no evidence of a king (*Western Civilization*, 9th ed., pp. 513–15 / 10th ed., pp. 510–12; Historical Thinking Skills—Contextualization, Analyzing Evidence: Content and Sourcing, Synthesis; Learning Objective OS-7, OS-8, IS-9; Key Concept 2.3).

6. **(C)** Evidence that this is a wealthy person's home included the numerous paintings and other artwork, comfortable chairs, carpeted floors, and the opulent clothing of the guests (*Western Civilization*, 9th ed., pp. 513–15 / 10th ed., pp. 510–12; Historical Thinking Skills—Contextualization, Analyzing Evidence: Content and Sourcing; Learning Objective PP-1, OS-10, IS-4, IS-7; Key Concept 2.4).

7. **(C)** Church records and government documents would not be written about salons, nor would they be mentioned scientific or enlightened writings. Participants at the salons, however, often kept journals or diaries, and they frequently wrote letters about what had been discussed at the parties (*Western Civilization*, 9th ed., pp. 513–15 / 10th ed., pp. 510–12; Historical Thinking Skills—Argumentation, Analyzing Evidence: Content and Sourcing; Learning Objective OS-7, OS-8; Key Concept 2.3).

8. **(C)** Historian Jackson Spielvogel sees the Industrial Revolution as a time of great economic change that forced change upon the political and social aspects of society as well. He sees it, not as totally bad nor as totally good (*Western Civilization*, 9th ed., pp. 596–97 / 10th ed., pp. 510–13; Historical Thinking Skills—Interpretation, Causation, Argumentation; Learning Objective PP-4, PP-6; Key Concept 3.1).

9. **(B)** According to the excerpt, the organization was changed to get the most production out of the factory as possible. This meant cramming as many people and machines into one room as possible (*Western Civilization*, 9th ed., pp. 596–97 / 10th ed., p. 592; Historical Thinking Skills—Patterns of Continuity and Change Over Time, Argumentation, Interpretation; Learning Objective PP-6; Key Concept 3.1).

10. **(A)** Although the excerpt does talk about 500 people working in one room, the person describing the situation sees it as a light-filled airy place. The negative example given in the text was the pregnant woman who was fined for sitting down on the job (*Western Civilization*, 9th ed., pp. 596–97, 616–20 / 10th ed., pp. 592, 598–99; Historical Thinking Skills—Argumentation, Analyzing Evidence: Content and Sourcing; Learning Objective PP-6, IS-3; Key Concept 3.2).

11. **(D)** William Cobbett, who describes the factory in such glowing terms, is most likely a factory owner or the owner/farmer of a large commercial farm. It is unlikely that a worker, and particularly a Luddite who hates machines and wants to break them, would positively describe a factory experience (*Western Civilization*, 9th ed., pp. 616–20 / 10th ed., pp. 592, 598–99; Historical Thinking Skills—Argumentation, Analyzing Evidence: Content and Sourcing; Learning Objective PP-6, IS-3, IS-5; Key Concept 3.2).

12. **(A)** The guillotine was the execution method of choice during the French Revolution. It was seen as a scientifically designed, more humane way to execute criminals (*Western Civilization*, 9th ed., p. 578 / 10th ed., p. 574; Historical Thinking Skills—Analyzing Evidence: Content and Sourcing; Learning Objective SP-7; Key Concept 2.1).

13. **(C)** Much of the Revolutionaries' anger and the excesses of the guillotine were fueled by the formation of public opinion, as more people became literate and newspapers, pamphlets, and other mass media forms accommodated their wish to know what was happening in their world (*Western Civilization*, 9th ed., pp. 578–79 / 10th ed., pp. 574–81; Historical Thinking Skill—Analyzing Evidence: Content and Sourcing, Synthesis; Learning Objective SP-7; Key Concept 2.1).

14. **(A)** Overthrowing a tyrannical monarch whose reign was marked by a lack of power by the lower classes would definitely have inspired Toussaint L'Ouverture to start a slave rebellion in Haiti (*Western Civilization*, 9th ed., p. 584 / 10th ed., pp. 580–81; Historical Thinking Skills—Causation, Patterns of Continuity and Change Over Time, Analyzing Evidence: Content and Sourcing; Learning Objective SP-9, INT-7; Key Concept 2.1).

15. **(D)** Louis XVI went to the guillotine BEFORE the Reign of Terror began (*Western Civilization*, 9th ed., pp. 577–81 / 10th ed., pp. 567–68, 574, 576; Historical Thinking Skills—Causation, Patterns of Continuity and Change Over Time, Periodization; Learning Objective SP-7; Key Concept 2.1).

16. **(D)** Versailles served many useful purposes, allowing King Louis XIV to contain his nobility and causing the French monarchy and court to become the envy of Europe. The palace, however, cost great amounts of money to build and maintain, increasing the national debt (*Western Civilization*, 9th ed., pp. 445–50 / 10th ed., pp. 441–45; Historical Thinking Skills—Contextualization; Learning Objectives SP-2, IS-7; Key Concept 2.1).

17. **(A)** The building of roads and canals improved communications and transportation of goods internally, increasing profits, but it was funded by the government (*Western Civilization*, 9th ed., pp. 445–50 / 10th ed., pp. 441–45; Historical Thinking Skills—Contextualization; Learning Objectives PP-1, SP-2; Key Concept 2.1, 2.2).

18. **(C)** Although some of the ceremonies, such as holding the king's candle, might have been demeaning to great nobles and churchmen, they participated in order to earn offices and titles from the king (*Western Civilization*, 9th ed., pp. 445–50 / 10th ed., pp. 441–45; Historical Thinking Skills—Contextualization; Learning Objectives SP-2, IS-7; Key Concept 2.1).

19. **(B)** Catherine the Great of Russia was able to take more Polish land than Austria or Russia. By the Third Partition of Poland in 1793, Poland no longer existed as a country at all (*Western Civilization*, 9th ed., pp. 539–42 / 10th ed., pp. 537–38; Historical Thinking Skills—Patterns of Continuity and Change Over Time, Analyzing Evidence: Content and Sourcing; Learning Objective SP-2, SP-4; Key Concept 2.1).

20. **(C)** Prussia's once widely scattered territories were united by the taking of Polish territory between Brandenburg and Prussia. Frederick II saw Prussia recognized as a great power before his death (*Western Civilization*, 9th ed., pp. 537–38 / 10th ed., pp. 537–38; Historical Thinking Skills—Causation, Analyzing Evidence: Content and Sourcing; Learning Objective SP-2; Key Concept 2.1).

21. **(D)** In spite of the fact that Charles VI made Maria Theresa his heir in the Pragmatic Sanction, Frederick II of Prussia did not accept her as Holy Roman Emperor (*Western Civilization*, 9th ed., pp. 539–42 / 10th ed., p. 540; Historical Thinking Skills—Patterns of Continuity and Change Over Time, Causation; Learning Objective SP-2, Sp-4; Key Concept 2.1).

22. **(D)** Although Hitler hoped that his forces could quickly eliminate the Soviet military and bring about the collapse of the Soviet government, the strength of the Soviet forces surprised Hitler's military, preventing Hitler from achieving his primary objective on the Eastern Front (*Western Civilization*, 9th ed., pp. 841–43 / 10th ed., pp. 836–41; Historical Thinking Skills—Contextualization, Causation; Learning Objectives SP-6, SP-8, SP-17, SP-18; Key Concept 4.1, 4.2).

23. **(B)** By the time Germany invaded the Soviet Union, France had already surrendered to the Germans (*Western Civilization*, 9th ed., pp. 841–43 / 10th ed., pp. 836–39; Historical Thinking Skills—Comparison; Learning Objectives SP-6, SP-8, SP-17, SP-18; Key Concept 4.1, 4.2).

24. **(C)** Although Germany had annexed large amounts of territory in the 1930s, it did not retain control of those lands after the war. As seen on the map, the nation, that annexed the most territory and kept it after the war was the USSR (*Western Civilization*, 9th ed., pp. 841–43 / 10th ed., p. 837; Historical Thinking Skills—Comparison; Learning Objectives SP-6, SP-8, SP-17, SP-18; Key Concept 4.1, 4.2).

25. **(B)** Although answer A might seem tempting, based on the map, the correct answer is B. The growth of national monarchies along the Atlantic seaboard led to exploration, new trade routes, and competition of global economic success (*Western Civilization*, 9th ed., pp. 357–61 / 10th ed., pp. 356–60; Historical Thinking Skills—Causation; Learning Objective SP-2; Key Concept 1.2).

26. **(C)** The lack of an urban society in Eastern Europe prevented the development of a strong merchant class that could challenge the bonds of feudalism (*Western Civilization*, 9th ed., pp. 357–61 / 10th ed., pp. 356–60; Historical Thinking Skills—Causation; Learning Objective PP-6; Key Concept 1.5).

27. **(D)** The Holy Roman Empire and France shared a sizeable border and neither wanted the other to gain territory and become more powerful (*Western Civilization*, 9th ed., pp. 357–61 / 10th ed., pp. 356–60; Historical Thinking Skills—Causation; Learning Objective SP-2; Key Concept 1.2).

28. **(A)** The Portuguese quickly engaged in regional trade between Japan, China, and Southeast Asia, transporting goods from Japan to other Asian nations and returning with items, such as silks from China. After the Chinese emperor prohibited direct trade with Japan, Portugal profited from being the intermediary in regional trade (*Western Civilization*, 9th ed., pp. 423–25 / 10th ed., pp. 419–21; Historical Thinking Skills—Contextualization; Learning Objective INT-6; Key Concept 1.4).

29. **(B)** The Japanese were interested in purchasing clocks, eyeglasses, tobacco, and firearms from the Portuguese, as well as commodities from China, such as silks that were carried on Portuguese ships (*Western Civilization*, 9th ed., pp. 423–25 / 10th ed., pp. 419–21; Historical Thinking Skills—Contextualization; Learning Objective INT-6; Key Concept 1.4).

30. **(D)** The interference of Catholic missionaries in local politics led to a Japanese backlash against Westerners, especially Christians. European missionaries and merchants were expelled, and several major trading posts were closed (*Western Civilization*, 9th ed., pp. 423–25 / 10th ed., pp. 419–21; Historical Thinking Skills—Contextualization; Learning Objectives INT-6, INT-11; Key Concept 1.4).

31. **(B)** The construction of sewers in large cities such as Paris, London, and Frankfurt greatly improved the public health in urban areas, removing the sewage from sources of drinking water and was one of the most important transformations in the infrastructure of late nineteenth-century urban centers in Europe (*Western Civilization*, 9th ed., pp. 716–19 / 10th ed., pp. 689–702; Historical Thinking Skills—Patterns of Continuity and Change Over Time; Learning Objectives PP-4, PP-13, PP-15, SP-5, IS-3, IS-7; Key Concept 3.1, 3.2, 3.3).

32. **(D)** Most people who moved to the cities did so because of economic necessity. Cities offered employment opportunities. Even if many of the jobs were low-paying and difficult, people who needed a job found them appealing and moved in hopes of a brighter future. Living conditions were also improving in urban areas by the late nineteenth century, and since many ordinary people did not have the means to acquire adequate amounts of land to make a living in rural regions, often they moved to the cities hoping for a brighter future (*Western Civilization*, 9th ed., pp. 716–19 / 10th ed., pp. 698–703; Historical Thinking Skills—Causation; Learning Objectives PP-4, PP-13, PP-15, SP-5, IS-3, IS-7; Key Concept 3.1, 3.2, 3.3).

33. **(C)** Although many of the old residential areas in large cities such as Paris were razed, they were not replaced with better housing for the poor; instead, they were replaced with wider streets, museums, cafes, theaters, parks, and department stores (*Western Civilization*, 9th ed., pp. 716–19 / 10th ed., pp. 698–703; Historical Thinking Skills—Patterns of Continuity and Change Over Time; Learning Objectives PP-4, PP-13, PP-15, SP-5, IS-3, IS-7; Key Concept 3.1, 3.2, 3.3).

34. **(A)** Children did not work in factories in New Lanark. They went to school (*Western Civilization*, 9th ed., pp. 636–38 / 10th ed., pp. 632–34; Historical Thinking Skills—Comparison, Analyzing Evidence: Content and Sourcing, Synthesis; Learning Objective PP-3, PP-6; Key Concept 3.3).

35. **(B)** Robert Owen, the owner of New Lanark, was a utopian socialist (*Western Civilization*, 9th ed., pp. 636–38 / 10th ed., pp. 632–34; Historical Thinking Skills—Analyzing Evidence: Content and Sourcing; Learning Objective IS-5, IS-7, PP-8, PP-10; Key Concept 3.3).

36. **(D)** Although they believed in setting up their societies somewhat differently, Saint Simon and Fourier were also utopian socialists (*Western Civilization*, 9th ed., pp. 636–38 / 10th ed., pp. 632–34; Historical Thinking Skills—Analyzing Evidence: Content and Sourcing, Synthesis; Learning Objective IS-5, IS-7, PP-8, PP-10; Key Concept 3.3).

37. **(C)** While children did not work, the factories (and in fact the entire town) were the property of the factory owner. Hours were somewhat shorter and pay a little better. The problem of boring work was solved by rotating jobs. However, workers still lacked ownership of the products they made (*Western Civilization*, 9th ed., pp. 636–38 / 10th ed., pp. 632–34; Historical Thinking Skills—Analyzing Evidence: Content and Sourcing, Synthesis; Learning Objective PP-3, PP-6; Key Concept 3.2, 3.3).

38. **(B)** Although elite women could participate in the informal scientific networks of their husbands and fathers, they were not yet enrolled in universities, so most got their knowledge of science from their families and their husbands (*Western Civilization*, 9th ed., pp. 490–91 / 10th ed., pp. 486–87; Historical Thinking Skills—Contextualization; Learning Objectives OS-4, IS-10; Key Concepts 2.1, 2.3).

39. **(A)** Most women in France and England who worked in the sciences came from aristocratic families that had provided them with a humanistic education and allowed them to participate in scientific gatherings hosted and attended by their male relatives, while most German women who participated in the sciences came from craft production backgrounds (*Western Civilization*, 9th ed., pp. 490–91 / 10th ed., pp. 486–88; Historical Thinking Skills—Comparison; Learning Objectives OS-4, IS-10; Key Concepts 2.1, 2.3).

40. **(D)** Although women in the sciences made many great contributions, they often faced obstacles to their scientific careers and were generally not allowed to join scientific societies (*Western Civilization*, 9th ed., pp. 490–91 / 10th ed., pp. 486–88; Historical Thinking Skills—Contextualization; Learning Objectives OS-4, IS-10; Key Concepts 2.1, 2.3).

41. **(A)** Although the Europeans had a great deal of economic and political control in China, they actually established spheres of influence and long-term leases of Chinese territory while allowing the Chinese government to maintain the nominal independence of the nation (*Western Civilization*, 9th ed., pp. 750–55 / 10th ed., pp. 742–48; Historical Thinking Skills—Causation; Learning Objectives IS-10, INT-3, INT-6, INT-7, INT-11; Key Concept 3.5).

42. **(D)** The Boxer Rebellion was an outburst of violence against foreigners that aimed at removing foreign influence in China. The allied powers responded with an attack against the Boxers that ended with concessions that forever weakened the imperial government (*Western Civilization*, 9th ed., pp. 750–55 / 10th ed., pp. 742–48; Historical Thinking Skills—Causation; Learning Objectives IS-10, INT-3, INT-6, INT-7, INT-10, INT-11; Key Concept 3.5).

43. **(C)** Due to extreme population growth in the nineteenth century, the number of poverty-stricken Indians grew rapidly. By the turn of the twentieth century, nearly two-thirds of Indians were malnourished and British occupation destroyed local industries, further limiting their opportunities (*Western Civilization*, 9th ed., pp. 750–55 / 10th ed., pp. 742–48; Historical Thinking Skills—Causation; Learning Objectives IS-10, INT-3, INT-6, INT-7, INT-11; Key Concept 3.5).

44. **(D)** Unlike old imperialism which largely involved the settlement of the Americas, new imperialism was focused on the colonization of Africa and Asia (*Western Civilization*, 9th ed., pp. 750–55 / 10th ed., pp. 742–48; Historical Thinking Skills—Causation; Learning Objectives IS-10, INT-3, INT-6, INT-7, INT-11; Key Concept 3.5).

45. **(A)** Coffeehouses were a new venue for sharing ideas and discoveries. Scientists and enlightened thinkers spent hours drinking coffee and arguing their points of view (*Western Civilization*, 9th ed., pp. 513, 521 / 10th ed., pp. 510, 516–17; Historical Thinking Skills—Argumentation, Analyzing Evidence: Content and Sourcing; Learning Objective OS-7, OS-8, OS-9; Key Concept 2.3).

46. **(D)** The Royal Society was for scientists only, while the rotary press and public schools are from a later time period. The rise in literacy made Diderot's *Encyclopedie*, along with dictionaries and lending libraries, necessary for the masses (*Western Civilization*, 9th ed., pp. 513, 521 / 10th ed., pp. 510, 506–07; Historical Thinking Skills—Contextualization, Synthesis; Learning Objective OS-8; Key Concept 2.3).

47. **(D)** Coffeehouses were popular among the urban middle classes and some members of the nobility who enjoyed drinking coffee, reading the newspapers that were provided free of charge, discussing issues, playing games, and completing business transactions. Political clubs sometimes emerged from coffeehouses, particularly in France immediately preceding the French Revolution (*Western Civilization*, 10th ed., pp. 517, 525, 572; Historical Thinking Skill—Contextualization; Learning Objective OS-8; Key Concept 2.3).

48. **(B)** Queen Elizabeth's speech at Tilbury, given in 1588, was designed to rally the troops to protect England from the attack of the Spanish armada (*Western Civilization*, 9th ed., pp. 397–400 / 10th ed., pp. 394–96; Historical Thinking Skills—Argumentation; Learning Objective SP-2; Key Concept 1.2).

49. **(B)** This speech, given by Queen Elizabeth I in 1588, was addressed to members of the British military in an attempt to rally them to fight against the attack of the Spanish armada (*Western Civilization*, 9th ed., pp. 397–400 / 10th ed., pp. 394–96; Historical Thinking Skills—Analyzing Evidence: Content and Sourcing; Learning Objective SP-13; Key Concept 1.2).

50. **(C)** Queen Elizabeth asserted the typical sixteenth-century view of women as being weak in body in her speech to her troops at Tilbury. The other choices all represent aspects of the queen that contradicted the standard view of women, in that day (*Western Civilization*, 9th ed., pp. 397–400 / 10th ed., pp. 394–96; Historical Thinking Skills—Patterns of Continuity and Change Over Time; Learning Objectives IS-6, IS-9; Key Concept 1.5).

51. **(D)** Queen Elizabeth was known as a *politique* who offered political toleration to citizens in return for political unity (*Western Civilization*, 9th ed., pp. 397–400 / 10th ed., pp. 394–96; Historical Thinking Skills—Contextualization; Learning Objective SP-13; Key Concept 1.2).

52. **(B)** The First International was not an influence on the ideas of Karl Marx, since it was an umbrella organization that promoted working-class interests. Although Marx served on its General Council, it was not an influence on the development of his ideas (*Western Civilization*, 9th ed., pp. 678–80 / 10th ed., pp. 673–75; Historical Thinking Skills—Contextualization; Learning Objectives PP-8, PP-10, PP-14, SP-5, IS-7; Key Concept 3.1, 3.3, 3.6).

53. **(D)** Because Marx believed that the bourgeoisie consistently exploited the proletariat, he asserted that society would be ideal if a classless society existed in which there would be no reason for exploitation. He believed this situation would be initially established by revolution (*Western Civilization*, 9th ed., pp. 678–80 / 10th ed., pp. 673–75; Historical Thinking Skills—Analyzing Evidence: Content and Sourcing; Learning Objectives PP-8, PP-10, PP-14, SP-5, IS-7; Key Concept 3.1, 3.3, 3.6).

54. **(C)** Although the organization was greatly influenced by the participation of Karl Marx, it disintegrated in 1872 due to internal dissension. Although it was resurrected in 1889, it had little significant influence (*Western Civilization*, 9th ed., pp. 678–80 / 10th ed., pp. 673–75; Historical Thinking Skills—Causation; Learning Objectives PP-8, PP-10, PP-14, SP-5, IS-7; Key Concept 3.1, 3.3, 3.6).

55. **(C)** Karl Marx believed that the history of all previous societies were characterized by class struggles, and that political struggles were only the manifestation of animosity between the bourgeoisie and the proletariat (*Western Civilization*, 9th ed., pp. 678–80 / 10th ed., pp. 673–75; Historical Thinking Skills—Contextualization; Learning Objectives PP-8, PP-10, PP-14, SP-5, IS-7; Key Concept 3.1, 3.3, 3.6).

ANSWERS FOR SECTION I, PART B: SHORT-ANSWER QUESTIONS

QUESTION 1

A) One of the most important developments that contributed to the success of overseas expansion was the invention of better ships and new navigational techniques. Using an axial rudder imported from China and lateen sails with a square rig, European shipbuilders began to make ships that were very maneuverable but also big enough to handle large cannons and sail against heavy winds. These ships, combined with the compass and astrolabe, made overseas expansion possible.

B) Overseas expansion was also made possible by the development of commercial capitalism and its corresponding new forms of commercials organization. The creation of joint-stock companies provided capital needed for overseas expansion, enticing individuals to invest in a company in hopes of receiving dividends on their investments. The success of joint-stock companies such as the Dutch East India Company that averaged a 30% return on investments over its first 10 years encouraged investors to risk their money and made it possible to raise enough money to fund world trade adventures.

C) One intellectual factor that contributed to the success of overseas expansion was the development of new maps and advances in cartography at the end of the fifteenth century, beginning in 1477 with a Latin translation of Ptolemy's *Geography*, a book that showed his map. Although the map was inaccurate, it did show that the world was spherical, convincing explorers like Columbus that they could sail west to get to Asia. As European explorers sailed further, they began to create new, more realistic maps. Finally, in 1630, Gerardus Mercator created a map using conformal projection that was much more accurate, giving sea captains much more accurate information for their voyages.

(*Western Civilization*, 8th ed., pp. 433–35 / 9th ed., pp. 406–07, 430–31 / 10th ed., pp. 400–403, 427–28; Historical Thinking Skills—Causation; Learning Objectives INT-4, PP-1; Key Concept 1.4)

Question 2

A) Eastern Europe became a cause of dispute between the superpowers because Americans believed that Stalin had imposed Soviet rule on the region and had prevented free elections and national self-determination which they had agree upon at the Yalta and Potsdam conferences. The Soviet Union wanted to maintain control of its Eastern European satellites in an attempt to secure its western border from another invasion, while the United States wanted to promote democracy in the region.

B) One piece of evidence used by the Soviet Union to show that the United States was responsible for the initial development of the Cold War was the belief that the United States wanted world dominance and was building its capacity to conduct a war against the Soviet Union. The Soviet Union used the friendly relations between the United States and England, along with American economic influence in Asia and the American expansion into the Arctic regions as evidence of American aggression and American plans to exclude the Soviet Union from influence in Asia and Europe. Truman asked Congress for money to aid the free governments of Greece and Turkey and help them fight off communist insurgents. In his speech to Congress, Truman announced that the United States would aid any free people who were being threatened by communists, and this policy was seen as a direct threat by the Soviet Union.

C) One piece of evidence that could be used by the United States to show that the Soviet Union was responsible for the initial development of the Cold War was the belief that the Soviet Union was committed to controlling many other nations directly, to destroying its rivals (particularly the United States), and to controlling people in the regions that they took over by underhanded and secret means. One example of this aggression was the Soviet Blockade of Berlin. When faced with the choice of cooperating with the West in the administration of post-war Germany or preventing the unification of the German nation, Stalin's choice to blockade West Berlin in an attempt to force the Western powers out of the city and to prevent the creation of a free West German nation. The ensuing airlift supplied the people of West Berlin with supplies, but Stalin had further poisoned his relationship with the Western powers.

(*Western Civilization*, 9th ed., pp. 868–72 / 10th ed., pp. 864–67. Historical Thinking Skills—Analyzing Evidence: Content and Sourcing, Causation; Learning Objectives SP-8, SP-13; Key Concept 4.1, 4.4)

QUESTION 3

A) One argument rejecting the traditional view of women in the seventeenth century was that women had rational minds that could expand with education. Believing that women were largely rational, chaste, and temperate beings, women argued that they no longer needed to be under male control and should, instead, be recognized as intellectual beings.

B) One argument supporting the traditional view of women in the seventeenth century was that women were inferior by nature, subordinate to men, in need of male guidance to help them control their base weak natures, and finally that they were best suited to be nurturing wives and mothers.

C) One piece of evidence used to support the argument in part B was that since women had different skeletal constructions with wider pelvises and smaller skulls, they were built to have children and were inferior to the large male minds. These physical differences were used to prove the intellectual superiority of men and the domestic role of women.

(*Western Civilization*, 9th ed., pp. 490–92 / 10th ed., pp. 486–88; Historical Thinking Skills—Contextualization; Learning Objectives OS-4, IS-10; Key Concepts 2.1, 2.3)

QUESTION 4

A) One demand advocated by British trade unions at the turn of the twentieth century was radical change in the economic system. Trade unions represented the working class, and members were frustrated with the failure of the government to adopt social reform policies. Consequently, trade unions began to demand collective ownership of the means of production, exchange, and distribution, and members began to strike for the adoption of a minimum wage and better conditions.

B) One demand advocated by British Fabian Socialists was universal male suffrage. The Fabians were not Marxists who wanted a violent overthrow of the existing society; instead, they demanded the right to vote so that they would be able to help shape a socialist state through parliamentary means. Sharing many of the goals of trade unions, the British Fabians hoped to improve the condition of the working class. In an attempt to gain enough power in government to achieve this goal, the Fabians eventually merged with some trade union representatives, forming the British Labour Party in 1900.

C) In response to the demands of the trade unions and the Fabian Socialists, British Liberals were forced to adopt policies that would originally have been considered unacceptable in previous decades. Challenged by the growth of the Labour party and not wanting to lose power, the Liberals adopted social welfare legislation rather than pursuing the traditional laissez-faire economic policies of previous years. The National Insurance Act of 1911 provided unemployment insurance for workers, and rich citizens were forced to pay more in taxes to support the growing "welfare state."

(*Western Civilization*, 9th ed., pp. 739–40 / 10th ed., pp. 735–37; Historical Thinking Skills—Patterns of Continuity and Change Over Time; Learning Objectives PP-8, PP-13, PP-15, SP-1, SP-4, SP-5, SP-9, IS-5; Key Concepts 3.2, 3.3)

ANSWER FOR SECTION II, PART A: DOCUMENT-BASED QUESTION (DBQ)

THE DOCUMENTS

Below are short analyses of the documents. The italicized words suggest what your margin notes might include:

DOCUMENT 1 This document is an editorial written by Lord Rothermere, publisher of the popular London newspaper, the *Daily Mail*. In it, Lord Rothermere *expresses his support for the Nazis and condemns his opponents as Communist sympathizers. Lord Rothermere is pro-Nazi and anti-Communist.*

DOCUMENT 2 This document is a letter to the editor *written by a pacifist*, the Rev. H. R. Sheppard of the Church of England. He boldly asserts that *war is not only un-Christian, but also "a crime against humanity."* Obviously Sheppard is against any notion of direct military confrontation against Nazi Germany.

DOCUMENT 3 This document is from a report by Anthony Eden, British foreign secretary from 1935 until his resignation in 1938. In it, Eden raises some interesting points regarding the German reoccupation of the Rhineland. He asserts that if Germany is forced out of the Rhineland by military action, the result might be *"Germany going Bolshevik."* He goes on to state that *many in the British military were anti-French and therefore would have little interest in fighting Germany over the Rhineland.* Finally, he claims that *most people in Britain see little harm in Germany's actions.*

DOCUMENT 4 This photograph, of *Sir Oswald Mosley saluting the ranks of British fascists, demonstrates British support for the fascist movement.*

DOCUMENT 5 This document is from an article in the *Manchester Guardian* newspaper describing a riot in the East End of London where anti-fascist supporters clashed with Sir Oswald Mosley and his Black Shirts. The document shows the *presence of a strong anti-fascist movement in Britain.*

DOCUMENT 6 This document includes *sections of government statute outlawing certain activities associated with fascist elements in Great Britain.* Specifically, the British government sought to prevent another riot similar to that which had occurred earlier in the year in the East End of London. The government was attempting to *limit the public activities of Sir Oswald Moseley and his fascist followers.*

DOCUMENT 7 This document is Winston Churchill's response to Chamberlain's policy of appeasement. Churchill was *appalled by the agreement and predicted trouble ahead* unless Britain exuded its "moral health and martial vigor."

YOUR ESSAY FOR THE DOCUMENT-BASED QUESTION

The key to answering this DBQ successfully is to pay attention to the prompt, which asks for *various* responses and reactions. Therefore, your thesis should compare different viewpoints. A good thesis will point to the multiple viewpoints in existence in Britain during the 1930s and demonstrate how contradictory they often were. In order to receive the first point, you must provide a clear thesis that touches on at least two different reactions or responses. For example, the essay could address the prevalence of parties that were interested in confronting Nazi Germany (7) and those opposed to confrontation (1, 3, 4, 5, 7). Other viewpoints would be those supporting the fascists (1, 4, 5) and those who were anti-fascists (5, 6). Finally, another conflict was between those in favor of (2, 3) and against appeasement (7). To earn the argument point, you will now need to write a coherent argument that directly answers the question and is supported by the documents and outside information. To earn all of the possible points for document analysis, it is important that you use at least six of the documents to support your thesis or relevant argument and also analyze the intended audience, purpose, historical context, or point of view in all of the documents that you use. This can be achieved several ways. One method is to relate authorial point of view to the author's place in society. In this DBQ, there are documents from high-ranking politicians including Anthony Eden and Winston Churchill, each of whom was an important decision maker. One could also make the argument of bias in that the peace movement was led by a clergyman. Other points of view you may want to consider include Lord Rothermere's letter to Churchill, in which he discouraged Churchill from pursuing an aggressive stance against Hitler (whom Rothermere supported). This DBQ lends itself to your using outside information, and the use of evidence beyond the documents is another required point on the rubric. For this DBQ, you could discuss events in Nazi Germany or the Soviet Union. A mention of *Lebensraum* would fit nicely, as would a summary of Western Europe's continued suspicion of the Soviet Union, and the fear of the spread of communism. Hitler's racial policy clearly influenced Britain's fascist movement, as evidenced by Mosley's march through a predominately Jewish section of London. Mention of the Spanish Civil War would be appropriate also, especially the reluctance of France and Britain to confront the fascist powers of Italy and Germany. Other factors that influenced public opinion regarding British foreign policy might include the lingering effects of World War I, the problems associated with the Great Depression, and the success of the Communist Party abroad.

A good response must also demonstrate an understanding of the broader context of the question, in order to earn the point for contextualization. For example, in this case, you could mention that although most modern historians point to the failure of appeasement as one of the factors that led to World War II, at the time, appeasement seemed like a heroic effort to avoid war and protect the citizens of Europe.

Finally, to earn the synthesis point, your essay must do one of the tasks listed in the final bullet in the directions for the document-based question. These include comparing/contrasting the topic of the question to another time or place, a different discipline, or a different course theme. Be sure to include a discussion of at least 2-3 sentences that fully explains the connections. An example of a way that you could earn that point for this essay would be to connect the topic of the question (reactions to the rise of Nazi Germany and the foreign policy decisions of German Chancellor Adolf Hitler during the period 1933–1939) to another geographical area, France. You could explain that just as there were people in Britain who supported a variety of views concerning appeasement, there were those in France who were adamantly opposed to appeasement, such as Charles de Gaulle, and others, such as Daladier, who actively promoted it.

ANSWERS FOR SECTION II, PART B: LONG-ESSAY QUESTIONS

QUESTION 1

This essay requires you to demonstrate the skill of analyzing causation by examining the fate of the Spanish empire between the years 1490 and 1650. Your thesis should note that Spain acquired wealth and power through its conquest of the New World and lost its wealth and power through a failure to adapt to a changing world. In particular, attitudes in Spain affected the economy and eventually brought about Spain's downfall.

Spain emerged at the end of the fifteenth century with a unified monarchy, having driven out the Moors in the 1490s. Christopher Columbus ushered in the age of exploration, sailing across the Atlantic and establishing colonies in the New World. Soon, Spain was exploring and colonizing territories throughout the Americas. Spanish conquistadors successfully subdued indigenous empires such as the Aztecs and Incas, helping to establish Spanish rule from the Caribbean to the southern tip of South America. At the same time, the Far East was colonized after Magellan's circumnavigation of the globe in 1519. This corresponded with the Golden Age of Spain, when the empire stretched across much of Europe, as well as around the world.

The rise of Spain was linked to the rule of Charles V, who became king of Spain in 1516 and Emperor of the Holy Roman Empire in 1519. Charles V spent most of his reign engaged in warfare, battling the French in Italy and Protestant forces in Germany. Nonetheless, Spain was able to afford its military adventures thanks to the massive imports from far-off territories, which enriched the Spanish monarchy. The Spanish treasury benefited from enormous amounts of bullion coming in from the New World.

Initially, the New World provided little in the way of trade, but with the discovery of silver mines in Mexico and Peru, the Spanish riches became legendary. Ultimately, the troves of gold and silver diverted Spain from investing in other industries and led to inflation by the end of the sixteenth century. The vast imports of gold and silver helped contribute to Spain's dependency on foreign sources for raw material and manufactured goods. The economy was additionally hurt by the expulsion of its commercial class through the dictates of the Inquisition. Most important was the prevalence of medieval attitudes, which viewed manual labor as dishonorable. Although well aware of the problems associated with inflation, the Habsburg rulers continued to spend money on military conflict, forcing Spain into bankruptcy several times.

Meanwhile, Charles V abdicated, dividing the Empire between his son and his brother. Philip II continued to oversee the Golden Age of Spain, gaining victories over the French and forming an alliance with England. Spain's supremacy was short-lived, however, as rebellions broke out in the Netherlands, forcing Philip to spend massive amounts of money to retain control over the valuable territory. With Queen Elizabeth I supporting Protestant causes in the Netherlands and Sir Francis Drake attacking Spanish ships and ports, Philip launched the Spanish Armada with the goal of subduing England. The Spanish fleet was turned away and England continued its ascent as a European power.

To earn the synthesis point, you need to do one of the tasks listed in the final bullet in the long essay directions. These include comparing/contrasting the topic of the question to another time or place, a different discipline, or a different course theme. Be sure to include a discussion of at least 2-3 sentences that fully explains the connections. For example, you might explain that after the death of Philip II, the Spanish monarchy experienced a long period of mediocrity, leaving the Spanish government struggling. The continued influence of the Spanish nobility, coupled with an overabundance of priests and monks, meant that Spain would experience difficulties throughout the seventeenth century. After its defeat in the Thirty Years' War, Spain would no longer play a decisive role in European affairs.

QUESTION 2

For this question, you need to present an argument based on a cause or reason for a particular event—in this case the Industrial Revolution, answering why the speed of industrialization was much slower on Continental Europe than in Great Britain. There are numerous factors that account for the discrepancy—some geographical, others political. A successful answer will address issues of infrastructure such as the lack of good roads and adequate river transit. Toll stations and custom barriers hindered trade across borders, increasing the costs of goods. Other problems included the continued influence and power of the guild system, which limited entrepreneurial opportunities. Cultural impediments also existed in Continental Europe, helping to discourage the entrepreneurial spirit that facilitated Britain's industrialization. For example, the nobility in many regions had a longstanding disdain for the commercial class. In addition, some cultures frowned on making the risky investments needed to nurture industrial growth. Finally, in many parts of Continental Europe, thriftiness was viewed as virtuous—even necessary to protect families from economic ruin.

Another important reason that Continental Europe was slow to industrialize was the effect of warfare on industrial development. Many regions transitioning from cottage industries to factories, including the Low Countries, France, and many German states, experienced major setbacks as a result of the upheavals caused by the French Revolution and Napoleon. For example, warfare disrupted communication between British industrialists and their counterparts on the Continent. By the time stability had returned to Continental Europe, British industry had grown so much that Continental industrialists found it hard to raise sufficient capital to compete. Not until the rise of the joint-stock investment banks such as the Banque de Belgique and Crédit Mobilier would Continental industrialists have access to needed capital resources.

Industrial development on the Continent was also hindered by difficulty in obtaining the knowledge and skills to build modern factories. The necessary skills and techniques were slow to enter Continental Europe, especially because the British enacted laws to prevent their importation. Until 1825, British artisans were prohibited from leaving the country. Only in the mid-1840s did Britain allow the export of certain kinds of machinery and parts.

To earn the synthesis point, you need to do one of the tasks listed in the final bullet in the long essay directions. These include comparing/contrasting the topic of the question to another time or place, a different discipline, or a different course theme. Be sure to include a discussion of at least 2-3 sentences that fully explains the connections. For example, you might explain that although Britain had the early advantage, Britain could retain its advantage for only so long. By the 1850s, Continental Europe had created environments conducive to industrial growth, including government policies promoting investment and education, along with protective tariffs that led to industrial success.

GLOSSARY

abbess the head of a convent or monastery for women.

abbot the head of a monastery.

absolutism a form of government in which the sovereign power or ultimate authority rested in the hands of a monarch who claimed to rule by divine right and was therefore responsible only to God.

Abstract Expressionism a post–World War II artistic movement that broke with all conventions of form and structure in favor of total abstraction.

abstract painting an artistic movement that developed early in the twentieth century in which artists focused on color to avoid any references to visual reality.

aediles Roman officials who supervised the public games and the grain supply of the city of Rome.

agricultural revolution the application of new agricultural techniques that allowed for a large increase in productivity in the eighteenth century.

Agricultural (Neolithic) Revolution *see* Neolithic Revolution.

alchemy a type of medieval and Renaissance science, similar to chemistry, which originally focused on turning metals into gold.

anarchism a political theory that holds that all governments and existing social institutions are unnecessary and advocates a society based on voluntary cooperation.

anticlericalism opposition to the power of the clergy, especially in political affairs.

anti-Semitism hostility toward or discrimination against Jews.

apartheid the system of racial segregation practiced in the Republic of South Africa until the 1990s, which involved political, legal, and economic discrimination against nonwhites.

appeasement the policy, followed by the European nations in the 1930s, of accepting Hitler's annexation of Austria and Czechoslovakia in the belief that meeting his demands would assure peace and stability.

Arianism a Christian heresy that taught that Jesus was inferior to God. Though condemned by the Council of Nicaea in 325, Arianism was adopted by many of the Germanic peoples who entered the Roman Empire over the next centuries.

aristocracy a class of hereditary nobility in medieval Europe; a warrior class who shared a distinctive lifestyle based on the institution of knighthood, although there were social divisions within the group based on extremes of wealth.

astrolabe an instrument used by mariners to measure the height of a star or the sun above the horizon to allow them to locate their position by calculating latitude.

astrology a popular science of the Renaissance that focused on interpreting the influence of heavenly bodies on people's lives.

atheism rejection of the belief in the existence of God or a supreme being.

Atlantic Economy the expansion of trade in the Atlantic during the 17th and 18th centuries, focusing on the growing economic dominance of European Atlantic powers and their trade with west Africa and the Americas.

audiencias advisory groups to viceroys in Spanish America.

Ausgleich the "Compromise" of 1867 that created the Dual Monarchy of Austria-Hungary. Austria and Hungary each had its own capital, constitution, and legislative assembly but were united under one monarch.

authoritarian state a state that has a dictatorial government and some other trappings of a totalitarian state but does not demand that the masses be actively involved in the regime's goals as totalitarian states do.

auxiliaries troops enlisted from the subject peoples of the Roman Empire to supplement the regular legions composed of Roman citizens.

balance of power a distribution of power among several states such that no single nation can dominate or interfere with the interests of another.

Baroque an artistic movement of the seventeenth century in Europe that used dramatic effects to arouse the emotions and reflected the search for power that was a large part of the seventeenth-century ethos.

benefice in the Christian church, a position, such as a bishopric, that consisted of both a sacred office and the right of the holder to the annual revenues from the position.

bicameral legislature a legislature with two houses.

Black Death the outbreak of plague (mostly bubonic) in the mid-fourteenth century that killed from 25 to 50 percent of Europe's population.

Blitzkrieg "lightning war." A war conducted with great speed and force, as in Germany's advance at the beginning of World War II.

Bolsheviks a small faction of the Russian Social Democratic Party who were led by Lenin and dedicated to violent revolution; they seized power in Russia in 1917 and were subsequently renamed the Communists.

bourgeoisie (burghers) inhabitants (merchants and artisans) of boroughs and burghs (towns).

boyars the Russian nobility.

Brezhnev Doctrine the doctrine, enunciated by Leonid Brezhnev, that the Soviet Union had a right to intervene if socialism was threatened in another socialist state; used to justify moving Soviet troops into Czechoslovakia in 1968.

Burschenschaften student societies in the German states dedicated to fostering the goal of a free, united Germany.

caliph the secular leader of the Islamic community.

capital material wealth used or available for use in the production of more wealth.

cartel a combination of independent commercial enterprises that work together to control prices and limit competition.

Cartesian dualism Descartes's principle of the separation of mind and matter (and mind and body) that enabled scientists to view matter as something separate from themselves that could be investigated by reason.

celibacy complete abstinence from sexual activity. Many early Christians viewed celibacy as the surest way to holiness.

centuriate assembly the chief popular assembly of the Roman Republic. It passed laws and elected the chief magistrates.

chansons de geste a form of vernacular literature in the High Middle Ages that consisted of heroic epics focusing on the deeds of warriors.

chivalry the ideal of civilized behavior that emerged among the nobility in the eleventh and twelfth centuries under the influence of the church; a code of ethics knights were expected to uphold.

cholera a serious and often deadly disease commonly spread by contaminated water; a major problem in nineteenth-century European cities before sewerage systems were installed.

Christian (northern) humanism an intellectual movement in northern Europe in the late fifteenth and early sixteenth centuries that combined the interest in the classics of the Italian Renaissance with an interest in the sources of early Christianity, including the New Testament and the writings of the church fathers.

civic humanism an intellectual movement of the Italian Renaissance that saw Cicero, who was both an intellectual and a statesman, as the ideal and held that humanists should be involved in government and use their rhetorical training in the service of the state.

Civil Constitution of the Clergy a law adopted by the French National Assembly in July 1790, that confiscated lands owned by the Roman Catholic Church and put the church under the control of the government.

civil disobedience a policy of peaceful protest against laws or government policies in order to achieve political change.

civilization a complex culture in which large numbers of humans share a variety of common elements, including cities; religious, political, military, and social structures; writing; and significant artistic and intellectual activity.

civil rights the basic rights of citizens, including equality before the law, freedom of speech and press, and freedom from arbitrary arrest.

Cold War the ideological conflict between the Soviet Union and the United States after World War II.

collective farms large farms created in the Soviet Union by Stalin by combining many small holdings into large farms worked by the peasants under government supervision.

coloni free tenant farmers who worked as sharecroppers on the large estates of the Roman Empire (singular: *colonus*).

Columbian Exchange the reciprocal importation and exportation of plants and animals between Europe and the Americas.

commercial capitalism beginning in the Middle Ages, an economic system in which people invested in trade and goods in order to make profits.

Commercial Revolution the European expansion of trade, banking, and other financial services that began in the late middle ages and lasted through the 18th century.

common law law common to the entire kingdom of England; imposed by the king's courts beginning in the twelfth century to replace the customary law used in county and feudal courts that varied from place to place.

commune in medieval Europe, an association of townspeople bound together by a sworn oath for the purpose of obtaining basic liberties from the lord of the territory in which the town was located; also, the self-governing town after receiving its liberties.

conciliarism a movement in fourteenth- and fifteenth-century Europe that held that final authority in spiritual matters resided with a general church council, not the pope; it emerged in response to the Avignon papacy and the Great Schism and was used to justify the summoning of the Council of Constance (1414–1418).

Concordat of 1801 an agreement made between Napoleon I and Pope Pius VII that restored peace between the Roman Catholic Church and the French government following the French Revolution.

condottieri leaders of bands of mercenary soldiers in Renaissance Italy who sold their services to the highest bidder.

confession one of the seven sacraments of the Catholic Church; it provided for the forgiveness of one's sins.

conquistadors "conquerors." Leaders in the Spanish conquests in the Americas, especially Mexico and Peru, in the sixteenth century.

conscription a military draft.

conservatism an ideology based on tradition and social stability that favored the maintenance of established institutions, organized religion, and obedience to authority and resisted change, especially abrupt change.

consuls the chief executive officers of the Roman Republic. Two were chosen annually to administer the government and lead the army in battle.

consumer revolution the emergence of an early consumer society that developed during the late 17th and 18th centuries and focused on luxury goods and foods, such as coffee, sugar, tobacco, and tea that were enjoyed by the middle and upper classes.

consumer society Western society that emerged after World War II as the working classes adopted the consumption patterns of the middle class, and payment plans, credit cards, and easy credit made consumer goods such as appliances and automobiles affordable.

containment a policy adopted by the United States in the Cold War. Its goal was to use whatever means, short of all-out war, to limit Soviet expansion.

Continental System Napoleon's effort to bar British goods from the Continent in the hope of weakening Britain's economy and destroying its capacity to wage war.

cosmopolitan the quality of being sophisticated and having wide international experience.

cottage industry a system of textile manufacturing in which spinners and weavers worked at home in their cottages using raw materials supplied to them by capitalist entrepreneurs.

council of the plebs a council only for plebeians. After 287 B.C.E., however, its resolutions were binding on all Romans.

Council of Trent a meeting of Roman Catholic Church officials that convened intermittently from 1545–1563 to address church policy in the face of Reformation challenges. It demanded improved clerical morality but did not change church doctrine.

Crusade in the Middle Ages, a military campaign in defense of Christendom.

Cubism an artistic style developed at the beginning of the twentieth century, especially by Pablo Picasso, that used geometric designs to re-create reality in the viewer's mind.

cultural relativism the belief that no culture is superior to another because culture is a matter of custom, not reason, and derives its meaning from the group holding it.

cuneiform "wedge-shaped." A system of writing developed by the Sumerians that consisted of wedge-shaped impressions made by a reed stylus on clay tablets.

curiales city councilors in Roman cities who played an important role in governing the vast Roman Empire.

Dadaism an artistic movement in the 1920s and 1930s begun by artists who were revolted by the senseless slaughter of World War I and used their "anti-art" to express contempt for the Western tradition.

de-Christianization a policy, adopted in the radical phase of the French Revolution, aimed at creating a secular society by eliminating Christian forms and institutions from French society.

decolonization the process of becoming free of colonial status and achieving statehood; it occurred in most of the world's colonies between 1947 and 1962.

deconstruction (poststructuralism) a system of thought, formulated by Jacques Derrida, that holds that culture is created in a variety of ways, according to the manner in which people create their own meaning. Hence, there is no fixed truth or universal meaning.

deism belief in God as the creator of the universe who, after setting it in motion, ceased to have any direct involvement in it and allowed it to run according to its own natural laws.

demesne the part of a manor retained under the direct control of the lord and worked by the serfs as part of their labor services.

denazification after World War II, the Allied policy of rooting out any traces of Nazism in German society by bringing prominent Nazis to trial for war crimes and purging any known Nazis from political office.

depression a very severe, protracted economic downturn with high levels of unemployment.

de-Stalinization the policy of denouncing and undoing the most repressive aspects of Stalin's regime; begun by Nikita Khrushchev in 1956.

détente the relaxation of tension between the Soviet Union and the United States that occurred in the 1970s.

developed nations a term used to refer to rich nations, primarily in the Northern Hemisphere, that have well-organized industrial and agricultural systems, advanced technologies, and effective educational systems.

developing nations a term used to refer to poor nations, mainly in the Southern Hemisphere, that are primarily farming nations with little technology and serious population problems.

dialectic logic, one of the seven liberal arts that made up the medieval curriculum. In Marxist thought, the process by which all change occurs through the clash of antagonistic elements.

Diaspora the scattering of Jews throughout the ancient world after the Babylonian captivity in the sixth century B.C.E.

dictator in the Roman Republic, an official granted unlimited power to run the state for a short period of time, usually six months, during an emergency.

diocese the area under the jurisdiction of a Christian bishop; based originally on Roman administrative districts.

divination the practice of seeking to foretell future events by interpreting divine signs, which could appear in various forms, such as in entrails of animals, in patterns in smoke, or in dreams.

divine-right monarchy a monarchy based on the belief that monarchs receive their power directly from God and are responsible to no one except God.

domino theory the belief that if the Communists succeeded in Vietnam, other countries in Southeast and East Asia would also fall (like dominoes) to communism; cited as a justification for the U.S. intervention in Vietnam.

Donatism a Christian heresy that argued that the sacraments of the church were not valid if administered by an immoral priest.

dualism the belief that the universe is dominated by two opposing forces, one good and the other evil.

dynastic state a state in which the maintenance and expansion of the interests of the ruling family is the primary consideration.

economic imperialism the process in which banks and corporations from developed nations invest in underdeveloped regions and establish a major presence there in the hope of making high profits; not necessarily the same as colonial expansion in that businesses invest where they can make a profit, which may not be in their own nation's colonies.

economic liberalism the idea that government should not interfere in the workings of the economy.

Einsatzgruppen in Nazi Germany, special strike forces in the SS that played an important role in rounding up and killing Jews.

empiricism the practice of relying on observation and experiment.

enclosure acts a series of laws passed by the British parliament between 1709 and 1869 that effectively eliminated common lands by allowing estate owners to fence off adjoining open fields.

encomienda in Spanish America, a form of economic and social organization in which a Spaniard was given a royal grant that enabled the holder of the grant to collect tribute from the Indians and use them as laborers.

Encyclopedia a heavily censored popular compilation of knowledge about nature, history, government, philosophy, and other scientific and intellectual topics. Edited by Diderot and D'Alembert, it was the first modern encyclopedia.

enlightened absolutism an absolute monarchy in which the ruler follows the principles of the Enlightenment by introducing reforms for the improvement of society, allowing freedom of speech and the press, permitting religious toleration, expanding education, and ruling in accordance with the laws.

Enlightenment an eighteenth-century intellectual movement, led by the philosophes, that stressed the application of reason and the scientific method to all aspects of life.

entrepreneur one who organizes, operates, and assumes the risk in a business venture in the expectation of making a profit.

Epicureanism a philosophy founded by Epicurus in the fourth century B.C.E. that taught that happiness (freedom from emotional turmoil) could be achieved through the pursuit of pleasure (intellectual rather than sensual pleasure).

equestrians a group of extremely wealthy men in the late Roman Republic who were effectively barred from high office but sought political power commensurate with their wealth; called equestrians because many had gotten their start as cavalry officers (*equites*).

estates (orders) the traditional tripartite division of European society based on heredity and quality rather than wealth or economic standing, first established in the Middle Ages and continuing into the eighteenth century; traditionally consisted of those who pray (the clergy), those who fight (the nobility), and those who work (all the rest).

ethnic cleansing the policy of killing or forcibly removing people of another ethnic group; used by the Serbs against Bosnian Muslims in the 1990s.

Eucharist a Christian sacrament in which consecrated bread and wine are consumed in celebration of Jesus's Last Supper; also called the Lord's Supper or communion.

Eurocommunism a form of communism that dropped its Marxist ideology. It was especially favored in Italy.

evolutionary socialism a socialist doctrine espoused by Eduard Bernstein who argued that socialists should stress cooperation and evolution to attain power by democratic means rather than by conflict and revolution.

exchequer the permanent royal treasury of England. It emerged during the reign of King Henry II in the twelfth century.

excommunication in the Catholic Church, a censure depriving a person of the right to receive the sacraments of the church.

existentialism a philosophical movement that arose after World War II that emphasized the meaninglessness of life, born of the desperation caused by two world wars.

family allowances one aspect of the welfare state whereby the state provides a minimum level of material assistance for children.

fascism an ideology or movement that exalts the nation above the individual and calls for a centralized government with a dictatorial leader, economic and social regimentation, and forcible suppression of opposition; in particular, the ideology of Mussolini's Fascist regime in Italy.

federates German troops enlisted in groups to fight as allies for the Romans.

feminism the belief in the social, political, and economic equality of the sexes; also, organized activity to advance women's rights.

fief a landed estate granted to a vassal in exchange for military services.

Final Solution the attempted physical extermination of the Jewish people by the Nazis during World War II.

Five Pillars of Islam the major tenets of the Muslim faith: belief in Allah and Muhammad as his Prophet; standard prayer five times a day and public prayer on Friday; observance of the holy month of Ramadan by fasting from dawn to sunset; making a pilgrimage (the *hajj*) to Mecca in one's lifetime if possible; and giving alms to the poor.

folk culture the traditional arts and crafts, literature, music, and other customs of the people; something that people make, as opposed to modern popular culture, which is something people buy.

free trade the unrestricted international exchange of goods with low or no tariffs.

Führerprinzip in Nazi Germany, a leadership principle based on the belief in a single-minded party (the Nazis) under one leader (Hitler).

functionalism the idea that the function of an object should determine its design and materials.

general strike a strike by all or most workers in an economy; espoused by Georges Sorel as the heroic action that could be used to inspire the workers to destroy capitalist society.

genocide the deliberate extermination of a people.

gentry well-to-do English landowners below the level of the nobility. They played an important role in the English Civil War of the seventeenth century.

geocentric (Ptolemaic) conception of the universe the belief that the earth was at the center of the universe and that the sun and other celestial objects revolved around the earth.

Girondins a faction in the National Convention during the French Revolution that favored keeping the king alive; so-called because their leaders came from the Gironde in southwestern France.

glasnost "openness." Mikhail Gorbachev's policy of encouraging Soviet citizens to openly discuss the strengths and weaknesses of the Soviet Union.

global economy an interdependent economy in which the production, distribution, and sale of goods are accomplished on a worldwide scale.

globalization a term referring to the trend by which peoples and nations have become more interdependent; often used to refer to the development of a global economy and culture.

global warming the increase in the temperature of the earth's atmosphere caused by the greenhouse effect.

Glorious Revolution the 1688 revolution in England in which Parliament invited William and Mary to replace James II and asserted parliamentary power and constitutionalism.

good emperors the five emperors who ruled from 96 to 180 (Nerva, Trajan, Hadrian, Antoninus Pius, and Marcus Aurelius), a period of peace and prosperity for the Roman Empire.

Gothic a term used to describe the art and especially architecture of Europe in the twelfth, thirteenth, and fourteenth centuries.

Gothic literature a form of literature used by Romantics to emphasize the bizarre and unusual, especially evident in horror stories.

Great Schism the crisis in the late medieval church when there were first two and then three popes; ended by the Council of Constance (1414–1418).

greenhouse effect the warming of the earth caused by the buildup of carbon dioxide in the atmosphere as a result of human activity.

guest workers foreign workers working temporarily in European countries.

guild an association of people with common interests and concerns, especially people working in the same craft. In medieval Europe, guilds came to control much of the production process and to restrict entry into various trades.

gymnasium in classical Greece, a place for athletics; in the Hellenistic Age, a secondary school with a curriculum centered on music, physical exercise, and literature.

Haitian Slave Revolt a revolt of Haitian slaves from 1791–1804 that resulted in the independence of Haiti and the abolition of slavery in the country.

Hanseatic League a commercial and military alliance of more than 100 North German cities and guilds that dominated Baltic Sea trade.

heliocentric conception of the universe the belief that the sun, not the earth, is at the center of the universe.

Hellenistic literally, "imitating the Greeks"; the era after the death of Alexander the Great when Greek culture spread into the Near East and blended with the culture of that region.

helots serfs in ancient Sparta who were permanently bound to the land that they worked for their Spartan masters.

heresy the holding of religious doctrines different from the official teachings of the church.

Hermeticism an intellectual movement beginning in the fifteenth century that taught that divinity is embodied in all aspects of nature; it included works on alchemy and magic as well as theology and philosophy. The tradition continued into the seventeenth century and influenced many of the leading figures of the Scientific Revolution.

hetairai highly sophisticated courtesans in ancient Athens who offered intellectual and musical entertainment as well as sex.

hieroglyphics a pictorial system of writing used in ancient Egypt.

high culture the literary and artistic culture of the educated and wealthy ruling classes.

Holocaust the mass slaughter of European Jews by the Nazis during World War II.

home rule in the United Kingdom, self-government by having a separate parliament but not complete independence.

hoplites heavily armed infantry soldiers in ancient Greece who entered battle in a phalanx formation.

Huguenots French Calvinists.

humanism an intellectual movement in Renaissance Italy based on the study of the Greek and Roman classics.

iconoclasm a movement against the use of icons (pictures of sacred figures) in the eighth-century Byzantine Empire.

iconoclast a member of an eighth-century Byzantine movement against the use of icons, which was condemned as idolatry.

ideology a political philosophy such as conservatism or liberalism.

imperium in the Roman Republic, the right to command troops that belonged to the chief executive officers (consuls and praetors); a military commander was known as an *imperator*.

In the Roman Empire, the title *imperator* (emperor) came to be used for the ruler.

Impressionism an artistic movement that originated in France in the 1870s. Impressionists sought to capture their impressions of the changing effects of light on objects in nature.

indigenous peoples people who are native to a particular region.

individualism emphasis on and interest in the unique traits of each person.

indulgence in Christian theology, the remission of part or all of the temporal punishment in purgatory due to sin; granted for charitable contributions and other good deeds. Indulgences became a regular practice of the Christian church in the High Middle Ages, and their abuse was instrumental in sparking Luther's reform movement in the sixteenth century.

infanticide the practice of killing infants.

inflation a sustained rise in the price level.

intendants royal officials in seventeenth-century France who were sent into the provinces to execute the orders of the central government.

interdict in the Catholic Church, a censure by which a region or country is deprived of receiving the sacraments.

intervention, principle of the idea, after the Congress of Vienna, that the great powers of Europe had the right to send armies into countries experiencing revolution to restore legitimate monarchs to their thrones.

isolationism a foreign policy in which a nation refrains from making alliances or engaging actively in international affairs.

Janissaries an elite core of eight thousand troops personally loyal to the sultan of the Ottoman Empire.

Jesuits (Society of Jesus) founded by Ignatius of Loyola, this new reform order of the Roman Catholic Church promoted a more humanist education, sent out missionaries to convert non-Christian peoples, and defended the Catholic church from the spread of Protestantism.

jihad "striving in the way of the Lord." In Islam, the attempt to achieve personal betterment, although it can also mean fair, defensive fighting to preserve one's life and one's faith.

joint-stock company a company or association that raises capital by selling shares to individuals who receive dividends on their investment while a board of directors runs the company.

joint-stock investment bank a bank created by selling shares of stock to investors. Such banks potentially have access to much more capital than private banks owned by one or a few individuals.

justification the primary doctrine of the Protestant Reformation, teaching that humans are saved not through good works but by the grace of God, bestowed freely through the sacrifice of Jesus.

Kulturkampf "culture conflict." The name given to Bismarck's attack on the Catholic Church in Germany, which has come to refer to conflict between church and state anywhere.

laissez-faire "let (them) do (as they please)." An economic doctrine that holds that an economy is best served when the government does not interfere but allows the economy to self-regulate according to the forces of supply and demand.

latifundia large landed estates in the Roman Empire (singular: *latifundium*).

lay investiture the practice in which someone other than a member of the clergy chose a bishop and invested him with the symbols of both his temporal office and his spiritual office; led to the Investiture Controversy, which was ended by compromise in the Concordat of Worms in 1122.

Lebensraum "living space." The doctrine, adopted by Hitler, that a nation's power depends on the amount of land it occupies; thus, a nation must expand to be strong.

legitimacy, principle of the idea that after the Napoleonic wars, peace could best be reestablished in Europe by restoring legitimate monarchs who would preserve traditional institutions; guided Metternich at the Congress of Vienna.

Leninism Lenin's revision of Marxism that held that Russia need not experience a bourgeois revolution before it could move toward socialism.

liberal arts the seven areas of study that formed the basis of education in medieval and early modern Europe. Following Boethius and other late Roman authors, they consisted of grammar, rhetoric, and dialectic or logic (the *trivium*) and arithmetic, geometry, astronomy, and music (the *quadrivium*).

liberalism an ideology based on the belief that people should be as free from restraint as possible. Economic liberalism is the idea that the government should not interfere in the workings of the economy. Political liberalism is the idea that there should be restraints on the exercise of power so that people can enjoy basic civil rights in a constitutional state with a representative assembly.

limited monarchy (constitutional monarchy) a system of government in which the monarch is limited by a representative assembly and by the duty to rule in accordance with the laws of the land.

major domus the chief officer of the king's household in the Frankish kingdom.

mandates a system established after World War I whereby a nation officially administered a territory (mandate) on behalf of the League of Nations. Thus, France administered Lebanon and Syria as mandates, and Britain administered Iraq and Palestine.

Manhattan Project a research and development project that produced the first nuclear weapons during World War II. It was led by the United States with the support of the United Kingdom and Canada.

Mannerism a sixteenth-century artistic movement in Europe that deliberately broke down the High Renaissance principles of balance, harmony, and moderation.

manor an agricultural estate operated by a lord and worked by peasants who performed labor services and paid various rents and fees to the lord in exchange for protection and sustenance.

Marshall Plan the European Recovery Program, under which the United States provided financial aid to European countries to help them rebuild after World War II.

Marxism the political, economic, and social theories of Karl Marx, which included the idea that history is the story of class struggle and that ultimately the proletariat will overthrow the bourgeoisie and establish a dictatorship en route to a classless society.

mass education a state-run educational system, usually free and compulsory, that aims to ensure that all children in society have at least a basic education.

mass leisure forms of leisure that appeal to large numbers of people in a society, including the working classes; emerged at the end of the nineteenth century to provide workers with amusements after work and on weekends; used during the twentieth century by totalitarian states to control their populations.

mass politics a political order characterized by mass political parties and universal male and (eventually) female suffrage.

mass society a society in which the concerns of the majority—the lower classes—play a prominent role; characterized by extension of voting rights, an improved standard of living for the lower classes, and mass education.

materialism the belief that everything mental, spiritual, or ideal is an outgrowth of physical forces and that truth is found in concrete material existence, not through feeling or intuition.

mercantilism an economic theory that held that a nation's prosperity depended on its supply of gold and silver and that the total volume of trade is unchangeable; its adherents therefore advocated that the government play an active role in the economy by encouraging exports and discouraging imports, especially through the use of tariffs.

Mesolithic Age the period from 10,000 to 7000 B.C.E., characterized by a gradual transition from a food-gathering and hunting economy to a food-producing economy.

Mesopotamia the valley between the Tigris and Euphrates rivers.

metics resident foreigners in ancient Athens who were not permitted full rights of citizenship but did receive the protection of the laws.

Middle Passage the journey of slaves from Africa to the Americas as the middle leg of the triangular trade.

militarism a policy of aggressive military preparedness; in particular, the large armies based on mass conscription and complex, inflexible plans for mobilization that most European nations had before World War I.

millenarianism the belief that the end of the world is at hand and the kingdom of God is about to be established on earth.

ministerial responsibility a tenet of nineteenth-century liberalism that held that ministers of the monarch should be responsible to the legislative assembly rather than to the monarch.

mir a peasant village commune in Russia.

mobilization the organization of troops and supplies for service in time of war.

Modern Devotion a movement founded by Gerard Groote in the fourteenth century, aimed at a practical mysticism based on leading lives serving the needs of fellow human beings.

Modernism the artistic and literary styles that emerged in the decades before 1914 as artists rebelled against traditional efforts to portray reality as accurately as possible (leading to Impressionism and Cubism) and writers explored new forms.

monasticism a movement that began in early Christianity whose purpose was to create communities of men and women who practiced a communal life dedicated to God as a moral example to the world around them.

monk a man who chooses to live a communal life divorced from the world in order to dedicate himself totally to the will of God.

monogamy the practice of being married to one person at a time.

monotheism the doctrine or belief that there is only one God.

Mountain a faction in the National Convention during the French Revolution that represented the interests of the city of Paris and favored the execution of the king.

multiculturalism a term referring to the connection of several cultural or ethnic groups within a society.

multinational corporation a company with divisions in more than two countries.

mutual deterrence the belief that nuclear war could best be prevented if both the United States and the Soviet Union had sufficient nuclear weapons so that even if one nation launched a preemptive first strike, the other could respond and devastate the attacker.

mystery religions religions that involve initiation into secret rites that promise intense emotional involvement with spiritual forces and a greater chance of individual immortality.

mysticism the immediate experience of oneness with God.

nationalism a sense of national consciousness based on awareness of being part of a community—a "nation"—that has common institutions, traditions, language, and customs and that becomes the focus of the individual's primary political loyalty.

nationalities problem the dilemma faced by the Austro-Hungarian Empire in trying to unite a wide variety of ethnic groups (Austrians, Hungarians, Poles, Croats, Czechs, Serbs, Slovaks, and Slovenes, among others) in an era when nationalism and calls for self-determination were coming to the fore.

nationalization the process of converting a business or industry from private ownership to government control and ownership.

nation in arms the people's army raised by universal mobilization to repel the foreign enemies of the French Revolution.

nation-state a form of political organization in which a relatively homogeneous people inhabits a sovereign state, as opposed to a state containing people of several nationalities.

NATO the North Atlantic Treaty Organization, a military alliance formed in 1949 in which the signatories (Belgium, Canada, Denmark, France, Great Britain, Iceland, Italy, Luxembourg, the Netherlands, Norway, Portugal, and the United States) agreed to provide mutual assistance if any one of them was attacked; later expanded to include other nations.

Naturalism a school of thought that advocated the realistic portrayal of subjects and their environments in art and literature and the philosophical belief in materialism.

natural laws a body of laws or specific principles held to be derived from nature and binding on all human societies even in the absence of written laws governing such matters.

natural philosophers a name given to medieval and Renaissance thinkers who studied the natural world prior to the Scientific Revolution.

natural rights certain inalienable rights to which all people are entitled, including the right to life, liberty, and property; freedom of speech and religion; and equality before the law.

natural selection Darwin's idea that organisms that are most adaptable to their environment survive and pass on the variations that enabled them to survive, while less adaptable organisms become extinct; "survival of the fittest."

Nazi New Order the Nazis' plan for their conquered territories; it included the extermination of Jews and others considered inferior, ruthless exploitation of resources, German colonization in the east, and the use of Poles, Russians, and Ukrainians as slave labor.

Neoclassicism a late-eighteenth-century artistic movement that emerged in France. It sought to recapture the dignity and simplicity of the classical style of ancient Greece and Rome.

Neolithic Revolution the shift from hunting animals and gathering plants for sustenance to producing food by sytematic agriculture that occurred gradually between 10,000 and 4000 B.C.E. (the Neolithic or "New Stone" Age).

Neoplatonism a revival of Platonic philosophy in the third century C.E., associated with Plotinus; a similar revival in the Italian Renaissance, associated with Marsilio Ficino, who attempted to synthesize Christianity and Platonism.

nepotism the appointment of family members to important political positions; derived from the regular appointment of nephews (Latin, *nepos*) by Renaissance popes.

New Economic Policy a modified version of the old capitalist system introduced in the Soviet Union by Lenin in 1921 to revive the economy after the ravages of the civil war and war communism.

new imperialism the revival of imperialism after 1880 in which European nations established colonies throughout much of Asia and Africa.

new monarchies the governments of France, England, and Spain at the end of the fifteenth century, whose rulers succeeded in reestablishing or extending centralized royal authority, suppressing the nobility, controlling the church, and insisting on the loyalty of all peoples living in their territories.

nobiles "nobles." The small group of families from both patrician and plebeian origins who produced most of the men who were elected to office in the late Roman Republic.

nominalist a member of a school of thought in medieval Europe that, following Aristotle, held that only individual objects are real and that universals are only names created by humans.

nuclear family a family group consisting only of a father, a mother, and one or more children.

nuns women who withdrew from the world and joined a religious community; the female equivalent of monks.

old order (old regime) the political and social system of France in the eighteenth century before the Revolution.

oligarchy rule by a few.

optimates "best men." Aristocratic leaders in the late Roman Republic who generally came from senatorial families and wished to retain their oligarchical privileges.

orders *see* estates.

organic evolution Darwin's principle that all plants and animals have evolved over a long period of time from earlier and simpler forms of life.

Paleolithic Age the period of human history when humans used simple stone tools (c. 2,500,000–10,000 B.C.E.).

pantheism a doctrine that equates God with the universe and all that is in it.

panzer division in the German army under Hitler, a strike force of about three hundred tanks and accompanying forces and supplies.

papal curia the administrative staff of the Catholic Church, composed of cardinals who assist the pope in running the church.

parlements provincial law courts in France.

pasteurization a process developed by Louis Pasteur for heating a product to destroy the microorganisms that might cause spoilage.

paterfamilias the dominant male in a Roman family whose powers over his wife and children were theoretically unlimited, though they were sometimes circumvented in practice.

patriarchal family a family in which the husband dominates his wife and children.

patriarchy a society in which the father is supreme in the clan or family; more generally, a society dominated by men.

patricians great landowners who became the ruling class in the Roman Republic.

patronage the practice of awarding titles and making appointments to government and other positions to gain political support.

Pax Romana "Roman peace." A term used to refer to the stability and prosperity that Roman rule brought to the Mediterranean world and much of western Europe during the first and second centuries C.E.

Pentateuch the first five books of the Hebrew Bible (Genesis, Exodus, Leviticus, Numbers, and Deuteronomy).

perestroika "restructuring." A term applied to Mikhail Gorbachev's economic, political, and social reforms in the Soviet Union.

perioikoi in ancient Sparta, free inhabitants but not citizens who were required to pay taxes and perform military service.

permissive society a term applied to Western society after World War II to reflect the new sexual freedom and the emergence of a drug culture.

Petrine supremacy the doctrine that the bishop of Rome (the pope), as the successor of Saint Peter (traditionally considered the first bishop of Rome), should hold a preeminent position in the church.

phalanstery a self-sustaining cooperative community, as advocated by Charles Fourier in the early nineteenth century.

phalanx a rectangular formation of tightly massed infantry soldiers.

philosophes intellectuals of the eighteenth-century Enlightenment who believed in applying a spirit of rational criticism to all things, including religion and politics, and who focused on improving and enjoying this world, rather than on the afterlife.

Pietism a movement that arose in Germany in the seventeenth century whose goal was to foster a personal experience of God as the focus of true religious experience.

pig iron a type of iron produced by smelting iron ore with coke; of lower quality than wrought iron.

plebeians the class of Roman citizens that included nonpatrician landowners, craftspeople, merchants, and small farmers in the Roman Republic. Their struggle for equal rights with the patricians dominated much of the Republic's history.

plebiscita laws passed by the council of the plebs.

pluralism the practice of holding several church offices simultaneously; a problem of the late medieval church.

plutocrats members of the wealthy elite.

pogroms organized massacres of Jews.

polis an ancient Greek city-state encompassing both an urban area and its surrounding countryside; a small but autonomous political unit where all major political and social activities were carried out centrally.

political democracy a form of government characterized by universal suffrage and mass political parties.

politiques a group who emerged during the French Wars of Religion in the sixteenth century, placed politics above religion, and believed that no religious truth was worth the ravages of civil war.

polytheism belief in or worship of more than one god.

Pop Art an artistic movement of the 1950s and 1960s in which artists took images of popular culture and transformed them into works of fine art. Andy Warhol's painting of Campbell's soup cans is one example.

popular culture as opposed to high culture, the unofficial written and unwritten culture of the masses, much of which was traditionally passed down orally and centered on public and group activities such as festivals. In the modern age, the term refers to the entertainment, recreation, and pleasures that people purchase as part of the mass consumer society.

populares "favoring the people." Aristocratic leaders in the late Roman Republic who tended to use the people's assemblies in an effort to break the stranglehold of the *nobiles* on political offices.

popular sovereignty the doctrine that government is created by and subject to the will of the people, who are the source of all political power.

populism a political philosophy or movement that supports the rights and power of ordinary people in their struggle against the privileged elite.

portolani charts of landmasses and coastlines made by navigators and mathematicians in the thirteenth and fourteenth centuries.

Post-Impressionism an artistic movement that began in France in the 1880s. Post-Impressionists sought to use color and line to express inner feelings and produce a personal statement of reality.

Postmodernism a term used to cover a variety of artistic and intellectual styles and ways of thinking prominent since the 1970s.

praetor a Roman executive official responsible for the administration of the law.

praetorian guard the military unit that served as the personal bodyguard of the Roman emperors.

predestination the belief, associated with Calvinism, that God, as a consequence of his foreknowledge of all events, has predetermined those who will be saved (the elect) and those who will be damned.

prefect during the reign of Napoleon, an official appointed by the central government to oversee all aspects of a local government.

price revolution the dramatic rise in prices (inflation) that occurred throughout Europe in the sixteenth and early seventeenth centuries.

primogeniture an inheritance practice in which the eldest son receives all or the largest share of the parents' estate.

principate the form of government established by Augustus for the Roman Empire; it continued the constitutional forms of the Republic and consisted of the *princeps* ("first citizen") and the senate, although the *princeps* was clearly the dominant partner.

procurator the head of the Holy Synod, the chief decision-making body for the Russian Orthodox Church.

proletariat the industrial working class. In Marxism, the class that will ultimately overthrow the bourgeoisie.

propaganda a program of distorted information put out by an organization or government to spread its policy, cause, or doctrine.

psychoanalysis a method developed by Sigmund Freud to resolve a patient's psychic conflict.

purgatory defined by the Catholic Church as the place where souls went after death to be purged of punishment for sins committed in life.

Puritans English Protestants inspired by Calvinist theology who wished to remove all traces of Catholicism from the Church of England.

quadrivium arithmetic, geometry, astronomy, and music; four of the seven liberal arts (the others made up the *trivium*) that formed the basis of medieval and early modern education.

quaestors Roman officials responsible for the administration of financial affairs.

querelles des femmes "arguments about women." A centuries-old debate about the nature of women that continued during the Scientific Revolution as those who argued for the inferiority of women found additional support in the new anatomy and medicine.

rapprochement the rebuilding of harmonious relations between nations.

rationalism a system of thought based on the belief that human reason and experience are the chief sources of knowledge.

Realism a nineteenth-century school of painting that emphasized the everyday life of ordinary people, depicted with photographic accuracy.

realist a subscriber to the medieval European school of thought that held, following Plato, that the individual objects we perceive are not real but merely manifestations of universal ideas existing in the mind of God.

Realpolitik "politics of reality." Politics based on practical concerns rather than theory or ethics.

reason of state the principle that a nation should act on the basis of its long-term interests and not merely to further the dynastic interests of its ruling family.

Reconquista in Spain, the reconquest of Muslim lands by Christian rulers and their armies.

relativity theory Einstein's theory that, among other things, (1) space and time are not absolute but are relative to the observer and interwoven into a four-dimensional space-time continuum and (2) matter is a form of energy ($E = mc^2$).

relics the bones of Christian saints or objects intimately associated with saints that were considered worthy of veneration.

religious pluralism the legal existence and toleration of more than one religion in a nation that resulted from the 16th and 17th century European wars of religion.

Renaissance the "rebirth" of Classical culture that occurred in Italy between c. 1350 and c. 1550; also, the earlier revivals of Classical culture that occurred under Charlemagne and in the twelfth century.

rentier a person who lives on income from property and is not personally involved in its operation.

reparations payments made by a defeated nation after a war to compensate another nation for damage sustained as a result of the war; required from Germany after World War I.

revisionism a socialist doctrine that rejected Marx's emphasis on class struggle and revolution and argued instead that workers should work through political parties to bring about gradual change.

revolution a fundamental change in the political and social organization of a state.

revolutionary socialism a socialist doctrine that violent action was the only way to achieve the goals of socialism.

rhetoric the art of persuasive speaking; in the Middle Ages, one of the seven liberal arts.

risorgimento a movement in Italy in the nineteenth century aimed at the creation of a united Italian republic.

Rococo an eighteenth-century artistic movement that emphasized grace, gentility, lightness, and charm.

Romanesque a term used to describe the art and especially architecture of Europe in the eleventh and twelfth centuries.

Romanization the process by which Roman culture and institutions were spread to the provinces; often accomplished through the Roman army as colonies of veterans were established wherever the legions were stationed throughout the empire.

Romanticism a nineteenth-century intellectual and artistic movement that rejected the emphasis on reason of the Enlightenment. Instead, Romantics stressed the importance of intuition, feeling, emotion, and imagination as sources of knowing.

sacraments rites considered imperative for a Christian's salvation. By the thirteenth century, these consisted of the Eucharist or Lord's Supper, baptism, marriage, penance, extreme unction, holy orders, and confirmation of children; Protestant reformers of the sixteenth century generally recognized only two—baptism and communion (the Lord's Supper).

salons gatherings of philosophes and other notables to discuss the ideas of the Enlightenment; so called from the elegant drawing rooms (salons) where they met.

sans-culottes "without breeches." The common people, who did not wear the fine clothes of the upper classes and played an important role in the radical phase of the French Revolution.

satrap a governor with both civil and military duties in the ancient Persian Empire, which was divided into satrapies, or provinces, each administered by a satrap.

scholasticism the philosophical and theological system of the medieval schools, which emphasized rigorous analysis of contradictory authorities; often used to try to reconcile faith and reason.

scientific method a method of seeking knowledge through inductive principles, using experiments and observations to develop generalizations.

Scientific Revolution the transition from the medieval worldview to a largely secular, rational, and materialistic perspective that began in the seventeenth century and was popularized in the eighteenth.

scriptoria writing rooms for the copying of manuscripts in medieval monasteries.

scutage in the fourteenth century, a money payment for military service that replaced the obligation of military service in the lord-vassal relationship.

secularism the process of becoming more concerned with material, worldly, temporal things and less with spiritual and religious things; a characteristic of the Italian Renaissance.

self-determination the doctrine that the people of a given territory or a particular nationality should have the right to determine their own government and political future.

senate the leading council of the Roman Republic; composed of about three hundred men (senators) who served for life and dominated much of the political life of the Republic.

separation of powers a doctrine enunciated by Montesquieu in the eighteenth century that separate executive, legislative, and judicial powers serve to limit and control each other.

serf a peasant who is bound to the land and obliged to provide labor services and pay various rents and fees to the lord; considered unfree but not a slave because serfs could not be bought and sold.

skepticism a doubtful or questioning attitude, especially about religion.

Social Darwinism the application of Darwin's principle of organic evolution to the social order; led to the belief that progress comes from the struggle for survival as the fittest advance and the weak decline.

socialism an ideology that calls for collective or government ownership of the means of production and the distribution of goods.

socialized medicine health services for all citizens provided by government assistance.

social security government programs that provide social welfare measures such as old-age pensions and sickness, accident, and disability insurance.

Socratic method a form of teaching that uses a question-and-answer format to enable students to reach conclusions by using their own reasoning.

Sophists wandering scholars and professional teachers in ancient Greece who stressed the importance of rhetoric and tended toward skepticism and relativism.

sovereignty supreme ruling power and authority.

soviets councils of workers' and soldiers' deputies formed throughout Russia in 1917 that played an important role in the Bolshevik Revolution.

sphere of influence a territory or region over which an outside nation exercises political or economic influence.

squadristi in Italy in the 1920s, bands of armed Fascists used to create disorder by attacking Socialist offices and newspapers.

stagflation a combination of high inflation and high unemployment that was prevalent in the United States and elsewhere from 1973 to the mid-1980s.

Stalinization the adoption by Eastern European Communist countries of features of the economic, political, and military policies implemented by Stalin in the Soviet Union.

Stoicism a philosophy founded by Zeno in the fourth century B.C.E. that taught that happiness could be obtained by accepting one's lot and living in harmony with the will of God, thereby achieving inner peace.

subinfeudation the practice whereby a lord's greatest vassals subdivided their fiefs and had vassals of their own, who in turn subdivided their fiefs, and so on down to simple knights, whose fiefs were too small to subdivide.

suffrage the right to vote.

suffragists advocates of extending the right to vote to women.

sultan "holder of power." A title taken by Turkish leaders who took command of the Abbasid Empire in 1055.

surplus value in Marxism, the difference between a product's real value and the wages of the worker who produced the product.

Surrealism an artistic movement that arose between World War I and World War II. Surrealists portrayed recognizable objects in unrecognizable relationships in order to reveal the world of the unconscious.

syncretism the combining of different forms of belief or practice, as, for example, when two gods are regarded as different forms of the same underlying divine force and are fused together.

tariffs duties (taxes) imposed on imported goods, usually to raise revenue and to discourage imports and protect domestic industries.

tetrarchy rule by four; the system of government established by Diocletian (284–305) in which the Roman Empire was divided into two parts, each ruled by an "Augustus" assisted by a "Caesar."

theocracy a government ruled by a divine authority.

Third Estate one of the traditional tripartite divisions (orders) of European society based on heredity and quality rather than wealth or economic standing, first established in the Middle Ages and continuing into the eighteenth century; consisted of all who were not members of the clergy or nobility (the first two estates).

three-field system in medieval agriculture, the practice of dividing the arable land into three fields so that one could lie fallow while the others were planted in winter grains and spring crops.

tithe a portion of one's harvest or income, paid by medieval peasants to the village church.

Torah the body of law in Hebrew Scripture, contained in the Pentateuch (the first five books of the Hebrew Bible).

totalitarian state a state characterized by government control over all aspects of economic, social, political, cultural, and intellectual life, the subordination of the individual to the state, and insistence that the masses be actively involved in the regime's goals.

total war warfare in which all of a nation's resources, including civilians at home as well as soldiers in the field, are mobilized for the war effort.

trade union an association of workers in the same trade, formed to help members secure better wages, benefits, and working conditions.

transformism the theory that societies evolve gradually.

transnational corporation another term for "a multinational corporation," or a company with divisions in more than two countries.

transubstantiation a doctrine of the Roman Catholic Church that during the Eucharist, the substance of the bread and wine is miraculously transformed into the body and blood of Jesus.

trench warfare warfare in which the opposing forces attack and counterattack from a relatively permanent system of trenches protected by barbed wire; a characteristic of World War I.

triangular trade a pattern of trade in early modern Europe that connected Europe, Africa, and the Americas in an Atlantic economy.

tribunes of the plebs beginning in 494 B.C.E., Roman officials who were given the power to protect plebeians against arrest by patrician magistrates.

trivium grammar, rhetoric, and dialectic or logic; three of the seven liberal arts (the others made up the *quadrivium*) that were the basis of medieval and early modern education.

Truman Doctrine the doctrine, enunciated by Harry Truman in 1947, that the United States would provide economic aid to countries that said they were threatened by Communist expansion.

tyrant in an ancient Greek *polis* (or an Italian city-state during the Renaissance), a ruler who came to power in an unconstitutional way and ruled without being subject to the law.

ultraroyalists in nineteenth-century France, a group of aristocrats who sought to return to a monarchical system dominated by a landed aristocracy and the Catholic Church.

uncertainty principle a principle in quantum mechanics, posited by Heisenberg, that holds that one cannot determine the path of an electron because the very act of observing the electron would affect its location.

unconditional surrender complete, unqualified surrender of a belligerent nation.

utopian socialists intellectuals and theorists in the early nineteenth century who favored equality in social and economic conditions and wished to replace private property and competition with collective ownership and cooperation.

vassalage the granting of a fief, or landed estate, in exchange for providing military services to the lord and fulfilling certain other obligations such as appearing at the lord's court when summoned and making a payment on the knighting of the lord's eldest son.

vernacular the everyday language of a region, as distinguished from a language used for special purposes. For example, in medieval Paris, French was the vernacular, but Latin was used for academic writing and for classes at the University of Paris.

viceroy the administrative head of the provinces of New Spain and Peru in the Americas.

volkish **thought** the belief that German culture is superior and that the German people have a universal mission to save Western civilization from "inferior" races.

war communism Lenin's policy of nationalizing industrial and other facilities and requisitioning the peasants' produce during the civil war in Russia.

War Guilt Clause the clause in the Treaty of Versailles that declared that Germany (with Austria) was responsible for starting World War I and ordered Germany to pay reparations for the damage the Allies had suffered as a result of the war.

Warsaw Pact a military alliance, formed in 1955, in which Albania, Bulgaria, Czechoslovakia, East Germany, Hungary, Poland, Romania, and the Soviet Union agreed to provide mutual assistance.

welfare state a sociopolitical system in which the government assumes primary responsibility for the social welfare of its citizens by providing such things as social security, unemployment benefits, and health care.

wergeld "money for a man." In early Germanic law, a person's value in monetary terms, paid by a wrongdoer to the family of the person who had been injured or killed.

world-machine Newton's conception of the universe as one huge, regulated, and uniform machine that operated according to natural laws in absolute time, space, and motion.

wrought iron a high-quality iron first produced during the eighteenth century in Britain; manufactured by puddling, a process developed by Henry Cort that involved using coke to burn away the impurities in pig iron.

zemstvos local assemblies established in Russia in 1864 by Tsar Alexander II.

ziggurat a massive stepped tower on which a temple dedicated to the chief god or goddess of a Sumerian city was built.

Zionism an international movement that called for the establishment of a Jewish state or a refuge for Jews in Palestine.

Zollverein the customs union of all the German states except Austria, formed by Prussia in 1834.

Zoroastrianism a religion founded by the Persian Zoroaster in the seventh century B.C.E., characterized by worship of a supreme god, Ahuramazda, who represents the good against the evil spirit, identified as Ahriman.